WATERFORD CITY AND COUNTY
KU-452-655

A History of the Bible

JOHN BARTON

A History of the Bible

The Book and Its Faiths

ALLEN LANE
an imprint of
PENGUIN BOOKS

ALLEN LANE

UK | USA | Canada | Ireland | Australia
India | New Zealand | South Africa

Allen Lane is part of the Penguin Random House group of companies
whose addresses can be found at global.penguinrandomhouse.com

First published 2019
004

Set in 10.2/13.87 pt Sabon LT Std
Typeset by Jouve (UK), Milton Keynes
Printed and bound in Great Britain by Clays Ltd, Elcograf S.p.A.

A CIP catalogue record for this book is available from the British Library

ISBN: 978–0–241–00391–6

www.greenpenguin.co.uk

Penguin Random House is committed to a sustainable future for our business, our readers and our planet. This book is made from Forest Stewardship Council® certified paper.

For Katie

Contents

PART FOUR
The Meanings of The Bible

List of Illustrations

1. The Near East in Old Testament times
Black Sea
HITTITE EMPIRE
Issus
Ras Shamra
Mediterranean Sea
LEBANON
Damascus
Tyre
CANAAN
Jerusalem
LEVA
EGYPT
R. Nile
SINAI
MIDIAN
Red Sea
0 100 200 miles
0 100 200 300 km

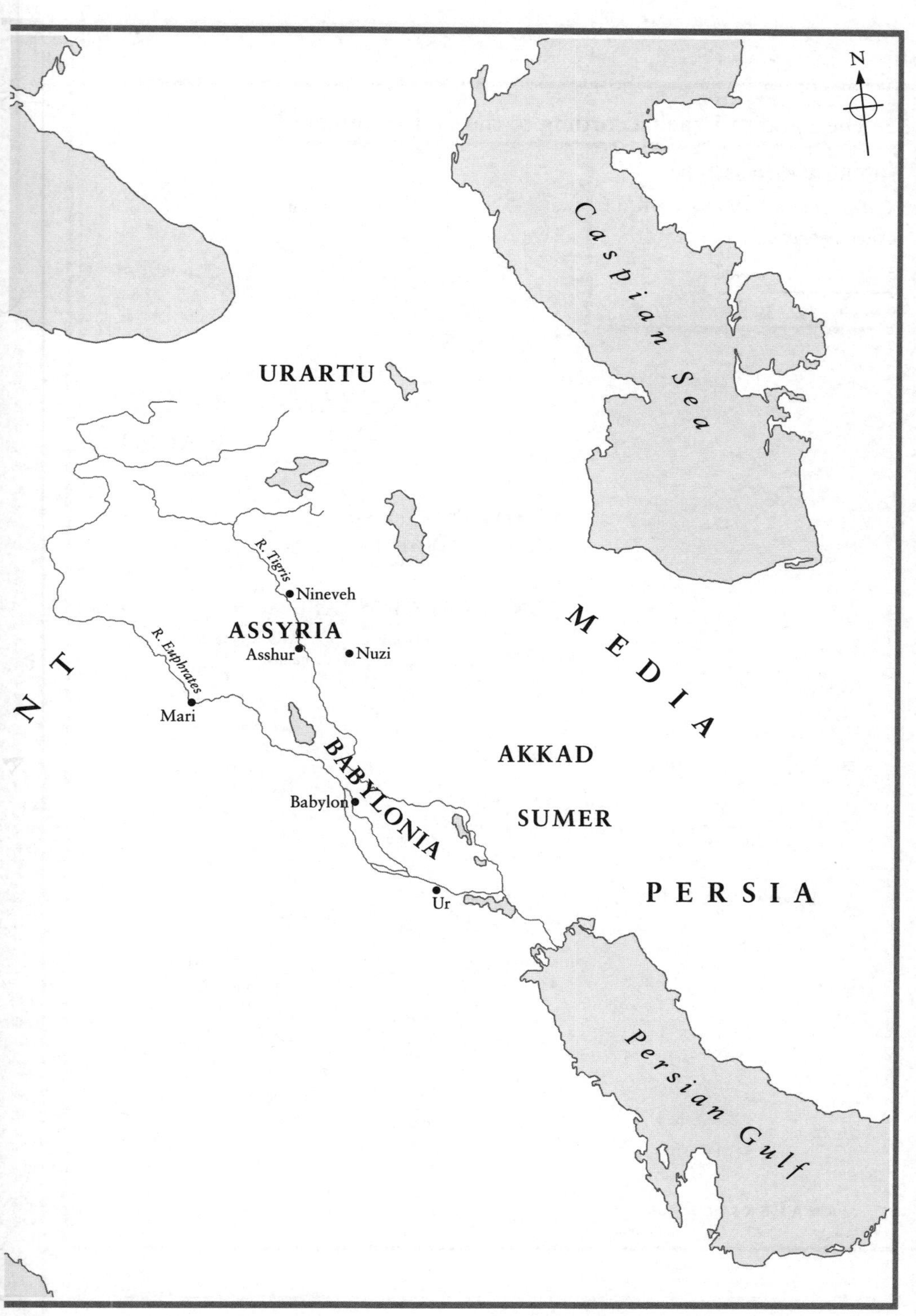

N
Caspian Sea
URARTU
R. Tigris
Nineveh
ASSYRIA
Asshur
Nuzi
MEDIA
R. Euphrates
Mari
NT
BABYLONIA
AKKAD
Babylon
SUMER
Ur
PERSIA
Persian Gulf

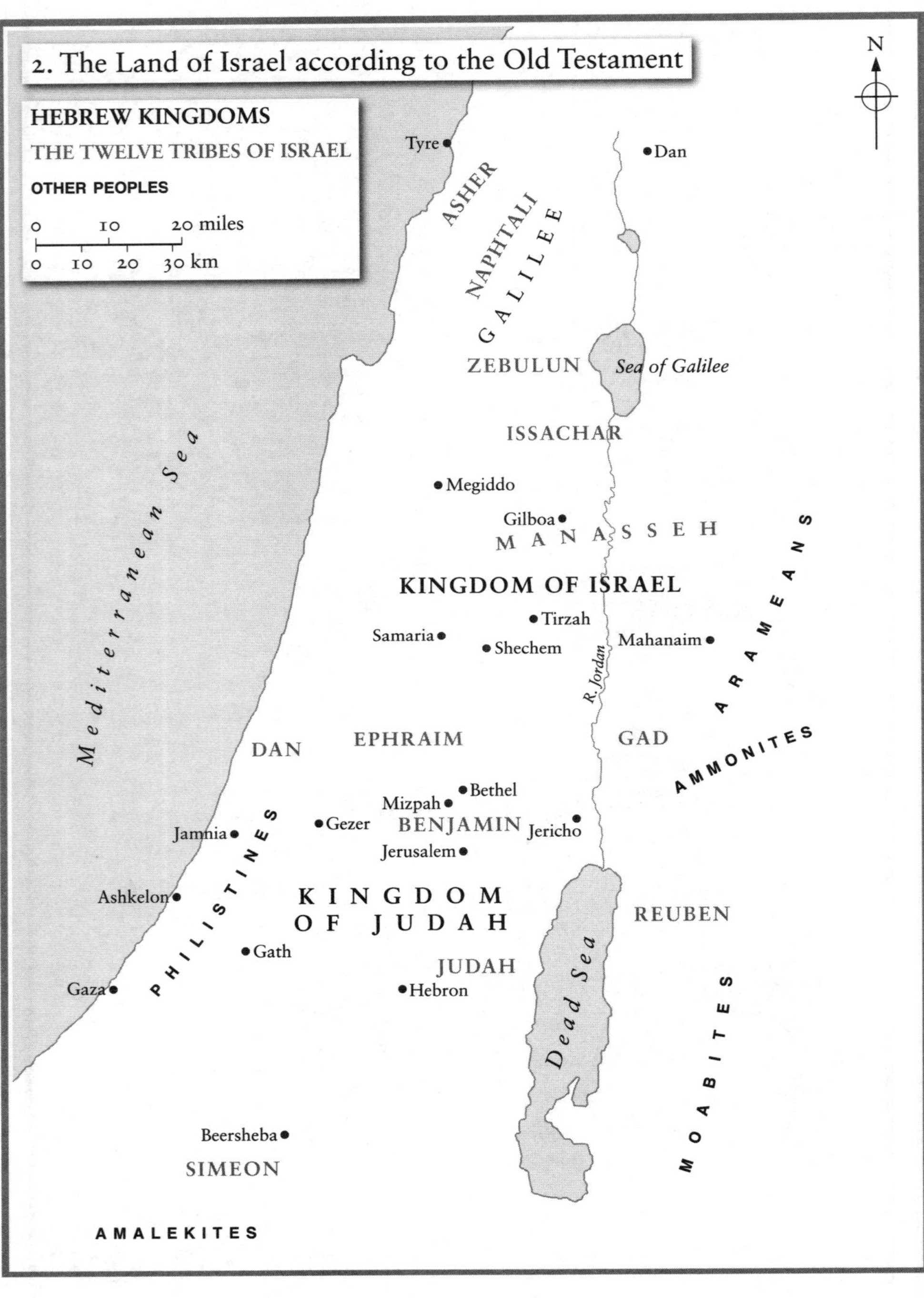

2. The Land of Israel according to the Old Testament
HEBREW KINGDOMS
THE TWELVE TRIBES OF ISRAEL
OTHER PEOPLES
0 10 20 miles
0 10 20 30 km
N
Tyre
Dan
ASHER
NAPHTALI
GALILEE
ZEBULUN
Sea of Galilee
ISSACHAR
Mediterranean Sea
Megiddo
Gilboa
MANASSEH
KINGDOM OF ISRAEL
ARAMEANS
Tirzah
Samaria
Shechem
Mahanaim
R. Jordan
DAN
EPHRAIM
GAD
AMMONITES
Bethel
Mizpah
Jamnia
Gezer
BENJAMIN
Jericho
PHILISTINES
Jerusalem
Ashkelon
KINGDOM OF JUDAH
REUBEN
Gath
JUDAH
Dead Sea
Gaza
Hebron
MOABITES
Beersheba
SIMEON
AMALEKITES

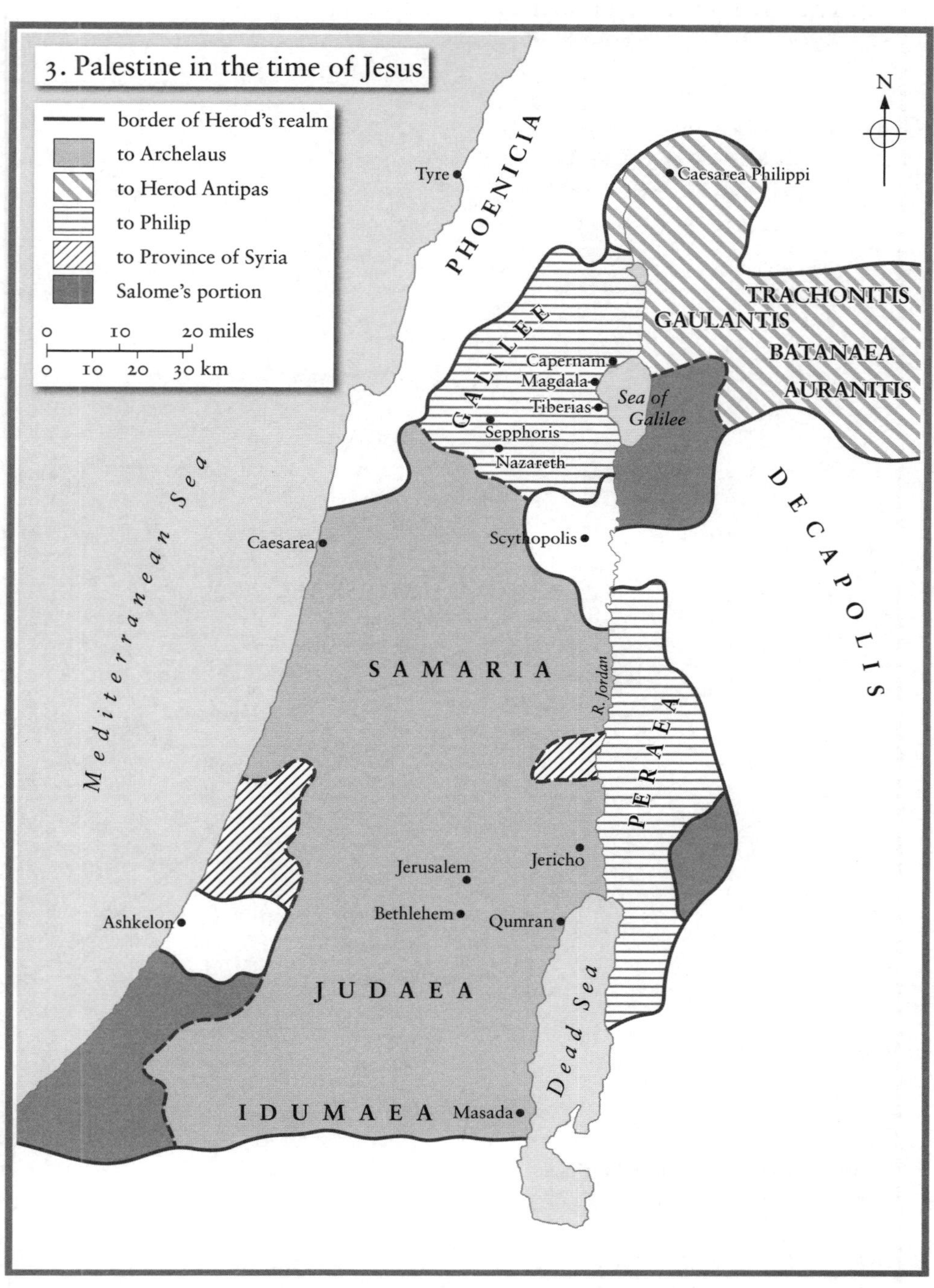
3. Palestine in the time of Jesus
border of Herod's realm
to Archelaus
to Herod Antipas
to Philip
to Province of Syria
Salome's portion
0 10 20 miles
0 10 20 30 km
N
PHOENICIA
Tyre
Caesarea Philippi
TRACHONITIS
GAULANTIS
BATANAEA
AURANITIS
GALILEE
Capernam
Magdala
Tiberias
Sepphoris
Nazareth
Sea of Galilee
DECAPOLIS
Mediterranean Sea
Caesarea
Scythopolis
SAMARIA
R. Jordan
PERAEA
Jerusalem
Jericho
Bethlehem
Qumran
Ashkelon
JUDAEA
Dead Sea
IDUMAEA
Masada

4. The Mediterranean under the Roman Empire
Lyons
Milan
Alcalá
Rome
Seville
Hippo
limit of the Roman Empire
division of its eastern
and western halves
0 100 200 miles
0 100 200 300 km

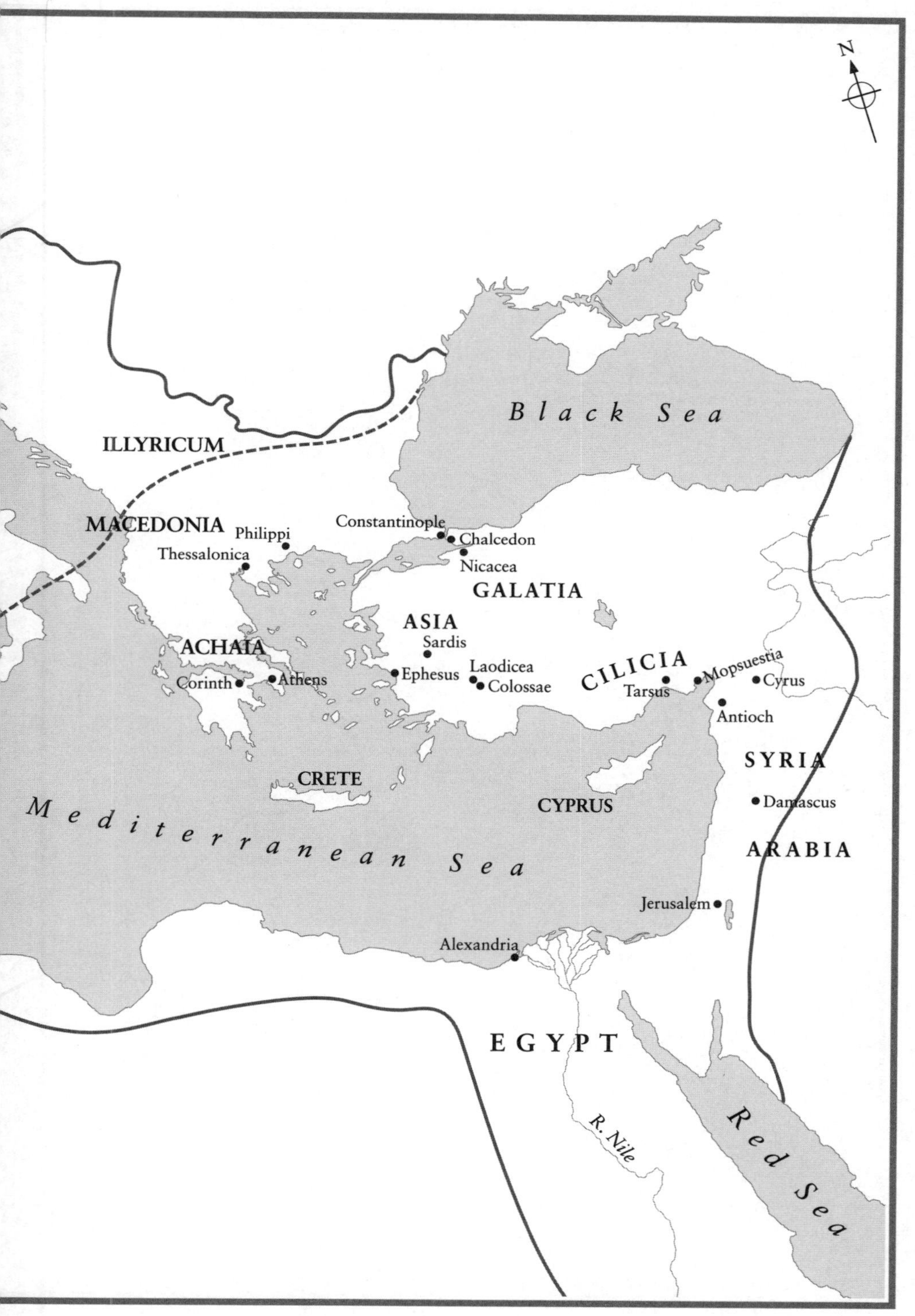
N
Black Sea
ILLYRICUM
MACEDONIA
Philippi
Thessalonica
Constantinople
Chalcedon
Nicacea
GALATIA
ASIA
Sardis
ACHAIA
Corinth
Athens
Ephesus
Laodicea
Colossae
CILICIA
Tarsus
Mopsuestia
Cyrus
Antioch
SYRIA
CRETE
CYPRUS
Damascus
Mediterranean Sea
ARABIA
Jerusalem
Alexandria
EGYPT
R. Nile
Red Sea

Acknowledgements

It is a pleasure to thank the many people who have helped me in writing this book. I am grateful to Stuart Proffitt for the invitation to undertake the work. He has commented minutely on the original draft, as has his colleague Ben Sinyor, saving me from many slips and infelicities and greatly improving the book. Grateful thanks to my copy-editor, Linden Lawson, for her exceptionally careful and thorough work. I must also thank Diarmaid MacCulloch and John Collins for reading the whole draft, and my agent, Felicity Bryan. Many colleagues have helped with advice and information, among whom I should mention particularly David Lincicum, Mary Marshall, Mark Edwards and Nicholas King SJ. The Oxford Faculty of Theology and Religion, and Campion Hall in Oxford, have provided a most congenial environment to work in. Special thanks are due to my wife Mary for her support, to my daughter Katie and her family who helped me to take time off from the project occasionally, and to numerous friends who have reminded me that life is more than writing.

The book is dedicated with much love to my daughter, Katie Walker.

John Barton
Campion Hall, Oxford
October 2018

Introduction: The Bible Today

The Canadian literary critic Northrop Frye (1912–91) wrote of the Bible: 'this huge, sprawling, tactless book sit[s] there inscrutably in the middle of our cultural heritage . . . frustrating all our efforts to walk around it'.[1] In a secular age, some might think it surprising how much interest there still is in the Bible, as the celebrations for the fourth centenary of the King James Version (KJV), sometimes known as the Authorized Version (AV), in 2011 showed clearly; even those who do not believe in Christianity continue to be fascinated by its presence. For believers, the Bible is often seen as inspired by God and having a high level of authority in matters of belief and practice. For non-believers, it is a central document of western culture: it continues to interest many readers as a collection of major literary works. The history of these works, and of how they have been disseminated and interpreted, is a central part of the history of western literature.

This book tells the story of the Bible from its remote beginnings in folklore and myth to its reception and interpretation in the present day. It describes the Bible's genesis, transmission and dissemination, and shows how it has been read and used from antiquity to the present, both in its original languages and in translation. Among other things, this will, I hope, dispel the image of the Bible as a sacred monolith between two black-leather covers, recapture the sense of it as the product of a long and intriguing process, and illustrate the extraordinary variety of ways in which it has been read over the centuries. Centrally, it also illustrates the difficulty in moving from the Bible to religious faith: neither of the two religions, Judaism and Christianity, that claim biblical books as their foundation can be read off from the Bible. Indeed, the Bible contains many elements that are problematic for Jewish and Christian belief. These include not only widely known morally objectionable features, such as God's destruction of innocent people in the stories of the Israelite conquest of the Promised Land, but also the variety of genres (narrative, prophecy, poetry), many of them not conducive to doctrinal definitions, and the setting in ancient cultures many of whose features we do not share. At the same time I aim to show that the Bible is an important source of religious insight, provided it is read in its original context and against the conditions prevailing when it was written.

The history will necessarily include a great deal of pre-history, as I explain how biblical books were composed, since few if any are the result of simple composition by one author: most are highly composite, and some even depend on others, so that there is a process of reception of older books going on in younger ones. The Bible is thus in itself already the record of a dialogue among authors and transmitters of tradition, and contains commentary in many of its books on many others. On the grandest scale, the New Testament frequently comments on the Old, nearly all of which was already regarded as 'Holy Scripture' (I will explain the meanings of that deceptively familiar term) in the world into which the New Testament came. The extent to which the Old Testament remains authoritative for Christians – and, if it does, how then it is to be read alongside the new ideas introduced by Jesus, Paul and others – is one of the main issues in Christian theology, and always has been. The New Testament speaks of the Old Testament as 'inspired by God' (literally 'God-breathed') in 2 Timothy 3:16, and Christians have extended that idea to the books of the New Testament too. It is not clear, however, how this affects the way the Bible actually functions, or the kind of authority it exercises over believers. To call the Bible inspired implies that God had a hand in its production, but exactly how that worked in practice is seldom defined.

A further purpose is to distil the current state of biblical scholarship. The Bible has been subject to the most minute scrutiny in modern times, and there is an ocean of theories about its origins, meaning and status, in which the general reader can drown. My intention is to describe the present consensus, where there is one, to discuss reasonable options in areas of dispute, and to indicate those where we might try harder.

Alongside these descriptive tasks, the book also makes an argument: that the Bible does not 'map' directly onto religious faith and practice, whether Jewish or Christian. I will propose that though the Bible – seen as a collection of religious texts – is irreplaceable for many reasons, Christianity is not in essence a scriptural religion, focused on a book seen as a single, holy work. Judaism, similarly, though it greatly reveres the Hebrew Bible, is also not so Bible-centred as is widely thought. Islam perhaps is the ideal type of book religion, and by comparison with it, Judaism and Christianity stand at a considerable distance from their central holy text. The Bible is very unlike a creed or a 'Confession', such as the great Protestant ones – the Confession of Augsburg for Lutherans or the Westminster Confession for some Calvinists. It is a mêlée of materials, few of which directly address the question of what is to be believed. The history of the Bible is thus the story of the *interplay* between the religion and the book – neither mapping exactly onto the other.

There are versions of Christianity that claim to be simply 'biblical' (no versions of Judaism do so), but the reality is that the structures and content of Christian belief, even among Christians who believe their faith to be wholly grounded in the Bible, are organized and articulated differently from the contents of the Bible. This can be seen most clearly in Christian fundamentalism, which idolizes the Bible yet largely misunderstands it.[2] Fundamentalists venerate a Bible that does not really exist, a perfect text that perfectly reflects what they believe. The description of the Bible (warts and all) which follows will necessarily make disconcerting reading for those who idealize it, but I will also show that it is not and cannot be the whole foundation of either Judaism or Christianity. I will thus also make the case for the kind of critical study that modern biblical scholars practise, which addresses the Bible without an assumption that whatever it says is to be regarded as authoritatively true.[3]

In truth, there are no versions of either Christianity or Judaism that correspond point for point to the contents of the Bible, which is often not what it has been made into and read as. In Christianity, for example, there are absolutely central doctrines, such as that of the Trinity, that are almost entirely absent from the New Testament; conversely, there are central ideas in the New Testament, such as St Paul's theory of 'salvation by grace through faith', that at least until the Reformation were never part of official orthodoxy at all, and even now are not in the creeds. Similarly, the elaboration of religious custom and tradition in Orthodox Judaism goes far beyond anything the Hebrew Bible itself implies: for example, the prohibition of eating meat and dairy at the same meal, with all its implications for the design of kitchens to avoid the two ever coming into accidental contact, is linked to Exodus 23:19 ('You shall not boil a kid in its mother's milk'), but exceeds anything that text in itself requires, as is generally acknowledged in Judaism.*

The Bible is centrally important to both Judaism and Christianity, but not as a holy text out of which entire religious systems can somehow be read. Its contents illuminate the origins of Christianity and Judaism, and provide spiritual classics on which both faiths can draw; but they do not constrain subsequent generations in the way that a written constitution would. They are simply not that kind of thing. They are a repository of writings, both shaping and shaped by the two religions at various stages in their development, to which later generations of believers are committed to responding in positive, but also critical, ways. To attribute religious authority to such a document stretches the word 'authority' to its limits, and can only be sustained by devising special ways of interpreting this book that differ from those in which others are interpreted.

To have as its holy text a mixture of works of many genres – predominantly narratives, aphorisms, poems and letters – introduces great complexity into Christianity. Catholicism has recognized other sources of authority besides the Bible, but has regarded the Bible as possessing a certain ultimacy; Protestants have developed theories according to which everything that matters to the religion is somehow present in the Bible, and some have even argued that nothing may be done or believed that the Bible does not explicitly sanction. This, I believe, is an abuse of these texts, which are deeply important for the Christian faith but cannot possibly bear the weight that is sometimes loaded upon them. Judaism has a more subtle approach to the Bible: while venerating it just as much as many Christians do, it does not claim that everything in the religion as actually practised is biblically derived, and recognizes development in new directions. Judaism thus has a holy book, and a set of religious beliefs and practices, but the two are known not to correlate exactly, despite being perceived as congruent; and this may be a better model for understanding Christianity too than the common Protestant perception of doctrine and practice as straightforwardly derived from the Bible. Because it allows a space between the Bible and the religion, this would in principle make it possible for the Bible to be heard on its own terms, and for religious faith to develop without being

* Quotations from the Bible are from the New Revised Standard Version (NRSV) Anglicized unless otherwise indicated. This has become the standard for academic quotation; other versions are discussed in Chapter 18.

totally constrained by it. The relationship between the two needs constant negotiation.

THE CULTURAL BIBLE

The Bible has two kinds of presence in the modern world. First, in western societies, it survives as a trace or ghost at the edges of both popular and literate culture, known in fragments as the source of quotations and allusions. Journalists can still assume that their readers will recognize the meaning of a 'David and Goliath' contest, or pick up references to the love of money as the root of all evil – though they may not know where the allusions come from, often thinking that some are from Shakespeare. Many people would recognize, for example, the following quotations:

Am I my brother's keeper? (Genesis 4:9)
Man does not live by bread alone (Deuteronomy 8:3)
The skin of my teeth (Job 19:20)
Three score years and ten (Psalm 90:10)
There is no peace for the wicked (Isaiah 48:22)
The salt of the earth (Matthew 5:13)
Pearls before swine (Matthew 7:6)
No room in the inn (Luke 2:7)
The powers that be (Romans 13:1)
A labour of love (1 Thessalonians 1:3)

But they would be unlikely to know the exact source, and more unlikely still to know what part they play in the various books they come from. Biblical literacy, as it is sometimes called, still exists, and advertisers (among others) can draw on it. Think, for example, of how ubiquitous the image of Eve is in advertising of all sorts, and how immediately visual and verbal allusions to apples, snakes and trees are picked up by consumers.[4]

The Bible has not died out of popular culture, as secularists might have predicted, and (as mentioned) the fourth centenary of the King James (Authorized) Version did show how widely it is still a cultural reference point for many literate people, even if often for style rather than for substance (see also Chapter 18). Oxford University Press alone sells a quarter of a million Bibles in the King James Version every year.[5] It is striking how often atheists commend it, even as they dissociate themselves from its religious claims: Richard Dawkins evidently approves of its cultural status and even exempts biblical scholars from his strictures on theology,[6] and Philip Pullman campaigns to retain the teaching of biblical stories and parables in schools, albeit alongside folk-tales and myths.[7] Pullman's own mythological system, in the trilogy *His Dark Materials*,[8] is at one level a deliberately anti-Christian reworking of the story of Adam and Eve, treating the acquisition of self-knowledge and awareness of sexuality as good rather than bad, as has sometimes been thought by Christian interpreters of the Genesis story.

The Bible still has major cultural importance in the USA, far more now than in Europe. A strong evangelical tradition in many areas of America has ensured that it remains highly significant even for people who are not religious, and for politicians to criticize or ignore the Bible is politically unwise. This does not necessarily mean that people in general *read* the Bible very much: it is an icon rather than an object of study.[9] Several states have declared a 'year of the Bible' from time to time – for example, Pennsylvania in 2012.[10] Despite the theoretical separation of Church and state in the USA, the Bible has a large public presence as a symbol of the essentially Christian basis of national life. In Britain, where attachment to the Bible is less strong, it still functions as a holy object – many people are still content to take oaths in court 'on the Bible', for example. And one can buy special Bibles in white-leather covers, to be carried by brides. The Bible remains a best-seller in most European countries, even though detailed study of it has become a minority interest as the appeal of Christianity wanes.

THE BIBLE IN FAITH COMMUNITIES

The Bible's second kind of presence in the modern world is within the faith communities of Christianity and Judaism, and here it retains a central importance. In recent decades in Judaism there has been an upswing of interest in the Bible, ushering in a new translation into English, the Jewish Publication Society's *Tanakh* Translation (1985 and 1999), and the large and impressive *Jewish Study Bible*.[11] (Orthodox Jews had tended to study the Talmud rather than the Bible, despite the prestige that the Bible of course enjoys within Judaism.) Within the practice of Christianity the Bible has also experienced a great resurgence over the last sixty years or so. Since the Second Vatican Council, inaugurated by Pope John XXIII in 1962 to reform and renew the Church, Roman Catholics have been encouraged to study it, and this has led to new Catholic translations in most European languages and a wide use of biblical study materials (commentaries and Bible-reading guides), on a scale never before seen in Catholicism. The documents of the Council have this to say about the Bible:

> Since everything asserted by the inspired authors or sacred writers must be held to be asserted by the Holy Spirit, it follows that the books of Scripture must be acknowledged as teaching solidly, faithfully and without error that truth which God wanted to put into sacred writings for the sake of salvation. Therefore 'all Scripture is divinely inspired and has its use for teaching the truth and refuting error, for reformation of manners and discipline in right living, so that the man who belongs to God may be efficient and equipped for good work of every kind' (2 Tim. 3:16–17, Greek text).
>
> However, since God speaks in Sacred Scripture through men in human fashion, the interpreter of Sacred Scripture, in order to see clearly what God wanted to communicate to us, should carefully investigate what meaning the sacred writers really intended, and what God wanted to manifest by means of their words.[12]

The twentieth century also saw a rise in Protestant churches focused explicitly on Scripture, especially Pentecostalism of various types in the 'old' west and, above all, in Latin America, South Korea and Africa. Many of these churches can be described as conservative (even fundamentalist) in their attitude to the Bible: they insist on its absolute truth, and maintain that God inspired every word of the text – not necessarily by verbal dictation, but certainly by influencing the minds of the writers so that what they produced was exactly the work God wanted the Church to have. What they call liberal biblical study – that which encourages a critical attitude to Scripture – strikes them as arid and uninspiring, even as faithless and essentially unChristian. In Britain and North America the churches that are growing tend to be those that adopt such a conservative approach to Scripture. They believe that the whole of the Christian faith can be derived from the Bible, which is seen as the only source of truth and inspiration. This produces at least five principles for reading the Bible, which more liberal Christians often endorse too, though in a watered-down version.

First, it is claimed, we should read the Bible in the expectation that what we find there will be *true*. For some Christians the truth that is sought is literal and historical, so that whatever the biblical text affirms is taken to be factually accurate. But even many who do not subscribe to this would agree that the Bible is to be read as true rather than as false. The truth it contains may sometimes be poetic or symbolic rather than factual, and this is particularly the case for more liberal Christians, but it is not an option to suggest that anything in the Bible is an expression of error. Even if the author of Genesis 1–2 did not accurately express the length of time it took God to create the universe, it is still unacceptable to say that he was therefore simply mistaken about the events he describes: there is bound to be some level at which what he wrote is true. For some biblical conservatives, it is important to believe that the chronology of the Old Testament, in which creation happened only some 6,000 years ago, is true – they are 'young earth' creationists. This has produced, mainly in the USA, the phenomenon of biblical theme parks, in which Adam and Eve walk among dinosaurs: the Creation Museum in Petersburg, Kentucky, is a good example.[13]

Secondly, Scripture is to be read as *relevant*. Even where Paul is discussing an issue that arose in the early Church but does not arise in the same form today (e.g. whether Christians are free to eat meat that has been sacrificed to false gods, as in Romans 14 or 1 Corinthians 8 and 10), this does not mean that the text in question has nothing to say to us. It is our task, as readers of Scripture, to discern what God is saying to us through the inclusion of such passages in the Bible. Because the Bible is canonical, that is, authoritative, it does not have passages that were once relevant but are so no longer: all that is written is there for *our* instruction:

> Whatever was written in former days was written for our instruction, so that by steadfastness and by the encouragement of the scriptures we might have hope.
>
> (Romans 15:4)

> These things . . . were written down to instruct us, on whom the ends of the ages have come.
>
> (1 Corinthians 10:11)

It is therefore not an option, when faced with a puzzling or difficult text, to conclude that it simply has nothing to say to us today. The fact that it was included in the Scriptures means that it is eternally relevant to the Christian believer.

The principle of relevance seems to be built into the idea of Scripture in most, perhaps all, religions that have a sacred book.[14] The early Christians believed in an even stronger version of the relevance of Scripture:

that everything was relevant in the very direct sense that their own life and times were actually predicted in the Scriptures of the Old Testament. It was indeed they 'on whom the ends of the ages ha[d] come'. God had inspired the scriptural writers to foretell coming events. Many conservative Christians still hold that to be true, believing that scriptural texts refer to the current world order, which its authors (or God speaking through them) foresaw in detail.

This can be seen particularly in the phenomenon of 'Christian Zionism', in which evangelical Christians support the state of Israel on the grounds that the return of Jews to the Holy Land is one of the precursors of the end-time prophesied in the Bible. (At the same time they often try to convert Jews to Christianity, a combination which Jews who welcome Christian support for Israel often do not understand.)[15] The events will begin with the 'rapture', the snatching from the earth of true believers to be kept safe with Jesus (along with the righteous dead, who will have been resurrected) during the tribulations that are to come on the earth, before Jesus returns to reign. The basis for this is 1 Thessalonians 4:17:

> Then we who are alive, who are left, will be caught up in the clouds together with them [the dead] to meet the Lord in the air.[16]

There are many 'prophecy novels' on the market that deal with these themes. The most famous and influential are the eighteen or so in the 'Left Behind' series.[17] The first, called simply *Left Behind*, envisages the rapture as happening all over the world at a single moment. Aeroplanes drop from the sky as their pilots are 'raptured', cars crash and there is immense suffering, but there are also conversions to Christian faith by those who recognize what is happening. The plot is tied up with other themes of modern American thought: the threat of Russia, the undesirability of pan-global organizations such as the United Nations, the need to keep American culture pure and pristine, safe from demonic influences such as the European Union. Naturally, by no means all Christian Americans who support Israel do so because they believe in this scenario, but a substantial number do. Pre-millennialism, as the system of thought is known technically, is a widespread evangelical strain in Anglophone Christianity.

More liberal Christians are more likely to see the relevance of the Bible as enduring – a matter of its having important things to say in any age, rather than as predicting the exact circumstances of the present day. Very many Christians attend Bible-study groups, at which participants read closely and try to discover what God is teaching them through the passage in question. 'Nothing' is not an acceptable answer.

Thirdly, everything in the Bible is *important* and *profound*. There is no triviality in Scripture, nothing that should be read as superficial or insignificant – in a way this is close to the previous point, about its relevance. The Bible is a book of divine wisdom, and it does not contain any unimportant texts. This can be difficult, because many people are likely to feel that some parts of Scripture are more important than others. Most Protestants make much more of the Letter to the Romans than they do of 2 John or Jude, especially since it was Romans, with its doctrine of 'justification by faith', that lay at the root of much of the Reformation in the sixteenth century (see Chapter 16). But strictly speaking, a conservative Bible reader will maintain, there is no hierarchy within Scripture: everything is inspired by God and therefore everything is important. Lutherans sometimes speak of a 'canon within the canon', a central core of really important texts inside a penumbra of less significant ones. But the majority of other Protestants, and of Catholics too, have not adopted this way of thinking.

Fourthly, Scripture is *self-consistent*. The Christian reader, it is believed, must not play one part of the Bible off against another. If there appear to be contradictions between two texts, more careful reading is required so as to show that they really cohere. A classic case of this would be the apparent discord in the New Testament between Paul and James over the question of good works, that is, actions that are meritorious. On the face of it Paul seems to deny that human beings are made righteous by good works (see Romans 3:21–4:12), whereas James affirms that good works are essential – indeed, that 'faith' apart from good works is empty and false (see James 2:14). There have been Christians who argued that this difference is irreconcilable: Martin Luther (1483–1546) proposed to exclude James from the core of the Bible because it contradicts Paul. But for conservative Christians this is not an option. They work to find ways of showing that Paul and James are not really at odds, but teach messages which, though different in emphasis, are ultimately compatible. In a way, the self-consistency of Scripture is already implied by saying that it is true, since two messages that are incompatible with each other cannot both be true. Because Scripture thus speaks with a single voice, obscure passages can always be elucidated from more transparent ones.

The self-consistency of Scripture seems to be a feature of all religions that have a holy text.[18] Certainly Judaism often works with an assumption that the Bible will cohere, and there are a number of discussions in rabbinic literature designed to show that apparent discrepancies are really reconcilable. In the Babylonian Talmud (Shabbat 13b), we read of the exploits of Hananiah the son of Hezekiah, who used up 300 barrels of oil to keep his lamp burning by night while he reconciled apparent discrepancies between the book of Ezekiel and the Pentateuch (the first five books of the Bible, Genesis–Deuteronomy). But Judaism also recognizes that texts of the Bible may sometimes be in dialogue with each other and that something positive may emerge from a kind of creative tension, whereas in Christianity this has not been a common view. Christians tend to think that all the holy texts must ultimately speak with the same voice. This belief lies behind harmonies of the Gospels, where a coherent account is believed to underlie the self-evidently different accounts in the different Gospels. There is a long tradition of this kind of work, going back into the earliest Christian centuries. Some Christians may think, as Augustine did,[19] that minor discrepancies among the Gospels do not really matter, since there is unanimity on the major issues of the truth of their message;[20] but more conservative readers would regard that as the beginning of a dangerous slippery slope that might end in general scepticism about the truth of the Bible.

Fifthly, Scripture is meant to be read as congruent with the content of Christian faith, with what the early Christians called 'the rule of faith' (see Chapter 13). This means something like a basic creed, or summary of what is to be believed. Some modern proponents of what is called a theological reading of the Bible thus say that our reading should be 'ruled', using this term in a technical sense to refer to its being controlled by the rule of faith.[21] Any interpretation of a biblical passage that makes it seem at odds with what Christians believe must be a misinterpretation. There are Jewish parallels to this idea, though the matter is not so much discussed in Judaism. But in both religions it is not acceptable to read the Bible as contradicting the basic tenets of the faith – especially as, in many forms of Christianity at least, what is to be believed is taken to be derived from the Bible in the first place. However exactly the relation of the faith to the Bible is conceived – and we shall see that this is a highly complex issue – they are assumed to be mutually supportive, not at odds.

Thus, to return to the Letter of James, if the theory of justification by faith alone really is central to Christian faith, then James must be read as supporting it, despite appearances. It must be saying, not literally that faith is dead without good works, but that the reality of faith can only be seen in the good works that people of faith perform: without good works their faith is not real but only apparent. (This may be a correct interpretation of James: my point here is simply that a commitment to the congruence of the Bible with Christian teaching more or less obliges one to adopt it.) Reconciling the Bible with the traditions of faith is a major undertaking, though those who do it would say that there is really nothing to reconcile, since the two are perfectly at one, but that it is sometimes necessary to show that this is the case because of doubts or worries that some believers experience. One of my purposes in this book is to demonstrate that there really are irreconcilables: that the faiths that appeal to the Bible are not totally congruent with it, though they are clearly closely related. In more conservative Christian and Jewish circles this would not be readily accepted, though there are both Jews and Christians who are more open to the idea that religion and holy text diverge. Some, indeed, do not pay much attention to the Bible at all. But the terms of debate tend to be set by the more conservative strands in both religions. In this book I shall try to engage with different styles of belief about Scripture, as I show how Bible and faith have been related down the ages.

ANCIENT AND MODERN

The Bible is thus absolutely not dead in the modern world. But it tends to be alive as either a cultural or a religious icon, distinguished from other books, and revered – in either a secular or a religious mode – rather than read as one might read other books. Both its cultural and its religious evaluation are alike in treating it as a uniquely special book; and as a result many of the questions we ask of other books are often ignored: how did it come to be written, who were its authors, above all what does it actually mean? There is an assumption in many Christian circles that it will speak to the present-day Christian community directly, and that questions about its origins and history are a secondary matter. Yet more secular readers, along with Christians of a less biblically conservative kind, sometimes do ask these questions. They may be surprised at how many of them can be answered.

The Bible may be a modern book, in the sense that it is still alive within the practice of Christianity and Judaism. But it is certainly also an ancient one, and cannot be understood except as the product of a long, often baffling history. Fundamentalist models of scriptural authority – and even official attitudes towards it in non-fundamentalist churches – elide this historical dimension by treating the Bible as in some sense a single book. Church reports on current issues, for example, frequently begin with 'the biblical background', treating the Bible as a single source, by comparison with the diversity of later writings. This is not only historically misleading, but diminishes the power of the various voices in the Bible to be heard – even while apparently honouring it as special. In the words of the great sixteenth-century Anglican writer Richard Hooker (1554–1600), 'as incredible praises given unto men do often abate and impair the credit of their deserved commendation, so we must likewise take great heed, lest, in attributing unto Scripture more than it can have, the incredibility of that do cause even those things which indeed it hath most abundantly, to be less reverently esteemed'.[22]

Hooker sets the scene for my treatment of the Bible in this book. I wish to show how it came into being, developed and was used and interpreted down the years, in both Christianity and Judaism. In the process I shall call in question the tendency of religious believers to treat it as so special that it cannot be read as any other book might be – 'attributing unto Scripture more than it can have', as Hooker put it. Yet at the same time I shall not seek to diminish the sense, shared by believers and many non-believers alike, that the Bible is a collection of great books. That it is not perfect (and what could be meant by a perfect book anyway?) does not mean it is of poor quality: on the contrary, these are some of the most profound texts humanity has produced. I have no intention to 'cause even those things which indeed it hath most abundantly, to be less reverently esteemed'. This may initially strike some readers as an uncomfortable balancing act, but I hope by the end to have shown that it is an approach that does justice to the Bible as it actually is, rather than to an imaginary Bible that exists only in some theoretical realm. As C. W. Goodwin put it 150 years ago:

> Admitting, as is historically and in fact the case, that it was the mission of the Hebrew race to lay the foundation of religion upon the earth, and that Providence used this people specially for this purpose, is it not our business and our duty to look and see how this has really been done? not forming for ourselves theories of what a revelation ought to be, or how we, if entrusted with the task, would have made one, but inquiring how it has pleased God to do it . . . It has been popularly assumed that the Bible, bearing the stamp of Divine authority, must be complete, perfect, and unimpeachable in all its parts, and a thousand difficulties and incoherent doctrines have sprung out of this theory.[23]

OUTLINE OF THE BOOK

The Old Testament/Hebrew Bible comes to us from the ancient Near East and cannot be understood without some knowledge of the history of Israel at that time, and the languages in which it circulated. I begin in the ninth and eighth centuries BCE, the age of major prophetic activity in the two kingdoms into which the Hebrew nation was divided, when the books began to take shape. All, or almost all, of the books were complete by the age of Alexander the Great (356–323 BCE).

I turn next to the contents of the Hebrew Bible, detailing its four major genres: prose narrative, law and wisdom, prophecy, and psalms and other poems. In the narrative books (Chapter 2) a variety of styles can be detected, and these help us understand their character and provide clues about their authors and the dates of their composition. Reading these books raises what will be a recurring theme: given that they tell a story rather than give instruction on what to believe or to do, the path from the biblical text to religious belief and practice in Judaism or Christianity today is far from straightforward. Legal and wisdom books (Chapter 3) appear more overtly to address the reader with demands or advice, but even such apparently universal texts as the Ten Commandments were written for and presuppose a society utterly different from our own, and cannot be applied today without extensive interpretation. This is even more obviously true of the books of the prophets (Chapter 4), which arose from various specific political crises in Israel's history, and in any case often seem to speak in riddles. Finally I examine poetic texts (Chapter 5), especially the Psalms and their obscure origins and uses. The Psalms have been attributed to a number of different periods in the history of Israel, from the time of King David (eleventh or tenth century BCE) down to the age of the Maccabees (second century BCE). One important theory suggests that they were used liturgically in the worship of Solomon's Temple, but many may also have arisen as personal prayers. What can be said is that they provide a digest of many religious themes characteristic of ancient Israelite thought – themes that recur in later Judaism and in Christianity.

Like the Old Testament, the New Testament makes sense only against its historical background. Chapter 6 describes the world in which Christianity emerged, and especially the blossoming in Judaism of various social and religious groups such as Pharisees and Sadducees, among whom the first Christians were to become the most successful. The earliest surviving texts of this new religion are not Gospels but letters, those of Paul deriving from the 50s CE, twenty years or so after Jesus' crucifixion. The interpretation of Paul is a major scholarly industry, and no consensus threatens, but it is possible to glean some essential elements in his thought-world and teaching – about human salvation, the relation of Christianity to Judaism, and the significance of the death and resurrection of Jesus and its relation to the climax of human history, which Paul thought was imminent. The Gospels and the Acts of the Apostles (Chapter 8) derive from the second half of the first century. Though there is general agreement that Mark is the earliest and John the latest, how the three Synoptic Gospels (Mark, Matthew and Luke) came to be written and where, what sources their authors used, and whether they were intended for all Christians or only for the community that produced them, are questions of unending interest to biblical scholars. Acts forms the second volume of Luke, but we cannot say whether it was written at the same time, or possibly much later. My concern in this chapter is to emphasize how little we know, in spite of a wealth of theories.

There is a widespread belief that the contents of the Bible were decided at a number of Church councils, no earlier than the fourth century CE, and that they excluded a substantial body of works that the Church authorities regarded as heretical. The third part of the book contests that belief. There were in fact hardly any decisions about what should or should not be canonical. All, or almost all, the books of the Old Testament/Hebrew Bible (Chapter 9) were accepted as Scripture by widespread consensus, in some cases probably not long after they were composed; only at the fringes was there any dispute. In the early Church (Chapter 10) as in Judaism, acceptance and citation of books long preceded any formal rulings about the limits of the canon. When there were such rulings, they usually simply endorsed what was already the case, while leaving a few books in a category of continuing uncertainty. The books which were actively excluded (Chapter 11) were in nearly all cases considerably later and less reliable than those that were accepted. That we have the Bible at all is due to generations of scribes who copied the texts by hand, and I proceed next (Chapter 12) to their transmission. There is a major contrast here: Judaism has long accepted a single text of the Hebrew Bible as authoritative, whereas Christians have never had an official text, only many different manuscript traditions. Printed Hebrew Bibles all derive from a single eleventh-century manuscript, whereas all printed New Testaments are based on the comparison of various different manuscripts. The art of making these comparisons is illustrated with examples, and I warn that appeal to the exact wording of the New Testament is fraught with difficulty because of the lack of an agreed text.

Does the Bible have an overall theme or meaning? Christians have generally thought so, and Chapter 13 examines attempts to define it, setting the scene for the chapters that follow, which spell them out in detail. Rabbinic readings of the Bible tend to treat it as a collection of sayings, any of which may illuminate any other, rather than as a continuous work, and this contrast is illustrated in Chapter 14. Jewish and Christian interpretations have at times influenced each other, but for the most part they form two separate systems, though both have traditionally interpreted Scripture so as to support their own religious beliefs. These beliefs are partly drawn from Scripture, partly not, and the interplay between the surface meaning of the biblical text and the meanings that have been read into it is part of the fascination of biblical study. In the medieval period (Chapter 15) the tendency to read the text in the light of one's prior beliefs becomes even more evident, but so does the emphasis on the Bible (interpreted correctly) as the source of all religious truth. The reading of the Bible at the Reformation (Chapter 16) inherited medieval methods and approaches, but it also paved the way for the critical questions that would come to characterize Enlightenment and modern biblical study. Martin Luther in particular pioneered a willingness to challenge parts of the Bible on the basis of theological principles.

My discussion of the Enlightenment and its heritage today (Chapter 17) begins with the ideas of Spinoza (1632–77). Spinoza questioned biblical miracles on the basis of natural science, but he also challenged traditional attributions of biblical texts, and introduced a distinction between the meaning of texts and their truth that was crucial for all subsequent biblical study. Critical biblical study developed through the eighteenth and nineteenth centuries to produce the types of argument and conclusions presented in the first half of this book. Chapter 18 surveys biblical translation from the third or second century BCE, when the Hebrew Bible was translated into Greek, to the present. I examine the King James Version and its legacy, and subsequent attempts to translate the Bible into English afresh. Translation raises questions not only about the meaning but also about the interpretation of the text, and this chapter discusses the ways in which some modern translations have entered into the interpretative debate.

Examining the Bible challenges as well as nourishes religious faith and practice, and my concluding chapter reflects on the relation of the Bible to its faiths, and the incomplete overlap between both Judaism and Christianity and its contents.

PART ONE

The Old Testament

I
Ancient Israel: History and Language

The Bible comes to us from the world of the eastern Mediterranean. Much of what Christians call the Old Testament was written in what is now Israel/Palestine, the majority probably in Jerusalem. Some may come from Mesopotamia (what is now Iraq), to which many Jews were exiled in the sixth century BCE, and some perhaps from Egypt, where a substantial Jewish community lived from the same period onwards. It is conceivable that there are passages in the Old Testament as old as the tenth or eleventh centuries BCE, but modern scholars tend to think that the eighth century – possibly the age also of Homer – is the earliest likely period; the latest Old Testament book (Daniel) comes from the second century BCE.

There may already be some surprises here. It is widely believed that large parts of the Bible are much older than this implies, with the stories about characters such as Abraham, Isaac and Jacob in the book of Genesis going back into the second millennium BCE. The story the Bible tells does indeed span a very long period; but the books that describe it almost certainly do not date back in written form to such remote antiquity themselves. For the early stories in Genesis, and even the accounts of the activity of Moses in Exodus, we probably have a written version of tales that originally circulated by word of mouth in a mostly illiterate culture, though some biblical scholars think they are deliberate fiction. (It is noticeable that Moses and his predecessors are scarcely mentioned again until literature that we are sure derives from the sixth century BCE, notably Isaiah 40–55.) The story of the origins of Israel, then, is at best folk-memory, which is unlikely to be accurate in any detail across more than a generation or so. This means that we have little access to the history of Israel in the times covered by the opening books of the Bible, the Pentateuch (Greek for 'five scrolls', and meaning Genesis, Exodus, Leviticus, Numbers and Deuteronomy).

At the other end of the chronology, it is also not generally known that there are Old Testament books more recent than Greek tragedies or the works of Plato and Aristotle. This is partly because later books tend to claim an older ancestry: Ecclesiastes (Qoheleth in Hebrew) seems to claim to be by Solomon, who lived in the tenth century BCE, and Daniel claims to be a near-contemporary of Jeremiah, living in the time of the exile in the sixth century BCE. But the general consensus now is that both books are the product of a much later period, and in the case of Daniel a time as late as the age of the Maccabees, Jewish freedom fighters in the second century BCE who went on to found a dynasty. Thus the Old Testament does not derive from a single period in the history of Israel, but from a wide range of dates as well as a variety of places. It is the national literature of a small nation: Israel is about the same size as Wales, or the state of Maine. Before modern times, Israel had a genuinely independent existence for only a few centuries, from perhaps the tenth to the seventh century BCE, and was otherwise subject to the main regional powers – Egypt, Assyria, Babylonia or the Hellenistic kingdoms that controlled the Middle East after the death of Alexander the Great in 323 BCE. Israel was itself a geopolitically unimportant state, but it lay at the heart of various trade routes in the Middle East and so was open to influences from its larger and more significant neighbours.

If we are to understand the development of its national literature, it is necessary to have in mind an outline history of Israel within the wider ancient Near Eastern world. But the history as reconstructed by modern historians differs markedly from the story the Old Testament itself tells. We begin by sketching this story, and then proceed to the modern reconstructions.

THE BIBLICAL STORY

The Old Testament gives the impression that the origins of the people of Israel do indeed go back well into the second millennium BCE. Abraham, Isaac and Jacob, and Joseph and his eleven brothers, live well before the time of Moses, which in turn is long before the first kings of Israel, Saul, David and Solomon. In Genesis, the ancestors migrate from Mesopotamia to the Promised Land but continue to have connections with their relatives to the east. They then move to Egypt in a time of famine, Joseph having gone ahead of them as a slave who becomes a major Egyptian official. Chronological notes in the Old Testament suggest that we are meant to think of this as happening in perhaps the fourteenth century BCE. The people return to the Land, this time from the west, from Egypt, under the leadership of Moses; after wandering in the desert for forty years and receiving the Ten Commandments and the other laws, they finally enter the Land with Joshua at their head. By the eleventh century or so they have settled down in the Land under the people the Old Testament calls the 'judges', tribal leaders who rose to rule the whole of Israel. They face opposition from other local peoples such as the Midianites. It is the Philistines, however, incomers who have settled in the west of the Land (where the Gaza Strip is now), who present the first major challenge; a local leader called Saul rises to the occasion, repels the Philistines and becomes the first king of all the tribes in the north of the Land, excluding the southern tribe of Judah. David, a Judahite from Bethlehem, takes over from Saul when Saul is killed in battle with the Philistines, and unites Judah and Israel to make a single kingdom with its capital at Jerusalem. The union is unstable, and always a source of tension. Under David and his son Solomon, Israel then expands to dominate the surrounding small nations such as Moab, Ammon, Edom and even Aram (now Syria), and we can speak of an Israelite empire. Solomon also constructs a royal temple in Jerusalem as a centre for the worship of God.

This is the high point of the history of Israel as the Old Testament sees it. After the death of Solomon the old north-south divide reasserts itself, and there are two kingdoms, Judah and the northern kingdom of Israel, sometimes referred to as Ephraim after the name of the main tribe that had settled in the area it covered. It is Judah that really interests the Old Testament writers, who (we may surmise) lived mostly in Jerusalem. Still there are stories of the north too, such as the tales of the prophets Elijah and Elisha, who work under various northern kings in the ninth century, including the notorious Ahab and his queen, Jezebel – regarded by the Old Testament's first book of Kings as apostates from the true Israelite religion and worshippers of the god Baal. Israel is continually at war with Aram, inconclusively so, throughout the century, but in the eighth century the rising power of Assyria, with its capital at Nineveh (near modern Mosul), snuffs out the northern kingdom:

> The king of Assyria invaded all the land and came to Samaria; for three years he besieged it. In the ninth year of Hoshea the king of Assyria captured Samaria; he carried the Israelites away to Assyria.
>
> (2 Kings 17:5–6)

Judah survives, the Bible tells us, as a tiny independent state until the beginning of the sixth century BCE when it in turn falls to the Babylonians, who have by now supplanted Assyria. The Temple is destroyed, and the land devastated. So begins the Jewish exile, with all the leadership either executed or transported to Babylonia, and only 'the poorest of the people of the land' (2 Kings 25:12) left behind.

The Old Testament speaks of a number of important figures from the exilic age, notably Jeremiah and Ezekiel, but tells us little of what the exiles in general did or suffered. Later in the sixth century the conquest of Babylon under its last king, Nabonidus, by the Persian monarch Cyrus the Great leads to a different imperial policy, under which exiled peoples are allowed to return to their homelands.

> 'Thus says King Cyrus of Persia: The LORD, the God of heaven, has given me all the kingdoms of the earth, and he has charged me to build him a house at Jerusalem in Judah. Any of those among you who are of his people – may their God be with them! – are now permitted to go up to Jerusalem in Judah, and rebuild the house of the LORD, the God of Israel.'[1]
>
> (Ezra 1:2–3)

Accordingly a number of Jews return to Judah and begin to rebuild the Temple (known usually as the Second Temple, to distinguish it from the original built by Solomon). We read of some of their activities in the books of Ezra and Nehemiah, who are presented as regulating Jewish life under the Torah – the great law book given by God, which we are probably meant to understand as the Pentateuch. After Nehemiah we learn little more of the Persian period, and the Old Testament gives the impression that the significant history of Israel, guided by its God, is more or less over. Only the book of Esther purports to tell of Jewish life under the Persians.

Persia was conquered by Alexander the Great (at the end of the fourth century, in 333 BCE, at the Battle of Issus), and there is more information about Jewish life in the Land under his successors in the books of Maccabees.* From them we learn that one successor of Alexander, Antiochus IV Epiphanes, tried to stamp out Judaism in the early second century BCE, but was resisted by Judah Maccabee and his brothers. From the Jewish historian Josephus we gather that their descendants established a new royal dynasty in Jerusalem, the first time

* Included in the Catholic Old Testament but not in the Bible of Jews or Protestants, the latter assigning them to the Apocrypha.

since the exile that the Jews had been ruled by a Jewish king. But this information does not come from the Old Testament itself, where the story of Israel peters out in the Persian age.

MODERN RECONSTRUCTIONS

There is probably not a single episode in the history of Israel as told by the Old Testament on which modern scholars are in agreement. Some take a conservative position, treating the Old Testament narrative as likely to be accurate unless there is proof to the contrary, and tend to regard even the stories of early Israel (before the monarchy) as broadly true.[2] Others, commonly referred to as minimalists, think that the story is mostly fiction; some even believe that little of it was written before the age of Alexander and his successors, in the fourth or early third century.[3] Most Old Testament scholars fall between these two extremes. Dating biblical material is extraordinarily difficult, and we have no manuscripts that go back into biblical times: the earliest are the Dead Sea Scrolls, from the second century BCE at the earliest, so dating can only be based on the contents of the biblical books, their style and their vocabulary – not on hard evidence such as the date of actual scrolls. So it is impossible to establish a complete consensus, and hard to avoid the impression that much reconstruction of the history of Israel depends on the temperaments of the scholars involved, whether sceptical or credulous, and often also on their religious stance – committed, indifferent, or hostile to the Bible as Scripture, that is, as a sacred text with the characteristics summarized above. We might despair of knowing anything worthwhile about the history, and hence (which is what concerns us here) of having a solid historical framework within which to decide when the various books of the Bible are likely to have been written. If there is no agreed history of the nation, then the history of its national literature cannot be written either.

This is unduly pessimistic. In fact the history of Israel can be reconstructed in some periods, and we can often tell when the biblical narrative approaches fiction and when it has roots in historical reality. The early history – that is, the period before the rise of the monarchy – is genuinely sketchy. The Bible presents the patriarchs (Abraham, Isaac, Jacob and his twelve sons) and the generation led by Moses as successive: Abraham comes to the Land, his descendants go to Egypt, then they return again under Moses. But we might detect here underlying, alternative traditions. Some of Israel's ancestors came from the east, from Mesopotamia or Syria, while others came from the west, from Egypt. Some scholars suggest that the Bible has arranged the traditions so as to give an impression that a single people had both experiences, but behind the unified story there lie two different stories belonging to two different groups.[4] Common to both groups is the belief that the Israelites were not native to Palestine, but were incomers from elsewhere, and this seems to be firmly fixed in the traditions behind the Pentateuch. But the stories reflect the experiences and folk-memories of people settling in the Land in the period we associate with the judges, the time just before the monarchy, rather than telling us much about the second millennium BCE. There is one reference to 'Israel' on a stele (victory inscription) found in Thebes in Egypt in 1896, belonging to the Egyptian pharaoh Merneptah and probably dated to about 1215 BCE, which indicates that a people calling itself by that name was already in Palestine in the thirteenth century, at that time under Egyptian rule. But we are told nothing more about them, and Israel is never mentioned again in any ancient Egyptian texts.

In the twentieth century some biblical archaeologists developed the theory that the stories of the patriarchs reflected customs known from second-millennium BCE texts – Mesopotamian documents, from the cities of Mari and Nuzi – rather than those current in later times in Israel. Hence, they argued, the stories must be genuine, or at least rest on traditions from that period. For example, there are three stories in Genesis where one of the patriarchs passes his wife off as his sister, which results in her being taken into the harem of a foreign ruler, to avoid his being killed (Genesis 12, 20, and 26):

> When he [Abram] was about to enter Egypt, he said to his wife Sarai, 'I know well that you are a woman beautiful in appearance; and when the Egyptians see you, they will say, "This is his wife"; then they will kill me, but they will let you live. Say you are my sister, so that it may go well with me because of you, and that my life may be spared on your account.'
>
> (Genesis 12:11–13)

It was argued that in Mari marriage between brother and sister did in fact occur, whereas in later times in Israel it was regarded as incestuous. Thus these stories would have to be 'pre-historic', and that would mean that we do have some information about the earliest ancestors of the Israelites.[5] More recently, however, this line of reasoning has been generally abandoned. In this particular case, the whole point of the story is that the woman in question is *not* the patriarch's sister: describing her as such is a ruse to protect him rather than a statement of fact, and hence presupposes that sisters could not also be wives – just as in historical times. We may still think that the patriarchal stories preserve some kind of folk-memory of earlier times, and indeed their names are notably not of a kind found later in Israel, suggesting that they are genuinely pre-monarchic. But exactly how old they are we cannot tell.[6]

Similarly, the names associated with the exodus from Egypt are in several cases unmistakably Egyptian. Moses occurs as an element in well-known Egyptian names such as Tut-mosis, and Aaron and Phinehas, other characters in the story, also bear Egyptian names. The exodus tradition must also preserve some kind of folk-memory that the Israelite ancestors spent time in Egypt; but these were not necessarily descendants of the patriarchal group that had originally come from the east, from Mesopotamia. Thus, as suggested above, we might be dealing with two parallel memories. It is not even clear which story is older than the other: if Merneptah's stele refers to a group that had settled under Moses' successor Joshua, while the patriarchal stories concern people settling under the leaders we call the judges, then the traditions in Exodus could actually be older than those in Genesis. The tribes ruled over by the judges bear the names of the twelve sons of Jacob, so the Genesis stories about these characters could easily reflect folk-tradition from the judges period. This is, however, speculative; it is possible that the narrative sequence the Bible offers us is correct.

All this may be felt to leave the biblical story of early Israel in tatters: what remains is the sense that the ancestors of the Israelites were not native to Palestine, but came in from elsewhere – much as did the Philistines in about the same period, probably from Crete. Recent archaeological work, however, has called even this in question.[7] Whereas the book of Joshua gives the impression that the Israelites conquered the Promised Land through a series of battles against the native Canaanites, excavations of early Israelite settlements reveal no break in population in the relevant periods: the population expanded, but there is no evidence of widespread destruction, and the crucial markers of identity such as pottery types continue uninterrupted. From this it seems that any incomers were probably few and far between. Unless some Israelites genuinely did owe their ancestry to people outside the Land, it is hard to see why such traditions should have developed, for it is hardly advantageous in most societies to present oneself as the child of immigrants.

But the archaeological evidence, combined with an analysis of the biblical narratives and what is known of how folk-memories are created, suggests that most later 'Israelites' were in fact Canaanites, that is, descendants of native inhabitants of the Land. The theological or ideological belief that all derived from those who had once come out of Egypt with Moses was the belief of a few, but was internalized by the nation at large in later times. So all Israel later celebrated the Passover and rejoiced in the deliverance from Egypt that Passover commemorates, even though many were the offspring of people who had never actually been there. Nation-building often involves the extension to all of folk-memories that originally affected only a few – much as Americans celebrate Thanksgiving, even though the majority are not the descendants of those who first did so, and indeed the historical background of most Americans follows a different trajectory.

Even when we come into the eleventh and tenth centuries BCE, the age of the first kings, it is not easy to be sure we have firm ground under our feet. Excavations in Jerusalem suggest that it was not a major city in this period,[8] even though it had been important as an administrative centre when Egypt ruled Canaan in the late second millennium BCE, the age of Merneptah's monument. The Bible's presentation of David and Solomon as emperors, subjugating all the surrounding nations and building on a lavish scale, therefore seems almost certain to be an exaggeration. The Old Testament contains copious stories about these two kings, as also about their predecessor Saul, but modern historians tend to think that the stories are quite novelistic in character, even though probably resting on some genuine historical information.

It is really only for the ninth and eighth centuries BCE that we have information in the Bible that can be substantiated from external records. Here the evidence shows the biblical account to be biased, but probably in touch with historical reality. The Assyrians record their relations with the northern kingdom of Israel, which they refer to as the 'house of Omri'. According to 1 Kings 16, Omri was a relatively unimportant king whose reign of twelve years was characterized chiefly by his disobedience to the God of Israel and his worship of foreign gods – a standard accusation against the kings of the north. But the Assyrian annals show that Omri was an important and powerful ruler: even into the eighth century the title 'house of Omri' continues as the name for Israel, and Jehu, a king who according to 2 Kings 9 actually overthrew Omri's dynasty, is identified as 'son of Omri' on the monument called the Black Obelisk (now in the British Museum in London), where he is shown doing homage to the Assyrian king, Shalmaneser III. The northern kingdom under Omri and his dynasty was prosperous and independent, and probably considerably more powerful than Judah, its poorer southern neighbour.[9]

The eighth century BCE is the moment when we have clear historical evidence for both kingdoms, and a majority of biblical specialists think that it is in this period that there were first significant writings. The stories of the earlier kings, as well as the folk-memories from the premonarchic age, were probably collected and edited around this time. From the eighth century too we have the words of prophets such as Amos, Isaiah, Hosea and Micah, however much their words have been overlaid with later additions, as we shall see in Chapter 4. It was a time when both kingdoms enjoyed a short respite from intervention by other powers. The Aramaeans, who had been so troublesome in the previous century, provided little opposition, while the Assyrians were preoccupied for some years with battles on other fronts, especially to their north where the state of Urartu was giving trouble. For a few decades, from about 760 to the 730s, Israel and Judah were free to enjoy peace and relative prosperity. The prophets, more far-sighted than others, already sensed that this prosperity would be short-lived; and so it proved. In 745 the Assyrian throne came to be occupied by Tiglath-pileser III, who had expansionist plans and began to push westwards; and by the end of the century the northern kingdom, always harder to rule than Judah and with no well-established dynasty, had been extinguished and turned into an Assyrian province. Judah (the size of an average English county) remained as the only viable part of the 'people of Israel', as the Judaeans continued to call themselves.[10]

In the seventh century we learn about the fortunes of Judah from the later chapters of 2 Kings, and also from extensive narrative sections of the book of Jeremiah, if these are reliable sources, as many Old Testament scholars think they are; certainly they tally well with Assyrian and Babylonian records. Assyria was conquered by Babylonia in 612 BCE (a victory reflected on in the biblical book of Nahum), but from the Judaean perspective this only made things worse. The last kings of Judah, before the Babylonian King Nebuchadnezzar finally annihilated it in the early years of the sixth century, seem to have believed they could avoid coming under the Babylonian yoke. Jeremiah, who prophesied during the last years of Judah, persistently told the leadership to accept Babylonian hegemony and not attempt foolhardy schemes to reassert their independence, but this was to no avail. In 598 BCE the

Babylonians invaded and took away the king, Jehoiachin, from Jerusalem, with many of his courtiers and officials.

> At that time the servants of King Nebuchadnezzar of Babylon came up to Jerusalem, and the city was besieged. King Nebuchadnezzar of Babylon came to the city, while his servants were besieging it; King Jehoiachin of Judah gave himself up to the king of Babylon, himself, his mother, his servants, his officers, and his palace officials. The king of Babylon took him prisoner in the eighth year of his reign.
>
> (2 Kings 24:10–12)

Eleven years later the king they set up in Jehoiachin's stead, his uncle Zedekiah, rebelled openly, egged on by unrealistic advisers, and this time the Babylonian army laid waste to Jerusalem, destroyed the Temple, and took Zedekiah away, blinding him after he had seen his sons executed. Judah ceased to exist as a state, though many people naturally remained in the Land, with a civil servant, Gedaliah, ruling over them from the city of Mizpah, north of the devastated Jerusalem. After only a few years Gedaliah was assassinated by a claimant to the throne, and after that we know no more of events in the homeland.

The exile in Babylonia probably involved only a fraction of the pre-exilic population of Judah, so there may be works in the Bible that derive from those who remained behind, such as the book of Lamentations (which is probably not by Jeremiah, as traditionally believed, but not far from his spirit). A leader of the exiled community seems to have been the prophet Ezekiel, and (as we shall see) significant literary work probably went on among the exiles. They were not imprisoned or punished, but were able to establish settlements: from then on there was always a Jewish presence in Babylonia. Jehoiachin was apparently still regarded as the legitimate king, and a cuneiform tablet (the Weidner Chronicle) records that provisions were allocated to him, confirming the account in 2 Kings 25:27–30:

> In the thirty-seventh year of the exile of King Jehoiachin of Judah, in the twelfth month, on the twenty-seventh day of the month, King Evil-merodach of Babylon, in the year that he began to reign, released King Jehoiachin of Judah from prison; he spoke kindly to him, and gave him a seat above the other seats of the kings who were with him in Babylon. So Jehoiachin put aside his prison clothes. Every day of his life he dined regularly in the king's presence. For his allowance, a regular allowance was given him by the king, a portion every day, as long as he lived.

From the next century we learn from the Murashu tablets (found in what is now southern Iraq) that the Jewish community had established businesses and even a bank, following Jeremiah's advice to settle down and acclimatize to the Babylonian environment (see Jeremiah 29).

How far there was communication with those left in Judah is unclear, though Ezekiel (exiled in 598) speaks of a messenger coming to him from Jerusalem when it fell in 587 (Ezekiel 33:21–2). But what is certain is that when Cyrus, king of Persia, defeated the last Babylonian king, Nabonidus, in 539, some Judaean exiles returned to the Land to re-establish national life there and even rebuild the Temple. The book of Ezra preserves what purport to be versions of a decree by Cyrus authorizing this, though many historians are sceptical about their authenticity.[11] At any rate, the Persian authorities evidently did not obstruct the initiative, and we learn from the prophets Haggai and Zechariah that by about 520 BCE the foundations of the new Temple were laid, and that the people were governed by a descendant of Jehoiachin called Zerubbabel and by a high priest called Joshua or Jeshua. From then on Jewish life had two foci: one in the diaspora – in Babylonia and other places, such as Egypt, to which Judaeans had fled after the fall of Jerusalem – and the other back in the homeland.

Of what happened during the long years of Persian rule over Israel we are badly informed. Various books of the Bible probably come from that time, including Job, Chronicles, probably indeed the whole Pentateuch in its finished form (many parts of it, as we shall see, are earlier in origin). But none reflects on the historical events of the period. Even the cataclysmic shift in power in the ancient Near East brought about by the rise of Alexander the Great is not commented on in the Bible, and it is only under his successors that we discover a palpable effect on the Jewish community. After Alexander died in 323 BCE, his empire was divided up among his generals. Palestine initially fell under the Ptolemaic rulers of Egypt, who appear to have governed the Jewish community benignly for all we can judge from the biblical evidence, scant as it is. But in the early second century BCE they were dislodged from their hegemony over the area by the Seleucid dynasty ruling in Syria.

In the 160s a ruler called Antiochus IV, who surnamed himself Epiphanes ('God made manifest'), decided that the Hellenization of the Jews – that is, their assimilation to Greek customs and ways of living – had not developed far enough, and began to enforce observance of practices that many Jews abhorred. Parents were forcibly prevented from circumcising their sons, the consumption of pork became mandatory as a test of loyalty to the empire, and Sabbath observance was forbidden. By now many Jews had assimilated and did not oppose these moves,[12] but a group of zealots, led by a family known as the Maccabees or 'hammers', took up arms against Antiochus. They rededicated the Temple, in which he had installed an image of Zeus, and for a time ruled over the Jewish state, which was thus independent for the first time in many centuries. Their dynasty was soon entangled in political wrangles, with the high priesthood up for sale, and in any case Jewish independence did not outlast the advent of the Romans in the Levant. Palestine became part of the Roman Empire, divided up under various local rulers all more or less vassals of the Roman power, until in 70 CE Jerusalem was sacked by the Roman army under Titus and the Jews no longer had a national state at all – just as had happened in the sixth century BCE.

When in this complicated history were the books of the Old Testament written? A rough consensus has arisen among specialists that biblical books are unlikely to go back much before the ninth or eighth century, the age of Omri, Elijah, Amos and Isaiah. As we have seen, before then 'Israel' was a vague entity with little centralized power: David and Solomon, who are said to have established a huge empire, have left almost no traces that archaeologists can examine, and receive no mention in the records of other nations in the region. Only in the ninth century do the Assyrians begin to speak of the 'house of Omri'. It seems improbable that Israel or Judah before then had the kind of royal administration that needed, and could train, scribes adept enough to write the biblical books.[13] Writing had indeed begun in Sumeria (southern Iraq) in the third millennium BCE, and around the same time in Egypt, so there is no reason in principle why even very early peoples should not have included those who could write. But writing in such societies was always the preserve of a specialized class of scribes: both cuneiform and hieroglyphic writing are too complex for widespread literacy to be plausible. The early Hebrew alphabet, by contrast, is quite simple, consisting of just twenty-two letters; yet still there is little evidence that literacy was widespread in ancient Israel before the seventh century BCE. (Almost our only earlier evidence is provided by the Gezer calendar, a brief text mentioning the seasons for various farming activities, discovered some twenty miles west of Jerusalem and generally dated to the tenth century BCE; but this does not demonstrate widespread literacy in this period.)

There is a lively scholarly debate about the importance of writing in ancient Israel, and of the possibility that scribal schools existed, as they certainly did in Mesopotamia and Egypt.[14] The books of the Old Testament are almost certainly the product of an urban elite, based in Jerusalem and perhaps other major cities such as Samaria, rather than folk-literature. They may well rest on earlier legends preserved orally and not only on earlier written documents such as state archives of the kind referred to in the books of Kings ('the book of the deeds of the kings of Israel/Judah'). Teasing out the development from oral tradition to written text is one of the most difficult tasks in biblical scholarship, and the results are at best tentative. As with any study of the classical world, we have no independent access to any oral traditions that may underlie the texts. Though it is fascinating to speculate on these, so far as the Bible as a book is concerned it is improbable that anything was written before the ninth century.

The books of what is now the Old Testament thus probably came into existence between the ninth and the second centuries BCE. This does not necessarily mean that the records of earlier ages are pure fiction, but it makes it hard to press their details as solid historical evidence. Many readers of the Bible would recognize that the stories of the early history of the world – Noah's Ark, the Tower of Babel – are mythical or legendary, but it may be more challenging to think that the stories of Abraham or Jacob or Moses are also essentially legends, even though people bearing those names may well have existed. No one is in a position to say they are definitely untrue, but there is no reasonable evidence that would substantiate them. This is also the case with the early kings, Saul, David and Solomon, even though the stories about them do make sense within a period (the eleventh and tenth centuries BCE) about which we know something, from the archaeological record. With the later, eighth- and seventh-century kings (for example, Hezekiah and Jehoiachin) there is definite corroboration from Assyrian and Babylonian records, and we are less in the dark. But even some of the stories of life after the exile, in the Persian period, may be fictional: most biblical scholars think that the book of Esther, for example, is a kind of novella rather than a piece of historical writing. A later date does not of itself mean that a given book is more likely to be accurate: much depends on its genre, as we shall see in the next chapter.

The biblical books of the Old Testament thus probably span a period of about eight centuries, though they may incorporate older written material – ancient poems, for example – and may in some cases rest on older, orally transmitted folk-memories. But the bulk of written records in ancient Israel seem to come from a core period of the sixth and fifth centuries BCE, with heavy concentrations in some particular ages: most think, for example, that the period of the exile was particularly rich in generating written texts, as was perhaps the early Persian age, even though we know so little about the political events of the time. The flowering of Israelite literature thus came a couple of centuries earlier than the classical age in Greece. The Old Testament, taken by and large, is thus older than much Greek literature, but not enormously so. Compared with the literature of ancient Mesopotamia or Egypt, however, Israelite texts are a late arrival.

THE TERM 'OLD TESTAMENT'

I have been referring to the body of texts in question here as 'the Old Testament', but the term is problematic. This is how Christians refer to it, by contrast with the New Testament (a term that goes back as far as Bishop Melito of Sardis (d. *c.*180 CE)). For Jews the New Testament is of course not part of their Scriptures at all, and so they tend to refer to the Old Testament as simply 'the Bible', or sometimes 'the Tanakh' (or Tenakh or Tanak), which is an acronym taken from the initial letters of the three sections into which the Bible is divided according to Jewish tradition: the Law (*torah*), Prophets (*nevi'im*) and Writings (*ketuvim*), including Psalms, Proverbs, Ezra-Nehemiah and Chronicles. In the world of academic biblical study there is much debate as to which term it is best to use. The problem with 'Old Testament' is that the word 'old' can be construed as negative or pejorative – 'these are the old Scriptures, but in the New Testament we now have some better ones'. This fits in with a long Christian tradition of what is known as supersessionism, the belief that Christianity has improved on and so supplanted Judaism, a view that is arguably implied in the New Testament Letter to the Hebrews, which describes Jesus as the 'mediator of a new covenant' (Hebrews 9:15) – *testamentum* is simply the Latin for covenant.

The solution in recent academic writing has tended to be to use the expression 'the Hebrew Bible' or 'the Hebrew Scriptures'. This has the advantage of not being a religious usage at all – it was coined, and is used, almost entirely within the academic world. It does leave the expression 'New Testament' somewhat stranded, since there is then nothing with which the word 'new' contrasts, but this is generally felt to be a price worth paying for a term that does not imply an adverse judgement on Judaism. As we shall see, it is inexact, because not everything in the Hebrew Bible is in fact in Hebrew. But it is a fair approximation to the truth. 'Old Testament', however, remains the normal term in popular usage, and within most Christian churches, and is the norm in printed Christian Bibles. This means that there is merit in continuing to use it, provided it is taken neutrally and without any implication of supersessionism; and there are Jewish scholars who are content to use it in that way. In this book 'Old Testament' and 'Hebrew Bible' are used more or less interchangeably, the former somewhat more in contexts in which these books are being seen as part of a larger Christian Bible, and the latter more when Jewish, or purely academic, perspectives are to the fore. But my own conviction is that 'Old Testament' is not tainted to the extent that it is unusable, and sometimes I treat it as the default term, given that this is what the majority of people in western culture have usually called these books.[15]

THE LANGUAGE OF THE OLD TESTAMENT

The word 'Hebrew', however, reminds us that most of these books were originally written in what is often called Biblical (sometimes Classical) Hebrew. Hebrew belongs to the Semitic language family, unrelated to European languages.* Semitic languages were spoken all over the ancient Near East, and this continues to be the case. The most important modern example is Arabic, which has developed into a major world language and, in its classical form, is known by many non-Semitic speakers because it is the language of the Qur'an. Hebrew belongs to the north-west branch of Semitic, along with other local languages of the southern Levant such as the now-defunct Ugaritic, Phoenician and Moabite. There are other branches: among East Semitic languages is Akkadian, the language of Assyria and the lingua franca of the whole Middle East until well into the first millennium BCE – Egyptians and Assyrians corresponded in Akkadian. (Sumerian, an earlier language in what is now Iraq, is not Semitic, and is not related to any other known language.) The ancient and modern languages of Ethiopia belong, like Arabic, to the South Semitic branch.

* 'Semitic' derives from the name Shem, one of the sons of Noah, who was thought of as the ancestor of the peoples of the Levant and Mesopotamia.

Another North-West Semitic language is Aramaic. There is sometimes a misapprehension that Aramaic derives from, or even is a late version of, Hebrew. In fact the languages are quite distinct though closely related, about as close as German and Dutch, or Spanish and Portuguese: clearly similar though not mutually comprehensible. But Aramaic is by far the more important in historical terms. It may have arisen in Syria (ancient Aram), but it too became a lingua franca across the Middle East, and in the first millennium even the Persians (whose own language was Indo-European) used it in correspondence and administration: this version is accordingly sometimes referred to as Imperial Aramaic. By the time of the New Testament it had replaced Hebrew as the language of everyday speech, and Jewish communities had begun to develop translations of the Hebrew Bible into Aramaic – these are known as targums (see Chapter 18). It is clear that Jesus and his followers would have spoken Aramaic, though they also knew the Bible in Hebrew. Aramaic survives as the liturgical language of the Assyrian Church of the East and the Syriac Orthodox Church, and in the form called Syriac[16] it is represented by a wide Christian literature, little known in the west but including much poetry and hymnology of high quality.

Knowledge of Hebrew never died out. It morphed into a form known as Mishnaic Hebrew, the language of the Mishnah, a collection of discussions of finer points of the Jewish Law or Torah that was codified in the early third century CE. There continued to be people able to speak and write Hebrew down to the twentieth century, when it was revived and developed in the form of Modern Hebrew, with many new words and constructions, as the national language of the state of Israel after 1947. In ancient times Hebrew was simply the local language of Israel and Judah, with no wider significance: it was the Bible that propelled it onto a larger stage.

The ability of many Jews in the first millennium BCE to read both Hebrew and Aramaic is strikingly illustrated in the Bible itself, because there are two biblical books that in their earliest extant states have passages in both languages: Ezra and Daniel (both among the later books of the Hebrew Bible).[17] In Daniel 2:4, the shift from Hebrew to Aramaic actually occurs in the middle of the verse, and the book then continues in Aramaic to the end of Chapter 7. There are various theories about why this should have happened, but it seems to indicate that the writer and readers could switch effortlessly from one language to the other, perhaps scarcely noticing the change, as multilingual people are known sometimes to begin a sentence in one language and finish it in another. Strictly speaking this means that the term 'Hebrew Bible' is a misnomer because the Bible is not exclusively in Hebrew, but it is an acceptable approximation to the truth.

As already mentioned, written Hebrew has only twenty-two letters, and these all principally indicate consonants. In ancient times, as also in modern Israeli Hebrew, vowels were not indicated. This might seem to make the language hard to read, but the vowels of Hebrew words are predictable more often than those in English ones, and in many sentences there is no more difficulty in reading a purely consonantal text than there would be in understanding an English sentence such as 'Hbrw wrtng ds nt hv vwls', especially when (as here) the context helps us to decipher it. Even so, from quite ancient times a custom arose of using a few of the letters to indicate vowels as well as consonants. Thus, for example, the letter *yodh*, which normally indicates the consonant *y*, could also stand for the vowels *e* or *i*, much as in English *y* can be either a consonant (as in *yellow*) or a vowel (as in *easy*). This practice became more common in later texts, and the Dead Sea Scrolls, originating in many cases from the first century BCE or so, make more use of these fuller spellings than does the Hebrew Bible in its now traditional form. Modern Hebrew continues this custom.

Well into the Christian era, Hebrew scribes began to develop a sophisticated system of marking vowels through dots and dashes over and under the letters ('vowel points'), which also happens in Arabic. This means that the Bible as we have it now does contain a full phonetic transcription of all the words. The fact that the system is much later than the texts it is used to write does not mean that it is unreliable: the pronunciation of the words was transmitted in the tradition of reading the Bible aloud, and what the Masoretes – the scribes who devised the system of vowel points – recorded was not invented by them. Modern biblical scholars tend to think that the vocalization, as it is known, is sometimes wrong, but overwhelmingly more often it is almost certainly right. The Masoretes, working in the sixth to tenth centuries CE in both Tiberias and Jerusalem in Palestine, and in Babylonia, developed techniques for making sure that their vocalization would be accurately transmitted by subsequent generations, with many marginal notes calling attention to anything surprising that scribes might be tempted to change. These notes are known as the Masorah.

Modern printed Bibles usually depend on a particular Masoretic manuscript, the Leningrad or St Petersburg Codex (referred to in biblical studies as L), from about 1008 CE. This is the oldest complete manuscript we possess, but much older fragments of many biblical books have been found among the Dead Sea Scrolls – in the case of the book of Isaiah, more or less the entire book was found there, and in more than one manuscript. These manuscripts, a good thousand years earlier than L, often differ in important ways from the texts familiar to us, though taken by and large they confirm that the transmission is remarkably accurate – we are clearly dealing with the same books, even if the wording is different in places or some passages are longer or shorter than in L. In two cases, Jeremiah and Psalms, there are really significant differences in the order and sometimes even the content of chapters, but this is the exception rather than the rule. Even the Dead Sea material is several centuries later than the original texts; as with writings from the world of Greece and Rome, so with the Hebrew Bible we do not have 'autographs', that is, texts from the hand of the original writers, but only later manuscripts. That is why there can be such controversy over the date of the original texts: they must be older than the Dead Sea Scrolls, but by how much is a matter for debate in each case.

Very little of what is set out in this chapter is controversial among biblical specialists. Some are much more optimistic about the reliability of the stories of early Israel in the Bible, but the general trend is towards scepticism about the accuracy of the narrative books of the Old Testament before the age of Amos and Isaiah, the eighth century BCE. What I have said about the Hebrew language, and the manuscript tradition, is not controversial at all. But the overall implications for the theme of this book are far-reaching, because the origins of the Bible, and particularly the Hebrew Bible, are thus rather obscure. Like any other collection of books from the ancient world, the Bible derives from many different periods and circumstances. Where it tells a historical story, it is not always accurate – partly because it contains legends, and partly because its account of history is governed by a commitment to various interests. The idea that the kingdom of Judah was more important than the kingdom of Israel, for example, is a theological or ideological rather than a historical judgement. The Hebrew Bible is not a book produced at one time, but an anthology of books, and, as we shall see, some of those books are themselves anthologies. Religious believers tend to think that it does have an overall coherence, as we saw in the Introduction, but this is hard to show empirically. When we dig back into the history of the Bible, what strikes us first is diversity and complexity.

2
Hebrew Narrative

There is great poetry in the Hebrew Bible; but more than a third is in prose – everything from Genesis to Esther. Prose narrative is the vehicle for relating the history of Israel and, indeed, that of the world, beginning with creation and ending in the period of Persian domination. The genius of classical Greek literature is the verse epic (Homer's *Iliad* and *Odyssey*), and the same is true of the epics of Mesopotamia such as *Gilgamesh*; but the characteristic mode of Hebrew literature is narrative in prose.[1]

The narratives tell a continuous story running from the creation of the world, Adam and Eve, Noah and the Flood and the Tower of Babel, through the history of Israel's ancestors, Abraham, Isaac and Jacob, the story of Joseph (all in Genesis), and the long accounts of the work of Moses (in Exodus, Leviticus, Numbers and Deuteronomy), on into the conquest of the Promised Land (Joshua). They go on to tell of the 'judges', who were local tribal leaders (Judges), and of the early kings (Samuel). The story continues into the periods of Assyrian and Babylonian domination (Kings), and ends with the exile. Chronicles offers an alternative account of the same period, from Adam to exile, though concentrating mostly on the time of the monarchy, and concluding with the possibility of exiled Jews returning to Jerusalem. After that the story is no longer continuous. Ezra and Nehemiah relate events under the Persian domination, as does Esther, but the sense of a coherent history is lost.

THREE STYLES OF HEBREW NARRATIVE

Hebrew narrative is not all of the same kind. We can easily distinguish three styles, which are quite apparent even in translation. Most of the narrative books, including nearly all the Bible stories most people know, are written in a plain, laconic style, in which hardly anything is said about the emotions or the appearance of the characters, and we are left to make our own deductions about what is going on beneath the surface.[2] God sometimes has a role in the plot, but often there is little about how he reacts to the events described: we are not told whether he approves or disapproves of what the characters do, but are left to infer it. I shall call this 'saga style', because it reminds me of the style of Icelandic sagas – and to some extent it also tends to deal with similar topics, such as family events. This is not a standard term in biblical studies, but the parallel with the clipped style of Icelandic saga seems to me to make it appropriate.

Here is an example, from the account of David becoming king over the northern kingdom of Israel in place of Saul's son, Ishbaal, through the actions of one of Saul's generals, Abner. David requires the restoration of his wife, who had been given to one of Saul's henchmen:

> Abner sent messages to David at Hebron, saying, 'To whom does the land belong? Make your covenant with me, and I will give you my support to bring all Israel over to you.' He said, 'Good; I will make a covenant with you. But one thing I require of you: you shall never appear in my presence unless you bring Saul's daughter Michal when you come to see me.' Then David sent messengers to Saul's son Ishbaal, saying, 'Give me my wife Michal, to whom I became engaged at the price of one hundred foreskins of the Philistines.'[3] Ishbaal sent and took her from her husband Paltiel the son of Laish. But her husband went with her, weeping as he walked behind her all the way to Bahurim. Then Abner said to him, 'Go back home!' So he went back.
>
> (2 Samuel 3:12–16)

As Jonathan Magonet comments, 'It is just a couple of sentences in the midst of these great negotiations and rivalries of kings – but in those sentences is summed up the tragedy of one man caught up in events beyond his control, whose life and love is destroyed in a moment, and who has no power at all to change things – he is simply dispensable.'[4] The writer makes no comment on any of this; he simply records the incident. Yet surely we are meant to get an impression of Paltiel's inconsolable state, of David's cruelty, and possibly also of his own love for Michal, who had stood by him in difficult times (see 1 Samuel 19:11–17).

Where saga style came from is a mystery. We possess almost no Hebrew texts outside the Bible until the Dead Sea Scrolls in the last couple of centuries BCE, apart from occasional inscriptions or fragments, so that the narratives in the Hebrew Bible are our only evidence for this style. This is very unlike the situation in Egypt or Mesopotamia, where there are thousands of texts in their original form, on papyrus or clay tablets respectively. For Israel, we have only the biblical texts, preserved in manuscripts much later than the original date of composition (see Chapter 12). We cannot say how the Israelites came to develop this sophisticated yet laconic style of narration in prose, and familiarity with the Bible can blunt our sense of how remarkable it is.

In other places we encounter narratives in which the divine attitude to human actions is made unmistakably clear, with overt judgements on whether the deeds of the characters in the story were right or wrong, though with little detail about what they actually did. This can be found in the frequent summarizing statements about the kings of Israel and Judah in the books of Kings. An example would be the treatment of Omri, king of the northern kingdom a century or so after David, in the first book of Kings:

> In the thirty-first year of King Asa of Judah, Omri began to reign over Israel; he reigned for twelve years, six of them in Tirzah. He bought the hill of Samaria from Shemer for two talents of silver; he fortified the hill, and called the city that he built, Samaria, after the name of Shemer, the owner of the hill. Omri did what was evil in the sight of the LORD; he did more evil than all who were before him. For he walked in all the way of Jeroboam son of Nebat, and in the sins that he caused Israel to commit, provoking the LORD, the God of Israel, to anger by their idols. Now the rest of the acts of Omri that he did, and the power that he showed, are they not written in the Book of the Annals of the Kings of Israel? Omri slept with his ancestors, and was buried in Samaria; his son Ahab succeeded him.
>
> (1 Kings 16:23–8)

We saw in the previous chapter that Omri was an important and successful king, so much so that the Assyrians were still calling Israel 'the house of Omri' a century later. Yet the author of Kings has little to say about him other than that he worshipped idols, and so caused Israel to be sinful – like his remote forebear Jeroboam, who reigned soon after Solomon in the tenth century. There is no descriptive narrative, only a summary of his deeds. The style of such passages is usually referred to as 'deuteronomistic', because they adopt criteria for judging people that seem to derive from the book of Deuteronomy, in which the importance of abolishing local sanctuaries where idols might be worshipped, and of centralizing worship at one place (presumably Jerusalem), is greatly stressed:

> You must demolish completely all the places where the nations whom you are about to dispossess served their gods, on the mountain heights, on the hills, and under every leafy tree. Break down their altars, smash their pillars, burn their sacred poles with fire, and hew down the idols of their gods, and thus blot out their name from their places. You shall not worship the LORD your God in such ways. But you shall seek the place that the LORD your God will choose out of all your tribes as his habitation to put his name there.
>
> (Deuteronomy 12:2–5)

Also characteristic of deuteronomistic style is the heaping up of synonyms for the law of God, for example:

> Now the word of the LORD came to Solomon, 'Concerning this house that you are building,[5] if you will walk in my statutes, obey my ordinances, and keep all my commandments by walking in them, then I will establish my promise with you, which I made to your father David. I will dwell among the children of Israel, and will not forsake my people Israel.'
>
> (1 Kings 6:11–13)

Later, in a prayer at the dedication of the newly built Temple, Solomon also speaks in deuteronomistic style himself:

> 'The LORD our God be with us, as he was with our ancestors; may he not leave us or abandon us, but incline our hearts to him, to walk in all his ways, and to keep his commandments, his statutes, and his ordinances, which he commanded our ancestors.'
>
> (1 Kings 8:57–8)

Deuteronomistic style also occurs frequently in the book of Jeremiah, and this may help to indicate that it arose in the seventh century, around the time of Josiah's reforms, which Jeremiah probably experienced. Its concentration on the law or *torah* of God as the focal point of religion is an early example of what became normal in Judaism and remains so to this day: the centrality of the right ordering of life according to divine direction in written ordinances. As we shall see in Chapter 5, this idea is celebrated in Psalms 19 and 119.

A third kind of style can be found in many passages, especially in the Pentateuch, and is normally dubbed priestly style. Here is an example, from the story of Israel's time in the wilderness under the leadership of Moses:

> On the day the tabernacle was set up, the cloud covered the tabernacle, the tent of the covenant; and from evening until morning it was over the tabernacle, having the appearance of fire. It was always so: the cloud covered it by day and the appearance of fire by night. Whenever the cloud lifted from over the tent, then the Israelites would set out; and in the place where the cloud settled down, there the Israelites would camp. At the command of the LORD the Israelites would set out, and at the command of the LORD they would camp. As long as the cloud rested over the tabernacle, they would remain in camp. Even when the cloud continued over the tabernacle for many days, the Israelites would keep the charge of the LORD, and would not set out. Sometimes the cloud would remain for a few days over the tabernacle, and according to the command of the LORD they would remain in camp; then according to the command of the LORD they would set out. Sometimes the cloud would remain from evening until morning; and when the cloud lifted in the morning, they would set out, or if it continued for a day and a night, when the cloud lifted they would set out. Whether it was two days, or a month, or a longer time, that the cloud continued over the tabernacle, resting upon it, the Israelites would remain in camp and would not set out; but when it lifted they would set out. At the command of the LORD they would camp, and at the command of the LORD they would set out.
>
> (Numbers 9:15–23)

We may feel that we had got the point somewhat before the end of this passage. This style is marked by ponderous repetition and a tendency to use set formulas, very different from the freedom and spontaneity of saga style. The association with priests is related to the fact that many of the biblical passages in this style concern matters of purity, worship and liturgy, rather than political or domestic events. The classic example of priestly style is the first chapter of Genesis:

> In the beginning God created[6] the heavens and the earth; the earth was a formless void and darkness covered the face of the deep, while a wind from God swept over the face of the waters. Then God said, 'Let there be light'; and there was light. And God saw that the light was good; and God separated the light from the darkness. God called the light Day, and the darkness he called Night. And there was evening and there was morning, the first day.
>
> And God said, 'Let there be a dome in the midst of the waters, and let it separate the waters from the waters.' So God made the dome and separated the waters that were under the dome from the waters that were above

the dome. And it was so. God called the dome Sky. And there was evening and there was morning, the second day.

And God said, 'Let the waters under the sky be gathered together into one place, and let the dry land appear.' And it was so. God called the dry land Earth, and the waters that were gathered together he called Seas. And God saw that it was good. Then God said, 'Let the earth put forth vegetation: plants yielding seed, and fruit trees of every kind on earth that bear fruit with the seed in it.' And it was so. The earth brought forth vegetation: plants yielding seed of every kind, and trees of every kind bearing fruit with the seed in it. And God saw that it was good. And there was evening and there was morning, the third day.

And God said, 'Let there be lights in the dome of the sky to separate the day from the night; and let them be for signs and for seasons and for days and years, and let them be lights in the dome of the sky to give light upon the earth.' And it was so. God made the two great lights – the greater light to rule the day and the lesser light to rule the night – and the stars. God set them in the dome of the sky to give light upon the earth, to rule over the day and over the night, and to separate the light from the darkness. And God saw that it was good. And there was evening and there was morning, the fourth day.

And God said, 'Let the waters bring forth swarms of living creatures, and let birds fly above the earth across the dome of the sky.' So God created the great sea monsters and every living creature that moves, of every kind, with which the waters swarm, and every winged bird of every kind. And God saw that it was good. God blessed them, saying, 'Be fruitful and multiply and fill the waters in the seas, and let birds multiply on the earth.' And there was evening and there was morning, the fifth day.

And God said, 'Let the earth bring forth living creatures of every kind: cattle and creeping things and wild animals of the earth of every kind.' And it was so. God made the wild animals of the earth of every kind, and the cattle of every kind, and everything that creeps upon the ground of every kind. And God saw that it was good. Then God said, 'Let us make humankind in our image, according to our likeness; and let them have dominion over the fish of the sea, and over the birds of the air, and over the cattle, and over all the wild animals of the earth, and over every creeping thing that creeps upon the earth.' So God created humankind in his image, in the image of God he created them; male and female he created them. God blessed them, and God said to them, 'Be fruitful and multiply, and fill the earth and subdue it; and have dominion over the fish of the sea and over the birds of the air and over every living thing that moves upon the earth.' God said, 'See, I have given you every plant yielding seed that is upon the face of all the earth, and every tree with seed in its fruit; you shall have them for food. And to every beast of the earth, and to every bird of the air, and to everything that creeps on the earth, everything that has the breath of life, I have given every green plant for food.' And it was so. God saw everything that he had made, and indeed, it was very good. And there was evening and there was morning, the sixth day.

Thus the heavens and the earth were finished, and all their multitude. And on the seventh day God finished the work that he had done, and he rested on the seventh day from all the work that he had done. So God blessed the seventh day and hallowed it, because on it God rested from all the work that he had done in creation.

(Genesis 1:1–2:3)

Here the same formulas are repeated – 'and it was so'; 'of every kind'; 'there was evening and there was morning' – and the narrative is carefully patterned: most days involve one act of creation, but the third and sixth each have two. (Some think that underlying this is a narrative of creation over eight days.) The prose is slightly mesmerizing as it takes its slow and stately course, and it altogether lacks the variety and freshness of saga style. The priestly writers seldom tell a story with varied characters and interesting incidents, but rather rehearse set pieces of ritualized events. The dignity and power of the writing is undeniable, as is the departure in style both from that of saga and from the work of the deuteronomistic school.

Priestly style presumably derives from those who controlled the Second Temple, or perhaps from their predecessors who, during the exile, worked to classify and elaborate the rules for Temple worship. The book of Ezekiel, who was a priest as well as a prophet and who worked among the exiles, has passages in a similar style, particularly in the regulations about life in the restored Promised Land in Ezekiel 40–48. The nearest modern analogy would be legal English, in which there is no attempt to avoid repetition or redundancy, since the essential thing is to be absolutely unambiguous.

We might expect to find whole books written in one or another of these styles, but this is not what we actually encounter in the Hebrew Bible. Even within a single account there may be two or even three different styles at work. An incongruous example is 1 Kings 2, which mixes saga and deuteronomistic styles to produce a puzzling speech by the dying King David:

When David's time to die drew near, he charged his son Solomon, saying, 'I am about to go the way of all the earth. Be strong, be courageous, and

> keep the charge of the LORD your God, walking in his ways and keeping his statutes, his commandments, his ordinances, and his testimonies, as it is written in the law of Moses, so that you may prosper in all that you do and wherever you turn . . .
>
> 'Moreover you know also what Joab son of Zeruiah did to me, how he dealt with the two commanders of the armies of Israel, Abner son of Ner, and Amasa son of Jether, whom he murdered, retaliating in time of peace for blood that had been shed in war, and putting the blood of war on the belt around his waist, and on the sandals on his feet. Act therefore according to your wisdom, but do not let his grey head go down to Sheol* in peace . . . There is also with you Shimei son of Gera, the Benjaminite from Bahurim, who cursed me with a terrible curse on the day when I went to Mahanaim; but when he came down to meet me at the Jordan, I swore to him by the LORD, "I will not put you to death with the sword." Therefore do not hold him guiltless, for you are a wise man; you will know what you ought to do to him, and you must bring his grey head down with blood to Sheol.'
>
> (1 Kings 2:1–3, 5–6, 8–9)

Whereas the basic speech (verses 5–9, the second paragraph above) seems to encourage Solomon, David's son and chosen heir, to settle old scores and kill David's arch-enemies (because he is a 'wise man'), the first paragraph, verses 1–3, tells him on the contrary to observe the law and commandments of Moses (which do not encourage political assassination), in a clearly deuteronomistic style. The best explanation of the contradiction is that the basic speech was composed earlier than the deuteronomistic passage, which was added by a later writer to tone down David's scandalous encouragement of bloody vengeance, and remake him in the mould of a preacher of the law. (Later stories about David in the books of Chronicles turn him into primarily a priest.) If this is correct, then 1 Kings 2 is not a unified, single text, but one that has been supplemented by a later writer. Such deuteronomistic insertions are not uncommon in the Hebrew Bible, and the German Old Testament scholar Martin Noth suggested in 1943[7] that the whole corpus of historical accounts from Joshua to 2 Kings had been thoroughly edited to make it read, taken as a whole, in a deuteronomistic mode: since his work it has been common to call these books, including Deuteronomy itself, the

* Sheol is the underworld, where people's spirits were thought to go after death, a place of shadows and no life.

'Deuteronomistic History'.[8] This editing or redaction did not by any means entirely purge the earlier material, and there are large portions of the text that are in saga style more or less throughout. The stories of Saul and David in 1 and 2 Samuel show very few signs of the deuteronomistic editing. Accordingly, both kings emerge as complex figures far removed from the stereotyping tendency of the deuteronomistic writers. They are presented as heroic yet flawed, and neither is an exemplar for how to obey God or act ethically. Elsewhere, especially in Judges and Kings, the deuteronomistic hand is more evident, perhaps most of all in the summary statements in which kings are either good or bad, according to whether or not they destroyed the local sanctuaries as Deuteronomy required.

Thus saga style seems to be older than deuteronomistic style: the more nuanced and complex stories preceded the more moralistic accounts and interpolations. Most scholars date the deuteronomistic style to the seventh or sixth centuries BCE, since the book of Deuteronomy itself (or some early version of it) has for a long time been thought to have a connection with the reforms of worship under King Josiah, dated according to 2 Kings 22:3 to about 621 BCE.[9] Josiah is said to have centralized the practice of sacrifice in Jerusalem, and this accords with the central requirement in Deuteronomy 12. Saga style, therefore, is earlier than this, and probably dates back to the eighth century, which, as we saw in Chapter 1, is about as old as Hebrew literature gets. This does not mean, however, that it did not continue to be used; it was not simply replaced with the deuteronomistic style, but rather overlaid with it in some cases. The Deuteronomistic History thus represents an editing of older stories to make them fit roughly the deuteronomistic agenda. Both styles are the work of learned scribes, but whereas the older saga writers were mostly drawing on old, perhaps largely oral materials or else composing freely, the deuteronomistic editors were taking existing writings and updating them in the light of their own concerns and preoccupations.

We encounter the priestly style most in the Pentateuch. Much material in this style consists of legal prescriptions, often about the details of Israel's worship: in fact the central section of the Pentateuch, from the middle of Exodus, through the whole of Leviticus and into the middle of Numbers, seems to have a priestly origin. In addition, there is priestly writing interwoven with older stories in saga style throughout Genesis and the first half of Exodus, where some of the well-known stories about the patriarchs and Moses exist in two versions, one in saga style and one in priestly. Genesis 2:4–25 preserves a saga-style version of the creation of the human race, which is different from Genesis 1:1–2:3 not only in details (man is created before woman, not at the same time, with the creation of the animals occurring between the two) but also, which concerns us more at present, in style: it is much more obviously a *story* than the priestly version. God talks to the man and gives him his orders (to avoid eating 'from the tree of the knowledge of good and evil'), and then experiments with creating the animals to be his companions; and when that fails to work, he creates the woman. God is much more a character in the story than the all-powerful figure in the priestly version of the creation. There are no repetitions or formulaic language in this second account.

INTERWEAVING

Confusingly, however, priestly and saga-style versions do not always stand alongside each other, but are sometimes conflated, to produce rather muddled stories. The classic example of this is the account of Noah's Flood[10] (Genesis 6–9), where there are discrepancies over the length of time the Flood lasted (forty days according to one version, a year according to the other), and also over how many animals went into the ark – a pair of each according to the priestly-style writer (Genesis 6: 19–20), but according to the other version seven pairs of ritually pure animals and one pair of impure ones (Genesis 7:2–3). Many details in both versions of the story go back into remote antiquity, and are already found in Mesopotamian versions of the Flood account such as the second-millennium Akkadian *Epic of Gilgamesh*[11] – for example, the dove and the raven that Noah sends out to see whether the waters have abated – so that neither of the Genesis writers is composing freely. But they do introduce their own nuances into the story. The priestly writer (conventionally known as P) is concerned with exact datings, fitting the account of Noah into a much larger chronological scheme that runs right through the Hebrew Bible, surfacing in later places such as 1 Kings 6:1. He also has a theory that none of the laws about purity were revealed until the revelation to Moses on Mount Sinai, and hence that the distinction between 'pure' and 'impure' animals made in the older account cannot yet have existed in the time of Noah. The result of the interweaving is that two coherent accounts have been added together to make one slightly incoherent one. The incoherence does not appear on a superficial reading, but as soon as one reads closely – imagining, for example, that one had to film the story, and hence attending to every detail – it soon becomes apparent that the account does not entirely hang together. Presumably (though no one really knows) the motivation for mixing the two versions is that the editor or editors of Genesis wanted to preserve both, which by their day were both venerable; but they could hardly set them down side by side as though there had been two great floods, so they wove one into the other. Whatever the motive, it seems clear that this is what they did. Textual weaving is something we shall encounter again in both the Old and New Testaments.

This gives us a key to how the Pentateuch was formed. If we leave aside the fifth book, Deuteronomy, which is largely a separate entity, Genesis-Numbers seems to be a combination of P and what is nowadays usually termed 'non-P' – the material in what I have been calling 'saga style'. Both P and non-P are traditionally seen as running right through Genesis-Numbers, and as having been continuous accounts of the early history of the Israelites. So the Pentateuch would have been compiled from at least three sources: P, non-P and Deuteronomy. We have already seen some of the characteristic vocabulary of deuteronomistic writing (statutes, testimonies, commandments, ordinances, laws), but P and non-P also differ in vocabulary as well as in style: P uses the expression 'to establish a covenant', non-P uses the curious formulation 'to cut a covenant'.

There is a further complication, in that non-P may itself be composite. Some scholars still follow a theory going back well into the eighteenth century,[12] according to which there were two distinct sources for the non-P material, one slightly older than the other. They differ on one major issue: the question when the Israelites began to use the name 'Yahweh' as the name of God.* One source (found in Genesis 4:26)

* 'Yahweh' is a modern surmise about the ancient pronunciation of the name of God, written YHWH in Hebrew. As explained in Chapter 1, in ancient times vowels were not marked; but once the dots and dashes that came to be used for vowels had been invented, a custom grew up (we do not know when) of indicating the vowels of *adonai* (Lord) on the consonants YHWH, since 'Lord' is what people by then had started to say. (Nowadays, observant Jews tend to say 'ha-shem', meaning 'the name'.) Christian attempts to pronounce this hybrid word as written resulted in the term 'Jehovah', a name which never existed in Judaism. The custom of saying 'the Lord', which passed into the Greek Bible, continues in modern Bibles in English, which generally indicate the name YHWH by translating it as 'the LORD' in capitals or small capitals ('the Lord'). There is some evidence that the name was anciently pronounced 'yahu' or 'yaho', since personal names ending in it often have this form (Hezekiah is in Hebrew *hizkiyahu*, for example), and some Greek texts speak of 'the god yao'. In Judaism the name may not be pronounced, and Christian commentators on the Bible often respect this prohibition by writing it in the unvocalized consonantal form YHWH.

thinks that people began using this name well before the patriarchs, whereas the other (in Exodus 3:13–15) holds that it was revealed for the first time to Moses, which is also the priestly theory (in Exodus 6:2–3). Consistently with this, the first source freely uses the name before Moses, whereas the second, like P, restricts it to the time after Moses has had it revealed to him at the burning bush. Because the name Yahweh is spelled *Jahwe* in German, and it was German scholars who developed and refined the theory of sources, the first source was called J. The second was called E, after the Hebrew word *elohim*, which is the Hebrew for 'God' rather than a proper name, and is the form used in the second source. If Deuteronomy, together with the occasional deuteronomistic passage in the earlier books of the Pentateuch, is called D, then we have the letters JEDP to describe the sources from which the Pentateuch was assembled.

In the nineteenth century much work was done to try to establish the relative dates of the four sources. The initial assumption had been that P, which contains all the legal rules for the sanctuary and its worship, and for forbidden foods, was the oldest source, but through the work especially of Julius Wellhausen (1844–1918)[13] it came to be thought that P actually postdated the other sources and was later than the return from exile, thus deriving from the sixth or fifth century BCE. This was chiefly because the historical books that recounted the history of Israel before the exile seemed unaware of the whole system of purity, sacrifices and dietary regulations found in P. This was a contentious conclusion at the time and remains so today, because P is in many ways the foundation of later Judaism, and in suggesting that it was so late Wellhausen seemed to some to be anti-Jewish or even anti-Semitic. He described P as the foundation document not of ancient Israelite religion but of Judaism, implying a lack of continuity between the two. There is no doubt that he regarded the Judaism of P as a decline from the religious insights of, for example, the great prophets, who were in his view nearer to the spirit of J and D. But this value judgement is essentially separable from questions of date: one could accept his late dating of P and yet regard it as religiously profound, even as an improvement on the rough-and-ready religious attitudes in J and E. There are large issues of theological belief and judgement at stake in the dating of P, and it remains one of the few areas of biblical study in which Christian and Jewish Hebrew Bible scholars often remain some distance from each other.

The theory of a separate J and E has been enjoying a revival in recent years from a group sometimes known as the neo-documentarians,[14] but probably a majority of scholars tend to talk merely of P and non-P, and to regard non-P as the earlier material. A widespread view in recent German scholarship[15] is that non-P never existed as a continuous source at all, but consists of blocks of formerly independent stories. The stories of Abraham, Isaac, Jacob, Joseph and Moses may not have originally existed as a continuous saga in any source, but may have circulated independently of each other in different groups until the editor of the Pentateuch, after the exile, arranged them in sequence. This would fit with the suggestion made in Chapter 1 that Abraham's arrival in Palestine from the east, and the trek of Moses and the people with him from the west, may not really have happened in that order, but may be contemporaneous – or even that Abraham and his descendants may have lived after Moses. They may belong to the period we normally call the time of the judges, in the eleventh century, when we hear of tribes named after the twelve sons of Jacob. But however the non-P material came together, its distinctiveness from P and from D is not in doubt; its style, as we have seen, is quite different from either, and my own view is that it is largely from pre-exilic times.[16]

Recently there has been a tendency among Old Testament scholars to propose later dates for large parts of the Hebrew Bible than had been usual, and accordingly some now date even non-P after the exile, during the period of Persian domination. If that were so, non-P and P might not be respectively earlier and later, but contemporaneous and deriving from different schools of thought.[17] Either way, it remains true that some scribes took it upon themselves to weave the two accounts together, while leaving much of each source intact.

The other narrative books also show signs of having been compiled from earlier materials, with inconsistent versions of the same story. How, for example, did David come to know King Saul? In 1 Samuel 16 he is introduced to Saul as a lyre-player, but in 1 Samuel 17, when he kills Goliath, it is clear that Saul has not met him before. Even so, there are long stretches of highly coherent narrative. In the so-called Court History of David in 2 Samuel 9–20,[18] which describes the palace intrigues involved in the succession to David,[19] the characterization and the complexity of the plot approach novelistic skill, and there is little evidence of multiple sources. As in so much non-priestly narrative in the Bible, the reader is strongly drawn into the story and shares the emotions of the characters, even though these are indicated only through actions rather than any authorial comment on their thoughts. When David's son Absalom rebels against him and is killed by Joab, one of David's generals, we see that it brings no joy to David:

> Then the Cushite [Ethiopian messenger] came; and the Cushite said, 'Good tidings for my lord the king! For the LORD has vindicated you this day, delivering you from the power of all who rose up against you.' The king said to the Cushite, 'Is it well with the young man Absalom?' The Cushite answered, 'May the enemies of my lord the king, and all who rise up to do you harm, be like that young man.'
>
> The king was deeply moved, and went up to the chamber over the gate, and wept; and as he went, he said, 'O my son Absalom, my son, my son Absalom! Would that I had died instead of you, O Absalom, my son, my son!'
>
> It was told Joab, 'The king is weeping and mourning for Absalom.' So the victory that day was turned into mourning for all the troops; for the troops heard that day, 'The king is grieving for his son.' The troops stole into the city that day as soldiers steal in who are ashamed when they flee in battle.
>
> (2 Samuel 18:31–19:3)

As described above, one passage in the Deuteronomistic History (1 Kings 2) represents a story in saga style that has been overlaid by the hand of the deuteronomistic writers, to make it more orthodox and complimentary in its teaching about the character of King David. The whole History probably passed through this process more than once. Most American scholars believe that there was a first edition in the seventh century, in the reign of King Josiah, and another after the beginning of the exile;[20] while in Germany the 'Göttingen school' holds that it went through at least two subsequent revisions, introducing respectively more prophetic and more priestly concerns.[21] In general there is reason to be sceptical of theories that posit a very large number of editions, since copying out a text in ancient times was a laborious process, and two or three major revisions, plus perhaps odd additions in the margin, are about as many as is credible.[22] It has to be remembered that we have no texts containing anything but the final version; all earlier editions are hypothetical, unless and until a manuscript is found containing one. That does not mean that the hypothesis is unreasonable, however; the evidence that biblical narrative is often composite, and hence must result from a scribe copying out an earlier text and introducing additions or changes, is plain to see, once we look closely.

A further example of interweaving may make this clearer. Take Exodus 24:

> 1. Then he said to Moses, 'Come up to the LORD, you and Aaron, Nadab, and Abihu, and seventy of the elders of Israel, and worship at a distance. 2. Moses alone shall come near the LORD; but the others shall not come near, and the people shall not come up with him.' 3. Moses came and told the people all the words of the LORD and all the ordinances; and all the people answered with one voice, and said, 'All the words that the LORD has spoken we will do.' 4. And Moses wrote down all the words of the LORD. He rose early in the morning, and built an altar at the foot of the mountain, and set up twelve pillars, corresponding to the twelve tribes of Israel. 5. He sent young men of the people of Israel, who offered burnt offerings and sacrificed oxen as offerings of well-being to the LORD. 6. Moses took half of the blood and put it in basins, and half of the blood he dashed against the altar. 7. Then he took the book of the covenant, and read it in the hearing of the people; and they said, 'All that the LORD has spoken we will do, and we will be obedient.' 8. Moses took the blood and dashed it on the people, and said, 'See the blood of the covenant that the LORD has made with you in accordance with all these words.' 9. Then Moses and Aaron, Nadab, and Abihu, and seventy of the elders of Israel went up. 10. And they saw the God of Israel. Under his feet there was something like a pavement of sapphire stone, like the very heaven for clearness. 11. He did not lay his hand on the chief men of the people of Israel; also they beheld God, and they ate and drank. 12. The LORD said to Moses, 'Come up to me on the mountain, and wait there; and I will give you the tablets of stone, with the law and the commandment, which I have written for their instruction.' 13. So Moses set out with his assistant Joshua, and Moses went up into the mountain of God. 14. To the elders he said, 'Wait here for us, until we come to you again; for Aaron and Hur are with you; whoever has a dispute may go to them.' 15. Then Moses went up on the mountain, and the cloud covered the mountain. 16. The glory of the LORD settled on Mount Sinai, and the cloud covered it for six days; on the seventh day he called to Moses out of the cloud. 17. Now the appearance of the glory of the LORD was like a devouring fire on the top of the mountain in the sight of the people of Israel. 18. Moses entered the cloud, and went up on the mountain. Moses was on the mountain for forty days and forty nights.
>
> (Exodus 24:1–18, slightly altered from the NRSV)

A casual reading leaves us with a general impression that Moses and others went up Mount Sinai, that he received laws which he passed on to the people, and that a select group had a meal in God's presence. But if we start to look more closely, there are oddities. How many times did Moses go up the mountain, without coming down again in between? If he went up in verse 9, how can he have been told to go up in verse 12; and again, if he went up in verse 15, how can he have gone up again in verse 18?

Who went up the mountain with him? According to verses 1 and 9, it was Aaron, Nadab and Abihu, with seventy elders; but according to verse 13 it was Joshua (not previously mentioned), while Aaron and Hur (also not previously mentioned) stayed with the elders, who did not go up with Moses. Then in verse 18 Moses seems to go up alone.

When did Moses receive the laws for the people? In verses 3–8 he already has a book that God has given him, and the people promise to obey its laws. Yet in verse 12 he is instructed to come up the mountain to receive the book, or, rather, tablets of stone.

There is also a difference in the way God is identified: in verses 9–11 he is 'God' (*elohim*), but in verses 15–18 he is 'the LORD' – Yahweh. As we have seen, this is one of the distinguishing marks between the sources of the Pentateuch.

As with the Flood narrative, so here there seem to be several more or less coherent stories that have been interwoven. Verses 12–15 give one straightforward account, in which Moses has his assistant Joshua with him, and the two of them are summoned to go up the mountain, leaving Aaron and Hur to act in their place. Verses 16–18 tell of a solitary ascent by Moses, when the mountain is shrouded in cloud, and God's presence is like fire. Verses 1–11 are a third story, in which Moses has already received the law, but then goes up with an entourage to enjoy a meal in God's presence; in this account not only Moses but all the leaders see God, and suffer no harm as a result. The chapter as it stands blends all these accounts together to create its impression of rather vague incidents happening in no particular sequence, but underlying it are three entirely simple stories, each with a different emphasis and even a different idea of God and his relation to the people to whom he reveals himself – besides a different recollection of who the important leaders were during Israel's time in the wilderness.

It can be argued that the account, however muddled, makes some religious points that are what really matter: about the authority of Moses, the centrality of the law, and the sublimity of God. No one of course is obliged to take an interest in the pre-history of the text. But once the difficulties have been noticed, anyone with an enquiring mind is likely to want to know how they came about, and some kind of analysis into several sources for the passage is likely to suggest itself. The question why a scribe wove the three stories together as he did, making an incoherent narrative in place of three coherent ones, follows. The best suggestion to date, as I see it, is that he wanted to ensure that no piece of tradition got lost. He was not writing a coherent story of Moses, like a modern biographer, but collecting pieces of Moses tradition and working them together to keep them safe.[23] This means that he did not see the finished text as a consistent work, as we do with novels or historical accounts, but as something more like an archive.

THE PRIMARY HISTORY AND OTHER NARRATIVES

Thus we have two great narrative works, the Pentateuch and the Deuteronomistic History, covering between them everything in the Hebrew Bible from Genesis to Kings – sometimes the whole of this is referred to as the Primary History. This distinguishes it from a compilation that is universally regarded as much later, the work of the Chronicler (1 and 2 Chronicles). Chronicles covers the same period as the Primary History, from creation (or at any rate Adam) to the end of the exile, though much of the history is dealt with simply by genealogies with minimal narrative – lists of significant names with tiny snippets of story intermingled. The story of Israel ends not with the exile, as does the Deuteronomistic History in 2 Kings 25, but with the permission by the Persian King Cyrus for the exiled nation to return to the Land: the last word of 2 Chronicles (36:23) is *veya'al*, 'then let him go up', that is, let anyone who wishes return from exile. In the Jewish arrangement of Scripture this is actually the final word in the Bible, speaking of hope after despair (see Chapter 13).

There is widespread agreement that the author of Chronicles had little independent material on which to draw, but largely simply rewrote the older history to bring it in line with his own concerns, concentrating on Israel's liturgical worship, and striving to show that people get what they deserve – rather more than the messier older stories do.[24] One problem for readers of the Deuteronomistic History, for example, is the case of King Manasseh of Judah, who lived in the seventh century. Second Kings 21 records that he was a king of almost unparalleled wickedness, who not only worshipped idols but actually burned his own son as a sacrifice.[25] Yet Manasseh had the longest reign of any

Judaean king (fifty-five years according to 2 Kings 21:1). For the Chronicler, this was a theological problem: surely God would not permit such an evil king to enjoy so long a reign? The solution is to invent a story about Manasseh's repentance. In 2 Chronicles 33 Manasseh is carted away to Babylon by the king of Assyria, as he thoroughly deserves; but

> While he was in distress he entreated the favour of the LORD his God and humbled himself greatly before the God of his ancestors. He prayed to him, and God received his entreaty, heard his plea, and restored him again to Jerusalem and to his kingdom. Then Manasseh knew that the LORD indeed was God.
>
> (2 Chronicles 33:12–13)

A much later text, the Prayer of Manasses, which is in the Greek Old Testament and hence in the Protestant Apocrypha, but not in either the Jewish or the Latin Bible, purports to be the very words of penitence that Manasseh spoke.

There are two other types of narrative in the Hebrew Bible. The books of Ezra and Nehemiah relate, in slightly garbled form, some of the events in the community that returned from exile, and in both cases some of the story is told in the first person (Ezra 7:27–9:15; Nehemiah 1–7 and 13). Biblical scholars have (perhaps credulously) often tended to trust the first-person narrative to be broadly reliable, accepting that it genuinely derives from these two figures, though exactly when and how they operated remains obscure. They must have been active in the fifth or, conceivably, fourth century BCE, and are presented as authorized by the Persian king to administer the affairs of what was by then the Persian province of Yehud (Judah). As with the books of Chronicles, the Hebrew of these books shows signs of its lateness as compared with the saga-style ones, with a number of loan words from Aramaic; and, as noted in Chapter 1, a couple of passages in Ezra are actually entirely in Aramaic.

Then there are what are now usually called Jewish novels,[26] the short tales about probably fictitious characters: Ruth, Jonah, Esther and the stories in Daniel 1–6 (and in the Apocrypha, Tobit and Judith). These books show every sign of having been composed as finished wholes, with a consistent narrative flow and well-constructed plots, and few signs that they rest on older folk-tales or oral traditions. They probably come from the Persian or even Hellenistic periods, that is, from somewhere between the fifth century and the second century BCE. Most modern scholarship treats them as deliberate fiction rather than as even potentially historical: they are on the whole 'tall tales', with Jonah swallowed by a great fish and then vomited up alive, Esther defeating a plot against the Jews in which vast numbers of people were to have been slaughtered, and Daniel escaping from a den of lions unharmed. Even comparatively conservative readers are not always convinced that the stories are historical, and are sometimes willing to see them more as parables or edifying tales rather than as history – though there are still many who continue to take an interest in supposed enormous fish in the Mediterranean, capable of swallowing a man.

Current scholarly study of the narrative books is polarized. Some scholars, especially in the German-speaking world, though also in North America and Israel, still concentrate on questions of origin and development, producing highly complex theories about the way oral and written materials have come together to form the books as we now have them.[27] Others, particularly in North America, are much more interested in literary aspects of these texts, and tend to read them synchronically, that is, as finished wholes and as great literature, without any regard to questions of origin or development.[28] In neither camp is there anything like consensus on the most fruitful conclusions these two approaches can achieve. The first is interested in how the Bible came into existence, the second with how it can be read in its finished form. If there is any agreement, it is that the narrative books are a highly important part of the Old Testament, and should not be subordinated, as they were in some traditional Christian readings, to the books of the prophets. (Early Christian writers cited the historical books rather little in comparison with the prophets.[29]) The fact that the Bible contains narrative is part of its particular character, differentiating it from later creeds and doctrinal definitions. Some of the narrative makes contact with history, providing us with evidence for the life of ancient Israel; but much is either fiction or artfully constructed story, even when there is a core of historical reality behind the accounts.

THE PURPOSE OF HEBREW NARRATIVE

How were the narrative books *used* in ancient Israel? Most scholars think that they were read aloud, since literacy was not widespread, and this may imply a liturgical context, perhaps at one of the annual festivals celebrated in Jerusalem both before and after the exile of the sixth century BCE. The stories of the decline and fall of the two kingdoms, Israel and Judah, in the books of Kings, may have functioned as a kind of national lament or confession of collective guilt.[30] During the Persian period synagogues – buildings where Jews assembled for prayer and study – seem to have come into existence, and certainly by New Testament times their liturgy included readings from the historical books, though in a selective way. Judaism was already moving in the direction of an emphasis on study of texts and non-sacrificial prayer at a local level, even while the Second Temple still stood and was functioning as a place of daily sacrifice. Early Christians too read some sections of the historical books in their own liturgical celebrations, as part of the record of God's history with his people from ancient times. Liturgy was indeed to be one of the main contexts in which later Jews and Christians encountered the Bible.

How can narrative books be *religiously* important, and how were they important for religious thought in ancient Israel? Certainly not as what we might call teaching: possibly as providing examples of how to live, but for this the Old Testament narratives are often too complex to be directly helpful. (It would, for example, be hard to draw out advice on living a good life from the story of Moses' various ascents of Mount Sinai discussed above.) They may well have functioned to draw people in and engage them in a narrative world that leads to no definite conclusions but illuminates the human condition obliquely. If so, this is very far from how they have been read in some strands of later Judaism and Christianity, where they have often been simply reduced to a source for ethical guidance and instruction.

Modern biblical scholarship has rediscovered the story element in what are traditionally called the historical books, recognizing that we cannot read off the history of Israel from them in any simple way. They are important as a way of establishing the identity of the people of Israel, rather than as archival material: they are national literature. The historical books often contribute to our understanding of the history of the nation through the insight they give into how events and social movements were understood in the time when they were written, rather than by providing reliable information about the history of the time they purport to describe. This realization arrived early in the case of Chronicles, which scholars for a long time have treated mainly as evidence for religious attitudes, and attitudes to history, in the Persian age, rather than as telling us much that is reliable about the sweep of history that it surveys. The idea that the Primary History was similarly a work of the imagination, informing us about Israelite thought from the eighth to the sixth or fifth century BCE rather than about the ancestors of

Israel and their kings from the second millennium onwards, arrived rather later, but is now commonplace. It is still sometimes shocking to committed Jews or Christians, who see it as an attack on the status and authority of the Bible. But most non-conservative believers long ago accepted that Genesis 1, for example, is not true in the sense of being an accurate account of the creation of the world, and scepticism about the details of the narrative books in general can coexist, as does this realization about Genesis 1, with continuing respect for the texts as religiously inspiring and informative. It leaves a question: how far can we go along a sceptical path before losing touch with traditional use and understanding of the Bible altogether? I shall return to this issue, and other great issues raised by the style of modern biblical study, at the end of the book.

3
Law and Wisdom

One of the reasons why people read the Bible is to find guidance on how to live. We have seen that the narratives in the Hebrew Bible only occasionally provide direct advice on this; most often they are more oblique in their approach. The Bible does, however, contain material that gives advice or even instructions in a much more unequivocal way. Two genres of literature can be seen to do this: wisdom and law.

WISDOM IN THE HEBREW BIBLE AND IN THE ANCIENT NEAR EAST

It has long been traditional to group together certain books in the Bible under the heading 'wisdom': Proverbs, Ecclesiastes and Job, and in the Apocrypha, Sirach or the Wisdom of Jesus son of Sira (also known as Ecclesiasticus) and the Wisdom of Solomon.[1] All these books contain many short sayings or aphorisms, summing up the fruits of experience or giving explicit advice on how to behave. Many seem to reflect life in a village or small community, and draw 'morals' from activities such as farming:

> The field of the poor may yield much food,
> but it is swept away through injustice.
>
> (Proverbs 13:23)

> Like vinegar to the teeth, and smoke to the eyes,
> so are the lazy to their employers.
>
> (Proverbs 10:26)

> The righteous know the needs of their animals,
> but the mercy of the wicked is cruel.

Those who till their land will have plenty of food,
  but those who follow worthless pursuits have no sense.

(Proverbs 12:10–11)

Many of these proverbs are paralleled in other cultures, and could be seen as part of a popular understanding of the world, like our own 'Too many cooks spoil the broth' or 'Look before you leap'.

But some sayings seem better suited to the culture of the royal court than that of the Israelite village:

When you sit down to eat with a ruler,
  observe carefully what is before you,
and put a knife to your throat
  if you have a big appetite.

(Proverbs 23:1–2)

Wise warriors are mightier than strong ones,
  and those who have knowledge than those who have strength;
for by wise guidance you can wage your war,
  and in abundance of counsellors there is victory.

(Proverbs 24:5–6)

Like the heavens for height, like the earth for depth,
  so the mind of kings is unsearchable.

(Proverbs 25:3)

Do not put yourself forward in the king's presence
  or stand in the place of the great;
for it is better to be told, 'Come up here',
  than to be put lower in the presence of a noble.

(Proverbs 25:6–7)

This has led to something like a consensus among biblical specialists that the collection of proverbs into books probably occurred at the king's court in Jerusalem, rather than in rural communities, even though some of the material originated there as a folk-wisdom or folk-morality. This is rendered all the more likely by the fact that we know that cities in ancient Egypt and Mesopotamia produced collections of aphorisms, a great number of which have been found in modern times. These collections were the work of scribes, people who were not merely literate but who made a living by writing, usually in royal employment.

The Egyptian material in particular spans a long period. If it really goes back to the royal vizier after whom it is named, the *Instruction of*

Ptah-hotep could come from the third millennium BCE, whereas the *Instruction of Amen-em-opet* is possibly from as late as the seventh century BCE. There is a section of the biblical book of Proverbs (Proverbs 22:17–24:22) that is so close to *Amen-em-opet* that it must have been borrowed from the Egyptian document, though this presents difficulties (were there Israelite scribes who could read Egyptian?). One striking parallel concerns the sanctity of boundaries:

> Do not remove an ancient landmark
> or encroach on the fields of orphans,
> for their redeemer is strong;
> he will plead their cause against you.
>
> (Proverbs 23:10–11)

> Do not carry off the landmark
> at the boundaries of the arable land,
> nor disturb the position of the measuring-cord;
> Be not greedy after a cubit of land,
> nor encroach upon the boundaries of a widow.
>
> (*Amen-em-opet* 6)

Furthermore, Proverbs 22:20 describes what follows as consisting of 'thirty sayings' (hard to demarcate exactly), which corresponds to the thirty 'chapters' in *Amen-em-opet*. In all about half the contents of the two documents are close enough for us to be sure there is a literary connection.

This opens up an important possibility about the social organization of Israel in the time of the kings. Though there is no explicit evidence for it, either textual or archaeological, it seems likely that Israel (both kingdoms, probably), like Egypt, must have had schools for the education of scribes. By scribes is meant not simply writers, but what we would call secretaries in every sense of that term, ranging from literate people who could write a simple letter up to Secretaries in the royal chancellery: the 'officials of King Hezekiah' who are said in Proverbs 25:1 to have written out various proverbs would probably come into this latter category. In other words, Israel in monarchic times had a civil service, and the people who produced collections of proverbs, like their Egyptian counterparts, belonged to this stratum of society. The attribution of the book of Proverbs to King Solomon would make sense in this context, with the king acting as a kind of patron for the works of his officials.

Even though Proverbs may thus go back to an apparently secular institution, the Israelite civil service, it often reflects theological thinking. True, none of the proverbs in the book is attributed to God as its source: these are not divine utterances, as the words of prophets claim to be, but human reflection on life. Yet such reflection often included thinking about the divine hand operating in human affairs. One theory suggests that the very oldest proverbs are purely secular observations on life, while later ones introduce a more moralizing tone, and the most recent stratum in the book becomes overtly theological.[2] A saying such as 'If you have found honey, eat only enough for you, or else, having too much, you will vomit it' (Proverbs 25:16) would be a purely empirically based observation; whereas 'Like snow in summer or rain in harvest, so honour is not fitting for a fool' (Proverbs 26:1) would belong to the moralizing stratum; while 'Do not be wise in your own eyes; fear the LORD, and turn away from evil' (Proverbs 3:7) would be part of the third, theological stage in the development of wisdom, when it ceased to be the preserve of either folk-teachers or royal officials and became part of the religious culture of Israel.

Tidy as it is, this is rather speculative. The Egyptian parallels, for what this is worth, tend in the opposite direction: the earliest Instruction (*Ptah-hotep*) is in many ways more openly theological than the latest (*Amen-em-opet*). We probably cannot arrange the proverbs on a timeline of this kind, though it is fair to note that it is definitely not until the Persian and even Hellenistic age that wisdom literature starts to refer to the specific experiences of Israel, and so to its unique theological traditions. Thus the Wisdom of Solomon, a book written in the first century BCE and found in the Apocrypha in most Bibles, surveys the history of Israel at length in chapters 10–19, and Ecclesiasticus or Sirach runs through the great heroes of the nation's history in chapters 44–9, the passage beginning 'Let us now praise famous men' (KJV/AV). But where God (or Yahweh) appears in Proverbs, it is never with reference to the exodus or the exile or any other historical experience of the nation, only to the place of the divine in the life of individuals or families. In that sense Israel's proverbs are timeless, not reflecting any particular period of the nation's history, and dating them is therefore difficult. In any case some of them probably go back to time immemorial, even though their collection into a corpus is much more recent.

Proverbs contains several smaller collections (1–9; 10:1–22:16; 22:17–24:22; 24:23–34; 25–29; 30; and 31) that have been included in the final version of the book, and these may have originated at different times. Chapters 1–9 are often regarded as the latest collection, consisting not of individual sayings but of short paragraphs making consecutive sense:

My child, if you accept my words
  and treasure up my commandments within you,
making your ear attentive to wisdom
  and inclining your heart to understanding;
if you indeed cry out for insight,
  and raise your voice for understanding;
if you seek it like silver,
  and search for it as for hidden treasures –
then you will understand the fear of the LORD
  and find the knowledge of God.

(Proverbs 2:1–5)

It would be difficult to extract a single 'message' from Proverbs. On the whole it teaches a temperate, equable lifestyle, rather as the Egyptian *Instructions* commend the 'quiet man' who 'lets his heart go into its shrine' and does not make a fuss. But beyond that its teaching is varied, one may say dialogical:[3] it often sets up opposing points of view without telling the reader how to choose between them. Thus bribery is condemned:

Those who are greedy for unjust gain
  make trouble for their households,
but those who hate bribes will live.

(Proverbs 15:27)

The wicked accept a concealed bribe
  to pervert the ways of justice.

(Proverbs 17:23)

Yet it is also observed that a bribe can ease the way in the necessary transactions of life:

A gift opens doors;
  it gives access to the great.

(Proverbs 18:16)

A gift in secret averts anger;
  and a concealed bribe in the bosom, strong wrath.

(Proverbs 21:14)

Getting rich is commended, and the poor are pitied as having no friends; yet excessive wealth is deceitful, and poverty with peace is to be preferred to riches with strife. The people commended by Proverbs are above all sensible and balanced, and this means that they can pick their way with skill through the minefield of opposing claims on their attention.

Extrapolating slightly precariously from the biblical text, and assuming the context in the royal court we have described above, E. W. Heaton gives this portrait of the person described in Proverbs:

> The man of Proverbs is a highly-motivated member of the lower middle classes ... He identifies himself neither with the rich nor yet with the poor ... and disapproves when men of different stations pretend to be what they are not ... He knows that money is not the be-all and end-all of life and he wants to get his priorities right. What is more, he has his home and family to think about, even though he is ambitious to give them security ... He is backed up by an extremely devoted and capable wife. Not only does she see to the meals and the children's clothes, but works all hours to earn a bit more. A wife, he holds, makes a world of difference to a man in his position. He is one who sets great store by domestic peace and feels sorry for men with 'a nagging wife and a brawling household', where the sons are always contradicting their father and getting their mother upset ... That is why he believes in being strict with his boys and knocking some sense into them ... The man of Proverbs is an open, cheerful character, who speaks his mind and does everything in his power to promote neighbourliness in the community at large ... The way to deal with enemies, he believes, is not by revenge but by the same sort of generosity a man ought to show to everybody in need. He would not want to deny that he has his principles, but he prefers to think of himself as a practical man, for whom getting results is all-important, even if sometimes it does mean compromise. There are occasions, for example, when a bribe works 'like a charm', and to turn a blind eye is the only sensible thing to do ... Such realism is the secret of his success ... What counts in the end is the 'know-how' which is born of experience and the rigorous use of a carefully-trained mind.[4]

Though this perhaps over-systematizes the rather mercurial teachings in Proverbs, which as we have seen often pull in different directions, it does pleasantly capture the urbane atmosphere of the book.

SCEPTICAL WISDOM

If there is implicit dialogue in Proverbs, the other two wisdom texts in the Old Testament proper, Job and Ecclesiastes, bring this out into the open. Both are much more overtly theological than even the more religious sayings in Proverbs, asking direct questions about the nature and character of God – who is named as Yahweh seldom in Job and not at all in Ecclesiastes. Job, almost certainly a work from the Persian period, is dialogic in a literal sense. Apart from the prose prologue and epilogue that tell the familiar story of a man persecuted by the Satan or 'adversary', a kind of heavenly devil's advocate, to test his piety, the main body of the book consists of three cycles of dialogue between Job and his three friends, Eliphaz, Bildad and Zophar, plus an interjection by a fourth character, Elihu (which may be an interpolation). It is rather like an early Greek tragedy of the Aeschylean school, with each character making a set-piece speech that does not necessarily connect with previous ones, but pursues its own path. After each speech Job replies, but again seldom directly answers what has been said. All the speeches use proverbial forms, sometimes apparently quoting from Proverbs and from the Psalms. In one striking quotation Job seems even to parody a psalm:

> What are human beings that you are mindful of them,
>   mortals that you care for them?
>
> (Psalm 8:4)

> What are human beings, that you make so much of them,
>   that you set your mind on them,
> visit them every morning,
>   test them every moment?
>
> (Job 7:17)

Where the Psalmist marvels at God's care for his human creation, Job complains that he takes an obsessive and unwelcome interest in it.

The topic under discussion throughout is why Job, an evidently innocent and pious man, is suffering extremes of illness, degradation and scorn. The friends propose answers to this conundrum that are in line with the general tenor of Proverbs. Job must have been more wicked than he seems ('Is not your wickedness great? There is no end to your iniquities', Job 22:5); or he is being tested ('How happy is the one whom God reproves; therefore do not despise the discipline of the Almighty', Job 5:17); or his sufferings will prove short-term and will soon be forgotten when God restores him to health and well-being ('Though your beginning was small, your latter days will be very great', Job 8:7). Job himself rejects all these spurious explanations of his plight. The climax of the book is an appearance by God (not unlike the *deus ex machina* in a Greek tragedy), in which God sarcastically tells Job that he knows nothing, since he is so puny compared with the power of the creator:

Where were you when I laid the foundations of the earth?
  Tell me, if you have understanding.
Who determined its measurements – surely you know!
  Or who stretched the line upon it?
On what were its bases sunk,
  or who laid its cornerstone
when the morning stars sang together
  and all the heavenly beings shouted for joy?

(Job 38:4–7)

But God also restores Job to health and blessing, and cryptically announces that Job has spoken 'what is right', whereas the friends have not (Job 42:8). The book thus remains enigmatic, showing that even in a wisdom text that openly thematizes the claims of the wisdom tradition itself we arrive at no final resolution of the theological issues involved. This contrasts with similar works elsewhere in the ancient Near East, such as the Babylonian text that begins, 'I will praise the Lord of wisdom',[5] which comes to the firm conclusion that the apparently righteous sufferer is in fact guilty of sins against the gods.

Ecclesiastes (Qoheleth) is even more the product of a kind of Hebrew scepticism than is Job. Overall the book is concerned with the possibility of finding a profound meaning in life, and it denies that any can be found: all is 'vanity', in Hebrew *hevel*, that is, pointlessness or absurdity – not vanity in the sense of personal pride, but in the sense in which we say that something has happened 'in vain', to no avail. Even the famous passage on the appropriate 'time' for things to happen turns out in context to be an illustration of the inevitability of pointless events – clear once we include the (often omitted) last line:

For everything there is a season, and a time for every matter under heaven:
a time to be born, and a time to die;
a time to plant, and a time to pluck up what is planted;
a time to kill, and a time to heal;
a time to break down, and a time to build up;
a time to weep, and a time to laugh;
a time to mourn, and a time to dance;
a time to throw away stones, and a time to gather stones together;
a time to embrace, and a time to refrain from embracing;

> a time to seek, and a time to lose;
> a time to keep, and a time to throw away;
> a time to tear, and a time to sew;
> a time to keep silence, and a time to speak;
> a time to love, and a time to hate;
> a time for war, and a time for peace.
> *What gain have the workers from their toil?*
>
> (Ecclesiastes 3:1–9; emphasis added)

Like Job, Ecclesiastes often seems to quote proverbs which in themselves suggest that there is order and worth in what happens on earth, but recontextualizes them to illustrate the futility of human striving:

> A good name is better than precious ointment,
> and the day of death, than the day of birth.
>
> (Ecclesiastes 7:1)

> Whatever your hand finds to do, do with your might; for there is no work or thought or knowledge or wisdom in Sheol,[6] to which you are going.
>
> (Ecclesiastes 9:10)

It is in effect a parody of a wisdom book, undermining the whole wisdom enterprise. Most think it was written in the Hellenistic period, partly because it has signs of later Hebrew, and if that is so then it may owe something to Greek scepticism. It is attributed to a 'son of David' (1:1), which has usually been taken to imply that (like Proverbs) it claims Solomon as its author, but could mean simply that it is supposed to be by a king of the Davidic line. Just as Job sets its proverbial wisdom within a narrative, so Ecclesiastes contains a few very short stories to illustrate how human affairs turn out badly and make no ultimate sense:

> There was a little city with few people in it. A great king came against it and besieged it, building great siege-works against it. Now there was found in it a poor, wise man, and he by his wisdom delivered the city. Yet no one remembered that poor man. So I said, 'Wisdom is better than might; yet the poor man's wisdom is despised, and his words are not heeded.'
>
> (Ecclesiastes 9:14–16)

It is possible that some or all of these tales contain veiled references to events in the history of Israel,[7] but they are anonymized to make them appear typical of 'the vanity of human wishes'.[8] An editor has added an epilogue to the book to wrench its teaching back into line with biblical orthodoxy:

> The end of the matter; all has been heard. Fear God, and keep his commandments; for that is the whole duty of everyone. For God will bring every deed into judgement, including every secret thing, whether good or evil.
>
> (Ecclesiastes 12:13–14)

For most readers today, this comes too late: the book has imprinted its scepticism on our mind before we reach this jarring envoi. The author's own aim seems to be to teach contentment with what human beings can achieve, rather than a doomed attempt to understand the world: as in Voltaire's novel *Candide*,[9] the moral is that we should simply get on with 'cultivating our garden' and enjoy the life we are given, not aim beyond what is achievable.

Wisdom literature thus invites the reader into a dialogue about human life and its patterns, rather than laying down the law. It tends to be open-ended rather than dogmatic: if it offers insight into the world and its ways, it is by proposing proverbs and wise sayings to ponder, not rigid diktats to be accepted and adhered to. Most typical, perhaps, are the short paragraphs in Proverbs 30 that draw analogies between human life and the world of nature, inviting us to reflect on the parallels between the two without necessarily drawing any particular practical conclusions:

> Three things are stately in their stride;
>   four are stately in their gait:
> the lion, which is mightiest among wild animals
>   and does not turn back before any;
> the strutting rooster, the he-goat,
>   and a king striding before his people.
>
> (Proverbs 30:29–31)

Whether it is good or bad for kings to stride at the head of their people, we are not told: it is simply an observation to be registered.

Who were the authors of the wisdom books? We have seen that Proverbs may derive from court scribes, collecting both folk and professional wise sayings. But Job and Ecclesiastes seem to be the writings of sophisticated individual writers, even though we do not know their names. Their social context is tantalizingly obscure to us. There must have been some setting in which such works could be read and discussed, but there is no evidence of philosophical schools such as existed in ancient Greece. We have only the evidence of the works themselves.

PERSONIFIED WISDOM

A later development in the wisdom tradition that would have important consequences for the Christian reading of the Bible is the personification of wisdom. In most of what are probably the older portions of Proverbs (chapters 10:1–22:16), 'wisdom' is simply an abstract noun meaning 'the property of being wise', just as it is in English. At some point, however, the idea arose that wisdom was a kind of being, something like a goddess, who favoured those who followed her precepts:

> Does not wisdom call,
>   and does not understanding raise her voice?
> On the heights, beside the way,
>   at the crossroads she takes her stand;
> beside the gates in front of the town,
>   at the entrance of the portals she cries out:
> 'To you, O people, I call,
>   and my cry is to all that live.
> O simple ones, learn prudence;
>   acquire intelligence, you who lack it . . .
>
> Take my instruction instead of silver,
>   and knowledge rather than choice gold;
> for wisdom is better than jewels,
>   and all that you desire cannot compare with her . . .
>
> By me kings reign,
>   and rulers decree what is just;
> by me rulers rule,
>   and nobles, all who govern rightly.
> I love those who love me,
>   and those who seek me diligently find me.
>
> (Proverbs 8:1–5, 10–11, 15–17)

Here wisdom is something like the Egyptian goddess *ma'at*, who was the principle of moral order in the world.[10] *Ma'at* was literally a goddess, the daughter of the sun-god Re, whereas in Israel wisdom was never worshipped, as *ma'at* was in Egypt.[11] But by a further move personified wisdom came to be seen as having been God's agent in creation, almost a kind of second, subordinate divine being:

The LORD created me at the beginning of his work,
  the first of his acts of long ago.
Ages ago I was set up,
  at the first, before the beginning of the earth.
When there were no depths I was brought forth,
  when there were no springs abounding with water . . .

When he established the heavens, I was there,
  when he drew a circle on the face of the deep,
when he made firm the skies above,
  when he established the fountains of the deep . . .

  then I was beside him, like a master worker;
and I was daily his delight,
  rejoicing before him always,
rejoicing in his inhabited world
  and delighting in the human race.

(Proverbs 8:22–4, 27–8, 30–31)

This development happened, probably, sometime after the exile, perhaps even in the Hellenistic period after 300 BCE or so. Later, in the first century BCE, in the Wisdom of Solomon, personified Wisdom becomes also the agent of God in directing the history of the world, and especially of Israel:

Wisdom protected the first-formed father of the world, when
  he alone had been created;
she delivered him from his transgression,
and gave him strength to rule all things . . .

When a righteous man was sold, wisdom did not desert him,
but delivered him from sin.
She descended with him into the dungeon,
and when he was in prison she did not leave him.

(Wisdom of Solomon 10:1–2, 13–14)

These passages refer clearly to Adam and Joseph; and all the major characters in the Pentateuch are dealt with in a similar way.

Wisdom is thus a kind of right-hand woman for God, acting as his agent in both creation and the history of the human race. In mainstream Judaism this did not become a particularly important line of thought, but in early Christianity it blossomed: the Christian conviction that

Jesus was in some sense divine, yet not simply identical with the one God, found the language of personified Wisdom an attractive model for describing the relationship of Jesus to God. In the great fourth-century CE debates about the nature of Christ, all the theologians involved took it for granted that the Wisdom referred to in Proverbs 8:22 meant Christ, but they disagreed over whether the verse should be translated 'the LORD created me' (as above) or 'the LORD possessed me', which would imply that Wisdom (that is, Christ) was uncreated. It did not occur to anyone that the text might not refer to Christ at all, or that they were arguing on the basis of the Greek translation rather than of the original Hebrew, and Proverbs 8:22 became a crucial text for Christology, that is, the doctrine of the nature of Christ. (See Chapter 14.)

HEBREW LAW IN ITS ANCIENT NEAR EASTERN CONTEXT

Judaism tends to regard all of the Hebrew Bible as constituting 'law' for the Jewish community, but 'law' here has a special sense. It stands for the Hebrew word *torah*, originally meaning 'teaching', which does not refer primarily to a legal corpus but to the instruction and advice given in ancient times by priests, and since the second century BCE or so by rabbis, scribes and other teachers. The Torah nowadays means the whole system of regulations by which observant Jews live, only some of which can be found in the Bible. It can also mean the Pentateuch, or occasionally the Bible as a whole, or the body of teaching built up over the centuries by rabbis (the 'Oral Torah'). In the Bible itself the word seems to have developed from meaning an individual ruling by a priest on a disputed matter (thus in Haggai 2:11–13) to referring to the whole way of life ordained by God for his people: it has the latter sense in, for example, the Psalms, especially Psalms 1, 19 and 119:

> Their delight is in the law of the LORD,
>   and on his law they meditate day and night.
>
> (Psalm 1:2)

> The law of the LORD is perfect,
>   reviving the soul;
> the decrees of the LORD are sure,
>   making wise the simple;
> the precepts of the LORD are right,

rejoicing the heart;
the commandment of the LORD is clear,
enlightening the eyes.

(Psalm 19:7–8)

Oh, how I love your law!
It is my meditation all day long.
Your commandment makes me wiser than my enemies.

(Psalm 119:97–8)

But within the Bible, considered as Torah, there are many individual laws and collections of laws in the more everyday sense of the term: directives on what is to be done in particular circumstances that come to court for adjudication, and also a number of general commandments or prohibitions given in the name of God. A major example of the latter is the Ten Commandments, sometimes known as the Decalogue, Greek for 'ten words'. The laws occur in the Pentateuch, which is why this is sometimes called the Torah, within the narrative framework of a revelation to Moses by God during the journey of the people of Israel towards the Promised Land. (I shall return to this point.) According to Exodus 19–20 this happened at Mount Sinai, vaguely located in the southern wilderness, where Moses passed the laws directly on to the people. According to Deuteronomy, Moses received laws at Sinai – though the mountain is called Horeb in Deuteronomy and other D passages – but did not communicate them to the people until they were in the plains of Moab across the Jordan, about to begin their push into the Land. In both Exodus and Deuteronomy, the Ten Commandments come first (in Exodus 20 and Deuteronomy 5), and so the more detailed laws that follow are presented as a spelling-out of the specific implications of these more general rules. But originally the detailed laws probably existed independently of the Ten Commandments, as codes of law in their own right.

There are three main collections of laws in the Hebrew Bible. The first is often referred to as the Book of the Covenant or the Covenant Code, and is found in Exodus 21–23. The general consensus is that this is the oldest of the biblical law codes. It presupposes a settled society, but one in which there is apparently no king, and for this reason is often thought to derive from pre-monarchic times. If the people of Israel did wander in the desert, it is not reflected here: those addressed have houses and domestic animals, and live in towns with local shrines. The popular belief, mirroring what the Old Testament tells us, that biblical legislation goes back to Moses and the wilderness is hard to accept once the details of this law code are pondered. Note in the following the italicized references that imply a settled, agrarian mode of life, with farmers living in houses:

> When you buy a male Hebrew slave, he shall serve for six years, but in the seventh he shall go out a free person, without debt . . . But if the slave declares, 'I love my master, my wife, and my children; I will not go out a free person', then his master shall bring him before God. He shall be brought *to the door or the doorpost*; and his master shall pierce his ear with an awl; and he shall serve him for life.
>
> (Exodus 21:2, 5–6)

> If someone leaves a pit open, or digs a pit and does not cover it, and *an ox or a donkey* falls into it, the owner of the pit shall make restitution, giving money to the owner, but keeping the dead animal.
>
> (Exodus 21:33–4)

> When someone causes *a field or vineyard* to be grazed over, or lets livestock loose to graze in someone else's field, restitution shall be made from the best in *the owner's field or vineyard.*
>
> (Exodus 22:5)

> You shall not delay to make offerings *from the fullness of your harvest and from the outflow of your presses.*
>
> (Exodus 22:29)

The second collection is found in the book of Deuteronomy, in chapters 12–26. It covers more topics than the laws in Exodus, but when it deals with the same topics it looks like an updated version of the laws in the Book of the Covenant. The clearest case of this can again be found in the law about Hebrew slaves:

> When you buy a male Hebrew slave, he shall serve for six years, but in the seventh he shall go out a free person, without debt. If he comes in single, he shall go out single; if he comes in married, then his wife shall go out with him. If his master gives him a wife and she bears him sons or daughters, the wife and her children shall be her master's and he shall go out alone . . . When a man sells his daughter as a slave, she shall not go out as the male slaves do.
>
> (Exodus 21:2–4, 7)

> If a member of your community, whether a Hebrew man or a Hebrew woman, is sold to you and works for you for six years, in the seventh year you shall set that person free. And when you send a male slave out from you a free person, you shall not send him out empty-handed. Provide liberally out of your flock, your threshing-floor, and your wine press, thus giving to him some of the bounty with which the LORD your God has blessed you.
>
> (Deuteronomy 15:12–14)

The theory mentioned in Chapter 2, that Deuteronomy was the law book promulgated in the reign of Josiah in the seventh century BCE (see 2 Kings 22:8–13), fits well with this evidence that the older laws have here been updated in line with later ideals.

The third legal corpus is Leviticus 19–26, generally known as the Holiness Code because it begins (19:2) with the injunction to be holy, as God is. This collection has some of the hallmarks of P about it, above all a concern with matters to do with ritual purity, and accordingly is usually dated to the exilic or post-exilic period like the rest of P; though indeed there is little about it to indicate any specific date, and it could be older than Deuteronomy 12–26. Consistent with its affinities to P, it is much more concerned than the other two codes with public worship and sacrifice, all carefully set in the time when Israel was in the desert and worshipping in a sacred tent (the tabernacle), though commentators mostly agree that the tent actually stands for the Temple in Jerusalem.

The Pentateuch also contains many more chapters of regulations and legislation, about the details of worship, dietary laws and other issues of purity: for example, Exodus 24–30, Leviticus 1–18 and Numbers 5–9. These are the sections of the Bible many modern readers (especially Christians) find least interesting, though they have their own fascination, for example, for the social anthropologist,[12] and also for anyone wishing to understand Judaism properly, since many of them lie at the root of the system of purity laws that still govern the life of observant Jews and give that life its distinctive style. Most of them probably came into being in their present form after the exile, but they may have much older roots in Israelite society.[13]

The three major law codes have particularly close links to other laws of the ancient Near East. A number of these, some dating back to the far reaches of the second millennium BCE, have been discovered in Mesopotamia, such as the Code of Hammurabi (eighteenth century

BCE), the Laws of Lipit-Ishtar (first half of the second millennium BCE), the Laws of Ur-Nammu (nineteenth century BCE) and the Middle Assyrian Laws (fifteenth century BCE). We have none from Egypt or, unfortunately, from the Levant. Some contain provisions so close to those in Hebrew law that there must be some connection. It is probably a matter of a common legal culture that persisted for centuries, unless Israelite scribes could read Akkadian and borrowed directly, for the Code of Hammurabi lived on in many copies over the centuries after its creation. The parallel that is most striking is the 'law of the goring ox':

> When an ox gores a man or a woman to death, the ox shall be stoned, and its flesh shall not be eaten; but the owner of the ox shall not be liable. If the ox has been accustomed to gore in the past, and its owner has been warned but has not restrained it, and it kills a man or a woman, the ox shall be stoned, and its owner also shall be put to death . . . If the ox gores a male or a female slave, the owner shall pay to the slave-owner thirty shekels of silver, and the ox shall be stoned.
>
> (Exodus 21:28–9, 32)

> If an ox, when it was walking along the street, gored a nobleman to death, that case is not subject to claim. If a nobleman's ox was a gorer and his city council had made it known to him that it was a gorer, but he did not pad its horns or tie up his ox, and that ox gored to death a member of the aristocracy, he shall give one half mina of silver.
>
> (Code of Hammurabi 250–51)

It could be argued that the similarity of this very ancient legal code to the laws in Exodus is due to the two having been written close together in time; though few indeed would date Moses as far back as the early second millennium. But Hammurabi's code consists of the laws of a city culture – one sufficiently advanced to have a municipal council – which bears no resemblance to the situation we would have to postulate for Moses and the wandering Israelites. For Israel to have been influenced by this, it must also have been a settled people living in towns and cities, with a scribal culture at least comparable to that of ancient Mesopotamia in Hammurabi's day. The Book of the Covenant is manifestly not the document of a group of nomads living in tents, and no such group, even if literate (which is itself almost inconceivable), would have borrowed from another society laws concerning how to deal with escaping oxen. Although the Bible associates the laws with Moses, once we think through its implications the connection is implausible.

THE TEN COMMANDMENTS

What then of the Ten Commandments? Here they are in the version in Exodus 20:2–17 (there is another in Deuteronomy 5:1–21):

> I am the LORD your God, who brought you out of the land of Egypt, out of the house of slavery; you shall have no other gods before me.
>
> You shall not make for yourself an idol, whether in the form of anything that is in heaven above, or that is on the earth beneath, or that is in the water under the earth. You shall not bow down to them or worship them; for I the LORD your God am a jealous God, punishing children for the iniquity of parents, to the third and fourth generation of those who reject me, but showing steadfast love to the thousandth generation of those who love me and keep my commandments.
>
> You shall not make wrongful use of the name of the LORD your God, for the LORD will not acquit anyone who misuses his name.
>
> Remember the sabbath day, and keep it holy. For six days you shall labour and do all your work. But the seventh day is a sabbath to the LORD your God; you shall not do any work – you, your son or your daughter, your male or female slave, your livestock, or the alien resident in your towns. For in six days the LORD made heaven and earth, the sea, and all that is in them, but rested the seventh day; therefore the LORD blessed the sabbath day and consecrated it.
>
> Honour your father and your mother, so that your days may be long in the land that the LORD your God is giving you.
>
> You shall not murder.
>
> You shall not commit adultery.
>
> You shall not steal.
>
> You shall not bear false witness against your neighbour.
>
> You shall not covet your neighbour's house; you shall not covet your neighbour's wife, or male or female slave, or ox, or donkey, or anything that belongs to your neighbour.

Surely these are the bedrock of Israel's laws, and they, at least, go back to Moses? Again we have to ask what situation the Commandments presuppose. The two listings, in Exodus 20 and Deuteronomy 5, differ little in content. They include moral principles common to almost every human society (prohibitions of theft, adultery and murder), which could come from any period in the history of Israel. But they also contain legislation implying, again, a settled agrarian community. The person who is addressed by the Sabbath law has slaves and domesticated animals to help him with his farm; his neighbour has a house that someone could covet. He is clearly not nomadic in lifestyle, nor does he live in the desert, but in a fertile land. The only theory that will preserve a Mosaic origin for such laws is the Bible's implication that Moses gave these laws as a matter of prophetic foresight: he knew that, once the tribes got into the Land, they would need them. But on any normal evaluation of the origins of legislation like this, we would judge that it came from a settled culture, the culture that prevailed in the days of the Hebrew kings, or just before it, as described in the book of Judges.

By the end of the nineteenth century it was usual for Old Testament scholars to think of the Ten Commandments as a distillation of the ethical teaching of the great prophets such as Amos, Hosea and Isaiah. In the twentieth century there was a conservative backlash against so late a dating, allied with the general sense that biblical archaeology had undermined scholarly scepticism about early Israel. As we saw in Chapter 1, this optimism about reconstructing early Israel proved short-lived, and the majority view would now be that we know little if anything about Moses as a historical figure, any more than we know about Abraham and his descendants. And with this goes a willingness again to contemplate the possibility that the Decalogue is a comparatively late arrival, probably later than the individual laws in the Covenant and Deuteronomic Codes that were arranged to look as though they are a detailed spelling-out of its implications. The Ten Commandments now appear in both contexts as a prologue to the detailed laws, but (like the Foreword to many books, usually written last) they were probably compiled later than those laws.

Even so, the Commandments may have passed through a series of stages in their composition. Some have tried to reconstruct an original core of just ten pithy rules, but this has led to no agreement, and has been largely abandoned in favour of seeing the texts as an amalgam of elements of differing date. The murder-adultery-theft section reflects a number of old texts such as Hosea 4:2 ('Swearing, lying, and murder, and stealing and adultery break out') and Jeremiah 7:9 ('Will you steal, murder, commit adultery, swear falsely, make offerings to Baal . . . ?'). The opening section, describing Yahweh as the God who brought Israel out of Egypt, looks more like a reflection on the stories in the Pentateuch after they had crystallized into their present form. The law about coveting seems an oddity, in that it prohibits a sin of thought rather than, like the others, a sin of action. The communities that revere the

Commandments cannot even agree on how they are to be divided into ten discrete rules: Jews and many Protestants distinguish the precept to have no other gods before Yahweh as the First Commandment and the prohibition of images as the Second, whereas Catholics and Lutherans run these together as two aspects of the same sin, and then divide the Tenth Commandment into (a) coveting your neighbour's house and (b) coveting anything else that is your neighbour's, so as to make up the requisite tally of ten. (The Jewish division seems more logical, since worshipping only one God and not using images are two separate issues, while there is no particular reason to introduce a division into the law against coveting.) This in itself shows that the text is not totally coherent as a list of exactly ten items, and must have some kind of history of growth, even if we cannot reconstruct it. It is also obvious that some of the Commandments have lengthy explanations and motivations, whereas others are short and crisp, and to any biblical specialist this immediately suggests a long period of transmission in which the text has been embroidered.

MOTIVATIONS FOR GOOD CONDUCT

Whatever the history of the laws in the Pentateuch, it may be felt, they are at least all laws – that is, they are clear and firm prescriptions and proscriptions of certain kinds of conduct. Observant Jews and Bible-believing Christians alike see the laws as authoritative pronouncements based on the sovereign will of God, and resist any relativizing tendency based on the study of their history that would remove the sense of absolute obligation from them. Two important features, however, need to be borne in mind.

One is that the laws often have 'motive clauses' attached, that is, incentives to obey the laws. Often these are related to future outcomes of obedience or disobedience – promises and threats. An obvious example of a promise is the motive clause added to the Commandment to honour one's father and mother, 'that your days may be long in the land that the LORD your God is giving you' (Exodus 20:12). At greater length, in Deuteronomy we find:

> If you heed these ordinances, by diligently observing them, the LORD your God will maintain with you the covenant loyalty that he swore to your ancestors; he will love you, bless you, and multiply you; he will bless

> the fruit of your womb and the fruit of your ground, your grain and your wine and your oil, the increase of your cattle and the issue of your flock, in the land that he swore to your ancestors to give you.
>
> (Deuteronomy 7:12–13)

The existence of threats is perhaps better known: God threatens punishment on those who disobey, as when Deuteronomy directs house-builders to put a parapet on the (flat) roof, 'otherwise you might have bloodguilt on your house, if anyone should fall from it' (Deuteronomy 22:8). Deuteronomy has large, generalized threats on disobedience to God in the lengthy curses of chapter 28:

> But if you will not obey the LORD your God by diligently observing all his commandments and decrees, which I am commanding you today, then all these curses shall come upon you and overtake you:
>
> Cursed shall you be in the city, and cursed shall you be in the field.
>
> Cursed shall be your basket and your kneading-bowl.
>
> Cursed shall be the fruit of your womb, the fruit of your ground, the increase of your cattle, and the issue of your flock.
>
> Cursed shall you be when you come in, and cursed shall you be when you go out.
>
> (Deuteronomy 28:15–19)

Moses is then presented as listing a very large number of specific curses that will be the consequence of disobedience: madness, blindness, theft of property, boils, enslavement, barrenness and cannibalism (see Deuteronomy 28:20–68).

But there are other kinds of incentive too, which are more common than this concern for future consequences. One type is reference back to Israel's past, urging that gratitude to God for his past blessings should motivate obedience to what he requires. This is particularly common in Deuteronomy, which repeatedly appeals to the exodus and the giving of the Land as motivations for obedience:

> You shall also love the stranger, for you were strangers in the land of Egypt. You shall fear the LORD your God; him alone you shall worship; to him you shall hold fast, and by his name you shall swear. He is your praise; he is your God, who has done for you these great and awesome things that your own eyes have seen . . . You shall love the LORD your God, *therefore*, and keep his charge, his decrees, his ordinances, and his commandments always.
>
> (Deuteronomy 10:19–21, 11:1; emphasis added)

The Ten Commandments begin with an implicit 'therefore' of this kind:

> I am the LORD your God, who brought you out of the land of Egypt, out of the house of slavery; you shall have no other gods before me.
>
> (Exodus 20:2)

Perhaps more surprising than appeals either to future consequences or past benefits is a tendency to argue that the laws are good in themselves, and that the reader can readily grasp the point of them. In Exodus there is a law regulating the pawning of goods, which refers to the extreme case of someone having nothing left to pawn but his outer cloak, and rules as follows:

> If you take your neighbour's cloak in pawn, you shall restore it before the sun goes down; for it may be your neighbour's only clothing to use as cover; in what else shall that person sleep? And if your neighbour cries out to me, I will listen, for I am compassionate.
>
> (Exodus 22:26–7)

Here there is an implied threat against the potential wrongdoer from God, who will listen to the poor person's cry and, presumably, avenge him. But there is also an attempt to reason with the wrongdoer: how can it be right to deprive someone of his only covering in bed? This is an appeal to shared human experience, and has the effect of making the law not an arbitrary command but a kind of natural moral principle. Deuteronomy explicitly states that the laws Israel has are good and just:

> See, just as the LORD my God has charged me, I now teach you statutes and ordinances for you to observe in the land that you are about to enter and occupy. You must observe them diligently, for this will show your wisdom and discernment to the peoples, who, when they hear all these statutes, will say, 'Surely this great nation is a wise and discerning people!' For what other great nation has a god so near to it as the LORD our God is whenever we call to him? And what other great nation has statutes and ordinances as just as this entire law that I am setting before you today?
>
> (Deuteronomy 4:5–8)

This implies some way of judging the merits of the laws that goes beyond the idea that they are simply commands that must be obeyed because they come from God. *Anyone can see* that the laws are good laws.

The other feature to be remembered is the fact that the laws are set in a narrative framework. We do not possess any 'raw' Israelite law, as we possess the law codes of Mesopotamia as entities in their own right. We have only the laws as contextualized by the writers of the Bible in the life of Moses and the people he led. That is, we encounter the law as part of a story, the story of God's association with Israel. Judaism, though it insists that the law is definitely to be obeyed, is more nuanced than conservative forms of Christianity in seeing it as part of a dialogue with the people of Israel – understood to embrace all generations of Jews down to the present. The law is not a series of bare demands, but one side of a partnership between God and his people. Torah, as we saw, is not 'law' in any simple sense. It has to be adapted to deal with changing circumstances, though it may not be abrogated. Christians who insist on a 'back to the Commandments!' stance are often less subtle than this, and ignore the contextualization of the law which the Bible presents.

But not only is a narrative framework offered for the laws in the Pentateuch; the laws themselves sometimes contain narratives. This is brought out by the Israeli lawyer and biblical scholar Assnat Bartor.[14] She cites the many passages in the laws where the lawgiver engages with the reader by narrating a (very short) story about an ethically challenging situation:

> If there is among you anyone in need, a member of your community in any of your towns within the land that the LORD your God is giving you, do not be hard-hearted or tight-fisted towards your needy neighbour. You should rather open your hand, willingly lending enough to meet the need, whatever it may be.
>
> (Deuteronomy 15:7–8)

> When you come upon your enemy's ox or donkey going astray, you shall bring it back. When you see the donkey of one who hates you lying under its burden and you would hold back from setting it free, you must help to set it free.[15]
>
> (Exodus 23:4–5)

This is true even in criminal cases: the situation is depicted as a narrative:

> Whoever strikes a person mortally shall be put to death. If he did not lie in wait for him,[16] but it came about by an act of God, then I will appoint for you a place to which the killer may flee. But if someone wilfully attacks and kills another by treachery, you shall take the killer from my altar for execution.
>
> (Exodus 21:12–14)

On the third passage, Bartor comments:

> The law as a whole describes three episodes. Three characters participate in the first: the assailant; the man who dies as a result of the latter's blows; and an additional, unidentified character whose role is to execute the death sentence. The second episode involves four characters: the man who 'did not lie in wait'; God; the lawgiver who is exposed through the phrase '*I* will appoint'; and the addressee, whose presence is indicated in the direct address 'for *you*'. The deceased receives no mention, and if not for the first episode it would not be apparent that the law deals with homicide; after all, the protagonist did not perform any action ('he *did not* lie in wait'), and we are not told what happened as a result of the divine intervention. The third episode, too, involves four characters: the slayer; the slain; the lawgiver, who reveals himself by mentioning '*my* altar'; and the addressee, who is drawn in as a participant via the command '*you* shall take [the killer]'.[17]

The deuteronomic law of unintentional homicide (Deuteronomy 19: 4–5) is even more vividly a story:

> Now this is the case of a homicide who might flee there[18] and live, that is, someone who has killed another person unintentionally when the two had not been at enmity before: Suppose someone goes into the forest with another to cut wood, and when one of them swings the axe to cut down a tree, the head slips from the handle and strikes the other person, who then dies; the killer may flee to one of these cities and live.

We are drawn into the situation envisaged, not presented with a set of rules. As with motive clauses, so in the way many laws are set out we find the legislators speaking to the community and encouraging them to imagine typical situations, on the basis of which they will form good judgements in analogous cases. The laws do not attempt to cover all possibilities, but simply provide examples from which to arrive at sound decisions by imagining similar situations. Jeremy Waldron comments as follows on the role of law in sophisticated societies: 'Having one's action guided by a norm is not just a matter of finding out about the norm and conforming one's behaviour to its specifications. It can involve a more complex engagement of practical reason than that. The use of a standard credits a human agent not just with the ability to comply with instructions but with the capacity to engage in practical deliberation.'[19]

Thus observing and enforcing the laws is not a simple matter of absolutes, but requires what in Christian moral tradition would be called casuistry, that is, the consideration of the requirements of each particular case. A school of 'law as literature' has arisen among those who study the Anglophone Common Law tradition, stressing that legal reflection is often more like reading and musing on narrative than it is like enforcing a rule. A leading exponent of this view, Bernard Jackson, has proposed that the biblical laws are more like wisdom than they are like statutes.[20] In fact he describes them as 'wisdom-laws'. They were not intended for judges and advocates, as a code to be enforced, but for people at large, as a statement of general legal principles: this may be equally true of the law codes of Mesopotamia. Judges probably made their own decisions rather freely, but they were informed by law codes, which set down what the lawgiver thought of as reasonable ways of proceeding in both civil and criminal cases, rather than absolute rules. Actual cases were probably decided mostly by precedent, and in ancient Israel more by town elders than by professional judges – their minds formed, but not constrained, by the items in the codes.

If this is correct, then in the very place where we are most inclined to see rulings, the Old Testament laws, we have in fact something closer to the open-ended observations of the wisdom writers. (Probably the scribes who wrote the law codes were in any case the same people who created the wisdom literature.) There are certainly absolute rules within the law codes: sometimes the laws are couched in an apodeictic, that is, absolute form, as in the case of the Ten Commandments – though even then there there are motive clauses, appealing to the reader's heart and mind, not merely demanding obedience, as we have seen. But much of the law is casuistic in form, proposing how to deal with various eventualities as they arise, and these are probably not to be construed as rulings but more as invitations to look for analogies and parallels in the case before the court, to general principles and precedents. Justice in ancient Israel seems to have been dispensed by the elders of local communities ('in the gate', that is, in the marketplace just inside the town gate) rather than by centralized courts, and the elders would pay attention to the rudimentary law codes, but not necessarily be bound by their strict letter.

So law and wisdom turn out to be closer together than at first appears, and both are to some degree dialogical in form, inviting the reader to enter into a moral discussion rather than closing off the debate from the start. Certainly there are some absolute commandments, but for the most part the literature is pragmatic and based on a consideration of individual cases.

THE CANONIZATION OF THE LAW

How did the diverse legal materials in the Hebrew Bible come to be joined together and combined with the narratives to form the Pentateuch as we now have it? If the priestly sections of Pentateuchal narrative (see Chapter 2) and the priestly laws such as the Holiness Code come from the very late pre-exilic, exilic or early post-exilic periods, that is from the sixth or fifth centuries BCE, as is widely agreed, then the final edition of the Pentateuch cannot be earlier than the late fifth century. Both Jewish tradition and critical scholarship as far back as the work of Baruch Spinoza (1632–77; see Chapter 17) have seen the priest and scribe Ezra as central in the forging of the Pentateuch or Torah in its final form. For in Nehemiah 8 we learn that the returned exiles assembled in Jerusalem to hear Ezra read over the course of a day the words of 'the law', while the Levites interpreted (or perhaps translated) it for the sake of the people who would not otherwise have understood it. It cannot be determined what 'the law' that Ezra read contained, and the story could be legendary anyway; but the idea that he read some version of the Pentateuch has become widely accepted. It is noteworthy that the reforms of Temple worship that the books of Ezra and Nehemiah ascribe to Ezra involve rules from all the collections of legal material in the Pentateuch, which might support this theory. Whether Ezra's 'law' also contained narrative is far less certain – and in any case, he could hardly have read the whole of the Pentateuch aloud in a single day, especially if it was simultaneously interpreted or translated.

As we shall see in Chapter 18, it was probably at some point in the fourth century BCE that the Pentateuch was translated into Greek in Egypt, so by then it must have been seen as an authoritative text for Jews in the Egyptian diaspora as well as in the Land. The exact date of Ezra's mission – assuming that it is historical fact – is uncertain, but sometime in the fifth century is likely, and this would fit well enough with a codification or canonization of both laws and narratives during this, the period of Israel's history when the province of Yehud was ruled by the Persians. Could the Persian authorities themselves have had a hand in imposing the Pentateuchal laws on the Jews? In the 1990s a widespread theory suggested that the Persians, while respecting the local laws of their subject peoples, tended to make sure they were properly codified and enforced, and some such procedure was hypothesized for the position of the Pentateuch in Yehud.[21] This is, however, speculative at best: it is hard to imagine that the Persian satrap of the great area of Transeuphrates, of which Yehud was such a tiny part, carefully checked the five books of Moses to ensure that they were in accordance with Persian principles of justice and law, still less that he read the narrative parts, and the many regulations for Temple worship. It seems on the whole more likely that it was Jews alone who decided that the Pentateuch was to function as their legal code, as well as being their historical foundation document. Judaism in the Persian period thus came to recognize the Torah as binding on it and as determining its institutions, customs and social arrangements. This does not mean that its text was as yet absolutely fixed and unchangeable. As late as the Dead Sea Scrolls we see variants in the text of the books of the Pentateuch, and a particular work, the so-called Temple Scroll, which sets out to reconcile differences between the different law codes and thus, probably, produce a document more authoritative than the already existing Pentateuchal laws.[22] But from the fifth century onwards Judaism would be a religion of law, in the technical sense of Torah.

Why did this shift occur? Deuteronomy already sees the respect and obedience that Israelites owe to God as encapsulated in the laws and admonitions Moses is said to have transmitted. The canonization of Torah in Judaism in the Persian period is a logical development of this trend, which may have roots even in pre-exilic times. But how Jewish thought came to include such a high valuation of law in the first place remains obscure.

THE PERSONIFICATION OF TORAH

A surprising development after the exile was a personification of Torah, rather similar to that of wisdom. We find this especially in Sirach (mid second century BCE). He first picks up the personification of Wisdom from Proverbs 8, developing it attractively:

> Wisdom praises herself,
>   and tells of her glory in the midst of her people.
> In the assembly of the Most High she opens her mouth,
>   and in the presence of his hosts she tells of her glory:
> 'I came forth from the mouth of the Most High,
>   and covered the earth like a mist.
> I dwelt in the highest heavens,

and my throne was in a pillar of cloud.
Alone I compassed the vault of heaven
and traversed the depths of the abyss.'

(Sirach 24:1–5)

But then he strikes a new note, associating Wisdom specifically with Israel:

'Over waves of the sea, over all the earth,
and over every people and nation I have held sway.
Among all these I sought a resting-place;
in whose territory should I abide?

'Then the Creator of all things gave me a command,
and my Creator chose the place for my tent.
He said, "Make your dwelling in Jacob,
and in Israel receive your inheritance."
Before the ages, in the beginning, he created me,
and for all the ages I shall not cease to be.
In the holy tent I ministered before him,
and so I was established in Zion.'

(Sirach 24:6–10)

And later in the chapter we discover that the divine Wisdom is actually identical with the Torah:

All this is the book of the covenant of the Most High God,
the law that Moses commanded us
as an inheritance for the congregations of Jacob.

(Sirach 24:23)

Thus divine Wisdom is, as it were, naturalized in Israel: true wisdom is to keep the Torah. By this means Torah comes out on top, and the tradition of wisdom, going back so far, is to some extent seen as surpassed by the specifically Israelite tradition of Torah: 'the author is claiming for the Jewish law a universal significance, and in so doing he no doubt is also concerned to answer charges of intellectual obscurantism and xenophobia directed at Jewish religious thought and practice which were in the air at that time.'[23] Non-Jews in the Persian and subsequent periods often regarded Jews with suspicion, particularly because they did not revere the gods as 'normal' people did, but insisted on their own, single God to the exclusion of all others. This made them singular and peculiar. The Jews' reaction, however, was to insist that they were the truly universal and normal ones, since they acknowledged a set of norms that surpassed all the ideas of other nations, and in those norms, set out in the Torah, true wisdom could be found.

Wisdom and law in the Hebrew Bible thus come nearest to providing the guidance for how to live that many people turn to the Bible for. Yet neither supplies a timeless code; both are rooted firmly in the institutional life of ancient Israel. That is not to deny that both exemplify moral principles that can often be seen also in modern discussions of ethics, and that were shared with other peoples of the ancient Near East. It does, however, make any direct application of biblical teachings difficult, and argues for a more oblique relationship between the Bible and modern Christian or Jewish faith.

4
Prophecy

PROPHETS AND THEIR BOOKS

Christians have always been enthusiastic about prophecy. The New Testament presents Jesus as the fulfilment of the prophecies about the Messiah in the Hebrew Bible, and (especially among evangelical Christians) a reading of the whole Bible focused on prophecies of the future and the signs of its coming is very popular. The classic messianic predictions include Isaiah 9:2–7:

> For a child has been born for us,
>   a son given to us;
> authority rests upon his shoulders;
>   and he is named
> Wonderful Counsellor, Mighty God,
>   Everlasting Father, Prince of Peace.
>
> (Isaiah 9:6)

Orthodox Judaism, on the other hand, has traditionally read the books of the prophets as a sort of commentary on the Torah, and has downplayed the predictive side of prophecy, though there are less mainstream types of Judaism that do focus on divine predictions of the future.[1] In ancient times, the community that produced the Dead Sea Scrolls, just like the early Christians a century or two later, saw their own life and history as the fulfilment of ancient prophecy.

Especially in the Gospel according to Matthew, passages from the prophets are cited after major events in the life of Jesus with a formula such as: 'this happened to fulfil what was spoken by the prophet'. For example, Matthew tells of the conception of Jesus by the Virgin Mary and adds (1:22–3), 'All this took place to fulfil what had been spoken by the Lord through the prophet: "Look, the virgin shall conceive and bear a son . . ."'. In one of the Dead Sea Scrolls,[2] a commentary on the prophet Habakkuk, we find the formula 'its interpretation is' (or 'interpreted, this concerns'), followed by a reference to something in the present experience of the community that produced the scrolls:

> Behold the nations and see, marvel and be astonished; for I accomplish a deed in your days but you will not believe it when told. (Habakkuk 1:5)

> Interpreted, this concerns those who were unfaithful together with the Liar, in that they did not listen to the word received by the Teacher of Righteousness from the mouth of God. And it concerns the unfaithful of the new covenant in that they have not believed in the covenant of God and have profaned his holy name. (1QpHab 2).[3]

In order to extract predictions of their own life and times from them, the Dead Sea community and Christians alike had to see the books of the prophets as essentially cryptic, because on the face of it they are about something else altogether, as we shall see. The books of the prophets can be divided into the 'Major' (i.e. longer) books of Isaiah, Jeremiah and Ezekiel, and the 'Minor' (i.e. shorter) books of the twelve prophets, Hosea, Joel, Amos, Obadiah, Jonah, Micah, Nahum, Habakkuk, Zephaniah, Haggai, Zechariah and Malachi. Daniel is also reckoned a Major Prophet in Christian understanding, though in Judaism his book appears in another part of the Bible, the Writings – see Chapter 9.[4]

These books may be the hardest part of the Bible for the modern reader because of their form as much as their content. It is not surprising that they were seen as cryptic, since it is not easy to extract any plain message from them. Most of them seem chaotic. The books of the Minor Prophets particularly appear to be arranged in no particular order, but even the Major Prophets are confused and muddled – we shall look later in the chapter at Isaiah, a particularly glaring example. Furthermore the contents are often obscure, and the prophets seem to speak in riddles. Some of the problem is caused by our sheer distance from the books, so that we do not easily pick up allusions which to the first readers were probably obvious; but there are also wild shifts from one topic to another that caused difficulties for ancient readers as much as they do for us. When Augustine of Hippo (354–430 CE) became a Christian he took advice from Bishop Ambrose of Milan (*c.*340–97 CE) on what to read, and was advised to start with the book of Isaiah. He reports that he found it simply incomprehensible.[5]

The key to understanding the prophetic books is to grasp that prophets did not write long, connected books, but delivered short, pithy sayings no longer than a paragraph, usually in verse. These oracles, as they are usually called, were gathered together later, either by the prophet himself or – more likely – by his disciples, and the resulting collections were then worked over by scribes, the same caste of learned people who also edited the narratives, laws and wisdom sayings, to produce the books we have now. They did not always know just when in the course of the prophet's life given oracles had been delivered, and they assembled them sometimes in what they thought was the correct chronological order, but sometimes thematically or on the basis of catchwords. Thus in Isaiah 1:9 and 1:10 there are two seemingly unrelated sayings that have been placed next to one another because they both happen to contain references to Sodom and Gomorrah:

> If the LORD of hosts
> had not left us a few survivors,
> we would have been like Sodom,
> and become like Gomorrah.
> Hear the word of the LORD,
> you rulers of Sodom!
> Listen to the teaching of our God,
> you people of Gomorrah!

The first oracle is about the destruction of Sodom and Gomorrah (see Genesis 19:24–5), the second about their wickedness; but they have been grouped together because of the occurrence of the names in both, even though the first probably makes sense in the context of the latest period in Isaiah's life, when Jerusalem was reduced almost to ruin, and the second in a much earlier time, when he was denouncing national sin.

What is more, words of later speakers or writers have often been included along with the utterances of the original prophet, either to augment or correct his words, or to gain authority from being ascribed to him. The result is the puzzling books we now find in the Bible, and there is no alternative to painstaking analysis if what we are interested in is the original words of the prophet whose name the book bears. (The possibility that we are not interested is discussed later in this chapter.)

Prophecy as a social phenomenon existed all over the ancient Near East, and there are many texts about people we would identify as prophets in ancient Mesopotamia, particularly in the archive of texts found at Mari on the Euphrates.[6] The prophet is a person (man or woman) who has privileged access to the gods because of special psychic powers, and who is consulted by rulers when planning some major undertaking – and sometimes even takes the initiative in warning or exhorting them to engage in or abstain from a military campaign, for example. Thus Letter 7 from Mari has a prophet opposing the making of a peace treaty by King Zimri-Lim with Eshnunna.[7] Sometimes prophets in Mari took the initiative in prophesying a bad outcome to some proposed course of action by the ruler,[8] though none that we know went so far as to oppose his or her king outright, as we find in Israel and Judah. One non-Israelite prophet familiar from the Hebrew Bible, Balaam (see Numbers 22–24), has turned up in a wall inscription in Syria.[9]

Prophets in Israel, whom we meet in the books of Samuel and Kings,[10] to some extent match the pattern known from Mari. They differ, though, in two important ways. First, they sometimes talk not of the outcome of one particular battle or campaign, but of the future of the nation or of the ruling dynasty as a whole:

> Samuel said to him [Saul], 'The LORD has torn the kingdom of Israel from you this very day, and has given it to a neighbour of yours [David], who is better than you.'
>
> (1 Samuel 15:28)

More significant still, they sometimes step out of their role as political advisers to comment on the morals and general behaviour of the kings of Israel and Judah, in a way unparalleled anywhere else in the ancient Near East. The classic case of this is Elijah, who uses his privileged position as a prophet to denounce and condemn King Ahab and his wife, Jezebel, and even consecrates another prophet, Elisha, whose task is to help eliminate Ahab's dynasty:

> Ahab said to Elijah, 'Have you found me, O my enemy?' He answered, 'I have found you. Because you have sold yourself to do what is evil in the sight of the LORD, I will bring disaster on you; I will consume and will cut off from Ahab every male, bond or free, in Israel . . . because you have provoked me to anger and have caused Israel to sin. Also concerning Jezebel the LORD said, "The dogs shall eat Jezebel within the bounds of Jezreel." Anyone belonging to Ahab who dies in the city the dogs shall eat; and anyone of his who dies in the open country the birds of the air shall eat.'
>
> (1 Kings 21:20–24)

> The LORD said to him [Elijah], 'Go, return on your way to the wilderness of Damascus; when you arrive, you shall anoint Hazael as king over Aram. Also you shall anoint Jehu son of Nimshi as king over Israel; and you shall anoint Elisha son of Shaphat of Abel-meholah as prophet in your place.

> Whoever escapes from the sword of Hazael, Jehu shall kill; and whoever escapes from the sword of Jehu, Elisha shall kill.'
>
> (1 Kings 19:15–17)

The accounts may be much exaggerated: our knowledge of dynastic struggles in Israel in the ninth century BCE, when these events are supposed to have happened, is sketchy. But the stories must have seemed plausible to later readers, and that implies that such actions were credible where important prophets were concerned.

Perhaps prophets such as Elijah could be presented in this unusual way precisely because of memories of the prophetic figures to whom books are ascribed, for the latter are definitely cast in this mould, as social critics and foretellers of disaster on the entire nation, and it may have been assumed that all prophets were of this kind. We meet such a figure for the first time in the earliest of the Minor Prophets, Amos, in the eighth century BCE.[11] Amos appears to have prophesied just as a period of relative prosperity for Israel was about to end, with the rise of Assyria (see Chapter 1). Far from being consulted by any kings, Amos speaks entirely unbidden, denouncing the king of the northern kingdom of Israel (Jeroboam II) and predicting the downfall of his 'house' (i.e. dynasty):

> Then Amaziah, the priest of Bethel, sent to King Jeroboam of Israel, saying, 'Amos has conspired against you in the very centre of the house of Israel; the land is not able to bear all his words. For thus Amos has said,
>
> "Jeroboam shall die by the sword,
> and Israel must go into exile
> away from his land."
>
> (Amos 7:10–11)

He also denounces not only a sequence of foreign nations (Amos 1:3–2:3), which was probably a standard prophetic task, but also Israel itself (2:6–8; 3:10; 5:21–4). He presents the social misdeeds in Israel (oppressing the poor by various legal ruses) as morally equivalent to the war crimes committed by surrounding nations, and foretells the complete collapse of the nation:

> Thus says the LORD:
> For three transgressions of Israel,
>   and for four, I will not revoke the punishment;
> because they sell the righteous for silver,
>   and the needy for a pair of sandals –
> they who trample the head of the poor into the dust of the earth,

and push the afflicted out of the way;
father and son go in to the same girl,
so that my holy name is profaned;
they lay themselves down beside every altar
on garments taken in pledge;
and in the house of their God they drink
wine bought with fines they imposed.[12]

(Amos 2:6–8)

Whether this reflects the reality of Amos' message or not, again the compilers of the Hebrew Bible must have thought that it was credible. A similar message can be found in Amos' younger contemporaries, Hosea (who also worked in the north) and in Micah and Isaiah, prophets in Judah; and it continues into the next centuries with the oracles of Jeremiah, Zephaniah and Ezekiel. All criticize the debased behaviour they see around them and prophesy the collapse of the nation under the onslaught of the Assyrians or, later, the Babylonians (see Chapter 1).

During and after the exile in the sixth century BCE we begin to find prophets foretelling restoration and peace for the Jews. This is part of the message of later oracles in Jeremiah and Ezekiel (see passages such as Jeremiah 31:10–14 and Ezekiel 34), both of whom lived through the disaster of the destruction of Jerusalem and deportation of king and ruling classes. It can be found especially in sixteen chapters of the book of Isaiah, 40–55, which we examine below. It is very clear in Zechariah, who worked around 520 BCE when the first steps were being taken to rebuild the ruined Temple, and who predicted blessing from God upon the renewed nation:

> Thus says the LORD, I have returned to Jerusalem with compassion; my house shall be built in it, says the LORD of hosts, and the measuring line shall be stretched out over Jerusalem. Proclaim further: Thus says the LORD of hosts: My cities shall again overflow with prosperity; the LORD will again comfort Zion and again choose Jerusalem.
>
> (Zechariah 1:16–17)

> Thus says the LORD of hosts: Old men and old women shall again sit in the streets of Jerusalem, each with staff in hand because of their great age. And the streets of the city shall be full of boys and girls playing in its streets.
>
> (Zechariah 8:4–5)

The consensus among Old Testament scholars has long been that, where oracles of blessing occur in the books of earlier prophets, they have been added by later scribes to an originally pessimistic core text. This cannot be proved, and some think that even very early prophets functioned more on the Mesopotamian model, mostly predicting success for the nation or king; only later, then, in the light of the exile, were prophecies of doom attributed to them.[13] But most scholars believe that early prophets – especially Amos, Isaiah and Micah – were prophets of doom, whose message has been lightened by later additions. We can see the process at work in passages such as the following, where I have italicized what seem to be additions qualifying the original message of doom:

> The eyes of the Lord GOD are upon the sinful kingdom,
> and I will destroy it from the face of the earth
> – *except that I will not utterly destroy the house of Jacob*,
> says the LORD.
>
> (Amos 9:8)

> For thus says the LORD: The whole land shall be a desolation; *yet I will not make a full end.*
>
> Because of this the earth shall mourn,
> and the heavens above grow black;
> for I have spoken, I have purposed;
> I have not relented nor will I turn back.
>
> (Jeremiah 4:27–8)

The tendency of prophets to preach good tidings, which is the image most Christians probably have of them, is in reality a post-exilic development that has been read back into earlier prophecy. Some even think that prediction was a minor theme in early prophecy anyway, and that social critique predominated – this is an interpretation especially common in the English-speaking world, and it has influenced some modern uses of the words 'prophet' and 'prophetic' to refer not to prognosticators of the future but to those who denounce the sins of society in the present. Probably, however, the great prophets of Israel were not so far removed as this from the normal role that ancient prophets had. Rather, they became convinced through a kind of second sight that trouble was coming – or even simply saw that it was, because they were politically better informed than most – and then explained this trouble as the result of national sin.

Whether the prophets thought disaster could be avoided is a moot point. Amos seems to hold out little hope for any national salvation,[14] while Hosea apparently predicts at least some kind of restoration after disaster even if not before it. Isaiah, as we shall see, is so complex a book that it is almost impossible to know which way the prophet's own teaching went. With Jeremiah, at least, we can feel sure that he spoke in terms of contingent results from the siege of Jerusalem by the Babylonians: if Judah surrendered, they would surely escape actual destruction, whereas if they did not, inevitable carnage would ensue – as it did. Yet later oracles in the book, whether or not they are by Jeremiah himself, speak of a glorious restoration under a new king of the line of David:

> In those days and at that time I will cause a righteous Branch to spring up for David; and he shall execute justice and righteousness in the land. In those days Judah will be saved and Jerusalem will live in safety.
>
> (Jeremiah 33:15–16)

Jeremiah is the one prophet who is said to have written a book of his oracles, or at least caused it to be written:

> This word came to Jeremiah from the LORD: Take a scroll and write on it all the words that I have spoken to you against Israel and Judah and all the nations, from the day I spoke to you, from the days of Josiah until today . . . Then Jeremiah called Baruch son of Neriah, and Baruch wrote on a scroll at Jeremiah's dictation all the words of the LORD that he had spoken to him.
>
> (Jeremiah 36:1–2, 4)

(The scroll is subsequently destroyed by King Jehoiakim, but then rewritten – see Jeremiah 36:5–32.) Since the production of a prophetic book seems to be presented as something remarkable, we may hypothesize that it was not the norm for prophets to write, or even to use a secretary to do so. In looking for the origin of the prophetic books we therefore seem to find ourselves back with the ubiquitous scribes, to whom in the end we owe the entire Hebrew Bible. Jeremiah's secretary Baruch is one of a handful we know by name. The prophetic books seem on examination to be the result of several stages of editing or redaction, which had a general tendency to soften the originally harsh message of judgement typical of the early prophets.

One type of prophecy introduced in these later, probably post-exilic, stages were oracles about a future king, such as the one quoted above from Jeremiah, who would reassert the rule of Yahweh over the kingdom of Judah (and even Israel, the long-lost north):

> Thus says the Lord GOD: I will take the people of Israel from the nations among which they have gone, and will gather them from every quarter,

> and bring them to their own land. I will make them one nation in the land, on the mountains of Israel; and one king shall be king over them all. Never again shall they be two nations, and never again shall they be divided into two kingdoms ... My servant David shall be king over them; and they shall all have one shepherd.
>
> (Ezekiel 37:21–2, 24)

The king would be, like David of old, an *anointed* king: Hebrew *mashiah*, from a verb meaning 'to smear' or 'anoint', later transliterated into Greek as *messias* and giving us the familiar word *messiah*. By the time of the New Testament some groups in Judaism had developed out of these hints the idea of a future saviour who would rule in the name of God over not just a restored Israel, but the whole world. But messianism in this sense scarcely exists within the Hebrew Bible itself, where the 'new David' is a literal new king of a liberated but limited Israelite or Judahite kingdom back within its old (or somewhat extended) borders. We have to move outside the Hebrew Bible, into later texts such as the *Psalms of Solomon* (eighteen Hellenistic Jewish texts from the second and first centuries BCE), to find detailed messianic hopes:

> Behold, O Lord, and raise up unto them their king, the son of David,
> At the time at which thou seest, O God, that he may reign over Israel thy servant.
> Wisely, righteously, he shall thrust out sinners from the inheritance ...
>
> With a rod of iron he shall break in pieces all their substance ...
>
> And he shall gather together a holy people, whom he shall lead in righteousness.
> And he shall have the heathen nations to serve him under his yoke;
> And he shall purge Jerusalem, making it holy as of old:
> So that nations shall come from the ends of the earth to see his glory,
> Bringing as gifts her sons that had fainted ...
>
> And he shall be a righteous king, taught of God, over them,
> And there shall be no unrighteousness in his days in their midst,
> For all shall be holy, and their king the anointed of the Lord.
>
> (*Psalms of Solomon* 17:23–38)

Expectations on a larger-than-life scale also occur in the type of prophecy generally known as apocalyptic, of which the main representative in the Hebrew Bible is the book of Daniel. Predictions of the imminent future (imminent at least in the mind of the writer) are projected back onto a figure of the remote past, very much as they were in the editing of the books of the prophets. The book of Daniel, for example, was certainly written no earlier than the second century BCE, but Daniel himself is presented as living at the time of the exile. These predictions often took on a larger scale and concerned themselves with the whole known world, not simply with Israel. Daniel 2, for example, uses the common ancient trope of four world empires, the last and eternally successful one proving – unsurprisingly – to be the empire of Israel, which the writer thinks is about to break in in his own day (the early second century BCE). He attributes the prophecy to the well-known traditional figure of Daniel, supposed to be a contemporary of Jeremiah and Ezekiel back in the sixth century. But apocalyptic texts such as this feel different from the genuinely earlier prophetic writings: they use the bizarre imagery, with symbolic animals and strange tableaux, that had begun to appear in Zechariah but are hardly to be found in any earlier prophetic works:

> I, Daniel, saw in my vision by night the four winds of heaven stirring up the great sea, and four great beasts came up out of the sea, different from one another. The first was like a lion and had eagles' wings. Then, as I watched, its wings were plucked off, and it was lifted up from the ground and made to stand on two feet like a human being; and a human mind was given to it. Another beast appeared, a second one, that looked like a bear. It was raised up on one side, had three tusks in its mouth among its teeth and was told, 'Arise, devour many bodies!' After this, as I watched, another appeared, like a leopard. The beast had four wings of a bird on its back and four heads; and dominion was given to it. After this I saw in the visions by night a fourth beast, terrifying and dreadful and exceedingly strong. It had great iron teeth . . .
>
> (Daniel 7:2–7)

> Then the angel who talked with me came forward and said to me, 'Look up and see what this is that is coming out.' I said, 'What is it?' He said, 'This is a basket coming out.' And he said, 'This is their iniquity in all the land.' Then a leaden cover was lifted, and there was a woman sitting in the basket! And he said, 'This is Wickedness.' So he thrust her back into the basket, and pressed the leaden weight down on its mouth. Then I looked up and saw two women coming forward. The wind was in their wings; they had wings like the wings of a stork, and they lifted up the basket between earth and sky.
>
> (Zechariah 5:5–9)

Apocalyptic books also have an even sharper sense than other prophetic works that everything is predetermined by God: kingdoms follow each other in prearranged succession, and no one can do anything to hasten or delay the divine plan. This is sometimes thought to correlate with the origins of the literature, which was no longer that of nationally influential people such as some of the old prophets had been, but of small and oppressed sects that recognized their own helplessness.[15] Be that as it may, it was the apocalyptic style that people in the age of the New Testament expected of prophecy; and when they read the prophetic books, they read them as though this was the kind of thing they were. We know the type of text any whose minds were formed in this mould would produce themselves, if they felt a prophetic spirit coming upon them: the book of Revelation. This is described as 'the book of the words of this prophecy', or 'the words of the prophecy of this book' (Revelation 22:18–19) – a gallimaufry of weird events taking place in heaven, with angels, strange beasts and white-robed elders bowing before God and his Lamb. It is magnificent, but it is not what Amos or Elijah meant by prophecy. For them, the prophetic message was anything but cryptic. It was meant to cause a rude awakening, not to set the reader or hearer a puzzle to solve.

THE GROWTH OF ISAIAH[16]

The book of Isaiah is probably the work whose composition spans the longest time of all among the prophetic texts. There is no reason to doubt that parts of it genuinely go back to the prophet Isaiah, who worked in Jerusalem in the days of the Kings Jotham, Ahaz and Hezekiah (Isaiah 1:1), beginning in 742 BCE, the year of the death of Uzziah (see Isaiah 6:1) and continuing at least until 701, when Jerusalem was besieged by the Assyrian King Sennacherib. The siege is described in the narrative material in Isaiah 36–9, which was either borrowed from or exported into 2 Kings 18–19, but it is the clear background of chapters 30 and 31. There were several political crises in which Isaiah seems to have been involved, doubling as a prophet and a royal counsellor or civil servant.

The first crisis was in the 730s, when there was an anti-Assyrian alliance forged between the northern kingdom of Israel and the Aramaeans of Damascus, which Judah was pressured to join. It was fronted by Rezin or Rezon of Aram and Pekah, son of Remaliah, in Israel (Ephraim, as Isaiah calls it), and the plan was to put a puppet ruler on the throne of Judah, someone we know only as the 'son of Tabeel'. This is the background of Isaiah 7–8, where we find King Ahaz of Judah tempted to appeal to the Assyrians themselves to resist the threats from the north, and Isaiah strongly opposing such a move. He apparently argued that the coalition would be snuffed out by the Assyrians anyway, without any need for Judah to draw their attention to itself by diplomatic appeals. In the event Ahaz did not listen and did approach the Assyrians, and the alliance was duly defeated. The cost was that the Assyrians took an interest in Judah from then on, though arguably they would soon have done so anyway, being bent on westward expansion (see Chapter 1).

> Then the LORD said to Isaiah, Go out to meet Ahaz, you and your son Shear-jashub, at the end of the conduit of the upper pool on the highway to the Fuller's Field, and say to him, Take heed, be quiet, do not fear, and do not let your heart be faint because of these two smouldering stumps of firebrands, because of the fierce anger of Rezin and Aram and the son of Remaliah. Because Aram – with Ephraim and the son of Remaliah – has plotted evil against you, saying, Let us go up against Judah and cut off Jerusalem and conquer it for ourselves and make the son of Tabeel king in it; therefore thus says the Lord GOD:
>
> It shall not stand,
> and it shall not come to pass . . .
>
> If you do not stand firm in faith,
> you shall not stand at all.
>
> (Isaiah 7:3–7, 9b)

Learning no lessons from the downfall of the coalition and the subsequent collapse of northern Israel in the 720s, during the years after about 710 the small remaining states around Judah were tempted into further anti-Assyrian politicking, involving the Philistines and, further west still, the Egyptians. Isaiah again advised against getting drawn in, telling the king (now Hezekiah) that Egypt was 'a broken reed' and could do its eastern allies no good:

> For Egypt's help is worthless and empty,
> therefore I have called her,
> 'Rahab who sits still'
>
> (Isaiah 30:7)

– referring here to an old myth of a monster killed by Yahweh. But again he was speaking to the deaf, and by 701 the Assyrians had invaded, and were at the gates of Jerusalem itself. The details of what happened are obscure. On the one hand, Hezekiah evidently had to pay tribute to the Assyrian king, Sennacherib, and lost a considerable measure of his independence (2 Kings 18:13–16). On the other hand, the city was not sacked, and the Assyrian army withdrew. Stories grew up that God had intervened, slaughtering the Assyrian army – see 2 Kings 18:17–19:37 and the parallel account in Isaiah 36–7. The story is retold in the poem 'The Destruction of Sennacherib' by Lord Byron (1788–1824), beginning, 'The Assyrian came down like the wolf on the fold':

. . . .

For the Angel of Death spread his wings on the blast,
And breathed in the face of the foe as he passed;
And the eyes of the sleepers waxed deadly and chill,
And their hearts but once heaved, and for ever grew still!

. . . .

And there lay the rider distorted and pale,
With the dew on his brow, and the rust on his mail:
And the tents were all silent, the banners alone,
The lances unlifted, the trumpet unblown.

And the widows of Ashur are loud in their wail,
And the idols are broke in the temple of Baal;
And the might of the Gentile, unsmote by the sword,
Hath melted like snow in the glance of the Lord!

Isaiah's part in it all is equally unclear: did he counsel capitulation and predict disaster if the king did not listen, or did he (rightly) foretell a great deliverance? Was he a prophet of doom, as generations of Old Testament scholars have believed, or was he a normal ancient Near Eastern prophet of (at least conditional) salvation? The answers depend on, but are in turn determinative for, our decision as to which of the sayings attributed to him in this crisis are really his own words, and which the work of later editors with theories of their own.

As matters stand, the text of Isaiah is a muddle. During the first crisis, at the time of the coalition, we find Isaiah appealing to the symbolic name he has given his son Shear-jashub, in Hebrew 'A remnant will return' – 'return' here may mean 'repent', 'come back (from exile)', or possibly 'remain'. Is the name meant as good news or bad? That depends on what people at large were expecting. If they thought Ahaz's policy of appealing to Assyria was likely to result in peace and prosperity, then the name is probably a name of ill omen: 'only a remnant of the nation will continue to exist' – compare Isaiah 6:13, 'Even if a tenth part remains in it, it will be burned again, like a terebinth or an oak whose stump remains standing when it is felled.' But if there was general fear and dread, then it is possible that Isaiah was giving at least some comfort – 'at least a remnant will survive' – though the comfort is at best somewhat cold. We can see the two possibilities juxtaposed in Isaiah 10:20–23:

> On that day the remnant of Israel and the survivors of the house of Jacob will no more lean on the one who struck them, but will lean on the LORD, the Holy One of Israel, in truth. A remnant will return, the remnant of Jacob, to the mighty God. [Hope and comfort]
>
> For though your people Israel were like the sand of the sea, only a remnant of them will return. Destruction is decreed, overflowing with righteousness. For the Lord GOD of hosts will make a full end, as decreed, in all the earth. [Threat]

Some of what Isaiah is reported as saying does make sense within the context of these various crises, as does his moral denunciation of the people around him, which continues in the tradition of Amos.

> Ah, you who join house to house,
> who add field to field,
> until there is room for no one but you,
> and you are left to live alone
> in the midst of the land!
> The LORD of hosts has sworn in my hearing:
> Surely many houses shall be desolate,
> large and beautiful houses, without inhabitant.
>
> (Isaiah 5:8–9)

Such a condemnation of exploitation of the poor by the rich could come from any period of Isaiah's activity, but belongs most probably in the time before the political crises began, when Judah like Israel was enjoying a time of reasonable prosperity.

Taken all together, this suggests that there are real sayings of Isaiah in chapters 1–8 and 28–31. But the rest of the book consists of material that may in some cases go back to his disciples (assuming he had any), or to the activity of scribes embellishing the book: sometimes by writing continuations of Isaiah's own words, sometimes by adding whole blocks of sayings that are in origin anonymous. To the first category – extensions – probably belong verses added to give Isaiah's originally negative message a more positive spin, just as happened to the other prophetic books:

> Then deep from the earth you shall speak,
> from low in the dust your words shall come;
> your voice shall come from the ground like the voice of a ghost,
> and your speech shall whisper out of the dust.
> *But the multitude of your foes shall be like fine dust . . .*
>
> (Isaiah 29:4–5; emphasis added)

To the second category belong several collections of oracles that together amount to more than two-thirds of the whole book. These are of various kinds.

First, in chapters 13–23 we find a phenomenon that occurs in several other prophetic books: oracles against foreign nations. There is already a collection of these in Amos 1–2, as we saw; but in the book of Isaiah they stretch beyond Israel's immediate neighbours to Babylon, which was not a power that emerged as a threat until the late seventh century, many decades after the lifetime of the eponymous prophet. Despite its importance in later thought – it contains the taunt that the king of Babylon is like the god of the morning star (in Latin, *lucifer*), who fell from heaven, which, combined with other Old Testament and later material about Satan and various demons, resulted in the Christian idea of the fall of the devil – the prediction of the fall of Babylon in 13–14 is thus very unlikely to go back to Isaiah himself. Isaiah 13–23 is a heterogeneous collection of oracles, some possibly based on genuine sayings of Isaiah but most reflecting later circumstances.

Secondly, chapters 24–7 have long been recognized as a collection of passages with an apocalyptic tone, dubbed 'The Isaiah Apocalypse'. These could be as late as the third century or even the second century BCE: they reflect the sorts of ideas we find in Daniel, with judgement in heaven as well as on earth, and even hints of life after death, a late arrival in Israel's literature:

> On that day the LORD will punish
> the host of heaven in heaven,
> and on earth the kings of the earth . . .
> Then the moon will be abashed,
> and the sun ashamed;
> For the LORD of hosts will reign
> on Mount Zion and in Jerusalem,
> and before his elders he will manifest his glory.
>
> (Isaiah 24:21, 23)

Your dead shall live, their corpses shall rise.
O dwellers in the dust, awake and sing for joy!
For your dew is a radiant dew,
and the earth will give birth to those long dead.
(Isaiah 26:19)

Whether this is truly a prophecy of literal resurrection is disputed; like Ezekiel's famous 'valley of dry bones' (Ezekiel 37), it may be a symbolic way of talking about the revival of the nation. But it is possible that it is thinking of the raising of the dead, as also in Daniel 12:2, 'Many of those who sleep in the dust of the earth shall awake.'

Thirdly, everything after chapter 40 makes sense only in the period when Jews in exile looked to the arrival of Cyrus II, the Persian king, to overcome Babylon and give permission for a resettlement of the Land. Cyrus is referred to by name in 44:28 and 45:1 (consecutive verses), and chapters 46–7 present a lengthy taunt against the Babylonians, deriding their gods as nothing but objects of wood and stone that have to be carted around on 'weary animals', and contrasting them with Yahweh, who on the contrary 'carries' Israel (Isaiah 46:1–4). There is a wide consensus that the second part of the book of Isaiah consists of two basic collections (both possibly augmented by even later scribes), 40–55 and 56–66. Of these the former is usually called Second or Deutero-Isaiah and the latter Third or Trito-Isaiah. The implication is that these are not merely expansions or extensions of the words of Isaiah, but originally independent books in their own right, which have been bolted onto chapters 1–39.

Second Isaiah is a significant section of the Hebrew Bible for several reasons. It speaks almost exclusively of blessings that will come on Israel, and so represents a new departure after the essentially gloomy message of the pre-exilic prophets up to and including Jeremiah. It does not play down the prophetic idea that the exile had been a punishment for the sins of Israel, but simply regards that as now lying in the past:

Rouse yourself, rouse yourself!
Stand up, O Jerusalem,
you who have drunk at the hand of the LORD
the cup of his wrath,
who have drunk to the dregs
the bowl of staggering . . .

These two things have befallen you
– who will grieve with you? –

devastation and destruction, famine and sword –
who will comfort you? . . .

Thus says your Sovereign, the LORD,
your God who pleads the cause of his people:
See, I have taken from your hand the cup of staggering;
you shall drink no more
from the bowl of my wrath.

(Isaiah 51:17, 19, 22)

Second Isaiah predicts not only a return of the exiles from Babylonia, but a gathering-in of dispersed Jews from all points of the compass, an influx so great that the walls of Jerusalem cannot contain the new inhabitants – in this it can be called the first manifestation of Zionism in the Bible:

Enlarge the site of your tent,
and let the curtains of your habitations be stretched out;
do not hold back; lengthen your cords
and strengthen your stakes.
For you will spread out to the right and to the left,
and your descendants will possess the nations
and will settle the desolate towns.

(Isaiah 54:2–3)

And, critical for later Jewish and Christian theological thinking, Second Isaiah contains the first explicit formulations of Jewish monotheism, the belief that only the God of Israel is the true God, and that all other pretended gods are nothing at all: not rivals, not even impotent rivals, to the one God, but simply non-existent:

Thus says the LORD, the King of Israel
and his Redeemer, the LORD of hosts:
I am the first and I am the last;
besides me there is no god.

(Isaiah 44:6)

This is a remarkable claim: Yahweh, who might have been thought to have been defeated by the gods of Babylon, is in reality the only God in existence, and actually controls both the Babylonians and Cyrus, their eventual conqueror. It became the bedrock for later thinking about the nature of God in both Judaism and Christianity. All the prophets are implicitly monotheistic, in that they do not reckon with any effective power in the universe other than that of the God of Israel, but Second Isaiah is the first to articulate this so overtly and unambiguously. Whether his work was originally completely distinct from the collection of the oracles of Isaiah (at whatever stage that had reached by the early sixth century BCE), or was consciously designed to be added to the Isaiah corpus, is unclear. A good case can be made for the latter theory, since there are places in 1–39 that seem to show editing in the manner of Second Isaiah. For example, Isaiah 12 is in tone very similar to Isaiah 40–55.[17] But either way Isaiah 40–55 represents a major block of material in the Hebrew Bible that moves theological thinking forward. (It is worth noting that the explicit monotheism here is roughly contemporary with the pre-Socratic philosophers in Greece, who were arriving at somewhat similar ideas. In neither case is it at all clear why such a distinctive development occurred.)

Third Isaiah is a less unified body of oracles than Second Isaiah, and can be divided into a number of smaller collections. Some of these (e.g. 57:1–13) revert to the older prophetic style of denunciation, commenting on religious practices (whose details are obscure) that the writer/prophet sees as disfiguring Judaism in his day – probably soon after the resettlement of the Land in the 530s BCE. Others (e.g. 60–62) continue and even enhance the rapturous tone of Second Isaiah, speaking of not only exiled Jews but even foreigners streaming into Jerusalem and initiating a new Israelite empire of peace and prosperity for all:

Lift up your eyes and look around;
  they all gather together, they come to you;
your sons shall come from far away,
  and your daughters shall be carried on their nurses' arms.
Then you shall see and be radiant;
  your heart shall thrill and rejoice,
because the abundance of the sea shall be brought to you,
  the wealth of the nations shall come to you.
A multitude of camels shall cover you,
  the young camels of Midian and Ephah;
  all those from Sheba shall come.
They shall bring gold and frankincense,
  and shall proclaim the praise of the LORD.

(Isaiah 60:4–6)

This finds a parallel in a famous passage of First Isaiah, 2:2–4, which is probably also from this late period – it also occurs in the book of Micah (4:1–4):

In days to come
  the mountain of the LORD's house
shall be established as the highest of the mountains,
  and shall be raised above the hills;
all the nations shall stream to it.
  Many peoples shall come and say,
'Come, let us go up to the mountain of the LORD,
  to the house of the God of Jacob;
that he may teach us his ways
  and that we may walk in his paths.' . . .

He shall judge between the nations,
  and shall arbitrate for many peoples;
they shall beat their swords into ploughshares,
  and their spears into pruning-hooks;
nation shall not lift up sword against nation.

(Isaiah 2:2–3, 4)

Zion (Jerusalem) as a focus for salvation to the whole world is a particular vision of this early post-exilic period, when hopes were buoyant and the mundane reality of everyday life in a minor province of the Persian Empire had not yet kicked in.

Again, we do not know whether Third Isaiah had an independent existence: it may have been deliberately added to the end of Second Isaiah, or it may be a collection that had already been formed into its present state before a scribe tacked it onto the growing Isaiah Scroll.

The study of Isaiah alone can be a life's work, so complex is its growth and development, but enough has been said to show that it can function as a small-scale illustration of how prophetic books came together. The other long prophetic books, Jeremiah and Ezekiel, offer similar evidence of addition and supplementation. Every prophetic book seems likely to have passed through several editions on the way to what we now have: this is true even of the shortest, Obadiah, which consists of a single chapter yet even so does not seem to come from a single hand.

THE EDITING OF THE BOOKS

Given all this variety in the component parts of books such as Isaiah, how did they come to be put together? German biblical critics in particular often suppose a complex process involving many editions of each book, and sometimes this produces hypotheses that are intricate to the point of self-defeat. As with the Pentateuch, so here it is probably best to think of only a few editions, though each time a book was copied, the scribe may have introduced small changes in individual verses. Most people who study the prophets think that the first edition of each of the early prophetic books was assembled by the prophet's disciples, and that a second edition was made during the period of the exile, when the gloomy predictions of these prophets were seen to have come about, and there was once again hope for the future. Some such process will account for most of what we find in Amos, Hosea, Micah, Isaiah, Jeremiah and Ezekiel. In the case of the post-exilic prophets (Haggai, Zechariah, Malachi), we could be dealing with written rather than spoken prophecy from the beginning, and in any case the prophecies are no longer predictions of unmitigated doom – though all three prophets have sharp criticisms to make of the people they are addressing.

But even here there are plenty of signs of later development. In the case of Zechariah, chapters 9–14 are so different from the rest of the book, and reflect so much later a situation, that they are often referred to as Deutero- or Second Zechariah. In the case of Isaiah, as we have seen, additional material is not only from the exilic and early post-exilic ages (40–66) but also, probably, from a still later time: in the case of the apocalypse in 24–7 we could have oracles from the Hellenistic period. So we must assume that in addition to the exilic editing of the pre-exilic prophets, similar processes of addition and revision happened among scribal circles after the exile, and indeed well down into the age of the Second Temple. Updating prophetic books was clearly an important industry among these scribes, who we may guess were attached to the Jerusalem Temple now that there was no longer a royal court, or else worked in the administration of the province of Yehud.

At some point indications were added to many prophetic books of the date of their activity, in the form of titles – for example:

> The vision of Isaiah son of Amoz, which he saw concerning Judah and Jerusalem in the days of Uzziah, Jotham, Ahaz, and Hezekiah, kings of Judah.
>
> (Isaiah 1:1)

> The words of Jeremiah son of Hilkiah, of the priests who were at Anathoth in the land of Benjamin, to whom the word of the LORD came in the days of King Josiah son of Amon of Judah, in the thirtieth year of his reign. It came also in the days of King Jehoiakim son of Josiah of Judah, and until

the end of the eleventh year of King Zedekiah son of Josiah of Judah, until the captivity of Jerusalem in the fifth month.

(Jeremiah 1:1–3)

THE FINISHED FORM

The kind of analysis just described has sometimes seemed to be harmful to the religious understanding and use of the prophetic books – just as source criticism of the Pentateuch has disturbed both Christian and Jewish readers. The reconstructed prophet Isaiah, for example, seems unlike the image of a prophet in either faith: he was neither a teacher of Torah nor a predictor of the coming Messiah, but a political player concerned with the catastrophic events of his day in Judah and Jerusalem. Even the additions to the book, which are many, do not focus much on the Messiah (9:2–7 and 11:1–9 are the only possible exceptions), but are overwhelmingly concerned with world events contemporary with the prophet, and their impact on the people of Israel and Judah. The same is true of most of the prophetic books, and of the prophetic figures who lie behind them. These people are part of the history of Judaism and Christianity, but what they taught does not approximate to either faith in the form we now know it.

However, analysis of the underlying components of the books of the prophets does not make for a complete study of them, for at some point they must have been stitched together to become the books we now have. After well over a century of breaking the books apart to see how they are constructed, biblical specialists in recent decades have started once again to take an interest in the 'final form', as it is sometimes called – that is, in the books as they now stand in the Bible. In a printed Bible (or for that matter in a Jewish Bible written by hand) there is no book of Second Isaiah or Third Isaiah, no Isaiah Apocalypse or Oracles against the Nations, but only a book called Isaiah. Surely its existing form also deserves study in its own right?

Pressure to re-examine the final form of the prophetic books has come from two quarters. Literary studies in the late twentieth century began to turn against what Robert Alter calls the archaeological model for analysing biblical texts, in which various textual layers are identified and sifted, and towards a more aesthetic interest in how the texts now present themselves to us. Someone must have meant us to read them as they stand; or, even if it was no one's intention, the books, just as they are, seem to invite a holistic reading. We shall say more about this turn to the final form on literary grounds in Chapter 17. But there is also a theological concern for the final form, driven by what is sometimes called a canonical approach to the Bible: that is, an interest in the texts as parts of the canon of Christian or Jewish Scripture, imparting a theological meaning that is more than simply the sum of the parts that, historically speaking, have come together to make the texts we now have. From either of these points of view, literary or theological, it makes sense to approach the texts again as they are, and to ask whether they map onto Christian or Jewish faith even if their component parts do not.

Someone who wanted to defend a traditional messianic interpretation of Isaiah, for example, could argue that the book is deeply concerned with kingship. It shows an interest in the doings of the kings of Judah, and contains oracles that foresee the coming of new kings (chapters 9:2–7 and 11:1–9 again). True, chapters 40–66 do not speak of any new king, though they do describe the Persian king, Cyrus, as Yahweh's anointed one in 45:1. But the prophecies of the return of the exiles and the gathering-in of foreigners do mesh with later Jewish and Christian ideas of the messianic age, even if a singular Messiah is not mentioned. Along some such lines the entire book might be understood as somehow in keeping with later messianism – which undoubtedly used texts from the book to validate its ideas, as we see in typical messianic texts such as the *Psalms of Solomon* (quoted above). Similarly, one could argue that Isaiah as it stands presents a number of ethical teachings that can still be relevant for later religious believers: from Isaiah's denunciations of sin, corresponding virtues can be derived:

> Ah, you who are heroes in drinking wine
>   and valiant at mixing drink,
> who acquit the guilty for a bribe,
>   and deprive the innocent of their rights!
>
> (Isaiah 5:22–3)

In both cases, however, such readings would seem to run against the grain of the book. Isaiah is more interested in the kings than most prophets, but the book does not foretell a single coming Messiah. Indeed, taking it as a finished whole makes this even less the case than if one concentrates, atomistically, on a few particular texts such as 9:2–7. As a whole, Isaiah is primarily about Judah and Jerusalem in their history, their disasters and triumphs, and only an allegorical interpretation which transforms Jerusalem into the heavenly city of God will remove this impression (see Chapter 15). The book likewise contains precious few imperatives telling the reader how to behave, so it can be seen as instruction in Torah only by imposing this as an external framework within which it is to be read, not by noticing any real internal features that tend in that direction. It can be made into either messianic prediction or ethical instruction, but only by doing a kind of violence to the impression it makes on the reader. Concentrating on the final form does indeed produce a reading different from concentrating on the minutiae of the component parts, but it does not bring the book any closer to a traditional Jewish or Christian understanding of Scripture.

The prophetic books, like the pieces of which they are composed, are for the most part subversive entities, undercutting the foundations of established religion, especially the state religious cults of the Hebrew kingdoms in pre-exilic times, and the political machinations of the times just before the exile. This element can be masked by selective quotation, but when the books are read in their entirety what emerges is a clear condemnation of what passed for religion in the communities the prophets addressed. Their predictions of disaster have been mitigated but not cancelled out by the addition of oracles of hope, which speak of the ways in which God will 'comfort his people' (Isaiah 40:1) *after* divine retribution has fallen on them, but hardly ever suggest that such retribution can be averted. Their condemnations of national sin are never tempered with any sympathetic understanding of what may have led people to behave so badly, but remain stark and clear. The prophets were not helpful people, and their books are not helpful texts: they do not say 'Peace, peace', where there is no peace (Jeremiah 6:14). Theirs are not the only words in the Hebrew Bible, and other texts, as we have seen, are much more encouraging. Later Judaism took to heart some features of the prophets' message, especially their condemnation of polytheism and the worship of images, but also domesticated them as teachers rather than denouncers, just as Christianity heard their critical voices but mainly saw them as heralds of good tidings, proclaiming a coming new age. But the prophets in all their original harshness have a distinctive witness to provide, and as we shall see, it does not feed easily into either of the religious systems that claim them as part of their Scriptures.

5
Poems and Psalms

Mesopotamian culture and the traditions of ancient Greece valued verse. Greece was the first culture to develop 'critical' history writing, in the works of Herodotus and Thucydides, who wrote in prose; but the traditional epics, the Homeric poems, just like the Mesopotamian *Epic of Gilgamesh*, are in verse. The 'historical books' of the Hebrew Bible, on the other hand, are almost entirely in prose, and the Bible contains no verse narrative whatever.

Nevertheless there is also plenty of verse in the Bible. Sometimes the prose narratives contain what seem to be older poems embedded in the story. A famous example is David's lament over the death of King Saul and his son Jonathan in battle with the Philistines on Mount Gilboa, in 2 Samuel 1:19–27, with its refrain, 'How have the mighty fallen!' It is said (2 Samuel 1:18) to have been known as 'The Bow':

Your glory, O Israel, lies slain upon your high places!
  How the mighty have fallen!
Tell it not in Gath,
  proclaim it not in the streets of Ashkelon;
or the daughters of the Philistines will rejoice,
  the daughters of the uncircumcised will exult.

You mountains of Gilboa,
  let there be no dew or rain upon you,
  nor bounteous fields!
For there the shield of the mighty was defiled,
  the shield of Saul, anointed with oil no more.

From the blood of the slain,
  from the fat of the mighty,
the bow of Jonathan did not turn back,
  nor the sword of Saul return empty.

Saul and Jonathan, beloved and lovely!
  In life and in death they were not divided;
they were swifter than eagles,
  they were stronger than lions.

O daughters of Israel, weep over Saul,
  who clothed you with crimson, in luxury,
  who put ornaments of gold on your apparel.

How the mighty have fallen
  in the midst of the battle!

Jonathan lies slain upon your high places.
  I am distressed for you, my brother Jonathan;
greatly beloved were you to me;
  your love to me was wonderful,
  passing the love of women.

How the mighty have fallen,
  and the weapons of war perished!

Together with another poem, this is supposed to have been recorded in 'the book of Jashar' (Joshua 10:13 and 2 Samuel 1:18); we read also of 'the Book of the Wars of the LORD' (Numbers 21:14) – books that no longer exist. There are other songs that have no name assigned them in the text, but are regarded by many as likely to be among the older sections of the Hebrew Bible, such as the song sung by Moses at the crossing of the Red Sea (Exodus 15:1–18) – sometimes called the Song of the Sea in modern times; Deborah's song in Judges 5; and the prayer of Hannah in 1 Samuel 2:1–10.

What I have said so far suggests that the dividing line between verse and prose is clear and sharp. In fact this is not so. In a traditional Hebrew Bible very few texts are set out as verse at all, Exodus 15:1–18 being one of the rare exceptions. (Printed Hebrew Bibles such as the *Biblia Hebraica Stuttgartensia*,[1] which is what most people studying the Old Testament use, introduce a verse arrangement in many places in prophets, Psalms and the historical books, but that is a modern convention, not one with ancient roots.) It is only since the eighteenth century that reasonably clear criteria have emerged for identifying verse, and there remain many texts where the distinction between verse and prose remains hard to apply. The biblical critic usually credited with establishing the salient characteristics of Hebrew verse is Robert Lowth, Bishop of London (1710–87), in his work *On the Sacred Poetry of the Hebrews*.[2]

Lowth's breakthrough was to see that neither rhyme nor rhythm was determinative, but an aspect of the *content* of poems, which he called parallelism (*parallelismus membrorum*). Verse in Hebrew typically works by setting up a pair of lines which say either the same thing, through synonyms, or opposite things, through antonyms. An example of synonymous parallelism is Psalm 91:1:

> You who live in the shelter of the Most High,
> who abide in the shadow of the Almighty.

Live/abide, shelter/shadow and Most High/Almighty form three neat pairs conveying exactly the same information but with variations in vocabulary.

The much rarer antonymous (usually called antithetical) parallelism can be seen in Proverbs 21:28:

> A false witness will perish,
> but a good listener will testify successfully.

Parallelism does not account for all the texts that can be identified as being in verse, but it is extremely common. As a criterion it is remarkable in that it survives translation into other languages perfectly well, with the result that we lose less of the original effect of Hebrew poetry when it is translated into English than might be the case with other systems.[3]

There are also more complex types of verse involving what is sometimes called 'step' parallelism, for example in the Song of Deborah's gloat over the death of the enemy warrior, Sisera, at the hands of Jael (see Judges 4 for details):

> She put her hand to the tent-peg
> and her right hand to the workmen's mallet;
> she struck Sisera a blow,
> she crushed his head,
> she shattered and pierced his temple.
> He sank, he fell,
> he lay still at her feet;
> at her feet he sank, he fell;
> where he sank, there he fell dead.
>
> (Judges 5:26–7)

Any reader would be able to recognize that this is verse, even if it were set out as prose. But in many cases the presence of poetry is less obvious, and Lowth's criterion of parallelism represented a leap forward in biblical studies. It helped identify many prophetic texts as poetry: in the King James Version they are printed as prose, but there is gain in recognizing where they are poetic. The section we know as Second Isaiah (Isaiah 40–55) contains many passages written with clear parallelism throughout:

> But now hear, O Jacob my servant,
> Israel whom I have chosen!
> Thus says the LORD who made you,
> who formed you in the womb and will help you;
> Do not fear, O Jacob my servant,
> Jeshurun whom I have chosen.
> For I will pour water on the thirsty land,
> and streams on the dry ground;
> I will pour my spirit on your descendants,
> and my blessing on your offspring.
> They shall spring up like a green tamarisk,
> like willows by flowing streams.
>
> (Isaiah 44:1–4)

Since Lowth many people who have studied Hebrew verse have pointed out that parallelism alone is not sufficient as a criterion for identifying verse, since there are lines of verse that do not display it:

> As for me, I am poor and needy,
> but the Lord takes thought for me.
>
> (Psalm 40:17)

> Why do you boast, O mighty one,
> of mischief done against the godly?
>
> (Psalm 52:1)

To cover such cases, the term 'synthetic parallelism' is sometimes used, but that is rather a desperate measure, trying to save the principle that verse always involves parallelism even when the evidence does not fit. In fact there is another criterion for identifying verse, and that is that the text can be broken up into short lines, as in the examples above. These lines tend to have a certain rhythmic pattern, typically three main beats: you who **live** in the **shel**ter of the Most **High**, who a**bide** in the **sha**dow of the Al**mighty** (an effect which also survives the transition to English, though not to all languages). It is hazardous to speak any more exactly than this of metre in Hebrew, but some kind of stress pattern does seem to be characteristic. In most cases there are two lines, each with three stresses, and where this is varied it is for a particular purpose. In the book of Lamentations, for example, we encounter many couplets in what has come to be known as *qinah* (lament) metre, where a three-stress line is followed by one with two stresses instead of three, so that the verse limps. Necessarily, here the parallelism is less complete. Here is a passage with the Hebrew stresses marked as well as the English will allow:

I am **one** who has **seen affliction**
  under the **rod** of God's **wrath**;
he has **driven** and **brought** me
  into **darkness** without any **light**;
against me **alone** he turns his **hand**,
  again and again, all day **long**.

(Lamentations 3:1–3)

The discovery of Hebrew verse has had important consequences. Not only is it valuable in itself, it also makes it possible to discern breaks between prose and verse, and so can contribute to theories about the composition of biblical books. The study of the book of Jeremiah, for example, has changed since it was seen that some passages are in verse and others in prose, which has led to hypotheses about the possibly separate origin of the two kinds of material: perhaps Jeremiah was a poet, and later editors added the extensive sections in prose (often 'deuteronomistic' prose – see Chapter 2).[4]

THE PSALMS[5]

The major collections of verse in the Hebrew Bible include Job and Proverbs, which we have already looked at as books of wisdom. But the Psalms are the classic examples of Hebrew poetry. The biblical psalms do not form a separate genre, as do wisdom, narrative and prophecy, but are a miscellaneous collection of poems of many sorts. The majority are prayers to God by either an individual or a group (or both), and are often classified as laments, though in some cases 'petitions' might be a better term.

Hear my prayer, O LORD;
  let my cry come to you.
Do not hide your face from me
  on the day of my distress.
Incline your ear to me;
  answer me speedily on the day when I call.

(Psalm 102:1–2)

O God, why do you cast us off for ever?
Why does your anger smoke against the sheep of your pasture?
Remember your congregation, which you acquired long ago,
which you redeemed to be the tribe of your heritage.

(Psalm 74:1–2)

As can be seen from these examples, the prayer in the psalm may be made in the name of an individual or of the collectivity of Israel. Consequently it is usual to speak of 'individual laments' and 'communal laments'. But it is more complicated than this, since some psalms move from one focus to the other. Psalm 102 is a case in point: the first twelve verses appear to be a prayer for God to help an individual suffering some kind of serious illness. Then we read:

You will rise up and have compassion on Zion,
for it is time to favour it;
the appointed time has come.
For your servants hold its stones dear,
and have pity on its dust.

(Psalm 102:13–14)

It seems that the personal lament has transmuted into a communal lament on the destruction of Jerusalem. This theme continues in the rest of the psalm, yet individual concerns break through again:

He has broken my strength in mid-course;
he has shortened my days.
'O my God,' I say, 'do not take me away
at the mid-point of my life,
you whose years endure
throughout all generations.'

(Psalm 102:23–4)

At the end, however, we revert to a corporate reference:

The children of your servants shall live secure;
their offspring shall be established in your presence.

(Psalm 102:28)

One possible explanation is that two psalms have been woven together – but in this case, at least, that does not seem likely, since the psalm gives a strong impression of unity and coherence. Another is that an individual lament has been 'communalized' or, alternatively, that a communal lament has been 'individualized', through the addition of extra material. But, again, the sense of unity makes that an unattractive theory, though there are psalms where such a hypothesis is indeed plausible – for example, Psalm 130:

> Out of the depths I cry to you, O LORD.
> Lord, hear my voice!
> Let your ears be attentive
> to the voice of my supplications!
>
> If you, O LORD, should mark iniquities,
> Lord, who could stand?
> But there is forgiveness with you,
> so that you may be revered.
>
> I wait for the LORD, my soul waits,
> and in his word I hope;
> my soul waits for the Lord
> more than those who watch for the morning
> more than those who watch for the morning.
>
> O Israel, hope in the LORD!
> For with the LORD there is steadfast love,
> and with him there is great power to redeem.
> It is he who will redeem Israel
> from all its iniquities.
>
> (Psalm 130:1–3, 5–8)

It seems that an individual prayer for forgiveness has here been augmented with two verses addressed to the nation. A similar pattern can be seen in Psalms 125 and 128, where blessings are pronounced on righteous individuals and their families, but the psalms end, 'Peace be upon Israel!' (Psalms 125:5, 128:6).

Perhaps in Psalm 102 – and also in other complex psalms – what we are dealing with is an identification of the needs of the individual with those of the nation, so that the text slides deliberately from an individual to a communal concern and back again. The speaker in Psalm 102 identifies his own calamity with that of his people, and vice versa, and sees no incongruity in mentioning first one and then the other. Some might suggest that this is a feature of an ancient mentality, but it seems to me that we are not far from the intense identification an individual today can have with a corporate entity, whether a nation, a political party, a church or a sports club. The boundaries between 'I' and 'we' can be fluid.

THE USE OF THE PSALMS

The oscillation between corporate and individual focus becomes even more complicated than just described once we start to ask how the Psalms were *used* in ancient Israel. There is little evidence in the Hebrew Bible for the actual use of psalmody, though Chronicles says that they were sung in the Temple during worship – evidence for the practice in the second, post-exilic Temple, but not for the Solomonic one, even though it is that Temple that the post-exilic Chronicler purports to be speaking of. (See 1 Chronicles 16, 2 Chronicles 5.) Even if the laments were used in the Temple, they were probably not sung communally: we should not imagine congregational singing, or even a large choir. The individual lament psalms were probably performed by an individual – not necessarily by the sufferers themselves, but more likely by a professional lamenter. Jeremiah tells us that there were 'mourning women' who could sing a dirge over the deceased: see Jeremiah 9:17–22, where they sing the words, 'Death has come up into our windows, it has entered our palaces.' But that may be equally true of the corporate laments, with a single singer standing for the whole community. Once we reckon with this possibility, the line between corporate and individual laments starts to blur further.

Were the Psalms *written* for use in worship? We do not know. In the modern world, lyric poems designed for private consumption are sometimes used in worship. A number of poems by George Herbert (1593–1633) are commonly sung as hymns in the Anglican/Episcopalian tradition, for example. Likewise, hymns intended for corporate singing can be reflected on and used in private prayer, as are many of Luther's hymns. There is no way of telling, given a bare text with no indications of intended use and context, what was the original purpose, and in any case many psalms may have changed their use over time.

So far we have been concentrating on 'laments', but the Psalter also includes many psalms of praise and thanksgiving, and with these too the question arises whether they are to be read as the expression of individual or communal sentiments. Some look clearly intended for a corporate, public context:

> Make a joyful noise to the Lord, all the earth.
> Worship the Lord with gladness;
> come into his presence with singing.
>
> Know that the Lord is God.

It is he that made us, and we are his;
we are his people, and the sheep of his pasture.

Enter his gates with thanksgiving,
and his courts with praise.
Give thanks to him, bless his name.

For the LORD is good;
his steadfast love endures for ever,
and his faithfulness to all generations.

(Psalm 100)

Rejoice in the LORD, O you righteous.
Praise befits the upright.
Praise the LORD with the lyre;
make melody to him with the harp of ten strings.
Sing to him a new song;
play skilfully on the strings, with loud shouts.

(Psalm 33:1–3)

Such psalms can be used by an individual, but only if understood as a member of 'Israel' as a whole. But there are also individual thanksgivings, such as Psalms 34 and 40:

I will bless the LORD at all times;
his praise shall continually be in my mouth.
My soul makes its boast in the LORD;
let the humble hear and be glad . . .

I sought the LORD, and he answered me,
and delivered me from all my fears . . .

This poor soul cried, and was heard by the LORD,
and was saved from every trouble.

(Psalm 34:1–2, 4, 6)

I waited patiently for the LORD;
he inclined to me and heard my cry.
He drew me up from the desolate pit,
out of the miry bog,
and set my feet upon a rock,
making my steps secure.
He put a new song in my mouth,
a song of praise to our God.

(Psalm 40:1–3)

Here again it is possible to imagine a group using a psalm that speaks of a single worshipper, since the individual may be understood as a representative of the group: and on the other hand, an individual using a corporate thanksgiving in private prayer, as many Jews and Christians have done and continue to do.

A number of biblical psalms are not directed to God in either lament or praise, but constitute teaching. Examples would be Psalms 1, 37, 49, 73, 112. Take Psalm 37:

> Do not fret because of the wicked;
> do not be envious of wrongdoers,
> for they will soon fade like the grass,
> and wither like the green herb.
>
> Trust in the LORD, and do good;
> so you will live in the land, and enjoy security.
> Take delight in the LORD,
> and he will give you the desires of your heart.
>
> (Psalm 37:1–4)

The speaker is a wise man rather than a professional singer, and it is hard to envisage a public setting for these psalms. If they appeared in the book of Proverbs it would not occur to anyone to relocate them into the Psalter. They have been and are sung in Christian worship (not so commonly in the Jewish liturgy), but they are slightly odd in that setting. Even odder is Psalm 119. Like some other psalms, this is an acrostic, but a complicated one: in each of its twenty-two sections each of the eight verses begins with the same letter of the alphabet. Thus there is an *aleph* section, a *beth* section, and so on all the way to *taw*, the last letter of the Hebrew alphabet. It is hard not to think that this was written for reading rather than for singing or recitation. It is an extended meditation on the beauty of observing the Torah, and every line contains a synonym for Torah – statutes, judgements, testimonies and so on. From a generic point of view it mixes prayer or lament with praise. Here is a representative section:

> The LORD is my portion;
> I promise to keep your words.
> I implore your favour with all my heart;
> be gracious to me according to your promise.
> When I think of your ways,
> I turn my feet to your decrees;

I hurry and do not delay
  to keep your commandments.
Though the cords of the wicked ensnare me,
  I do not forget your law.
At midnight I rise to praise you,
  because of your righteous ordinances.
I am a companion of all who fear you,
  of those who keep your precepts.
The earth, O LORD, is full of your steadfast love;
  teach me your statues.

(Psalm 119:57–64)

Some find the psalm boring – certainly, its 176 verses are somewhat relentless – but I would agree with C. S. Lewis that it is a thing of beauty, the Hebrew equivalent of a perfect sonnet.[6] In Christian tradition it has long been recited at the 'little hours', that is, services of prayer between morning and evening prayer, which are more widely observed in religious communities than by ordinary laypeople. In that context it helps to affirm the community's commitment to keeping God's law in every aspect of life.

LITURGICAL INTERPRETATION OF THE PSALMS

What has been said so far represents a common-sense reading of the Psalms as sometimes intended for, or used in, public worship, in one of the two Temples of ancient Israel (the one built by Solomon or the Second Temple, built after the exile) or, for that matter, at local places of worship which by the first century BCE had become recognizable as what are now called synagogues – houses for prayer and study. We do not know when synagogues originated, but by the first century BCE the institution certainly existed both in Palestine and in the diaspora, and was the context for the reception and study of what would become the biblical texts. Some public use of the Psalms is plausible, but what we can really know about this is extremely vague. Any context of use earlier than the synagogue is a matter of speculation. Nor do we know who wrote the Psalms, or when. One or two clearly presuppose the exile – for example, Psalm 137, 'By the rivers of Babylon – there we sat down and there we wept when we remembered Zion'. Others, such as Psalm 72, imply that there is still a king on the throne. But most could come from a variety of periods in the history of Israel, and they could have been produced by scribes, temple singers or other poets whose role in society is unknown to us.

During the twentieth century, however, a school of interpretation of the Psalms developed, mainly in Scandinavia but also in Britain, which claimed that we could know much more precisely how and when the Psalms were used. It took its rise from the work of the German Old Testament scholar Hermann Gunkel (1862–1932).[7] Gunkel was among the first to study the Psalms with attention to their possible use in ancient Israel. He regarded them all as religious lyrics – not as public texts at all – but, crucially, argued that they were *modelled on* texts that had had a public use in earlier times. He produced a taxonomy of the various types of psalm, which I have drawn on in speaking, for example, of individual and corporate laments. His student, the Norwegian scholar Sigmund Mowinckel (1884–1965),[8] suggested that Gunkel's account was too timid: why should the psalms we have not be public texts themselves? As we have seen, this is quite plausible. Mowinckel then went on to devise a method of studying them that promised much more insight into their public use. His approach has only recently begun to give way to different questions about the Psalter.

Mowinckel's account represents the conflation of two approaches. One is the comparative study of worship in other cultures of the ancient Near East, and especially the Mesopotamian civilizations of Assyria and Babylonia. From cuneiform texts we know a good deal about the religious rites of these cultures, and in particular that they celebrated a New Year festival at which the epic of creation was recited, and the king was ritually humiliated before being re-enthroned for the coming year. Mowinckel proposed that this *akitu* festival, as it was known, would surely have had parallels in Israel, and so he hypothesized a New Year festival in Jerusalem before the exile, comprising similar features. A number of the psalms could fit well into such a festival: those, for example, that speak of the royal rule of Yahweh over the nation and over the world, such as 93 and 96–99, and perhaps those concerned with the creation, such as 104.

The other key to reconstructing the Israelite liturgy, according to Mowinckel, was Gunkel's pioneering work in what is called form criticism. This method (important also in study of the Gospels, as we shall see in Chapter 8) consists in identifying the genre of texts that reflect an underlying oral tradition, and then theorizing about their likely use in a given social setting (German *Sitz im Leben*). Some of the stories in

Genesis, for example, can be understood as answers to a child's question. 'Why is that pillar of salt there?'; 'It's Mrs Lot, who looked behind her when Sodom and Gomorrah were destroyed.' Such stories are classified form-critically as *aetiologies*: explanations of origins. Genesis 1 is an aetiology of the world, a theory of everything, but most biblical aetiologies are much slighter. They explain place names (e.g. in Genesis 32:30, Peniel, where Jacob sees God face to face, means 'face of God'), natural phenomena (such as the pillar of salt in Genesis 19:26), and customs (e.g. the food taboo mentioned in Genesis 32:32, which explains that because Jacob's thigh was injured in his wrestling match with God, or his angel, therefore Israelites do not eat a particular part of the thigh of animals). Texts such as the Psalms can also be classified according to possible settings, in which they might have had a practical use. As we have already seen, they can be identified as individual laments, corporate laments, songs of thanksgiving, and so on. But we can also speculate about the way in which they were used in Israel's public worship.

For example, careful reading shows that some psalms combine both lament or petition and thanksgiving, such as this text about victory in a coming battle:

> The LORD answer you in the day of trouble!
> The name of the God of Jacob protect you!
> May he send you help from the sanctuary,
> and give you support from Zion.
> May he remember all your offerings,
> and regard with favour your burnt sacrifices.
>
> May he grant you your heart's desire,
> and fulfil all your plans.
> May we shout for joy over your victory,
> and in the name of our God set up our banners.
> May the LORD fulfil all your petitions.
>
> Now I know that the LORD will help his anointed;
> he will answer him from his holy heaven
> with mighty victories by his right hand.
>
> (Psalm 20:1–6)

Treated psychologically as a lyric poem, this is odd: how does the concluding assurance of victory relate to the opening lines praying for it? Interpreted liturgically, however, the psalm might actually be two psalms, and between the two there might have been an oracle or blessing from a priest or prophetic figure, assuring the worshipper(s) of a successful outcome. One psalm indeed seems to preserve the oracle as well as the reaction to it (Psalm 60), but there are many where the change from petition to thanksgiving could be explained as being due to some intervention in the liturgy between the two parts of the psalm (e.g. Psalms 6, 7, 10, 12, 13, 22, 28, 31, 54, 59, 69, 71). Here is Psalm 28:

> To you, O LORD, I call;
> my rock, do not refuse to hear me . . .
>
> Hear the voice of my supplication,
> as I cry to you for help,
> as I lift up my hands
> towards your most holy sanctuary.
>
> Do not drag me away with the wicked,
> with those who are workers of evil,
> who speak peace with their neighbours,
> while mischief is in their hearts . . .
>
> Blessed be the LORD,
> for he has heard the sound of my pleadings.
> The LORD is my strength and my shield;
> in him my heart trusts;
> so I am helped, and my heart exults,
> and with my song I give thanks to him.
>
> (Psalm 28:1, 2–3, 6–7)

The sense of assurance at the end that God will indeed help is sudden and unmistakable. It could be a psychological shift, but it seems more likely that something happened during the recital of the psalm to produce it.

Once one has learned the trick of this kind of interpretation, many psalms yield detailed information about liturgy. Take Psalm 118, where there are several shifts in point of view and, probably, in speaker. It seems to be intended for a procession to the Temple, for at verse 19 the procession arrives at the gates and the congregation prays:

> Open to me the gates of righteousness,
> that I may enter through them
> and give thanks to the LORD

to which the priests reply in verse 20:

> This is the gate of the LORD;
> the righteous shall enter through it.

Similarly, in verse 26 they bless the congregation:

> Blessed is the one who comes in the name of the LORD.
> We bless you from the house of the LORD.

None of this rests on any hard evidence, but it does make sense of the frequent changes of tone and speaker in the Psalms.

If we combine the form-critical approach with comparative study of liturgy in the ancient Near East, we can go even further. Psalm 89 speaks of the humiliation of the king of Judah, in apparent contravention of Yahweh's promises to him (see verses 38–45). This is traditionally interpreted as a reflection on the experience of the exile, with the king in question being Jehoiachin or conceivably Zedekiah, both exiled in the sixth century when Jerusalem fell to the Babylonians. Mowinckel's method throws up a wholly different possibility: that no specific king is meant, but rather every Judaean monarch, who was subjected to annual ritual humiliation at the New Year festival, just as in Mesopotamia at the *akitu* festival. The psalm is then not the reaction to a specific historical event, but a reusable text to be applied to the king every year. Once one has seen this possibility, a number of features fall into place: there is no reference to any identifiable enemies in the psalm; nothing in it offers any foothold for dating the text; and the king remains not only unnamed but unidentifiable.

Mowinckel and those who followed him offered detailed reconstructions of the worship in Solomon's Temple, based on his twin concerns for comparative method and for form criticism, and these reconstructions are all appealing and persuasive. Not a single one, however, can be demonstrated: they rest on arguments of a 'what if?' and 'surely!' type. The strength of the Mowinckel school's approach is not so much the specific reconstructions, which are necessarily speculative, as in two realizations. One is that Israel existed in a world of formal cultic festivals, which it must have known about and therefore quite possibly imitated; the other, that liturgical texts such as the Psalms may well belong in concrete contexts of worship, and may offer us hints for reconstructing those contexts. Once one has read Mowinckel, the Psalms never seem the same again.

THE ORDER OF THE PSALMS

All academic fashions pass; and Mowinckel's theories have not lasted for ever. There has been no general rejection of the liturgical interpretation of the Psalms, and scholars still interested in reconstructing pre-exilic Israel remain invested in the Mowinckel school, which provides possible information about the liturgical life of Israel that cannot be come by in any other way. But with a shift of focus to the post-exilic or Second Temple period in Old Testament scholarship in general, an interest has grown in the Psalter as a compiled book, rather than in the individual psalms and their original *Sitz im Leben*.[9]

The complete book of Psalms, or Psalter, can scarcely have come into existence before about 300 BCE, since there are individual psalms in it that are probably no earlier than the late Persian period (which ended with the conquests of Alexander the Great in the 330s). This is true of Psalm 119, in celebration of the Torah, mentioned above, but also of such Psalms as 49, which shows points of contact with Ecclesiastes, or Psalm 1, which again has the Torah as its theme and seems designed as an introduction to the Psalter. Everything suggests that the growth of the Psalter was immensely complicated. As it stands it is like the Pentateuch or Torah divided into five 'books' (Psalms 1–41; 42–72; 73–89; 90–106; 107–50). But the divisions do not correspond to breaks in theme or sense – for example, Psalm 107 stands at the start of a new book, yet it is most like Psalms 105 and 106 in beginning, 'O give thanks to the LORD'.

Then there are smaller pairs of psalms such as, indeed, Psalms 105 and 106, two 'historical' psalms; Psalms 103 and 104, both beginning 'Bless the LORD, O my soul'; and Psalms 20 and 21, about the victory of the king. The headings to the psalms, which are probably later than the texts themselves, show that there must have been earlier small collections, such as 'Psalms of David' (3–41, 51–70, 108–10, 138–44 with a few exceptions), 'Psalms of the Korahites' (42–9, 85, 87–8), and 'Psalms of Asaph' (73–83), which *partly* correspond with the division into books. These collections must have been disturbed when the Psalter was organized into its present form, with the addition of a lot of psalms that have no headings at all, especially those in book 5.*

* *The numbers of the Psalms.* Jewish and Protestant Bibles, on the one hand, and Catholic and eastern Orthodox ones on the other, have different ways of numbering the Psalms. These go back respectively to the Hebrew and the Greek and Latin Bible. Psalms 1–8 are numbered identically. Psalms 9 and 10 are treated in Catholic and Orthodox Bibles as a single

In short, the Psalter is a mess. What is more, there is evidence for different orders in antiquity. The Psalms Scroll from cave 11 at Qumran arranges book 5 quite differently from the Masoretic tradition, as follows: 101, 102, 103, 109, 105, 146, 121–32, 119, 135, 136, 118, 145, 139, 138, 93, 141, 133, 144, 142, 143, 149, 150, 140, 134. It has sometimes been suggested that this is merely a liturgical reordering: that is, the Qumran community knew the Psalms in the same order as we do, but produced this variant order because it was the one in which they sang or recited them – much as a modern Jewish or Christian community may produce a prayer book with the Psalms printed in the order they are prayed, without thereby implying that the biblical order is 'wrong'. But most scholars think that the Qumran order is genuinely an alternative arrangement: not necessarily opposed to the Masoretic order, if that already existed, but rather showing that the order was still fluid in the time of the Dead Sea Scrolls, probably the last two centuries BCE. (Even the number of the Psalms is not absolutely fixed: the Greek version of the Bible contains a Psalm 151, and the Syriac version Psalms 152–5.)

Like the current interest in the finished books of the prophets, finding coherence where earlier scholars saw only loose anthological works, the Masoretic order has become the object of study in its own right. So popular is the quest for the order of the Psalter that it has, for now at least, displaced the interest in liturgical reconstruction that had been going full-pelt since Mowinckel's work. As is generally true of the current interest in the 'final form of the text', there can be two motivations. One is a literary concern: this is an ancient and respected text, and it seems altogether likely that it would have been assembled on some coherent principles, if only we could discover what they are. The other is a theological motive: the Masoretic ordering is what the Jewish and Christian communities have received, and it should be assumed that there is a religious message, not just in the text of each psalm taken in turn or in isolation from others, but in the complete assemblage of the finished Psalter.

---

psalm (Psalm 9), and thereafter all the numbers are reduced by one: Psalm 11 (Hebrew) becomes Psalm 10 (Greek and Latin), and so on. Psalms 114 and 115 (Hebrew) are also treated as a single psalm in the Greek and Latin Bibles. But before this can reduce the numbering further, Hebrew Psalm 116 is divided in two in the Greek and Latin tradition, until Hebrew Psalm 147, which is also divided in two in the Greek and Latin Bibles, becoming 146 and 147, so that the numbering is then identical in the two traditions for the last three psalms, 148–50. Thus the overall number of 150 psalms is maintained. Some Bibles helpfully print the alternative numbering in brackets. It is important when reading works from early Christian writers to remember that they generally cite the Psalms in the Greek/Latin numbering.

It cannot be said that the quest for an underlying meaning in the Psalter taken as a whole has been very successful, but some striking observations have been made. Psalms 1 and 2 (which have no headings) seem to be a prologue to the Psalter, and to belong together: there is ancient evidence that they were seen as a single psalm by some. The early Christian writer Justin Martyr (100–165 CE) quotes them as a single continuous text in his *First Apology*, Chapter 40. In Acts 13:33, Paul quotes a line from Psalm 2 and identifies it as from 'the second psalm' in most manuscripts, but there is an alternative tradition in others that reads 'in the first psalm', probably implying that the two psalms were regarded as a single one.[10] They encompass two themes that will recur throughout the Psalms: the Torah and the king. Book 1 then continues with a morning hymn (Psalm 3), an evening hymn (Psalm 4) and another morning hymn (Psalm 5), though the alternating sequence does not seem to be sustained after that. At the end of the Psalter any reader can see that Psalms 147–50 form a crescendo, building up to a call to praise God in every verse of the final psalm. And there are more subtle cases of deliberate ordering: for example, Psalms 111 and 112 treat God and the righteous man respectively in remarkably similar terms, suggesting that the pairing is not an accident. But there is little evidence of larger-scale organization in the Psalter, such as would make it possible to read the book through with any sense of cumulative meaning. Rather like Proverbs, it is essentially an anthology. Anthologies may well show some internal ordering, with thematic links, but it is a mistake to look for a continuous sense in them. And, as with many anthologies, the Psalms seem to come from diverse periods and to express differing theological standpoints, so that it would be impossible to corral them into some kind of single, coherent whole.

In this the Psalter is a kind of microcosm of the Old Testament in general. Only a strong determination to find order and unity can succeed in overcoming the effect that most readers feel of encountering a slightly random work. The Psalms, like the contents of the Old Testament as a whole, share many theological ideas, just as they share the conventions of the Hebrew verse system: they speak of the kingship of God, of the righteous and the wicked, and of God's creative and redemptive providence. But they do not tell a wholly consistent story. Nor does the Old Testament as a whole: it is full of loose ends and surprising turns. This is one reason why it is so hard to treat it as a unitary Holy Scripture.

THEMES IN THE PSALMS

The Psalms deal with a wide range of religious issues that are found all over the Old Testament.

Creation. Most people think of Genesis as the main account of creation in the Bible. But there are references to it elsewhere, for example in Job (Job 38), which are easily overlooked. The Psalter also contains a number of passages that tell us how the creation was thought of in ancient Israel, some of them not exactly in accordance with the account in Genesis. Psalm 104 reflects at length on God's creation of the earth, and his provision for both animals and human beings to eat and prosper:

> You cause the grass to grow for the cattle,
> and plants for people to use,
> to bring forth food from the earth,
> and wine to gladden the human heart,
> oil to make the face shine,
> and bread to strengthen the human heart.
>
> (Psalm 104:14–15)

It lists a whole range of creatures God has made – birds, cattle, storks, wild goats, coneys, lions – though nothing is said about when or how God made all these things.

But there is another tradition about creation, absent from Genesis, that surfaces occasionally in the Psalms, which traces the origins of the world back to a contest among the gods. We find it also in the Babylonian Creation Epic, known, from its first words, as *Enuma elish* ('When on high'). This text goes back to the early second millennium BCE. Here the physical world is created by the chief god, Marduk, from the body of a conquered goddess called Tiamat or Tiamtu, who stands for the waters of chaos that existed before an ordered world was made. There is possibly an echo of this in Genesis 1 in the waters over which the spirit of God hovered in 1:2, which are called *tehom* in Hebrew, a word which may be related to Tiamat; but there is no divine battle here, since God seems to control everything effortlessly. However, in the Psalms the myth is still active:

> You rule the raging of the sea;
> when its waves rise, you still them.
> You crushed Rahab like a carcass;

you scattered your enemies with your mighty arm.
The heavens are yours, the earth also is yours;
the world and all that is in it – you have founded them.

(Psalm 89:9–11)

You divided the sea by your might;
you broke the heads of the dragons in the waters.
You crushed the heads of Leviathan . . .

Yours is the day, yours also the night;
you established the luminaries and the sun.
You have fixed all the bounds of the earth.

(Psalm 74:13–14, 16–17)

Rahab and Leviathan are monsters like Tiamat, though both male: Leviathan is familiar from texts in Ugaritic, a language quite close to Hebrew, found in Syria, while Rahab is not known outside the Hebrew Bible (and is not to be confused with the woman of that name in Joshua 2).

The conflict with the dragon-god as the basis for the creation of the world is, needless to say, a much less monotheistic account of how things came into being than that in Genesis, implying as it does that God had to conquer hostile forces in order to shape and fashion the universe.

God and Israel. Many psalms reflect on the special relationship between God and Israel, recalling the covenants made through Abraham or Moses and celebrating Israel's status as God's own people. Psalm 74, quoted above, concludes with a plea for God to remember the covenant, and equates Israel's enemies with the hostile forces he overcame in the creation:

Have regard for your covenant,
for the dark places of the land are full of the haunts of violence.
Do not let the downtrodden be put to shame;
let the poor and needy praise your name . . .

Do not forget the clamour of your foes,
the uproar of your adversaries that goes up continually.

(Psalm 74:20–21, 23)

Psalm 136 records all the great deeds of God on Israel's behalf, listing the death of the firstborn in Egypt, the exodus, the parting of the Red Sea and the overthrow of Pharaoh and his army, the conquest of

Canaanite kings such as Sihon and Og, and the settlement of Israel in the Land. And in Psalm 115 we hear of how God will bless Israel and its component parts, such as the house of Aaron (Psalm 115:12–13).

Throughout the Psalter there is an assumption that Israel is the people of God, and that Israel's enemies are his enemies and vice versa:

> O that you would kill the wicked, O God,
> And that the bloodthirsty would depart from me . . .
>
> Do not I hate those who hate you, O LORD?
> And do not I loathe those who rise up against you?
> I hate them with perfect hatred;
> I count them my enemies.
>
> (Psalm 139:19, 21–2)

This equation of the speaker's own enemies with God's is one of the major problems for modern Jews and Christians in using the Psalms. It rests on the idea that God has a special people whom he fosters and protects, but this has the drawback that it can make God appear indifferent or even hostile towards other peoples. In both religions there have been strains that have accentuated the theme of divine hostility to outsiders, but also others in which the specialness of Israel (or the Christian community) has been seen as a means for extending knowledge of God and the benefits of that knowledge to all humanity. Despite their sometimes vindictive tone, that theme is present even in the Psalms. Psalm 148, for example, runs through all the aspects of creation that are called upon to praise God (angels, sun and moon, stars, sea monsters, fire and hail, snow and frost, mountains and hills), and then continues:

> Kings of the earth and all peoples,
> princes and all rulers of the earth!
>
> (Psalm 148:11)

There is here evidently no sense that foreigners are cut off from the possibility of praising God. Nevertheless, the psalm still ends:

> He has raised up a horn for his people,
> praise for all his faithful,
> for the people of Israel who are close to him.
>
> (Psalm 148:14)

God and the Individual. Although the primary relationship of God in most of the Hebrew Bible is with the people of Israel considered as a collectivity, there are many laments and thanksgivings in the Psalter that seem to imply a close relationship with the individual – even though, as we have seen, the 'I' in the Psalms can sometimes stand for the group. Personal cries of distress seem to reflect a genuine sense that God is interested in the individual at prayer:

> My heart is in anguish within me,
> the terrors of death have fallen upon me.
> Fear and trembling come upon me,
> and horror overwhelms me.
> And I say, 'O that I had wings like a dove!
> I would fly away and be at rest.'
>
> (Psalm 55:4–6)

This psalm seems to reflect a situation that can only be that of an individual:

> It is not enemies who taunt me –
> I could bear that;
> it is not adversaries who deal insolently with me –
> I could hide from them.
> But it is you, my equal,
> my companion, my familiar friend.
>
> (Psalm 55:12–13)

It is taken for granted that God will be interested in and concerned for the speaker's plight.

One might expect that the individual in distress would think about God's relationship to Israel as a whole, but there is virtually no evidence of this. With the exception of Psalm 77, the individual laments almost never contain any reflection on what God has done for the nation. The individual is not seen primarily as a subset of the collective entity that is the nation, but has a relationship with God unconnected to national fortunes. God is concerned for individuals:

> You have kept count of my tossings;
> put my tears in your bottle.
> Are they not in your record?
>
> (Psalm 56:8)

God is here pictured as keeping an account of the misery of his worshipper, and there is no suggestion that it is part of any larger national record.

Prosperity and suffering. The 'wisdom' psalms in particular reflect on the suffering of the good and the success of the bad, in a way sometimes reminiscent of the book of Job, but never coming to the sceptical conclusions we find there. Psalms 37 and 73 both weigh up the prosperity of the wicked, but come to the conclusion that it is either short-lived, or worth less than the sense of communion with God enjoyed by the righteous, or both:

> Do not fret because of the wicked;
> do not be envious of wrongdoers,
> for they will soon fade like the grass,
> and wither like the green herb.
>
> (Psalm 37:1–2)

> . . . when I thought how to understand this,
> it seemed to me a wearisome task,
> until I went into the sanctuary of God;
> then I perceived their end.
> Truly you set them in slippery places;
> you make them fall to ruin . . .
>
> . . . I am continually with you;
> you hold my right hand.
> You guide me with your counsel,
> and afterwards you will receive me with honour.
> Whom have I in heaven but you?
> And there is nothing on earth that I desire other than you.
>
> (Psalm 73:16–18, 23–5)

Psalm 49, in tone more like Ecclesiastes, reflects that good and bad come to the same fate, so there is nothing for the wicked to gloat about: 'Mortals cannot abide in their pomp; they are like the animals that perish' (Psalm 49:12, 20). Nevertheless, the good live longer than the wicked, since God 'ransoms them' from the power of the underworld (Psalm 49:15), whereas the wicked descend 'straight to the grave' (Psalm 49:14).

Other psalms reflect the standard belief in the Old Testament that God blesses the righteous: Psalms 1, 5, 16 and 112 are all confident assertions of this. There is no psalm that discusses the sufferings of good people in a theoretical way, though many psalms are clearly pleas to be delivered from suffering by a person who believes in his own goodness. And there are penitential psalms that ask for forgiveness for sins committed, the classic example being Psalm 51, famous in its setting by Gregorio Allegri (1582–1652):

Have mercy on me, O God,
  according to your steadfast love;
according to your abundant mercy
  blot out my transgressions.
Wash me thoroughly from my iniquity,
  and cleanse me from my sin.

(Psalm 51:1–2)

There are traditionally said to be seven penitential psalms, one for each of the seven deadly sins: 6, 32, 38, 51, 102, 130 and 143. Not all are really penitential: Psalm 6 is an individual lament that makes no mention of anything the Psalmist has done wrong, and instead asks for deliverance from attacks by enemies. The Psalms contain relatively little about wrongdoing on the part of the individual who is cast as the one praying, far more about the iniquity of his ill-natured enemies.

The Nature of God. The God of the Psalms is certainly a vengeful God (see Psalm 94:1: 'O LORD, you God of vengeance, you God of vengeance, shine forth!'), but is also merciful and forgiving to those who pray to him. Above all, he is thought to be worthy of ceaseless praise, as the many psalms of praise and thanksgiving bear witness. Several psalms offer extended reflections on God's character, providence and splendour:

Bless the LORD, O my soul,
  and do not forget all his benefits –
who forgives all your iniquity,
  and heals all your diseases,
who redeems your life from the Pit,
  who crowns you with steadfast love and mercy,
who satisfies you with good as long as you live
  so that your youth is renewed like the eagle's.

(Psalm 103:2–5)

The LORD is gracious and merciful,
  slow to anger and abounding in steadfast love.
The LORD is good to all,
  and his compassion is over all that he has made . . .

The eyes of all look to you,
  and you give them their food in due season.
(Psalm 145:8–9, 15)

Thus God sustains everything he has made, and also saves those who trust him from various afflictions. All this is part of the traditional Jewish and Christian idea of God, and the Psalms provide many contributions to it. There is also, of course, an assumption that such a God deserves to be worshipped: hence the large number of psalms of praise and adoration, specially the last five psalms in the Psalter, each of which begins, 'Praise the LORD' (*hallelu-yah* in Hebrew).

There is no distinction between the God of creation and providence, who directs the course of the whole world and 'gives food to all flesh' (Psalm 136:25), the God who chooses and protects Israel, and the God who cares for the individual worshipper. These functions are not shared out among different gods, as they might be in a polytheistic system, but are all aspects of the one and only God. In this way the Psalms are in practice monotheistic, even though there is no theoretical discussion of monotheism in them – or indeed elsewhere in the Old Testament, unless perhaps in Second Isaiah.

God and David. Traditionally the Psalter is called 'The Psalms of David', even though only some of them are attributed to him within the text itself, and some are attributed to others – for example, Psalm 72 is ascribed to Solomon, and Psalm 90 to Moses. But there is certainly a connection with the monarchy in the case of many psalms, and David is mentioned on a number of occasions. This is not surprising if some psalms were used in ceremonies at the Temple of Solomon, which was in effect a royal chapel for the kingdom of Judah, and part of whose raison d'être was to celebrate the monarchy. The psalms that rejoice in the fact that 'The LORD is king' (Psalms 93, 97 and 99) may well be meant to underpin the monarchy: God is king, so the human king is thereby authenticated and supported in his kingship. The opposite reading is also possible: God alone is king, so there is no place for a human one. And in 1 Samuel 12:12 the prophet Samuel rebukes the Israelites for demanding a monarch 'though the LORD your God was your king'. In the ancient world in general, however, human kings were seen as the earthly representatives of the heavenly one.

Two psalms – 89 and 132 – are explicitly concerned with God's promises to David, the first recalling how God said that he would never forsake David's line, but then going on in verses 38–51 to complain that he appears to have done so. Presumably the reference is to the exile and the concomitant loss of the monarchy, unless Mowinckel was right and this refers to a ritual humiliation of the king in an annual ceremony. Other psalms allude less obviously to David. Psalms 2 and 110 both played a major role in early Christian writing because the references to the king in them were thought to be messianic, and the New Testament applies them to Jesus:

> I will tell of the decree of the LORD:
> He said to me, 'You are my son;
>   today I have begotten you.
>
> (Psalm 2:7)

> The LORD says to my lord,
>   'Sit at my right hand
> until I make your enemies your footstool.' . . .
>
> The LORD has sworn and will not change his mind,
>   'You are a priest for ever according to the order of Melchizedek.'
>
> (Psalm 110:1, 4)

Here the king is addressed by God and assured of an exalted, almost semi-divine status. The reference to Melchizedek, the ancient priest-king of Jerusalem (see Genesis 14:18–20), probably signals that the king of David's line has inherited all the rights of the kings of Jerusalem who reigned there before the Israelites annexed it.

Thus the king has a high status in the Psalms, and none of them is critical of the monarchy. As we saw above, some may well have been used in royal rituals, but we cannot be sure.

Jerusalem. Closely linked with the monarchy is the position of Jerusalem, the 'city of David'. As Psalm 122 tells us,

> Jerusalem [is] built as a city
>   that is bound firmly together . . .
>
> For there the thrones for judgement were set up,
>   the thrones of the house of David.
>
> (Psalm 122:3, 5)

A number of psalms glorify Jerusalem as the centre and citadel of the kingdom, and several refer to the tradition that it was impregnable because God would always defend it – a belief that has some connection with the prophet Isaiah; it is very difficult to know whether he believed it or attacked it. Psalm 48 is the classic exposition of the theme usually referred to in Old Testament scholarship as 'the inviolability of Zion':[11]

> Great is the LORD and greatly to be praised
> in the city of our God.
> His holy mountain, beautiful in elevation,
> is the joy of all the earth,
> Mount Zion, in the far north,[12]
> the city of the great King . . .
>
> Then the kings assembled,
> they came on together.
> As soon as they saw it, they were astounded;
> they were in panic, they took to flight.
>
> (Psalm 48:1–2, 4–5)

Psalm 76 attests to the same theory about Jerusalem, the place where God 'broke the flashing arrows, the shield, the sword, and the weapons of war' (verse 3).

What was the context for using psalms with this theme? We could imagine them being recited just before a battle, or alternatively on a regular basis to reinforce confidence in the royal city. Arthur Weiser[13] suggested that there was an annual 'royal Zion festival' at which they were sung, but that has gone the way of all the scholarly reconstructions of festivals. The theme of the sacrosanctity and consequent safety of Jerusalem certainly entered the thought of many readers of the Psalms, and it is nowhere more strongly stressed than in Psalm 46, the model for Martin Luther's famous hymn 'Ein feste Burg ist unser Gott', 'A safe stronghold our God is still':

> God is our refuge and strength,
> a very present help in trouble . . .
>
> God is in the midst of the city; it shall not be moved;
> God will help it when morning dawns.
> The nations are in an uproar, the kingdoms totter;
> he utters his voice, the earth melts.
>
> (Psalm 46:1, 5–6)

The Torah. Finally, some of the psalms have the Torah as a central theme. We have already noted this in Psalms 1 and 119. The second half of Psalm 19 also concentrates on the Torah, and seems to parallel it with the sun, which is the theme of the first half. Some think these are two psalms subsequently stitched together, but, even if that is so, someone must have seen a connection between the two themes: as the sun gives light to the world, so the Torah gives light to a well-lived life:

> The law of the LORD is perfect,
> reviving the soul;
> the decrees of the LORD are sure,
> making wise the simple;
> the precepts of the LORD are right,
> rejoicing the heart;
> the commandment of the LORD is clear,
> enlightening the eyes;
> the fear of the LORD is pure,
> enduring for ever;
> the ordinances of the LORD are true,
> and righteous altogether.
> More to be desired are they than gold,
> even much fine gold;
> sweeter also than honey,
> and drippings of the honeycomb.
>
> (Psalm 19:7–10)

Psalm 119 is in effect a spelling-out in more detail of the excellence of the Torah as presented here, using the same range of synonyms; while Psalm 1 celebrates the man who is faithful to it, and promises him prosperity. On the whole, however, the Psalms are probably older than this kind of reflection on the Torah, which has not left its mark on many other psalms than these three. In general terms, the Psalmists approve of a well-ordered life, but do not yet have the technical vocabulary of Torah-observance to describe it with.

These themes cannot all be added together, as though there were a unified theology of the Psalms; but they cover a great deal of what the Hebrew Bible as a whole discusses, so that in this respect we can see the Psalter as the Hebrew Bible in miniature.

JEWISH AND CHRISTIAN READINGS OF THE PSALMS

The Psalms raise in an acute form the question of biblical authority. With law and wisdom, much of the material is imperative in form, so that it is at least possible to see what could be meant by regarding it as having authority, even divine authority. But the Psalms, like the narrative books, do not take the form of divine address to human readers, but for the most part are clearly human discourse, sometimes to other people (most obviously with the 'wisdom' psalms), but most often to God. How can we read a collection of texts that are addressed from human beings to God as some kind of divine address to us? Christians and Jews have typically adopted different strategies. Christians have tended to read the Psalms, like the other books of the Hebrew Bible, as prophecy. In the New Testament David (the supposed author of the Psalms) is often referred to as a prophet (e.g. Acts 2:25–36; 4:23–8), and individual verses are singled out as examples of his prophetic powers – meaning his ability to foretell the coming of the Messiah in the person of Jesus:

> Since [David] was a prophet, he knew that God had sworn with an oath to him that he would put one of his descendants on his throne. Foreseeing this, David spoke of the resurrection of the Messiah, saying, 'He was not abandoned to Hades, nor did his flesh experience corruption' [a quotation from Psalm 16].
>
> (Acts 2:30–31)

Jews, on the other hand, have tended to assimilate the Psalms to the model of Torah, regarding even verses that address God as essentially divine instruction to Israel, to encourage the keeping of the Torah and to interpret it better. For example, in the early-third-century CE compilation of Jewish teachings known as the Mishnah we find:

> Whence do we learn that on the Day of Atonement anointing is equal to [i.e. as bad as] drinking? Although there is no proof of the matter, there is an indication, in that it is written, 'And it came into his inward parts like water and like oil into his bones' [Psalm 109:18].
>
> (Mishnah Shabbat 9:4)

> It was ordained that a man should salute his fellow with the [use of the] name [of God], for it is written . . . 'It is time to work for the Lord: they have made void thy law' [Psalm 119:126].
>
> (Mishnah Berakhot 9:5)

Neither of these approaches strikes most readers of the Psalms today as natural, yet both seemed intuitively obvious to their respective communities in the past, and they continue to be respected within traditional Jewish and Christian groups. As we shall see in Chapter 14, both are understandable responses to the need to build a bridge from the variegated text of Scripture, with its deficit of divine imperatives or definitions of doctrine, to the practical needs of the religions that embrace it as their foundation document. The Psalter has been important to both faiths, but for different reasons. Though both have been alike in using it for performance in liturgy, when it comes to interpretation they go their separate ways.[14]

For a modern reader, whether Christian or Jew or neither, the value of the Psalms does not lie obviously in either of these approaches, but in their coverage of so many biblical themes. They may not be divine revelation, but they are deeply revealing – about many different aspects of the God of the Bible and that God's relationship with the human race.

PART TWO

The New Testament

6
Christian Beginnings

In Christian Bibles, the Old Testament and the New seem to be simply two sections, unequal in length but belonging to the same overall genre: sacred writings or Scripture. We have begun to see that this does not do justice to the variety of material in the Old Testament, and shall go on to show how diffuse the New Testament also is. This view also overlooks some important differences between the Old Testament and the New. The Old Testament is the literature of a nation, written over some centuries, and having a certain official character. The New Testament is the literature of a small sect, distributed all over the eastern Mediterranean world, and in its origins unofficial, even experimental writing. It was written in less than a century, from the 50s to perhaps the 120s CE. In Christian printed Bibles Matthew follows Malachi, just as Malachi follows Zechariah: but this misleads, at least on the historical level. The New Testament is a radically different thing from the Old.

The Christian movement began in Palestine with the life, teachings and death of Jesus himself. He must have been born around 4 BCE if his birth took place during the lifetime of Herod the Great as Matthew 2:1 asserts, and by most reckonings his crucifixion took place in the early 30s CE. The Gospels in the New Testament constitute almost all our evidence for him, though he is mentioned, as 'Christus', by the Roman historian Tacitus.[1] His followers were, to begin with, a small group of Jews. Soon after his death the movement spread, both geographically, to Syria and Asia Minor (modern Turkey), and then to Greece and even Rome, and ethnically, to Gentiles (non-Jews). Not until the reign of Constantine (306–37 CE), however, was it any kind of official religion. It existed on the fringes of society in all the areas where it became established, and from its infancy encountered persecution – in the early years from other Jews, but then increasingly from the officials of the Roman Empire. Its literature was written against the backdrop of this persecution, and constituted the writings of a small, oppressed group which nevertheless thought of itself as destined to triumph in God's good time. The only parallels to be found in the Old Testament are the writers behind apocalyptic literature, in so far as that too is the product of persecution. But the Christians went even further. They believed not only that deliverance was coming but that to a significant extent it had already arrived, in the resurrection of Jesus. Their home-grown literature bore witness to this conviction, and thus diverged completely from its Jewish antecedents. The assertion that in Jesus something profoundly new had happened, which broke the bounds of existing Scripture, was fundamental to early Christian writers, and it meant that the two Testaments could not be seen as simply continuous with each other.

THE HISTORICAL CONTEXT

The backdrop to the rise of the Christian movement is the Roman Empire. After the successes of the Maccabees in the second century BCE (see Chapter 1), the Jews enjoyed a period of independence such as they had hardly ever known before, and were ruled by the Hasmonean kings, named after an ancestor of the Maccabees. The kings, however, started to take over the high priesthood too, even though they were not of the traditional high-priestly family, and this caused strife and resentment, though it was eventually accepted by most. It was this issue that first brought the Romans into Palestine, to arbitrate between the brothers Hyrcanus II and Aristobulus II, who both sought the high priesthood. The Roman general Pompey was then campaigning in Syria, and in 63 BCE he came into Jerusalem, where he besieged and eventually entered the Temple – even the Holy of Holies, which was out of bounds to everyone except the high priest. The Romans did not assume direct control of Palestine, but from then on they were the effective power in the region. Probably this would have happened even if they had not been called in to sort out the quarrel between the two Hasmonean brothers, rather as was the case with the Assyrians many centuries earlier; Palestine was small but strategically important, and Rome must have had its eye on it.

So there was no real national freedom for the Jews after 63 BCE, though this is not to say that the Roman presence was at all times invasive or oppressive. After a brief period under the last Hasmonean king, Antigonus, who had been installed by the Parthians after they had briefly ousted the Romans from Palestine, the country was ruled from

37 to 4 BCE by Herod the Great, a former governor of Galilee, as a client king – recognized by the Roman Senate as 'king of Judaea'. Though unpopular with some as a non- or half-Jew (he came from Idumaea, anciently Edom), he rebuilt the Temple, and was by no means a despotic ruler by the standards of the time. The Romans were content for him to govern the Jewish state without much interference from them.

When Herod died, his territory was split among three of his sons. Herod Antipas inherited Galilee and Peraea, Philip inherited Batanea, Trachonitis, Auranitis, Gaulanitis and Panias (all north of the Sea of Galilee), and Archelaus governed Judaea. Archelaus struggled to rule Judaea, and in 6 CE it came under direct Roman rule, along with Samaria and Idumaea, of which he had also been 'ethnarch'. The political situation was turbulent and complicated. Talk of the 'Roman occupying army' in comments on the New Testament is not always accurate: Judaea was indeed occupied, but Galilee was still a client kingdom governed by its own ruler and without Roman troops regularly stationed there. In any case the Roman presence was not always oppressive: the Roman Empire worked by allowing subject peoples to live largely under their own laws, provided these did not conflict with Roman law, and to be ruled by their own kings where it was deemed safe. Even in Judaea, the Roman touch was reasonably light – the reason why such low-grade administrators as Pontius Pilate were appointed was precisely because the area was not seen as troublesome.[2] Batanea and the other territories ruled by Philip were eventually added to the Roman province of Syria. There continued to be high priests, but they were appointed by the Romans, and turnover was so high that in John's Gospel (18:13) the high priesthood is (incorrectly) presented as an annual office.

All Herod the Great's descendants used the name 'Herod', in much the same way that Roman emperors adopted the name 'Caesar'. This produces confusion in the New Testament over which 'Herod' is meant. The following chart, constructed by E. P. Sanders, presents the different 'Herods' clearly:[3]

Herod the Great: Matthew 2:1–22; Luke 1:5

Antipas (Herod's son, tetrarch of Galilee): Matthew 14:1–6; Mark 6:14–22; 8:15; Luke 3:1, 19; 8:3; 9:7, 9; 13:31; 23:7–15; Acts 4:27; 13:1

Agrippa I (Herod's grandson): Acts 12:1–21

Agrippa II (Herod's great-grandson): Acts 23:35

Archelaus (Herod's son, ethnarch of Judaea): Matthew 2:22

In Jesus' lifetime Galilee proved relatively easy to govern, and Antipas was a successful tetrarch for forty-three years. His downfall came only when, egged on by Herodias, his second wife, he sought the title 'king' – never a good move in the eyes of Rome. Judaea was far less stable, and after Archelaus' dismissal a Roman governor was appointed with some 3,000 troops – not enough to keep the peace when Jerusalem was thronged with visitors at major festivals, though even there effective day-to-day rule was exercised by local leaders, a small group of town or village elders, one of whom acted as magistrate. The Roman governor ('prefect' from 6 to 41 CE, then 'procurator') did not normally interfere, and for any major threat he had to call on the legate of Syria, his superior, who commanded much larger forces.

Jerusalem itself was governed by the high priest and his council, which included other priests and leading laymen, all of course subject to the higher jurisdiction of the Roman governor, who also appointed the high priest. From about 6 to 66 CE the system worked reasonably well, with the Roman authorities respecting the high priest, who commanded the allegiance of most of the population and operated his own police force, the Temple guards. Joseph Caiaphas, the high priest at the time of Jesus' crucifixion, was a successful ruler who served for seventeen years, ten of them in tandem with Pontius Pilate, with whom he seems to have co-operated smoothly. 'Rome's interests', as E. P. Sanders puts it, 'were quite limited: a stable region between Syria and Egypt.'[4]

Still, Roman governors, including Pilate (who ruled as prefect 26–36 CE), sometimes acted with insensitivity towards Jewish customs and practices in Judaea and Jerusalem; and a build-up of anger and resentment eventually resulted in a Jewish revolt in 66–70 CE. In 66 the then procurator, Florus, had robbed the Temple: the Temple authorities then ceased to offer sacrifices for the emperor, and people refused to pay the Roman tribute, and there was an uprising. All-out war followed after Florus had crucified the rebels. It lasted four years, complicated by the many changes of emperor at Rome after the death of Nero and by infighting among various factions on the Jewish side. But when Vespasian took the throne in Rome his son, Titus, led an assault on the Jews and destroyed Jerusalem in 70 CE on the ninth of the Jewish month of Ab (July or August), which is still a day of mourning and lamentation in the Jewish calendar today. The Temple was burned down, and so the book of Lamentations, originally written for the destruction of the first Temple by the Babylonians in 586 BCE, is read in the synagogue service. Even then some resistance continued in the Judaean desert, and ended only with the Roman attack on the fortress of Masada, to which Jewish freedom-fighters had retreated. The revolt ended in 74 CE when the defenders of Masada committed mass suicide.[5]

In 132 CE there was a further revolt, led by Simeon bar Koseba, to resist the Emperor Hadrian's intention of building a shrine to Jupiter on the site of the ruined Temple. Simeon was apparently believed by Rabbi Akiba, a great authority of the time, to be the one foretold in Numbers 24:17 ('a star shall come out of Jacob'), and was renamed Bar Kochba, 'son of a star'. The Romans crushed the revolt without mercy, and there were no further attempts to re-establish Jewish independence.

HELLENISM

All the areas bordering the Mediterranean were by the turn of the era under some kind of Roman power, whether as provinces or client kingdoms: only in remote parts of Europe and the Middle East did the Roman writ not run, or not run clearly – east and north of the Rhine, or in Armenia. Culturally much of the Roman Empire was Hellenistic, that is, it had inherited the Greek culture imported by Alexander the Great and his successors. Where rulers in Egypt and Mesopotamia had corresponded in Akkadian, and then in Aramaic, they now used, not Latin, but Greek. Hellenistic culture united the Mediterranean world, and meant that wherever Paul travelled, for example, he was never exactly 'abroad': as a Hellenized Roman citizen he could expect to find certain customs and practices constant in most countries he visited, and to be treated with respect because of his citizenship (see Acts 16:35–9, 22:25–9). (Note, however, that Paul never refers to his citizenship in his own letters.)

Earlier generations of scholars, before the mid twentieth century, often drew a sharp contrast between Judaism and Hellenism. Judaism in Egypt, with its base in Alexandria, was acknowledged to have been heavily Hellenized. We can see from the book in the Apocrypha called the Wisdom of Solomon, a work written in Greek in the first century BCE, that its author believed in personal immortality, an idea not found clearly in the Hebrew Bible, and saw virtue as better than long life; while he thought of the body as an encumbrance to the purity of the soul:

> The righteous who have died will condemn the ungodly who are living, and youth that is quickly perfected will condemn the prolonged old age of the unrighteous.
>
> (Wisdom of Solomon 4:16)

> But the souls of the righteous are in the hand of God, and no torment will ever touch them. In the eyes of the foolish they seemed to have died, and their departure was thought to be a disaster, and their going from us to be their destruction; but they are at peace. For though in the sight of others they were punished, their hope is full of immortality. Having been disciplined a little, they will receive great good.
>
> (Wisdom of Solomon 3:1–5)

> . . . a perishable body weighs down the soul, and this earthly tent burdens the thoughtful mind.
>
> (Wisdom of Solomon 9:15)

In Palestine, it was believed until recently, Judaism continued in a non-Hellenized form. Since the pioneering work of Martin Hengel, however, it has become clear that, in this period, 'all Judaism was Hellenistic Judaism'.[6] Jesus' recorded teaching stresses the difference between soul and body just as does Wisdom:

> 'Do not fear those who kill the body but cannot kill the soul; rather fear him who can destroy both body and soul in hell.'
>
> (Matthew 10:28)

There is a long tradition, especially among Jewish scholars, of seeing Paul as the one who took the basically Jewish (Hebrew) teachings of Jesus and turned him into a Hellenized figure, and in particular altered him from a teacher, like many another rabbi or wandering Galilean charismatic, into the Son of God incarnate. Paul is thus understood as having imposed alien Greek ideas on the underlying Hebrew traditions to which Jesus was heir, and which he lived and breathed. This has been in part a reaction to a Christian attitude, dominant in the nineteenth century, to extol the virtues of Hellenism by contrast with Judaism – an attitude not far removed in some of its expressions from anti-Semitism. There may be something in this contrast, but it operates with an exaggerated idea of the gap between Hebrew and Greek ideas in this period.

The Judaism of Galilee and Judaea in any case owed much to its Hellenistic milieu. The thought-world of the New Testament is thoroughly Hellenistic, and trying to reconstruct an early form of the Christian message as yet untainted by Hellenism is likely to be fruitless. A Galilean artisan, even if he grew up in the small town of Nazareth rather than in one of the highly Hellenized cities of Galilee such as Tiberias (founded when Jesus was in his twenties) or Sepphoris, couldn't have been immune to the Hellenized culture that permeated all the areas around the Mediterranean. By all the accounts in the Gospels, Jesus was an educated man who could read the Hebrew Bible, and was clearly regarded as a serious teacher, aware of currents in the Judaism of his day that were indebted to Hellenism, whether he detected this influence or not.

JOSEPHUS

In 37 CE, not long after Jesus' crucifixion, a Jerusalem priest was born who exemplifies the cross-fertilization of Jewish and Graeco-Roman culture, as well as being our main source for most of the events described above. His Hebrew name was Joseph, Hellenized as Iosephous (in Latin Josephus), and he lived till about 100 CE, both experiencing the Jewish War as a general on the side of the rebels, and then chronicling it as a Roman citizen after he had been captured and turned his coat. As a Jewish aristocrat he was involved in politics from an early age, and a few years before the war (in about 61 CE) he visited Rome to appeal on behalf of friends who had been sent there as prisoners by the governor of Judaea. When the war began he joined the rebels and was put in charge of defending Galilee. After his capture, as early as the spring of 67 CE, he decided to surrender to Rome, but rather than being ill treated, as he feared, he profited from a vision he had that predicted the rise of Vespasian, the general commanding the Roman troops in Judaea, to emperor. This made him important in Vespasian's eventual success and ensured that he would be released; and from 69 CE onwards he was given Roman citizenship and a pension. After the war he stayed in Rome to write a study of it (in Greek) as an eyewitness and historian who had thoroughly researched the events. He also wrote a complete history of the Jews (the so-called *Antiquities*), summarizing the biblical account and extending it down to his own day, and an autobiography that offered an apologia for having been among the rebels.[7] (As we shall see, his *Against Apion*, a diatribe against a Hellenistic critic of Judaism, informs discussion of the biblical canon, since it contains valuable evidence of his own beliefs about the extent and contents of Jewish Scripture.)

As Martin Goodman points out, because of Josephus 'the story of Jerusalem in the years up to 70 CE can be told in far more depth than that of any other city in the Roman Empire at this time, apart from the story of Rome itself.'[8] Josephus was a rational Graeco-Roman historian, trying to work in the mould of Thucydides or Livy; yet he was also a visionary, and believed himself to have received prophetic inspiration from the Jewish God, whom he continued to worship. He regarded the Jewish Scriptures as vastly better than all the literature of Greece and Rome, and treated them as utterly reliable historically. He shows us just how Hellenized the elite in Jerusalem could be, even as they clung tenaciously to their ancestral traditions.

PHILO

Another, more elusive, Jewish figure to feel the embrace and influence of Hellenism belongs to an older generation than Josephus. This is the Alexandrian philosopher Philo (Jewish name Jedidiah), who was born around 25 BCE and died in about 50 CE, thus being partly contemporary with both Jesus and Paul.[9] He is known to have made one visit to Rome as part of a Jewish delegation to the Emperor Caligula (Caius) in 40 CE, representing the Alexandrian Jewish community following a dispute between them and the Greek community there: he described the event in his book *Embassy to Caius*, some of which is still extant. But otherwise we know about his life only through Josephus.[10]

Philo's own writing consists mainly of a lengthy commentary on the Greek version of the Pentateuch from the standpoint of Greek philosophy, mainly Stoic and Platonic. Like Josephus, he wrote in an educated Greek. Unlike the rabbis, he interpreted the Bible allegorically, seeing the patriarchs as philosophers before their time, and treating the food laws, for example, as metaphors for various spiritual and moral realities, thus pushing them well beyond their literal meaning, while still insisting that they must be observed. His work is at least partly an attempt to explain Judaism to interested non-Jews who thought in philosophical categories. It was to become important in Christianity rather than, on the whole, in Judaism, greatly influencing Christian writers such as Origen (185–254 CE) and Clement of Alexandria (*c.*150–215 CE).

It is from Philo that the idea derives of Greek philosophers having borrowed from the Hebrew Bible: Plato read Moses! Implausible as this is historically, it was a notion that took on a life of its own, and helped early Christian writers to justify arguing philosophically about doctrines deriving from the Bible, especially where the status of Jesus as Son of God was concerned. Philo's idea of the *logos* ('word'), the principle of divine reason inherent in the world, was pressed into service to explain how Jesus already existed as God's 'word' before the creation of the universe – as in the Gospel according to John 1:1–18. So Philo is in significant ways the father of later Christology, the doctrine of the nature of Christ, even though he himself was an Orthodox Jew who had, so far as we know, no personal contact at all with early Christians.

Philo's allegorical style can be seen in the following passage from his treatise *On the Migration of Abraham*, prefaced here with the account given in the Bible:

> And the Lord said unto Abraham, Depart out of thy land, and out of thy kindred, and out of thy father's house, into the land which I shall shew thee; and I will make thee a great nation and will bless thee and make thy name great, and thou shalt be blessed. And I will bless them that bless thee, and them that curse thee I will curse, and in thee shall all the families of the earth be blessed.
>
> (Genesis 12:1–3)

> God begins the carrying-out of his will to cleanse man's soul by giving it a starting-point for full salvation in its removal out of three localities, namely, body, sense-perception and speech. 'Land' or 'country' is a symbol of body, 'kindred' of sense-perception, 'father's house' of speech. How so? Because the body took its substance out of earth (or land) and is again resolved into earth. Moses is a witness to this, when he says, 'Earth thou art and unto earth shalt thou return' [Genesis 3:19]; indeed he also says that the body was clay formed into human shape by God's moulding hand, and what suffers solution must needs be resolved into the elements which were united to form it. Sense-perception, again, is of one kin and family with understanding, the irrational with the rational, for both these are parts of one soul. And speech is our 'father's house', 'father's' because mind is our father, sowing in each of the parts of the body the faculties that issue from itself, and assigning to them their workings, being in control and charge of them all; 'house' – because mind has speech for its house or living room, secluded from the rest of the homestead. It is mind's living-place, just as the hearthside is man's. It is there that mind displays in an orderly form itself and all the conceptions to which it gives birth, treating it as a man treats a house.
>
> (Philo, *On the Migration of Abraham* 1–4)

Philo does not deny that the events described actually happened, but what matters for him is that they symbolize general truths about human nature and especially about its inner constitution. Abraham is a symbol of the soul in its journeyings. We shall see that this kind of biblical interpretation was highly influential in both Judaism and (even more so) in Christianity, particularly among interpreters in Philo's own city, Alexandria.

LANGUAGE

Greek was the lingua franca of the Roman Empire, and the whole New Testament was written in Greek. It is not the classical Greek of Plato or Thucydides, but what had come to be known as the *koine* or 'common' Greek: a form of the classical language that had developed over the few centuries that separated the Mediterranean world of the first century CE from the golden age of Athens. 'Common' has both positive and negative connotations: on the one hand, universal, common to all educated speakers; on the other, vulgar, down a register or two from the pure classical norm.[11]

The changes from classical to koine Greek are a matter of detail, but most reflect a tendency to simplify – eliminating grammatical complexities – and to standardize: the many inflections at the ends of nouns and verbs tend to be reduced in number, and clauses come to be linked more with a simple 'and', rather than with the multitude of nuanced adverbs and particles of classical Greek. The underlying purpose of the changes is to make it possible for communication to take place between two people neither of whom may have Greek as their first language.

Even though koine is a simplified version of classical Greek, it can still be spoken or written correctly or incorrectly. In the New Testament, Mark's Greek has notable deficiencies by comparison, say, with Luke's, which is far more stylish, at least when Luke is composing freely, as in the opening prologue (Luke 1:1–4), rather than copying Mark. And Revelation is often in positively incorrect Greek, with grammatical errors that are noticeable by any standards. The author was almost certainly more fluent in a Semitic language – probably Aramaic – than in Greek of any kind.

Paul's Greek is less Semitized than that of the Gospel writers, suggesting that he thought fluently in the language. He could obviously read Hebrew and presumably also Aramaic, but Greek is his natural habitat. He was familiar with some at least of the conventions of Greek rhetoric:

> ... suffering produces endurance, and endurance produces character, and character produces hope, and hope does not disappoint us ...
>
> (Romans 5:3–5)

The Old Testament is of course quoted in Greek in the New Testament, and the quotations show that Greek was already evolving by the time the Hebrew Scriptures were being translated into Greek. The Greek translation or Septuagint (see Chapters 1 and 18) is not in classical Greek, but in the Greek of the last few centuries BCE, though with the complication that it is full of 'Semitisms', that is, places where the Greek is distorted by the desire to remain as close as possible to the underlying Hebrew (and Aramaic).

All the New Testament writers are sufficiently fluent in koine Greek to suggest that they wrote in that language: there is no evidence that any New Testament book is a translation from any other language. Bits of Aramaic, when they occur, are always translated into Greek. In Mark 5:41 Jesus speaks to a dead girl and says, 'Talitha kumi', which the evangelist translates as 'which means, "Little girl, get up!"', suggesting that the audience for the books did not know Aramaic. The very first disciples would certainly have spoken Aramaic; whether or not they (or indeed Jesus) knew any Greek is unclear.[12] But all the people to whom the books of the New Testament were addressed seem to have known Greek and no Aramaic, a sign of how soon the Christian message moved into the Gentile world and away from its Palestinian, Aramaic-speaking homeland.

With the exception of the odd phrase such as *talitha kumi*, we do not possess any of the sayings of Jesus in the Aramaic he would have spoken himself,[13] but only in Greek translation. This ought to be seen as a problem if one is appealing, as to a ruling, to anything he is recorded as saying, since we can never press the exact wording – it may have been distorted in the translation. It is very common for Christians to argue from the exact wording of Jesus' sayings, for example on subjects such as divorce, while forgetting that he uttered them in a language different from that in which we have them in the New Testament. This is also true of a sentence over which much ink, and indeed blood, has been spilled in Christian history, the words, 'This is my body' at the Last Supper. Christians have argued about the exact meaning of 'is' – but in the original Aramaic there will have been no verb in the sentence, since in Semitic languages such sentences have simply the pronoun and noun ('This my body' or 'My body this').

Latin did not play a major role in the early transmission of the Christian message, despite the fact that this all happened in the Roman Empire. But Latin was not an international language so early. Romans used it to communicate with each other, but their subject peoples did so in Greek, and all educated Romans had competence in Greek. Even early Christian worship in Rome was conducted in Greek, and that is the reason why a few words of Greek remain in the liturgy, notably *kyrie/christe eleison* ('Lord/Christ, have mercy'). Nevertheless, some Latin (written in Greek letters) does appear in the New Testament, mostly in technical terms that would have been known from the ubiquity of the Roman army: words such as *praetorium*, *centurion*, *speculator* (executioner), *denarius* and names of other coins. (See also Chapter 18.)

SECTS AND PARTIES

The early Christians were described above as a sect, meaning by this a small, focused group aware of itself as exceptional in relation to a larger, more mainstream body. The distinction between open-ended organizations and more exclusive, and therefore more easily defined, groups goes back to Max Weber, and, before him, to Ernst Troeltsch.[14] The characteristics of a sect are well summed up by Joseph Blenkinsopp:[15]

> (1) The sect is a voluntary association. To become a member of a sect one must satisfy criteria and qualifications dictated by the purpose of the group . . .
>
> (2) The sect is characterized by a strong sense of boundaries, of an insider-outsider differentiation . . .
>
> (3) The sect will either be introversionist and withdrawn from 'the world' outside as corrupt and corrupting or it will be reformist and undertake a mission to transform and save the world.
>
> (4) . . . the sect will tend either to define itself with reference to the parent body from which it has dissociated itself or from which it has been forcibly dissociated, or it will stake an exclusive claim to be the authentic heir and possessor of the traditions cherished by the parent body . . .
>
> (5) . . . a sect will generally arise and function at the margins of the society in which it is embedded, and will therefore be deprived of access to the sources of political and religious power in that society.

There were various groupings in the first century CE among Palestinian Jews: Pharisees, Sadducees, scribes and Essenes, to name just four, and they may have overlapped – someone could be both a Pharisee and a scribe. Sadducees were mostly priests, and therefore well integrated into Jewish society – not at all sect-like in character, even though they had some distinctive ideas, apparently rejecting the quite widespread belief in life after death, for example (see Acts 23:8). Essenes, according to Josephus, Philo and the Roman writer Pliny the Elder, led a somewhat ascetic life, involving many purification rituals and, at least for some, celibacy.

The Pharisaic movement was focused on stricter standards of observance of the Torah than was usual among most Jews – something like modern ultra-Orthodox Judaism.[16] Pharisees were Jews who took their religious obligations more seriously than most. They had no intention, however, of splitting off from the main body of their fellow-believers, and they lived a public life and were not 'introversionist'. We might call them a semi-sect, an important Pharisaic institution being the *haburah* or fellowship group, to join which one had to take on certain obligations to a higher standard of ritual purity than the average Jew. 'In a sense the pharisaic *haburah* was an enclave of holiness, in which priest and layman alike shared the same degree of holiness.'[17] The Pharisees shared with the first Christians their interest in eschatology – the coming great change in the course of history that God would bring about, which would include the resurrection of the dead. Their religious life focused on the synagogue rather than the Temple; though some Pharisees were indeed priests, their spirituality was one of the study-house rather than of the Temple cult, which placed emphasis on animal and vegetable sacrifices. Pharisees were in no way opposed to the Temple, but they developed a piety that was able, in the long run, to survive its destruction and become recognizably the ancestor of modern Orthodox Judaism.

Only two of these groups really qualify for the title 'sect': early Christians, and the community at Khirbet Qumran to whom we owe the preservation of the Dead Sea Scrolls. (The latter may be identical, or may overlap, with the Essenes: this is much discussed among experts.[18]) The Dead Sea community may or may not have been largely celibate; certainly some members of it were. But in any case it observed very high standards of ritual purity, requiring frequent bathing and a fierce community rule prescribing various penalties for ritual infringements, which went well beyond what the Torah required. Its members lived in acute expectation of the irruption of the rule of God, in this being very like the earliest Christians.

These two groups were also alike in operating with clear boundary markers to distinguish members from non-members. They had rather similar attitudes towards the Hebrew Bible, regarding it as predicting what had happened in the life of the community in question. Both the group at Qumran and the early Christians tended to see themselves as the true 'Israel', in contradistinction to the main body of Jews who claimed that title. Thus Paul:

> For a person is not a Jew who is one outwardly, nor is true circumcision something external and physical. Rather, a person is a Jew who is one inwardly, and real circumcision is a matter of the heart – it is spiritual and not literal.
>
> (Romans 2:28–9)

Somewhat more stridently in Hebrews:

> We have an altar from which those who officiate in the tent [in other words, the Temple] have no right to eat.
>
> (Hebrews 13:10)

They regarded themselves as the faithful ones – it was everyone else who had erred: a classic sectarian attitude, as suggested by Blenkinsopp, above. It was they who had taken over the promises made to Israel. The Dead Sea community similarly saw itself as the true Temple, performing the correct rituals in the desert while the priests in the actual Temple had gone astray.[19]

Christianity was the one successful Jewish sect that survived and flourished after the Qumran group had long ceased to exist, as sects tend to do, especially if they depend on a particular location. In its early days the Christian group was a Galilean movement, and its adherents were fishermen and other largely uneducated people, but after Jesus' crucifixion it grew apace, undoubtedly because of the disciples' belief that Jesus had risen from the dead and empowered them with the spirit of God. By Paul's day it had spread into Syria, assuming that the account of his conversion on the road to Damascus, and reception there by Christian believers, is essentially historical (see Acts 9:1–22). Its great success, however, came when it widened its scope to include Gentiles – anyone in fact who professed faith in Jesus – offering a form of Judaism (which many non-Jews already respected) that did not entail circumcision and the observance of the food and purity regulations; and then turned itself into what Weber defined as a 'church', that is, a group with more porous boundaries than a sect and embracing far more people in its remit. It is not certain whether the move to welcome Gentiles was chiefly on Paul's initiative: Acts 10–11 portrays Peter as the first to make it, the same Peter who, according to Galatians, later backtracked (see Galatians 2:11–14). It was probably Paul who transformed what had been, at most, a proselytizing mission to spread a novel form of Judaism into the promotion of what was in effect a new religion open to all, with its own

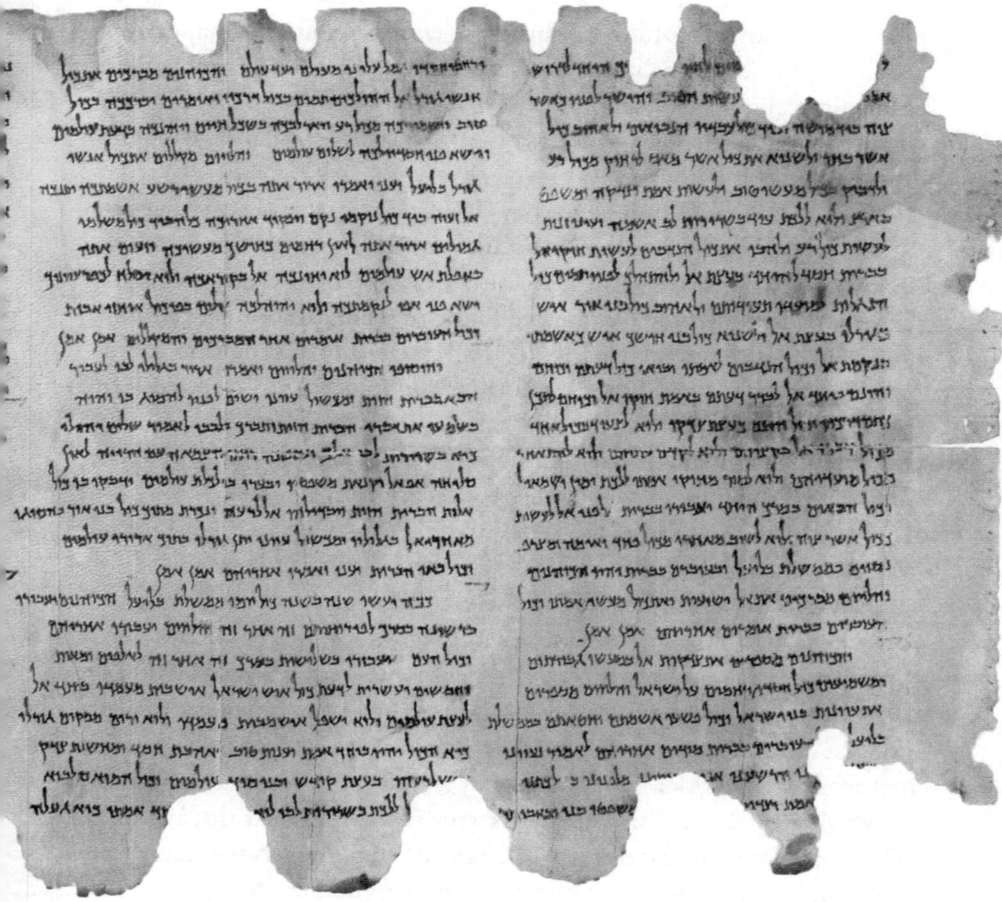

The 'Community Rule' from the Dead Sea Scrolls, setting out requirements for members of the group.

terms of reference that were no longer identical with those of nascent rabbinic Judaism. But imagining 'Christianity without Paul' is a speculative exercise.[20] We do know, from Paul's own witness, that the church in Rome was not founded by him: his letter to that church is his lengthiest discussion of the balancing act involved in uniting Jews and Gentiles in a single community. So it is likely that preaching to the Gentiles really did antedate Paul's own mission.

Nevertheless, there is always a tension in Christianity between an open and a closed attitude to outsiders, with some denominations, or groups within denominations, insisting on the boundaries, and others caring little about them, and this goes back to the time of Paul. The very earliest Christians, however, clearly fell on the sectarian side of this divide. They could not have survived otherwise.

There is another feature shared by the Dead Sea sectaries and the first Christians: they produced a sizeable body of their own literature, which supplemented, and gave rules for interpreting correctly, the existing Hebrew Scriptures. At Qumran we find commentaries on the Hebrew Bible (such as the great *Habakkuk Pesher* cited in Chapter 4), documents about the coming intervention of God and how to respond to it (for example the War Scroll), and rules for the life of the community (the 'Community Rule'). Christianity was also to generate its own texts, some of which would become the New Testament.

CHRISTIAN WRITINGS: THREE STAGES

Christian writing began with the letters of Paul, within a couple of decades of the crucifixion of Jesus, that is, in the 50s CE. It never stopped, though eventually a body of early Christian literature came to be delineated from later works by its definition as the New Testament. Within the writing of these works it makes sense to distinguish three stages, even though to some extent they overlap, and not every New Testament book can be unhesitatingly assigned to one or another of them.

The earliest stage is represented by the genuine letters of Paul, beginning with 1 Thessalonians. Their order depends on correlating events and places mentioned in them with what we can establish of Paul's life from the Acts of the Apostles. We shall see in the next chapter that this can be difficult, but most New Testament specialists agree on the order: 1 Thessalonians, 1 Corinthians, 2 Corinthians, Galatians, Romans, Philippians, Philemon. The other letters are widely regarded as inauthentic, though there is no agreement on this in the case of 2 Thessalonians, which would need to have been written soon after 1 Thessalonians, and Colossians, which would have followed Philippians. The issue of pseudonymous letters will be addressed in Chapter 7.

The sayings of Jesus, in so far as they genuinely go back to him, must be earlier than anything in Paul, coming from the 20s or 30s CE. But the books in which the sayings are contained, the Gospels, are agreed by most to be later than the whole corpus of Paul's letters (see Chapter 8). Some think that Mark, the earliest Gospel, was written before Jerusalem fell to the Romans in 70 CE, but it is still later than Paul's letters; while Matthew, Luke and John are generally seen as composed after 70, with John conceivably at the beginning of the second century. The Gospels thus represent a second phase in the production of Christian writings; a whole generation of Christians practised their faith without having access to them. This is not to imply that the Gospels are late fictions: almost certainly they rest on memories passed down by word of mouth, and perhaps sometimes jotted down in informal documents, collections of sayings such as the putative Q, which I shall discuss in Chapter 8. The fact remains, however, that the first generation did not apparently find a need to record the traditions about Jesus in formal books, and much seems to have been transmitted orally. Paul indeed refers to the tradition he had received about the crucifixion and resurrection, as also about the Last Supper and the origins of the Eucharist:

> For I handed on to you as of first importance what I in turn had received: that Christ died for our sins in accordance with the scriptures, and that he was buried, and that he was raised on the third day in accordance with the scriptures, and that he appeared to Cephas [i.e. Peter], then to the twelve. Then he appeared to more than five hundred brothers and sisters at one time, most of whom are still alive, though some have died. Then he appeared to James, then to all the apostles. Last of all, as to someone untimely born, he appeared also to me.
>
> (1 Corinthians 15:3–8)

> I received from the Lord what I also handed on to you, that the Lord Jesus on the night when he was betrayed took a loaf of bread, and when he had given thanks, he broke it and said, 'This is my body that is for you. Do this in remembrance of me.' In the same way he took the cup also, after supper, saying, 'This cup is the new covenant in my blood. Do this, as often as you drink it, in remembrance of me.'
>
> (1 Corinthians 11:23–5)

Paul does not suggest that there was any written record of these things, nor does he tell us from whom he heard them.

The third phase, towards the end of the first or at the beginning of the second century CE, saw the writing of a diverse collection of Christian documents. One is the Acts of the Apostles, presented as the second volume of Luke's Gospel (see Acts 1:1) but not necessarily by the same author as Luke, and another may be the book of Revelation, though some think it much earlier than this.[21] The majority of the later works are in the form of letters, either attributed to Paul (2 Thessalonians, Colossians, Ephesians, 1 Timothy, 2 Timothy, Titus)[22] or ascribed to various of Jesus' followers (Peter, James, John, Jude). There is also Hebrews, traditionally thought to be by Paul but actually anonymous: the title in the King James Version, 'The Epistle of Paul the Apostle to the Hebrews', does not correspond to anything in any ancient manuscripts. By general consent 2 Peter is the latest of the New Testament books to be written, early in the second century. Some of its content derives from Jude, which is another latecomer.

By then other Christian works also existed, and we are faced with the question why they were not also eventually accepted into the canon, the official list of biblical books. Some were, in some communities: thus we have manuscripts that contain the work called *The Shepherd*, by an otherwise unknown Christian writer called Hermas, as well as the Gospels, notably the great *Codex Sinaiticus* of the fourth century. There are scholars who think that *The Teaching of the Twelve Apostles* (the *Didache* as it is called in the Greek) is older than some Gospels and is indeed one of the sources of Matthew. Even if this is not so, it is at the latest from the very early second century, and so probably earlier than at least some of the New Testament books. There is also the *Gospel of Thomas*, which some believe preserves a few genuine sayings of Jesus, even though as a whole it is unlikely to be very early. It should be stressed, however, that no other Gospels are anything like as early as those now in the New Testament: the theory that the Church suppressed works early enough to be authentic records of Jesus' teaching is wild speculation.[23] (There will be more on these questions in later chapters.)

The dating of the New Testament books has been described as like a line of drunks, propping each other up, with no fixed wall to lean on.[24] The only ones that are really secure are the dates of Paul's letters, which must have been written between the 40s and the 60s. Where other books are concerned, there is wide variation. James, for example, may be seen as a late, pseudonymous work, or as a very early Jewish writing that has been only slightly Christianized. The date of John's Gospel is disputed, too: the consensus is that it is later than the Synoptics (Matthew, Mark and Luke), whether or not its author knew them; but there are scholars who think it much earlier than this. Acts, which is pivotal in establishing the relative dates of Paul's letters, is regarded by some as an early account of the mission of the Church in its first years and an authentic record of the missionary journeys of Paul, but by others as a late fiction, presenting an idealized story of early Christianity, and falsely claiming that its author was present with Paul on his travels.

Often these conflicting opinions correlate with scholars' attitudes towards the status of the Bible. Conservative approaches to the authority of Scripture – emphasizing its divine inspiration – tend to go hand in hand with early datings for the biblical books; more liberal ones often manifest at least hospitality towards later datings. One may spin this differently and say, for example, that those of a conservative bent have minds open to evidence of early dating, whereas liberals have closed their minds to this in advance.

As so often with the Bible, even such apparently innocuous questions as the dates of books can be informed by a prior concern for a particular way of reading and reacting to these books. In the end one can only try to weigh the evidence, aware all the time of one's own bias, and hope to be as objective as possible.

7
Letters

'If anyone is in Christ, there is a new creation: everything old has passed away; see, everything has become new!' (2 Corinthians 5:17). Early Christians' belief that the resurrection of Jesus Christ had renewed and refreshed the whole of creation released a huge wave of energy and innovation within this initially small and politically insignificant movement. This was expressed not only in the corporate life of the young churches, but also in the literature they produced; and not only in the content of that literature, but even in its form: letters and Gospels.

The letters or epistles of Paul are the earliest Christian literature we possess. Nothing is known of Paul except from the New Testament. The book of Acts presents him as a zealous Pharisee from Asia Minor who had studied in Jerusalem and was an early persecutor of the Christian movement, until he was converted to it himself through a vision while on the way to Damascus (see Acts 9:1–30). It is clear both from Acts and from his own letters that he travelled widely around the Mediterranean, preaching the news about Jesus to both Jews and Gentiles, but predominantly the latter. At the end of Acts he is under house arrest in Rome, and Christian tradition holds that he was martyred there, though there is no direct evidence for this.

Paul is a good example of the Hellenization of Jewish culture described in Chapter 6. A highly observant Jew, he was fluent in Greek, and the corpus of his letters gives us insight not only into early Christian thought, but also into the assumptions a Hellenized Jew of his time shared with his co-religionists.

Letters were a familiar phenomenon in the Graeco-Roman world and had a set form, with formulaic opening and closing greetings. In a context where writing materials were expensive and most letters were actually penned by a secretary, letter-writing was not a casual activity, and often writers aimed at literary excellence: some collections of letters, such as those of Cicero (106–43 BCE), were published. Paul's letters are similarly carefully wrought, not casual pieces. But they are distinctive in many ways against the background of the time.[1]

The letters of Paul that have survived were mostly written not to individuals but to Christian communities. Paul expected his letters to be read aloud when the community came together to worship and share meals. And the letters are long, by contemporary standards, and often quite involved, requiring several readings to be fully understood and absorbed. They also have a characteristic form. There is an opening greeting identifying the writer and his associates:

> Paul, an apostle of Christ Jesus by the will of God, and Timothy our brother, To the church of God that is in Corinth, including all the saints[2] throughout Achaia: Grace to you and peace from God our Father and the Lord Jesus Christ.
>
> (2 Corinthians 1:1–2)

Then follows (in all except Galatians) a section giving thanks for the faith and goodness of the particular Christian community being addressed. This is an innovation in letter-writing:

> We always give thanks to God for all of you and mention you in our prayers, constantly remembering before our God and Father your work of faith and labour of love and steadfastness of hope in our Lord Jesus Christ.
>
> (1 Thessalonians 1:2–3)

The body of the letter then concentrates on the matters Paul wants to take up with the addressees, usually concerned with the ordering of their community life or what they are to believe, and in the process he discloses much about his own theological thought. A number of letters end with a section of ethical exhortation, and then closing greetings, including on one occasion a greeting from the scribe who had acted as Paul's secretary and actually written the letter in the physical sense: 'I Tertius, the writer of this letter, greet you in the Lord' (Romans 16:22). One letter, the short letter to Philemon, is addressed to an individual, but it still exhibits the same form, which taken in all its elements is an innovation on Paul's part.

Paul's letters were nearly all addressed to churches he himself had founded through his missionary activity around the Mediterranean, in what we would now call Greece and Turkey – according to the Acts of the Apostles, Paul himself came from Turkey (Asia Minor), from Tarsus. Only the Letter to the Romans is meant for a church he had not founded, and in consequence it is more restrained than the other letters when it comes to giving advice and instruction. Paul begins by saying that he is coming to visit the Roman church to benefit it, but then seems to draw back and reflect that it is not 'his' church:

> I am longing to see you so that I may share with you some spiritual gift to strengthen you – or rather so that we may be mutually encouraged by each other's faith, both yours and mine.
>
> (Romans 1:11–12)

In the other letters Paul considers himself as having the authority to command those he had converted to the new faith as to what they should believe and do. In one case, the Letter to the Christians of Galatia, he was faced with what he saw as such a misunderstanding of the gospel message that he even omits the opening praise of his readers, and after the initial greeting (in which he reminds them at once of his authority) pitches straight into an attack on them:

> Paul an apostle – sent neither by human commission nor from human authorities, but through Jesus Christ and God the Father, who raised him from the dead – and all the members of God's family who are with me, To the churches of Galatia: Grace to you and peace from God our Father and the Lord Jesus Christ, who gave himself for our sins to set us free from the present evil age, according to the will of our God and Father, to whom be the glory for ever and ever. Amen. I am astonished that you are so quickly deserting the one who called you in the grace of Christ and are turning to a different gospel – not that there is another gospel, but there are some who are confusing you and want to pervert the gospel of Christ.
>
> (Galatians 1:1–7)

We know there were other letters that are now lost, since the first letter to the church in Corinth refers to at least one other letter (1 Corinthians 5:9). It is also possible that 2 Corinthians is not a single letter, but an amalgam of sections from more than one, which could explain why it is less coherent than is generally the case with Paul, with odd breaks and inconsequentialities.[3]

There is fairly broad agreement on the order of Paul's authentic letters, though, as we shall see, most specialists regard some of them as pseudonymous. Partly the order depends on our knowledge of where Paul was at various stages of his peripatetic mission, and that in turns depends on the Acts of the Apostles, which is a problem in itself. But the order 1 Thessalonians, 1 and 2 Corinthians, Galatians, Romans, Philippians,

Philemon is, as we have seen, relatively uncontroversial. The correspondence with Corinth and Galatia comes from the earlier part of Paul's work, with Romans following when he was still hoping to visit Rome on his way to Spain. In the end he made it there only as a prisoner awaiting trial and, probably, martyrdom. Philippians and Philemon would then date from his imprisonment, though just where he was at the time is uncertain: he will have been held in various places on his way to Rome. It is also possible that they come from an earlier incarceration, since we know from his own account that he had several spells in prison (see 2 Corinthians 11:23).

From these few genuine letters of Paul we learn what he had taught those he converted, and what he himself believed, though this is never presented systematically, but piecemeal as the argument of each letter requires. Deferring for a moment the major topic of 'justification by faith', which has been the focus of much academic writing on Paul, we can see from two examples, the resurrection of Jesus and his status as Son of God, that Paul differs considerably from what later became Christian orthodoxy; and this sets up a difficulty in treating the Pauline letters as a source for Christian doctrine.

PAUL AND THE RESURRECTION

Paul assumes in all his letters that Jesus has been raised from the dead and is now alive eternally:

> I handed on to you as of first importance what I in turn had received: that Christ died for our sins in accordance with the scriptures, and that he was buried, and that he was raised on the third day in accordance with the scriptures.
>
> (1 Corinthians 15:3–4)

In the Gospels, which are much later compositions, various people find Jesus' tomb empty, and are then confronted by the resurrected Jesus: in Matthew, Mary Magdalene and another Mary (Matthew 28:1–10); in Luke, the women who had followed Jesus from Galilee (Luke 24:1–24); in John, Mary Magdalene (John 20:1–18). Paul by contrast never mentions the empty tomb. He does refer to resurrection appearances, but they are very different from those recorded in the Gospels:

> He appeared to Cephas [i.e. Peter], then to the twelve. Then he appeared to more than five hundred brothers and sisters[4] at one time, most of whom

> are still alive, though some have died. Then he appeared to James, then to all the apostles. Last of all, as to someone untimely born, he appeared also to me.
>
> (1 Corinthians 15:5–8)

There is no mention here of the women who, according to the Gospels, were the first at the tomb, and the 'five hundred' disciples are not referred to anywhere else in the New Testament. Furthermore Paul seems to imply that his own vision of the risen Jesus was the same as that of all the other early witnesses, even though according to Acts (9:3–5) he saw only a light and heard a voice. As to the nature of the resurrection itself, he seems to differentiate it from physical resuscitation, emphasizing that 'flesh and blood cannot inherit the kingdom of God' (1 Corinthians 15:50) and that what any resurrected person possesses is a 'spiritual body' (15:44), which sounds like a deliberate contradiction in terms, attempting to grasp a new reality that cannot really be captured in words. It would be wrong to say that Paul's picture of the resurrection is actually incompatible with the accounts in the Gospels, but it certainly stresses quite different aspects. Attempts to ground faith in the resurrection of Jesus by emphasizing the empty tomb, or the appearance of the risen Lord to the women, cannot appeal to Paul for support: he seems to have quite different concerns.

For Paul the resurrection of Jesus belongs in an eschatological context, that is, the breaking-in of the 'last days', the time foretold by the prophets when God would inaugurate his royal rule over the world. We already see the concern with the end-time in this sense in 1 Thessalonians, where Paul grapples with the fact that his own preaching had so stressed the imminence of the End that his converts were worried that recently deceased adherents would miss out on the benefits of God's kingdom. For Paul, the resurrection of Jesus is a sign that the kingdom is nearly present: Christ, he says, is the 'first fruits', that is, the first sheaf in the harvest of the earth, and a sure sign that the full harvest will soon follow (1 Corinthians 15:23). Resurrection was believed in by many Jews, but it was to happen only when God brought in his kingdom, not on an occasional or random basis.[5] Paul's argument is that the kingdom is about to dawn, and the resurrection of this one person, Jesus, is the sign of this. He does not argue, as many Christian apologists might, that Jesus' resurrection proves that resurrection is possible, but rather that resurrection must be possible, or else we could not believe in the resurrection of Jesus (1 Corinthians 15:12–19). What the resurrection of

Jesus proves is that the End is near, and Christian believers can look forward to sharing his risen life when the End comes. The answer to the Thessalonians' concern is that those who die before the End will not be disadvantaged, but will join those who are still alive to 'meet the Lord in the air' (1 Thessalonians 4:13–18). (As we saw in the Introduction, this passage is the source of the theory of the 'rapture' believed in by many evangelical Christians worldwide, though they integrate it into a wider eschatological scheme that draws on other parts of the Bible too.)

JESUS AS SON OF GOD IN PAUL

In traditional Christianity Jesus is believed to be the incarnation of the Second Person of the Trinity, which means that he is God. Common sense suggests that such an idea must have arisen slowly, as a Galilean peasant preacher gradually turned, in the minds of his followers over several generations, into a divine being. But in fact there is evidence that Paul and his associates were already developing a high Christology – meaning an exalted status for Jesus – within the lifetime of some people who had actually known him. Paul does not make the simple equation Jesus = God, but he speaks of Jesus in elevated terms, and thinks that Christians ought to give him honour very little different from the honour they pay to God. This can be noticed already in the opening greetings in Paul's letters, 'from God our Father and the Lord Jesus Christ' (1 Corinthians 1:3; compare 2 Corinthians 1:2, Galatians 1:3, Philippians 1:2), and in the final greeting in 2 Corinthians 13:13, 'The grace of the Lord Jesus Christ, the love of God, and the communion of the Holy Spirit, be with all of you' – hinting at a Trinitarian formula already in Paul's lifetime.

Many readers notice that Paul has little interest in Jesus' earthly life or deeds: there are no references to the miracles, and virtually none to the teachings. Paul denies, or at least appears to deny, that he should be interested in the human side of Jesus – 'even though we once knew Christ from a human point of view [Greek: after the flesh], we know him no longer in that way' (2 Corinthians 5:16). What interests him is Jesus as the Messiah (*christos* in Greek), and not only Messiah but also Son of God. This is an old title for the Messiah, deriving from a term used of the king in early Israel, which does not of itself imply that the Messiah is on a par with God, but does place him far above ordinary mortals. In Philippians 2 Paul describes how Christ descended from

God and became mortal, and was then exalted by him (through the resurrection):

> ... though he was in the form of God, [he] did not regard equality with God as something to be exploited, but emptied himself, taking the form of a slave, being born in human likeness. And being found in human form, he humbled himself and became obedient to the point of death – even death on a cross. Therefore God also highly exalted him and gave him the name that is above every name, so that at the name of Jesus every knee should bend, in heaven and on earth and under the earth, and every tongue should confess that Jesus Christ is Lord, to the glory of God the Father.
>
> (Philippians 2:6–11)

Some think that Paul is here quoting an already existing hymn to Jesus;[6] if that is so, then the belief the passage expresses must be even earlier than Paul himself, and must have come into being within a decade or two after the crucifixion. What exactly was meant by Christ 'being in the form of God' is unclear, but it must at least imply that he existed in some form before he was born on earth. This is sometimes seen as an example of Paul applying Greek categories, such as Plato's concept of invisible and heavenly 'forms', to the originally Jewish gospel message, perhaps to explain the message to non-Jewish converts. But there are Jewish texts that already see the Messiah as at least semi-divine.[7] *Second Baruch*, a Jewish book probably originally written in Hebrew in the late first century CE, for example, speaks of the Messiah (the 'anointed one') as a supernatural figure:

> And it will happen after these things when the time of the appearance of the Anointed has been fulfilled and he returns with glory, that then all who sleep in hope of him will rise. And it will happen at that time that those treasuries will be opened in which the number of the souls of the righteous were kept, and they will go out and the multitudes of the souls will appear together, in one sole assembly, of one mind ... The souls of the wicked, on the contrary, will waste away completely when they shall see all these things.[8]
>
> (2 *Baruch* 30:1–2, 4)

Second Corinthians (8:9) also implies that Jesus had a pre-earthly existence: 'you know the generous act of our Lord Jesus Christ, that though he was rich, yet for your sakes he became poor, so that by his poverty you might become rich.' This does not mean that Jesus had been particularly affluent and then become impoverished, but that he had possessed a divine status and had then come to earth, becoming 'poor' in the sense of becoming mortal. It is important to notice that this far-reaching teaching is put forward as what 'you know', something taken for granted and which must have been part of Paul's original proclamation of the gospel to the people in Corinth. And it is quoted almost as an aside, in a passage that actually concerns a practical issue, the collection that Paul was gathering up from his churches to help Christians in Jerusalem. The humility of Jesus in taking on human flesh can be referred to as something so well known that it can form the basis for an appeal for generosity.

A third passage confirms that Jesus is the Son of God, but represents a different approach to the question. In the greeting at the beginning of Romans Paul contrasts Jesus as son of David (i.e. Messiah), which he was 'according to the flesh', with Jesus as Son of God:

> Paul, a servant of Jesus Christ, called to be an apostle, set apart for the gospel of God, which he promised beforehand through his prophets in the holy scriptures, the gospel concerning his Son, who was descended from David according to the flesh and was declared to be Son of God with power according to the spirit of holiness by resurrection from the dead, Jesus Christ our Lord.
>
> (Romans 1:1–4)

This passage, however, has what would later be referred to as an *adoptionist* tone, that is, it seems to think of Jesus as *becoming* Son of God rather than having been so from all eternity. The resurrection is identified as the moment at which his adoption as God's Son occurred.[9] This was a variety of Christian belief quite common in the early centuries, though eventually condemned as a heresy. In Paul there are as yet no hard-and-fast doctrines that can be judged orthodox or heretical: he is trying out various ways of capturing the sense he has of the exalted character of Jesus as risen from the dead. In fact the passage is a bit equivocal: it speaks of Jesus as being designated Son of God *with power*, which might mean he already was Son of God but this only became apparent at the resurrection. Understanding Paul often involves ambiguities and uncertainties of this kind, and using his writings as the basis for well-defined doctrines is a very fragile approach. In the letters one can see him feeling his way towards adequate formulations for a reality he could not yet properly define. If we could ask Paul, 'Was Jesus the Second Person of the Trinity?', he would not have had an answer: such a way of putting the question developed after his time. Even so, we have already noticed the inchoately Trinitarian formula in 2 Corinthians 13:13, and here in Romans Father and Son are named alongside 'the spirit of holiness'. (NRSV in a footnote speculates that we should perhaps print 'Spirit' with a capital S.)

Fourthly, there are places where Paul is what would come to be called subordinationist: he regards Jesus, though in some sense divine, as subordinate to God the Father. We find this in 1 Corinthians 15:28:

> When all things are subjected to him [i.e. Jesus], then the Son himself will also be subjected to the one who put all things in subjection under him, so that God may be all in all.

Again, this would in later times have seemed slightly heretical, but for Paul, apparently, it is natural to think that Jesus Christ, though highly exalted, has a lower rank than God himself. Jesus is the Son, very much with a capital S, but not the Father. Later generations would grapple to get a coherent doctrine out of this, but for Paul it implies an extremely high evaluation of the identity of Jesus:

> Even though there may be many so-called gods in heaven or on earth – as in fact there are many gods and many lords – yet for us there is one God, the Father, from whom are all things and for whom we exist, and one Lord, Jesus Christ, through whom are all things and through whom we exist.
>
> (1 Corinthians 8:5–6)

Though this may seem to ascribe a lower status to Jesus than in the later formulations of the doctrine of the Trinity, it represents an extraordinarily high Christology a couple of decades after the crucifixion. Jesus is the one 'through whom we exist', akin to God's wisdom, by which he made the world (see Chapter 3). This theme is developed in Colossians, but many commentators think this is not really by Paul. There Christ 'is the image of the invisible God, the firstborn of all creation; for in him all things in heaven and on earth were created . . . He himself is before all things, and in him all things hold together . . . For in him all the fullness of God was pleased to dwell' (Colossians 1:15–17, 19).

CHURCH ORDER

On a number of topics to do with Christian belief and life, then, Paul provides a great deal of information, even though what we learn from him may conflict with later beliefs. But there are other questions we might like to know about which Paul simply does not discuss. This applies particularly to the way the churches he founded were ordered and organized. We can see from the letters that Paul set up some form of organization in his churches: there were evidently leaders, though they have no fixed titles, and there is no telling what their activities consisted of. Philippians 1:1 speaks of the *episkopoi kai diakonoi*, traditionally translated as 'bishops and deacons', but there is no way of telling what relation such people have to later bishops and deacons. A small church such as that at Philippi would hardly have had a multitude of 'bishops' in the later sense of the word, and the NRSV note, 'overseers and helpers' may capture the sense better. In 1 Corinthians it is clear that Stephanas *and his family* have a central role (16:15–16), and we find believers who seem to 'host' the church, which meets in people's houses (16:19). There are also odd references to 'apostles' (*apostoloi*), one of whom may be female (Junia, mentioned in Romans 16:7). They are clearly not identical with the twelve original disciples. But what Paul meant by *apostolos* is impossible to say; in 2 Corinthians 8:23 he refers to the *apostoloi* of the churches, meaning simply 'those sent by the churches' (*apostolos* means originally 'sent one' or 'envoy') – 'the messengers of the churches', as NRSV translates it.

Nor do we know whether the leaders of the churches were in charge of their liturgical life. Nothing at all is said about who may preside at the Lord's Supper or Eucharist, as it came to be known, and there is nothing about who may baptize. Paul at one point actually denies that he himself had done this to any significant extent (1 Corinthians 1:16–17), saying that his task was not to baptize but to preach the gospel, a distinction that would not have appealed to later generations of Christian leaders. The idea that these were in some sense priests, like the priests of ancient Israel, arrived later than Paul's day: indeed, throughout the New Testament 'priest' (*hiereus*) means either the priests in the Old Testament or the priestly caste of contemporary Judaism, and is never applied to any Christian minister or leader. In Hebrews it is Jesus who is the true high priest:

> We have such a high priest, one who is seated at the right hand of the throne of the Majesty in the heavens, a minister in the sanctuary and the true tent that the Lord, and not any mortal, has set up.
>
> (Hebrews 8:1–2)

Where the contents of Christian worship are concerned, Paul again provides virtually no information. 1 Corinthians 11 and 14 are the main sources, which speak of the importance of everything being done in an orderly way (14:40), but imply that members of the Christian congregation each come with contributions they wish to make and that they must allow them to be arranged, so there is not a cacophony:

> When you come together, each one has a hymn, a lesson, a revelation, a tongue, or an interpretation.
>
> (1 Corinthians 14:26)

Nothing is said, for example, about readings from Scripture (i.e. the Old Testament), though we get the impression from all the letters that Paul's converts are broadly familiar with it – whether they would have picked up all his allusions is another question. Try as we may, we cannot extract any specific regulations for Christian worship from Paul.

How far did Paul's churches know the story of Jesus, which would later come to be incorporated into the Gospels? If, as seems likely, it circulated by word of mouth for a generation before the Gospel writers began their work, then probably the Pauline churches were familiar with it. But Paul makes tantalizingly few references to Jesus as a historical figure, as we have seen. Perhaps the Corinthians recounted incidents from his life, or sayings of his, when they met for worship; but, if so, we could not work this out from Paul. All we learn from him is that Jesus was born, was crucified, and rose again from the dead. We also learn that baptism in his name was thought to effect incorporation into him, such that the baptized Christian in some mystical sense died and rose with Jesus:

> Do you not know that all of us who have been baptized into Christ Jesus were baptized into his death? Therefore we have been buried with him by baptism into death, so that, just as Christ was raised from the dead by the glory of the Father, so we too might walk in newness of life.
>
> (Romans 6:3–4)

Christians corporately formed the 'body' of Christ, and could be compared to the limbs and organs of a human body (1 Corinthians 12). This represented a new style of religious belief and practice, very different from any version of Judaism known to us, even though it continued to revere the God of Judaism and to make at least some use of the Jewish Scriptures.

PAUL AND THE ACTS OF THE APOSTLES

So far we have tried to establish Paul's teachings, and some details of his life, without paying any attention to the Acts of the Apostles. By general consent Acts comes from much later than Paul's day (probably some thirty or forty years later), even though it may preserve some historical memories – especially if it really is by Luke, who was perhaps one of those who accompanied Paul on his missions. A number of passages about Paul's travels are in the first-person plural (generally known as the 'we' passages), implying that the author was part of Paul's entourage.* For most of Christian history it has been assumed that the letters and the account in Acts could be used to complement each other in a straightforward way, so that one could work out where Paul was when he wrote each letter.

A sea-change in this approach came about with the publication in 1950 of the short book *Chapters in a Life of Paul* by the American New Testament scholar John Knox.[10] Knox made the point, until then almost entirely neglected, that the evidence of Acts is secondary evidence, while that of the letters is primary evidence from Paul himself, and hence the two sources should not be treated as equally accurate and simply harmonized. Knox argued that it was indeed possible to reconstruct the life of Paul from Acts and from the letters (in both cases with many gaps), but that the two versions were radically at odds with each other.

In Acts, Paul is based in Jerusalem, from where he undertakes three great 'missionary journeys' around the eastern Mediterranean. In the letters, there is no suggestion of these carefully planned excursions, and Paul seems to be based, if anywhere, in Damascus. Furthermore the chronologies do not tally. In Galatians 1–2 Paul tells us that three years after his conversion he was still unknown to the leaders of the church in Jerusalem, but then made just a single journey to Jerusalem to meet Peter and James. Then there was a period of fourteen years until he went there again. Fitting these fourteen years into the structure of Acts is almost impossible, since they would have to precede the missionary journeys, with the result that Paul's activity has to be stretched over a very long period. There is a fixed point towards the end, the accession to power of Porcius Festus as procurator of Judaea (Acts 24:27) in about 55 CE,[11] and if everything is to be fitted in before that, Paul's conversion has to be moved back extremely close to the crucifixion of Jesus, perhaps as early as 33 CE. It seems much more likely that the silent fourteen years were in fact filled with Paul's journeyings – more bitty than the idea of three great missionary journeys implies – and that

* The 'we' passages are Acts 16:10–17; 20:5–15; 21:1–18; and 27:1–28:16.

we know less than we might think (on the basis of Acts) about the chronology and geography of Paul's movements.

For example, one of his letters, Philippians, is clearly written from prison, and basing ourselves on Acts we would have to conclude that it dates from the time when he was imprisoned and taken to Rome for trial and, probably, execution. But from 2 Corinthians 11:23–9 we learn that Paul had often been in prison, as well as punished by flogging, shipwrecked, and subject to all kinds of other hardships and calamities, something we would not guess from Acts, where only one single night in prison is reported (Acts 16:19–40) before Paul's final arrest in Jerusalem. If we follow Paul's own statement, then it becomes impossible to know where he was when he wrote Philippians. Similarly, even the order of the letters is no longer easy to establish, once we abandon the framework provided by Acts and attend simply to the internal evidence of the letters themselves. As Knox points out, even solidly established hypotheses such as the idea that 1 Thessalonians is the first of Paul's letters can start to look shaky when we do this. First Thessalonians 1:8–9 says, 'For the word of God has sounded forth from you not only in Macedonia and Achaia, but in every place where your faith in God has become known, so that we have no need to speak about it. For the people of those regions report about us what kind of welcome we had among you', which implies quite a long period since Paul evangelized in Thessalonica, rather than that the letter followed soon after his visit, as is normally assumed. (Some think that these verses were added by a later editor.)

Above all, the Paul of the letters is not the same as the Paul of Acts. In Acts Paul operates under the authority of the church leaders in Jerusalem and is always careful to make sure he is in concord with them, eventually taking part in a fairly formal council, reported in Acts 15, on the question of the legitimacy of Gentile Christians. The 'council of Jerusalem', as it is sometimes known, is chaired by James, and Paul and Barnabas are treated as delegates to it from the church in Antioch. The council agrees, after debate, that the mission to the Gentiles is legitimate, provided that Gentile converts observe a few basic rules about morality and the consumption of meat. As James summarizes it:

> 'We should write to them to abstain only from things polluted by idols and from fornication and from whatever has been strangled and from blood.'
>
> (Acts 15:20)

In other words, Gentile Christians do not need to become Jews, but do need to observe a kind of junior version of Jewish purity rules. According to Acts, the council takes place relatively early in Paul's career. If we follow the letters, however, then Knox is probably correct in arguing that Paul's visit to Jerusalem to confer with the leaders is more likely to have taken place towards the end of his life, and that it led chiefly to his agreeing to take a collection from the Gentile churches for the impoverished Christian community in Jerusalem. A couple of years later he was delivering this collection when he was arrested, and his freedom came to a decisive end. The Paul who visited Jerusalem for this consultation – surely not a 'council' in a formal sense – did not see himself as under anyone's authority, but rather as fully equal with the Jerusalem leaders. We may recall that on the issue of the Gentiles he had withstood Peter to his face in Antioch (Galatians 2:11–14).

The Paul of the letters is thus a much more independent, wilder figure than Acts has made him, less concerned with maintaining harmony in the nascent Church, and convinced of his own rightness, especially over the Gentile issue. He claims to be an apostle in the fullest sense, defined as one who has seen the risen Jesus, and does not cede primacy in this to those who had been Jesus' disciples in his lifetime. This is a rather extraordinary claim, and the author of Acts does not seem to recognize it: he nowhere calls Paul an apostle, and in chapter 13 he actually has the community in Antioch laying hands on Paul and Barnabas to authenticate their mission to Jerusalem, something we may suspect Paul himself would have scorned. He can be humble enough, seeing himself as 'the least of the apostles' because he had persecuted the Church (1 Corinthians 15:9), but on the question of his apostolic authority he yields to no one.

Once we recognize that Acts is a late and secondary source of evidence for Paul's career, then we are left with a much vaguer outline into which to slot the letters, and we cannot date them absolutely at all, though the relative dating 1 Thessalonians, 1 and 2 Corinthians, Galatians and Romans remains defensible, with Philippians and Philemon floating uncertainly since we do not know which of Paul's 'many' imprisonments they belong to. What we do gain, however, is a body of genuinely very early evidence for the life and thought of the churches in the first generation after the crucifixion. This evidence comes from Paul as the leader of a number of Gentile churches in Greece and Asia Minor: we learn very little about the core Christian community in Jerusalem or Galilee, or about Jewish converts to the new faith. The question of the relationship of Jews to Gentiles within God's scheme of things as revealed through Jesus Christ does, however, come high on the agenda of topics the early Church was concerned about, and Paul's contribution to that issue is central to his thought, as we shall now see.

PAUL AND JUSTIFICATION BY FAITH

Since Martin Luther rediscovered Paul as an inspiration for his own theology, the interpretation of Paul has been dominated by Lutheran themes. In the Middle Ages Paul's thought had been integrated into a wider theology in which he appeared only as a comparatively minor contributor, much as his life story had been integrated with the outline provided by Acts. Paul's teaching that Christians are accepted by God not on the strength of their deeds but only because of God's grace, which they appropriate by having faith in God through Christ, had fallen from attention, because it was stressed that acceptability to God depended on one's actions. These actions were deemed to include various 'good works', meaning chiefly religious acts such as pilgrimages, saying and hearing Mass, taking part in religious processions, and the like. As is well known, Luther opposed this whole structure of religious works as a basis for salvation, and sought to show that the Bible did not require or teach it. Key to his reinterpretation of the Bible as teaching salvation only by the grace of God, obtained by faith in him rather than by good works, were the letters to the Romans and the Galatians, which became the linchpins of Reformation theology:

> 'No human being will be justified in his sight' by deeds prescribed by the law, for through the law comes the knowledge of sin. But now, irrespective of law, the righteousness of God has been disclosed, and is attested by the law and the prophets, the righteousness of God through faith in Jesus Christ for all who believe. For there is no distinction, since all have sinned and fall short of the glory of God; they are now justified by his grace as a gift, through the redemption that is in Christ Jesus.
>
> (Romans 3:20–24)

> [The promise to Abraham] depends on faith, in order that the promise may rest on grace and be guaranteed to all his descendants, not only to the adherents of the law but also to those who share the faith of Abraham.
>
> (Romans 4:16)

> We have come to believe in Christ Jesus, so that we might be justified by faith in Christ, and not by doing the works of the law, because no one will be justified by the works of the law.
>
> (Galatians 2:16)

Paul, like Luther, was seen as having struggled with the demands of God in the Old Testament law, only to be led eventually to the conviction that no amount of obedience to legal requirements could ever produce salvation. Paul at times confessed that he was incapable of the necessary obedience to God ('I do not do the good I want, but the evil I do not want is what I do', Romans 7:19); and at other times that he had been obedient (Philippians 3:4–6), yet had come to see that this was not enough. The matter was complicated by a certain ambiguity over what exactly is meant by 'works': ethical behaviour in general, or obedience to the specific ritual requirements of Judaism and, by analogy, of Catholicism. But it was agreed that neither was sufficient to earn salvation.

In the twentieth century there began to be what is usually called a New Perspective on Paul, associated especially with the American scholar E. P. Sanders, and in the United Kingdom with James Dunn and N. T. Wright.[12] This approached the theme of salvation by grace through faith not from the point of view of 'the introspective conscience of the West',[13] but by situating Paul in his historical context. Paul was not in truth struggling with his own failures or successes in observing the law, but was concerned mainly with the issue of Gentile admission to the Christian community and the relation of Gentile Christians to Jews – the issue that took him to Jerusalem to confer with Peter and James and the other leaders. The question was not how people in general are saved (meaning, individually rescued from eternal death, as in the Reformation debate), but whether Gentile converts to Christianity need to observe all the details of the Jewish law if they are to be saved (meaning, become part of the Christian community that is destined for eternal life with Christ). Paul's argument, which in places becomes strident, is that the Gentiles who have turned to Christ are not obliged to keep the Jewish law, because their faith in Christ is a fully sufficient substitute for the works of the law. Indeed, he suggests that Jews too are 'justified' (reckoned as righteous by God) through faith rather than through the works of the Torah ('law') – though he does not go so far as to suggest explicitly that Christian Jews should abandon the Torah.

But Paul never suggests that Christians do not need to observe basic moral precepts, although, like Jesus, he tends to reduce them to a few simple formulas:

> 'You know the commandments: "You shall not murder; You shall not commit adultery; You shall not steal; You shall not bear false witness; You shall not defraud; Honour your father and mother."'
>
> (Mark 10:19)

> '"You shall love the Lord your God with all your heart, and with all your soul, and with all your mind." This is the greatest and first commandment. And a second is like it: "You shall love your neighbour as yourself."'
>
> (Matthew 22:37–9)

> Owe no one anything, except to love one another; for the one who loves another has fulfilled the law. The commandments, 'You shall not commit adultery; You shall not murder; You shall not steal; You shall not covet'; and any other commandment, are summed up in this word, 'Love your neighbour as yourself.'
>
> (Romans 13:8–9)

Later generations sometimes drew the conclusion that faith was a substitute for moral behaviour in general, so that it did not matter what Christians did. Christ had abolished all moral constraints: Christians were free to do anything they liked. This belief, known technically as antinomianism (meaning 'opposition to the law'), was probably expressed by a few people in the second century. Much more often, however, it became a stick with which to beat one's opponents, by arguing that this or that attitude to faith and works would lead in an antinomian direction. Like many heresies, it existed mainly in the eye of the beholder. Paul in particular cannot possibly be called antinomian: the letters end with a list of moral exhortations which readers are expected to observe. Many are very demanding, perhaps few as much as the list at the end of Galatians:

> Now the works of the flesh are obvious: fornication, impurity, licentiousness, idolatry, sorcery, enmities, strife, jealousy, anger, quarrels, dissensions, factions, envy, drunkenness, carousing, and things like these. I am warning you, as I warned you before: those who do such things will not inherit the kingdom of God. By contrast, the fruit of the Spirit is love, joy, peace, patience, kindness, generosity, faithfulness, gentleness, and self-control.
>
> (Galatians 5:19–23)

The New Perspective on Paul has been important in resituating Paul in his own context and refusing to make him answer our questions. For Christians there continues to be a discussion about how people are saved, but it can no longer proceed as though Paul had provided us with a timeless answer in terms of faith as a substitute for ethics. Paul was focused on the needs and the status of his Gentile churches, and staunchly defended their standing before God against those (including perhaps Peter) who wanted to insist that Gentiles must become Jews before they could be Christians. If there are lessons to learn from this for the modern Church, they will be about inclusion and exclusion rather than about the relation of faith and works.

Not everyone has accepted the New Perspective, but it has opened up a fresh way of seeing Paul against the background of his time, and the debates he was actually engaged in, rather than issues highlighted in much later times. A general interpretation of Paul's thought informed by the New Perspective is offered by David Horrell:

> Paul's theology, his gospel, is profoundly and thoroughly Jewish: it tells the story of how the God of Abraham, Isaac and Jacob, the God who spoke through Moses and the prophets, has now acted to fulfil the promises made long ago and to enable God's people to inherit their long-awaited blessings through the coming of the Messiah. Yet according to Paul's gospel, the people who inherit these blessings, the people who are the true 'children of Abraham', are not all who are Jewish, but all who have faith in Christ, whether they be Jew or Gentile. Indeed, 'in Christ', according to Paul, 'there is no longer Jew or Greek' (Gal. 3:28, cf. 1 Cor. 12:13; Col. 3:11). So Paul's theology is essentially Jewish, yet it claims Israel's identity, blessings and salvation for a community which is not comprised solely of Jews, but of Jewish and Gentile believers in Christ. There is then in Paul's theology a fundamental tension between continuity and discontinuity: Paul's message did not represent a rejection of his Jewish 'past', but neither was it simply a straightforward continuation of it. While Paul saw his gospel as the announcement of what the God of Israel had now done in order to fulfil the promise to bless all nations through Abraham (Gen. 12:3), many of his Jewish contemporaries regarded it as dangerous, false and heretical – hence Paul's rejection by his own people and his repeated punishment in their synagogues (2 Cor. 11:24; 1 Thess. 2:14–16).[14]

From a wider perspective we might see Paul as engaged in a discussion about the relation between old and new in the Christian message. Though he decries the works of the law as a basis for salvation for

Gentile Christians, he never repudiates the Old Testament/Hebrew Bible, which he sees as coming to fruition in Christ. Yet the Gentiles' relationship to it is bound to be ambiguous. It is a true revelation of the one God who is both the God of Israel and the Father of Jesus Christ; but it is also surpassed by what has been seen of God in Christ, and Gentiles at least do not need to observe its mandates scrupulously. Christ is 'the end [Greek: *telos*] of the law' (Romans 10:4), meaning both its abolition and yet also its consummation or goal. There is a tension here which characterizes Christianity from this point onwards. The second-century teacher Marcion of Sinope (85–160 CE) sought to resolve it by declaring that the Old Testament was simply abrogated for Christians, and even cleaning up the Gospels to remove any reference to it. That was one extreme, which some followed for generations, but which was eventually declared heretical. At the other extreme have been those in the ancient world, and some more conservative Christians in the present, who simply deny the tension and treat the Old Testament as in all respects as binding as the New. Paul treads a difficult line between these two extremes, sometimes tying himself in knots: reading Romans 9–11 will convince most people that his position was highly complex and not very consistent. These chapters argue both that Gentile Christians have been accorded the place in God's promises that non-Christian Jews have forfeited, yet also that Israel as a whole will in due course be saved. There is something to be said for the idea that Paul was simply contradicting himself,[15] but to me it seems that he is struggling with equally strong arguments that pull in opposite directions. If we are to treat Paul as authoritative in some sense, it must involve trying to think through this issue, with which he himself wrestled, rather than treating his words in the same way as his opponents did the Old Testament – as totally binding and required for salvation.

AUTHORSHIP

So far we have referred only to those letters that most scholars think are authentically Paul's. This leaves several others as more likely to be pseudonymous, attributed to Paul but not genuinely by him. The most obvious case is the so-called Pastoral Letters, 1 and 2 Timothy and Titus. These, like the authentic Philemon, are addressed not to churches but to individuals we know to have been associated with Paul in his mission. But they seem unPauline for two reasons.

First, the Greek style is unmistakably different from Paul's own, much more polished and refined. It is possible that Paul changed his style over time, and some have argued that the Pastorals come from late in his life, supposing that he escaped execution and took up his mission again till, in old age, he wrote to his old colleagues in these letters. But this strikes most as a desperate ploy to 'save' the letters for Paul.

Secondly, the structures of the church that are implied in the Pastorals resemble much more those of the second century than those of Paul's day. In Paul's letters, as we have seen, church order is still inchoate; in the Pastorals there is a Christian polity, with bishops who have some standing in society in general[16] and who are supposed to be heads of a family; and there is an order of widows in which elderly women can be enrolled (1 Timothy 5:3–16). The position of women is clear: they are to be subordinate to men:

> Let a woman learn in silence with full submission. I permit no woman to teach or to have authority over a man; she is to keep silent.
>
> (1 Timothy 2:11–12)

Paul had been more ambiguous over this. He insisted that women should be veiled in church, but at the same time he assumes that they will pray and prophesy when the assembly meets for worship (see 1 Corinthians 11:2–16). At the same time, in another passage in 1 Corinthians (14:33b–36), we read that 'women should be silent in the churches . . . For it is shameful for a woman to speak in church'. NRSV prints the whole paragraph in parentheses, probably implying the widespread belief that it is a later addition to 1 Corinthians, since it disrupts the argument of the chapter, which is about prayer and prophesying in the Christian assembly but not about who is permitted to speak. If it is genuinely by Paul, then one reason for being doubtful about 1 Timothy is diminished, but it certainly seems to be an insertion, twisting Paul's teaching in the same direction as that of the Pastorals. For elsewhere Paul seems robustly in favour of the inclusion of women, like slaves and Gentiles, on equal terms in the churches:

> There is no longer Jew or Greek, there is no longer slave or free, there is no longer male and female; for all of you are one in Christ Jesus.
>
> (Galatians 3:28)

Next comes 2 Thessalonians. Most, though not all, scholars[17] think that it reflects the failure of the end-time, which Paul had thought was imminent, to arrive, and the need to deal with this. A complicated scheme had been worked out involving various stages in the progression towards the End, with some person acting as a 'restraining' power keeping it from breaking in (see also Chapter 18). The letter is rather obscure, and the exact details of its eschatological scheme are hard to decode. It seems marked by the opposite anxieties to 1 Thessalonians.

Colossians is accepted as Pauline by many. Part of the case against is that, as we saw, it represents an extremely high Christology, analogous to that in John's Gospel, which is widely held to be much later than Paul. I am less sure about this, since already in Philippians his Christology is elevated, as we have seen. There is a complication: Colossians shares some material with Ephesians, which is likewise widely seen as pseudonymous.[18] The mention of Ephesus in its superscription is not in many manuscripts, and it is possible that it was a kind of encyclical sent to several churches, or deliberately written as a covering letter summing up Paul's teaching and intended to introduce an early collection of his letters. That said, it has recently been argued that there is a Pauline core to the letter, which has been supplemented by a later editor.[19] Douglas A. Campbell goes further, arguing that Ephesians is really the Letter to Laodicea which is mentioned in Colossians 4:16 (he thus thinks that both letters are authentically Pauline).[20]

But the New Testament contains other pseudonymous letters, attributed to other apostles: James, Peter, John, Jude. There is also Hebrews, which has no attribution even though anciently many people thought it was by Paul; Origen showed on stylistic grounds that it is not, though the King James Version describes it as 'The Epistle of Paul the Apostle to the Hebrews'. All the pseudonymous letters except James clearly seem to reflect a situation much later than that of the apostles they are named for. James is thought by some to be a Jewish work thinly Christianized, but even then probably from late in the first century, though it could be earlier. One issue with it and with all the other 'apostolic' letters is that they are in Greek, and whereas Paul was clearly a Greek speaker it seems highly unlikely that Jesus' original disciples, such as Peter or James, could have written long letters in correct Greek, even if they could speak it a little.

For many practical purposes, the fact that some letters in the New Testament are pseudonymous does not matter. These works are just as important to any search for the theological themes of the New Testament as the authentic ones. On the other hand, in the case of Paul we get a clearer picture of what he believed and taught if we can remove later letters falsely attributed to him. But there is a major problem about pseudonymity, hinted at by the word 'falsely'. It is not a matter of later readers having ascribed letters to people who were not claimed in the text to have been their authors, as happened with Hebrews, but that the letters *themselves* make a clear claim to be by this or that apostle. In the case of the Pastorals there are explicit references within the text of the letters to circumstances in Paul's life, adding verisimilitude to the claim that they are by Paul: he greets particular people, and refers by name to those people who are opposing his mission, such as Alexander the coppersmith (2 Timothy 4:14). How should we deal with this phenomenon?

It has been common for New Testament scholars to say that the attribution of texts to people who were not their actual authors was a matter of convention in the ancient world. In the case of the Bible, they point to the ascription of the Psalms to David, or the wisdom books to Solomon, or the Pentateuch to Moses. This, it is argued, does not mean that anyone was being deceived: people knew that it was customary to attribute one's own writings to figures from the past. The analogy is however an imperfect one. In fact, very few Old Testament books are actually ascribed *within the text itself* to the figures whose names we know them by, and when this does occur, it is the use of a hallowed name from the remote past to give a kind of seal of approval to a recent work. This is true also of the large number of Jewish works outside the Hebrew Bible that have come down to us in various languages: they are almost always ascribed to an ancient prophet or seer, not to a contemporary of the actual author. In the case of the New Testament, we are talking about an attribution to a figure from the last or last-but-one generation, one that is surely meant quite literally. People in antiquity knew about forgery, and abhorred it, as we can see from 2 Thessalonians itself, where 'Paul' cheekily tells his readers not to take any notice of letters fraudulently ascribed to him (2 Thessalonians 2:2), and at the end adds: 'I, Paul, write this greeting with my own hand. This is the mark in every letter of mine; it is the way I write' (3:17). (Compare 1 Corinthians 16:21, Galatians 6:11.) This is an unambiguous claim to real Pauline authorship. Bart Ehrman, in a major study of the subject, speaks plainly of 'forgery' in such cases, and the term can scarcely be avoided.[21] Matters may be different where an original letter of Paul or some other figure has been edited by adding passages or tweaking the text: scribes did that kind of thing a lot, without thereby falsifying the naming of the text. But the fabrication of a completely new letter which is then attributed to Paul or James or Peter is surely something else.[22]

What difference does this make for those who venerate the New Testament? Liberal readers of the Bible may either consciously or subconsciously take less notice of the pseudonymous texts, while still being interested in their content and open to finding aspects of them illuminating; but for more conservative readers the problem is acute, since they are committed to the full inspiration of these texts. The normal procedure for conservative Christians is to deny that they are pseudonymous: however implausible this may be, it is worse to acknowledge that there are forgeries in the Bible. Indeed, it may be argued that the fact that a book of the Bible claims to be by Paul, etc., is the best possible evidence that it really is, since the Word of God does not lie. A milder version of this is to argue that the deutero-Pauline letters are written 'in the spirit' of the apostle or by his immediate disciples, and that this makes the false attribution less serious. Certainly most would agree that some of these works do have a flavour of Paul about them, notably Colossians and Ephesians, and that they contain among the most inspiring passages in the New Testament:

> I have fought the good fight, I have finished the race, I have kept the faith. From now on there is reserved for me the crown of righteousness, which the Lord, the righteous judge, will give to me on that day, and not only to me but also to all who have longed for his appearing.
>
> (2 Timothy 4:7–8)

That a text is uplifting doesn't mean that it is not also fraudulent, and when such letters refer to incidents allegedly happening to Paul in the present, it is hard to see them otherwise, even if they are written in Paul's spirit.

Perhaps a more important issue is whether a pseudonymous work that is indeed a forgery can none the less contain valuable ideas and teachings. An art forger may produce a beautiful picture, very close to the style of the painter being imitated. Our knowledge that it is a forgery detracts from our valuation of it in many ways, but from an aesthetic point of view we can still admire it. Similarly with a forged document: it may contain material that is of literary or theological value, however much we may regret that its author chose to commend it by ascribing it to someone else. The Pastorals have no place in attempting to reconstruct the thought of Paul, but there is nothing to prevent our studying the thought of the Pastorals, and finding it interesting and perhaps persuasive. This is far removed, however, from treating it as being on a par with the thought of Paul himself. And the taint of forgery cannot be removed.

How far can pseudonymous works be religiously authoritative? A lot depends on how we define the authority of biblical books. Are Paul's letters authoritative because they are by Paul? If so, then establishing that one of them is in fact pseudonymous presumably reduces or even annuls its authority. Or are they authoritative because they are in the Bible? If so, the question of who wrote them might be regarded as irrelevant. For most Christians, the answer is probably a blend of both factors, though this is arguably incoherent. What would we say about a newly discovered letter that there was reason to think authentically Pauline? Would that have the same authority as Romans, or more authority than the Pastorals? It is hard to say.

In practice, many readers of the New Testament do attribute more effective authority to some letters than to others. Lutherans have notoriously tended to promote Romans and Galatians over James, Luther indeed calling James 'an epistle of straw' because it appears to teach 'salvation by works'. That the question of priority among the letters is shaped by ideological concerns can be seen from the issue of women's leadership in the Church, where the arguments of conservative opponents who appeal to Paul tend to rely on 1 Timothy, and more liberal believers reply that this letter is not really by Paul anyway. Along these diverging lines, little meeting of minds is possible. The question of authenticity in the New Testament letters is thus not a technical, theoretical issue, but one with great practical consequences for the churches.

8
Gospels

Paul refers to no details of the life of Jesus beyond that he was born, instituted the Lord's Supper (1 Corinthians 11:23–6), died by crucifixion, and rose again from the dead (Galatians 4:4; 1 Corinthians 15: 3–4). Only very occasionally does he quote sayings of Jesus. The principal example is his citation of Jesus' words at the Last Supper:

> For I received from the Lord what I also handed on to you, that the Lord Jesus on the night when he was betrayed took a loaf of bread, and when he had given thanks, he broke it and said, 'This is my body that is for you. Do this in remembrance of me.' In the same way he took the cup also, after supper, saying, 'This cup is the new covenant in my blood. Do this, as often as you drink it, in remembrance of me.' For as often as you eat this bread and drink the cup, you proclaim the Lord's death until he comes.

In outline this corresponds with the traditions in the Gospels of Matthew, Mark and Luke, though it is nearest to Luke.[1] Paul's teaching about divorce and remarriage he also traces back to Jesus (1 Corinthians 7:1–11), though it is not clear there whether he is referring to sayings of Jesus during his lifetime, or to teaching Paul believed had been revealed to him by the risen Lord. But at all events we can fairly say that Paul hardly ever quotes Jesus, surprising as this must seem.

Yet it is inconceivable that Paul can have evangelized so many people without having passed on to them at least some account of who Jesus had been, and this is inseparable from what he had taught. The converts must have learned enough about Jesus to feel that his resurrection was good news: the restoration to life of, for example, Pontius Pilate would not have struck any of them as a matter for celebration. So we must assume that the early Christian churches received some outline, however rudimentary, of Jesus' life and work and teaching. (This is implied in the speeches in the Acts of the Apostles, such as Acts 2:14–36, where Peter describes Jesus as 'a man attested to you by God with deeds of power, wonders, and signs'.) This means that Christian evangelists such as Paul must have transmitted both sayings and narratives, based on the accounts of eyewitnesses, and it is hard to imagine that these were radically different from the basic accounts we have in the Gospels; hence the foundations of the Gospels must go back into the earliest Christian movement.

None of this means that the Gospels are themselves eyewitness accounts. The Gospels are often thought to rest on the memories of four separate eyewitnesses, and that this explains why they differ from each other. But only two of them (Matthew and John) are even ascribed to members of the twelve apostles, and even here the attribution is much later than the Gospels themselves: the titles ('according to Matthew', 'according to Mark', and so on – not including the word 'Gospel') are not an integral part of the text, but were added later during the copying of the manuscripts – we do not know exactly when. In subsequent tradition, Mark was taken to be the 'John Mark' referred to in Acts 15:37, and Luke 'Luke, the beloved physician' of Colossians 4:14; but even if this is true, neither would have been anything like eyewitnesses of the events they record. This has always been acknowledged. We can see it from the attempt to connect Mark, at least, with a real eyewitness in a saying of Papias, Bishop of Hierapolis[2] in Asia Minor (70–163 CE): in his *Exposition of the Sayings of the Lord* Papias is said to have reported that, according to 'John the Elder', Mark acted as Peter's interpreter and wrote his Gospel on the basis of Peter's reminiscences.[3] Even if this were true, it would still put Mark at some distance from the events he narrates. Luke, by his own account (Luke 1:1–4), consulted widely to find out the truth about Jesus:

> Since many have undertaken to set down an orderly account of the events that have been fulfilled among us, just as they were handed on to us by those who from the beginning were eyewitnesses and servants of the word, I too decided, after investigating everything carefully from the very first, to write an orderly account for you, most excellent Theophilus, so that you may know the truth concerning the things about which you have been instructed.

This implies not only that he belonged to a later generation than the apostles themselves, but also that by his day a number of different written accounts were already circulating.

The question of the origins of the Gospels, and in particular the interrelation among them, is the most intricate in biblical studies, even more perplexing than the origin of the Pentateuch. How did the stories about Jesus and his sayings come to be recorded and ordered in such different ways, and why did the four different versions acquire a status such that they are all part of the Church's Scriptures, even though they are often incompatible with each other in so many points of detail?

THE SYNOPTIC GOSPELS

The first thing to notice is that the Gospels are not four independent works, but fall into two groups: Matthew, Mark and Luke on the one hand, and John on the other. The first three Gospels are alike in significant ways, presenting a Jesus who teaches mainly in short, pithy sayings about how people should live, and proclaims the imminence of the 'kingdom of God'; whereas John's Jesus teaches in long discourses, and talks mainly about his own status as God's son. There are also major differences in the narrative. In John, Jesus works in both Galilee and Jerusalem throughout his career, whereas in the other three Jesus goes to Jerusalem only once as an adult, at the end of his life. The date of Jesus' death in relation to Passover is different in John as against the other Gospels,[4] and one crucial incident, the 'cleansing of the Temple', when Jesus kicked out the moneychangers and sellers of animals, is quite differently dated: in Matthew, Mark and Luke it is part of the run-up to Jesus' arrest and is possibly thought of as the last straw that turned the Jewish authorities against him[5] (Matthew 21:12–13, Mark 11:15–18, Luke 19:45), whereas in John it comes early in his career (John 2:13–22). A recognition of these differences is registered in the traditional description of the first three Gospels as 'Synoptic', meaning that they have a similar perspective on the life of Jesus, as distinct from John, the Fourth Gospel. There is near-unanimity among New Testament specialists that the Fourth Gospel was also written later than the others, probably towards the end of the first century or beginning of the second century CE, though the original reason for this dating was the theory that it depended upon them, which is not now universally granted: if John is independent of the Synoptics, it could be no later than Matthew and Luke, or even Mark.

Even the Synoptics, however, are products at the earliest of the second generation of Christians. Paul shows no awareness of them, and they all represent an individual way of ordering the raw material about Jesus, which evidently must have been transmitted by word of mouth.

In the mid twentieth century there was intensive study of how this might have occurred.[6] Form critics examined the individual stories and sayings in the Synoptic Gospels to determine what role they may have played in the teaching and preaching of the gospel message during the years before there were any written Gospels. By and large, the yield was fairly meagre. Classifying stories produced the insight that different types had different conventions: for example, a miracle story would typically end with a reference to the astonishment of the crowd (e.g. Mark 5:35–42), and other types of tale might culminate in a memorable saying (e.g. Matthew 12:46–50). This tended if anything to undermine the historical reliability of the accounts, since they 'had to be' told in this particular way whether they were true or not. But form criticism did have the virtue of showing the contexts in which stories and sayings might plausibly have been transmitted, in preaching and teaching, and we can easily imagine that each individual short section into which the Synoptics can be broken down had its own history of transmission before it reached the evangelists. Thus we can get behind the finished Gospels to the separate reminiscences on which they rest. Form critics tended to see the Gospel writers as mere collectors of these fragmentary bits and pieces, very few of which, they believed, actually went back to Jesus himself. They were evidence for the teaching of the early Church rather than for Jesus' own life and work.

More recently it has come to be thought that the Gospel writers exercised some narrative skill in joining the fragments together, and did not simply write them down in a random way. Each of the Synoptics has its own profile, so that a reader familiar with them all can usually tell which Gospel a passage is from by its style or theological concerns.

Yet to say that the Gospel writers exercised skill also implies that the narratives are not simply an accurate account of the life of Jesus, but are written with a degree of artifice. This is apparent as soon as we begin to notice not just that the Synoptic Gospels are so similar that they form a cluster, but also that in significant ways they differ from each other, not just in detail but in broad outline – not as glaringly as they do from John, but still enough to be noticeable. Mark, now almost universally agreed to be the earliest (as it is also the shortest), lacks any nativity story at the beginning; while Matthew and Luke each have one, but they are incompatible with each other. Popular expressions of Christianity such as carol services and nativity plays mix them up, so that the baby Jesus is adored both by shepherds (only in Luke 2:8–20) and by wise men from the East (only in Matthew 2:1–12). In Matthew the impression is given that Mary and Joseph live in Bethlehem, where they have a house, and only later move to Nazareth, whereas in Luke they live in Nazareth and travel to Bethlehem for the census (see Matthew 2:22–3, where Joseph's intention, after being in Egypt, is to go back to Judaea, but he is diverted to Galilee; and Luke 1:26, where Mary lives in Nazareth all along and travels to Judaea in 2:4–5). There are also major discrepancies in the accounts of the trial of Jesus, with Luke including a trial before Herod, which is lacking in Matthew and Mark (Luke 23:6–12 – no parallels in the other Gospels).

In finer detail also there are discrepancies. Compare, for example, these two accounts:

> Then they came, bringing to him a paralysed man, carried by four. And when they could not bring him to Jesus because of the crowd, they removed the roof above him; and after having dug through it, they let down the mat on which the paralytic lay.
>
> (Mark 2:3–4)

> Just then some men came, carrying a paralysed man on a bed. They were trying to bring him in and lay him before Jesus; but finding no way to bring him in because of the crowd, they went up on the roof and let him down with his bed through the tiles into the middle of the crowd in front of Jesus.
>
> (Luke 5:18–19)

Obviously this is the same story; but Mark's version is in a rather Semitized Greek, beginning with a vague 'they' and only spelling out the 'four' later (I have adjusted NRSV here better to reflect the Greek), whereas Luke's is in a purer Greek. And whereas Mark speaks of a roof that can be 'dug through', Luke's roof is tiled, perhaps reflecting the rather better houses he was used to.

Or consider the following parallel accounts in Mark and Matthew:

> As he was setting out on a journey, a man ran up and knelt before him, and asked him, 'Good Teacher, what must I do to inherit eternal life?' Jesus said to him, 'Why do you call me good? No one is good but God alone.'
>
> (Mark 10:17–18)

> Then someone came to him and said, 'Teacher, what good deed must I do to have eternal life?' And he said to him, 'Why do you ask me about what is good? There is only one who is good.'
>
> (Matthew 19:16–17)

The discrepancy in Jesus' response when he is addressed as 'Good Teacher': 'Why do you call me good? No one is good but God alone'; ('Why do you ask me about what is good? There is only one who is good' probably represents Matthew's toning-down of a saying which originally implied that Jesus was not to be identified with God). The early Church would have been uneasy about Mark's wording, since Jesus' divine status had come to be widely accepted among Christians. Mark would thus preserve an older version of the saying, perhaps the original one: no one in the early Church would have altered Matthew's blander statement into it, thereby casting doubt on Jesus' divinity. We do not *know* that any of the sayings attributed to Jesus in the Gospels are genuinely original, that is, that he actually uttered them. But one such as this, in its Marcan version, is highly unlikely to have been made up in the early Church.[7]

On an even larger scale, the Gospels order their material in different ways. In Matthew, for example, there are five collections of sayings, starting with the Sermon on the Mount in chapters 5–7, interspersed with blocks of stories about Jesus' miracles and other acts. The breakdown is as follows:

5–7	Sermon on the Mount
10	Instructions to the disciples
13	Parables of the kingdom
18	Directions for life in the Church
22–25	Parables, controversies and predictions of the end-time

One attractive theory is that Matthew's Gospel is structured to be a kind of Christian Pentateuch, with its five divisions,[8] and this may be supported by the fact that for the first block of teaching Jesus, like Moses, goes up a mountain (Matthew 5:1). The deliberate ordering of the material makes it unlikely that Jesus really delivered his teaching in exactly this order, or that the Sermon on the Mount, for example, was literally a sermon uttered all at the same time. Rather, it represents a sample of what he taught at various times and places, which Matthew has brought together into a single whole. The subsequent collections of sayings are similarly ordered thematically, as the descriptions above indicate. Even Christians who are committed to the authenticity and authority of the Gospels usually have little problem in accepting this degree of ordering by the evangelists. Neither of the other Synoptics reproduces Matthew's scheme. In Luke, in particular, the narrative sequence is quite loose, with anecdotes about Jesus that are not set in any particular narrative context: for example, 8:22, 'One day he got into a boat with his disciples'. Mark and Matthew imply a consecutive story (Mark in particular often connects events with 'and immediately'), but Luke does not.

THE SYNOPTIC PROBLEM

Yet, for all their differences, the Synoptics manifestly tell the same story, and from ancient times readers have wondered how they are interrelated. The earliest theory, reflected in the order of the Gospels in our Bibles, was that Matthew (who was after all supposedly one of the twelve disciples) wrote first, that Mark produced an abbreviated version of Matthew – the motivation for doing so was never clear – and that Luke then compared the existing two Gospels in writing his own. Modern critics have almost all agreed that Mark's shorter Gospel was the first to be written, but that leaves a question about the other two. Did Matthew revise Mark, and Luke then consult both, or did both Matthew and Luke revise Mark independently? (No one, apparently, thinks that Matthew used Luke.)

In favour of the second option is the existence of much additional material that is common to Matthew and Luke, yet is located by them in different places within the Marcan outline which they both broadly follow. Some of this material seems to be preserved in its original form in Luke. For example, Luke has Jesus say, 'Blessed are you who are poor, for yours is the kingdom of God. Blessed are you who are hungry now, for you will be filled' (Luke 6:20–21), as against Matthew's 'Blessed are the poor in spirit, for theirs is the kingdom of heaven . . . Blessed are those who hunger and thirst for righteousness, for they will be filled' (Matthew 5:3, 6). The general hypothesis has been that Jesus' original words are likely to have been about literal poverty and hunger, rather than spiritual need and desire; so the saying in Luke would be the older version. (How we know that Jesus spoke of literal rather than metaphorical hunger is unclear, but that is how the argument runs.) This has led a majority of critics to see the option that Luke revised Matthew as unsustainable: why would he have changed the order so perversely, and how could he have recorded versions of Jesus' sayings older than those in Matthew, if Matthew was his only source? These questions resulted in one of the most important hypotheses of New Testament scholarship, analogous to the four-source theory of the Pentateuch: that there was a common written source, now lost, on which both Matthew and Luke drew, and which contained most of the material they share that was not in Mark, though it may have been as old as (or even older than) Mark. This hypothetical source is known as Q, from the German *Quelle*, 'source'.[9] Q would have been almost entirely a selection of Jesus' sayings, including a number of parables, with little narrative. No one knows where or when it originated. It can be reconstructed from the material shared by Matthew and Luke that is not in Mark, but whether it was transmitted in writing or orally, and what order its material was in, we do not know.

Q gives us a simple model for understanding the origin of Luke. Rather than Luke having had two Gospels before him (Mark and Matthew), and needing to compare them and copy out bits from one or the other with changes in order, he simply had one Gospel (Mark), into which he spliced extracts from Q, which consisted only of sayings of Jesus, not narratives. (There are very few narratives in Luke that are not in Mark.) Matthew, similarly, also had just Mark and Q, so he will have worked in the same way, though the combination he produced was strikingly different. Both evangelists also drew on material of their own which was in neither Mark nor Q, and this they inserted at what they felt to be appropriate points.

Almost all scholars in the German-speaking world accept the Q hypothesis as the best explanation for the curious relationship among the Synoptics. In English-speaking scholarship, however, there is some support for the older idea that Luke revised Matthew. This anti-Q movement derives from my own teacher, Austin Farrer,[10] and has been continued by John Muddiman and his student Mark Goodacre,[11] who argue strongly that the Q hypothesis is unnecessary: wherever Luke changes the order of Mark and Matthew there is a good reason for it, and similarly when he appears to preserve a 'more original' version of a saying it is in fact his own preferred change to the Matthaean version.

There is also a problem that has long been known about, the 'agreements of Matthew and Luke against Mark'. There are numerous places where Matthew and Luke seem to be following Mark (that is, not Q passages), yet they both differ from Mark in the same way. For example, Mark 4:30–32 has the parable of the mustard seed:

> And he was saying, 'How shall we liken the kingdom of God, or in what parable shall we put it? Like a grain of mustard seed, which when it is sown upon the earth is the smallest of all seeds on the earth and when it is sown, it grows and becomes the greatest of all the vegetables, and it produces great branches, so that the birds of heaven are able to rest under its shade.[12]

Both Matthew and Luke reproduce this parable (Matthew 13:31–2; Luke 13:18–19), but both say, '*which a person having taken it* sowed in his field/garden'; 'it *becomes a tree*'; and '*in its branches*' instead of 'under its shade'. How is this to be explained, if Luke and Matthew were independent of each other? Conceivably the passage was in Q as well as in Mark – but that is a very complicated solution; or perhaps Matthew and Luke knew a version of Mark different from the one we now have – but that piles conjecture on conjecture. The simplest solution is clearly that Luke knew Matthew (or Matthew knew Luke).[13]

This dispute, however it may be eventually resolved, shows just how complex Synoptic relationships are, and that all hypotheses are fragile. The Mark-Q theory for the origin of Matthew and Luke (sometimes called the Two Source Theory) also leaves loose ends: what about the material that is only in Matthew (such as the parable of the labourers in the vineyard, Matthew 20:1–16) or only in Luke (such as the parable of the Prodigal Son, Luke 15:11–32, or the Good Samaritan, Luke 10: 29–37)? Critics used to attribute these to 'M' and 'L', as two further sources;[14] but for all we know they could be free compositions by Matthew and Luke respectively.

This raises an important point. Though there are some good reasons for accepting the Q hypothesis, it may sometimes serve a conservative religious agenda. To say that Matthew and Luke derive their shared but non-Marcan material from an earlier source is an implicit denial that they made any of it up themselves. The M and L hypotheses work in the same way, reassuring us that the material we value in Matthew and Luke is genuinely older than those Gospels, and hinting that it may go back to Jesus himself. And indeed it may; but Gospel criticism cannot show that. Modern approaches to the Gospels have tended increasingly to stress the typically 'Lucan'/'Matthaean' character of the Lucan/Matthaean version of Jesus, and especially of the passages that occur only in one of those Gospels; and this tends to reduce the case for thinking that they are real reminiscences of Jesus himself. If Jesus says things that go against the drift of a Gospel, we may be more confident that they are authentic, since the evangelist would not have made them up (the principle of dissimilarity, as it is known); but if they are typical of the evangelist's interests and emphases, we have to remain agnostic about whether or not they go back behind the evangelist to Jesus.

Luke's parables, for instance, are long and complex stories with complicated points to make. In the Prodigal Son there is not only the pardoning of the 'bad' son but also the rebuke, accompanied with blessing, to the 'good son' – quite unlike the much shorter and simpler parables in Mark and Matthew:

> Jesus said, 'There was a man who had two sons. The younger of them said to his father, "Father, give me the share of the property that will belong to me." So he divided his property between them. A few days later the younger son gathered all he had and travelled to a distant country, and there he squandered his property in dissolute living. When he had spent everything, a severe famine took place throughout that country, and he began to be in need. So he went and hired himself out to one of the citizens of that country, who sent him to his fields to feed the pigs. He would gladly have filled himself with the pods that the pigs were eating; and no one gave him anything. But when he came to himself he said, "How many of my father's hired hands have bread enough and to spare, but here I am dying of hunger! I will get up and go to my father, and I will say to him, 'Father, I have sinned against heaven and before you; I am no longer worthy to be called your son; treat me like one of your hired hands.' " So he set off and went to his father. But while he was still far off, his father saw him and was filled with compassion; he ran and put his arms around him and kissed him. Then the son said to him, "Father, I have sinned against heaven and before you; I am no longer worthy to be called your son." But the father said to his slaves, "Quickly, bring out a robe – the best one – and put it on him; put a ring on his finger and sandals on his feet. And get the fatted calf and kill it, and let us eat and celebrate; for this son of mine was dead and is alive again; he was lost and is found!" And they began to celebrate. Now his elder son was in the field; and when he came and approached the house, he heard music and dancing. He called one of the slaves and asked what was going on. He replied, "Your brother has come, and your father has killed the fatted calf, because he has got him back safe and sound." Then he became angry and refused to go in. His father came out and began to plead with him. But he answered his father, "Listen! For all these years I have been working like a slave for you, and I have never disobeyed your command; yet you have never given me even a young goat so that I might celebrate with my friends. But when this son of yours came back, who has devoured your property with prostitutes, you killed the fatted calf for him!" Then the father said to him, "Son, you are always with me, and all that is mine is yours. But we had to celebrate and rejoice, because this brother of yours was dead and has come to life; he was lost and has been found." '
>
> (Luke 15:11–32)

This seems so peculiar to Luke that we could well doubt whether it goes back behind him to Jesus.[15] The characters are not stylized, but there is a depth of characterization; and more than one point is made, since the story concerns both the father's forgiveness of the prodigal son and also the elder brother's resentment. It lacks the formulaic aspect of some of the parables in Mark and Matthew – we feel the three characters are real people, not ciphers.

Another relevant factor is what is known as Luke's 'great omission'. Luke on the whole follows Mark's outline rather than Matthew's; yet there is a whole passage in Mark which Luke leaves out, Mark 6:45–8:26 (nearly all of which also occurs in Matthew). This might suggest that the version of Mark that Luke was consulting lacked this section, and thus that there was an earlier version of Mark, proto-Mark as it is sometimes known (German: *Urmarkus*), which was shorter than the Gospel we know today. Luke itself may also have gone through more than one revision. Luke 3:1–2 reads very much as though it was originally the beginning of the Gospel:

> In the fifteenth year of the reign of the Emperor Tiberius, when Pontius Pilate was governor of Judaea, and Herod was ruler of Galilee, and his brother Philip ruler of the region of Ituraea and Trachonitis, and Lysanias ruler of Abilene, during the high-priesthood of Annas and Caiaphas, the word of God came to John son of Zechariah in the wilderness.

Like Mark, this would have been a Gospel opening with the work of John the Baptist and with nothing about the origins of Jesus. The birth narratives and stories of Jesus' (and John's) childhood in chapters 1–2 would then be a later addition: interestingly, as we have seen, they show no points of contact with Matthew's infancy stories, and they are written in a quite distinct style, mimicking that of the Greek translation of the Old Testament. On the other hand, Luke 4:23 also suggests the existence of earlier stories, not now recorded in Luke, about Jesus' early ministry:

> [Jesus said,] 'And you will say, "Do here also in your home town the things that we have heard you did in Capernaum."'

On this basis some have argued that there was a 'proto-Luke' that contained some stories not now in our Gospel but also omitted the birth stories, which have been added by a later reviser.[16] As Luke's birth narratives are never referred to anywhere else in the New Testament, there is no telling when or where this reviser might have worked.

A further issue in the case of Luke is the relationship with the Acts of the Apostles. Luke-Acts is normally seen as a single work in two parts, and this interpretation is encouraged by the prologues to the two books (Luke 1:1–4, Acts 1:1–2), which stress the identity of both the author and the addressee, Theophilus (who may be a real person – but the term could also mean 'lover of God' and so refer to any pious reader). The prologue to Luke was quoted above; that to Acts reads:

> In the first book, Theophilus, I wrote about all that Jesus did and taught from the beginning until the day when he was taken up to heaven . . .

Luke presumably had materials about the life of the early Church, and about the career of Paul, similar to those he had for the life of Jesus, and he draws implicit parallels: the second half of Acts is an account of Paul's mission and eventual arrest, which is constructed so as to recall the sufferings of Jesus, though it stops short of Paul's actual martyrdom (assuming he was indeed martyred, which we do not know for sure). This makes Luke unlike the other Gospels. But it is possible that the two, the Gospel and Acts, are really quite distinct, and that a later editor has joined them together by appending the prologues – though the Greek of the two works is similar, a notch above much New Testament Greek for style. (It approaches the Greek of the Letter to the Hebrews, which some in both ancient and modern times have speculated, for just this reason, could be by Luke.) In the Church of the second and third centuries Luke-Acts was rarely treated as a single work, because the Gospels were seen as having a status higher than other Christian books.

WHEN, WHERE AND FOR WHOM WERE THE GOSPELS WRITTEN?

If all this gives the impression that we know less for certain about the Synoptic Gospels than we should like, that is no more than the truth. Despite centuries of research they remain an enigma, and those who revere them should be aware of how much we do not know about their composition. Further important issues are when and where they were written. A significant detail for the dates is the reference in Mark 13:14 (cf. Matthew 24:15) to the 'desolating sacrilege' standing in the Temple ('where it ought not to be'). This is universally taken to be a reference to the Roman occupation of the Temple in Jerusalem, and implies that even Mark, the earliest Gospel, cannot have been written much before 70 CE, when the Temple was stormed, even if he foresaw this by a few years. Matthew and Luke definitely seem aware of the Roman sack of Jerusalem in 70 (Luke speaks of Jerusalem 'surrounded by armies', Luke 21:20), and so must have been composed later. What is more, there is no evidence that Luke's Gospel was known in the early second century. Traditionally Luke has been dated to approximately the same period as Matthew – because if he wrote much later, it would be odd for him not to show knowledge of Matthew, which according to the Q hypothesis he does not. If there was no Q, then Luke could be dated considerably later than Matthew, and Luke-Acts could be a second-century work. But on any hypothesis, even Mark was written at least some twenty years later than the final letters of Paul.

Equally hard is the question *where* the Synoptics were written. The fact that they are all in Greek, even if – in the case of Mark – somewhat rough Greek, means that they are unlikely to derive from Palestine or from communities of Jewish Christians there, who would more likely have written in Aramaic. Attempts to argue that the Gospels are translations from Aramaic have largely failed, though the individual sayings of Jesus, if authentic, will of course have been uttered in Aramaic in the first place (see Chapters 6 and 18). Probably we should think of the various Gentile churches that Paul and his fellow-workers had established or inspired as the source for the Gospels. The best guesses at the moment are that Mark derives from the Syrian church: older suggestions that it was written in Rome, because of Papias' linkage of Mark with Peter, and the presence of some Latin words in the Gospel, are now mostly rejected. Matthew may also be Syrian, from Antioch, Luke more likely from Asia Minor, perhaps Ephesus as a major early Christian centre, where John is also often located. In truth we simply do not know where any of the Gospels originated, and these are only guesses. I shall say more about the Gospels' locations below.

In all theories of the composition of the Synoptics, one evangelist changed the text of another, and this is not reflected upon enough. Mark must have had sufficient prestige for Matthew to have taken it as his basis, yet not so much that he could not feel free to revise it. Though there is a basic outline of Jesus' life (ministry in Galilee, move to Jerusalem, teaching in the Temple, arrest, trial, death, resurrection), there cannot have been any sense that the detail was fixed, and many incidents, just as the form critics proposed, were presumably free-floating and could be slotted in wherever a given Gospel writer chose. So in 'improving' Mark's account, Matthew was probably not conscious of contradicting him: this was simply, to him, a new way of telling the story that gave a better picture of Jesus – and had the advantage of including more material that had come down in one or more other sources alongside Mark. Matthew blended Mark with Q – not too difficult a task, in that there was probably little overlap: Q was simply a set of sayings, with no narrative, so that 'wove together' might be a better way of putting it. Luke, presumably, did just the same as Matthew, though if (as opponents of Q believe) he had both Mark and Matthew before him, then he had a harder task, still taking Mark as his template but fitting in distinctive material from Matthew where he thought it would be more effective – which for some reason was always in a different place. At any rate, Matthew and Luke are alike in having treated Mark with respect, yet sought to improve on it. When we continue to read Mark, we are in a way contradicting what both Matthew and Luke intended: they wanted us to read only *their* version of the Gospel, and to leave Mark behind.

I have written as though the distinctive characteristics of each Gospel reflected the personal interests of the writer, and this seems to me a natural way of interpreting the data. It does not mean that the Gospels are fiction, but it does imply that each evangelist had a good deal of freedom to change and nuance the traditions he had inherited. It has been usual in recent scholarship, however, to see the distinctive features of the Gospels as reflecting not simply the writer, but also his local community. Mark's Gospel is seen as an expression of 'the Marcan community' in Antioch (or Rome). Not only so, but it is generally believed that each Gospel was *intended* purely for the community in question. John, it is widely thought, was written in Ephesus, and is the product of a 'Johannine community'[17] which shared the mystical and highly distinctive theology we find in that Gospel; but it would not have been used in any other church. So there would have been 'Lucan Christians' and 'Johannine Christians', just as there were 'Pauline Christians' – though the latter were spread out all around what we now call Greece and Turkey.

If the Gospels were indeed local Gospels, then the communities that used them did not have the problem that has existed ever since the early second century, when all of them were in general currency in all the churches: the question of how to deal with several different, and partly incompatible, accounts of the life and teaching of Jesus. We know that this difficulty was acutely felt, since there was at least one attempt to produce a coherent reconciliation of the four Gospels, Tatian's *Diatessaron* (160–75 CE), which in Syria was used instead of the separate Gospels down into the fifth century. But if each local church had its own

Gospel, then originally this problem did not exist. This interpretation – which, given the mobility of early Christians seems inherently rather implausible – has been sharply challenged by Richard Bauckham,[18] who argues that each Gospel was written for any Christians who might encounter it. Each may in some measure reflect the concerns of the originating community, just as it owes much to the personality and interests of the writer, but it was not meant simply for that community – any more than it was written for the writer's own private use.[19] It was intended to be universal in appeal. As Bauckham points out, the very fact that Matthew and Luke are so clearly updated versions of Mark must mean that Mark was available to them; and unless they all lived in the same place, that in turn implies that Mark had circulated beyond the community where it originated.

Furthermore, Matthew and Luke are presumably meant to be *improvements* on Mark, and thus of value to the 'Marcan community', if one existed, as much as to the Matthaean and Lucan ones. Luke, in his prologue, implies that he had examined a number of sources for the life of Jesus. This could be merely a literary convention; but more probably it reflects a situation in which more than one version of the life of Jesus was indeed available to him. Bauckham suggests that the evangelists, like many of their fellow-Christians, may have been on the move and lived in more than one community, just as Paul did. He also points out, on the other hand, that the Gospels are not like the letters of Paul, which were necessarily addressed to the concerns of a particular community, but were inherently of interest to any Christians who might come to read them. In short, they were not meant for a closed group, but for an open church without definite borders.[20] Mark and Matthew were both known to Papias in Hierapolis, in western Asia Minor, around 110 CE: neither Gospel is at all likely to have been written there. Certainly all the Gospels soon became widely known: a papyrus fragment of John that turned up in Egypt can be dated to the early second century, not so long after the Gospel's composition, probably in Asia Minor, which 'attests to the remarkably rapid and wide circulation of the text'.[21] To John we now turn.

JOHN

Mark and Matthew were probably composed later than the fall of Jerusalem in 70 CE; Luke is perhaps considerably later still. That they none the less contain traditions about Jesus that are likely to be early and, indeed, to go back to Jesus himself, is evident from the fact that many of the stories, and especially the sayings, belong to a time when Jesus was the one who proclaimed the kingdom of God and challenged people to live in accordance with the values of God's kingdom, rather than being concerned with their attitude towards himself. A shift of emphasis from the former to the latter is already under way in Paul, who talks very little about the message *of* Jesus and much more of the message *about* Jesus. The Synoptics preserve traditions from before that happened, and therefore are likely to go back to Jesus. This distinction is important, because when we turn to John we find that the process is complete, and the whole Gospel is primarily about Jesus and who he is, with hardly any ethical teaching apart from the call to follow him.

> Jesus said to them, 'I am the bread of life. Whoever comes to me will never be hungry, and whoever believes in me will never be thirsty. But I said to you that you have seen me and yet do not believe. Everything that the Father gives me will come to me, and anyone who comes to me I will never drive away . . . I am the living bread that came down from heaven. Whoever eats of this bread will live for ever; and the bread that I will give for the life of the world is my flesh.'
>
> (John 6:35–7, 51)

John thus parts company with the Synoptics, and picks up where Paul left off. In John, as Rudolf Bultmann (1884–1976) put it, 'The Proclaimer became the Proclaimed.' This is in some measure true of all the Gospels, in that they are written to encourage faith in Jesus, not simply to report his teaching and deeds, and the elements of which they are made up were transmitted orally with that in mind, too. Mark already begins, 'The beginning of the good news of Jesus Christ' (and some manuscripts add 'the Son of God'). But in John it is clear that the historical figure of Jesus, the ethical teacher, has receded behind someone who primarily reveals the nature of his own status in relation to God.

John's difference from the Synoptics is enormous. Where the sayings of Jesus are concerned, there is more or less no overlap at all. The miracles (which John calls 'signs') include the feeding of the 5,000, which is also in the Synoptics, but otherwise there is nothing in common, except that the healing of the royal official's son in John 4:46–54 is reminiscent of that of the centurion's slave in Matthew 8:5–13. John has seven 'signs', which include the turning of water into wine at the wedding in Cana (John 2:1–11), a kind of magic not really found in the Synoptics, and the raising of Lazarus, the healing of the man born blind and the healing of the paralysed man at the pool of Beth-zatha (John 11:1–44; 9:1–41; 5:2–18). Where Synoptic miracles sometimes result in a chorus of approval from the crowd (one of the typical features of miracle stories worldwide, according to the form critics), John's signs characteristically lead into a long discourse by Jesus (e.g. John 5:19–47). As we have already seen, one crucial event in the Synoptics, the 'cleansing of the Temple', as it is traditionally known, appears right at the end of Jesus' career, whereas in John it is near the beginning.

John's passion narrative differs widely from the Synoptic accounts, too, as will be familiar to anyone who knows the two Bach Passions. John's Jesus is not silent before Pontius Pilate but engages in a dialogue with him (John 18:33–8; 19:8–12), and gives the impression of being in charge of the events as they unfold: in the garden of Gethsemane (John 18:6) the soldiers fall to the ground when he utters the words, 'I am', which are probably meant to be seen as his self-identification with God, whose name is 'I am' in Exodus 3:14. (There are, indeed, a number of sayings beginning, 'I am' throughout the Gospel: 'I am the true vine', 'I am the bread of life', 'I am the good shepherd'.) Even on the cross the dying Jesus does not utter the cry of despair, 'My God, my God, why have you forsaken me?' but the serene, 'It is finished' (John 19:30). He commends his mother to the care of the 'disciple whom he loved' (John 19:26–7), traditionally identified as John, son of Zebedee, who seems to be thought of as the author or at least source of the Gospel. The disciple 'whom Jesus loved' also makes an appearance in the story of the Last Supper, where he reclines next to him (John 13:23), and in the resurrection story, in which he is the first at the empty tomb after Mary Magdalene (John 20:8). None of this is in the Synoptics.

It is disputed whether John borrowed from the Synoptics (or one of them) any of the small amount of material he has in common with them, and the question is probably unanswerable. There is a curious relationship with Luke in particular. Both have the story of the miraculous catch of fish, not found in Mark or Matthew, but in Luke it occurs during Jesus' early career (Luke 5:1–11), whereas in John it is part of a resurrection appearance (John 21:1–14). Both have Jesus appearing to the disciples in Jerusalem rather than Galilee, as in Matthew. And both share little inconsequential touches: that there was a second Judas among the Twelve (Luke 6:16; John 14:22), that the slave of the high priest lost his *right* ear in Gethsemane (Luke 22:50; John 18:10), and that Joseph of Arimathea's tomb had never previously been used (Luke 23:53; John 19:41). It is thinkable that Luke could even be later than John, and depend on him: that would put Luke (and presumably also Acts) into the early second century CE, if we accept the usual date for John, around 90 CE – though that date depends partly on the argument that John is later than the Synoptics, including Luke, and hence is fragile. Thinkable, too, that there was a document that was known to both John and Luke containing these shared features – a sort of Q(LJ). But apart from these small overlaps, John goes his own way. The Fourth Gospel is not a new version of Mark, as Matthew and Luke are, but a wholly different conception of a Gospel, bringing out the inner meaning of Jesus' life and teaching: a 'spiritual Gospel', as Clement of Alexandria put it.

We have referred so far to the author of the Fourth Gospel as John, but we do not know his name, any more than we know the names of the authors/compilers of the Synoptics.[22] Furthermore, it is not certain that the Fourth Gospel is the product of a single writer. Most New Testament scholars think it is the endpoint of a long process of compilation and revision in which a number of people had a hand, perhaps as members of a school or group that may have evolved over time. This might help to explain the fact that the Fourth Gospel, for all its compositional skill, has dislocations in its narrative that suggest that no individual exercised final control over its finished state. For example, at the Last Supper Jesus delivers a long discourse (chapters 14–16), followed by a prayer (chapter 17); but at the end of chapter 14 he says, 'Rise, let us be on our way' (14:31), apparently implying that he has finished talking. Chapter 5, which recounts the healing of the paralysed man, is set in Jerusalem, but at the beginning of chapter 6 Jesus crosses the Sea of Galilee, evidently from a starting point in Galilee. There have been numerous attempts to reorder the Gospel and make it more coherent, but there is no consensus.

What does unite the Gospel is not its narrative coherence, but its style and its theology. The style has a masterly simplicity, hinting at great depths of meaning through a very restricted vocabulary and simple syntax. At the Last Supper Judas, dismissed by Jesus to 'Do quickly what you are going to do', goes out of the room, 'And it was night' (in Greek three syllables, *en de nux*) – no mere indicator of time, but a reflection on the spiritual darkness that surrounds Judas (John 13:27, 30). There is a strange echo in Luke, where Jesus tells the people who come to arrest him, 'this is your hour, and the power of darkness' (Luke 22:53).

The theology represents a high point even in the New Testament's high Christology, with Jesus presented as the Word of God that existed from the beginning of time yet became incarnate in this one man. It develops the Pauline theme found in Philippians and Colossians of Christ as the one who descended from God to live a human life on earth, but sees this as expressed, not only in the initial moment of incarnation, but in everything Jesus did and said. His teaching, indeed, mostly concerns his own nature: how God is his Father and how he existed before the world began,[23] and how he is the supreme example of every major symbol in Christian theology: bread, shepherd, light, vine, and so on.

How did such a different Gospel come to be put together in a world where the Synoptics, or some of them, already existed? Those who speak of a Johannine school tend to think that this was a Christian community with its own very distinctive ethos, somewhere in Asia Minor – probably Ephesus, as mentioned above. Its atmosphere can be seen not just in the Fourth Gospel, but also in the three Letters of John, which share many stylistic traits with the Gospel, and in some measure in Revelation too, which tradition equally ascribes to John. In all there is the same emphasis on Jesus as the supreme representative of God, the 'word of life' as 1 John 1:1 puts it. The Johannine church would have been markedly different from those founded by Paul and his companions, with an emphasis on the mystical and indeed the mysterious side of Christian faith. It is hard to know how far it rejected features of the sorts of church represented by the Synoptics. There is no description of Jesus' inauguration of the Eucharist, for example: John's Last Supper is focused on the foot-washing and makes no mention of the bread and wine, as the Synoptics do. This could mean that John's community rejected the Eucharist and perhaps even that it held foot-washings instead. Equally it could mean that the Eucharist was already coming to be thought of as something so awesome that it must be concealed from outsiders, and therefore not mentioned in case a non-Christian should come to read the Gospel. In that case we should probably see it hinted at in the long discourses on Jesus as the bread of life in John 6, for insiders with eyes to see and ears to hear.

THE PURPOSE OF THE GOSPELS

This raises a question about the purpose of all the Gospels. To put it in technical terms, are they *kerygma* – proclamation of the faith to make it known to non-Christians, what we should call evangelism; or are they *didache* – teaching intended to build up and inform those who are already believers? One reason why it is hard to know is that it is possible for the same text to serve both purposes; but still the distinction is a meaningful one. John certainly presents itself as kerygma: 'these [signs] are written so that you may believe' (John 20:31), which could explain its reluctance (if it is reluctance) to describe the origin of the early Christian 'mystery', the Eucharist. Yet surely the believer, too, is meant to meditate on the stories and sayings in the Gospel, as on those in the Synoptics. The fact is, we do not know the social function of any of the Gospels, or how they were meant to be read.

Can we get help from any parallels to the Gospels in the ancient world? As we saw, Paul and the other letter writers were adapting and transforming what was already an existing tradition of letters in the Graeco-Roman context. Can anything similar be said about the Gospels? For most of the twentieth century it was argued that the Gospels were *sui generis* and had no parallels. But recent study has tended to reinstate an older view, arguing that they resemble the genre known as the *bios* or life, a type of biography, of which the best examples are the *Lives* by Plutarch (*c.*46–120 CE);[24] and the Gospels bear some similarity to that. Biography in the ancient world was, as Richard Burridge puts it, 'a type of writing which occurs naturally among groups of people who have been formed around a certain charismatic teacher or leader, seeking to follow after him';[25] its purposes often include the encouragement of imitation of the great man, but sometimes (as with Plutarch's *Caesar*) simply admiration for him.[26]

The idea that the Gospels are a form of biography is perfectly compatible with their resting on oral tradition. But whereas early-twentieth-century critics often saw no further than the oral traditions, treating the individual Gospels as little more than repositories for sayings and stories, a biographical approach is more open to the shaping hand of each evangelist, and builds on the movement known as redaction criticism, which flourished in the study of both Old and New Testaments in the second half of the twentieth century.[27] This approach stresses that editors ('redactors', as they are usually called in biblical studies) did not simply collect or transcribe material from the past, but actively shaped and rewrote it in the interest of their own guiding ideas. Once we look at the Gospels in that way, we can see important differences among them that do indeed make them look rather more like ancient biographies than mere assemblages of older material. For example, Luke highlights certain themes, such as

Jesus' interest in the poor and outcast (6:20–21; 7:11–17) and his concern for women (7:36–50; 20:47). Even in the infancy stories, it is not exotic wise men, as in Matthew 2:1–12, but poor shepherds who are the first outside Jesus' family to learn of his birth (Luke 2:8–20). Matthew pays particular attention to controversies with Jewish interlocutors and presents Jesus as a new Moses, giving a sermon on a mountain (Matthew 5:1), as we have seen. These differing emphases imply that the evangelists were creative writers, not mere transcribers or compilers. The point is most obvious in the case of John, which has its own style and concerns that control its whole presentation of Jesus' life and teaching, with its long discourses (so unlike anything in the Synoptics) and its different chronology of his career and its end.

Ancient biographies were intended to be read by the literate: they were the kind of work that reasonably well-off people might aspire to possess copies of. It is generally thought that the early Christians did not belong to that class but were poor and, probably, illiterate. If that is so, then we should have to think of the Gospels as meant to be read aloud in public when the Christian community assembled for worship – just the same context as form critics assumed for the individual stories and sayings in their pre-written state. We might speculate that after a time in at least one such Christian community people became concerned that oral memory was dying out, and encouraged the writer we call Mark to commit it to writing, thus bringing into being the first Gospel. In British New Testament scholarship there have been some who proposed that the Gospels were actually compiled as lectionaries, that is, as texts to be read in weekly portions round the year, much as the Torah is read in Jewish synagogues to this day (though we do not know for sure that this practice goes back to the first century CE).[28] Even without going that far, it remains plausible that the Gospels were meant for public reading. However, we should not rule out the possibility that some early Christians were literate and rich enough to possess a Gospel manuscript. The first generation of disciples, certainly, were fishermen and probably not highly literate (if literate at all). But in the next generations, as the gospel message spread to communities beyond Palestine and acquired adherents such as Paul, it may have attracted middle-class people who could afford libraries. Paul admittedly tells his converts in Corinth that not many of them were powerful or of noble birth (1 Corinthians 1:26), but on the other hand the Letter to Rome ends by listing a great many of his friends and colleagues who have travelled to Rome from other places he had visited (Romans 16), and that could not be accomplished without a certain amount of money. Burridge suggests that only the very top and bottom levels of society were unrepresented in the Pauline churches, which certainly included both masters and their slaves, as we see in 1 Corinthians 7:21–4 and Philemon.

That Matthew and Luke represent alternative updates of Mark seems clear; whether John is the same kind of exercise is less obvious, since its dependence on any of the Synoptics is hard to demonstrate. As we have seen, the miracles ('signs') are mostly different from those in the Synoptics, and the teaching scarcely overlaps at all. If John is meant to replace the Synoptics, it cannot be by way of augmentation and small adjustments, as arguably is the case in Matthew and Luke, but by wholesale replacement. Perhaps instead it represents a wholly alternative set of traditions, which (somewhat against Bauckham) we might think of as the version of Jesus' life that circulated in Asia Minor rather than in Greece or Palestine, and which may have preserved memories that had been lost in other places. It is sometimes suggested, for example, that John's chronology for Jesus' last days on earth is more accurate than that in the Synoptics;[29] so even if John is a late work (from the end of the first century), it still retains details from much earlier tradition. John is also well informed about places in Jerusalem, such as Gabbatha ('The Stone Pavement', John 19:13). Most scholars remain doubtful that Jesus' long discourses in John can possibly go back to the same person who uttered the pithy sayings in the Synoptics: it is rather like trying to reconcile the Paul of Galatians, say, with the Paul of 1 Timothy. Nevertheless, John cannot be simply written off as an ahistorical document. Its intention seems, like the Synoptics, to be to provide a life of Jesus; even though it embroiders a good deal, we cannot say that it does so more than they do, since we have no independent source of information about Jesus with which to compare any of the Gospels.

FOUR GOSPELS

If the purpose of the Gospels is, in each case, to offer a biography of Jesus, what is the purpose of the four Gospels as a collection? Because all four are so familiar, it is not always noticed just how odd it is that they stand alongside each other, offering alternative pictures of Jesus and his life and work. Both redaction criticism, and the recent interest in the 'community' of each evangelist, have had the effect of highlighting the differences among the Gospels, reminding us that it is not only that John differs from the Synoptics, but that the Synoptics differ radically among themselves. If each Gospel was intended as an improvement on, and replacement for, its predecessors, then the conceptual problem of how to read the four divergent accounts arose after the actual composition of the Gospels. Matthew's Gospel was written not to be read alongside Mark, but rather to supersede it as a kind of second edition, while Luke's two-volume work was also meant to supersede Mark and any other Gospels Luke may have been familiar with. The eventual four-Gospel canon of the Church resulted from a recognition that all the Gospels were so established that none could be omitted. In some ways this is reminiscent of the acceptance of all the sources of the Pentateuch, allowed to stand alongside each other even when radically incompatible. But in other ways it is very different, for the Pentateuchal redactors wove the sources together – as Tatian wove together the four Gospels – whereas in the canonical New Testament the four Gospels stand side by side, unreconciled. Where Matthew and Luke had actually changed Mark to produce their own Gospels, later Christians did not feel the freedom to do the same, but simply accepted them all, despite the problems that brought when they diverged. In later chapters we shall look at the techniques Christian writers used to deal with these problems.

Modern Christians probably do not spend much time reflecting on this issue. Long familiarity with the Gospels prevents people from noticing just how strange it is to have divergent *official* versions of the life and sayings of the founder of Christianity, and even atheist critics of the faith seldom batten onto this problem. Historically the diversity is what we should expect, given that the stories and sayings in the Gospels circulated orally over a long period before being written down; but it is remarkable that the Church decided to canonize all four versions and not to attempt to reconcile them. It is possible, however, to see this as an advantage:

> As the second century superscriptions remind us, none of the Gospels is *the* Gospel. They are all fallible human witnesses. Their theological subject-matter lies beyond the text and beyond anything the historian can draw from these sources. The biggest danger of the so-called quest of the historical Jesus is the suggestion that the historian's conclusions might provide not simply one critical norm amongst others but the foundation and substance of Christian faith. This critical reduction to a single norm, like Tatian's solution to the plurality of the Gospels, would be in danger of

> making *the* Gospel into a new law. The variety of witnesses (which include the other New Testament writers) to the one Lord is one way of ensuring that this Lord transcends not only these witnesses but also all subsequent Christian theological and ethical positions and decisions . . .
>
> A normative portrait of Jesus would perhaps facilitate theological criticism of unsatisfactory faith images and judgements. But any simple measuring of these against that would rapidly extinguish the freedom of the spirit. It would also imply that the Christian gospel could be identified with any one formulation of it. Perhaps Matthew, and certainly later harmonizers, wanted this. One can understand why. The Christian church has always had to exercise some control over the enthusiasms of faith. Perhaps that is why the Gospels were composed. But it seems to have been a higher wisdom which resulted in a plurality of Gospels in the canon.[30]

Going even further, Francis Watson says:

> Faced with this dissonant plurality, there are just two possibilities: either to select one of the gospels as a historically reliable guide and to disregard the others, or to accept that the truth of the four is not to be found at the literal-historical level . . . Thus the fourfold gospel marks the end of all attempts to reconstruct the life of the historical Jesus.[31]

But the original reason for the tolerance of the plurality may lie elsewhere, in early Christian practice, as the next chapter will illustrate.

PART THREE

The Bible and Its Texts

9
From Books to Scripture

AGREEMENT ABOUT THE HEBREW SCRIPTURES

Writing around the beginning of the second century CE, Josephus defended Judaism against attack by a pagan opponent by pointing to the restricted range of holy books the Jews accepted, and the prestige they accorded to these books:

> Among us there are not thousands of books in disagreement and conflict with each other, but only twenty-two books, containing the record of all time, which are rightly trusted. Five of these are the books of Moses, which contain both the laws and the tradition from the birth of humanity up to his death; this is a period of a little less than 3,000 years. From the death of Moses until Artaxerxes, king of the Persians after Xerxes, the prophets after Moses wrote the history of what took place in their own times in thirteen books; the remaining four books contain hymns to God and instructions for people on life. From Artaxerxes up to our own time every event has been recorded, but this is not judged worthy of the same trust, since the exact line of succession of the prophets did not continue.[1]

Josephus' presentation does not exactly square with any other known arrangement or understanding of the Scriptures[2] we know as the Old Testament or Hebrew Bible. It attributes most of them to 'prophets' and it counts them as twenty-two (one for each letter of the Hebrew alphabet), whereas later Jewish tradition holds that there are twenty-four. He does not specify what the books are, but most readers have thought that he is probably describing more or less those that are now in the Hebrew Bible. Like some other ancient authors, he may be counting Jeremiah and Lamentations as a single book, likewise Judges and Ruth, to produce the lower headcount. If this is correct, then by the early second century the Hebrew Bible contained at least the books we now think of as scriptural.

The usual way of reckoning the books in Judaism today is as follows, and we shall see that aspects of it go back to the time of Josephus, even though it does not correspond exactly to his description:

The Torah
Genesis
Exodus
Leviticus
Numbers
Deuteronomy

The Prophets
Joshua
Judges
Samuel
Kings

Isaiah
Jeremiah
Ezekiel
The Twelve Minor Prophets: Hosea, Joel, Amos, Obadiah, Jonah, Micah, Nahum, Habakkuk, Zephaniah, Haggai, Zechariah, Malachi

The Writings
Psalms
Proverbs
Job
Song of Songs
Ruth
Lamentations
Ecclesiastes
Esther
Daniel
Ezra-Nehemiah
Chronicles

Josephus' account is broadly confirmed by early Christian lists from the second century.[3] Melito, Bishop of Sardis, in what is now Turkey, who died in about 180 CE, visited the Holy Land on a fact-finding mission to establish which ancient books the Jews there considered Scripture, because this was disputed among the Christians in his own community. His findings were that the Jews accepted as authoritative the books we now recognize as being in the Old Testament, except that he does not mention Nehemiah, Lamentations and Esther – he may, like other writers, think of Ezra-Nehemiah as a single book,[4] and Lamentations as part of Jeremiah. He also reverses the order of Leviticus and Numbers.[5] A little later Origen also confirms much the same list, and gives the Hebrew names of the books.[6] He also counts them as twenty-two – though he in fact lists only twenty-one, omitting, apparently accidentally, the Twelve Minor Prophets, which are reckoned as a single book in the Hebrew Bible. And in the fourth century Jerome (347–420 CE) has essentially the same list. These various authorities differ in the *order* in which they list the books, a subject we shall return to. Jerome says that most Jews count twenty-two books – again referring to the alphabet – but some twenty-four.

From the Jewish side there is little discussion of the contents of the Bible. It is particularly important to register that in Judaism there was never any kind of official council or synod, as there was later in the Church, that ruled on the contents of the Bible, only a few piecemeal discussions of individual books. But there are two substantial pieces of evidence which strongly suggest that all the books now in the Hebrew Bible were accepted by Jews by the middle of the second century CE at the latest – and possibly a good deal earlier. One is the Mishnah, a collection of legal rulings and discussions that was put together from older materials in the early third century CE. It contains no list of the Scriptures, but it frequently quotes them: and more or less all the books in the present Hebrew Bible are cited, indicating that all were regarded as authoritative, capable of clinching an argument. The other is a section in the Babylonian Talmud. The Talmud is a much later work, but sections of it are believed to be early traditions that have been incorporated into the finished collection. One of these sections explicitly discusses the contents of the Bible.[7] It does not mention the Pentateuch, which it probably takes for granted, but it does list all the other books we now know. (It also mentions only six of the Twelve Minor Prophets by name, but this is not remarkable given that they were felt to form a single book.) Scholarly opinion is that this section of the Talmud may well also date from the second century CE.

No less important is the New Testament, which quotes from every single book of the Old Testament with the possible exception of the

Song of Songs and Esther. Some books are much more important than others: Paul, for example, uses Genesis, Deuteronomy, Psalms and Isaiah far more than any other ones. But virtually all of them are cited, often with the formula, 'it is written' or 'Scripture says'. The books now in the Old Testament were thus virtually all authorities for the New Testament writers, which means we can push the date of 'canonization' of these books back from the second well into the first century CE.

The Dead Sea Scrolls enable us to go back further still, since some of them date from the first century BCE, and they include copies (often fragmentary) of all the biblical books except Esther. What is more, the scrolls also include a number of biblical commentaries, known technically as *pesharim* (singular *pesher*). In these a biblical verse is cited, and then the writer explains that 'its interpretation' (*pishro*) is as follows, continuing with some reference to the life of the community that composed the scroll in question. Thus, for example:

> *Because of the blood of men and the violence done to the land, to the city, and to all its inhabitants* [Habakkuk 2:8b]
>
> Interpreted, this concerns the Wicked Priest whom God delivered into the hands of his enemies because of the iniquity committed against the Teacher of Righteousness and the men of his Council, that he might be humbled by means of a destroying scourge, in bitterness of soul, because he had done wickedly to His elect.[8]

Clearly, for this writer the book of Habakkuk was an authoritative text that had implications well beyond its own time. Like early Christians, the Qumran community looked to holy books to explain the events it was involved in.

'DEFILING THE HANDS'

It is often suggested that at the end of the first century CE there was still debate among rabbinic authorities about a few of the books that ultimately were accepted into the Scriptures. The books in question are the Song of Songs and Ecclesiastes (Qoheleth), and perhaps also Esther. The argument is a technical one, and depends on the meaning of a curious expression, that 'holy scriptures defile the hands', in the Mishnah (early third century CE), in the tractate Yadaim (meaning 'hands')

3:5. The tractate is concerned with various items that render anyone touching them ritually impure, requiring ceremonies of cleansing; and among these items, counterintuitively, are the texts of the Scriptures. Rather than, as we might expect, conveying holiness, contact with the Scriptures instead conveys contagion.[9] Perhaps this is meant to have a deterrent effect, to discourage too irreverent a handling of these holy objects; later rabbinic discussion (also beginning from puzzlement about the ruling) suggests that it may indeed have been the motivation. The passage in Yadaim 3:5 reads:

> All holy scriptures defile the hands. The Song of Songs and Qoheleth defile the hands.
>
> Rabbi Judah says: The Song of Songs defiles the hands, but there is a dispute concerning Qoheleth.
>
> Rabbi Yose says: Qoheleth does not defile the hands, but there is a dispute concerning the Song of Songs.
>
> Rabbi Simeon says: Qoheleth is among the lenient decisions of the school of Shammai and among the stringent decisions of the school of Hillel.
>
> Rabbi Simeon ben Azzai says: I have heard a tradition from the seventy-two elders on the day that they seated Rabbi Eleazar ben Azariah in the academy, that the Song of Songs and Qoheleth defile the hands.
>
> Rabbi Akiba said: God forbid! No man in Israel ever disputed the status of the Song of Songs saying that it does not defile the hands, for the whole world is not worth the day on which the Song of Songs was given to Israel. For all the writings are holy, but the Song of Songs is the holiest of the holy. If there was a dispute it concerned Qoheleth.
>
> Rabbi Johanan ben Joshua, the son of Rabbi Akiba's father-in-law, said: Ben Azzai's version of what they disputed and decided is the correct one.

The rabbis who are recorded as arguing with each other are not all contemporaries, and span the period from the early to late second century CE: this is a common way of proceeding in the Mishnah and Talmud, in which various conflicting opinions are lined up even though they may not all have been held at the same time. Clearly, 'defiling the hands' is a desirable quality for a text to have. The question is whether these two works possess it, and there is more of a majority for the Song of Songs than for Qoheleth.

There are two ways of taking this. The majority view has been, and still is, that where texts are concerned, 'making the hands unclean' means 'being canonical', so that to question whether the Song of Songs, say, defiles the hands is equivalent to questioning its status as Scripture. In that case we should have to conclude that the 'debate' referred to was about whether or not to include the two books mentioned among the Scriptures. Earlier scholars even spoke of a 'council' of Yavneh, where the rabbinic academy met after the Romans sacked Jerusalem, ruling on the question of what should be in Scripture. Though this term is now considered anachronistic, the opinion is still in general that what the rabbis debated was indeed the scriptural status of the two books, and that these would therefore have been of uncertain canonicity until at least the second century CE.

A minority view argues that 'defiling the hands' does not *mean* 'being canonical', but is a normal characteristic of books that are biblical. The question arises precisely for these two books (and in another rabbinic discussion, also for Esther) because they are agreed to be biblical or 'canonical'. There must have been something about all three books that made it dubious whether they had the power to defile the hands. My own tentative suggestion is that it may be because these books lack the holy name YHWH, which appears in every other book in the Hebrew Bible. But if that is not the reason, then there is some other feature that means they do not defile *even though* they are 'Holy Scriptures'. The Mishnah, after all, does not say that 'all holy scriptures defile the hands, and Song of Songs and Ecclesiastes are holy scriptures' – as if someone doubted that; it says, 'all holy scriptures defile the hands, and Song of Songs and Ecclesiastes defile the hands' – implying that they are just like other holy scriptures in this respect, though for some reason you might expect them not to do so.

The issue, in fact, is not about canonicity, but about the ritual prescriptions to be carried out in relation to the scrolls that contain these particular books. This is confirmed in the regulations around the passage in question, which rule about the power of the biblical scrolls as material objects – spaces in the text, wrappings, etc. – to cause ritual impurity. The content of the scrolls, in the sense of their meaning or message, is not a factor. The passage is not a judgement on Song of Songs and Ecclesiastes as not being sufficiently religious, or something of that kind. It is concerned with physical features of the scrolls on which they are written. Given that the same question arose about Esther,[10] which is read liturgically at the festival of Purim and is surely as scriptural as anything in the Bible, it seems likely that the issue is the absence of the divine name in these scrolls, rather than their canonical status.

In this light, the argument that there was still doubt at the beginning of the second century CE about the status of any of the books that are now in the Hebrew Bible looks suspect. All our evidence points to the existence of a canon or collection, containing the very same books that now appear in printed Hebrew Bibles, by the middle of the first century CE at the latest. And – assuming that Yadaim 3:5 is concerned with physical scrolls – there is no evidence of any disagreement about any of these books at any time. The books had assembled themselves without debates or rulings being necessary. The New Testament writers, like the rabbis who put together the Mishnah, took them for granted as holy texts. No one ever canonized them, in the sense of taking a positive decision that they should be regarded as authoritative, still less insisted on this against opposition. They were simply accepted.

EARLY STAGES IN THE FORMATION OF THE HEBREW BIBLE

Can we nevertheless trace any earlier stages in the process by which the books gained this acceptance? Scholars in the early twentieth century often referred to the three divisions of the Jewish Bible – Torah, Prophets and Writings – and proposed that they bore witness to a three-stage canonization process. The Law or Torah (that is, the Pentateuch) was holy as early as the time of Ezra, in the fifth century BCE, when it was imposed on the people who had returned from exile (see Nehemiah 8) – not so long after it was compiled, if we follow the JEDP theory outlined in Chapter 2. But the community in Samaria, which had become the semi-Jewish community called the Samaritans by New Testament times, accepted only the Torah as Scripture (and still does today). This suggests that the other parts of the Hebrew Bible came together somewhat later than the Torah, which must have been all the Bible there was at the time of the Samaritan schism. Unfortunately no one knows just when this was,[11] but whenever it happened, the growth of the Prophets and the Writings must have been later. Where these two sections are concerned, it was sometimes argued that the Prophets must have been complete before the writing of Daniel in the early second century BCE, since that book would surely have been included among the Prophets, had that still been possible. The Writings would thus have come into being last – and their edges were still fuzzy at the end of the first century CE, as witness the disputes over Song of Songs and Ecclesiastes that we have just surveyed.

If this three-stage hypothesis has been largely abandoned, it is not because there is hard evidence against it, but simply because there is very little in its favour. It is a series of guesses – not, admittedly, a rare thing in biblical studies. We do not know why the Samaritans accept only the Torah. We can be certain that it must have existed at least as early as the schism, or the Samaritans would not have been able to adopt it; but we cannot say that it must have had a special scriptural status for all Jews by then, or that everything else in the Bible must be later. Ezra, assuming he existed, is supposed to have read 'the law' to the assembled people, but that this was more or less our present Pentateuch is only a surmise, and (as mentioned above) he would have had to be a fast reader to get through it in a single morning. Again, there may be many reasons why Daniel was not placed among the prophets: the book itself never describes him as a prophet, but as a wise man, and it is a modern judgement that his book 'ought to be' in the Prophets section of the biblical canon. And the Writings were not fuzzy, if the hypothesis about Ecclesiastes and the Song of Songs just outlined is correct; and even on the majority view they were only slightly fuzzy. There is a pleasant logic about thinking that Law, Prophets and Writings were assembled in that order, but it was never more than a rather ramshackle theory.

The truth may be more untidy, yet in some ways also more traditional. Probably different parts of the Hebrew Bible achieved authoritative status at different times, irrespective of which section they now stand in. One can well imagine that the books of the prophets, or some of them, came very soon after their composition to be seen as the utterances of God that they claimed to be, and so were accorded a special status – even, perhaps, before some parts of the Torah. Unless that happened, it is hard to see how they would have survived at all. Similarly, some legal sections of the Pentateuch may have attained an authoritative status almost immediately. Deuteronomy, in particular, may well have been accorded credence right from the start, if, as many still think, it was indeed the 'book of the law' found in the Temple in the reign of Josiah (see Chapter 3). The Psalms, or some of them, similarly acquired prestige from their use in the Temple, and the ascription of the whole book to David, like that of the wisdom books to Solomon, was a bid for canonicity that may have swiftly succeeded. Among the historical books and sections, the tales in the Pentateuch probably did become normative soon after being written. The Deuteronomistic History – the first four books of the Prophets in the Hebrew Bible – is an official history of Israel, not a piece of free-lance speculation, and may well have been accepted as such as soon as it was written, perhaps in the sixth century BCE. Thus the canonicity of much in the Hebrew Bible may well be even earlier than on the three-stage model. The cultures of the ancient Near East were familiar with canonical literature, and the Hebrew Bible is Israel's canon.[12] Of course, books cannot have become authoritative before they were written: if Daniel or Qoheleth were composed only in the second century BCE, that is the earliest they can have become canonical. However, I am doubtful of a model in which material was written but became canonical only centuries later. Little of the Old Testament is occasional literature; most of it seems designed for official recognition, and probably received it almost at once.

That does not help us much with absolute dates. In the case of the finished Pentateuch, the general consensus puts it in the fifth or fourth century BCE, not far from the work of Ezra, so the connection to him could still be valid. It is, however, almost inconceivable that the earlier stories, and some of the old laws, in Genesis or Exodus respectively, had to wait for Ezra in order to become official, national literature. Similarly, it was probably only in the Second Temple period, maybe as late as the third century BCE, that some of the Psalms were written – take, for example, the one dedicated to the law, Psalm 119 – and the whole collection (as opposed to some individual psalms) began to be described as Psalms of David. But there may be much older psalms that had already acquired authority as expressions of national sentiment back in the time of Solomon's Temple, in the eighth or seventh centuries BCE. Once we stop thinking of canonization as the attribution of official status to already existing texts from the ancient past, and allow that it may have followed shortly after a text was written, then it is no longer necessarily a process separate from and following the composition of the Old Testament books. The complete silence in Jewish texts about the process of canonization seems to me to be telling. These were texts no one could remember *not* being canonical.

SCRIPTURE AND CANON: THE APOCRYPHA

Canonization of texts has two aspects, and so far we have dealt with only one of them. What we have been examining is the definitive inclusion of some texts in the sacred literature of Israel: that *at least* these books belong to the Hebrew Scriptures, and cannot be removed. The other question, so far left aside, is the process by which it came about that *at most* these books were to be seen as Scripture. This is canonization in a narrower but perhaps more accurate sense of the word: the establishment of an exclusive list, from which nothing may be subtracted but also to which nothing may be added: a closed canon. Some writers, myself included, have argued that it would be helpful to distinguish these two aspects by talking in the first case of scripture, meaning a potentially open-ended collection of texts – and only in the second case of canon, as a completed list which is exclusive.[13] The Bible is nowadays a canon in that narrower sense for all the religious communities that recognize it, though one does occasionally hear voices asking why other, more modern, works could not be added to it. But it is quite conceivable that there was a time when the Bible (not yet so called, as though it were a single work) was an open collection, with many more books clamouring for admission than were eventually included.

Most Bibles in the English-speaking world contain two sections, the Old Testament and the New, but sometimes between them there is a third section, usually called the Apocrypha. These are books that many Christians in ancient times regarded as authoritative, but which the churches of the Reformation decided should be excluded from the main canon of the Bible. Some Protestants, especially Lutherans and Anglicans (Episcopalians), treat them as important and edifying, though secondary to Scripture proper, and some Anglicans read them in the liturgy; others, notably Reformed Christians, reject them altogether and see them as having no more importance than purely secular books. In Catholic and Orthodox Churches, on the other hand, they are treated as fully scriptural, although as a recognition of their slightly anomalous status they are described as 'deutero-canonical' – belonging to a second tier of Scripture. But they do not appear as a separate collection: they are integrated into the Old Testament, each book standing next to the Old Testament books it most closely resembles. Thus Tobit and Judith are grouped with Esther, and Sirach and the Wisdom of Solomon with Proverbs and Ecclesiastes. The title 'Apocrypha' was given to these books at the Reformation: in ancient times 'apocryphal' meant hidden (that is the original meaning of the Greek word), in other words, secret books belonging to sects such as the Gnostics. In the early Church there was no special term for the books now known as either apocryphal or deutero-canonical.

The contents of the apocryphal/deutero-canonical books are not precisely defined, since more books are accepted in the eastern Orthodox churches than in the Roman Catholic Church, and still more in Ethiopia. But they consist of at least the following books:

Tobit
Judith
Additions to the Book of Esther
Wisdom of Solomon
Wisdom of Jesus son of Sira/Sirach/Ecclesiasticus
Baruch
Letter of Jeremiah (= Baruch 6)
Additions to the Book of Daniel:
    The Prayer of Azariah and the Song of the Three Jews
    Susanna
    Bel and the Dragon
1 Maccabees
2 Maccabees

What distinguishes these books from those in the Jewish canon of Scripture? The distinction is not one of content or quality. Tobit and Judith, for example, are tales about Jewish heroes and heroines very similar to Esther; Wisdom of Solomon and Sirach are books of teaching that roughly resemble Proverbs. The additions to Esther and Daniel bring out the divine involvement in the plot more clearly than the original texts. The distinction is twofold. First, the 'apocryphal' books are relatively late by comparison with the books in the Jewish canon. There is some overlap, in that Tobit, for example, could be slightly older than Daniel; but in general these are works from the Hellenistic period. What is more important is that they were known in ancient times only in Greek, not in Hebrew or Aramaic. In some cases at least they were evidently composed in Hebrew or Aramaic: Hebrew fragments of Tobit and large portions of Sirach have been found in modern times.[14] Others, such as the Wisdom of Solomon, were certainly composed in Greek in the first place, probably in the Jewish community in Alexandria, in Egypt. All the apocryphal books are Jewish in origin, but it seems to have been mainly Christians who accepted them as Scripture. They are lacking in the lists of the Jewish Scriptures as recorded by Melito and Origen, in the second and third centuries CE. We saw that the Mishnah, in the early third century, quotes from all the books now in the Jewish canon: equally, it does not quote at all from any of the books of the Apocrypha. Nor, in later times, does the Talmud. There is some evidence that rabbinic authorities discussed the book of Sirach, which they will have known in Hebrew, but decided it was too recent to be canonical – they did not know that Qoheleth, for example, may well be almost as late, because they thought it was by Solomon.[15] We have no other evidence that Judaism ever considered these books as scriptural.

Yet Christians for the first few centuries seem to have had no difficulty in accepting and using the books that would come to be called the Apocrypha, even when they knew that the Jews did not. Some thought that the Jewish rejection of the books was of a piece with their (alleged) mutilation of the Old Testament to remove passages conducive to Christianity. (Justin Martyr falsely believed that Psalm 96 had had a reference to God reigning 'from the tree' excised.) Not until the time of Jerome and Augustine in the fifth century do we find overt discussion of the Apocrypha. Jerome knew well that the Jews did not accept the deutero-canonical books, and urged that Christians ought to reject them too – though that did not prevent him from translating them into Latin, since he thought they were perfectly edifying even though not scriptural. Augustine responded with the argument that the Church had always used these books, had regarded them as divinely inspired, and ought to continue doing so: Jewish practice could not be binding on the Church.[16] Augustine won the day, and it was not until the Reformation[17] that the argument resurfaced that only the books extant in Hebrew, and regarded as holy by the Jews, should be accepted into the canon. (What they would have made of the rediscovery of the Hebrew text of Sirach is anybody's guess.)[18]

There is a paradox here. The books in question are universally agreed to be Jewish in origin, yet they are accepted only by (some) Christians. Two of them, the books of Maccabees, even explain the origins of the Jewish festival of Hanukkah, which celebrates the rededication of the Temple in the second century BCE after it had been defiled by Antiochus IV Epiphanes – yet even they are not regarded by Jews as part of the Scriptures. If we try to understand this paradox, however, it may lead us to a subtler understanding of what is meant by 'Scripture'.

On the one hand, it is perfectly true that Christians before Jerome accepted the inspiration and authority of the deutero-canonical books, and when they cited them they used the same formulas – 'it is written', 'as Scripture says' – as they did with citations from the Hebrew books. They show every sign of having thought of all the books, both those shared with the Jews and those that were deutero-canonical, as equal in prestige and importance. One such book in particular, the Wisdom of Solomon, was held in great esteem by many early Christian writers. Wisdom 7:22–8:1, a lengthy description of the wisdom of God, was frequently regarded as disclosing the nature of the Holy Spirit:

There is in her a spirit that is intelligent, holy,
unique, manifold, subtle,
mobile, clear, unpolluted,
distinct, invulnerable, loving the good, keen,
irresistible, beneficent, humane,
steadfast, sure, free from anxiety,
all-powerful, overseeing all,
and penetrating through all spirits
that are intelligent, pure, and altogether subtle.
For wisdom is more mobile than any motion;
because of her pureness she pervades and penetrates all things.
For she is a breath of the power of God,
and a pure emanation of the glory of the Almighty;
therefore nothing defiled gains entrance into her.
For she is a reflection of eternal light,
a spotless mirror of the working of God,
and an image of his goodness.
Although she is but one, she can do all things,
and while remaining in herself, she renews all things;
in every generation she passes into holy souls
and makes them friends of God, and prophets;
for God loves nothing so much as the person who lives with wisdom.
She is more beautiful than the sun,
and excels every constellation of the stars.
Compared with the light she is found to be superior,
for it is succeeded by the night,
but against wisdom evil does not prevail.
She reaches mightily from one end of the earth to the other,
and she orders all things well.

Wisdom of Solomon's influence reaches back into the first generation of Christians. Its account of the way sin came into the world through Adam's disobedience seems to underlie Paul's argumentation in Romans 5, which is the scriptural basis for the later doctrine of original sin. There is no Old Testament text that interprets Genesis 3, the garden of Eden story, in this way, and Judaism never developed a doctrine of original sin from it. So Wisdom was an important text for Christians:

God created us for incorruption,
and made us in the image of his own eternity,
but through the devil's envy[19] death entered the world.

(Wisdom of Solomon 2:23–4)

Not only the deutero-canonical books, but even books of a lower status are cited in the New Testament and in the Christian Fathers. The Letter of Jude quotes the work known as *1 Enoch*:

> Enoch, in the seventh generation from Adam, prophesied, saying, 'See, the Lord is coming with tens of thousands of his holy ones, to execute judgement on all, and to convict everyone of all the deeds of ungodliness that they have committed in such an ungodly way, and of all the harsh things that ungodly sinners have spoken against him.'
>
> (Jude 14–15)[20]

Jude also refers to the *Assumption of Moses*, a first-century CE Jewish pseudonymous work that never became canonical anywhere. Paul too shows awareness – though mostly without actual quotation – of works that go beyond even the deutero-canonical books.[21] This seems to nudge us in the direction of thinking that the Old Testament of the early Christians was what Albert C. Sundberg Jr, one of the most important writers on the early canon, called 'a wide religious literature without definite bounds'.[22]

On the other hand, the deutero-canonical books, and those not even close to canonicity, are not nearly so frequently cited by early Christian writers as the books in the Hebrew canon. Wisdom of Solomon is the only exception to this, and even that comes nowhere near the frequency of use we find for Genesis or Isaiah or the Psalms. Franz Stuhlhofer, who has carried out a statistical analysis of the use of the Bible from Jesus to Eusebius, shows clearly that, in proportion to their length, the deutero-canonical books are of quite minor importance in most early Christian writing.[23] This will be confirmed intuitively by anyone who knows the Old Testament and Apocrypha well and who works through the New Testament and the writings of the first few Christian centuries: quotations from the books of the Hebrew Scriptures are noticeably more common than those from the other books. The evidence does not enable us to say that these other books were definitely uncanonical, but it does show that they were simply not as important or central as those now in the Hebrew Bible. So far as the New Testament is concerned, deutero-canonical books are never preceded with a citation formula, as are the books of the Hebrew Bible.

Jewish writers too use the deutero-canonical books very little. Josephus draws freely on those of Maccabees in retelling the history of the Jews, but it is not clear what kind of authority he attributed to them: he may simply have seen them as useful sources, and it is hard to include them in his count of twenty-two books in *Against Apion*. But he uses other deutero-canonical books hardly at all. Nor does Philo, the first-century Jewish philosopher and commentator on the Torah.

Yet these are certainly Jewish books. Older scholars used to think that the longer Greek Bible represented the biblical canon of the Jews of Alexandria, whereas the Hebrew one was Palestinian, but this theory has been largely abandoned. It is not as though Hebrew was unknown in Alexandria or Greek in Palestine, and the neat division does not do justice to the variety of Judaism found throughout the eastern Mediterranean and in Mesopotamia in the last centuries BCE and the first century CE. We have no evidence that the Egyptian Jewish community used the deutero-canonical books more than their contemporaries in Palestine. A better explanation is called for.

The question, 'What was the biblical canon for Jews or Christians in the first century CE?' may be the wrong one to ask: the concept 'biblical canon' did not yet exist. There can be no doubt that there was a core of books that were regarded as centrally important by both groups, and these included most or indeed all of what we now think of as the Old Testament, though some books in it were of a different order of importance than others. No one took as much notice of Obadiah as they did of the Psalms, though there are still surprises: the community at Qumran treated the rather brief and obscure book of Habakkuk as a major source of inspiration and information about their own circumstances, as we have seen. There was also a large number of books that were thought of as either unimportant or positively to be rejected, 'outside books' as the rabbinic sources such as the Mishnah call them – *antilegomena*, 'books spoken against', to Christians. But in between there was a range of works that were held in respect but not used or quoted nearly as much as the core, and here Jews and Christians came to diverge: Jews tended to move them into the 'outside' category, while Christians often embraced them, though still without promoting them to the core. The 'core', however, was not a 'canon' in the sense of a fixed and determinate list, but simply a repository of much-used books.

By the end of the second century it does make sense to speak of a Jewish canon of the Hebrew Scriptures and a Christian canon of the Old Testament, which differed from each other in the matter of the deutero-canonical books. For those in both faiths, certain books had established themselves as belonging to a core of holy texts, by repeated usage and frequent citation (see further in Chapter 10). But in the first century, the century when most of the New Testament was being written, things were more fluid. Jews and Christians (some of whom, of course, were still

Jews) drew on a wide range of books that were on their way to becoming a Bible but had not yet been described as such: they were 'holy writings', and no one had formally decided which, exactly, they were. In Judaism there never was a formal decision; Christians, more given to conciliar rulings, did eventually make official lists, but not until the fourth century. Most people would have known which the holy books were, in a general way, but not necessarily with the precision needed to be sure whether a relatively obscure book was in or out: 'in' and 'out' had not yet been defined. As the biblical scholar James Barr once put it, 'In what we call "biblical times", or in much of them, there was as yet no Bible.'[24] The first century CE saw the development from 'books' to 'Scripture', but the process was not complete until the second.

The actual term 'canon' itself is even later. In early Christianity it meant a rule, usually the 'rule of faith' – something like an early creed. Not till Athanasius, in the fourth century, do we find the expression that certain books are *ouk ek tou kanonos*, 'not of the canon'.[25] By the time there were rulings, people mostly agreed anyway: we shall find that this applies to the contents of the New Testament too. And Judaism never developed a term corresponding to canon, though from Josephus onwards, as we saw, an interest did grow in enumerating and identifying the holy books.

JEWISH AND CHRISTIAN PERCEPTIONS OF THE BIBLE

At a theoretical level there is a further distinction to be seen between Jewish and Christian perceptions. In Christianity there never seems to have been much difference in status among the different books of the Old Testament. In the New Testament the commonest designation for what we call the Hebrew Bible is 'the law and the prophets', with just one threefold description, 'the law of Moses, the prophets, and the psalms' in Luke 24:44. This shows that there was an awareness that the 'law' – the Pentateuch or Torah – had some kind of pre-eminence among the holy books. But nothing is made of this: we do not find any reflection on the difference of status, or passages from the Torah privileged in any way above those from elsewhere. When Christians come to list the books of the Old Testament, as did Eusebius of Caesarea (265–340 CE), they do so in a simple, linear way, not marking any kind of break at the end of Deuteronomy but running straight on through into Joshua and the other historical books and prophecies. Jewish writers, on the other hand, show an awareness of the special status of the Torah. We see this even in Josephus, who treats the works of the prophets (which for him, as for other Jews, probably included what we call the historical books) as similar in content to the Torah, yet still marks out the works of 'the lawgiver', Moses, as special.

We find the same thing earlier in the first century CE in Philo, whose major works are a lengthy commentary on the Pentateuch, treated as the foundation document of Judaism, rather like the Homeric epics for the Greeks. His division of the Pentateuch into sections, on each of which he writes a treatise (in all, amounting to several volumes in recent editions), may reflect the beginnings of the Jewish practice of reading a long section from the Torah in the synagogue service each Sabbath, though not for certain. All this indicates that in Judaism the Pentateuch was a closed corpus by the first century, even though we cannot argue that it came to be regarded as the most important part of the holy writings before any others were accepted as authoritative – some prophetic books and the Psalms, for example, could have achieved this status just as early, as we saw above.

In practice the greater weight of the Torah, and the inferior status of what would become the Prophets and the Writings, is not yet very marked in Judaism in this early period, so that its difference from nascent Christianity can easily be exaggerated. In the Mishnah, for example, one of the major sources of biblical quotations is the book of Proverbs, regarded in the Jewish arrangement of the Hebrew Bible as among the Writings – the third division. Also in the Writings section are the 'five scrolls', Esther, Lamentations, Song of Songs, Ruth and Ecclesiastes (Qoheleth), which came to be read on various holy days of the Jewish year. By contrast, some of the Prophets are barely used in Jewish writings or liturgy – this is true, for example, of Kings. The functional core of the Hebrew Bible in Judaism thus does not correspond exactly to its theoretical shape. In Christianity, on the other hand, where there is no theoretical shape but simply a list, it is also true that some books are much more important than others, so much so that we could speculate that many early Christian communities possessed only a selection of the biblical books, whether in Hebrew or Greek, which would have been in the form of scrolls. A given community might thus not even have known which books it ought theoretically to possess – another reason why it is hard to know exactly what the 'canon' contained, and why we should probably not use the term before the late second century.

The Jewish organization of the Scriptures into Law, Prophets and Writings is clear by the time of the Babylonian Talmud, where there is every reason to think it was long established, even if it did not function as much of a distinguishing mark when books were being cited. In the

Mishnah we tend to find a twofold distinction into Torah and 'tradition' (*kabbalah* – not to be confused with the medieval Jewish mystical philosophy that goes by that name), rather like the New Testament's division into 'law and prophets'. But that does not necessarily mean that the threefold division was unknown, only that it was not functional when citing texts in support of an argument.

The reason for the distinction between Prophets and Writings is completely obscure. The latest books of the Hebrew Bible (Daniel, Ecclesiastes, Song of Songs, Chronicles, Ezra-Nehemiah, according to most datings) are in the Writings. But so are Proverbs and Psalms, which, as we have seen, may be as old as some of the material in the Prophets section. In the later synagogue liturgy, after the long reading from the Torah, there is a shorter one (called the *haftarah*) from another book, and this is always taken from the Prophets, never from the Writings. But we do not know how old this custom is, or what is its rationale.[26] Nowadays it is sometimes said by Jewish teachers that the Writings are not revealed by God but rather are human reflection on God's revelation; but this clearly seems to be a theory established after the event rather than the original reason for the sorting of texts into Prophets and Writings. The distinction remains mysterious. Early Christian writers seem wholly unaware of it.

Christian lists have two striking features. First, they run together the Pentateuch and the historical books with no regard for the higher status of the Pentateuch, to produce the list Genesis-Exodus-Leviticus-Numbers-Deuteronomy-Joshua-Judges-Ruth-Samuel-Kings-Chronicles-Ezra-Nehemiah-(Tobit-Judith)-Esther. Notice that Chronicles and Ezra-Nehemiah are added – even though for Judaism these stand in the Writings – together with the deutero-canonical books Tobit and Judith. Sometimes we find other '-teuch' words applied to the combination of Pentateuch and histories: Pentateuch + Joshua can be called the 'Hexateuch' (Greek *hex* means six), or the list going all the way to Kings may be the 'Enneateuch' (Greek *ennea* = nine). In Judaism these coinages would be impossible, because of the different *level* of the Pentateuch/Torah. The medieval Church often spoke of the Octateuch, the eight books Genesis, Exodus, Leviticus, Numbers, Deuteronomy, Joshua, Judges and Ruth.

Secondly, Christian lists consistently place texts that in Judaism are among the Writings – the Psalms and the wisdom books – *between* the historical books (what Jews now call the 'Former Prophets', though the term is not ancient), and what Christians call the prophets (Jewish 'Latter Prophets') Isaiah, Jeremiah, Ezekiel and the Twelve Minor Prophets.

They usually also insert Daniel after Ezekiel, among the prophets. Thus instead of the Jewish scheme (1) Law, (2) Prophets, (3) Writings, Christians operate with an arrangement of (1) histories (beginning with Genesis), (2) teaching books (including Psalms, Proverbs, Job, Ecclesiastes, Sirach, Wisdom of Solomon) and (3) prophets. Thus a typical Christian listing will be something like this:

Histories
Genesis
Exodus
Leviticus
Numbers
Deuteronomy
Joshua
Judges
Ruth
1 Samuel
2 Samuel
1 Kings
2 Kings[27]
1 Chronicles
2 Chronicles
Ezra
Nehemiah
Tobit
Judith
Esther

Poetic or teaching books
Job
Psalms
Proverbs
Ecclesiastes
Song of Solomon
Wisdom of Solomon
Sirach (Ecclesiasticus)

Prophetic books
Isaiah
Jeremiah
Lamentations

Baruch
Ezekiel
Daniel
Twelve Minor Prophets (in varying order)

The exact order varies a great deal, but the general structure tends to be agreed. Unlike in Judaism, there is no sense of any gradation of authority, simply a different order. But one effect is that prophecy moves to the end of the Old Testament, and this is probably significant. Christianity in general stressed the prophetic side of the Old Testament: we see this on many occasions in the New Testament, where texts that do not strike the casual reader as prophetic at all – from the Psalms or the histories, for example – are treated as foretelling Jesus' life, death and resurrection. It is probably consistent with this to arrange the biblical books so that they climax with the prophetic texts. The effect becomes really clear once a New Testament is appended to the end of the Old: if the Twelve Minor Prophets conclude the prophetic collection, as they often do, then the last words of the Old Testament, in Malachi 4:5, are about the coming of Elijah to prepare the way of the Lord, and this is taken up near the beginning of Matthew with the story of John the Baptist's proclamation of the coming Christ. It is impossible to be sure that the arrangement is deliberate, but if it is a coincidence it is certainly a striking one. Manuscripts of the Greek translation of the Old Testament, nearly all of Christian origin, fairly consistently follow the history-wisdom-prophecy scheme, though (so far as I know) it is never commented on as significant by early Christian writers.

The order of the books in both the Hebrew Bible and the Christian Old Testament was not always as described here: over the centuries all sorts of alternative arrangements can be found in manuscripts. For example, there are Hebrew copies of the Torah that incorporate the five short books read at festivals, in places near the Torah passages read around the same time of year. The order of the Latter Prophets can vary: the Babylonian Talmud[28] states that it is Jeremiah-Ezekiel-Isaiah rather than the normal Isaiah-Jeremiah-Ezekiel, on the grounds that Jeremiah is all about disaster (following Kings, which ends in disaster), Ezekiel begins in disaster but ends in hope, and Isaiah is all hope – so they are placed in that order, like matching dominoes. There is no known manuscript that actually follows the Talmudic order. Since only one prophetic book would normally fit on a scroll, 'order' (Hebrew *seder*) must have meant the order of scrolls in a library rather than the order within a single volume, but that is something the rabbis may well have been interested in. (It is only in Christian circles that biblical books were copied into codices, that is, what we call books, sewn down a spine, rather than scrolls: this development will be examined in Chapter 10.) Christian lists, as we have already noted, can even scramble the order in the Pentateuch, reversing Leviticus and Numbers, and are not consistent in their arrangement of the 'teaching' books. In general, it seems that the order of biblical books did not matter much to Christians.

CANONICAL AND NON-CANONICAL BOOKS?

As we have seen, describing books as biblical or canonical in the first centuries BCE and CE is likely to be something of an anachronism. There were books about whose status there was no doubt – Genesis or Isaiah, for example – but there were others that were held in respect and about whom no one had yet ruled that they were either in or out. When, from the 1950s, the various scrolls found at Qumran began to be classified, some of them were described as biblical scrolls – and have now been published all together in *The Dead Sea Scrolls Bible*[29] – because they are manuscripts of books that now appear in our Bibles; others were said to be reworkings of biblical books, or to be non-biblical. But this may be teleological, defining the beginning from the perspective of the end. One Dead Sea Scroll, the so-called Temple Scroll, is an interesting case in point.[30] This consists of a reworking of some sections of the Pentateuch as we know it to make the laws about the Temple more consistent and coherent. Interpreters initially saw it as a kind of commentary on the Pentateuch. But the possibility ought to be allowed that it was meant to *replace* the relevant parts of the Pentateuch – in other words, that it was claiming authoritative status superior to that of the familiar Torah.[31] In so far as anything we could call Scripture existed in this period (probably the first century CE), the Temple Scroll may have been regarded by the Qumran community as fully scriptural – and the relevant sections of the Pentateuch itself perhaps as not scriptural, or no longer scriptural. It is also possible that they somehow managed to hold both as authoritative, just as later Jews and Christians have managed to live with both Samuel-Kings and Chronicles despite their glaring inconsistencies, or Christians, as we have seen, with four mutually incompatible Gospels. What is not possible is to say that the Pentateuch was already so fully canonical for the Qumran community that the Temple Scroll *cannot* have been intended to replace it. That is to read later definitions back into a period in which they may not yet have obtained.

A further complication is this. It is not as though all the biblical books were written, then they all became Scripture, and then they were all delimited as a fixed canon of the Hebrew Bible. The three processes overlap. All three must have happened in the case of each canonical book, but they were already complete for some books while others had still not yet been written. Long after Deuteronomy had become undoubted Scripture, books were still being written that would eventually attain scriptural status: Daniel, for example, dates from the early second century BCE; and though it probably came to be seen as sacred in quite a short time, since it is quoted a good deal in the New Testament, yet it was not in origin a piece of Scripture, but a freelance prophetic and wisdom book. But by then it was probably already regarded as illicit, at least in some circles, to add to or take away from anything in the Pentateuch, which was already in that sense a canon (though maybe not at Qumran, as we have just seen).

There are many non-canonical texts from Jewish sources, some of which (for example, *1 Enoch*) are almost certainly earlier than the New Testament but did not find their way into the Hebrew Bible. Just as there were groups that existed on the fringes of Christianity and revered works such as the Gnostic Gospels and Epistles (as we shall see in Chapter 11), so in Judaism there were many books that arrived too late for inclusion in the canon of the Hebrew Bible, but were taken seriously by many generations of Jews. Most are pseudepigrapha, that is, writings pseudonymously attributed to great Old Testament figures: Enoch, Noah, Moses, Isaiah, the twelve sons of Jacob, even Adam and Eve. Some nearly made it into the Hebrew canon, and for certain Jews in the last two centuries BCE, such as the community that produced the Dead Sea Scrolls, the books of Enoch and Jubilees (the latter a retelling of Genesis and Exodus) were held in great esteem, and can perhaps be said to have been Scripture.[32] *First Enoch*, as we saw above, is quoted in the New Testament Letter of Jude (Jude 14) and is apparently being treated as an authoritative book, on a par with others in the Hebrew Bible. By now it will be clear that the question, 'Was *1 Enoch* canonical for Jude?' is unanswerable, because the whole idea of a canon is a later one. We can at least say that Jude does not seem to make any distinction between the way it treats *1 Enoch* and the way it treats the other books that are now definitely canonical.

Outside the Qumran community, we have no evidence for Jews revering *1 Enoch*, but it is likely that some did – though its preservation came about through Christian hands. Many of the pseudepigrapha show clear signs of Christianizing additions: this is specially true of the *Testaments of the Twelve Patriarchs*, into which prophecies about Jesus have been inserted:

> The heavens will be opened,
> and from the temple of glory sanctification will come upon him,
> with a fatherly voice, as from Abraham to Isaac.
> And the glory of the Most High shall burst forth upon him,
> and the spirit of understanding and sanctification
> shall rest upon him in the water.
>
> (*Testament of Levi* 18:6–7)[33]

(The reference here is to Jesus' baptism, as reported in Mark 1:9–11 and parallel passages in the other Synoptic Gospels.) The difficulty of knowing how Jews regarded the various books that existed in the last centuries BCE and the first century CE can be illustrated, again, from the Dead Sea Scrolls. By the end of the first century CE there probably was broad agreement that at least the books we now have as the Hebrew Bible had an established status, though this does not mean that the canon was definitively closed. But we need only go back to the group at Qumran to find a more complex picture. Among the Qumran Scrolls there are fragments of almost every book that is now regarded as biblical, with the exception of Esther. But there are also works that generally go by the name 'Rewritten Bible'[34] – reworkings of biblical texts to bring out features particularly attractive to the Qumran sect. The term tends to assume that the underlying texts were authoritative – that they were part of the Bible – and that the Dead Sea community were producing special editions of them for their own use, just as they also produced commentaries on the biblical books. But we do not know how far the rewritten texts were really seen as merely parabiblical, and how far, as with the Temple Scroll, they may have been intended to *replace* the texts they reworked: we have only the rewritten texts, no critical notes to tell us how they were regarded. Was the status of these books still somewhat fluid, so that perhaps it was a given that there was a book called Genesis, but its exact content was still negotiable? 'Part of the Bible' is after all an anachronistic term: the Qumran community, and Jewish groups in general, had a variety of books, but no unified Bible.

How soon any given book came to be accorded a special status is a question that has to be posed separately in each case, and often we cannot answer it. It is important to remember that in ancient cultures the fixing of anything in writing tended to confer a certain status on it, given the expense and difficulty of writing. So even when a canon is nearly fixed, a newly discovered writing has some *prima facie* claim to attention; while on the other hand, a given community might not have possessed all the scrolls that were theoretically sacred, and simply had to manage without them. The synagogue at Nazareth, for example, may not have owned a full set of what are now the Hebrew Scriptures, and Jesus quotes mainly from what I have called the basic core (Pentateuch, Psalms, Isaiah). Perhaps for him there was as yet no 'canon' – and perhaps that should make Christians sit more lightly to the Bible, or at least be willing to prioritize among its books.

For most Christians there is indeed an effective canon that includes only parts of the 'official' one. Most Protestants, for instance, place much more weight on Romans than on James (which Luther, as we shall see, actually wanted to downgrade from the New Testament); most Catholics probably read the Gospels as more central than Paul. Few Christians in practice think of Leviticus as on a par with Isaiah, let alone with the Gospels. Given the diversity of the biblical books, it must be nearly impossible to give them all equal status in practice. Attempts to do so, as we shall see, usually involve some special techniques for getting all the texts to speak with a single voice – such as treating many Old Testament books as allegorical in character. (These techniques will concern us in Chapter 13.) In Judaism, on the other hand, though there is a 'canon within the canon' in the form of the Pentateuch (Torah), there is no sense that any part of the Hebrew Bible is dispensable or unimportant. It is a clearly bounded work, and there is an absolute answer to the question as to what is in and what is out. As we have seen, in Christianity the canon of the Old Testament is a more fuzzy concept. As one might expect, for Christians it is the New Testament that is exactly defined – though this was not the decision of a moment, any more than the fixing of the canon of the Hebrew Bible was in Judaism. The next two chapters will trace the winding route to a clearly defined New Testament. Here too we shall find that the Bible, even when its contents were agreed, still functioned as a set of core texts with a penumbra of less important ones, rather than as a monolith.

10
Christians and Their Books

By the end of the first century CE the books now in the Hebrew Bible – the accumulated literature of ancient Israel – had acquired an official status for Jews, which Christians (whether Jewish or non-Jewish) took for granted. When they are quoted, in either Christian or Jewish sources, it is with formulas such as 'it is written' or 'as Scripture says'. There is a certain formality and weight about these books, many of which even from the start claim authority as a word from God. This is particularly clear, for example, in Deuteronomy:

> See, I have set before you today life and prosperity, death and adversity. If you obey the commandments of the LORD your God that I am commanding you today, by loving the LORD your God, walking in his ways, and observing his commandments, decrees, and ordinances, then you shall live and become numerous, and the LORD your God will bless you in the land that you are entering to possess. But if your heart turns away and you do not hear, but are led astray to bow down to other gods and serve them, I declare to you today that you shall perish.
>
> (Deuteronomy 30:15–18)

The possibility that further books might still be added to the collection was not yet fully excluded, but there was no doubt about the status of the books that have come down to us as the Hebrew Bible.

The New Testament, on the other hand, did not begin life as a collection of sacred writings at all, but as occasional literature – highly important, but not sacrosanct. Each of Paul's letters is addressed to a specific situation in one of the local churches; and, though he no doubt intended his letters to be kept, and reread, they were not holy in the way that the Hebrew Scriptures unequivocally were. The Gospels, treated so solemnly in later Christian life and liturgy, are the distillation of traditions about Jesus, and as such were also naturally highly regarded and copied for subsequent generations, but they were not seen by the first Christians as verbally exact: there was no tradition, as there was in Judaism, of precise copying of the text – with the consequence that New Testament manuscripts vary greatly, and none is authoritative.

Yet eventually what we call the New Testament books did become Scripture in much the same sense as the Old Testament: that is, after all, how most Christians see them today. When did this change occur? There is a widespread belief that it did not happen until the fourth century, which is the period from which we have the first official lists of New Testament books. My argument in this chapter is that, though indeed listing of that kind is a later development, it was in the second century that the New Testament books began to be seen not as informal documents but as scriptural texts.

IRENAEUS AND THE NEW TESTAMENT AS HISTORICAL RECORD

There is clear evidence that for the first few generations the Gospels did not operate as sacred Scripture, but were seen as collections of material about Jesus which could be drawn on in retelling his story: just as Matthew retold Mark with additions and omissions, so an early Christian preacher could in some measure extemporize from the Gospel he or she knew best, or perhaps already from a mental harmony of more than one Gospel.[1]

We still see this in Irenaeus, the late-second-century Christian Bishop of Lyon and a leading theologian, who was martyred in about 202 CE. Irenaeus emphasizes the importance of the four Gospels. He claims that there cannot be more or fewer than four, drawing analogies with the four winds and (for the first time in Christian writing) with the four 'living creatures' of Ezekiel 1:5–10 and Revelation 4:6–7:

> . . . the first living creature like a lion, the second living creature like an ox, the third living creature with a face like a human face, and the fourth living creature like a flying eagle.
>
> (Revelation 4:7)

Traditionally these creatures are identified, in order, with the evangelists Mark, Luke, Matthew and John.

Some think this may mean that acceptance of just four Gospels was a recent development, or why would he have needed to find such far-fetched reasons for it? It seems to me that the argument works the other way: finding contrived reasons for a custom implies that the custom is firmly embedded and cannot be changed. But for our present purposes a much more interesting fact about Irenaeus' treatment of the Gospels is that he does not regard them as Scripture, as he does the Old Testament, but as historical sources for the life and teaching of Jesus.

Irenaeus follows the earlier writer Justin Martyr in ascribing ultimate authority not to the Gospels in their finished form, but to the words and deeds of Jesus that they record. Both clearly knew these words and deeds from the Gospels, but they do not treat them as deriving their authority from this. The sayings of Jesus and the story of his life, death and resurrection are not authoritative because they are preserved in a holy book, but have, as we might say, a life of their own apart from any written version. Indeed, Justin is wary of talking of what we call the Gospels as 'Gospels' (*euangelia*), referring to them as 'the memoirs of the apostles': there is still a sense that 'gospel' means the central message of Christianity, rather than being the name of a literary genre. Irenaeus has moved to accepting the later usage whereby it refers to books; but he still treats the Gospels as sources rather than as sacred literature. The point is made by C. H. Cosgrove:

> The second-century church tended not to conceive of the Gospels as discrete, theologically-shaped literary entities; this is a more modern notion of them. Narrative and sayings material even in Justin's day represented separate streams of oral tradition, and these strands of Gospel material continued to have a life of their own separate from their joint literary incorporation into written Gospels. Consequently, it is possible, even natural, for the second-century [c]hurch of Justin's time to think of the logia [sayings] of Jesus or the events of his life quite apart from the evangelical [i.e. Gospel] literature and to conceive of the Gospels as mere guardians of such tradition. The 'orthodox' Gospel literature represents not so much right interpretation, although this is not entirely absent, as correct circumscription and preservation.[2]

This comes out strikingly in Irenaeus precisely because he is so insistent on the authority of the four Gospels. When, in the second and third books of his work *Against Heresies*, he sets out what is known about Jesus, it is highly likely that he is drawing on the Gospels; but readers who did not know this might more naturally form the impression that he had two collections, a 'sayings-source'[3] (like Q) without narratives, and a narrative source without sayings, since he treats the sayings of Jesus as though they had an existence entirely independent of the

Gospels – which are to be seen primarily as evidence for the teaching of each of the four evangelists.

Irenaeus outlines his methodology for vindicating the true faith from four authorities:[4] the preaching of the apostles, the teaching of the Lord, the predictions of the prophets and the pronouncements of the Law – in effect, therefore, from what we would call the New and the Old Testaments. For the first two authorities, what he needs is a tradition of what the apostles taught, and one of the words of Jesus. What he has, however, is the four Gospels, Acts and a collection of letters. He deals with this mismatch in a rather muddled way. In the third book of *Against Heresies* he starts by trying to assimilate the Gospels to 'the preaching of the apostles' by talking simply about the *beginning* of each Gospel as evidence for the teaching of the four evangelists (not all of whom, as we might object, were apostles anyway, even in Irenaeus' eyes), outlines the teaching of the apostles who are mentioned in Acts, and finally moves on to Paul's letters. But in the fourth book he turns to the words of Jesus, paying no attention at all to the fact that they actually occur in the Gospels he has previously discussed. He treats them as an independent source of authority, but because he draws on the Gospels, some narrative material creeps in too. Retrospectively, he explains that he has now outlined not only the teaching of the apostles but also what Jesus taught *and did* – though he had not intended to bring in what Jesus did at this stage. Then he says he will go on to deal with the rest of the Lord's sayings (those in which he spoke plainly, as opposed to the parables, which he has already discussed) and with Paul's letters – now detached from his place with the other apostles.

The reason for the muddle is not hard to find. Irenaeus is working with a traditional Christian appeal to the sayings of Jesus and the 'memoirs of the apostles', which was how Christian memory was organized in the days when it was still transmitted as oral tradition – or, conceivably, in written documents that were the precursors of the Gospels – at a time when these two types of information had been codified in four Christian biographies of Jesus, combining sayings and narratives into a seamless whole. Matthew to some extent preserves the old distinction, with his alternating blocks of sayings and narratives, but even there they are not entirely discrete; only Q, if it existed, was composed purely of sayings.[5] However, the tradition that that is how the material about Jesus had been transmitted in these two separate categories outlasted the advent of Gospels that organized it differently. Irenaeus was trying to apply the older system to a reading of something very like our present

New Testament, and the fact that it does not work confirms that times had changed.[6] The existence of Gospels combining narrative and sayings into biographies of Jesus meant that the old model was outdated.

The Gospels surely originate, as the form critics argued, in oral testimony to Jesus, and their fixing in writing, though momentous in the long term, was at first – and perhaps still for Justin and even Irenaeus – thought of as providing a kind of aide-mémoire for later circles of preachers and teachers. Indeed, we still find this attitude in Clement of Alexandria, who 'continues to represent an older inclusive account of the gospel in which the content is more important than its precise textual location'.[7]

This, perhaps, is the true reason for the Church's tolerance of four different Gospels, as well as for the diversity of New Testament manuscripts. In the first few generations Christians did not write commentaries on the Gospels as though they were holy books, but used them as sources for preaching and teaching. Though actually books, they were theoretically 'non-books', more notebooks than works of literature. As we saw in Chapter 8, as a matter of fact they *were* literary works, biographies like others of the time, but they were not so perceived. It was in the course of the second century that they (along with the New Testament letters) came to be seen as scriptural texts like the books of the Old Testament. There are five pointers to the stages in this development.

SCROLLS AND CODICES

The first relevant phenomenon, still not wholly explained, is that virtually every manuscript of a New Testament book ever discovered has the form of a codex rather than a scroll. A codex is what we think of as a book, written on separate sheets and fastened along one edge so that it can be opened at any point. In scrolls, on the other hand, the text is written in vertical columns which are accessed by holding the scroll in both hands and turning it around two rollers: to find a given place one has to wind the scroll backwards or forwards. To us the greater convenience of the codex form seems obvious,[8] but in the ancient world scrolls were regarded as of much higher status, and people developed great facility in turning them. The codex was not used for important texts, but only as we might use a notebook, to make jottings or write drafts.

In Judaism the use of the scroll for the Scriptures was as universal as it was for high literature in the Graeco-Roman world generally: no one would have thought of writing Homer or Virgil in a codex, and

Fragments of Chester-Beatty papyrus p45, from the late second or early third century, showing Matthew 25:41. Christian texts came in codex form from the very beginning.

similarly no Jew would have produced a codex of the Pentateuch. The Roman poet Martial tried, in a set of epigrams written between 84 and 86 CE, to popularize the codex, representing it as much handier than the scroll, ideal for travel – rather the way we think of paperbacks:

> You who are keen to have my books with you everywhere, and want to have them as companions for a long journey, buy these ones which parchment confines within small leaves. Provide cylinders for great authors: one hand can hold me. So that you may not fail to know where I am for sale, and wander aimless throughout the whole city, with me as your guide you will be certain: look for Secundus, the freedman of learned Lucensis, behind the threshold of the Temple of Peace and the Forum Palladium.
>
> (I, ii)

But the idea did not catch on till much later. Christians, however, routinely wrote codices containing the Gospels or the works of Paul.[9] The earliest fragments of papyrus codices, dating from the second and third centuries CE, are a fragment of the Gospel of John, fragments of the Gospels and the Pauline Epistles in the so-called Chester-Beatty papyri, and the Bodmer papyri, containing Luke, John, Matthew and fragments of the Catholic Epistles.[10]

Evidently, the Christian writings were not then Scripture. As we have seen, this is confirmed by the fact that they are hardly ever cited with the formula 'as it is written' by early Christian writers, which on the face of it might suggest that these Christian works had a lower status than the Jewish Scriptures. Even into the second century, Justin Martyr refers to the Gospels as the 'memoirs' (*apomnemoneumata*) of the apostles. He tells us that in Christian worship they were read alongside 'the prophets',[11] probably meaning the Old Testament in general. But proximity does not necessarily entail equality, and it is entirely possible that they did not have the same status. The Gospels were not fixed Scripture but simply the reminiscences of the apostles. The codex/scroll distinction marks this opposition. A codex, to repeat the formulation above, is a 'non-book', and it is certainly not 'Scripture'.[12]

We should not, however, equate 'not being Scripture' with 'having a lower status than Scripture'. What was crucial was not the external form of the Christian writings, which were certainly more informal by far than the Old Testament Scriptures, but their content. Eventually the sense of the non-scriptural character of the New Testament writings was in any case lost, and they came to be treated as the same kind of thing as the Old Testament. This must have happened by the time of

Origen, who began the tradition of writing Gospel commentaries, just like his commentaries on Old Testament books. But it is already anticipated within the New Testament itself, with late 2 Peter (probably early second century CE) referring to the writings of Paul as containing 'some things ... hard to understand, which the ignorant and unstable twist to their own destruction, as they do *the other scriptures*' (2 Peter 3:16; emphasis added).

But at least until Irenaeus, a tradition persisted that it was not the New Testament writings as books that were holy, but the traditions preserved in them – the stories about Jesus, and his sayings. The loss of this sense meant, paradoxically, that they were in a way demoted from being the all-important source of knowledge about Jesus and the faith he taught and embodied, and turned into parts of a larger Bible. The earlier feeling that they were not Scripture (here meaning the Old Testament) *and yet contained truths more important than those in Scripture* was lost. We see this in the way early Christian writers quote more from what would become the New Testament than from the Old, even though they generally do not use citation formulas such as 'it is written' with New Testament material.[13] Rather than seeing Jesus, known through the Gospels, as a reference point even more important than the Old Testament Scriptures, Christians after Irenaeus started to see the Gospels, the Letters and the Old Testament as all equally authoritative, parts of a unified Holy Bible. 'Bible' is in origin a plural – *ta biblia* in Greek, 'the books' – but a sense developed, certainly by the end of the third century, that the books were in reality a single one with many parts. This marked a departure from the earliest Christian perception.

Thus in time, the New Testament came to be regarded as Scripture in the same way as the Old; but in origin it was not so understood. As I have argued, this does not mean that its contents were not authoritative. From the early second century CE we find writers citing sayings of Jesus as having an ultimate authority. But, crucially, the authority derives from their author – that is, Jesus – not from the fact that they occur in a sacred book. Early Christian writers sometimes quote *agrapha* ('unwritten things'), that is, sayings of Jesus that do not occur in any of the four Gospels, as having the same authority as ones that do. Thus Justin Martyr writes: 'our Lord Jesus Christ said, *In whatever things I apprehend you, in those I shall judge you*' (Justin, *Dialogue with Trypho*, 47); and Origen: 'But the Saviour himself says, *He who is near me is near the fire; he who is far from me, is far from the kingdom*' (Origen, *Homilies on Jeremiah*, 20:3) – this *agraphon* actually appears also in the *Gospel of Thomas*, discovered only in the twentieth century.[14] Justin also says that

Jesus' mother was descended from David (rather than that Joseph was, as in Matthew and Luke), and that Jesus was born in a cave – which has remained the usual understanding in the Orthodox churches.[15] These two traditions are also found in the *Protevangelium of James*, which we shall encounter in Chapter 11. Some of the sayings may have been culled from Gospels or other texts no longer regarded as canonical, such as the *Gospel of the Egyptians* or the *Gospel of Peter*.[16] But it is clear that Christian teachers in the first couple of centuries actually knew about Jesus mainly from the four now-canonical Gospels. Any other information they might come upon would, however, strike them as equally important: the significant criterion was not whether it was in a Gospel, but whether it went back to Jesus. Thus the attitude of early Christians to what we call the Old and New Testaments was in the beginning radically different, and only over time did the collections even out and come to be seen as two components, on an equal level, of a 'Holy Bible'.

By the beginning of the third century CE the Hebrew Scriptures had become for Christians the first part of a two-part Bible and therefore can understandably be called the 'old' portion of it – not necessarily implying a hard form of what is nowadays termed supersessionism, the belief that Christianity has replaced Judaism, though this is certainly sometimes present. This is the period of what has come to be called 'the parting of the ways' between Judaism and Christianity, their development into distinct religions, rather than there being simply varieties of Judaism of which the Christian sect was one.[17] Various early Christian writings coalesced into a second canonical collection, known from the second century onwards as 'the books of the new covenant'. This perception of the relation of 'old' and 'new' differs from that of the first Christians and values these writings in a quite different way. Although it is usual for Christians to appeal to early Christianity as a basis for their life and actions today, on the question of the Bible they generally operate with theories formed at the Reformation or even later, rather than examining how the first Christians perceived the matter. If an attempt were made to take seriously the relative status of Old and New Testaments for the earliest Christians, the Bible would be seen in a new way.

What might that be? In early Christianity, it was believed, on the one hand, that God had intervened in human history through the life, teachings, death and resurrection of Jesus of Nazareth. This new divine input had radically realigned religious belief and practice and issued new ethical challenges. On the other hand, the God who had done this was not a new, previously unknown deity (this idea was quickly seen as heretical), but the one already known in Israel and worshipped by the Jews – who was also, it was believed, the only God in existence, the creator of everything. Christianity was defined by the dialectical relationship between its new revelation and the older traditions of the Judaism from which it emerged, and working out some kind of equilibrium was tremendously difficult, as we saw in Paul's writings. The relationship between the Old Testament and the Gospels, as accounts of Jesus' life, teaching, death and resurrection, was also hard to define: the Gospels were in some ways more than Scripture, in some ways less. A Christian theory of the Bible needs to grapple with these tensions. The question is not primarily the relation between two bodies of texts, though that is how it may present itself, but that between two belief systems. Christianity is not Judaism, yet it derived from Judaism and affirms that the knowledge of God which Judaism claimed and claims is indeed true; while at the same time asserting that something genuinely new happened through Jesus Christ. The two-part Christian Bible of Hebrew Scriptures plus New Testament, which were originally two different types of writing rather than sections of a larger whole, symbolizes this complicated relationship. Franz Stuhlhofer sums up the matter clearly:

> We see here a paradox. The early Church cited the Old Testament as 'Scripture', but to begin with tended to possess it only in fragmentary form. The New Testament, on the other hand, was widely available and was used much more heavily, but it was not yet cited as 'Scripture'.[18]

Nevertheless, as we have seen, the New Testament did in time come to be seen as Scripture, and this is a development of thinking that was not wholly absent even when it was being formed. Paul makes it clear that, for the communities he is writing to, his own words have complete authority; he surely intended his letters to be retained and mulled over more than once, not simply read and then discarded. Writing, whether on scroll or codex, was a complex and expensive task performed by professional scribes, some of whom must have existed within the Christian community – such as Tertius, who tells us he penned the Letter to the Romans (Romans 16:22). Paul's letters were meant to remain as a source of authoritative guidance for the community in this or that church. Indeed, it was not long before there came into existence a Pauline 'corpus', that is, a 'collected works of Paul': the papyrus fragment p46 shows this, and probably dates from the late second century, the age of Irenaeus. The letters of Paul were not Scripture in the technical sense, but they were authoritative writings; by the time of the *First*

Letter of Clement (very early second century) they can already be referred to as a source of teaching. Clement, an early Bishop of Rome, writes to the church in Corinth and refers back to what Paul had said to Christians there in 1 Corinthians.

Or take the Gospel according to John. It begins, 'In the beginning was the Word' (John 1:1), in an obvious reference to Genesis ('In the beginning God created the heavens and the earth', Genesis 1:1), which can be understood as an attempt to provide a kind of Christian equivalent to the Pentateuch or Torah. This is not simply occasional literature, any more than Paul's letters are casual or meant only for the moment: it is solemn writing, intended to be kept and reflected on over generations – which is, more or less, what we mean by 'Scripture'.[19] Whatever the theoretical position may have been – and Christian writers do not discuss the status of the various works they know and refer to, whether scriptural or non-scriptural – in practice Paul and John soon had a higher authority for Christians than the Old Testament Scriptures.

The use of the codex, to return to our current theme, may fit with this. Far from indicating that the first Christians regarded their own writings as having a low literary status, the use of the codex that Christians pioneered may have been a deliberate way of distinguishing their writings from the classics (of either Jews, or Romans and Greeks) as having a new and special character. It was part of the Christian tendency to reinvent Jewish custom in a novel form,[20] which can be seen in other spheres too: baptism replaced circumcision, Sunday instead of Saturday came to be celebrated as a new, Christian Sabbath. It belongs to the Christian sense that the old religion has been surpassed by something new, which expresses itself in embracing customs that contradict those of Judaism – even down to apparently trivial details such as who must pray with covered heads (men in Judaism, women in Christianity [see 1 Corinthians 11:2–16]), and on which days of the week fasting is to be observed (Wednesdays and Fridays in Christianity, Mondays and Thursdays in Judaism, according to the *Teaching of the Twelve Apostles* or *Didache*,[21] a late first- or early second-century work). The idea that Christianity has superseded Judaism is a problem for modern Christians and Jews, and most Christians would now reject it. But it cannot be denied that it was prevalent in early Christianity – a sect that had to differentiate itself from its parent.[22] The codex may belong to this way of thinking: our writings are in a different form from theirs. So far as I am aware there is no ancient text that reflects explicitly on the replacement of the scroll by the codex in Christianity, so all this must remain speculation; but it would fit with how we know early Christians thought and reasoned. I shall return to this theme in Chapter 14, when examining attitudes to Scripture in the second and third centuries.

How far such attitudes were prevalent among the very early Christians who were still Jews we do not know: almost all our evidence comes from Gentile Christianity, for Paul already in the 50s is writing in Greek to churches whose members are nearly all non-Jews. For Paul himself, the Gentile mission that he spearheaded helped to show the true meaning of the Old Testament text. It is noticeable that, in writing to Gentiles, Paul actually cites Hebrew Scripture rather little as an authoritative text; but when he does it is often on the theme of the inclusion of non-Jews in the kingdom of God (thus especially in Romans 9–11). He claims that the events in which he himself is caught up, and indeed helping to inaugurate, are a fulfilment of the old Scriptures – much as the Qumran sectarians argued was the case for the events they were involved in. This in turn entails that the meaning of those Scriptures is now for the first time revealed. It is Christians 'on whom the ends of the ages have come' (1 Corinthians 10:11). As readers, Paul's churches do not go to the Old Testament to understand what Paul means; they go to Paul to understand what the Old Testament means. And that implies that at a functional level, whatever may be true at a theoretical level, it is Paul with whom authority lies. Similarly with Jesus in the Gospels: the Old Testament means what he says it means, and so he is the ultimate authority, greater than Moses, as John intimates:

> Then Jesus said to them [the people for whom he has just multiplied the loaves], 'Very truly, I tell you, it was not Moses who gave you the bread from heaven, but it is my Father who gives you the true bread from heaven. For the bread of God is that which comes down from heaven and gives life to the world.' They said to him, 'Sir, give us this bread always.' Jesus said to them, 'I am the bread of life.'
>
> (John 6:32–5)

The question of whether the New Testament was written as – or was believed by its earliest readers to be – Scripture is thus a good deal more complicated than it seems at first sight. It was, in one sense, not Scripture, a term reserved for the writings of ancient times that we call the Old Testament or Hebrew Bible. Yet in another sense it was more than Scripture, just as Jesus, for Christians, was more than Moses. What is certainly not the case is that the two Testaments were on a level. The New Testament, as it came to be known, was from the start of greater *practical* authority within Christian communities (especially perhaps Gentile ones) than the Old Testament; yet at the same time it was not defined as a corpus of holy writings in the way that the Old Testament was.

These ambiguities and paradoxes are concealed from us by the fact that we get our Bibles packaged in such a way that the Old and New Testaments are presented in exactly the same way, giving the impression that all these works are equally authoritative because all are 'Scripture'. If we could see a complete early Christian Bible, assuming such a thing had existed, it would be (1) a set of scrolls of the Old Testament in Hebrew or Greek (possibly including more books than in our present Old Testament – on this see Chapter 9 – but perhaps with some that we now recognize accidentally missing from the collection), and (2) a collection of codices of early Christian writings, looking to a contemporary far less impressive than the scrolls, yet to their users even more valuable because they were believed to contain words of life about Jesus and, incidentally, the truth about the meaning of the scrolls, too. Whether we should describe the tattered codices as less or more than Scripture depends on how the question is being posed. What is clear is that they are not the same kind of thing. They are not another chunk of the Bible, alongside the Prophets or the Torah. A word of Jesus, or even Paul, clinched any argument, whether or not we say that the books containing these words were 'scriptural'.

In time the relative status of Old and New Testaments evened out in Christianity. The Old Testament became a subject of study and interest in its own right, not only as a precursor of Jesus Christ. And the New Testament came to be seen as Scripture in the same way as the Old. By the time of Origen we find that the process is more or less complete, and there is a Bible consisting of two Testaments of equal standing. But in the beginning it was not so. Modern approaches to interpreting the Bible, and especially to using it as an authoritative source, might be quite different if we returned to the early understanding of Old and New Testaments not as two different portions of a uniform Bible but as two different kinds of material: the ancient, received traditions of pre-Christian revelation, and the records of a new revelation which both trumped the old and yet exposed its true meaning. We should have a hard task to avoid appearing to claim that the Old Testament had been *improved on*, but at the same time we should not be seeing it as *abolished*. The task might be difficult, but it was one that early Christians felt compelled to carry out.

The great shift in approach I have been describing here did not occur in the fourth century, but was a second-century phenomenon. By the end of that century a Christian codex of the Gospels or Pauline letters was no longer an informal notebook, but a holy text. A century later, such codices might be written with the highest skill a scribe could command, on expensive parchment, with Old and New Testaments combined in a single document such as *Codex Sinaiticus*, which we shall examine in Chapter 12.

THE NEW TESTAMENT AS SCRIPTURE

I want to suggest three steps in the process by which the New Testament books morphed from highly important sources into Scripture in a sense similar to that in which the Hebrew Bible is Scripture in Judaism, and in which both Testaments are Scripture in modern Christianity. These three steps did not occur simply in succession; they overlap to some extent, but they are conceptually distinct.

(1) The argument from prophecy

The first is the so-called 'argument from prophecy'. Early Christian writers, including Paul and the writers of the Gospels, place great emphasis on the argument that Jesus is the fulfilment of the Scriptures of the Old Testament. The classic illustration of this is the Gospel according to Matthew, which a number of times describes an event in the life of Jesus and then says, 'this took place to fulfil what was spoken by the prophet', followed by an Old Testament quotation. Examples are Matthew 2:18, where the massacre of the innocents by Herod fulfils what was spoken by Jeremiah; or Matthew 12:15–21, where Jesus' healing of the sick fulfils the prophecy in Isaiah 42:1–4.[23]

> Many crowds followed him, and he cured all of them, and he ordered them not to make him known. This was to fulfil what had been spoken by the prophet Isaiah:
>
> 'Here is my servant, whom I have chosen,
>   my beloved, with whom my soul is well pleased.
> I will put my Spirit upon him,
>   and he will proclaim justice to the Gentiles.
> He will not wrangle or cry aloud,
>   nor will anyone hear his voice in the streets.'
>
> (Matthew 12:15–19)

Anyone today who attends a Christmas carol service will be aware of this argument, since passages that early Christians believed were fulfilled in Jesus are read – for example, Isaiah 9:2–7 or Micah 5:2–5.[24] Most scholars today believe that the passages in question mostly had a relevance to the time in which they were written or uttered, and that the application to Jesus is a forced reading of them. Be that as it may, the logic of the argument is that the Old Testament prophecies have an authority such that if Jesus can be seen to correspond to what they were predicting, then his status as the Messiah is vindicated. That the Old Testament is Scripture, in the sense of being an authoritative text, is taken for granted; that authority then spills over into the early Christian message of salvation through Jesus. In arguing with Jews about the claims of Jesus, as Paul did (if we are to follow the evidence of Acts, for example Acts 28:23), it was crucial for Christians to proceed on the shared ground that the Old Testament/Hebrew Bible was divinely inspired; if it could be shown that it actually looked forward to Jesus, then Jesus was vindicated. For this argument, the New Testament is not 'Scripture', since that term refers exclusively to what we call the Old Testament. For a Christian it may, as I have been suggesting, have been in some ways more important than Scripture, but it is not the same kind of thing as the Old Testament.

(2) The argument from Christ

But in the second century, when almost all Christians were non-Jews, the argument changed direction. Gentile Christians had come to accept the Old Testament only at the same time as they accepted faith in Christ, and many never got to know more than selected portions of it: parts of Genesis, Isaiah, Psalms and beyond that probably mainly isolated messianic passages from other books. For them belief in Jesus came first, with the acceptance of the Jewish Scriptures as a corollary. From their perspective, Jesus was the known factor, the Saviour in whom they had come to believe. It was great news that he fulfilled some old prophecies, but that had the effect of making them believe in the old prophecies because he had fulfilled them. The argument from prophecy thereby ceased to be a way of showing that Jesus was a valid revelation of the God already known in Judaism, and became on the contrary a way of showing that the Jewish Scriptures were important and ought not to be abandoned, because they were about the God who had now been revealed in Jesus. There was a real risk that Gentile Christians might have abandoned them, under the influence of Marcion of Sinope, who taught at Rome in the mid second century CE. Marcion regarded the Jewish Scriptures as the work of a demonic, evil god, from whom Jesus had come to save humankind, and he rejected all the Gospels except Luke, which he purged of all references to the Old Testament. For a time it seemed possible that Christianity would become Marcionism: Marcionite churches had great success for some generations. To combat Marcion it was necessary to argue that the Old Testament was an authentic revelation of the one true God, a task undertaken with relish by Tertullian (155–240 CE) in his *Against Marcion*.

We can see what may be an early anti-Marcionite argument in Justin Martyr's *Dialogue with Trypho*. Justin apparently tries to follow in the steps of Paul, and demonstrate to a Jew that Jesus fulfils the Old Testament Scriptures. But in all probability the subtext is the converse: to prove to Christians, from the fact that Jesus fulfils the Scriptures, that the Scriptures are authentic and authoritative. '[T]he aim is not so much to demonstrate the validity of faith in Christ from the Scripture as conversely to re-establish the threatened authority of Scripture in the light of Christ.'[25] The Pseudo-Clementine *Recognitions*, also from the second century, put it frankly: 'Jesus is not to be believed because the prophets foretold him, but rather the prophets are to be believed to be true prophets, because Christ bore witness to them.'[26]

For people who thought like this, the authority of the New Testament – or at least of the main *content* of the New Testament – was clearly already established. It was not that they were demoting the Old Testament, but more that it was not their primary datum: as Gentiles, they had never 'owned' the Old Testament in the first place. New Testament writings, in the novel codex form, were for them more important than the Jewish scrolls, which they may have possessed only in a fragmentary way. When they referred to them, it was with great reverence, using formulas such as 'it is written'; but it was the writings of the New Testament that really animated their life and faith. Almost certainly there were handy collections of important passages from the Old Testament, constituting what are sometimes called in Latin *testimonia* – testimonies to Christ. As we have seen, the traditional way of describing the development of the canon of Scripture is that early Christians began by accepting the Old Testament, but the New Testament writings gradually gained strength until they were seen as having an equal status. However, the process just described suggests that, although in some kind of theoretical sense this is true – if you had asked an early-second-century

Christian whether Isaiah and Matthew were Scripture, he would have said that Isaiah was and Matthew wasn't – yet from a functional point of view it was the New Testament writings that called the tune. The reversal of the argument from prophecy is the clearest indication that Christians came to place more emphasis on the Gospels and Paul than on the Old Testament. Official lists of the contents of the New Testament, certainly, still lie a couple of centuries ahead. But books are Scripture if they *function* as Scripture, and the New Testament books clearly did so once the argument from prophecy was reversed into an argument from Christ.

(3) The divine plan in the Old and New Testaments

Eventually (certainly by the time of Origen) the argument from prophecy stopped lurching between proving Christ from the Scriptures and proving the Scriptures from Christ, and settled into an equilibrium in which it came to work in both directions at once. It became an invitation to consider the divine *plan* in which important events were foretold and came to be. The providence of God is revealed through the matching of prophecy and fulfilment. For this perspective, both Old and New Testaments need to be fully accepted, and it seems to me likely that it is linked to the acceptance of Scripture as a bipartite work, consisting of both Testaments considered as essentially the same kind of thing; in other words, when we find such a perspective we can talk of the existence of the Bible as we now know it. Such a way of thinking is certainly present in Origen. By his day, neither part of the Bible was under threat for most Christians (though there were still Marcionites around), and each was seen as harmonizing with the other. As we noted, Origen wrote commentaries on the books of both Testaments, with no sense that they were different kinds of work. Thus by the middle of the third century there was something like what we mean by the Bible, and its unity was not controversial.

THE OLD TESTAMENT AS A CHRISTIAN BOOK

A third way of approaching the question of when the New Testament came to be accepted as Scripture alongside the Old, rather than as something different in kind, is to observe a shift in early Christian thought from seeing the Old Testament as in itself a Christian book to regarding it as a companion piece to the New. This involves some surprising trains of thought. In the earliest days of Christianity it was possible to tell the story of Jesus almost without reference to the Old Testament. Whereas Matthew, as we have noted, is full of references to how Jesus fulfilled the prophecies of the Old Testament, Mark, the earliest Gospel, makes little use of it: his passion narrative, for example (Mark 14–15), scarcely quotes from the older Scriptures. Some have concluded from this that the Marcan community (if there was one – see Chapter 8) did not use the Old Testament, or that it was marginal for them. A more likely reason is that they saw the Old Testament as already containing a Christian message – that the Scriptures had been written with Christians and their beliefs in mind. To read the Old Testament was to read a coded account of Jesus.

Paul repeats, from the tradition he had received, the belief that Christ died and rose from the dead 'in accordance with the scriptures' (1 Corinthians 15:3–4), yet he himself makes little use of the argument from prophecy. This does not mean that he treated the Old Testament as valid 'on its own terms', in the sense of leaving it to have the meaning Judaism found in it. On the contrary, everything in it was for him to be interpreted from a Christian standpoint. He had no sense of distance from the Old Testament, such that one could compare the new revelation with the old; rather, the new revelation was already present in the old Scriptures. The true meaning of the entire Old Testament was a Christological one. Thus in 1 Corinthians 10:4 he speaks of the rock containing fresh water that, according to Jewish tradition, had followed the Israelites around when they were wandering in the desert on their way to the Promised Land, and says simply that that rock 'was Christ'. Everything in the old Scriptures was written 'to instruct us' (1 Corinthians 10:11). The Old Testament, it had become clear to Paul, was already a Christian book through and through, now that the veil had been removed from it – see 2 Corinthians 3:14–15, which speaks of a veil lying over the minds of Jews when the Old Textament is read, a veil that is only removed through Christ. It did not just contain specific passages capable of bearing a Christian meaning – discrete prophecies of the coming Messiah that had been fulfilled in Jesus – while the rest remained purely Jewish. Rather, it was a Christian book in its entirety.

We can see this idea still at work in two texts from the second century. One is the so-called *Epistle of Barnabas*, falsely attributed to one of Paul's fellow-workers, or possibly genuinely by some other Barnabas.

Reflecting on Genesis 1, the author of *Barnabas* alleges that this passage is not really about the creation of the world, but about the new 'creation' that Christians experience in Christ:

> When [God] turned us into new men by the remission of our sins, it made us into men of a wholly different stamp – having so completely the souls of little children that it seemed as though he had created us all over again. It is with reference to *our* refashioning that Scripture makes him say to his Son, 'Let us make man in our own image and likeness; and let them rule over the beasts of the earth, and the fowls of the air, and the fishes of the sea'; adding, as he contemplated the beauty of *our* refashioning, 'Increase, and multiply, and fill the earth.'[27]

Genesis is not simply providing images that can be drawn on in describing the Christian new creation, as in the later approach known as typology, in which some Christian event is 'prefigured' in the Old Testament; no, Genesis is actually describing the Christian new creation, without remainder. For *Barnabas* there is no description of the creation of the world in Genesis 1: it is simply about the new creation in Christ. Where Marcion and others attempted to abolish the Old Testament as Christian Scripture, *Barnabas*, at the other extreme, simply annexes it as a completely Christian text – a different way of resolving the dialectic between old and new. In a way there is no need for a New Testament so long as the Old can be read as describing the Christian faith so fully, and it is not surprising that the Gospels were not seen as Scripture themselves, or that *Barnabas* scarcely quotes anything from them.

Another example of this tendency can be found in the Easter Homily of Melito, the Bishop of Sardis in what is now western Turkey, who died in about 180 CE and whom we have already encountered because of his interest in the Jewish canon of Scripture. For him, the passage in Exodus 12 that describes the preparation of the Passover lamb is not meant to be read alongside the Gospel accounts of the Last Supper and the crucifixion, as prefiguring Christ: properly understood, it is *already* an account of what Jesus did and suffered. The Old Testament is not, as in the argument from prophecy, a proof of the reliability of the New Testament; once read through properly enlightened (that is, Christian) eyes, it virtually is a New Testament already. When it is read in church, it is a symbolic description of the passion of Jesus.

This is not to suggest that the author of *Barnabas*, or Melito, did not know one or more Christian Gospels; they almost certainly will have done. It is to say that they did not need to cite such texts as if they were scriptural, since for them the existing Scriptures, the Old Testament as we call them, were already to be read as essentially Christian works.

Perhaps this helps to explain a strange phenomenon in some early Christian writers: accusations that the Jews have falsified the Old Testament text by removing references to Christ or inserting misleading passages. Thus Justin Martyr alleges that Psalm 96:10 originally said that God reigned 'from the tree' – a clear reference to the cross of Christ. There is no reason at all to think that this is true: 'from the tree' is in fact a Christian addition to the text of the psalm. But for Justin, Christ was already present in the text of the Old Testament before his incarnation, and would have said nothing there incompatible with what he afterwards said as the earthly Jesus.[28]

So Christians had the right, and indeed the duty, to correct the Old Testament in the light of the revelation through Christ. The Old Testament was a complete, and completely true, revelation of Jesus Christ, not merely some preliminary disclosure. Where the Old Testament seemed in some way non-Christian, a theory was developed that the false passages that had been introduced into it needed to be removed or corrected: this is another idea we find in the Pseudo-Clementines, and also in the Letter of Ptolemy *To Flora*, found at Nag Hammadi in Egypt, which distinguishes the divine revelations in the old Scriptures from 'false pericopes'* added by human beings.

Now, surely, there has been a shift when we find that writers no longer see the Old Testament in these terms, but present it as the document of a pre-Christian time, containing some things that continue to be in force but others that have been superseded or else fulfilled in Christ. There is a difference between thinking that the Old Testament matters because everything in it was spoken by Christ (even if not by the incarnate Christ), with a primary meaning that is Christian, and which the Jews have blindly misunderstood; and thinking that it is a pre-Christian revelation by God, preparing the ground for Christ. On the first interpretation, the only true Jew is actually a Christian, as Paul comes close to saying (Romans 2:28–3:2). On the second, Christians may have supplanted the Jews in God's affections, but they are aware of Judaism as a continuing entity with its own Scriptures.

The first attitude – the Old Testament as essentially a fully Christian book – ceases to work once there is an accepted body of Christian

* A pericope is a short section of text, something like a paragraph.

literature that is beginning to function for Christians as the old Scriptures did for Jews. Then it becomes apparent that the teachings of the Gospels and of Paul represent a fresh stage in revelation, and thus that Christians need to think in terms of an Old and a New Testament.

Thus ideas about the Old Testament as a Christian book in early Christianity help to confirm what we have already argued on other grounds: that it was sometime in the course of the second century CE that there came to be a New Testament, conceived of as like the Old Testament. The books that constitute it are older than this, of course – Paul's letters go back to the 50s CE – but its articulation as a body of material similar to the Old Testament lies somewhere between the time when people could still treat the Old Testament as a Christian book and the time when it fell into the past, as a consciously pre-Christian (though still authoritative) collection of texts.

HARMONIZATION

A fourth indication that it was in the second century that the New Testament started to be something like a Bible, rather than a collection of texts that was not yet fixed, can be found in the evidence of harmonization. From early times readers have noticed that there are discrepancies among the Gospels, running all the way from minor differences of wording up to major variations in the life of Jesus and in the way his story is told. As we saw in Chapter 8, there was at least one attempt to solve the problem this posed for Christians in the form of Tatian's *Diatessaron* (Tatian lived approximately 100–180 CE), which wove the Gospels together to produce a single work, consistent in itself. This was so successful that it was still widely used in Syria two centuries later. For our present purposes its importance is that it shows that the Gospels were already significant (or why would anyone go to the trouble of harmonizing them?), yet not so important that they could not be changed (or how would Tatian's work have been permissible?). It implies that the Gospels were still perceived as a source of information, as repositories of stories and sayings that could be reblended, rather than as fixed works.[29] The situation was very different when Augustine came to write his *On the Consensus of the Evangelists* (*De consensu evangelistarum*) in the fourth century. This is an extended attempt to show that the Gospels *already* tally with each other in all important respects: that alleged discrepancies between them are illusory.

Augustine's is the line taken in subsequent 'harmonies of the Gospels', of which many have been produced throughout Christian history, and especially around the time of the Reformation. It implies that the Gospels are canonical Scripture and so cannot be changed, and that any conflicts between them are only apparent. But for Tatian this is not yet the case: the materials in the Gospels are fluid and can be altered – just as Matthew was free to change Mark. Although I have suggested that the Gospels were originally discrete works conceived on the analogy of Graeco-Roman biographies, that is not how Christians in the early second century saw them: they regarded them as sources of information about Jesus that could still be corrected and reordered. In a sense, Tatian is simply a fifth evangelist. It is after him that the idea of the Gospels as fixed entities must have arrived, and it is already fully in place in the work of Origen, with his commentaries on the Gospels as separate works, long before Augustine. Thus again it seems to be to the (late) second century that we must look for the idea that the books of what we call the New Testament are fixed and 'biblical'.

NOMINA SACRA

A fifth piece of evidence about the transition of the New Testament texts from important sources to Scripture by sometime in the second century CE may be seen in the phenomenon known as *nomina sacra*, 'holy names'. In almost all early Christian manuscripts (but in practically no non-Christian ones) certain words are written in an abbreviated form: these include the words that make up the early Christian acronym ICHTHUS ('fish'): IESOUS CHRISTOS THEOU UIOS SOTER, 'Jesus Christ, Son of God, Saviour', and also some other special terms: 'heaven', 'spirit', 'mother' and 'cross', for example.[30] There is remarkable consistency in the contraction (use of the first and last letters) or 'suspension' (use of the first two letters) in manuscripts of the books now in the Christian Bible. For example, when the word *theos* ('god') means a pagan god, it is not abbreviated, nor is *uios* ('son') when it refers to an ordinary son rather than to Jesus as Son of God. The custom is a bit like our practice of capitalizing holy terms: 'God', 'Spirit', 'Son', or, in some books, 'He' and 'His' when they refer to God or Jesus. We know that the custom of using *nomina sacra* is as old as *Barnabas*, because the writer reflects on the numerical value of the name 'Jesus' (numbers in Greek are rendered by letters of the alphabet) when written as *IE*:

> Circumcision was given to us in the first place by Abraham; but he, when he circumcised himself, did so in a spiritual prevision of Jesus. He got his instruction in three letters of the alphabet; for the Scripture tells us that *out of his own household Abraham circumcised eighteen and three hundred.* How does his spiritual intuition come into this? Well, notice how it specifies the eighteen first; and then, separately from this, the three hundred. Now, in writing eighteen, the ten is expressed by the letter I and the eight by E; and there, you see, you have IE(sus).
>
> (*Barnabas* 9)

(The writer did not pause to reflect that Abraham did not speak Greek.) The practice marks out Christian manuscripts as special, though despite much speculation no one knows when, where or why it originated. Like the use of the codex, this may be one of the ways in which Christians distinguished themselves from Jews, who treated the divine name of God (YHWH) with special reverence in their manuscripts, and wrote it out in full with great care; Christians, on the other hand, contracted or suspended holy words, perhaps equally as a mark of respect. We do not know for sure when the *nomina sacra* were created, but it cannot have been later than the early second century, given the reference in *Barnabas*. It marks out certain manuscripts as sacred.

THE NEW TESTAMENT IN THE SECOND CENTURY

In this chapter I have argued for one main point: that as early as the second century the majority of the books that would come to constitute the New Testament already had enormous prestige in the churches, and their authority for Christians was not in doubt. Whether we say they were already Scripture, or the Bible, is a matter of definition. I have suggested that we shall bring them more sharply in focus by saying that they were not yet Scripture – not meaning by this that they were unimportant; quite the opposite. They were in many ways more important than the Old Testament for the nascent Christian Church, and when they did become Scripture in the same sense as the Old Testament, that involved a diminution as well as a promotion.

From our own perspective – seeing the beginning in the light of the end – we can discern a clear move in the direction of our present New Testament books becoming canonical Scripture, a process that was complete by the time Origen was writing commentaries on the books of both Old and New Testaments as if they were the same kind of thing. But if we go back just a little in time, we find an earlier perception of the New Testament books as historical and theological resources, but not actually Scripture in the sense that the Old Testament was; and my suggestion has been that we would do well to reflect on that early stage in the development of the Bible, since it offers a more nuanced approach to the material Christians have come to regard as scriptural. It explains, for example, why there has never been a single, authoritative text of the New Testament, analogous to the Masoretic Text of the Hebrew Bible, but only a multiplicity of manuscripts. And it calls in question, for just that reason, attempts to appeal to the exact wording of, for example, the sayings of Jesus recorded in the Gospels. Very early Christian writers did not (could not) do that: they had to appeal to the gist of Gospel stories and sayings, which they communicated with considerable freedom of expression. The idea of exact verbal inspiration arose later – even when the New Testament had come to be thought of as Scripture, it was still not seen as a perfect, and perfectly precise, text. How much more was this so in the days when it was still seen as essentially a collection of source material, a kind of aide-mémoire for preachers of the gospel, recorded in that informal format, the codex.

In Chapter 9 we saw how the canonization of the Hebrew Scriptures involved two processes: a wide agreement that *at least* certain books had authority, and a decision that *at most* certain books had it. In the first sense, virtually the whole of our present Hebrew Bible was already canonical Scripture in the first century CE, in that there were few if any doubts in Judaism about the status of any of the books now accepted; in the second sense, there were still books that might have been accepted, and were eventually accepted by Christians, though Jews rejected them. If we adopt the terminology I prefer, we would need to say that everything now in the Hebrew Bible was already *Scripture* in the first century CE, but that it was not until the second or third century that there was a defined *canon*, officially excluding other books. We are beginning to see that a similar distinction might be useful for the New Testament too. Almost everything that is in our present New Testament was accepted as having authority for the Christian Church by the end of the second century CE.[31] *At least* these books were, by the time of Origen, Christian Scripture. But that does not mean there was a barrier to other books: no one had yet established the principle that these books *at most* were canonical, for we have seen that Christian teachers could still quote other Gospels, and even *agrapha*, unwritten traditions, in support of their arguments. The position is similar to that of the Hebrew Bible in the first century CE: an agreed core, but a penumbra of other writings that might yet be accepted as having at least some degree of authority. In the next chapter we shall look at the growth of the idea that books other than those now in the New Testament should be positively excluded, a process that was not complete until the late fourth century, and indeed in some ways is not fully complete even now.

11
Official and Unofficial Texts

It is frequently claimed that it was not until the fourth century CE that the Church decided on the contents of the New Testament, and that when it did so the decision was arbitrary, or even malicious – many works were deliberately excluded because they were not in favour with the ruling party in the Church but were of a 'heretical' nature. Dan Brown popularized this view in *The Da Vinci Code*, but the idea has a long lineage.[1] As we shall see, this theory greatly exaggerates the evidence of official rulings on the canon. It depends upon the confusion between Scripture and canon – between believing that there is a basic core which constitutes Scripture, and believing that the canon of Scripture is closed, so that no more books can be included. I summed this up in Chapter 10 in a distinction between the idea that certain books at least are scriptural, and the belief that certain books at most are scriptural. It is the second feature that we do not find very much until the fourth century; but the first, the belief that there is a core accepted by virtually all Christians, was already established in the second century CE. There were many books which Christians read, some of which would eventually be proscribed; but none was anything like as central, for Christian teachers and writers, as the four Gospels, Acts, the major Pauline letters, 1 Peter and 1 John. The position is strikingly similar to that in Judaism in the first century CE (examined in Chapter 9), where books that Christians would eventually call deutero-canonical or apocryphal were still possible candidates for scriptural status, yet the central core formed by the Pentateuch, the historical books, the prophets and the Psalms and Proverbs, was overwhelmingly more important.

DEFINING THE CANON

The fourth century saw the first sustained official rulings on the complete contents of the New Testament. The primary one is found in

Athanasius' *Festal Letter* of 367 CE – the oldest surviving document in which exactly the present New Testament books are listed. By this time the Church had changed from a small sect of Judaism into a large and predominantly non-Jewish religious movement, with a sophisticated organization controlled by bishops. Athanasius (296–373 CE), Bishop of Alexandria in Egypt, sent this encyclical to his diocese in time for Easter:

> . . . it is not tedious to speak of the books of the New Testament. These are, the four Gospels, according to Matthew, Mark, Luke, and John. After these, the Acts of the Apostles and the Epistles called Catholic, of the seven apostles: of James, one; of Peter, two; of John, three; after these, one of Jude. In addition, there are fourteen Epistles of Paul the apostle, written in this order: the first, to the Romans; then, two to the Corinthians; after these, to the Galatians; next, to the Ephesians; then, to the Philippians; then, to the Colossians; after these, two of the Thessalonians; and that to the Hebrews; and again, two to Timothy; one to Titus; and lastly, that to Philemon. And besides, the Revelation of John.
>
> These are fountains of salvation, that he who thirsts may be satisfied with the living words they contain. In these alone the teaching of godliness is proclaimed. Let no one add to these; let nothing be taken away from them.[2]

This statement is less an intervention than a recognition of what was largely already the case: it is not innovative in any way. The books listed are simply those that we know were in practice authoritative in the Church. The four Gospels identified by Athanasius are the four Gospels all Christian writers quoted and referred to, and had done since they were written. And by the mid to late second century, as we have seen, these Gospels were regarded as having the same kind of authority in the Church as the Old Testament, and in earlier times arguably an even higher one.

I have based my arguments so far on evidence of how the New Testament writings were used in the Church. But there are earlier lists of the New Testament books that confirm that the great majority of them were accepted, though not necessarily to the exclusion of all others, from the early third century at the latest. The lists tend to have a tripartite form, mentioning those books on which everyone agrees (the great majority), those that are generally rejected or regarded as heretical, and those about which there is dispute – usually the second and third of the Letters of John, sometimes James, Jude and 2 Peter. The only major books that seem to have been disputed are Revelation, which the eastern churches were slow to accept (and which to this day is not read in the Byzantine liturgy), Hebrews (see below), and the Gospel according to John,[3] which some in the Roman church apparently had some doubts about for a time, though many Latin writers freely quote it.

Thus a few decades before Athanasius we find Eusebius of Caesarea, the Church historian, commenting as follows:

> At this point it seems appropriate to summarize the writings of the New Testament which have already been mentioned. In the first place must be put the holy quaternion of the Gospels, which are followed by the book of the Acts of the Apostles. After this must be reckoned the Epistles of Paul; next in order the extant first Epistle of John, and likewise the Epistle of Peter must be recognized. After these must be put, if it really seems right, the Apocalypse of John, concerning which we shall give the different opinions at the proper time. These, then, are among the recognized books. Of the disputed books, which are nevertheless familiar to the majority, there are extant the Epistle of James, as it is called, and that of Jude; and the second Epistle of Peter; and those that are called the Second and Third of John, whether they belong to the evangelist or to another person of the same name.
>
> Among the spurious books must be reckoned also the Acts of Paul, and *The Shepherd*, as it is called, and the Apocalypse of Peter; and, in addition to these, the extant *Epistle of Barnabas*, and the Teachings of the Apostles, as it is called. And, in addition, as I said, the Apocalypse of John, if it seems right. (This last, as I said, is rejected by some, but others count it among the recognized books.) And among these some have counted also the Gospel of the Hebrews, with which those of the Hebrews who have accepted Christ take a special pleasure.
>
> Now all these would be among the disputed books; but nevertheless we have felt compelled to make this catalogue of them, distinguishing between those writings which, according to the tradition of the Church, are true and genuine and recognized, from the others which differ from them in that they are not included in the Testament, but disputed, yet nevertheless are known to most churchmen. This we have done in order that we might be able to know both these same writings and also those which the heretics put forward under the name of the apostles; including, for instance, such books as the Gospels of Peter, of Thomas, of Matthias, or even of some other apostles besides these, and the Acts of Andrew and John and the other apostles. *To none of these has any who belonged to the succession of*

> *ecclesiastical writers ever thought it right to refer in his writings.* Moreover the character of the style also is far removed from apostolic usage, and the thought and purport of their contents are completely out of harmony with true orthodoxy and clearly show themselves that they are the forgeries of heretics. For this reason they are not even to be reckoned among the spurious books, but are to be cast aside as altogether absurd and impious.[4]

Here is a clear tripartite division, which corresponds closely to the evidence of the actual use of the New Testament texts as calculated by Stuhlhofer. Eusebius, it is true, is not entirely clear about which of the two categories a few books belong in: Revelation may be canonical or 'spurious', though it is certainly not to be listed in the third category as one of the 'heretical' books that are not to be read at all.[5] The evidence from contemporary art confirms the knowledge of books that would eventually not be regarded as canonical. Thus the tomb of Junius Bassus in Rome (359 CE) shows many biblical scenes – the sacrifice of Isaac, Christ led before Pilate, Adam and Eve and the snake, Job on the dunghill – but also includes Paul being led off to execution and Peter striking a rock to produce water, in the manner of Moses, which come from books that the later Church did not regard as canonical.[6]

There is one important list that might establish a very early date for the decisive canonization of the New Testament, the so-called Muratorian Fragment. This is a fragment of a manuscript found in the Ambrosian Library in Milan by Ludovico Muratori (1672–1750). The general opinion is that it is a Latin translation from a Greek original, though this is not certain. The text reads:

> . . . at which nevertheless he was present, and so he placed [them in his narrative]. The third book of the Gospel is that according to Luke. Luke, the well-known physician, after the ascension of Christ, when Paul had taken him with him as one zealous for the law, composed it in his own name, according to the general belief. Yet he himself had not seen the Lord in the flesh; and therefore, as he was able to ascertain events, so indeed he begins to tell the story from the birth of John [the Baptist]. The fourth of the Gospels is that of John, one of the disciples . . . Moreover, the acts of all the apostles were written in one book . . . As for the Epistles of Paul, they themselves make clear to those desiring to understand, which ones they are, from what place, or for what reason they were sent. First of all, to the Corinthians, prohibiting their heretical schisms; next, to the Galatians, against circumcision; then to the Romans he wrote at length, explaining the order of the Scriptures, and also that Christ is their main theme. It is

> necessary for us to discuss these one by one, since the blessed apostle Paul himself, following the example of his predecessor John, writes by name to only seven churches in the following sequence: to the Corinthians first, to the Ephesians second, to the Philippians third, to the Colossians fourth, to the Galatians fifth, to the Thessalonians sixth, to the Romans seventh. It is true that he wrote once more to the Corinthians and to the Thessalonians for the sake of admonition, yet it is clearly recognizable that there is one Church spread throughout the whole extent of the earth. For John also in the Apocalypse, though he writes to seven churches, nevertheless speaks to all. Paul also wrote out of affection and love one to Philemon, one to Titus, and two to Timothy . . . There is current also an epistle to the Laodiceans, and another to the Alexandrians, forged in Paul's name to further the heresy of Marcion, and several others which cannot be received into the catholic Church . . . Moreover, the Epistle of Jude and two of the above-mentioned (or, bearing the name of) John are counted in the catholic Church . . . We receive only the apocalypses of John and Peter, though some of us are not willing that the latter be read in church. But Hermas wrote the *Shepherd* very recently, in our times, in the city of Rome, while bishop Pius, his brother, was occupying the episcopal chair of the city of Rome. And therefore it ought indeed to be read; but it cannot be read publicly to the people in church either among the prophets, whose number is complete, or among the apostles, for it is after their time . . .[7]

Like Eusebius, the author of the Fragment recognizes a central core, consisting of more or less the books that are now in the New Testament. Then there is a penumbra of a few that deserve discussion though in the end they cannot be admitted, such as *The Shepherd*, a well-respected text in the early Church, and the *Apocalypse of Peter*.[8] Finally there is an outer ring of books that some read, but which should be dismissed as heretical. Thus we have here the same tripartite pattern as in Eusebius.

But there is a major dispute about the date of this text.[9] The manuscript is not ancient – it comes from no earlier than the seventh century CE – but the text itself is certainly older than this. Often it is regarded as originating early in the second century, earlier even than Irenaeus: if that is correct, the New Testament canon was fixed remarkably soon, and some of the more tentative moves towards seeing the New Testament as Scripture that I have outlined become rather hard to understand. More recently, the case has been made for a fourth-century date, which would put it not far in time from Eusebius or from Athanasius' Letter, and this seems to me on the whole more likely.

The argument centres on the expression, 'very recently, in our times', applied to *The Shepherd*. Does this mean that *The Shepherd* was written just a few years or months before, in which case the list would need to be early; or does it mean that *The Shepherd* was written in 'modern times', as opposed to the 'ancient days' to which the other New Testament books belong, in which case the list would need to be late? The case is finely balanced. There are no other canonical lists anything like as old as would be implied by the early dating of the Fragment. If it is indeed that early, then Christians became interested in defining the exact contents of the New Testament already in the second century, and the 'at most' approach would be practically as early as the 'at least' approach to Scripture. The Fragment does not, even in that case, suggest that they saw the New Testament as on a par with the Old Testament; on that issue it is silent. But if it comes from the fourth century, then it accords with our other evidence. It is noteworthy that it lists the letters of Paul as we have them, but does not mention the Letter to the Hebrews, which some, particularly in the western churches, disliked for its rigorist theory that there could be no repentance after baptism. In this it is in accordance with *The Shepherd* of Hermas:

> For if we wilfully persist in sin after having received the knowledge of the truth, there no longer remains a sacrifice for sins, but a fearful prospect of judgement, and a fury of fire that will consume the adversaries. Anyone who has violated the law of Moses dies without mercy 'on the testimony of two or three witnesses'. How much worse punishment do you think will be deserved by those who have spurned the Son of God, profaned the blood of the covenant by which they were sanctified, and outraged the Spirit of grace?
>
> (Hebrews 10:26–9; cf. 6:4–8)

Whether the Fragment is from the second or the fourth century, there was in any case already a wide consensus by the end of the second century that the books we now know as the New Testament formed a central core of the Church's texts; while as late as the fourth century – certainly still in Eusebius – there remained a certain fuzziness about the edges of the canon. In very broad terms, it is fair to say that the New Testament writings grew through the first and into the second century, and were only finally restricted – codified or canonized – in the fourth, though if the Fragment really is early, the fourth-century development was anticipated in the second. But by the end of the second century the core was immensely stable, and Christian writers were quite prepared to reject some documents as unacceptable; while even as late as the fourth century there was still not complete clarity over the status of a few books, such as the shorter letters and even Revelation. It is not as though the New Testament first grew freely, with no attention to issues of authority and authenticity, and then was absolutely delimited without remainder, in a neat two-stage process. Already within the New Testament there is a warning against spurious letters (2 Thessalonians 2:2 – itself possibly spurious), and even as late as the fourth century people are still encouraged to read such works as *The Shepherd*, even though by then it was defined as not part of the New Testament. The growth of Scripture and its delimitation overlapped in the case of the New Testament, just as with the Hebrew Bible.

What cannot be said for either period is that there was a huge mass of miscellaneous literature, any or all of which could have become the Church's New Testament Scripture had it not been for a conspiracy by certain bishops or other leaders to suppress it. Such a theory is encouraged by such works as J. R. Porter's *The Lost Bible: Forgotten Scriptures Revealed*, which provides an attractive introduction to much apocryphal early Christian literature, yet manages to give a misleadingly exaggerated impression of just how fluid the growth of the New Testament was:

> . . . the New Testament was selected from a body of literature that included the apocryphal works considered here . . . The New Testament canon was settled only in the fourth century CE . . . Before the [Jewish and Christian] canons were finalized, several of the works in *The Lost Bible* would probably have been widely accepted as authoritative. Certainly, on the grounds of character and content alone, it is not really possible to draw a sharp distinction between the non-canonical books on the one hand and the Hebrew Bible and the New Testament on the other.[10]

'Selected' is entirely the wrong word to use. Athanasius was not faced with ten or twenty or thirty Gospels, from which he selected four; he was faced with four Gospels that had long been normative, and some others which had already been widely rejected. Sometimes criteria were suggested according to which the non-canonical books fell short of the quality required to have been accepted. For example, books needed to have apostolic authority in some manner, whether they were (supposedly) written by apostles (Matthew, John) or had authors who were in touch with apostles (Mark, Luke). Also, they had to be 'orthodox' in their teaching. We can see both these criteria being referred to in the account of Eusebius, above: 'the character of the style [of the non-canonical books] also is far removed from apostolic usage, and the thought and purport of their contents are completely out of harmony with true orthodoxy'.[11] But these two criteria tended to prop each other up. Apostolic works could be assumed to be orthodox, so John was accepted, at least by most, despite its having a few tendencies that in other books might have led to an accusation of 'Gnosticism' (see below). And orthodox works could be assumed to be apostolic unless there was evidence to the contrary, so that *The Shepherd* would have been canonical, for the writer of the Muratorian Fragment, if it had not been known to be non-apostolic; while those who supported Hebrews as theologically sound tended also to ascribe it to Paul. Origen can even define 'apostles' as those who produced Gospels, rather than defining Gospels as the writings of apostles.[12] What all this suggests is that both criteria operated after the event; they are part of the Church's reflection on the scriptural status that was already ascribed to certain works, rather than principles on which these works were selected in the first place.[13]

Perhaps the major issue in accepting the canonicity of texts was continuity of use in the Church, as again in the quotation from Eusebius: 'To none of these [that is, the non-canonical books] has any who belonged to the succession of ecclesiastical writers ever thought it right to refer in his writings'. Not mere antiquity but long use was the essential characteristic of a holy book – a test that most of the Gospels and Epistles rejected by the likes of Athanasius could not possibly have passed. Such use certainly included the reading of a text in the liturgy, which was an attestation of its sanctity and normative character. The comments in the Muratorian Fragment about *The Shepherd* suggest that there was opportunity in the liturgy for public reading of non-canonical books, but that they were distinguished from the books of the New Testament, perhaps by being read in a different place in the service, rather than among 'the prophets' (the Old Testament books?) or 'the apostles' (the New Testament books?).

To put it bluntly, as C. E. Hill does, the answer to the question, 'Who chose the Gospels?' is 'No one.'[14] They began to be used, they became indispensable, they were defended against attack, and they became an essential resource for the Church, but no one ever 'chose' them according to this or that criterion. The justifications for accepting them are all retrospective: books are canonical if apostolic, but also are apostolic if canonical. They were accepted because they had always been accepted. The point is put well by Stuhlhofer:

> If we think of the countless continuities in early Christian use of the New Testament books, we are impressed by the 'deep silence, for observers from later generations, in which the canon came into existence' (Franz Overbeck). It is a history quite without any revolutions. All the essentials are there from the beginning, and the tiny changes occur so gradually that no one notices them.[15]

THE EXCLUDED BOOKS

What, then, of the books that were excluded? On the whole they are considerably later than those accepted as canonical, and also of lower quality – although this is a matter of opinion, it is not hard to feel that Christians would react with dismay if asked to accept most of them as Scripture. Take, for example, the *Infancy Gospel of Thomas*, a second-century book about the early life of Jesus (not to be confused with the *Gospel of Thomas*, see below), in which Jesus curses people who give him trouble. Even if such texts were suppressed by the Church, one can see why. Some were clearly used in the early Church, though not nearly as often as the canonical books; many fell entirely into disuse and have only been discovered in modern times, often sparking sensationalist publicity campaigns – thus especially the *Gospel of Judas* and the *Gospel of Mary*, two other Gnostic texts that are no earlier than the late second century CE.

The most significant archaeological find of parabiblical Gospels and letters is that at Nag Hammadi in Egypt in 1945, which yielded a number of interesting texts in Coptic. Just one of these, the *Gospel of Thomas*, is thought by some scholars possibly to contain a few genuine sayings of Jesus, one or two of which were previously known as *agrapha* through the writings of Christian teachers, as we saw in Chapter 10. Origen and Eusebius certainly knew of *Thomas*. It is not a narrative Gospel but purely a collection of sayings, rather like Q (if that ever existed) – some of them quite enigmatic:

> (3) Jesus said, 'If those who lead you say to you, "Lo, the kingdom is in heaven", the birds of heaven will precede you. If they say to you, "It is in the sea", then the fish will precede you. Rather, the kingdom is within you and outside you. When you know yourselves, then you will be known, and you will know that you are sons of the living Father. But if you do not know yourselves, then you are in poverty and you yourselves are the poverty.'

> (7) Jesus said, 'Blessed is the lion which the man shall eat, so that the lion will become man; and cursed is the man whom the lion shall eat, and the lion will become man.'

(11) Jesus said, 'This heaven will pass away, and that which is above it will pass away, and the dead are not alive, and the living will not die. In the days when you ate what is dead, you made it alive; when you come into the light, what will you do? On the day when you were one you became two. But when you have become two, what will you do?'

(22) Jesus saw some infants being suckled. He said to his disciples, 'These children who are being suckled are like those who enter the kingdom.' They said to him, 'If we are children, shall we enter the kingdom?' Jesus said to them, 'When you make the two one, and when you make the inner as the outer and the outer as the inside, and the upper as the lower, and when you make the male and the female into a single one, so that the male is not male nor the female not female, when you make eyes in place of an eye, and a hand in place of a hand, and a foot in place of a foot, an image in place of an image, then you shall enter the kingdom.'

(42) Jesus said, 'Become passers-by.'

Others seem to be borrowed from (or else to be the sources for) sayings in the four canonical Gospels:

(9) Jesus said, 'Behold, the sower went out; he filled his hand, he sowed. Some seeds fell on the road. The birds came and gathered them up. Others fell on the rock and did not take root in the earth and did not produce ears up to heaven. Others fell among thorns. They choked the seed and the worm ate them. But others fell on good ground and it brought forth good fruit to heaven. These yielded sixty per measure and one hundred and twenty measures.'

(20) The disciples said to Jesus, 'Tell us, what is the Kingdom of Heaven like?' He said to them, 'It is like a grain of mustard seed, smaller than all seeds. But when it falls on cultivated ground the soil puts forth a large branch and provides a shelter for birds of heaven.'

(65) He said, 'A good man had a vineyard. He leased it to some farmers so that they would cultivate it and he would receive the fruit from them. He sent his servant so that the tenants would give him the fruit of the vineyard. They seized his servant, beat him, and almost killed him. The servant returned and told his master. His master said, "Perhaps they did not recognize him." He sent another servant. The tenants beat him also. Then the owner sent his son. He said, "Perhaps they will respect my son." Those tenants knowing he was the heir of the vineyard seized him and killed him. He who has ears, let him hear.'

(86) Jesus said, '[The foxes have] their earths and the birds have their nests but the Son of Man has nowhere to lay his head and rest.'

(90) Jesus said, 'Come to me, for my yoke is easy and my lordship is gentle and you will find repose for yourselves.'[16]

The date of *Thomas* is a matter of great dispute. If the analogy with Q is pressed, it can be argued that it is earlier than the canonical Gospels, just as Q must have been: this would assume that collections of Jesus' sayings preceded narrative accounts of his life, which is thinkable. On the other hand, parallels with the canonical Gospels could be an indication of later origin, with the author excerpting from them sayings that suited his purpose. Dates offered thus range between the mid first century (contemporary with Paul) and the mid second century (not much before Irenaeus). On the whole, *Thomas* is the only non-canonical work that a significant number of scholars think could be as old as the canonical Gospels, and hence could contain sayings genuinely going back to Jesus.[17]

Other Nag Hammadi texts are the *Gospel of Truth*, the *Apocryphon of James*, the *Apocryphon of John*, the *Gospel of Philip*, the *Gospel of the Egyptians*, the *Hypostasis of the Archons* and the *Acts of Peter and the Twelve Apostles*. Most of these texts are 'Gnostic' in character – that is, linked to a form of religion that has affinities with the kind of Manichaeism that Augustine famously embraced and then rejected in later times. Gnostics taught that the world and everything in it is evil, and that only extreme asceticism is an adequate human response to this. They were highly negative about 'the flesh', and pessimistic about the character of the creator God whom Christians worshipped. Most present a Jesus very different from the one described in the canonical Gospels. There is no denying that early Christian leaders opposed Gnosticism. But the now-canonical New Testament books were making their way into the minds of Christians well before most of the Gnostic texts were even written. These (mostly second-century and later) texts are witnesses not to an early alternative Christianity, but rather to a late development largely at odds with the Christianity of Paul and, indeed, with the teachings of Jesus. They illustrate the tendency of people influenced by the Christian gospel to take authentic elements to extremes, and also to interpret it in the light of a dominant philosophy, forcing it into an alien mould.[18]

In recent years there have been two Gnostic Gospels – not from Nag Hammadi – that have caught the public interest. In 2006 *National Geographic* magazine published a translation of the *Gospel of Judas*, a text that had turned up on the antiquities market in Geneva in 1983 but had allegedly been found in the 1960s. Like the Nag Hammadi finds, it is in Coptic, and purports to record conversations Judas had with Jesus, which seem to imply that it was Jesus' idea for Judas to betray him. The line that became salient in public discussion is 'You shall sacrifice the man that clothes me.' This is a typically Gnostic idea of Jesus as only apparently human, a spirit 'clothed' by a human body, and belongs to a movement of thought known as Docetism (from Greek *dokein*, 'to appear': Jesus only appeared to be human), which was later influential in Islamic thought. There is no reason to think that this text is older than the second century, nor to suppose that it preserves any genuine reminiscences about Jesus and Judas; but, like the Nag Hammadi finds, it prompted a number of conspiracy theories: this, so the word went, was the truth about Jesus and Judas at last, which the Church had suppressed.

The *Gospel of Mary* is another Coptic text, discovered in 1896. There is widespread agreement that it comes from the middle of the second century, but not all regard it as Gnostic in character. In it Jesus instructs Mary (almost certainly Mary Magdalene) about the nature of the soul, so that his teachings are presented as a path to interior spiritual knowledge. He also says that he values her above his other disciples, a saying that incenses Peter but has ensured that the text is of interest to modern Christian feminists, who argue that it shows there was an alternative to the patriarchalism of early Christianity. So far as I know there have not been any suggestions that the *Gospel of Mary* should be added to the canon, but Karen L. King has proposed that it could be as old as the canonical Gospels,[19] although it is not mentioned by early writers and its existence was unknown in modern times before the discovery of the three manuscripts which contain (parts of) the text. The major one of these is the manuscript known as Papyrus Berolinensis (BG 8502), now housed in the Papyrology Collection of the National Museums of Berlin. This codex contains four works in Coptic translation: the *Gospel of Mary* is the first. The original language was almost certainly Greek.[20]

THE APOSTOLIC FATHERS

Arguably more important than the (mainly Gnostic) works discussed so far is another set of second-century texts, the so-called Apostolic Fathers. Eusebius and Athanasius both mention two of these, the *Epistle of Barnabas* (which I discussed in examining the argument from prophecy in Chapter 10) and the *Teaching of the Twelve Apostles* or *Didache*, probably written in Syria, together with another early work, possibly from Rome, *The Shepherd* by Hermas. These, though little known to conspiracy theorists, nearly did get into the New Testament. The fourth-century *Codex Sinaiticus*, a great Greek Bible roughly contemporary with Athanasius (and now in the British Library), includes in its New Testament section both *Barnabas* and *The Shepherd*; how its scribes regarded their status, whether as canonical or not, we simply do not know, but it was evidently high enough to include them in a prestige edition of the Bible.

The *Didache* consists mainly of directions for organizing the Church, explaining the rights and duties of different ministries, including 'prophets' and 'apostles', who appear to be itinerant preachers, and regulating prayer and, especially, the Eucharist. It seems to reflect a time when the Eucharist was still a real rather than a symbolic meal, which it had certainly ceased to be by the mid second century, and this makes it a very early text, perhaps earlier than some of the New Testament books (see Chapters 8 and 10 on the dating of the New Testament). When it refers to sayings of Jesus, it seems to know them in a form that precedes their fixing in the Gospels. There is no agreement on the place of writing, major candidates being Egypt and Syria; similarities with the Gospel according to Matthew might tend to support the latter, if Matthew is indeed a Syrian work. But it was known in Egypt in later times: Clement of Alexandria seems to refer to it as Scripture, and, as we saw above, Athanasius was familiar with it. It provides important evidence for the ordering of Church life in, perhaps, the last years of the first century CE.

The Lord's Prayer appears as a regular part of the prayer life of the congregation in the *Didache* (8), which is the first source to describe it as being said three times a day, and there are prayers for the Eucharist which give every impression of being older than most of the others we know:

> (9) At the Eucharist, offer the eucharistic prayer in this way. Begin with the chalice: 'We give thanks to thee, our Father, for the holy Vine of thy servant David, which thou hast made known to us through thy servant Jesus.'
>
> *'Glory be to thee, world without end.'*
>
> Then over the broken bread: 'We give thanks to thee, our Father, for the life and knowledge thou hast made known to us through thy servant Jesus.'
>
> *'Glory be to thee, world without end.'*
>
> 'As this broken bread, once dispersed over the hills, was brought together and became one loaf, so may thy Church be brought together from the ends of the earth into thy kingdom.'
>
> *'Thine is the glory and the power, through Jesus Christ, for ever and ever.'*

But there is also a provision that a prophet should be free to use his own words, implying a Church order in which prophets were particularly honoured and were to be given a livelihood in virtue of their gifts (they are your 'high priests' (13)), and in which Eucharistic presidency was by no means the prerogative of the ancestors of later bishops and presbyters or priests. We have no way of knowing how far the influence of the *Didache* reached, given that we do not even know where it was compiled; but it does undermine any idea of the early Church as hierarchically ordered everywhere.

Comically, the writer interprets Jesus' command, 'When you fast, do not be like the hypocrites' (Matthew 6:16) as follows: 'Do not keep the same fast-days as the hypocrites. Mondays and Thursdays are their days for fasting, so yours should be Wednesdays and Fridays' (8). It is hard not to feel that the fervent atmosphere of the Sermon on the Mount has here been replaced with something much more flat-footed. But this is, after all, a Church order, and therefore it is only to be expected that it would be more pedestrian than a sermon. And there is plenty of wisdom on offer:

> If any prophet, speaking in the spirit, says, 'Give me money (or anything else)', do not listen to him. On the other hand, if he bids you give it to someone else who is in need, nobody should criticize him (11).

The *Epistle of Barnabas* shares some material with the *Didache*, a short treatise on the two paths (of good and evil conduct: *Didache* 1–6, *Barnabas* 18–20). But the bulk of the text is an interpretation of parts of the Old Testament in a Christianizing way, as I tried to illustrate in Chapter 10. As Andrew Louth puts it:

> His concern is not to show that with the coming of Christ the Old Testament Scriptures now have a new and deeper meaning, but to show that apart from Christ they cannot be understood at all. Their *only* meaning is that revealed in Christ; the Jews have *always* misunderstood their Scriptures by interpreting them literally.[21]

Since the author is aware of the destruction of the Temple in Jerusalem, *Barnabas* must have been composed after 70 CE, but it could be considerably later. It was known to Clement and Origen, so cannot be later than around the end of the second century. Because of its treatment of the Old Testament as in effect a Christian book, it is probably relatively early, rather than belonging to the time when the old Scriptures came to be consciously allegorized, but this is a matter of rather subjective impressions. It was at any rate old enough for there to be a real question in the fourth century about including it in the canon of the New Testament, and, though Athanasius rejected it, the scribe of *Codex Sinaiticus* may have had other ideas.

Barnabas scarcely quotes the New Testament, only the Old, which may also suggest a relatively early date. But often the author seems to be drawing on lists of proof texts for the status of Jesus, *testimonia*, which often turn up in later works too and probably circulated independently, rather as did collections of the sayings of Jesus (if the Q hypothesis is true). Some of the texts cited in *Barnabas* purport to show in particular that Jewish worship has been superseded in Christ, rather as is argued in Hebrews. There is a section (16) on the Temple, which assembles Old Testament texts that speak of God's rejection of the Temple in favour of the spiritual worship inaugurated through Christ:

> I will show you how mistaken those miserable folk were in pinning their hopes to the building itself, as if that were the home of God, instead of to God their own Creator . . . For mark how completely the words of the Lord himself dispense with it . . . *The heaven is a throne for me, and the earth a stool for my feet. What sort of house, then, will you build for me, and where is the spot that can serve me for a resting-place?* [Isaiah 66:1] . . .
>
> But what we have to ask next is, Can there be such a thing as a temple of God at all? To be sure there can – but where he himself tells us that he is building and perfecting it . . . When we were granted remission of our sins, and came to put our hopes in his Name, we were made new men, created all over again from the beginning; and as a consequence of that, God is at this moment actually dwelling within us in that poor habitation of ours . . . This is what the building up of a spiritual temple to the Lord means.

We know from Justin's *Dialogue with Trypho* that Christians collected Old Testament texts that could be used in anti-Jewish polemic, and could also be deployed in what was probably a more immediate and important battle, that with 'Judaizers' in the Church – that is, those who interpreted the Old Testament literally. Some did this to argue for a Jewish form of Christianity; but others, of whom Marcion was the foremost, in order to show how unfit the Old Testament was to be Christian Scripture. Texts such as *Barnabas* provided ammunition against the literal interpretation, and in favour of a spiritual reading that made the Old Testament yield a Christian meaning.

The Shepherd is an altogether different kind of work. It is a series of revelations, mostly in symbolic form, organized for Hermas, the hero and purported (perhaps also actual) author, by the Shepherd, an angelic being. Much of it concerns the building of a tower, symbolizing the Church, and the incorporation into it of various kinds of stone, standing for different types of Christian. The overall purpose is to encourage perseverance in faith and good works, and also to deal with an issue that greatly preoccupied some early Christians: could there be a second repentance of sins after baptism? The Letter to the Hebrews had maintained that there could not (see Hebrews 6:4–8 and 10:26–31, discussed above). Hermas, however, puts forward the view that there can be one further repentance, but that is the last chance:

> 'The Lord, therefore, being merciful, had mercy on his creation, and established this repentance, and to me was the control of this repentance given. But I tell you,' said he, 'after that great and holy calling, if a man be tempted by the devil and sin, he has one repentance, but if he sin and repent repeatedly it is unprofitable for such a man, for scarcely shall he live.' (*Shepherd*, Mandate IV.3.5–6)

> 'Those who have no knowledge of God and do wickedly, are condemned to death, but those who have knowledge of God and have seen his great deeds, and do wickedly, shall be punished doubly, and shall die for ever.' (*Shepherd*, Similitudes IX.18.2)[22]

In general the moral teaching of *The Shepherd* is familiar from other Jewish and Christian sources. The good person refrains from adultery and fornication, drunkenness, luxurious living and gluttony, pride, lying, hypocrisy and blasphemy (Mandate VIII.3). Instead he attends to the 'deeds of goodness':

> To minister to widows, to look after orphans and the destitute, to redeem from distress the servants of God, to be hospitable . . . to resist none, to be gentle, to be poorer than all men, to reverence the aged, to practise justice, to preserve brotherhood, to submit to insult, to be brave, to bear no malice, to comfort those who are oppressed in spirit, not to cast aside those who are offended in the faith, but to convert them and give them courage, to reprove sinners, not to oppress poor debtors. (*The Shepherd*, Mandate VIII.10)

It is hard to find anything in this that Paul or any other early Christian writer would have disagreed with.

Hermas also tried to bring clarity to one issue that is notoriously obscure in the Gospels (see Chapter 12): Jesus' teaching on divorce and remarriage:

> 'Sir,' said I, 'if a man have a wife faithful in the Lord, and he finds her out in some adultery, does the husband sin if he lives with her?' 'So long as he

> is ignorant,' said he, 'he does not sin, but if the husband knows her sin, and the wife does not repent, but remains in her fornication, and the husband go on living with her, he becomes a partaker of her sin, and shares in her adultery.' 'What then,' said I, 'sir, shall the husband do if the wife remain in this disposition?' 'Let him put her away,' he said, 'and let the husband remain by himself. But "if he put his wife away and marry another he also commits adultery himself."' 'If then,' said I, 'sir, after the wife be put away she repent, and wish to return to her own husband, shall she not be received?' 'Yes,' said he; 'if the husband do not receive her he sins and covers himself with great sin; but it is necessary to receive the sinner who repents, but not often, for the servants of God have but one repentance. Therefore, for the sake of repentance the husband ought not to [re] marry . . .' (*The Shepherd*, Mandate IV.1.4–8)

Here the issue of second repentance arises again in a different context. It was clearly a great preoccupation in the circles in which Hermas moved, probably in Rome if the Muratorian Fragment is to be believed.

How far *The Shepherd* is from any tinge of Gnosticism can be seen near the beginning, where the goodness of God's creation is affirmed:

> I remembered the last words, for they were profitable for us and gentle: 'Lo, "the God of the powers", whom I love, by his mighty power and by his great wisdom "created the world", and by his glorious counsel surrounded his creation with beauty, and by his mighty word "fixed the Heaven and founded the earth upon the waters", and by his own wisdom and forethought created his holy Church, which he also blessed.' (*The Shepherd*, Visions I.3.3–4)

The Shepherd is on the whole a gentle book, though extremely long-winded and repetitive. It is not surprising that a number of the Church Fathers thought it a candidate for the canon, and that as late as the fourth century it was still possible for it to be included with the New Testament texts in *Codex Sinaiticus*.

OTHER NON-CANONICAL TEXTS

Non-canonical texts continued to be important throughout Christian history, those of an apocalyptic type enjoying a resurgence after the Renaissance and in periods when people were looking for an overthrow of the existing order.[23] They form a significant penumbra around the canonical scriptures, to the extent that some have contributed to popular belief about what is actually in the Bible. Examples would be the ideas that Joseph was an old man who already had children when he married Mary, whose parents were called Joachim and Anna, that Mary rode to Bethlehem on a donkey (all in *Protevangelium of James*, *c.*150 CE, attributed to Jesus' brother James), and that the three wise men were kings, called Caspar, Melchior and Balthazar (first attested in a Greek manuscript probably composed in Alexandria *c.*500 CE, translated into Latin as *Excerpta Latina Barbari*). The royal character of the magi is so well established that in German the feast of Epiphany is known as *Dreikönigstag*, 'Three Kings' Day', and Cologne Cathedral allegedly houses the kings' bones.

The additional Gospels, letters and apocalypses that continued to be written in antiquity nearly always show clear dependence on the canonical texts. The apocryphal Gospels essentially fill in details of the life of Jesus, or other figures about whom people were naturally curious:

> A good example is the Gospel of Nicodemus, a Gospel narrative that concentrates on the passion of Christ. It begins with the trial of Jesus by Pontius Pilate, and most of the life of Christ, concentrating on his miracles, is narrated as a flashback by witnesses at the trial. After Christ's crucifixion and resurrection, the Gospel relates various disputes between the Jews and three secret disciples of Christ: Nicodemus, Joseph of Arimathea, and Gamaliel. This culminates in the testimony of two sons of Simeon, who rose from the dead at Christ's crucifixion and who give a vivid description of Christ breaking open the gates of hell and leading various Old Testament patriarchs out of hell into heaven. This apocryphal Gospel spread widely in the Middle Ages and was the principal source for dramatic depictions of the scenes preceding the resurrection of Christ, the so-called harrowing of hell. It also gave names to some otherwise anonymous figures in the Gospel, such as Longinus, the soldier who pierced Christ on the cross, and Veronica, the woman who was healed from a haemorrhage in Luke 8:44 and was thought to have wiped Christ's face on his way to the cross.[24]

Texts of this kind raise at least two questions. First, how far the details of some stories in the canonical Gospels are similarly the result of a desire to fill in missing information. This could well apply to the birth narratives in Matthew and Luke, with their cast of characters – Zechariah, Elizabeth, the shepherds, the magi – in stories for which it is hard to imagine any historical source. Readers of the New Testament, even biblical scholars, tend to shy away – at least overtly – from treating these stories with the same scepticism that everyone shows towards such works as the *Gospel of Nicodemus*. There is much speculation, especially around Christmas, about the nature of the star followed by the magi; and the date of Jesus' birth is calculated by everyone, it seems, by relating it to the reign of Herod the Great, who appears in Matthew 2. Yet we should immediately regard such features as legendary if they appeared in an apocryphal Gospel. That two sons of Simeon rose from the dead at Jesus' crucifixion seems obviously legendary; but then we recall Matthew 27:52–3, where many bodies of holy people rose when Jesus died on the cross, entered Jerusalem after the resurrection, and appeared to many, surely an equally legendary addition, though of course a much earlier one. The apocryphal Gospels thus remind us that the canonical ones, though much older and accepted as authoritative in the Church well before some of their non-canonical counterparts were even written, spring from some of the same motives, and despite being relatively 'early' are still decades later than the events they chronicle.

Secondly, what were the intentions of those who wrote Gospels that were, to use Bart Ehrman's blunt term, forgeries? Were readers meant to believe that the text just mentioned was really by Nicodemus, or is a literary convention involved, just as is alleged, for example, for the deutero-Pauline letters? And were they meant to believe the additional details such as the post-resurrection debates recorded in *Nicodemus*, or is this simply pious story-telling for entertainment or edification? Again, exactly the same question arises with the canonical Gospels. Assuming that Matthew (or whoever wrote Matthew 2) invented the travelling star (which I think very likely), was he trying to delude readers into thinking it real, or was it simply a vivid way of indicating that God leads people of all races and creeds to worship Christ, as so many Christmas and Epiphany sermons tell us?

Studying apocryphal Gospels reminds us how hard it is to understand the frame of mind of authors such as these; and that, in turn, should make us reflect on the mindset of the canonical evangelists, too. As we have already seen, popular ideas about the events surrounding Jesus' birth not only blend Matthew and Luke; they also incorporate apocryphal elements, not least because it is difficult to say that those elements are less plausible than the canonical ones. If the apocryphal infancy and resurrection narratives contain legendary or invented material, then so, probably, do the canonical versions, which are also in that sense forgeries – written by people who must have known they were recording unevidenced details. We simply do not know whether they intended readers to believe literally in the stories they, or some predecessor, had created. From a religious perspective, the two easy options are either to believe that the stories are historically true, or to deny that they are making actual historical claims and are meant 'symbolically' (or allegorically – see Chapters 12 and 13). But what if the truth is that they were intended to persuade the reader of something that the writer knew had not actually happened? In that case their canonicity is surely no answer, however much the Church Fathers affirmed it, as we have seen that they did.

I argued in Chapter 8 that the Gospels are generically biographies, and this seems to me true of the apocryphal ones as much as the canonical. That classification does not imply that everything in them is true, or historiographical in intent. Biographies – modern as well as ancient – may contain anecdotes that are probably not historically accurate but do capture or illuminate the character of the subject. In a modern biography they will be identified as such, but in ancient times this was often not done: notoriously, speeches in ancient writers present what it would have been appropriate for a character in the narrative to have said rather than what he actually did say, even in critical history writing such as that of Thucydides. How much more is this true of the biblical narratives, which seamlessly blend historiography with legend. But it does, for us, raise questions about credibility and about the intentions of the authors, and these questions are no easier where the canonical Gospels are concerned than with the apocryphal texts that the early Church rejected as 'spurious'. If for them it would have been all too easy to accept fake Gospels – had they not known, as they mostly did, that these were late arrivals – for us it would be only too easy to reject the canonical ones as full of legendary and imaginative accretions.

In trying to show that the canonicity of the four Gospels now in the Bible was accepted at a very early date, I thus do not mean to claim that they are therefore 'true' accounts: that has to be examined in the ways discussed in Chapter 8. A text could be very early, and universally accepted as authoritative, yet still be inaccurate or even fictitious. My purpose in this chapter is not to vindicate the canonical Gospels as compared with the apocryphal ones; it is simply to show that the former were widely accepted from an early period in the history of Christianity, and the latter were not. Yet even those the Church rejected have often influenced later generations on points of detail in the stories they tell; for unofficial texts can still be significant, especially to people who are not clear as to the exact limits of the canon, even though the bishops and theologians think they should be.

Some of the apocryphal Gospels have considerable appeal, none more so than the *Protevangelium of James*, with its description of the moment when Joseph sees the world pause suddenly for the birth of Jesus to Mary (who is in a cave – still part of the nativity tradition in eastern Orthodoxy):

> Now I, Joseph, was walking, and yet I did not walk, and I looked up to the air and saw the air in amazement. And I looked up at the vault of heaven, and saw it standing still and the birds of the heaven motionless. And I looked down at the earth, and saw a dish placed there and workmen reclining, and their hands were in the dish. But those who chewed did not chew, and those who lifted up did not lift, and those who put something to their mouth put nothing to their mouth, but everybody looked upwards. And behold, sheep were being driven and they did not come forward but stood still; and the shepherd raised his hand to strike them with his staff but his hand remained upright. And I looked at the flow of the river, and saw the mouths of the kids over it and they did not drink. And then suddenly everything went on in its course. (*Protevangelium of James* 18:2)[25]

Such embellishments of the Gospel stories posed no threat to Christian orthodoxy, but they were still not included in any canon of the Scriptures, simply because the *Protevangelium* was too late: the New Testament had already achieved more or less its finished form before the end of the second century, and nothing could be added. Works such as the *Protevangelium* continued to be held in high regard, and exist in at least 100 Greek manuscripts, but were not Scripture, for all that they contributed considerably to the traditions surrounding the nativity story.[26] Formally non-canonical, the *Protevangelium* has a kind of canonicity in at least some parts of the Christian imagination.

12
Biblical Manuscripts

The road that led to the formation and canonization of the Bible was a long and winding one. But how do we come, today, to have the Bible at all? In the centuries before printing, only through the copying and transmission of manuscripts, with all that that implies about errors in transcription and the possibility of deliberate changes to the text. The same is true of classical texts. Only in ancient cultures that wrote on materials such as stone and clay – thus chiefly in Mesopotamia – or whose climate could preserve even a perishable material like papyrus, such as Egypt, do we have documents as they left the original writer; though even then we are often dealing with copies. For ancient Israel and the early Church there are no autographs in the technical sense of manuscripts actually written out by Isaiah or Paul, while Jesus did not write anyway, so far as we know.[1]

On the whole we are well served by ancient manuscripts of the Bible, in that many aspects of the biblical text seem quite secure, and all of them preserve what are clearly the same stories, in broad outline at least. But there are sharp differences between the Old and New Testaments in this respect.

THE NEW TESTAMENT

There are several thousand New Testament manuscripts from the first few centuries CE, from early papyrus fragments to the great elaborate fourth-century manuscripts such as *Codex Sinaiticus*. As well as manuscripts in Greek, the original language of the New Testament writers, there are many of translations into other languages, including even languages of northern Europe such as Gothic (see Chapter 18). The work of New Testament textual critics is painstaking and difficult, and earlier attempts to establish 'the original text' of any book have now largely been set aside in favour of tracing the history of different manuscript 'families', and so establishing various parallel traditions as to what, in detail, the books contain.

Thus there is not, and never can be, a text of 'the New Testament' as it left the hands of Paul, Luke or John: we have only variants. The implications of this for theories of the inspiration and authority of the New Testament have scarcely begun to be worked out. Where the words of Jesus are concerned, for example, we often know only roughly what he is supposed to have said (and whether he really said it is of course yet a further question).

Manuscripts of the New Testament,[2] or of parts of it – some are mere fragments – are classified according to a system that is internationally agreed and administered by the Institute for New Testament Textual Research in Münster, Germany. The manuscripts fall into four categories, and are numerous: for example, nearly 2,500 preserve all or some parts of one or more Gospels. (This far outweighs the number of manuscripts of non-canonical works that have survived from antiquity, which could mean that they were suppressed, as in the Dan Brown conspiracy theory, but could also mean that they were far less used and copied.)

The first category[3] consists of papyri, which are given the letter P and a number, sometimes written superscript – thus p45 or p^{45}, a papyrus document found in Egypt that contains parts of all four Gospels and comes from the late second or early third century. P66 has most of John, and p73 large sections of Luke and John. Papyrus was the common writing material in this period, manufactured from the papyrus reed, laid out in strips and criss-crossed. It is highly perishable, like paper, whose name derives from it. But in Egypt it was able to survive because of the exceptionally dry conditions, so that is where most surviving papyrus manuscripts come from. New Testament papyri derive from the second to the seventh century CE, and thus include the very earliest manuscripts we have.

Famous codices such as *Codex Sinaiticus*, written in the late fourth century and perhaps in Rome, belong to a second category, usually known as uncials from the style of lettering – what we should call capital letters – used throughout. This is true also of the papyri, but the uncials are distinctive in being written on parchment rather than papyrus. These texts are given a number beginning with zero, and *Sinaiticus* is 01; but they also have a letter by which they are usually known, and

Codex Sinaiticus, one of the great uncial codices. John 7:52 is followed by 8:12 at the top of the left column, omitting the story of the woman taken in adultery found in most modern Bibles (see pp. 293–6).

Sinaiticus has a Hebrew letter, *aleph* (א), whereas the others have Latin or Greek letters. Other important uncials are *Codex Vaticanus* (B), a slightly earlier manuscript though possibly also Roman, and *Codex Bezae* (D), a fifth-century work possibly written in Italy or France. These contain not only the New Testament but also the Old Testament in Greek (the Septuagint or LXX – see Chapter 18), and in the case of *Sinaiticus*, as noted in the previous chapter, also some books that are not now canonical. The *Codex Sinaiticus* in the British Library is nearly complete, though a few pages are elsewhere – some still in the monastery of St Catherine in Sinai, where the manuscript was discovered in the nineteenth century and sent to St Petersburg 'on loan' (subsequently sold to the British Museum by Stalin in 1933), and some in other locations. *Codex Vaticanus* comes from Egypt, but has been in the Vatican library since the fifteenth century, and *Codex Bezae* is in Cambridge, having been presented to the university by Theodore Beza in 1581: it contains the Gospels and Acts in both Greek and Latin, on facing pages. As we saw earlier, the codex form is typical of, and distinctive to, Christian manuscripts of the Bible, and scarcely any early manuscripts show evidence of having had the form of scrolls – even the papyri clearly come from codices. Interestingly enough, this is often not true of non-canonical books, which are at least sometimes scrolls. As we saw in Chapter 10, it suggests that Christians early on decided that the codex was the form for their own special writings, possibly as a deliberate contrast with Greek, Roman and Jewish books, though (as discussed in Chapter 10) the matter is obscure. There are 196 extant uncial codices (some extremely fragmentary) containing some parts of the Gospels.

From the tenth century onwards there was a great demand for Bibles in the Byzantine Empire, and a more informal cursive or 'minuscule' (lower-case) hand was developed which made copying quicker. There are nearly 3,000 minuscule manuscripts of the New Testament, each simply given a running number, from 1 to 2,856. Most of these documents are on parchment but some are on paper, which began to be manufactured in the west in the thirteenth century. By now the text of the New Testament had settled down into a standard form, known as the Byzantine or Koiné. One might assume that earlier manuscripts would be closer together, and that more and more variants would creep in over time. But, if anything, the reverse is the case: the earliest papyri show the greatest variation, and with the passage of time an agreed text developed. This is not to say that there are no important variations in

Byzantine manuscripts: many were copied from much older documents and so preserve early readings, which textual critics now try to identify. But in general manuscripts converged rather than diverged over time.

The fourth type of manuscript is the lectionary. These are texts that do not follow the order of the Bible, but set out the passages to be read in the liturgy on particular days. Such books still exist in all the churches that follow a set liturgy, and avoid the reader having to locate the relevant passage in a Bible – hard enough now, but very difficult indeed in a world with no page numbers and large, cumbersome codices. Lectionary texts, mostly on parchment or paper, are identified with an italic *l* followed by a number; there are about 2,500 of them, mostly minuscule in style, and dating from no earlier than the eighth century. Mostly they contain Gospel passages. The text can be interesting, since what is read in liturgy tends to be conservative, and so may preserve older readings. One lectionary was often copied from another rather than from a whole Bible, so they have their own tradition.

There are other important sources for the text of the Bible. Citations in early Christian writers can tell us what wording the writer in question was familiar with, and this may differ from any extant manuscripts. Sometimes it may represent an otherwise lost tradition, but it is always hard to know how far the differences may be the result of citation from memory – or even derive from a sense, still active in the first couple of Christian centuries, that a preacher was free to improvise a little on the basis of the written text (as discussed in Chapter 10). Nevertheless, there are places where we can identify a distinctive reading.

A further source is ancient translations of the Bible, which exist in many languages: Latin, Syriac, Coptic, Armenian, Georgian, Old Church Slavonic, even (as noted above) Gothic. Where there is a deviation from the Greek text familiar to us, it is always possible that the translator was looking at a different text rather than changing the one we are familiar with. The ancient translations are usually known as the 'versions'. A really competent textual critic needs to know many languages.

Further sources are amulets – short passages of the Bible designed to be worn as charms against evil – and copies of the Gospels designed for fortune-telling, with marks against appropriate verses. Like lectionaries, these are not whole Bibles, but it is always possible that they preserve genuinely ancient readings.

Modern printed New Testaments always represent a critical and eclectic text: that is, the editor (or, usually, panel of editors) decides which of the many readings often attested in a given case is likely to be the oldest. This is often mainly a matter of intuition, but there are broad general principles that can be applied. For example, where two manuscripts preserve different wordings, the critic will prefer the one that seems less likely to have been changed into the other, perhaps because it makes a less obvious point, or is less orthodox when seen from a later vantage point. This is not unlike the 'principle of dissimilarity' that I described in the study of the Gospels, where we tend to think that a saying is original to Jesus if we cannot see how anyone could plausibly have made it up, since it differs from what the early Church would have wanted Jesus to have said. The textual point is a similar one: if one of the versions of a saying is angular in some way, and another rather more bland, we may decide that the bland one is a toning-down of the angular one, since no one would have taken perfectly smooth sayings and made them more angular, whereas it is easy to see why an awkward saying might have been smoothed over.

In Chapter 8 we observed this happening from one Gospel to another in the case of the Marcan and Matthaean versions of Jesus' reply to the man who asked about the conditions for inheriting eternal life:

> As he was setting out on a journey, a man ran up and knelt before him, and asked him, 'Good Teacher, what must I do to inherit eternal life?' Jesus said to him, 'Why do you call me good? No one is good but God alone.'
>
> (Mark 10:17–18)

> Then someone came to him and said, 'Teacher, what good deed must I do to have eternal life?' And he said to him, 'Why do you ask me about what is good? There is only one who is good.'
>
> (Matthew 19:16–17)

The principle of dissimilarity tells us that the Marcan version is more likely to go back to what Jesus actually said, since the wording in Matthew seems to tone down a saying in which Jesus sharply differentiates himself from God, whereas the early Church was keen to propound his oneness with God. Faced with Matthew's version, no one in the Church would have emended it into Mark's apparent denial that Jesus is divine; hence, Mark is more likely to preserve the original version of the saying.

The same principle operates at the level of which version of a passage is likelier to represent what the original scribe wrote. At the beginning of the Fourth Gospel, we read in the NRSV:

> But to all who received him, who believed in his name, he gave power to become children of God, who *were* born, not of blood or of the will of the flesh or of the will of man, but of God. And the Word became flesh and lived among us.
>
> (John 1:12–14; emphasis added)

This seems to speak of the spiritual rebirth, a rebirth unlike their original physical birth, of those who believe in the Word of God, who became incarnate in Jesus. But a few ancient translations (in Latin and Syriac), and quotations in Tertullian and Irenaeus, have:

> But to all who received him, who believed in his name, he gave power to become children of God; who *was* born, not of blood or of the will of the flesh or of the will of man, but of God. And the Word became flesh and lived among us.

Here it is the Word who had no normal human birth but was born of God alone. This is, most scholars think, a reference to Jesus' virginal conception, commonly referred to as the Virgin Birth – the doctrine that he had no human father, but was 'conceived by the Holy Spirit and born of the Virgin Mary', as the Christian creeds express it.

How are we to decide which is the original reading, or closer to it? Something akin to the principle of dissimilarity suggests the following argument: no one faced with a text that affirms the Virgin Birth would have changed it into a statement about the rebirth of believers, since they would be appearing thereby to deny a central plank of Christian doctrine. It is much likelier therefore that the first reading set out above is older, and that it has been tinkered with to produce a witness to what was later considered orthodox Christian doctrine. The augmentation represents what Bart Ehrman calls the 'orthodox corruption of Scripture',[4] the theory that 'scribes occasionally altered the words of their sacred texts to make them more patently orthodox and to prevent their misuse by Christians who espoused aberrant views'.[5]

In this case there is anyway overwhelming evidence from all Greek manuscripts in favour of the first rendering above.[6] But even if this were not so, we should still probably prefer it, on the grounds that it is more likely to have been changed into the second version than vice versa. This argument did not prevent the Jerusalem Bible (see Chapter 18) from printing 'was born', without indicating in a note how fragile the reading is. The same doctrinal pressure that resulted in the singular translation in the first place was probably still operating on the translators in the 1960s.

Another, similar example is the saying of Jesus recorded in Matthew 24:36:

> But about that day and hour no one knows, neither the angels of heaven, nor the Son, but only the Father.'

The majority of manuscripts lack 'nor the Son', although it is present in the best and earliest, despite being found in the parallel passage in Mark (Mark 13:32). We can argue that the manuscripts that preserve it are more reliable in general, so it should be retained on that basis. An even stronger argument arises from thinking again about which reading is likely to have been turned into the other. People in the early Church usually believed that Jesus was, like God himself, omniscient, because, indeed, he *was* God. If the text lacked any reference to the Son's ignorance of the last days and said that only the Father knew such things, an orthodox Christian would hardly have been likely to introduce such a reference. Far more probable is that scribes of an orthodox disposition would have removed it, so as not to imply ignorance in the Son and call into question the divinity of Jesus. The manuscripts that leave out the phrase are thus examples again of the 'orthodox corruption of Scripture'. (In this case the argument is bolstered by the syntax of the verse: without 'nor the Son' we are left with 'neither the angels of heaven but only the Father' – a 'neither' with no 'nor' to complete it, just as striking in Greek as in English.)

Codex Sinaiticus shows the cycle of corruption and restoration by flip-flopping on the issue, as one can see that the manuscript originally included 'nor the Son', that it was then erased, and that a further scribe then reinstated it. The omission occurs very early, since Origen already attests the shorter version of the verse, but this does not mean it is therefore correct: we can see good reasons why the text has been curtailed, but it is almost impossible to imagine circumstances in which anyone would have inserted words that seem to imply a 'low' Christology.[7]

When we have established the oldest reading *available to us*, we should not delude ourselves that we have therefore got back to the words Jesus uttered, or to the exact historical details of something he did, or even to what the author originally wrote. Certainty about any of those things is beyond the textual critic's reach. The best that can be achieved is to establish the earliest version of a story or saying that we are able to reconstruct. Where sayings are concerned, we must remember that Jesus probably taught in Aramaic, so that any Greek version of his sayings, however old, is a translation, and one that is earlier than any extant Gospel manuscript – just as the Gospels themselves are in any case decades later than the time of Jesus. The textual history of the Gospels, or of the letters for that matter, is far from totally chaotic, for it is a unified tradition in many ways; but the nature of the material does not permit us to talk with certainty or assurance that we have access to the words of Jesus himself. Here are two examples of textual criticism in practice.

Example 1: the Woman Taken in Adultery

The Gospel according to John as we have received it contains a story that for many sums up the compassionate and non-judgemental quality of Jesus, and his astute way of dealing with his opponents: that of the woman taken in adultery, John 7:53–8:11:

> Then each of them went home, while Jesus went to the Mount of Olives. Early in the morning he came again to the temple. All the people came to him and he sat down and began to teach them. The scribes and Pharisees brought a woman who had been caught in adultery; and making her stand before all of them, they said to him, 'Teacher, this woman was caught in the very act of committing adultery. Now in the law Moses commanded us to stone such women. Now what do you say?' They said this to test him, so that they might have some charge to bring against him. Jesus bent down and wrote with his finger on the ground. When they kept on questioning him, he straightened up and said to them, 'Let anyone among you who is without sin be the first to throw a stone at her.' And once again he bent down and wrote on the ground. When they heard it, they went away, one by one, beginning with the elders; and Jesus was left alone with the woman standing before him. Jesus straightened up and said to her, 'Woman, where are they? Has no one condemned you?' She said, 'No one, sir.' And Jesus said, 'Neither do I condemn you. Go your way, and from now on do not sin again.'

The NRSV gives the basic textual facts about this passage in a footnote, as well as enclosing it in double square brackets:

> The most ancient authorities lack 7:53–8:11; other authorities add the passage here or after 7:36 or after 21:25 or after Luke 21:38, with variations of text; some mark the passage as doubtful.

'The most ancient authorities' in fact amount to almost all ancient manuscripts, among them *Codex Sinaiticus* and *Codex Vaticanus*, many papyri and Latin versions, and translations into Coptic. One ninth-century minuscule manuscript, 565, includes a note that the passage was in the manuscript the scribe was copying from, but he has omitted it as being spurious. It is present only in very few manuscripts, and as noted it occurs at different places in the Gospels, in Luke as well as in John. It is in the place in John familiar to us in *Codex Bezae*, and in the Byzantine text, but it seems clear from the evidence that it was a piece of 'floating' tradition about Jesus, not securely anchored at any particular point in the Gospel narrative. Yet it was known early in the second century, as is clear from citation in one early Christian writer, Papias of Hierapolis (70–163 CE) (according to Eusebius' *Church History*), who says it existed in the *Gospel of the Hebrews*, a text no longer extant though occasionally quoted by early writers. Papias lived at the beginning of the second century, not so long after the Gospels were completed, on most datings. It is he who claimed that Mark was Peter's amanuensis. And a variant version exists in a tenth-century Armenian Gospel book:

> A certain woman was taken in sins, against whom all bore witness that she was deserving of death. They brought her to Jesus (to see) what he would command, in order that they might malign him. Jesus made answer and said, 'Come ye, who are without sin, cast stones and stone her to death.' But he himself, bowing his head was writing with his finger on the earth, to declare their sins; and they were seeing their several sins on the stones. And filled with shame they departed, and no one remained, but only the woman. Saith Jesus, 'Go in peace, and present the offering for sins, as in their law is written.'[8]

This is clearly the same story in essence, but it no longer specifies adultery as the sin, and it presents a different conclusion, more in line with what Jesus says to the lepers he has healed in Luke 17:14. In addition, it tells us what Jesus was writing on the ground – the sins of the woman's accusers – which resolves a puzzle most readers wonder about.

The overwhelming weight of evidence suggests that it is misleading to print this story as part of John's Gospel: rather, it should at most appear as an appendix to the Gospels. Indeed, one family of manuscripts locates it after the end of John, while there is an eleventh-century Gospel manuscript (1,333) that places it after the end of Luke. (As a matter of fact, the themes of the passage, concerning divine compassion exercised through Jesus and a concern for the well-being of women, are more typically Lucan than Johannine.) If it were less lengthy, and less well loved, it is unlikely that the story would appear in modern printed Bibles at all, but there is great resistance to removing it.

Does the story itself go back to a genuine reminiscence of Jesus? That is a quite different question. The lack of secure anchorage in the Gospels suggests that it is, in effect, a piece of oral tradition, just as all the stories of Jesus were before the Gospel writers fixed them in writing. It was, as we saw, known about just as early as most of the other Gospel stories: if it had not got into one or two manuscripts, we should treat it as an *agraphon*, an unwritten story cited in early Christian writers; and *agrapha* may perfectly well be genuine. That may remind us, however, that there is also no way of being sure of the veracity of anything in the Gospels, if by 'sure' we mean established beyond all reasonable doubt. The likelihood that stories in the Gospels are true does not rest on undertaking an examination of each one in detail, but is a cumulative case involving the coherence of the whole narrative; and the story of the woman taken in adultery seems as likely a candidate for truth as most of the stories about Jesus. The odd incident in which he twice writes on the ground tends if anything to support the veracity of the account, in that it presented a problem to ancient interpreters (and still does today): the Armenian version is clearly an attempt to make sense of it and to pull the whole story together more coherently. Why would anyone invent a detail that no one can adequately account for?

Thus to say that the story in question is not part of the original Gospel is not, in itself, to say that it is fictitious: it may be a piece of genuinely old tradition that was transmitted orally and missed being included in what John (or Luke) wrote in his Gospel. But there is a sting in the tail here. For, by the same token, the fact that a story *is* an original part of a Gospel does not prove that it is true. The story of the woman taken in adultery could be true; the story of the woman who wiped Jesus' feet with her hair (Luke 7:36–50), which contains the same themes of Jesus' compassion as a model of God's, could be false, a composition by the evangelist:

> A woman in the city, who was a sinner, having learned that he was eating in the Pharisee's house, brought an alabaster jar of ointment. She stood behind him at his feet, weeping, and began to bathe his feet with her tears and to dry them with her hair. Then she continued kissing his feet and anointing them with the ointment . . . [Jesus said] ' . . . her sins, which were

many, have been forgiven; hence she has shown great love. But the one to whom little is forgiven, loves little.' Then he said to her, 'Your sins are forgiven.' But those who were at the table with him began to say among themselves, 'Who is this who even forgives sins?' And he said to the woman, 'Your faith has saved you; go in peace.'

(Luke 7:37–8, 47–50)

Both stories come down to us from the early Church: in neither case can a link with Jesus himself be absolutely demonstrated.

Example 2: Divorce and Remarriage

The evidence that both Jesus and Paul had occasion to talk about questions to do with divorce is overwhelming. All the Synoptic Gospels contain sayings about the subject (Mark 10:2–12; Matthew 5:27–32 and 19:3–9; Luke 16:18), and Paul discusses marriage and divorce in 1 Corinthians 7. The text-critical issues have been discussed with the greatest clarity by D. C. Parker,[9] and I shall summarize his arguments here.

There are three issues: (1) differences between the Gospels; (2) differences between manuscripts; (3) interpretation of the meaning of the sayings. Through these we can see that textual criticism is inseparable from the study of the Gospels in general, and from understanding what Jesus may or may not have meant.

First, then, differences between the Gospels. Following the NRSV, we can note:

'Whoever divorces his wife and marries another commits adultery against her; and if she divorces her husband and marries another, she commits adultery.'

(Mark 10:11–12)

'Anyone who divorces his wife, except on the ground of unchastity, causes her to commit adultery; and whoever marries a divorced woman commits adultery.'

(Matthew 5:32)

'Whoever divorces his wife, except for unchastity, and marries another commits adultery.'

(Matthew 19:9)

> 'Anyone who divorces his wife and marries another commits adultery, and whoever marries a woman divorced from her husband commits adultery.'
>
> (Luke 16:18)

Two differences are immediately obvious. Mark allows for the possibility that a woman might divorce her husband, whereas the other Gospels do not; and Matthew has what is traditionally called the 'Matthaean exception', permitting divorce on the grounds of 'unchastity' by the wife. As for the first point, we know that in Jewish law it was impossible for women to divorce their husbands – indeed, this is still the case among Orthodox Jews – but that Roman law permitted it, and this has been a reason for thinking that Mark may have been written in Rome. (The Roman rule would have been known throughout the empire, so it is probably a weak reason for locating Mark in one place rather than another.) The Marcan formulation is unlikely to go back to Jesus, who was speaking in a Jewish context, not laying down rules for the operation of Roman law. On the second matter, an exception clause looks like a later adjustment of an originally unconditional statement; and it is worth noting that there are no manuscripts of Mark that have been adjusted to include it. It seems to be peculiar to Matthew. More generally, there are differences in the exact situation envisaged. Mark 10 says that remarriage after divorce constitutes adultery, as does Matthew 19; Matthew 5 says that divorcing one's wife makes her an adulteress, and that marrying a divorced woman is adultery; and Luke 16 combines ideas from both Mark and Matthew, saying that remarriage after a man's own divorce is adultery and that marrying a divorcee is also adultery.

The matter is already complicated, but when we bring in the evidence of the manuscripts it becomes extremely fraught. To take just Mark 10, NRSV follows *Codex Sinaiticus* (א). But there are many other readings:

> 'If a woman divorces her husband and marries another, she commits adultery; and if a man divorces his wife, he commits adultery.'
>
> (The Freer Gospels, W)

> 'If a woman divorces her husband and marries another, she commits adultery; and if a man divorces his wife and marries another, he commits adultery.'
>
> (Minuscules 1 and 209)

'Whoever divorces his wife and marries another commits adultery, and if a woman divorces her husband and be married to another, she commits adultery.'

(*Codex Alexandrinus*, A)

'If a man divorces his wife and marries another, he commits adultery against her; and if a woman separates from her husband and marries another, she commits adultery against him; likewise also he who marries a woman divorced from her husband commits adultery.'

(Three Old Latin manuscripts)

One difference, seemingly small but of tremendous significance, is whether the woman in question is said to 'marry' (W and א) or to 'be married' (A and the Byzantine text). The last reading cited above, from some Latin manuscripts, seems to combine Mark and Luke by adding Luke's provision about marrying a divorcee. Even more significantly, the reading in W appears to suggest that divorcing one's wife is in itself adultery, not just remarriage after divorce – a very rigorist position. The version in W also places the woman divorcing her husband first, as though that were the greater danger, as do 1 and 209. Thus within manuscripts of Mark – let alone the other Synoptic Gospels – there is a range of teaching.

A third important aspect is to ask interpretative questions that go beyond the realm of either textual criticism or attempts to reconstruct the earliest Gospel traditions. What, for example, is 'unchastity' in the Matthaean exception? In Greek it is *porneia*, which can have a range of meanings, from adultery to prostitution. In the early Church it was certainly taken here to mean adultery. It can be argued, as does Parker, that the exception clause is not meant to specify a condition under which divorce is permissible so much as to emphasize that divorcing a faithful wife is wrong – we need to recall that divorcing one's wife was comparatively easy under Jewish law, and could be done for trivial reasons, such as bad cooking. As to remarriage, it was also easy for a family to force a divorced woman into a perhaps unwanted second marriage: the sayings, in all their forms, safeguard against that. (Hence the importance of the variant 'be married' for 'marry' in the woman's case, stressing the passivity of the woman.) 'We can . . . see that the problem addressed is the opposite of the use to which the passage is often put. It is employed to hinder divorced people who wish to remarry. It was intended to protect vulnerable people who wished not to remarry.'[10] In fact, nearly all versions of the sayings seem to have the protection of the woman as their primary concern, making it illicit to divorce except in extreme circumstances, and ruling out exploitative remarriage. The context of Jesus' teaching is one in which there is a clear imbalance of power between men and women in respect of marriage and divorce: by describing even regular divorce as a form of adultery the sayings offer women more protection than did the law.

Recovering the original form of Jesus' saying(s) on this subject is clearly impossible. The Gospels differ, and manuscripts differ within each Gospel. But, as Parker puts it, 'We have no excuse for claiming simplicity where there is confusion.'[11] This does not mean that we cannot extract some truths about the teaching of Jesus: on this topic, it is clear that he must have talked about divorce and remarriage and that he wanted to guard women against exploitation. But we cannot know enough in detail to extract a quasi-legal principle from his teaching, such as has been done in Church law in many Christian traditions. Parker is worth quoting at length:

> The quest for a Law in the teaching of Jesus cannot be pursued in the face of the evidence that, for those early Christians who passed the tradition to us, there was – no law, but a tradition whose meaning had to be kept alive by reflection and reinterpretation.[12] What we have is a collection of interpretative rewritings of a tradition. It would be unscientific to claim, on the basis of these few passages, that there was no such thing as a Gospel in the sense of a recension, an attempt to produce a fixed form. But any writer who crystallizes a point in a changing tradition (which he thereby also changes) must accept that his writing may also be liable to alteration by somebody else. And once this is acknowledged, then the concept of a Gospel that is fixed in shape, authoritative, and final as a piece of literature has to be abandoned. The invitation to pay heed to the words of Jesus is then freed from the demand to accept the authority of that shaped and final text.[13]

This suggests that the search for Jesus' exact words – which in any case would have been in Aramaic, not in Greek – is inimical to what we know about the Gospels, and that we could do better to look for the general effect of his teaching. On the question of divorce and remarriage, there would be no sayings at all if he had not had things to say that were felt to go beyond generally received wisdom; and it is clear that in all their forms they are meant to protect women's place in marriage. But turning them into canon law is quite another matter: for that, we would need access to the exact original forms, something we certainly cannot have. Who can say whether Jesus in any case intended his sayings to be turned into universal rules?[14]

THE HEBREW BIBLE

There are many manuscripts of the Old Testament/Hebrew Bible, but they tend to stand in a recognizable tradition because from quite ancient times there was a single, carefully curated text. Here it makes sense to start at the end rather than at the beginning, because almost all modern printed Bibles derive from a single manuscript, rather than being the result of modern editors comparing many divergent mansucripts, as is the case with the New Testament. That one manuscript is the Leningrad or St Petersburg Codex, known as 'L', which was written in the eleventh century and preserves the readings of the family of Ben Asher, who worked in Tiberias on the Sea of Galilee and whose life's work was the accurate copying and correction of biblical manuscripts. L is the only complete text of the Hebrew Bible to have come down from the early Middle Ages, though there is another, earlier one preserving everything except the Pentateuch (which was destroyed in a fire): the Aleppo Codex (A) from Syria, which dates from the tenth century (perhaps 925 CE).[15]

Printed editions of the Hebrew Bible ever since the Rabbinic Bibles of the sixteenth century have been technically known as 'diplomatic editions', that is, exact copies of L, rather than critically reconstructed editions as is normal with the New Testament. In more recent times printed Bibles have recorded readings that differ from L, taken from other manuscripts, from the ancient versions, and from the editors' conjectures, but these have appeared only as footnotes, not incorporated into the text itself. Thus, whereas we cannot speak strictly of 'the New Testament' at the textual level, where the Old Testament/Hebrew Bible is concerned there is an agreed text. The people who worked on the biblical text in Tiberias and elsewhere are known as the Masoretes (or Massoretes), meaning 'handers-on of tradition', and the text they produced is known as the Masoretic Text (MT). There are more than 6,000 manuscripts from the Middle Ages that follow the same text as L. Naturally they contain errors, but it is clear that all are attempts at reproducing the same text.

To say that there is now an agreed text of the Hebrew Bible is not, of course, to say that this has always been the case.[16] Even leaving aside later errors in copying L (usually only at the level of minute detail), it has always been realized that there must have been earlier manuscripts that might preserve a different text, though none was known until the twentieth century. This changed dramatically with the discovery of the Dead Sea Scrolls in the Judaean desert, beginning in 1947, both at

The Leningrad Codex, showing Deuteronomy 32. The Masorah can be seen in the margins and at the head and foot of the page.

Qumran and at other sites, especially Nahal Hever and Wadi Murabba 'at, which have been variously dated to between 250 BCE and 115 CE. Among them are some 200 fragments or longer texts from all the biblical books except Esther, and some books are represented by several more or less complete manuscripts – famously Isaiah, of which a replica of the Qumran 'a' scroll (1QIsa[a]) is displayed in the Shrine of the Book in Jerusalem. The analogy with the New Testament would probably lead one to expect these materials to show a range of diverse texts, but this is by no means so: nearly all the Dead Sea books are 'proto-Masoretic', that is, they are extraordinarily close to L in basic text. There are many differences in spelling, and hundreds of tiny variations in detail, but there can be no doubt that we are basically dealing with what was to become the Masoretic tradition. There is a rabbinic claim that there was a single copy of the Torah kept in the Temple in Jerusalem; if that is true (and it may be only a pious legend), then that scroll may have served as the exemplar from which most biblical texts were copied.[17] If so, then the Masoretic Text would go back to the second century BCE, providing independent evidence, incidentally, that the contents as well as the text of the Hebrew Bible were more or less agreed as early as that. But even if we do not accept this idea, the Dead Sea evidence shows at least that the biblical text was in something approaching a standardized form much earlier than might be expected.

One of the differences between Dead Sea texts and L (or A) is that the former do not indicate vowels: the texts are purely consonantal. So far as we know, the indication of vowels was not practised until the early medieval period, when there was a desire to fix the traditional pronunciation of the text and a system of dots and dashes was developed to make sure that it was not lost (see also Chapter 2). In that sense L and A represent a considerable departure from the Dead Sea Scrolls. But the vowel 'points', as they are known, only make explicit what the reading tradition of the Hebrew Bible had preserved through oral tradition. (They are still not used in scrolls intended to be read in worship, but only in study editions: in public reading from an unpointed text the reader has to supply the vowels from memory.) To draw an analogy, most New Testament manuscripts do not have word divisions: the text runs on continuously, which for a modern reader makes for a difficult read. But when printed texts introduced separation between words, no one perceived this as changing the text, only as clarifying it. In a similar way, the introduction of vowel points simply records an already existing tradition, and was not felt to be changing anything – quite the reverse. It was ensuring that traditional understandings of the text were not lost.

Whereas New Testament manuscripts can, as we have seen, differ in including or excluding whole passages in the Gospels, the differences between Dead Sea manuscripts and the later Masoretic tradition tend to be at the level of individual words or even letters. These can be at a minute level, such as the frequent confusions between the letters *daleth* ד (d) and *resh* ר (r), which in Hebrew script look almost identical. If one is studying the Hebrew of Isaiah, numerous Dead Sea variants have to be taken into account, and modern translations such as NRSV occasionally record them in footnotes. But none is of such moment that the reader who does not know about them will come away from Isaiah with a misleading impression of what the book is saying. For anyone looking for assurance that modern Bibles represent a version of a reliable ancient text, this is likely to come as good news.

On the other hand, even a text that has been reliably transmitted since the second century BCE is not the same as one that goes back to Isaiah, or the editors of the Pentateuch, or the compilers of the Psalms, or any other original biblical writer. We cannot, however, look back behind the Dead Sea Scrolls with the same confidence. We do not know whether there was ever an 'original' form of (say) Isaiah: there may have been different editions, none of which could claim superiority – the analogy with the New Testament would then have been closer than it was in later times. Indeed, in one case there definitely was a variant tradition, and that is the book of Jeremiah, where fragments from Cave 4 at Qumran suggest a much shorter book than the Masoretic tradition has preserved. Taken on its own, this is compatible with several hypotheses. Perhaps the Qumran texts represent an abbreviation of the original; perhaps MT is an expansion of the Qumran version; or perhaps there were two editions of Jeremiah, neither older or more original than the other. But alongside this evidence we need to take into account the Greek translation of the book.

The Greek translation of the Hebrew Bible, normally referred to as the Septuagint (LXX), from the legend that it was carried out by seventy translators, seems to have been begun in the mid third century BCE and to have been completed by the beginning of the second (for more details see Chapter 18). For the most part it sticks quite closely to its Hebrew original, which must have been similar to what has come down to us as the Masoretic Text, though there are thousands of differences in the minutiae of the text. But sometimes it diverges sharply, and the book of Jeremiah is the most obvious example. Greek Jeremiah is about 20 per cent shorter than Jeremiah in MT, and some of the chapters are in a different order – the oracles against foreign nations, for example, come in the middle of the book rather than at the end. Thus the Septuagint and the texts from Cave 4 both support the existence of a distinctly shorter Jeremiah Scroll, and most scholars have concluded that there was a pre-Masoretic edition which later Hebrew tradition rearranged and lengthened. The books of Samuel also contain sections where Qumran evidence supports the Septuagint against MT.

Because the Greek version of the Bible is older even than the texts from Qumran, as we shall see, most textual critics treat it as a potential witness to a more ancient Hebrew text when it differs from MT. It is generally recognized that the Greek translators did not normally change or emend the Hebrew they were translating, but strove to provide an accurate rendering, not importing (except accidentally) their own ideas into the text. When the Septuagint diverges seriously from the Hebrew we know, it is therefore a reasonable hypothesis that a Hebrew text existed that corresponded to the Greek, and we try to reconstruct it by translating back from Greek into Hebrew, a procedure referred to as retroversion.

Strangely, many biblical critics have become rather more conservative in recent decades, and respect the Masoretic Text where older scholars had been more prone to emend in the light of the Greek: one can even speak of a 'Masoretic fundamentalism' that resists all emendation of the received Hebrew text. But in most commentaries and translations of the Bible one will find still many places where what is being translated is a variant reading attested in the Greek. Only the Jewish Publication Society Bible follows the principle that the MT is never to be emended, which can easily be defended on the basis that this translation is meant to be a rendering of the traditional Jewish Bible – the English-language equivalent of a diplomatic edition of the Leningrad or St Petersburg Codex. Other English-language Bibles feel free to emend in the light of the Greek translation, though it has to be remembered that what they are producing by that is a text allegedly older than MT, but not necessarily the 'original' text as it left the pen of the first scribe: that is just as unrecoverable as the autograph of the Gospels or Paul.

Of course the Greek translation of the Hebrew Bible itself also exists in many different manuscripts. *Codex Sinaiticus*, for example, contains not only the whole New Testament plus *Barnabas* and *The Shepherd*, but also the Old Testament in the Greek version. Most Septuagint manuscripts are Christian in origin, since in time the Jewish community – for whom the Bible had been translated into Greek in the first place – ceased to use the Septuagint and reverted to the Hebrew, leaving the Septuagint to be the Old Testament of the Christian churches. Even before this, in the late second century CE, three scholars of Jewish origin, possibly working in Asia Minor, had produced alternative Greek versions that they thought superior to the Septuagint, being on the whole more literal: Aquila, Symmachus and Theodotion. The Septuagint also contained the apocryphal/deutero-canonical books that Judaism in time came to reject, but which the Christian churches continued to use (see Chapter 9).

As we shall see in Chapter 18, there are other ancient translations of the Bible: the Old Latin, which is a second- or third-century translation from the Greek; Jerome's late-fourth-century Latin translation from the Hebrew Old Testament and Greek New Testament, now usually called the Vulgate; and the Peshitta, a translation into Syriac, a version of Aramaic. The Peshitta Old Testament was probably translated directly from the Hebrew, and the New Testament from the Greek, in the second century. Occasionally one or other of these will throw up a reading that could just reflect a variation in the underlying Hebrew or Greek; but they are on the whole more interesting in their own right than as evidence for the history of the biblical text. All, naturally, exist in various manuscripts that also differ from each other.

As with the New Testament, there are quotations of Old Testament books in other works. Rabbinic and ecclesiastical writers cite passages from Scripture which can sometimes suggest possible emendations to the Masoretic Text. A striking example is 1 Samuel 10–11, where the Jewish historian Flavius Josephus (37–*c.* 100 CE; see his *Jewish Antiquities* VI:5:1) attests the existence of a section that makes sense of what is otherwise a puzzling transition, and what he says has now been found in a scroll from Qumran (4QSam[a]). The Hebrew text as we have it runs awkwardly, but gains in clarity if we insert the extra section, as is done in the NRSV (the insertion is indented below):

> Saul also went to his home at Gibeah, and with him went warriors whose hearts God had touched. But some worthless fellows said, 'How can this man save us?' They despised him and brought him no present. But he held his peace.
>
> Now Nahash, king of the Ammonites, had been grievously oppressing the Gadites and the Reubenites. He would gouge out the right eye of each of them and would not grant Israel a deliverer. No one was left of the Israelites across the Jordan whose right eye Nahash, king of the Ammonites, had not gouged out. But there were seven thousand men who had escaped from the Ammonites and had entered Jabesh-gilead.

> About a month later, Nahash the Ammonite went up and besieged Jabesh-gilead; and all the men of Jabesh said to Nahash, 'Make a treaty with us, and we will serve you.' But Nahash the Ammonite said to them, 'On this condition I will make a treaty with you, namely that I gouge out everyone's right eye, and thus put disgrace upon all Israel.'
>
> (1 Samuel 10:26–11:2)

The insertion makes it clear that Nahash has form in inflicting these injuries, and the story runs more smoothly with it, since he presumably has in mind the men who have escaped him previously. (It is not clear why the insertion was lost, but it may simply reflect a copying error.) The incident helps to explain the background to the rise of Saul and his successful war against the Ammonites. This is probably a case where the shorter MT is later than the Qumran version, which was known to Josephus, probably from a pre-MT text.

TEXTUAL VARIATION AND THE ORIGINAL TEXT

This chapter may have given the impression that there is nothing one can call 'the Bible' because the text varies so much from one manuscript to another, but that would be a rather nihilistic conclusion. Even in the New Testament, where the textual variation is much wider than in the Old, there are whole blocks of text where the general drift of the passage is not in serious doubt. What the existence of textual variation rules out, it seems to me, is appeal to the exact wording of biblical sayings as if they were legal rulings, since for that a precise text would be essential. We have seen that that has significant consequences when it comes, for example, to Jesus' sayings on divorce and remarriage. But, for all the variation between manuscripts, we can still identify certain features of Mark as Marcan or of Luke as Lucan: Mark's tendency to short, clipped descriptions of events, and Luke's to long, circumstantial stories remain evident through all the vicissitudes of manuscript transmission. Even with the extreme case, Jeremiah, the longer Hebrew version and the shorter Greek (and Qumran) one are still recognizably Jeremiah. So in general terms we can feel assured that there is still a Bible.

Harder is the question of how far any of the material in the Bible goes back to the people to whom it is attributed. We have manuscripts of the Hebrew Bible probably from as early as the second century BCE, and of the New Testament from the second century CE; but we do not have autographs. Even when Paul says that a greeting at the end of one of his letters is written in his own hand (Galatians 6:11: 'See what large letters I make when I am writing in my own hand!'), we cannot see it, only what he wrote as copied out by a later scribe. Study of biblical manuscripts can never get us back reliably to the original author, only to the earliest point in the transmission of the text that can be reconstructed, which will always fall short of the original. Considered against the background of all study of the ancient world, the Bible is no special case. We hardly ever have autographs for any ancient author: yet no one seriously supposes that it is impossible to know about Plato's philosophy, or Julius Caesar's life and wars, because the manuscripts are all later than the classical authors themselves.

PART FOUR

The Meanings of the Bible

13
The Theme of the Bible

King's College, Cambridge, holds a 'Festival of Nine Lessons and Carols' every Christmas Eve, broadcast throughout the English-speaking world and imitated in very many churches, especially Anglican/Episcopalian ones. As the title indicates, it includes nine readings from the Bible, interspersed with hymns and carols. The carols change a little from year to year, but the readings are more or less constant. At the beginning of the service there is a 'bidding' – a call to listen and to pray – which includes what amounts to an interpretation of the whole of the Bible in one sentence:

> Let us read and mark in Holy Scripture the tale of the loving purposes of God from the first days of our disobedience unto the glorious Redemption brought us by this Holy Child.

The Bible – 'Holy Scripture' – is seen here as telling a story of disobedience and redemption, of sin and salvation, of paradise lost and paradise regained, concerning the whole human race ('our' disobedience). The main characters in the story are Adam and Jesus Christ, Adam who sinned in the garden of Eden (part of Genesis 3 is always the first reading in the service) and Jesus Christ, whom St Paul called the 'last Adam' (1 Corinthians 15:45), who obeyed God and through his obedience, even up to the point of death, conferred salvation on the whole of humanity. The Bible is thus understood as a story about a disaster followed by a rescue mission, and this fits with the nature of Christianity as a religion of salvation.

CHRISTIAN READING OF THE BIBLE

This idea of what the Bible is essentially about is so ingrained in western culture that it seems to most people with any kind of Christian background to be simply obvious. It results in a very particular way of understanding the Old Testament – which, on this interpretation, begins in history but ends in prophecy. It starts with the disobedience of Adam and then the tale of how the people of Israel continued to slide away from the moral values God demanded, and ends with the predictions of the coming saviour, such as we find in Handel's *Messiah*. The King's College service always contains two of these, both from the book of Isaiah. One is the prediction of a royal son who will be the 'prince of peace' (Isaiah 9:6–7):

> For a child has been born for us,
>   a son given to us;
> authority rests upon his shoulders;
>   and he is named
> Wonderful Counsellor, Mighty God,
>   Everlasting Father, Prince of Peace.
> His authority shall grow continually,
>   and there shall be endless peace
> for the throne of David and his kingdom.
>   He will establish and uphold it
> with justice and with righteousness
>   from this time onwards and for evermore.
>
> (verses 6–7)

The other is the prophecy about the 'peaceable kingdom' in which the 'wolf shall live with the lamb' (Isaiah 11:1–6):

> A shoot shall come out from the stock of Jesse,
>   and a branch shall grow out of his roots.
> The spirit of the LORD shall rest on him . . .
>
> The wolf shall live with the lamb,
>   the leopard shall lie down with the kid,
> the calf and the lion and the fatling together,
>   and a little child shall lead them.
>
> (verses 1–2, 6)

As we saw in Chapter 9, it fits with this way of thinking that the Christian Old Testament – always written as a codex, as we have seen – is arranged so that the prophetic books such as Isaiah come at the end, immediately before the Gospels in which the prophecies find their fulfilment.

This is how Christians have read the Bible since at least the second century CE, the age of Justin and Irenaeus. The King's College system of readings[1] is really a modern descendant of the ancient tradition of making excerpts from the Old Testament of the passages that were thought to point to Jesus Christ – known technically as *testimonia*, 'testimonies' (see Chapters 10 and 11). Many early Christians will not have had access to the whole Old Testament, and will have known it mainly through *testimonia*-books, whose contents they may have learned by heart, and which may well have contained some texts that are not actually in the Old Testament at all, such as the one quoted in Matthew 2:23, 'He will be called a Nazorean.'[2]

This understanding of the Old Testament as a story of disaster calling out for rescue goes back to Paul, for whom the Scriptures (meaning of course the Old Testament) are teleological, running from Adam to Christ and then on to the Second Coming. The pattern is already implied in 1 Thessalonians and 1 Corinthians in the first couple of decades after the crucifixion, and is spelled out explicitly in Romans:

> Sin came into the world through one man, and death came through sin, and so death spread to all because all have sinned ... If the many died through the one man's trespass, much more surely have the grace of God and the free gift in the grace of the one man, Jesus Christ, abounded for the many ... For just as by the one man's disobedience the many were made sinners, so by the one man's obedience the many will be made righteous.
>
> (Romans 5:12, 15, 19)

Christ undoes Adam's sin, and this is good news not only for Jews but for the whole human race, Adam's descendants. The Old Testament is to be read as a description of the sin into which Adam precipitated humankind and as a prophecy of the salvation from that plight that would be brought by Jesus Christ. The Old Testament thus runs seamlessly into the new dispensation described in the New.

Christian theologians of the first few centuries CE take this scheme for granted and elaborate it. Not content with seeing disobedient Adam as paralleled and reversed in obedient Christ, they develop a more complex typology, that is, a series of correspondences between Genesis (and the rest of the Old Testament) and the Gospels. Take, for example, John Chrysostom, the fourth-century Bishop of Constantinople (349–407 CE), in one of his homilies:

> If you reflect upon the Scriptures and the story of our redemption, you will recall that a virgin, a tree and a death were the symbols of our defeat. The virgin's name was Eve: she knew not a man. The tree was the tree of

> the knowledge of good and evil. The death was Adam's penalty. But now those very symbols of our defeat – a virgin, a tree and a death – have become symbols of Christ's victory. In place of Eve there is Mary; in place of the tree of the knowledge of good and evil, there is the tree of the cross; and in place of the death of Adam, there is the death of Christ.[3]

To most Christians from the second century CE onwards this has seemed an obvious and rather beautiful way of reading the Bible: the New Testament completes the story told in the Old by showing how God rescued the human race from the disaster into which it had fallen, and to which the Old Testament bears witness. Old Testament characters are often a foreshadowing of people and events in the New Testament and in Christian history. Of course, the Old Testament had other kinds of importance too, for example as providing a basic moral code; but as a narrative it was taken to be about the human lapse into sin, sin's continuation through the history of disobedience in the life of Israel, and the restoration of the human race through the death and resurrection of Christ, who will then come again for the final judgement of the world.

JEWISH READINGS OF THE BIBLE

It can therefore come as a shock to Christians when they first encounter a mainstream Jewish reading of the Hebrew Bible, which contains mainly the same books as what Christians call the Old Testament.[4] In Judaism, to generalize a little, the Bible is not a story of disaster and rescue, but much more of providential guidance. The main character is not Adam: in Judaism, as it has developed down to modern times, there is no emphasis at all on the garden of Eden story as an account of the 'fall' of the human race, as Christians call it. Much more central is Abraham, the founder of the people of Israel, and the biblical story is that of how his descendants lived in the land that God gave them, were expelled from it when they sinned, but were afterwards allowed back and given an ongoing existence. There is no emphasis on 'salvation', at least not in the otherworldly and individual sense that Christians have often given that word, but rather on divine leadership and guidance of the people as a corporate entity through the winding paths of history. The prophets are there, but they are seen as guides for the path, and the predictions of the Messiah, though there are a few, are not in any way central or very important – they are a minority interest. The difference in the way the

Bible is read in Judaism can be seen in how the books are arranged: the last book in the Bible is not a prophetic book, as it is for Christians, but the book of Chronicles, which ends with the exiled Jews being given permission by the Persian ruler Cyrus to return to the Promised Land. The final word of the Bible on this arrangement is the Hebrew word *veya'al*, 'let him go up', that is, let anyone who wishes return to the Land. (This is the reason why immigration of Jews to Israel is now known as *'aliyah*, 'going up', from the same Hebrew verb *'alah*.)

For Jews therefore, at least throughout much of history, the Bible has been not at all about fall and redemption, but about how to live a faithful life in the ups and downs of the ongoing history of the people of Israel. The first eleven chapters of Genesis, from creation through Adam and down to Abraham, are a prologue to the history of Israel, rather than setting the main themes of the collection of books that follow. Christians have tended to treat all of the Old Testament as a kind of prophecy – even the Psalms have often been read as predicting the Messiah, and the books of Moses, Genesis to Deuteronomy, have been mined for predictions. Jews, by contrast, tend to treat it all as a form of instruction in living a good and observant life, in other words as *torah*, the Hebrew word for instruction or teaching (misleadingly translated 'law' – see Chapter 4). As Alexander Samely puts it:

> Rabbinic texts contain details of a human project which could be described in modern terms as follows. Everyday life is an infinite series of opportunities for obedience to God, whose will is articulated and implied in Scripture, a book filled to the brim with instructions and information.[5]

It is sometimes said that Jews and Christians share the Old Testament, and differ simply in whether or not they regard the New Testament as part of the Bible. Although this is strictly speaking true, it misses out a great deal. Jews and Christians do indeed share these books, but traditionally construe them in such diverse ways that it is almost as though they were different works: and the difference in arrangement signals this diversity. For Jews the Torah or Pentateuch is overwhelmingly important; alongside it there are the Prophets and the Writings, but these are of far less significance. It would be an odd form of Judaism nowadays that foregrounded the Prophets in the way that Christians have done, and treated them as the interpretative key to reading the Bible. The Jewish Bible is definitely not one but three collections, one of them far more important than the other two. This was certainly true by the early third century CE at the latest, since the Mishnah presupposes this arrangement. For Christians the Old Testament is a single work. As we saw in Chapter 10, for them the Pentateuch runs on into the other historical books to make what some of the Fathers actually call an Enneateuch (nine books; see Chapter 9). Then, after a kind of interlude constituted by the 'teaching' books such as Psalms and Proverbs, the work finds its climax in the words of the prophets, foretelling the coming Messiah. If we are to talk at all of 'the meaning' of a corpus of literature as long and varied as the Old Testament, we have to use some kind of overarching scheme of interpretation; and, given the difference between the Christian scheme of fall and prophesied redemption on the one hand, and the Jewish theme of providential guidance and instruction on the other, it is indeed almost as though they were two different collections.

Having set up this stark contrast, I must now qualify it slightly. What I have been saying is true for the way Judaism and Christianity have developed over the centuries. But if we go back to the time of Paul, that is, to the first century CE, we actually find that Jewish conceptions were more varied than they later became, and that Christian perceptions were not yet so fixed on the disaster-and-rescue model. Two books that were too recent to get into the official Jewish Bible, but can be found among the apocryphal/deutero-canonical books, reflect the same kind of interest in Adam's fall that Christians were to pick up. One is the so-called Wisdom of Solomon, a work from the first century BCE, well known to Christians, even those who do not regard it as Scripture, for the line, 'the souls of the righteous are in the hand of God' (Wisdom 3:1). The other is the slightly earlier book of Ecclesiasticus/Sirach, which gives us 'Let us now sing the praises of famous men' (Sirach 44:1). In both, sin and death result from the disobedience of Adam and Eve, and the Wisdom of Solomon at least thinks of God as able to reverse them, and so grant immortality – much closer to the Christian model:

> God created us for incorruption,
> and made us in the image of his own eternity,
> but through the devil's envy death entered the world . . .
>
> (Wisdom of Solomon 2:23–4)

– a clear reference to the garden of Eden story, with the snake as the devil, just as in later Christian imagination, though not (at least not explicitly) in Genesis 3. The author goes on to say that the 'hope [of the righteous] is full of immortality' (3:4), and to claim that their souls are indeed 'in the hand of God' (3:1). Ben Sira, the author of Ecclesiasticus, blames Eve for the loss of immortality:

From a woman sin had its beginning,
and because of her we all die.

(Sirach 25:24)

A third book, where the importance of the sin in the garden is clearest of all, is 2 Esdras, which comes from the end of the first century CE and so could depend on Christian ideas – though most commentators agree that its core is purely Jewish, despite its having been placed within a Christian framework.[6] It is not, strictly speaking, canonical for any Christians, though it appears as a supplement in the Latin Bible, while being unknown to the Greek tradition. It was probably written in Aramaic or Hebrew, but is now extant mainly in Latin. In it Ezra, the putative author of the books, says:

> 'This is my first and last comment: it would have been better if the earth had not produced Adam, or else, when it had produced him, had restrained him from sinning. For what good is it to all that they live in sorrow now and expect punishment after death? O Adam, what have you done? For though it was you who sinned, the fall was not yours alone, but ours also who are your descendants.'
>
> (2 Esdras 7:46–8/116–18)

This is much closer to Paul's conception – and to that of subsequent Christian authors – than to what became normal in Judaism. Thus a Christian understanding of the fall and of redemption does have Jewish roots: they lie in the last couple of centuries BCE, when Judaism changed quite radically, rather than in the Hebrew Bible as it was read in earlier times and as it has been read by later Jews. Christians inherited a style of Jewish thinking about Adam and Eve and about the need for salvation that developed only towards the end of the Second Temple period, and they persisted in teaching it, after mainstream Judaism had largely abandoned it again.

Similar things can be said about messianic prophecy. The idea of the coming of a great king after the model of David certainly occurs in the Hebrew Bible, in books such as Zechariah, where he is called the *mashiah*, 'messiah', meaning anointed one. But it is a comparatively minor theme in the Old Testament. Many passages that Christians later interpreted as messianic prophecies probably referred originally to something much more mundane, the birth of a royal child in the normal course of events. This is likely to be the case in Isaiah 9:2–7, the passage about the prince of peace, which originally concerned the coming birth of the king's son. Towards the end of the Second Temple period some groups did become greatly interested in messianic prophecy, as we see from the Dead Sea Scrolls.

> His [that is, the Messiah's] kingdom is an everlasting kingdom, and all his ways truth. He will judge the earth with truth, and all will make peace. The sword will cease from the earth, and all cities pay him homage. The great God will be his strength.
>
> (4Q246)

But rabbinic Judaism, the style of Judaism that is the precursor of what we now think of as Orthodox Judaism, tended to lose interest in messianic prophecy except in certain periods of tension or heightened expectation. It saw the Messiah as promised, certainly, but not as a subject of great interest for practical purposes.

Thus the whole model of a disaster and rescue mission, as I have called it, was not completely a Christian invention or discovery. It occurred within Judaism. But by making it the universal way of reading Old Testament Scripture, Christians ensured that Christianity would develop along quite different lines from Judaism. Christians soon came to see Judaism as having thoroughly misread its own Scriptures and even, according to some writers, as having falsified those Scriptures, removing allusions to the Messiah and to Jesus Christ as the saviour of lost humanity. We recall again how the second-century CE teacher Justin Martyr insisted that the Jews had changed the text of Psalm 96, which had originally read 'the Lord reigns *from the tree*', a reference to the cross. He also claimed that they had deleted from Jeremiah a reference to what is called the harrowing of hell, Christ's visit to Hades after his death but before his resurrection to preach to the pre-Christian righteous. According to Justin the text had read, 'The Lord God of Israel remembered his dead who slept in the earth of a grave, and he descended to them to preach to them his salvation.'[7] There is no truth in either accusation, as there is no evidence that either of these passages was ever in the Hebrew Bible. But they confirmed the Christian feeling that Christians understood the Old Testament better than the Jews, and could even correct its text.

RECONCILING JEWISH AND CHRISTIAN READINGS?

So the New Testament is not just an addition to the Old: it radically rewrites it in many ways. Subsequent Christian thinkers, though they inherited the Old Testament as part of their Scriptures, read it in quite a different way from their Jewish contemporaries. Christians believed that in and through Jesus Christ something new had happened, which could not be wholly understood in terms of the existing Scriptures; and this meant that when those same Scriptures were read, they were read differently. Even so, the Christians drew on contemporary Judaism for models to understand what they saw as this new revelation. Judaism itself very soon took a different course, and read the Bible primarily as sustenance for a journey of faith and obedience that was continuous from the time of Abraham through to the present, without any disruption of the kind represented for Christians by the disobedience in the garden of Eden. The Babylonian exile was a major hitch in the story, but it did not ultimately call into question God's faithfulness to his people; and there is no suggestion, as there has so often been in Christian thought, that any event, whether the disobedience in the garden or some other, renders human beings entirely unable to respond to God. There is no doctrine of original sin in Judaism, no sense that humankind is irretrievably lost without divine grace. That is a Pauline idea that subsequent Christian thinkers developed, but not one that most Jews ever envisaged.

The difference between Jewish and Christian readings of the Bible is the theme of an important short book by R. Kendall Soulen, *The God of Israel and Christian Theology*.[8] Much as I have been arguing myself, he suggests that for Jews and Christians respectively the main plot of the Bible has been quite differently articulated. Since the second or third Christian generation, Christians have read the Bible as concerned with four essential elements in a large-scale story: not the story of Israel, but the story of the world. The four elements are the creation; the fall; the redemption brought by Christ; and the final consummation of all things, as described in Revelation at the end of the two-Testament Christian Bible.[9] The fall of humankind as a whole, which scarcely figures at all in a Jewish reading (and this is not surprising, since outside Genesis 3 the Hebrew Bible never mentions it), has been for Christians an absolutely central element in this structure, since it defines the question to which redemption in Christ provides the answer. This question is not how Jews should live, but how the whole human race can relate to a God whom it radically displeases.

Soulen shows how this fourfold schema can be found in Christian theologians from Justin and Irenaeus in the second century CE to Karl Barth (1886–1968) and Karl Rahner (1904–84) in the twentieth.

Nothing much is made of the history of Israel, other than as the stage on which the messianic promises, one day to be fulfilled in Jesus, were set. The Bible is seen as being primarily not about Israel and its history, but about the redemption of the world from sin. To this end the two Testaments relate different stages in the process of redemption. The subject of the Hebrew Bible, on this interpretation, is 'us', meaning either the whole human race or the people who are the forerunners of Christians, such as the patriarchs and prophets: not the great mass of the Jews, who are simply not in focus at all. Soulen argues that this amounts to supersessionism, the doctrine that Christianity has replaced Judaism. Such an idea is inherent not in specific features, such as whether the covenant with Abraham has been improved on in Christ – which, though important, are relatively small-scale matters – but in the whole way of construing the history told in the Hebrew Bible. There can only be mutual understanding between Jews and Christians, he believes, when they come to see how irreconcilably different have been their characteristic ways of reading it.

But there is another element in his work, and that is to argue that Christians ought to abandon their own traditional fourfold scheme and get back to reading the Bible in the Jewish manner. They would then see that God's dealing with the human world works on the basis that there are always to be Jews and Gentiles on earth, and that neither can ever be subsumed into the other. The New Testament offers the hope that some Gentiles and Jews alike can come to see that God has done a really new thing through Jesus, which changes world history; but in the process nothing requires them to cease to be, respectively, Gentiles and Jews. The central theme of the Hebrew Scriptures, Soulen argues,

> is the God of Israel's work as Consummator and . . . God's work as Consummator engages the human family by opening up an 'economy of mutual blessing' between those who are and who remain different. God consummates the human family by electing it into an historical and open-ended economy of difference and reciprocal dependence, the identifying characteristic of which is the divinely drawn distinction between Israel and the nations. Jewish and gentile identity are not basically antithetical or even 'separate but equal' ways of relating to God. They are, rather, two mutually dependent ways of participating in a single divine *oikonomia* of blessing oriented toward the final consummation of the whole human family in God's eschatological *shalom*.[10]

For most Christians, this would be an entirely novel way of reading the Bible, one not found at all in the history of Christian biblical interpretation.

Central to such a reading is God's covenant relation with Israel: a relationship added to through Christ, in revealing more to Gentiles than they had previously known, but not in any way abrogated. The usual Jewish way of construing Scripture as the story of Israel is here affirmed, not set aside. To it is added that Scripture is also about the story of the other nations (the Gentiles or *goyim*) in relation to Israel, a point which Jewish readers would be unlikely to want to deny. But the Gentiles are not presented as those who will one day take over the promises to Israel through a new and better covenant. Rather, they are portrayed as people to whom the God of Israel also relates. This is, after all, inherent in the story of the blessing of Noah, the ancestor of the entire human race, as traditional Jewish readings have always affirmed. But the model of fall and redemption, which Christians have traditionally used to structure their own reading of the whole Bible, is seen as too easily bypassing the story of Israel and the nations, and introducing a falsely universalizing theme into a book which is closely bound up with a specific people, Israel, and its relations with the outside world.

Soulen's work challenges Christians to listen to the witness of the Hebrew Bible without imposing on it a prearranged theological schema based in the New Testament. It could lead, after much theological reflection, to a robust Christian use of the Hebrew Bible, in which supersessionism is overcome, yet the newness of Christ is truly celebrated as good news for the whole world, for Gentiles and Jews alike. Jews would be under no pressure whatever to abandon their Judaism. On the contrary, Christians would want them to celebrate and affirm it as being of eternal value. While the proposal is attractive, I do not think it corresponds to anything that has existed before in the Christian reading of the Hebrew Bible, which has always (since Paul) followed the disaster and rescue-mission model that universalizes the message of the Bible while relativizing its Jewish character. It does, however, open up the intriguing question how Jesus himself read the Jewish Scriptures. Did he see himself as the one who would deliver the world from its sins – the later Christian model – or essentially as a Jewish teacher who sought to improve Jewish adherence to Torah by radical moral teaching? The second understanding has characterized the modern 'Jesus the Jew' movement in scholarship,[11] which drives a wedge between Jesus and Paul and views Paul as having 'de-Judaized' the message of Jesus. If this is correct, then Soulen's argument could be seen as a return to Jesus' own understanding of the logic of the Hebrew Bible, across the intervening doctrinal development of the four-stage scheme that he rightly thinks has determined most Christian Bible-reading since the second century CE. It does, however, tend to ignore the question of Jesus' own claims for his own status as inaugurating a new stage in God's dealings with Israel, or perhaps as bringing in the close of the age. It is not so easy to remove from the traditions in the Gospels Jesus' sense of his own divinely ordained destiny, and to leave us with him as simply a Jewish teacher, however great.

INTERPRETATION OF THE HEBREW BIBLE IN JUDAISM

In fact, the contrast between Jewish and Christian approaches to the Bible is in some ways even more stark than indicated above, in that mainstream Judaism has not typically read the Hebrew Bible as having an overarching grand narrative at all. In the synagogue liturgy[12] only the Pentateuch is read right through, and the Prophets (which include the histories) are read only in small excerpts to accompany the readings from the Pentateuch. The vast majority of passages from the Prophets are left unread, and thus are unfamiliar to many highly observant Jews. The Writings – the third part of the Hebrew Bible, including Psalms, Proverbs, Ezra-Nehemiah and Chronicles – are not read at all except for the five scrolls, Lamentations, Esther, Ecclesiastes, Song of Songs and Ruth, which are read at five major festivals, and particular psalms are used on a regular basis. There is no ideal of publicly reading through the whole Bible, as there has been in Christian traditions such as Anglicanism, or in Christian monastic practice. The sense that the Bible forms a narrative whole is, in contrast to the Christian view, altogether lacking.

In rabbinic commentary, pieces of the Bible are interpreted in an atomizing way, often with no regard for their context in Scripture; and though there are many stories in the midrashim (the plural form of midrash), the traditional Jewish commentaries on the biblical books, they are usually individual anecdotes, not part of any overall narrative framework. Overwhelmingly the stories in Scripture are mined for what they have to teach about obedience to Torah, not for their contribution to any teleological scheme of salvation or redemption, which is largely lacking. It is possible for Jewish scholars to write articles subtitled, 'Why Jews don't read Books',[13] implying that Jewish biblical interpretation does not focus on whole books, still less on the scriptural collection as a whole, but on fragmentary bits. In traditional Jewish exegesis, all of Scripture is like an enormous anthology of sayings (rather like the book of Proverbs), with no particular order or flow – according to one very important rabbinic maxim, 'there is no before or after in Scripture'[14] – so that one may interpret an earlier passage in the light of a later one just as much as the reverse, as though all the books had been written at the same time – in God's eternity, in fact. The rabbinic approach to the Bible has been characterized as involving 'the segmentation of the Hebrew Bible into micro-Scripture. Each sign can be considered on its own, each word can have different meanings, each sentence different topics, and each story can have many links to other stories.'[15] We shall return to this way of seeing the Bible in Chapter 14.

Thus it is not so much that Judaism uses the Scriptures to tell a different overall story from Christianity, but that the concern for an overall story is in itself a largely Christian preoccupation. Of course, it is obvious to anyone who reads the whole Old Testament that it does tell a continuous story from the creation to the end of the exile, and then after that provides at least sporadic information about life under the Persians and under the Hellenistic rulers of Egypt and Syria. But reading the whole Old Testament through is mostly a Christian interest. If one reads only the Torah – the Pentateuch, the first five books from Genesis to Deuteronomy – one reads about God's faithfulness to the patriarchs, the giving of the law through Moses, and the gift of the Promised Land, which will be fulfilled under Joshua. But the story of how that in fact happened, along with the subsequent history of divine guidance, Israel's rebellion and God's mercy, all lies outside the Torah and does not have the same centrality to Judaism. Many Jews knew the rest of the Scriptures extremely well – it is clear from rabbinic literature that most sages committed almost the whole of the Prophets and Writings to heart, just as they had the Torah – but that knowledge is not as essential a part of the religion for everyone as knowledge of the Torah.

In modern Judaism – we do not know how far back the custom goes, but certainly into Talmudic times – on the Sabbath known as *simchat torah*, 'rejoicing in the law', the final section of Deuteronomy is read, with Israel on the brink of the Promised Land, and then is immediately followed by the first section of Genesis, starting up the annual cycle of Torah-reading again. The story does not continue into Joshua as it does in the Christian Bible; Joshua is the first book in the Prophets, the second, and less important, division of the Jewish Bible. The Christian feeling that Deuteronomy is followed by Joshua just as much as Genesis is followed by Exodus is lacking in Judaism, which retains a sense that these are all separate scrolls.

Indeed, studying the Bible at all has tended to develop in modern times in Israel rather than in the diaspora, as part of giving the state not so much a religious as a cultural identity – new recruits to the army, for example, are presented with a pocket Hebrew Bible. Orthodox Jews had traditionally studied the Talmud, not the Bible, even though the Talmud constantly refers to biblical texts. The bland assertion that Jews and Christians 'share the Old Testament', even though they disagree about the New, fails to see how distinctively these books function in the two religions, and have done at least since the second century CE. Christianity developed a wholly different idea of divine salvation from Judaism, and one that was linked with exactly the scheme Soulen has identified: creation, fall, redemption, final consummation, all affecting the entire human race. In Judaism ideas of salvation were bound up instead with the fortunes of Israel, which it saw as lying in observance of the divine Torah.

One may press this point further by saying that Judaism, unlike Christianity, is not really a religion of salvation at all. An article in the English weekly newspaper the *Church Times* began as follows:

> Religions are concerned, above all, with salvation – with what is awry in the human condition, and its remedy. Their beliefs centre, therefore, on what we need to be saved *from* and *for*, and how this can be achieved.[16]

The case of Judaism, Christianity's closest relative, shows how far this is from being universally true. Not all religions are about rescue from the human plight: it is perfectly possible to have a religion that does not see the human race or the individual as sunk in misery from which salvation is needed, and Judaism is just such a one. As Dietrich Bonhoeffer (1906–45) put it, 'the faith of the Old Testament is not a religion of redemption'.[17] Judaism, like many religions, recognizes human sin and weakness. Unlike Christianity, however, it does not propose that these are at such a pitch that God needs to intervene dramatically to rescue humanity from them. Furthermore, it is not in general very concerned with humanity as a whole. Judaism does have theories about the well-being of, and the ethical obligations incumbent on, non-Jews, such as the theory of the so-called Noachite laws, supposedly made known to all humanity through Noah; and it has an awareness that there are prophecies about the gathering-in of the Gentiles at the last day. But such questions are marginal, not something that Jews spend a lot of time thinking about, any more than they do about the sin of Adam. Christians tend to assimilate Judaism to the model of Christianity, asking what Jews have to say about the fall, about original sin and about salvation, and it is perfectly possible to find Jewish teachings on such matters if one looks hard. But the heart of Judaism does not lie there, and to establish a set of Christian questions to which one then seeks Jewish answers is to misunderstand the different genius of the two faiths. As we have seen, there were strands in Judaism in the time of the New Testament that did take more interest in such matters, but they did not continue into what became rabbinic Judaism. Thus Judaism and Christianity diverged over time in their way of reading the Hebrew Bible, just as they did in so many other ways.

OLD AND NEW

The idea of a substantial difference between the Testaments is not acceptable to all Christians, and is easily dismissed with the word 'Marcionism', referring to the famous second-century heretic who taught that the gods of the two Testaments were simply two different gods, an evil god who created the world (Old Testament) and a good God who redeemed it (New Testament).[18] Marcionism was rejected in the second century by the dominant party in early Christianity. That the God of Jesus Christ is also the creator, who was already known in Israel, seemed crucial to Christian writers. Jesus himself obviously believed in this God. By the time the Church had assimilated both Jesus' teaching and Paul's, it had a religion that understood the Bible in something quite close to the four stages identified by Soulen. The second- and third-century Christians who developed this view were not inventing something new, but drawing the consequences of what Jesus and Paul had taught. It is a reading that extends beyond the natural sense of the Hebrew Bible, and makes fresh claims and proposals about the relation between God and the human race that do not contradict the Old Testament, but do move outside it.

Christians then proceeded to read the Old Testament as though it already taught these new ideas, and in the process they distorted its natural meaning, because they wanted the two Testaments to hang together as a seamless whole, despite the fact that they tell significantly different stories; and for Christians the New Testament story always trumped the Old Testament one. This was worked out in practice by a creative rereading of the Old Testament as though it spoke with the New Testament's voice. As we saw, in early times that could sometimes be accomplished by arguing that it was really a Christian book all along – that is the solution, for example, in the *Epistle of Barnabas*.[19] But by the later second century more sophisticated methods of reading the Old Testament had been developed, in which it was seen as having a natural surface sense, yet also a deeper meaning that pointed forward to Jesus and to the New Testament. We shall examine this in Chapter 14.

Ultimately, there is no one correct way of reading the Old Testament/Hebrew Bible: it is a huge, heterogeneous collection of material that can only be given a unity by imposing some interpretative scheme on it. Jews and Christians have done this in different ways, but neither takes account of everything contained in the books, and it is not easy to see how any scheme could do so, given the variety within the collection. Both faiths have at times insisted on the Old Testament telling the story they wanted to tell anyway. Such insistence pretends that the Bible determines what we believe, when really the belief system in both faiths is to some degree independent of the Scriptures, which each reads according to its core tenets. Scripture is for both a resource, but it is not determinative of either as it has in fact developed.

READING THE NEW TESTAMENT

This chapter has mostly been about the Old Testament/Hebrew Bible, since it is over that that Jewish and Christian interpreters have disagreed, identifying different themes as salient. But for Christianity there is also a question about the thematic unity of the New Testament. Here too we find at best a loose fit between what the Church taught as the essentials of Christian faith, and the Scriptures that were its main resource in locating them. At the latest from the time of Irenaeus in the late second century CE, appeal can be made to something called the 'rule of faith', which is a summary of the basics of Christian belief, analogous to the creeds and, indeed, lying at their root. The rule of faith is both a key for interpreting the Bible and also a summary of its contents: there is a kind of feedback loop between the two. When the New Testament is read, the rule of faith provides an interpretative framework that tells one where to place the emphasis, what are the main themes of the books, what is at the core of the faith and what is at the margins. At the same time, the Bible feeds into the rule of faith and fleshes it out in detail. 'The rule of faith', writes Eugen J. Pentiuc, 'can be compared to a frame for a canvas made of various scriptural texts. Interpreters can enjoy a great deal of liberty provided they pay attention to the framework.'[20]

An early statement of the rule of faith would be this, from Irenaeus, who says that Christians believe

> in one God, the Father Almighty, who made the heaven and the earth and the seas and all the things that are in them; and in one Christ Jesus, the Son of God, who was made flesh for our salvation; and in the Holy Spirit, who made known through the prophets the plan of salvation, and the coming, and the birth from a virgin, and the passion, and the resurrection from the dead, and the bodily ascension into heaven of the beloved Christ Jesus, our Lord, and his future appearing from heaven in the glory of the Father to sum up all things and to raise anew all flesh of the whole human race.

Obviously this derives from the New Testament; but, perhaps less obviously, it places the emphasis differently from the New Testament, read as a whole.

First, it is Trinitarian in character, organized – as the creeds would later be – around the nature of God as Father, Son and Holy Spirit. There is only one explicit reference to God as Trinity in the New Testament, Matthew 28:19, where after the resurrection Jesus commands his disciples, 'Go therefore and make disciples of all nations, baptizing them in the name of the Father and of the Son and of the Holy Spirit.'[21] Many scholars think this command has been added in the light of the later doctrine of the Trinity. There is also 2 Corinthians 13:13, 'The grace of the Lord Jesus Christ, the love of God, and the communion of the Holy Spirit be with all of you.' But it could not easily be argued that the doctrine of the Trinity is central to the New Testament, as it clearly is in Irenaeus' formulation. There are places, for example, where Jesus is presented as definitely subordinate to God the Father in a way that would later have been regarded as heretical: thus in 1 Corinthians 15:28 we read, 'When all things are subjected to him, then the Son himself will also be subjected to the one who put all things in subjection under him, so that God may be all in all.' But, even apart from this problem, references to God as Trinity are largely missing from the New Testament.

Likewise, 'the coming, and the birth from a virgin' emphasizes the birth stories of Jesus at the beginning of Matthew and Luke, but these are never referred to elsewhere in the New Testament. Paul, in particular, never mentions the virginal conception of Jesus, and nor do any of the other books of the New Testament, including Mark and John, Acts and the non-Pauline letters. '[T]o sum up all things' is a peculiarity of Irenaeus' own theology: he sees Jesus as repeating and completing in himself God's guidance of the people of Israel and, indeed, the whole universe. But this idea does not clearly appear as a theme within the New Testament.

On the other hand, much of what the Gospels do tell us about Jesus, his teaching, healings and other miracles, are not mentioned in Irenaeus' rule of faith and would not be mentioned in the later creeds either. Rudolf Bultmann claimed that in John's Gospel, 'the Proclaimer became the Proclaimed', in other words that Jesus went from being the one who spoke of the coming kingdom of God, and taught people how to live in its light, to being himself the content of the Christian proclamation. Instead of a gospel preached *by* Jesus, Christians came to believe in a gospel *about* Jesus. This development had certainly advanced even further by the time of Irenaeus, whose rule of faith sees Jesus as the person the Christian message is about. In the process the content of Jesus' own teaching is played down. We know that Irenaeus knew and valued the teaching in the Gospels, but he does not present it as central to basic Christian beliefs: what Christians are to believe in are the virginal conception, the resurrection, the ascension of Jesus and his Second Coming in judgement. This recalls Paul, who similarly says virtually nothing about Jesus' teaching, or his healings and other miracles, which has the effect of downgrading much of the content of the Gospels.

Thus the theme of the New Testament, as it emerges from the Church's rule of faith, is heavily Pauline and Johannine, and makes far less of the Synoptic Gospels. As with Christian and Jewish understandings of the Old Testament/Hebrew Bible, it is not a complete distortion of biblical ideas, but it is selective, and puts the emphasis in a different place than might be expected from a straightforward reading of the Bible. What God has done, according to the New Testament, is seen as part of a rescue plan for the human race, in accordance with the way the Old Testament was being read. Jesus Christ saves human beings by his coming as man, dying, rising and ascending, and will come again in glory at the last judgement. This has been the core of Christian teaching since the second century. Before Irenaeus it is already there in Justin Martyr:

> He was born of a virgin as a man, and was named Jesus, and was crucified, and died, and rose again, and ascended into heaven.[22]

But it does not capture the drift of the New Testament taken as a whole, which has much more on Jesus as a teacher than the rule of faith allows.

Also noteworthy is the focus on God as creator, which is a very minor theme in the New Testament, though one can argue that it is assumed there. This emphasis in second-century writers may reflect the need to combat Marcionism, and other systems of thought that denigrated the created world or even ascribed it to the work of a second-rate or evil god (as Marcion apparently did, and was certainly believed to have done). In New Testament times the creatorship of the one God was taken for granted, and was not yet a controversial issue.

Thus the rule of faith as we find it in second-century Christian teachers is certainly compatible with the New Testament, but is not exactly what readers of the New Testament might arrive at, left to their own devices. The emphasis falls in rather different places. Underlying it is the same fourfold scheme Soulen identifies in Christian reading of the Old Testament/Hebrew Bible: creation, fall, restoration in Christ, consummation at the last judgement. All these elements appear in the New Testament, but one would not get them, as four equal elements in an overall scheme, from a simple reading, for example, of the Synoptic Gospels, or the non-Pauline letters. The scheme is essentially drawn from John and Paul. That is not to say that it has been artificially imposed on the New Testament, as it arguably has on the Old; but it does shift the emphasis away from Jesus as the Proclaimer to Jesus as the Proclaimed, and places him in a Trinitarian context that the New Testament itself is as yet barely aware of.

THE QUEST FOR A THEME IN THE BIBLE

Finding a single theme for a work as long and varied as the Bible is a difficult task, perhaps even a fool's errand. As we have seen, many strands in Judaism do not even attempt it where the Hebrew Bible is concerned, but see the unity of Judaism as a religion as lying in certain patterns of belief and, above all, practice, that relate at best obliquely to the biblical text. Judaism is not, and does not claim to be, essentially a biblical religion, but can perhaps be defined as 'a literature and a set of related practices',[23] with no implication that the practices derive directly from the literature and little sense that the literature prescribes what is to be believed. Christianity as it has developed since the second century CE has been much more focused on belief, and so has had to define the relation of correct belief to the biblical canon.

In that process Christians necessarily had to establish a hermeneutic, that is, a framework of understanding within which the Bible is to be interpreted; it came up with the rule of faith, which captures those aspects of the biblical texts that early Christians saw as central, and downplays others. For a modern Christian the selection is less obvious. Why, for example, was the bodily ascension of Jesus – which is mentioned only twice in the New Testament, at the end of Luke and the beginning of Acts[24] (Luke 24:51 – in some manuscripts – and Acts 1:9) seen as important enough to get into the rule, while his teaching and healings are not mentioned, even though they take up a huge portion of the Gospels and are emphasized in the speeches in Acts? Why did Trinitarian language become so central to the rule's structure, when the New Testament hardly knows it? The answer is that these were all issues for the second-century Church, which therefore read the New Testament in their light. The New Testament becomes an answer to questions that are not exactly those its authors originally raised. Like any text that persists over time, it came to be seen through successive, and different, lenses. Perhaps it is only in modern times that we have become aware of this, and have been able to detach the original text from the layers of interpretation that have been superimposed on it – or, at least, to think that we have.

14
Rabbis and Church Fathers

The *Mekhilta of Rabbi Ishmael* is a Jewish commentary on the second half of the book of Exodus. It was probably produced, by synthesizing material from various dates, sometime in the second century CE.[1] It is concerned primarily with how to observe the various pieces of legislation in Exodus, which from chapter 20 onwards consists of laws and precepts about life in society and the worship of the sanctuary. This kind of teaching is known in Judaism as *halakhah*, from the Hebrew verb *halakh*, meaning 'to walk' – in other words, advice or instruction on how to live. (It is usually contrasted with *aggadah*, 'narration', which refers to teaching that is illustrative of the good life through narrating stories or anecdotes.) The *Mekhilta* is one of the oldest collections of rabbinic teaching in the form of scriptural commentary. It is meant to be read alongside the Mishnah, codified in the early third century CE, which is arranged by theme rather than as a commentary on a biblical text, and contains rather little biblical material. By this period Judaism, having lost its Temple, had become concentrated on the study and observance of the biblical text and the establishment of a style of living that is recognizably the ancestor of modern orthodoxy. Its spiritual leaders were the rabbis, primarily teachers who transmitted their instruction orally to groups of disciples. Those who worked from the first to the mid third century CE are known as the Tannaim, meaning 'transmitters'.

A typical passage in the *Mekhilta* concerns the Jewish custom of binding on one's forehead and left arm a small scroll containing certain biblical texts, before beginning prayer.[2] This is seen as enacting the instructions about keeping the Passover in Exodus 13:6–9:

> For seven days you shall eat unleavened bread . . . You shall tell your child on that day, 'It is because of what the LORD did for me when I came out of Egypt.' It shall serve for you as a sign on your hand and as a reminder

on your forehead, so that the teaching of the LORD may be on your lips; for with a strong hand the LORD brought you out of Egypt.

The phrase 'a sign on your hand' is understood as meant literally rather than metaphorically, and as referring to the arm rather than the hand, for various reasons that the *Mekhilta* spells out. Then it comes to the question, why the *left* arm? 'You say it is the left,' runs the text, 'but perhaps not, perhaps it is the right?' Although there is no direct proof, there are two texts that point to the left hand being meant. In Isaiah 48:13 we read, 'My hand laid the foundation of the earth, and my right hand spread out the heavens', and in Judges 5:26, where Jael is killing the enemy commander Sisera, 'She put her hand to the tent-peg and her right hand to the workman's mallet.' How do these passages help? In both, the right hand is explicitly mentioned when it is intended, so that 'the hand' without further designation must surely mean the left hand. Hence the 'sign on your hand' must mean, 'on the left hand' – or arm.[3]

To most modern readers this line of argument will seem extremely strange. First, the text in Exodus 13:9 is surely intended metaphorically: the remembrance of the exodus is to be as close to the Israelite *as if* it were written on his hand. Still, it is understandable that a physical expression of the command came to be customary. Much more puzzling is the argumentation about the left hand (or arm). For one thing, in the Isaiah 48 quotation we surely have parallelism: the two halves of the verse balance, and it seems likely that in both halves the right hand is intended, rather than God's being imagined as using both hands. In general in the Bible God does powerful things with his right hand, and creating the world shall fall under this heading. In Judges there is perhaps parallelism too, though since Jael kills Sisera by hammering a tent-peg through his temple as he lies asleep, she would have needed both hands. But it seems obvious that neither passage has anything to do with the custom of wearing *tefillin*, as the little scrolls are called. How can the texts in Isaiah or Judges demonstrate which arm they are to be worn on, even if it is true that in them the unspecified 'hand' means the left hand (or arm)?

RABBINIC PRINCIPLES OF INTERPRETATION

What we see here are some principles of early rabbinic interpretation. First, any passage in the Bible can illuminate any other passage, regardless of whether it was known to the author of the other or not. A modern interpreter would ask whether the author of Exodus 13 could have known Isaiah 48 or Judges 5, and so have been referring to them. For the rabbinic commentator this is not an issue. Any passage in Scripture can aid in the interpretation of any other passage, since Scripture forms a kind of interlocking web of texts among which there is what might nowadays be called intertextuality: that is, all are interrelated, irrespective of date or authorship (see Chapter 13).

Secondly, there need not be any connection of thought among the texts: verbal similarity is sufficient. Any passage that contains the word 'hand' is potentially evidence for its use in the Exodus text, even though it may not be referring to the same topic at all. It is as though the Bible were a kind of dictionary, in which all the texts containing the word 'hand' could be drawn on as evidence for its meaning in the particular passage in question. What is more, the verbal similarity may extend to homonyms, words which are only partly similar. Thus in a rabbinic homily about Abraham's near-sacrifice of Isaac in Genesis 22, Abraham's being tested (Hebrew *nissah*) is linked to a verse in Psalm 60:4, 'You have given a flag (*nes*) to those who fear you', and the writer develops the theme that Abraham is elevated, like a flag, through his obedience to the test.[4]

Thirdly, every feature of the texts being discussed is significant. In the case of Isaiah 48:13, the fact that 'hand' and 'right hand' are mentioned in the two halves of the verse is probably not important in the context of the story of creation: God is pictured as using his powerful hand to create the world, and the fact that he does not specify which hand he is using in the first half of the verse does not matter. But for rabbinic interpreters there is nothing in the Bible that does not matter. If the specification of the hand is omitted, that is because something is being communicated by that omission, and in this case what is being communicated is that it refers to God's left hand. Perhaps, in the mind of the interpreter, God chose to leave out 'left' precisely so that the verse would be available later to help resolve the issue about which arm to use for the *tefillin*.

Fourthly, there is no sense of each biblical book as a separate entity. There is no meaningful level of the text between the individual verse (or even the individual word) and the whole of Scripture: the boundaries between the books are of no real significance for interpretation. The modern sense that each book has its own integrity and meaning is scarcely to be found in rabbinic reading. Alexander Samely writes:

> The complete biblical episode, prophetic speech, legal code, psalmodic song, and so forth, in which a biblical sentence has its function, are often

> ignored when interpreting it. The literary whole is not treated as if it were necessarily greater than the sum of its parts . . . the rabbis locate meaning primarily in that dimension of Scripture which *can be quoted* or which constitutes some syntactical unit.[5]

Fifthly, customs and practices all demand a biblical warrant. The custom of binding on *tefillin* for prayer needs to be justified from the Bible, even though in fact no (literal) reference to it can be found there, and the passages used in support of binding them on the left arm are not in fact relevant. But my use of 'in fact' would have been disputed by the rabbis, who see their way of using the Bible as attributing authority to the Bible. Conversely, all the Bible is about custom and practice – it is all *torah*.[6] It is generally impossible to determine whether a scriptural text gave rise to a certain ruling, or whether the ruling was, as a modern scholar would put it, 'read into' the biblical text. The rabbis lived, on the one hand, in a world wholly permeated by biblical phraseology, and on the other hand had a Bible which they read in accordance with the customs and practices of their form of Judaism. The lack of fit, at a literal level, between the biblical text and their own practices was invisible to them.

All this means that the Bible was being read very differently from how one would read any other book; probably the rabbis themselves would not have read other books in this way. There is what in modern times would be called a 'special hermeneutic' for reading Scripture – a set of reading techniques unique to the Bible. The Bible is seen as carrying an enormous weight of meaning, in which every tiniest feature is potentially important. Nothing is without significance, and one can never tell when one passage will suddenly become useful in helping to decide on the meaning of another. There is no redundancy – no feature of the text simply 'happens' to be so; and there are no insignificant omissions – thus the fact that the left hand is not specified, in the present case, cannot be without its importance. Scripture is like an enormous crossword puzzle, or a complex tapestry: it is nothing at all like any other book someone might write. A simple, surface reading is bound to be a false reading.

This kind of commentary on the Bible is known as midrash, from the verb *darash*, which means 'to seek out': it is a matter of getting ever deeper into the biblical text. To practise midrash one needs to know the Bible virtually by heart, so that a word that needs explanation immediately recalls the same word elsewhere, and even the same combination of words or (as in the example about the left hand) some particular feature of the wording that suggests a resemblance.

Rabbinic works are open to each other in much the same way as they see the different books and verses in the Bible as open to each other. The rabbis who appear in midrashic literature tend to be thought of as existing in one time frame, to the extent that they occasionally dine together, even though they are unlikely to have been contemporaries at all, and any rabbinic text may quote from any other. The rabbis see the Bible as having the same characteristics as their own texts, and their own texts as having the same characteristics as the Bible. There is 'no before and after' in rabbinic texts, any more than there is in Scripture; and 'readers whose ingenuity goes too far in constructing thematic unity where none was intended are not reined in by mere juxtaposition; and readers who fail to recognize unity where it was intended are not enlightened by it.'[7]

It is not exactly clear when midrashic interpretation of the Bible began, but there is evidence of it already in the New Testament. Thus in the Letter to the Hebrews we find a discussion of the text from Psalm 95:7–11, in which God is presented as saying that he was angry with the generation of Israelites who left Egypt with Moses: because of their persistent disobedience he swore that 'They shall not enter my rest.' There follows (Hebrews 3:12–4:11) a long homily that circles round the term 'rest', seeking to demonstrate that the passage was in fact a prediction of the 'rest' that Jesus would offer his followers. The reader, it is argued, might think that Joshua (in Greek, the same name as Jesus – *Iesous*) already gave the people 'rest' by taking them into the Promised Land. But if that were so, the text would not say, 'They shall not enter my rest', which shows that there must still be a 'rest' to be entered into. And that 'rest' is the possession of the eternal Sabbath that God will give the disciples of Jesus. This interpretation is of course different from what any rabbi would have produced, since it assumes that Jesus is the crucial figure; but the way of arguing is akin to that in later rabbinic texts, ruling out *prima facie* interpretations of a biblical verse, and arguing for a different one by foraging Scripture, comparing text with text.

Midrash as a phenomenon occurs in all types of Jewish writing, including the great legal collections, the Mishnah (compiled in the early third century CE) and the later Talmuds, collections of commentary on the Mishnah: the Babylonian Talmud or *Bavli* and the Palestinian (Jerusalem) Talmud or *Yerushalmi*. These are arranged primarily by theme, drawing on scriptural texts as and when they are deemed necessary to the argument. But there are also lengthy texts known specifically as midrashim, of which the *Mekhilta* is one of the earliest, along with *Sifra* and *Sifre*.[8] From the early Middle Ages we have the 'Great Midrash', *Midrash Rabbah*, on the books of the Pentateuch and the five scrolls that are read in the liturgy: Song of Songs, Lamentations, Esther, Ecclesiastes and Ruth, as well as other midrashim.

Much of the material in the midrashim is not halakhic in character but aggadic.[9] The rabbis develop small stories on the basis of the biblical text, often, indeed, tall stories that were probably not meant to be taken too seriously. In the *Pirke de Rabbi Eliezer*, which may come from the Tannaitic period – the second or third century CE – there is a tale about the fate of the ram that was sacrificed by Abraham according to Genesis 22. God had instructed Abraham to sacrifice Isaac, his favourite son, but at the last moment, as Abraham was about to do so, God stayed his hand through a message sent by an angel, and substituted a ram instead:

> From that ram, which was created at the twilight, nothing came forth that was useless. The ashes formed the foundation of the inner altar used for the expiatory offering on the Day of Atonement. The sinews of the ram were the strings of the harp on which David played. The ram's skin was the girdle around the loins of Elijah . . . The horn of the ram of the left side was the one which marked the revelation at Mount Sinai . . . The horn of the right side, which is larger than that of the left, is destined in the future to be sounded in the world that is to come and at the ingathering of the exiles, as it is said 'And it shall come to pass in that day, that a great trumpet shall be blown' (Isaiah 27:13), and it is said 'And the Lord shall be king over all the earth' (Zechariah 14:9).[10]

Evident here is the rabbinic principle that 'there is no before and after in Scripture'. Abraham, David, Elijah, the revelation to Moses on Sinai, the Temple and the world to come all exist in one dimension, and the one ram contributes to all of them. This can also be seen from the following excerpt from the *Mekhilta*, where past, present and future are blended together:

> You find that the prayers of the righteous are heard in the morning. Whence do we know about Abraham's morning? It is said: 'And Abraham rose early in the morning' [Genesis 22:3; other examples from the past follow] . . . Whence do we know about the mornings of the prophets destined to arise in the future? It is said: 'O Lord, in the morning shalt Thou hear my voice; in the morning will I order my prayer unto Thee, and will look

> forward' [Psalm 5:4; other examples follow from passages taken to be predictions] . . . Whence do we know about the morning of this world in general? It is said: 'They are new every morning; great is Thy faithfulness' [Lamentations 3:23].[11]

The early midrashim are the work of the generations of rabbis (the Tannaim), who worked in both the land of Israel and in Babylonia in the first three centuries of the Christian era. There are variations among them: there is, for example, another *Mekhilta*, the *Mekhilta of Rabbi Shimon bar Yohai*, which has subtle differences in the way it treats Scripture that it shares with other rabbinic commentaries such as *Sifre* and *Sifra*.[12] But to the outside observer, midrashic approaches have a substantial unity. James Kugel summarizes them as based on four assumptions about the Bible, which overlap with what we have already seen.

The first assumption is that the Bible is a cryptic text, and needs to be deciphered by the reader. Though it appears to be a consecutive account of events, or of laws, or of songs of praise, in reality it is a tissue of interconnected clues to a deeper sense. Each individual verse bears a meaning, and so does the interconnection of each verse with, potentially, each other verse, regardless of which books the verses appear in. There is little sense of the books as continuous discourse. As Benjamin Sommer points out, since the Middle Ages Jews have recognized certain salient stories in the Bible, such as the near-sacrifice of Isaac in Genesis 22, traditionally called the Binding of Isaac (in Hebrew, *Akedah*). But no such conception exists in earlier Jewish texts, where Genesis 22 is just a collection of individual verses, to be interpreted in relation to other verses that may not be in Genesis at all.[13]

The second assumption is that the Bible is always relevant, a belief shared by most Jews and Christians in all periods. To the question, 'Does the Bible illuminate the problem at hand?' the answer is always yes. It is simply a matter of getting the Bible to speak, and this can be done by the decipherment just described. To declare the biblical text outdated or irrelevant is simply not an option. This is a rabbinic idea, found also in early Christian writers, that has persisted to this day.

Thirdly, the Bible contains no contradictions but is perfectly harmonious. Much trouble is taken in midrash to reconcile differences between passages or verses that seem to challenge this assumption, particularly if they affect matters of practice. I already referred, in the Introduction, to the alleged efforts of Hananiah son of Hezekiah, who used 300 barrels of oil as he sat up late reconciling Ezekiel with the Torah – and thus averting the danger that Ezekiel might be declared non-canonical.

Fourthly, according to the rabbis the Bible is divinely inspired, not a merely human product. It is unlike all other books in its origin, not only in its content. That is why it can be treated in the ways just outlined, as no other book would be. This too confirms that for the early rabbis it did form a canon, a fixed list of books, since all the books within the canon are treated in these special ways and no books outside are – better evidence than any theoretical list of holy books.

These assumptions led to a number of detailed principles for interpretation. The earliest codification of them is attributed to Hillel, a near-contemporary of Jesus, who is said to have propounded seven *middot* or rules; in subsequent centuries the number was expanded, Rabbi Ishmael (of the *Mekhilta*) counting thirteen, and later interpreters still more. Some of them are generally recognized 'laws of thought' – for example, that one can argue from a lesser case to a greater one, what we call arguing *a fortiori* ('if one should avoid anger, how much more murder!'). But the *middot* are really codifications after the event of the way rabbis interpreted the Bible, rather than rules that they set out to apply; most of their work was instinctive, or learned by analogy, rather than rule-driven. We shall see that the same is true of Christian rules for interpretation.

Rabbinic biblical interpretation can strike the outsider as arbitrary and even perverse in the way it handles Scripture, with a determination to find the conclusions it seeks by hook or by crook. Such adverse judgements, which have in the past even fed anti-Semitism, are predicated on the assumption that Judaism is determined by the Bible. But though Judaism is a religion that is certainly a descendant of the Bible, it is by no means limited to its biblical heritage; and it uses the biblical text, often in a consciously playful way, to illustrate its practices and beliefs. In doing so it tries to imply that these practices and beliefs are already present in the biblical text, but this is not a literal claim. The ingenuity in finding other passages that seem to help interpret the one at hand, often by what look like almost random word associations, is part of a great love of Scripture, even though to some non-Jews it seems uncontrolled and, indeed, arbitrary. It has come to enjoy a new lease of life in recent literary readings of the Bible,[14] for which random association is no longer necessarily seen as a drawback, and more particularly in readings driven by psychoanalysis. As Alexander Samely points out, midrash is a kind of postmodernism *avant la lettre*.

CHRISTIAN MODES OF INTERPRETATION

For early Christians, too, the Bible (for them, of course, including the New Testament) was a special book that required special principles of interpretation. As we have seen, already within the New Testament itself there are readings of Old Testament passages that we could call midrashic. But there are also important differences from Jewish styles of interpretation. Christians had a strong sense (as I showed in Chapter 13) that the Scriptures told a coherent story about God's involvement in human affairs. They sometimes interpreted texts piecemeal in something like the rabbinic manner, but more often they were interested in the general drift and meaning of continuous passages, and this gives Christian biblical interpretation a different flavour from its Jewish counterpart, by at least the end of the second century. What it shares with rabbinic interpretation, however, is the belief that the Bible forms a single whole rather than being merely a collection of individual books, and that one book can be used in the interpretation of another. It is also, as we shall see, similar to midrash in concentrating on difficulties or inconsistencies in the text, though to a lesser extent.

At about the same time as the *Mekhilta of Rabbi Ishmael* was being compiled, the greatest early Christian scholar and teacher, Origen,[15] was working in his catechetical school in Alexandria, where he had been born to Christian parents. His father was martyred in 202 CE. Unlike so many of the early Christian writers whose works have come down to us, Origen was not a bishop. Late in life he was ordained priest, but this was a fateful decision, since it happened in Caesarea during his travels in the Holy Land, to the disapproval of his bishop in Alexandria. Origen moved to Caesarea and taught there, till he was caught up in the persecutions under the Emperor Decius and tortured, dying shortly after from the effects of his ill-treatment. (It was in Caesarea that he prepared the Hexapla, discussed below.[16])

At first sight, much of Origen's biblical interpretation is similar to rabbinic methods. For example, he is alert to any apparent redundancy in the wording of passages, and gives explanations of it very like those of the rabbis. Thus:

> The apparent redundancy of Genesis 24:16 in saying both that Rebekah was a 'virgin' *and* that 'no man had known [her]' in fact makes the point

> that she was holy both in body *and* spirit (*Hom. Gen.* 10.4). When God says, 'I have received the Levites from the midst of the sons of Israel' (Num. 3:12), the words 'the midst of' seem unnecessary. A careful search for other uses of the same expression in Scripture reveals its significance: to *stand* 'in the midst' is never to turn aside to the right or to the left, that is, to be sinless. This can only be affirmed of Christ (according to John the Baptist, Christ 'stands *in the midst of* you' [John 1:26]). The righteous (who, admittedly, are not sinless) may nonetheless be said to '*dwell* [not "stand"] in the midst' (so 2 Kings 4:13), and it is from their number that the Levites were chosen (*Hom. Num.* 3.2.3).[17]

Any rabbi would have been content with arguments of this kind, I believe. Also in a rabbinic manner, Origen finds deep meaning in passages that look repetitious and arid. To take a famous example: in his homily on the Old Testament book of Numbers, he deals with Numbers 33:1–49. This passage lists the forty-two places where the Israelites halted in their progression through the wilderness on the way to the Promised Land. Each time we read, 'They set out from A and encamped at B. They set out from B and encamped at C' – and so on, almost, the modern reader is likely to feel, ad infinitum, and certainly ad nauseam. Most readers today will skip this passage, but that is not a luxury that early Christian readers felt they could afford: Numbers was inspired Scripture, and the passage must have a significant meaning of some sort. Origen interprets it as teaching that there are forty-two stages in the life of the Christian, just as there were forty-two generations from Abraham to Jesus, according to Matthew 1:17. (Note that finding related passages, in the manner of the rabbis, now for a Christian commentator spans both Testaments.) Each of the place names has a symbolic sense; though Origen was not always able to suggest what a given name meant, he found meanings for most and was sure that all the names were significant in some way.[18]

The criss-crossing over several books to find details such as the number forty-two is typically rabbinic, and we might think that Origen was influenced by Jews: he was undoubtedly in touch with some, as we shall see. But there are also significant differences. Origen, like the rabbis, works with a model in which the whole Bible is a single network of interlocked meanings: any part can be elucidated from any other part. And for both the meanings uncovered by tracing cross-references can be cryptic: without Matthew 1:17 no one could have guessed that the forty-two stopping places were a symbol of the stages in the Christian life. But the rabbinic approach rarely uses the idea of symbols, or suggests a deeper, spiritual sense for texts. The rabbis tend to find parallels between parts of biblical stories: thus in *Genesis Rabbah* 55, discussed above, the binding of Isaac and the circumcision of Ishmael, Abraham's other son, are treated as corresponding to each other, while Abraham's action in saddling his donkey (Genesis 22:3) recalls that of Balaam in Numbers 22:21.[19] Origen, on the other hand, wrote, 'We ought not to suppose that historical events are types of other historical events and material things of other material things; rather material things are types of spiritual things and historical events of intelligible realities.'[20] The correspondences, we might say, are vertical for Origen – earth corresponds to heaven – rather than horizontal, as for the rabbis.

Taking the text literally is often, for Origen, a sign of stupidity. Writing on Genesis, he comments:

> Could any man of sound judgement suppose that the first, second, and third days [of creation] had an evening and a morning, when there were as yet no sun or moon or stars? Could anyone be so unintelligent as to think that God made a paradise somewhere in the east and planted it with trees, like a farmer, or that in that paradise he put a tree of life, a tree you could see and know with your senses, a tree you could derive life from by eating its fruit with the teeth in your head? When the Bible says that God used to walk in paradise in the evening, or that Adam hid behind a tree, no one, I think, will question that these are only fictions, stories of things that never actually happened, and that figuratively they refer to certain mysteries.[21]

The usual way of describing Origen's approach is to call it allegorical. He takes people, places and things in the text to point, not to other people, places and things, but to realities on a higher plane or in a symbolic world. If he is indebted to a Jewish writer, then it is to the first-century Alexandrian Jewish scholar Philo, who wrote in Greek, rather than to rabbis writing in Hebrew or Aramaic (on Philo see Chapter 6). Philo was a Platonist, who believed as Plato had that there was a world of ideas or eternal forms above and beyond the world of sense. Origen is probably not to be thought of as a Platonist,[22] but he borrowed some of his interpretative tools from Philo. For such thinkers the mundane physical realities the Bible referred to were really pointers to heavenly or spiritual things, and this could often be discerned by analysing their names, or other apparently unimportant things about the way they are described.[23] Thus Philo comments on the words Adam speaks in Genesis 2:23 on being presented with Eve, 'This now is bone of my bones and flesh of my flesh', asking why he says 'now':[24]

> The explanation is, external sensation exists now, having its existence solely with reference to the present moment. For the mind touches three separate points of time; for it perceives present circumstances, and it remembers past events, and it anticipates the future. But the external sensations have neither any anticipation of future events, nor are they subject to any feeling resembling expectation or hope, nor have they any recollection of past circumstances; but are by nature capable only of being affected by that which moves them at the moment, and is actually present.
>
> (Philo, *Allegorical Interpretation*, 2:42–3)

Eve is thus interpreted as a symbol or allegory for the world of sensation, as opposed to the mental or spiritual world of thought associated with the masculine figure of Adam (for Philo, women are obviously less rational than men – this was a familiar trope in antiquity). Philo treats the literal sense of the Bible as much inferior to its latent spiritual meaning: 'Probably there was an actual man called Samuel, but we conceive of the Samuel of the Scripture not as a living compound of body and soul, but as a mind which rejoices in the service and worship of God.'[25]

Origen uses allegory in a rather similar way: in his exposition of the parable of the Good Samaritan, the Samaritan who stopped to help the injured man is to be understood as Christ; the man's journey from Jerusalem to Jericho is our own decline from heavenly to earthly things; the bandits who attacked the man are hostile spiritual forces or demons; the inn to which the Samaritan took the man for safety and restoration is the Church; and so on.[26] Irenaeus had earlier followed a similar line of thought,[27] and much the same interpretation would appear later in Augustine.[28] The literal meaning did not present a problem for these writers, nor was it trivial – on the contrary – but they thought in terms of an additional symbolic or metaphorical dimension as part of the richness of the text. Augustine would take an analogous line with the exodus story: 'the people, according to the Old Testament, are liberated from Egypt; the people, according to the New Testament, are liberated from the devil . . . Just as the Egyptians pursue the Jews as far as the sea, so Christians are pursued by their sins as far as baptism.'[29]

In explaining the claim that Joshua wrote a copy of the law in the presence of the sons of Israel (Joshua 8:32), Origen takes the literal, physical action as an impossibility. So the 'letter' of the text must be a clue to an underlying meaning: Deuteronomy, in Greek the 'second law', is written by God on believers' hearts:

> How can he write so long a book with the sons of Israel remaining there to the end, or even, how could the stones of the altar bear the contents of such a long book? . . . [O]ur Lord Jesus does not need much time to write Deuteronomy, that is, the second law, in the heart and spirit of believers who are worthy of being chosen for the construction of the altar; to inscribe there the law of the spirit.[30]

One of the features that Origen shares with the rabbis is that, just as with them, so with him there is a desire to read the Scripture so that it accords with the precepts of the faith he professes. In the Jewish case, this means primarily to ensure that the (Hebrew) Bible is read as conforming to the established customs of the Torah: practical discrepancies have to be reconciled, as we have seen. In Origen's case it is more a matter of squaring the Scriptures with Christian doctrine, and ensuring that they are read in accordance with the 'rule of faith'. Given that the Old Testament, at least, comes from a Semitic rather than a Greek philosophical world, this often requires a tour de force. For example, at a literal level the Old Testament seems to imply that God has a physical body with hands, arms and a face.[31] For Origen, as for Christians in general, this is simply untrue; such passages must therefore be interpreted metaphorically. (The rabbis also believed that God was non-physical, but the issue was not of central concern for them, since it had no implications for the practice of Jewish life.)

Origen's allegorical method results in the implication that the Old Testament is really a Christian text – much as we saw to be true for *Barnabas* in an earlier generation.[32] Like Paul, Origen thought that references to the crossing of the Red Sea by the Israelites coming out of Egypt really referred to Christian baptism: 'What the Jews supposed to be a crossing of the sea, Paul calls a baptism; what they supposed to be a cloud, Paul asserts is the Holy Spirit' (*Homily on Exodus*, 5; cf. 1 Corinthians 10). The whole ritual and sacrificial system of the Old Testament is a veiled allusion to the sacrifice of Christ, just as the Letter to the Hebrews implies: its mundane form has ceased to be, but it lives on in the realm of symbol. It is hard to resist the conclusion of Soulen, discussed in Chapter 13, that this is a form of supersessionism: Judaism ceases to have any independent validity, and Christianity takes over its texts and reads them as foreshadowing the true reality, Jesus Christ. That is what most of the Christian Fathers believed, and it is a problem today for Christians who wish to affirm the continuing importance of Judaism and to reject the idea that it has been superseded by Christianity. The 'spiritual' reading, which is what Origen calls it, decontextualizes the Old Testament. A particularly striking instance of this is his discussion of Psalm 137, 'By the rivers of Babylon':

> O daughter Babylon, you devastator!
>   Happy shall they be who pay you back
>   what you have done to us!
> Happy shall they be who take your little ones
>   and dash them against the rock!
>
> (Psalm 137:8–9)

Origen comments:

> Blessed is the one who seizes . . . the little ones of Babylon, which are understood to be nothing else but these 'evil thoughts' that confound and disturb our heart. For this is what Babylon means. While these thoughts are still small and just beginning, they must be seized and dashed against the 'rock' who is Christ [cf. 1 Corinthians 10:4], and, by his order, they must be slain, so that nothing in us 'may remain to draw breath' [Joshua 11:14].
>
> (Origen, *Homily on Joshua*, 15:3)

Allegorization removes a scandalous aspect of this psalm, its apparent encouragement of killing babies in time of war; but the price is that the psalm is lifted out of its ancient Israelite context and brought into the Christian ambit with its concentration on 'spiritual' matters. The opposition to the Old Testament that had been expressed by such as Marcion is thus deftly avoided: read properly – that is, allegorically – there is nothing in the psalm to offend Christian belief or ethics. Marcion had opposed allegorizing readings that made offensive passages in the Old Testament less offensive to Christian sensibilities: not because he had Jewish sympathies, but precisely because he did not, and because he thought that allegorizing made it possible for Christians to go on affirming texts that they ought to be rejecting. But Marcion had lost, and more than half a century later Origen was able to build on his defeat, and undertake a systematically allegorical reading of the Old Testament text.[33]

Allegorization extended even to the New Testament, and not only to the parables, which clearly are in some sense symbolic anyway, but also to New Testament narratives and sayings. In Matthew 16:28, which directly precedes the story of Jesus' transfiguration, Jesus says that 'there are some standing here who will not taste death before they see the Son of Man coming in his kingdom'. This, too, presents problems: surely the disciples did die before the coming of the Son of Man, if that is interpreted to mean what Christians have called the Second Coming? Origen deals with the difficulty in two ways. First, he explains (*Commentary on Matthew*, 12:32) that at a simple and literal level one may see the word of Jesus here fulfilled in the transfiguration – that it was a kind of 'coming in his kingdom' – which the three disciples Peter, James and John did indeed 'see'. Secondly, there is a higher sense, more appropriate for mature Christians: those who stand beside Jesus see him coming, not in humility and suffering as in his passion, but in glory and kingship on the 'high mountain' which is his divine majesty. Thus here, just as in his interpretation of the Old Testament, Origen looks for a higher level, a reference to heavenly things, above the literal sense of Scripture. The classic and most systematic example of this mode of interpretation is in his commentary on the Song of Songs, which he is among the earliest writers to treat as an allegory of the relation between the soul and God, rather than as the love between a human man and woman, as most modern commentators suppose was its original meaning.[34]

Allegory was not invented by Origen, nor even by Philo. It had long been deployed in interpreting the works of Homer, as a way of dealing with the scandalous aspects of the activities of the gods, who behave in many respects like immoral human beings. Interpreters, especially in Alexandria, Origen's (and Philo's) home town, had explained the human foibles of the gods as pointing to spiritual realities, thereby neutralizing the offence the stories could give. The epics of Homer had a somewhat canonical status in Hellenistic culture, and needed to be sanitized for innocent readers. As Martin Goodman points out, 'no one in the first century CE wished to live literally in the moral universe of Achilles or Odysseus'.[35] Hence such figures were given a symbolic interpretation. Origen inherited this tradition, which had been used before him by Christian writers, and applied it extensively to the Bible. Though the God of the Bible was not immoral in the ways that the Olympian gods were in Homer, nevertheless he often did and said things that seemed unworthy of his exalted status, and (especially in the Old Testament) was presented as all too human in losing his temper, changing his mind, and generally acting as an earthly tyrant might act. Allegory could remove all these problems at a stroke.

But Origen went further than resorting to allegory as a defensive device. He commended it as positively sublime. A book that required it was higher in status and authority than any lowly, literal work could be.

We find this in his reply to the pagan philosopher Celsus, who had criticized Christians for having (in both Testaments) a scripture unworthy of any god worth worshipping. Celsus points to the scandal of the angry god of the Old Testament and also to such problems as the discrepancies among the Gospels – matters that anti-Christian writers were to continue to insist on throughout the generations, down to our own day. Origen's reaction was not to go on the defensive and try to deny or justify the charges, but rather to argue that they are to be seen as clues pointing to deeper meanings. And a book that contains such things is sublime – just like the works of Homer, which in Hellenistic culture were agreed to be so. Thus Origen seizes the high ground. The more problems there are in the Bible, the more it requires allegorizing interpretation, and therefore the more exalted it is.

A modern reader is likely to view this as somewhat disingenuous, even cynical, but Origen appears really to have believed it. Problems in the text mark the existence of buried treasure. This can be seen, for example, in the food laws of Leviticus and Deuteronomy, still the basis for Orthodox Jewish practice. These cannot, Origen believed, be taken seriously at face value, and consequently they point to deeper truths about purity and holiness of soul. A Jewish reader is bound to find Origen unconvincing on this, failing to see the moral seriousness with which the kosher regulations are taken in Jewish life, and altogether blind to their spiritual value. (Philo had been content to detect allegorical meanings beyond the letter of the regulations, but he explicitly denies that the letter of the law therefore does not need to be observed.[36]) By now, Judaism and Christianity had truly diverged, and one did not understand the other.

Origen's interpretative principles are not only demonstrated in his practice of commenting on specific texts; he is also the first Christian author to have written a reflective treatise on biblical interpretation, book IV of his *On First Principles*.[37] Here he argues that

> Divine wisdom took care that certain stumbling-blocks, or interruptions, to the historical meaning should take place, by the introduction into the midst (of the narrative) of certain impossibilities and incongruities; that in this way the very interruption of the narrative might, as by the interposition of a bolt, present an obstacle to the reader, whereby he might refuse to acknowledge the way which conducts to the ordinary meaning; and being thus excluded and debarred from it, [h]e might be recalled to the beginning of another way, in order that, by entering upon a narrow path, and passing to

> a loftier and more sublime road, he might lay open the immense breadth of divine wisdom. This, however, must not be unnoted by us, that as the chief object of the Holy Spirit is to preserve the coherence of the spiritual meaning, either in those things which ought to be done or which have been already performed, if He anywhere finds that those events which, according to the history, took place, can be adapted to a spiritual meaning, He composed a texture of both kinds in one style of narration, always concealing the hidden meaning more deeply; but where the historical narrative could not be made appropriate to the spiritual coherence of the occurrences, He inserted sometimes certain things which either did not take place or could not take place; sometimes also what might happen, but what did not: and He does this at one time in a few words, which, taken in their 'bodily' meaning, seem incapable of containing truth, and at another by the insertion of many. And this we find frequently to be the case in the legislative portions, where there are many things manifestly useful among the 'bodily' precepts, but a very great number also in which no principle of utility is at all discernible, and sometimes even things which are judged to be impossibilities. Now all this, as we have remarked, was done by the Holy Spirit in order that, seeing those events which lie on the surface can be neither true nor useful, we may be led to the investigation of that truth which is more deeply concealed, and to the ascertaining of a meaning worthy of God in those Scriptures which we believe to be inspired by Him.

Finding a meaning 'worthy of God' is always Origen's primary concern, and that, for him, often entails a non-literal interpretation.

Sometimes our assumption that Origen allegorized literal texts can hit a surprise, where suddenly he super- or re-allegorizes a text that we regard as allegorical (parabolic or metaphorical) from the start. Take the parable of the labourers in the vineyard (Matthew 20:1–16):

> 'For the kingdom of heaven is like a landowner who went out early in the morning to hire labourers for his vineyard. After agreeing with the labourers for the usual daily wage, he sent them into his vineyard. When he went out about nine o'clock, he saw others standing idle in the market-place; and he said to them, "You also go into the vineyard, and I will pay you whatever is right." So they went. When he went out again about noon and about three o'clock, he did the same. And about five o'clock he went out and found others standing around; and he said to them, "Why are you standing here idle all day?" They said to him, "Because no one has hired us." He said to them, "You also go into the vineyard." When evening came, the owner of the vineyard said to his manager, "Call the labourers and give them their pay,

> beginning with the last and then going to the first." When those hired about five o'clock came, each of them received the usual daily wage. Now when the first came, they thought they would receive more; but each of them also received the usual daily wage. And when they received it, they grumbled against the landowner, saying, "These last worked only one hour, and you have made them equal to us who have borne the burden of the day and the scorching heat." But he replied to one of them, "Friend, I am doing you no wrong; did you not agree with me for the usual daily wage? Take what belongs to you and go; I choose to give to this last the same as I give to you. Am I not allowed to do what I choose with what belongs to me? Or are you envious because I am generous?" So the last will be first, and the first will be last.'

To the modern reader the labourers are simply characters in an illustrative story, a parable or, if you prefer, an allegory. But Origen further interprets them as standing for five stages in the history of Israel: the first men hired represent the generations from Adam to Noah, those hired at nine o'clock those from Noah to Abraham, those hired at noon the generations from Abraham to Moses, those at three in the afternoon those from Moses to Jesus Christ, and those at five o'clock people from Christ to the present day.[38] This is a reminder – a point that will arise again in the next chapter – that the 'literal' sense of a text can be already 'allegorical'. Parables intentionally use the characters in the story they tell as symbols or metaphors, and Origen is so committed to allegorical reading that he is not content to leave them there, but metaphorizes what are already metaphors.

ORIGEN AS A BIBLICAL SCHOLAR

I have deliberately called the first part of Origen's Bible the Old Testament, because it is in no sense the Hebrew Bible he is concerned with in his interpretations. What he interprets – what all the Fathers interpret – is the Greek Old Testament, including the apocryphal/deutero-canonical books. But Origen did not naively embrace the Greek Scriptures, which he knew from childhood: he knew well that they were a translation of a Hebrew original, and he took steps to learn some Hebrew from Jewish contemporaries. Origen was the first Christian writer whom we can reasonably call not just a biblical interpreter, but a biblical scholar, and even, in something approaching a modern sense of that term, a biblical critic, who asked difficult questions about the coherence and history of the original text.

As a scholar, Origen was aware of differences between manuscripts of the Gospels and of the Old Testament books, and also that, in the case of the Old Testament, the Greek translation was not always an exact rendering of the Hebrew original. He knew about 'the Three', that is, the three Hellenistic scholars of Jewish background who had in the second century CE retranslated the Hebrew Bible into Greek in an attempt to improve on the Septuagint version: Aquila, Symmachus and Theodotion (see Chapters 12 and 18). All of them produced noticeably more word-for-word renderings of the Hebrew than the Septuagint translators had done, Aquila particularly so.[39] Origen constructed a book in six parallel columns, known as the Hexapla, containing the Septuagint, the Hebrew text, the Hebrew in a transliteration into Greek letters, and the versions of the Three. The Hexapla in its entirety is lost: it will have consisted of about fifteen volumes, totalling some 6,000 pages. Parts can be reconstructed from the fragments that remain in citations in the writings of early Christian teachers.

This massive work, of which there may only ever have been a single copy, was meant to make it possible to check the Septuagint translation against the other texts and versions, with a view to arriving at the best readings. Origen marked, in the Septuagint text, places where there was significant variation from the Hebrew original, either omissions or additions. This was the kind of work that literary scholars in the library of Alexandria practised on the Greek classics, but Origen was the first to apply it to the Bible. He was fully aware that the New Testament writers mostly followed the Septuagint rather than the Hebrew, and suggested that sometimes Paul in particular quoted the Old Testament text from memory, or even adjusted it slightly to fit his purpose.[40]

As a biblical critic, Origen anticipated many of the findings of modern times. For example, he noticed discrepancies between the Gospels – possibly more freely than others might have done, because he was then able to argue that they pointed to spiritual meanings, whereas anyone with a more literal mind might have been embarrassed. Stephen and Martin Westerholm cite the following examples:

> If, as the Synoptic Gospels relate, Jesus' baptism was followed ('immediately', according to Mark 1:12–13) by forty days of fasting in the wilderness and temptation by Satan, it is noteworthy that John's Gospel not only fails to mention the temptation, but that its chronology ('the next day' after Jesus' baptism, 'the next day' after that, 'on the third day' [John 1:35, 43; 2:1]) apparently excludes it (*Com. John* 10.10). John the Baptist is said

> to have been arrested 'about the time of Jesus' temptation' in Matthew (Matt. 4:1–12); but he is active 'for a long time' in the Gospel of John (*Com. John* 10.35). Events that, in the Synoptics, are said to have taken place on a single trip to Jerusalem (e.g. the triumphal entry and the cleansing of the temple), are divided up, in John, between two trips separated from each other by a host of other deeds and travels (*Com. John* 10.129). 'On the basis of numerous other passages also, if someone should examine the Gospels carefully to check the disagreement so far as the historical [i.e. literal] sense is concerned . . . he would grow dizzy' (*Com. John* 10.14).[41]

Sometimes Origen argues that contradictions can be reconciled, but for the most part he is content to observe them and then to contend that they show that the Gospels are not to be understood at a merely historical level: the discrepancies do not matter for a spiritual reading. 'In order to achieve their mystical end, [the evangelists] transposed some episode or other and placed in some setting an event accomplished elsewhere, or even . . . reversed the order of the times and modified the terms of the discourse.'[42]

Many modern Christians would concur, being unfazed by differences among the Gospels because they feel that the Jesus who appears in them has a clear profile which is unaffected by discordant details. Modern critics generally use the discrepancies to argue for the separate integrity of each Gospel as a constructed work, so that they become part of an argument against the historical accuracy of any of the Gospels and in favour of seeking to reconstruct the historical reality through such endeavours as the 'quest for the historical Jesus' (see Chapter 17). Origen was much less inclined than we are to think of each of the evangelists as having a separate story to tell, and for him everything in the Gospels was true, at some level, whether literal or spiritual. But he was sensitive to differences of style and approach, having been trained in literary appreciation. He produced, for example, what is still the standard set of arguments for thinking that Hebrews is not by Paul, on stylistic grounds, when so many of the Fathers simply assumed that it was Pauline.

THE SCHOOL OF ANTIOCH

Origen's importance for subsequent biblical interpreters is incalculable. More or less all of them accepted and applied his allegorical method of reading the Old Testament, and benefited from his scholarship as shown in the compilation of the Hexapla. In the following century, however, a school of interpreters arose in the Syrian city of Antioch which departed significantly from his approach. Three important representatives of the Antiochene school are John Chrysostom, Theodore of Mopsuestia (a small town in Cilicia, now Turkey, 350–428 CE), and Diodore of Tarsus (d. 390 CE).[43] A later writer in the same tradition is Theodoret of Cyrus (393–457 CE).

It has become usual to say that the Antiochenes rejected allegorical reading in favour of literalism. They tend to avoid messianic interpretations of prophetic and psalmic texts, preferring to see them – as do Jewish commentators – as fulfilled in Jewish history, and so not still awaiting fulfilment in Christ. This led to accusations of 'Judaizing' from contemporaries of a different persuasion. But at other times their interpretation can seem just as allegorical as Origen's, and they owed him a great debt. For example, Theodoret refers to the title of Psalm 30, 'A Psalm. A song at the dedication of the Temple' and takes it to refer to 'the restoration of human nature that Christ the Lord accomplished by accepting death on behalf of us, destroying death and giving us hope of resurrection'[44] – hardly a literal interpretation. The Antiochene concern was that the text should be read as morally and spiritually edifying, and not collapse into symbols; it somewhat resembles Jewish reading, not in being non-allegorical but in sharing the Jewish concern for ensuring that the text had something to say about *halakhah*, that it was relevant to everyday life.

As part of this concern, Antiochene interpreters attended to questions of genre and to the flow of argument in a text, indebted for this to their training in rhetoric. They were all serious intellectuals who could have had careers in public life in Antioch, a large and prosperous city with an administrative class and in which Christians could lead a respectable life, no longer the persecuted sect of the early years. The Antiochenes had much experience in studying classical texts, and did not see them as collections of fragments, but as continuous and well-structured arguments, and they applied the same principles to the Bible. Frances Young writes:

> Origen was happy to decode symbols without worrying about textual or narrative coherence, and the symbols were tokens . . . But this meant the wording of the text found its significance in jots and tittles over-exegeted, rather than in context and flow. The Antiochenes sought a different kind of relationship between wording and content, style and meaning. The narrative sequence and flow of argument mattered. The text was not a pretext for something else.[45]

> So neither literalism as such, nor an interest in historicity as such, stimulated the Antiochene reaction against Origenist allegory, but rather a different approach to finding meaning in literature which had its background in the educational system of the Graeco-Roman world. Perhaps we could say that it was not 'allegory' as such that they objected to; for allegory was a standard figure of speech, and, if the text carried some indication of its presence, even allegory could be allowed. What they resisted was the type of allegory that destroyed textual coherence.[46]

The Antiochenes were concerned, as Irenaeus had been in an earlier generation, with what was called the *hypothesis* of Scripture, meaning its overall thrust or drift, rather than its minute detail. (How was one to establish this? Mainly, Christian interpreters agreed, by attention to the Church's rule of faith, which provided, as we have seen, an interpretative framework within which to read the Bible.) At the time, Antiochene insistence on the 'historical' or 'plain' sense of the text rather than any possible allegorical or metaphorical meaning was sometimes seen, like their interest in the historical fulfilment of prophecy, as rather Jewish. But, as discussed above, most rabbinic biblical interpretation is actually far from interested in any 'plain' sense of the text, and is certainly not concerned with its argumentative or narrative flow; on the contrary, the rabbis tend to divide the text into verses, or even words, and interpret them out of context. In this respect rabbinic reading is much closer to Origen's allegorical reading than it is to Antiochene concern for a holistic interpretation of the text.

The differences between Origen and the Antiochenes should not be exaggerated. When interpreting obscure parts of the Old Testament, especially those traditionally understood as foreshadowing Christ, they do diverge significantly; but in reading the Pauline letters or, indeed, the Gospels, which have a clear flow of discourse or narrative, the gap between them narrows. Origen did not allegorize Paul, but explained his train of thought, and so did the Antiochenes. In interpreting discursive texts such as the letters, all alike were concerned with the flow of the argument – what in Greek was called the *akolouthia*, the 'sequence'.

Surveying even some of the most bitter arguments about biblical interpretation in the patristic age – the period from the end of New Testament times to the Council of Chalcedon in 451 CE[47] – the modern reader is likely to be struck more by what united than by what divided the major figures. The period was dominated by debates about the nature of Christ: was he divine as well as human, and, if so, in what sense? A major controversy that erupted around the time of the Council of Nicaea (325 CE) was waged between those who would later be regarded as orthodox in their doctrine and the followers of Arius (256–336 CE). Arius maintained that Jesus, though in a sense divine, was ultimately the greatest of God's creatures – a kind of super-archangel, while his opponents claimed that he was 'of one being' (Greek *homoousios*) with God the Father himself.

Alongside the philosophical issues involved was a discussion of biblical evidence. The main proof text used by the Arians was Proverbs 8:22, where personified Wisdom (see Chapter 3) says, 'The LORD created me at the beginning of his work, the first of his acts of long ago.' They argued that this clearly implied that the Son was a creation of God rather than himself divine. The Arians' opponents engaged in various interpretative ploys to avoid this conclusion. But on two points the two sides did not differ. First, they took it for granted that the text did indeed refer to Christ – where a modern biblical scholar would tend to say that it is about wisdom as personified in the thought of the ancient Israelite wisdom tradition, and has nothing to do with Jesus. Secondly, they all argued on the basis of the Greek verb *ektisen*, 'created': it did not occur to anyone to ask about the meaning of the underlying original Hebrew. Rather as the fact that the King James Bible is a translation, not the very Word of God in every letter, does not trouble some contemporary 'King James Bible fundamentalists' (see Chapter 18), they seem to have been oblivious to the fact that the Bible they were all using was a Greek translation.

The hallowed tradition of a particular version of the Bible overrides any awareness that it is, after all, a translation, with all the room for inexactness that that implies. Origen had been acutely aware of this, of course – as the compiler of the Hexapla and as one who knew at least some Hebrew, he could not fail to be. Yet he too interpreted always on the basis of the Greek text, pressing its exact wording as if it were itself inspired Scripture. Indeed, he believed it *was* inspired. This is no less true for the Antiochenes: though working in a region, Syria, where the local language was Semitic, they were mostly monoglot Greek speakers, and treated the Septuagint simply as the Bible. (Where the New Testament is concerned, naturally both sides were on firmer ground, since they read that in the Greek in which it was originally written – even though we must recall that the sayings of Jesus in the Gospels were almost certainly spoken in Aramaic.)

Thus ancient Bible readers, however much they differed, often shared certain assumptions that are not current today. It was taken as a given that the Old Testament spoke of Jesus. For Origen, it did so through allegorical use of language; for the Antiochenes, through overt prophecy, which was to be interpreted more literally. But the idea that the Old Testament did not speak of Jesus *at all* would have struck them all as shocking, and not to be contemplated. Modern readers may wish to venerate these great interpreters, who had sharp minds (and sometimes also sharp tongues); yet their Bible-reading worked on different principles from almost anyone's today.[48]

BIBLICAL INTERPRETATION IN THE WEST

So far we have considered the Greek east, to which even Irenaeus, though he worked in what is now Lyon, originally belonged. It was in the eastern Mediterranean that the major intellectual development of Christian thought took place in the first three centuries of the Church's life. With the division of the Roman Empire into eastern and western halves in the late third century CE, Christian traditions began to develop differently: the most obvious sign of this is the wide divergence between eastern Orthodox and Roman Catholic liturgy that is still familiar today. The Greek east was the home of intricate philosophical thought about the Christian faith, while in the Latin west more energy was put into the practical organization of the Church. The Emperor Constantine made Christianity the official religion of the empire, and in 325 CE convened the Council of Nicaea, himself converting to Christianity on his deathbed in 337. The official recognition of the Christian faith made great differences to the administration and prosperity of the Church, and encouraged the growth of Christian literature. Constantine commissioned fifty copies of the Bible from Caesarea alone. The interpretation of the Bible, however, was little affected: the traditions already established continued.

Biblical interpretation in the west developed less subtly than in the east, and many of the controversies among different groups of interpreters passed western Christians by. By the fifth century, however, we do find one major treatise on the interpretation of the Bible in the form of the work *On Christian Teaching* (*De doctrina christiana*) by Augustine of Hippo, in Roman North Africa, and perhaps the most significant contribution to biblical study in the Latin world, Jerome's new translation of the whole Bible into Latin, which we will discuss in Chapter 18.

Augustine often follows Origen's lead in accepting the need to interpret metaphorically when the text is obscure, inconsistent, or factually false;[49] but he adds a general principle that had not occurred to the earlier scholar. This is that the Bible is not only to be interpreted in line with the Church's rule of faith, but also that it must be read so as to encourage love – love of God and neighbour. Scripture accommodates itself to the capacity of every reader, and the non-expert will sometimes not understand the text at the literal level, but yet will be enabled by it to increase in love. Any interpretation that does not promote love can only be a misinterpretation, however learned it may be. So if the literal sense of the text offends against the principle of love, we may be sure that some deeper sense is intended. One consequence of this is that Augustine can at times sit quite loosely to the details of the text: for example, he says it does not matter just what Genesis 1 means by the 'firmament'. 'Our authors knew about the shape of the sky, whatever may be the truth of the matter. But the Spirit of God who was speaking through them did not wish to teach people about such things, which would contribute nothing to their salvation.'[50] At the same time, Augustine was not indifferent to contradictions in Scripture, and (as already observed) wrote an extensive work on the differences between the Gospels, arguing that they could all be harmonized by one means or another. Occasionally the differences are treated as trivial, but normally he finds ways of showing that they are apparent rather than real. This work, *On the Consensus of the Evangelists* (*De consensu evangelistarum*), is the first major attempt in a long line down to the present.

Augustine's concern for the ordinary reader comes out in his comments about the Song of Songs, which he treats as obviously allegorical. On the one hand he thinks that the fact that God expresses his teaching in the Song through metaphor and allegory makes it more attractive to the reader, who is consequently more likely to read it with interest and remember it; on the other hand, the text expresses through allegory nothing that cannot be found plainly stated elsewhere in the Bible. 'It is much more pleasant to learn lessons presented through imagery, and much more rewarding to discover meanings that are won only with difficulty . . . Virtually nothing is unearthed from these obscurities which cannot be found quite plainly expressed somewhere else.'[51] Like the Greek Fathers, Augustine believed in the inspiration and authority of the Greek translation of the Old Testament, even though he thought that ideally one would consult the Hebrew original (but he himself knew no Hebrew). He also believed that the longer Greek canon of the Old Testament should be accepted as authoritative. He and Jerome clashed over this: Jerome believed that Christians should follow the Hebrew canon, even though he translated the apocryphal/deutero-canonical books and used them in his own writings. For Augustine the longer Greek canon had simply come down to the Church and should not be questioned.[52]

THE FATHERS' APPROACH

For all the apparent wilfulness, to modern sensibilities, of their interpretative approaches,

> The Fathers did preserve what might be called the framework of the message of the Bible, the doctrines of creation, of the choice of the Jewish people by God, of the Incarnation, of the Atonement, of the resurrection and of judgement. They did not abandon what is today called the concept of *Heilsgeschichte* ['salvation history']. They may have undervalued the historical books and the messages of the prophets to their contemporaries, but they did not reject or completely obscure them. And they understood perfectly well the necessity of defending and valuing the historical career of Jesus, even though they may have conceived of the humanity of Christ very unimaginatively.[53]

Despite the piecemeal interpretation, which they sometimes share with rabbinic commentators, they remain concerned with the flow of the text. The Antiochenes are probably the best representatives of this approach, but it is not wholly lacking in any patristic authors:

> [Their aim in handling Scripture] was not to produce an entirely consistent system of doctrine which would somehow fit in every little detail of the Bible, nor was it to set up a biblical literalism which would treat the Bible as one treats a railway timetable. It was to discover, and to preach and teach, the burden, the purport, the drift, the central message of the Bible . . . Irenaeus describes this as the *hypothesis* of the Scriptures, Tertullian as the *ratio*, Athanasius as the *skopos*. They are aware that their treatment of details may be open to question . . . But they realise that what matters is, what the Bible comes to, where the main weight of its evidence lies, in what direction its thought thrusts.[54]

In short, the Fathers operate with the kind of interpretative framework described in Chapter 13, and it is this that controls even their most baroque flights of fancy in reading the detail of the text. They keep a grasp on what Luther, a millennium later, would describe as the 'matter' of Scripture (*res scripturae*) – what Scripture is ultimately about. In order to maintain this, however, they inevitably sometimes interpret individual parts of the Bible in forced ways, just as the rabbis do. It is part of the price which both Judaism and Christianity pay for having such a long, complex and internally inconsistent set of Scriptures.

15
The Middle Ages

THE BIBLE AS A BOOK[1]

When Charlemagne was enthroned as emperor in Aachen in 800 CE, Alcuin of York (735–804), his chief adviser on matters educational, presented him with a copy of the Latin Bible that he had revised at Charlemagne's direction.[2] The gift was a symbol of the emperor's commitment to the revival of learning. The choice of the Bible, rather than, say, a code of laws is an indication of the importance it was to have throughout the succeeding centuries. Like its near-contemporary, the great Book of Kells, a richly illustrated manuscript of the Gospels now housed in Trinity College, Dublin, Alcuin's Bible reminds us of the importance attributed to the Bible throughout the Middle Ages.

In Christian circles the Bible was revered as a holy object as well as reflected on for its content. There is an old stereotype that the laity were denied access to it until Protestants began to assert their right to read it. In reality, for most of the Middle Ages the Bible was accessible in principle, though the majority of people, being illiterate, could not read it for themselves. Bibles were also expensive to produce. But it was heard in the Church's liturgy, expounded in sermons, and illustrated in murals and stained-glass windows. Biblical stories were widely known, not only through formal instruction in church, but also through mystery plays and their equivalents throughout Europe. What was thought to be taken from the Bible was, however, sometimes really extra-biblical: we saw earlier how important a text such as the *Protevangelium of James* was in informing popular ideas of the nativity story, with Jesus' birth in a cave, Mary riding on a donkey, and Joseph as an old man who already had children. Few in medieval times would have known that these were not in Scripture – and that remains the case. The notion of an absolutely fixed and closed canon had still not fully arrived, for all that Fathers such as Athanasius had offered rulings on it. Not till the Council of Trent (which met between 1545 and 1563 in Trento and Bologna and sought to establish a Catholic response to the Protestant Reformation) was there a final ruling on its contents, though most whole Bibles (*pandects*, as they are known) in the Middle Ages included no material outside what is now recognized as canonical by Catholics. (They therefore always included the deutero-canonical books, but not works such as *The Shepherd* or *Barnabas*, unlike the earlier *Codex Sinaiticus*.)

Pandects, however, were for a long time the exception rather than the rule. Most manuscript Bibles contain only some portion of the whole – the Pentateuch, the wisdom books, or the Gospels.[3] The last are often found in decorated books intended for use at Mass, where the Gospel book was carried in procession before it was solemnly read to the congregation, as is still the practice in Catholic and Orthodox (and some Anglican/Episcopalian) churches. The older perception of the Bible as a collection of books rather than as a single book persisted for a long time. A fine early complete Bible, indeed the earliest complete Latin Bible extant to use the text of the Vulgate, Jerome's translation (see Chapter 18), is the *Codex Amiatinus*. This was written in the monastery of Wearmouth-Jarrow in the north-east of England, where Bede would spend his life in the early eighth century. Prepared as a gift for Pope Gregory II (669–731), it now resides in Florence. It was probably modelled on a pandect using the pre-Jerome Latin text, translated from the Greek rather than from the Hebrew, which was brought to Wearmouth-Jarrow from the library of Cassiodorus, who died in 585. He was a Roman statesman who became a monk in his old age, and founded a monastery on his estate in southern Italy called the Vivarium. This housed an impressive library containing more than one set of Bibles, including a pandect he called his *codex grandior*, his 'rather large' codex, comprising over 1,500 pages, which may well be the exemplar that found its way to Britain at the hands of Abbot Ceolfrith (d. 717). Cassiodorus' *Institutes*, written for the monastic community, contain much material on the Scriptures, which he too still treated as essentially a library of individual books rather than as a single text, despite having them all copied into single volumes. The *Institutes* provides a guide to the contents and correct interpretation of the Bible, and an account of the Fathers who had expounded it. Cassiodorus was a contemporary of Benedict (480–547), founder of the Benedictine order of monks, but unlike Benedict he considered the task of the monk to be focused less on

The *bible moralisée*: the Annunciation to the Virgin Mary and her response as an example of humble obedience, from an illuminated manuscript commissioned perhaps by Blanche of Castile to mark the marriage of her son Louis IX in 1234.

meditation on Scripture for the cultivation of virtue and more on study for the sake of theological learning. It is a contrast which, as we shall see, would characterize the respective attitudes of monks and friars in later centuries.[4] The two ideals do not necessarily conflict, but they represent different ways of approaching the Bible.

In the eleventh century there developed a taste for huge, so-called Atlantic Bibles (named for Atlas, the giant in Greek mythology who carried the world on his shoulders), usually in more than one enormous volume. These were in part luxury objects, but most were intended as gifts for monasteries, where they might serve as lectern Bibles. Some accordingly lack both the Psalms and the Gospels, which would have had their own books for liturgical use; had these gigantic Bibles been intended for study, the omission of these central texts would be much more surprising. Some large Bibles, being copied particularly carefully, also served as exemplars against which other biblical manuscripts could be checked and corrected.[5] They sometimes have marginal notes giving instructions to scribes, as we shall see that Jewish Bibles also do, and to a far greater extent. About 100 Atlantic Bibles still exist, in whole or part, and are often of exceptional beauty in both script and illumination.

Whole Bibles, in a much smaller format, became more common towards the end of the twelfth century, when they were needed by the new religious orders of friars, Franciscans and Dominicans (founded respectively in 1209 and 1216), who preached as they moved from place to place rather than being static in their monasteries as the older orders had been. Technology developed to facilitate this itinerancy, with thinner vellum and smaller handwriting giving rise to Bibles that even today appear minute, small enough to put in a pocket. Although the popular image of Bibles being not only used but also copied by monks is accurate for an earlier period, from the mid twelfth century at least Bibles were also produced in secular scriptoria and workshops, and sold like any other goods to a ready market. Even the earlier giant Bibles had often required local or peripatetic craftsmen to supply skills not possessed by the scribe, such as illumination and work with gold leaf. The friars' small portable Bibles were all commercially produced.

These broad developments in the twelfth and early thirteenth centuries were accompanied by some striking experiments, such as the creation of the *bible moralisée*. This 'moralized Bible', of which just four copies remain, was a lavishly illustrated manuscript containing pictures only of the narratives – of both Old and New Testaments – condensed into medallions. Each page had four of these, accompanied by another four medallions giving the moral interpretation of each story, sometimes through typological connections – for example, between Old and New Testament stories – but sometimes with illustrations of scenes from contemporary life that show obedience or disobedience to the message of the biblical incident in question. Thus the moral sense of the text was given pictorially rather than in words. Such Bibles were luxury items, in many cases intended for the French and Spanish aristocracy or royalty,[6] and lay at one extreme of the pictorial Bibles produced in the thirteenth century, often with superb illustrations and only brief captions in French or Latin.

In the late thirteenth and early fourteenth centuries another kind of illustrated Bible came into being, the so-called *biblia pauperum*, 'Bible of the poor', of which about eighty examples survive. The name is misleading (and does not appear in the Bibles themselves), since they were designed for lay Christians of the literate middling classes, and probably also for clergy who had to preach on the Bible from time to time. They focused on the mystical and meditative dimensions of the text, mediated through an illustrated life of Christ enhanced, again, with typological parallels – pictures of the near-sacrifice of Isaac next to the crucifixion, for example. These were mostly produced in German-speaking areas, and the text was often a mixture of Latin and German, commonly still including material from non-canonical books. Biblical references are given, implying that the reader could look up the relevant passages in his or her own Bible.

Early Latin Bibles (and Greek ones, for that matter) were generally written without spaces between the words. This is slightly less inconvenient in a language with many inflections than in one such as English, because when you spot an inflection you know that it is the end of a word; but even so the lack of word division could slow down reading and lead to ambiguities. Medieval Bibles introduced spaces and other devices to aid the reader. Punctuation made slow progress, though phrases and sentences were often marked off with a space, a custom already recommended by Jerome. But other marks were common, and in Bibles intended for liturgical use it is usual to find indications of where readings are to begin and end. Chapter division is also a medieval invention, thought to have occurred for the first time in England (and traditionally ascribed to Archbishop Stephen Langton [1150–1228]), though the chapters were shorter than our current ones.[7] It was in Paris that chapter-numbering became general. (In *Codex Amiatinus*, older marginal chapter numbers have been crossed out and replaced with a newer system of longer chapters.) The twelfth- and thirteenth-century portable Bibles have prominent chapter numbers as well as running heads, so that finding a given text is no harder than in a modern printed Bible. Verse-numbering is a still later addition to the Latin Bible, deriving from the Paris printer Robert Estienne, a Protestant who had fled from persecution in Paris to the safety of Geneva, in 1534 – though Hebrew Bibles had had such subdivisions, but without numbers, from much earlier times, and the Latin versions of the Psalms had long been divided into verses for singing and recitation.

Twelfth- and thirteenth-century Bibles were produced in great numbers, implying a wide literate readership that wanted a standardized and convenient format, with running heads and prologues to the biblical books (often adopted from Jerome) as well as notes to explain biblical names. They were produced by a growing book trade, especially in Paris. 'More Bibles survive from the thirteenth century than any other artefact, except perhaps coins and buildings.'[8] Scribes acquired great facility in writing Gothic script, often small enough for a Bible to be no larger than a typical modern one.

INTERPRETING THE BIBLE: CHRISTIAN APPROACHES

In many ways, medieval Christian attitudes to the Bible are continuous with those of the Fathers. They share the same underlying assumption that what the Bible teaches is in line with Christian doctrine, and that the text must be interpreted so as to ensure that that is so. It did not occur to anyone to read the text on its own terms outside the framework of the Christian faith: to do so would have made it irrelevant to the Christian reader. But much effort went into defining just how faith and text were related, and the Middle Ages is the great period for conscious reflection on the nature of biblical authority, inspiration and interpretation.[9]

We saw how Origen in particular pursued an allegorical sense in many scriptural passages. Where the straightforward meaning of the text was unproblematic, Origen accepted it. But where it was difficult, and especially where it seemed to him absurd, he argued that it must be meant in some other, metaphorical or allegorical sense. This sense, however, might take a variety of forms: it might refer to the soul's relation to God, or to a moral issue, or be a prediction of the end-time. Origen did not systematize the possible non-literal senses, which he described simply as 'spiritual'. And even in places where the literal meaning was fully acceptable, we might draw metaphorical conclusions; thus from the story of the exodus of the Israelites from Egypt, which to Origen's way of thinking certainly happened at a literal level, we could also be led to consider the 'exodus' of humankind from bondage to sin and the freedom conferred by Christ, or the liberation of the individual soul. 'God's ways in the guidance of the soul are the same as those by which he guides his people and hence we have the right to draw spiritual teaching from Exodus.'[10] Later writers continued to think that 'absurdities' in the text pointed to a deeper meaning, but they were even more inclined than Origen to suppose that all of Scripture might have a hidden sense. This was eventually formalized into a fourfold scheme, whereby biblical passages could be interpreted as (1) literal, (2) allegorical, (3) moral and (4) anagogical.[11] Their meaning is summed up in a famous mnemonic verse:

> Littera gesta docet, quid credas allegoria,
> moralis quid agas, quo tendas anagogia.[12]

> The literal sense teaches historical truths; the allegorical, what you are to believe;
> the moral, what you are to do; the anagogical what you are to strive for.

According to this principle, any passage in the Bible can either be interpreted in its obvious literal meaning, or else treated as a guide to doctrine, morals[13] or eschatology. In practice, few if any commentators managed to extract all four senses out of every passage they commented on – it is more a matter of a repertoire of possibilities. Confusingly, all three non-literal senses are sometimes described as allegorical, just as Origen would have described them all as spiritual or mystical. A classic example of the fourfold sense was a common medieval interpretation of 'Jerusalem' in the Old Testament, where the historical or literal sense is a reference to the city of the Jews, the allegorical to the Christian Church, the anagogical to the city of God in heaven, and the moral or tropological to the human soul.[14]

We saw in the previous chapter, with Psalm 137 and striking babies against the rock, the advantages conferred by a metaphorical reading of passages that are morally objectionable. It became normal in the Middle Ages to interpret the 'little ones' here not as literal Babylonian babies, but as human vices that should be crushed and destroyed against the 'rock' that is Christ himself, just as Origen had argued. Thus a text that, read literally, seemed to conflict with Christian teaching on the importance of forgiveness, could be transformed by a tropological or moral reading into something spiritually fruitful.

The kind of interpretation that allegorization can lead to can be seen in Gregory the Great's *Moralia in Job*,[15] written in the 580s in Constantinople. Here is a summary of the beginning of his exposition of the book of Job:

> The allegorical interpretation of Job 1:1–5 begins with a Christological reference . . . The name 'Job' means 'the one who suffers' and Uz means 'the counsellor'. Thus Job's name points to Christ, who suffers, and who lives in the land of Uz when he reigns in the hearts of believers, to guide and counsel them. The number of Job's children (seven sons and three daughters) gives rise to various speculations. Seven is a number of perfection, as shown by the fact that God rested on the seventh day, and that the seventh day was the sabbath. Further, seven represented the apostles, since seven is comprised of 3 plus 4 which amount to 12 when multiplied. 3 and 4 also signify that the Trinity is preached to the four corners of the earth. The three daughters can be linked to the three saints of Ezekiel 14:14, Noah, Daniel and Job. These three men represent respectively the priests (Noah guided the ark as priests guide the church), the celibate (Daniel abstained from the luxuries of Babylon) and the faithful married.[16]

This kind of interpretation is to modern eyes simply absurd: by it, anything whatever can be proved from the biblical text. We might say of such Christian readings what G. W. H. Lampe wrote about the interpretation of the Hebrew Bible in the Dead Sea Scrolls, that they 'depend upon the belief that the Scriptures are an assortment of oracles whose meaning is revealed to those who have the insight to discern it and apply it to the contemporary scene . . . the ingenuity of the allegorist comes by a kind of inspiration.'[17] The author has in his mind a set of doctrines or ideas on which he wants the text to shed light, and he turns the text this way and that until it does. The implication must be that God planted in the text various features, such as numbers, for which there is no obvious reason, and that these are present in order to elicit this kind of allegorical interpretation. Implicit in this, in turn, is the idea that there is nothing trivial in biblical texts: if we are told that Job had seven sons, that cannot be simply a random historical fact (or, as we might think today, part of the verisimilitude of the story): it must have a deeper significance. (Compare the discussion of rabbinic interpretation in Chapter 14.)

Most medieval exegesis of this kind concentrated on the Old Testament, but the New Testament too was sometimes allegorized. The parables of Jesus, for example, were often taken to be not only metaphorical in the obvious sense of being stories with a moral, but also coded references to the life of Jesus or to features of the Church. We saw this in the patristic period, as far back as Origen and Augustine, with the allegorization of the parable of the Good Samaritan to make it deliver a message about the Church and the sacraments.[18] There are of course parts of the New Testament that have a natural depth analogous to allegory, particularly the Gospel of John, in which things are seldom what they seem on the surface. To return to an example from Chapter 8: when Judas goes out from the room where Jesus and his disciples have been eating, the author adds, 'And it was night' (John 13:30). Few readers would hear this as merely a helpful indication of the time of day, so clearly does it draw on the imagery of darkness to depict the situation of Jesus' imminent betrayal. Medieval interpreters were aware of such passages, where a deeper meaning is obvious to any sensitive reader, but they ranged much more widely, and also imputed allegorical senses to many more texts than those.

Sometimes Christian writers followed in the steps of the New Testament itself (and of the Dead Sea community, though they could not have known that) in interpreting details in Scripture as referring to the present day – as when they read the Bible as pointing to the crusades, affirming that Isaiah's prophecy 'to bring your children from far away' (60:9) foretold the victory of the Franks over the Saracens.[19] But this was a specialized form of interpretation, not at all widespread in most of the medieval exegesis that has come down to us, and it was often seen as rather suspect by Church authorities, since it might be linked to the idea that the Bible provided a warrant for insurrection or revolution. Hence the suspicions about the eschatological interpretations of the revered theologian and monk Joachim of Fiore (1135–1202), who derived from the Scriptures a scheme of history in which the end-time was about to break in, inaugurating a new age in which there would be no need for a church.[20]

Even in antiquity there had been commentators who preferred the literal sense to the various spiritual ones, but by the Middle Ages the kind of interpretation provided by the Antiochene school, which regarded only a few psalms as messianic prophecies, and treated most as referring to the experiences of the Jews in their history, had largely died out, as the spiritual sense gained more hold on the Christian imagination. There was, however, a revival of attention to the historical sense in the work of the Victorines, scholars who belonged to the Abbey of St Victor in Paris in the twelfth century. Hugh of St Victor (1096–1141), the founder of this school of interpretation, examines Isaiah 4:1:

> Seven women shall take hold of one man in that day, saying, 'We will eat our own bread and wear our own clothes; just let us be called by your name; take away our disgrace.'

He comments:

> The words are plain and clear enough. You understand each separate clause . . . But perhaps you cannot understand what it means as a whole . . . And, so it happens, you think that a passage whose literal meaning you do not grasp should be understood only in a spiritual sense. So you say that the *seven women* are the seven gifts of the Holy Spirit, who *shall take hold of one man*, that is Christ . . . who alone 'takes away their reproach' that they may find in him a refuge . . .
>
> Lo! you have expounded spiritually and you do not understand what it means literally. But the prophet could mean something literally too by these words.[21]

Hugh goes on to explain, much as would any modern commentator on Isaiah, that the prophet is talking about a time of national ruin in which many men are dead, and the widowed women are looking for a man to marry them on any terms because widowhood and childlessness are reckoned a 'reproach' in that society. This could hardly be further from the approach of Gregory the Great. Only when Christian tradition sanctions a spiritual reading – especially if it is supported by the New Testament – does Hugh abandon the historical/literal sense: for example, with Joel's prophecy of the pouring-out of the Spirit upon all flesh (Joel 2:28), which is explicitly quoted in Acts 2 as a reference to the empowering of the disciples of Jesus on the day of Pentecost.

The Victorine approach found its climax in the next generation in the work of Andrew of St Victor (d. 1175) (to whom Beryl Smalley devoted a long chapter in her classic *The Study of the Bible in the Middle Ages*).[22] A passage of Isaiah long dear to Christians was the description of the 'Suffering Servant' (Isaiah 52:13–53:12), which seemed to match the sufferings of Christ at so many points that it had long been read almost as if it were part of the New Testament, with no further meaning being even thought of. (It is still regularly read in Christian churches on Good Friday, and parts of it are used in Handel's *Messiah*.)

> See, my servant shall prosper; he shall be exalted and lifted up, and shall be very high. Just as there were many who were astonished at him – so marred was his appearance, beyond human semblance, and his form beyond that of mortals – so he shall startle many nations; kings shall shut their mouths because of him; for that which had not been told them they shall see, and that which they had not heard they shall contemplate. Who has believed what we have heard? And to whom has the arm of the LORD been revealed? For he grew up before him like a young plant, and like a root out of dry ground; he had no form or majesty that we should look at him, nothing in his appearance that we should desire him. He was despised and rejected by others; a man of suffering and acquainted with infirmity; and as one from whom others hide their faces he was despised, and we held him of no account. Surely he has borne our infirmities and carried our diseases; yet we accounted him stricken, struck down by God, and afflicted. But he was wounded for our transgressions, crushed for our iniquities; upon him was the punishment that made us whole, and by his bruises we are healed. All we like sheep have gone astray; we have all turned to our own way, and the LORD has laid on him the iniquity of us all. He was oppressed, and he was afflicted, yet he did not open his mouth; like a lamb that is led to the slaughter, and like a sheep that before its shearers is silent, so he did not open his mouth. By a perversion of justice he was taken away. Who could have imagined his future? For he was cut off from the land of the living, stricken for the transgression of my people. They made his grave with the wicked and his tomb with the rich, although he had done no violence, and there was no deceit in his mouth. Yet it was the will of the LORD to crush him with pain. When you make his life an offering for sin, he shall see his offspring, and shall prolong his days; through him the will of the LORD shall prosper. Out of his anguish he shall see light; he shall find satisfaction through his knowledge. The righteous one, my servant, shall make many righteous, and he shall bear their iniquities. Therefore I will allot him a portion with the great, and he shall divide the spoil with the strong; because he poured out himself to death, and was numbered with the transgressors; yet he bore the sin of many, and made intercession for the transgressors.

Jews, naturally, had contended that this was a description of Isaiah himself, or perhaps of a personification of Israel, suggestions which are common in modern commentators too. Most Christians, following the direction pointed to in Acts 8:26–40, read it as obviously a prediction of the sufferings and vindication of Christ. But Andrew simply adopts the Jewish reading without so much as mentioning the Christological possibilities.[23] He treats the Old Testament as making sense on its own terms, without bringing in questions of the fulfilment of prophecy, or any possible spiritual meanings.

The literal meaning of a passage can of course be an allegorical one, if a text is written as a deliberate allegory – just as the literal meaning of a parable is metaphorical. The parable of the Prodigal Son (Luke 15: 11–32) does not imply, at any level, that there really was such a person and that the ring his father put on his hand might one day turn up in an archaeological dig. We recognize the parable as a story, not a piece of history. In the same way the strange beasts described in Daniel 7 – one like a lion with eagles' wings, one like a leopard with four bird's wings and four heads – will never be found in a zoo: they are symbols or illustrations of the nature of evil. Medieval interpreters were perfectly aware of this point, and the Victorines are no exception (any more than were the Antiochenes). But making such distinctions implies in principle an interest in the intention of the author. This we find in Andrew: 'What distinguishes him from contemporaries is his awareness that some personality is there. He does not lose sight of the prophet in the prophecy.'[24] This represents a change from what had been usual in interpretation of the biblical text, where, as Smalley observes, readers 'took less interest in the mind of the author and more in the author's product . . . The text was more alive than its author.'[25]

It was by pursuing an explicit distinction between what the author intended, and what the text might be taken to mean if read without that question in mind, that Thomas Aquinas (1225–74) made a breakthrough in the understanding of the Bible. Aquinas, a Dominican friar, had studied and taught in Paris and Cologne as well as in Rome, and despite his immense work in philosophy and theology – he is widely regarded as the greatest Christian teacher of the Middle Ages – he saw his primary work as the exposition of Scripture. In reading the Bible, authorial intention was to be the interpreter's guide. What the author meant was to be described as the literal sense:[26] this might, as we have seen, be allegorical if the author was deliberately writing an allegory. It remained true that the ultimate author was the Holy Spirit, but the agency of the human author was not to be bypassed in the interests of non-literal reading. Aquinas also argued (as had Augustine) that there were no truths that could be revealed through allegorical reading that were not to be found plainly expressed somewhere else in the Bible – so that understanding the biblical revelation was not reserved to those whose learning enabled them to spot possible allegorical meanings, but was available to the simplest reader. He thus demolished the sense that only special readers could access the deeper meaning of Scripture – part of his general tendency to see the Bible's teaching, like his own, as freely available to ordinary people.[27]

For Aquinas the textual sense is whatever was intended by the writer, whether that was literal in the ordinary sense of the word, or metaphorical as in the case of parables or visions. He wrote: 'The literal sense is that which is first intended by the words, whether they are used properly or figuratively.'[28] The spiritual sense (a better term than allegorical) was the meaning intended by God, which might not have been apparent to the scriptural writers themselves – that would be the case, for example, with some messianic prophecies.[29] Digging out the spiritual sense took theological and religious acumen. This simple distinction avoids many of the complications into which some earlier medieval theories of interpretation had fallen. Attention to authorial intention would come to be crucial in later study of the Bible; in recent times it has become much contested, as we shall see in Chapter 17.

Aquinas is best known as a massively productive philosopher and theologian, whose *Summa theologiae* fills many volumes. But in his day he was thought of as primarily a biblical exegete, and expounding the Scriptures was his daily work. Christian doctrine for him is, in theory, drawn from the Scriptures, not independent of them.[30] Like many before and since who have adopted that theory, however, there is a great deal in his teaching that derives not at all from the Bible, but from his philosophical background in the study of Aristotle. To him there seemed no conflict between the Philosopher, as he calls him, and the teaching of the Bible.

COMMENTARIES AND THE GLOSS

Much medieval teaching, in monasteries, churches and the early universities such as Paris, Oxford and Cambridge, took the form of commentary on the Bible. Only with the coming of the friars, Dominicans and Franciscans, in the thirteenth century, did theology come to be a discipline to some extent separate from biblical exposition, with non-biblical topics expounded and debated in their own right. Even then, competent theologians would be expected to have a sound grasp of biblical knowledge, as did Thomas Aquinas. But life was too short for every scholar to study the books of the Bible systematically for himself, and so there grew up reference works that contained what were thought to be the best comments of the Fathers on the books of Scripture.

Already before the eighth century this tradition can be seen in the production of *florilegia*, 'bouquets' of quotations from the Fathers to accompany an anthology of biblical excerpts: a classic example is the *Sentences* of Isidore of Seville (560–636). *Florilegia* drew on the Fathers of east and west, together with Gregory the Great, widely regarded in the early Middle Ages as the master of biblical interpretation. But by the twelfth century the custom developed of producing Bibles with such comments – culled from *florilegia* that were known as 'expositors' – incorporated between the lines and in the margins. The comments were widely called glosses, and a Bible containing them was also called a Gloss (*glosa* or *glosatura* or *glosatus*). The arrangement was probably borrowed from what was already customary in lectures in the liberal arts, where it was common for texts to be written leaving spaces for students to add notes.[31] In the cathedral schools of northern France a similar method came to be applied to the text of the Bible.

In time there developed a more or less agreed version of the Gloss, known as the *Glossa Ordinaria* ('Standard Gloss'). This seems to have been started by Anselm of Laon (d. 1117) and other teachers in northern France.[32] For many lecturing on the Bible, some version of the *Glossa Ordinaria* would come to be taken as a prerequisite of biblical study: students would bring a copy to lectures. From the twelfth century we have thousands of copies of glossed Bibles, more than of the plain text. From about 1120 there was a complete Gloss on every book of the Bible, and lectures were no longer given only on selected books, but on the whole of Scripture: this is the background to the Victorine school already discussed. A notable lecturer on the entire Bible was Stephen Langton, later Archbishop of Canterbury. A complete edition of the *Glossa Ordinaria* is reckoned to have spanned some twenty-one volumes. It became such a semi-official text that late in the twelfth century we find Peter Comestor (d. 1178/9) producing glosses on the Gloss itself.

The Gloss was not, however, a single, completely standardized work as it might have been in an age of printing, but existed in many versions.[33] Typically it consisted of the text of the biblical book in question, with comments (short glosses) between the lines, and longer glosses in the margins or above and below the text. Longer passages of discussion and comment (seldom with any disagreements, but presenting different nuances) were placed between chapters or after the main text, while each biblical book was preceded by the appropriate section of Jerome's prologues: these soon acquired such authority that they came to be glossed themselves, and were treated as more or less scriptural. Indeed, there was a tendency which we have already observed in Christian commentaries in general for the Gloss to take precedence over the text being commented on. The Gloss became the 'voice' of the biblical text, which was dumb without it,[34] and readers took the meaning of the biblical text to be that implied by the Gloss. It was perhaps an awareness of the way power relations between supposedly authoritative text and supposedly secondary commentary tend in practice to invert that led Francis of Assisi to insist that his Rule, setting out how the friars were to live, should never be glossed.

The effect of the Gloss could be very marked. The interlinear glosses in particular often give the text a quite radical shift from the natural meaning towards a 'spiritual' reading. 'The Gloss reads the text, especially of the Old Testament books, as a spiritual lesson about Christ and the living of the Christian life.'[35] Many passages are given a Christological slant, with allegorized readings of the New Testament parables, and attention to the natural sense tended to be lost altogether. The text became the vehicle for expounding Christian doctrine, and there was no sense that it had its own story to tell apart from the teachings of the Church, or in criticism of them. If we think in terms of there being two entities, the Bible and the Christian faith, then in the Gloss the two are simply merged.[36] Theology is identified with biblical exposition, but this means that in practice theological themes and ideas take over the interpretation of the biblical text.

By the later Middle Ages there was a contrast between the kind of Bible-reading practised in monasteries – generally known, then and now, as *lectio divina*, 'divine reading' – and the pursuit of what would nowadays be called systematic theology, the attempt to summarize and analyse the whole Christian faith in a philosophically rigorous way. *Lectio divina* is not primarily analytical, but meditative or ruminative, and it is part of a quest for wisdom, rooted in thinking about Scripture. Passages are read slowly and peacefully. The study of systematic theology, which begins seriously in the work of the friars, is a quest for knowledge: for a well-ordered account of what Christians are to believe,

The *Glossa Ordinaria* on Genesis 9, the building of the Ark.

which draws on Scripture but exists alongside it. Its characteristic form is not the biblical commentary, but the disputation or treatise, and its ascendancy 'threatened to turn the individual struggle to know God into a matter for the syllabus and the examination'.[37] Jean Leclercq formulates the contrast as follows:

> The basis of the influence of Holy Scripture was the elementary fact that it was read; but the precise meaning of the term *lectio* needs to be established. It is applied to two different activities. In the schools, especially those where clerics were trained for pastoral duties, Scripture was read mainly to gain light on intellectual and moral problems. The text was examined, *quaestiones* were propounded, and these were answered by means of the *disputatio*. Knowledge is the principal object of the search . . . On the other hand, in monasteries of the various rules, all of which were centres of an intense spiritual life, the monks pursued the traditional *lectio divina* of Scripture. Here it is not so much the text itself that is considered most important as the fact of reading it and gaining personal benefit from it. The aim is not so much to acquire ideas, since knowledge of the faith is presupposed, but rather to taste and savour the Word of God; thus the contemplative life of prayer and union with God might be strengthened. These two ways of reading Scripture were practised throughout the middle ages: the first developed primarily in twelfth-century scholasticism, the second remained in favour in the monasteries.[38]

The Gloss allows us to see on the same pages the distinction between the contents of the Bible and the belief system of Christianity, precisely because it was one massive attempt to demonstrate the coherence between the two, by interpreting the biblical text through the sayings of those Fathers thought to have taught orthodox theology. Treatises on theology, such as Aquinas' *Summa theologiae*, operate in the opposite direction, expounding the faith in a philosophical manner but trying to show how it derives from Scripture. Both approaches share the assumption that the Bible and the faith are congruent. In reality this is not always so. In monastic *lectio divina* this problem is perhaps less marked, since meditation on the text is free-ranging and not part of an attempt to establish Christian doctrine; but in the school-tradition represented by the Gloss, obscuring the lack of fit between the Bible and the faith at times involves doing violence to the biblical text, as when Christological concerns lead to forced readings of the Old Testament.

Northern France was again significant for biblical interpretation in the fourteenth century, when a leading scholar was Nicholas of Lyra

(1270–1349).[39] Born at Lyre in Normandy, where he was able to learn from Jewish teachers, Nicholas joined the Franciscans in 1300 and was soon sent to Paris to study and, in due course, to teach. His two major works, both of which draw extensively on the *Glossa Ordinaria*, are *postillae* (commentaries) on the whole Bible, one 'literal' (written 1323–31) and one 'moral' (1333–9). We see here again that by no means all scholars tried to produce a fourfold sense for all of Scripture, and Nicholas preferred the literal and the moral senses. The literal sense, as he uses the term, is 'that which does not need to be explicated in order to be understood',[40] in other words, what an intelligent reader would take the text to mean if not given additional information. This might be a parabolic or allegorical meaning if the text is clearly a parable or an allegory, but it would not be an allegorizing reading of one intended by its author to convey simple historical truth. Nicholas' decisions as to which texts were intended to be allegories, however, might differ from ours. Like all other medieval interpreters, he took the Song of Songs to be in intention an allegorical work – not about Solomon and his queen (or about two anonymous lovers, as modern commentators tend to think), but about God and the Church. This was not, for Nicholas, an *additional* allegorical meaning derived from the literal text; it was the literal meaning.[41] Nicholas was an important figure down into the Reformation period, and in the sixteenth century his *Postilla literalis* was sometimes printed with the *Glossa Ordinaria*.[42]

Even when interpreting the literal sense in its most basic historical form, Nicholas uses a hermeneutical framework, as do all medieval writers. He takes as a given the 'system of sin and redemption, which frames the Old and New Testaments, and which forms the unifying message and purpose of the scriptural witness'.[43] The idea that one might interpret the text *so* literally as to ignore its whole scriptural context, as the Church understood that, had not yet arrived – and when it did, it would always be a minority interest. Nevertheless, Nicholas is in some ways a precursor of later, self-consciously non-confessional biblical interpretation, in that he often concerns himself with the factual and historical, rather as Andrew of St Victor had done, and the Antiochenes before him. In his commentary on Ruth, Nicholas is not so concerned with theological meanings, but more with geography, history and what we might call anthropology or ethnography – the customs revealed by the narrative. It is easy to see why he was described as *doctor planus et utilis*, 'a plain and useful teacher'. But his emphasis on what the text meant on its own terms, rather than according to the tradition of its interpretation, was to be more far-reaching than he could have known. In Martin Luther it was to turn into the principle that Scripture is its own interpreter, and is 'clear' in its meaning to the Christian reader, without the need of intermediaries such as popes or priests. Thus Nicholas is traditionally claimed as one of the forerunners of the Reformation, as summed up in the jingle, *si Lyra non lyrasset, Lutherus non saltasset*: 'if Lyra had not played his lyre, Luther would not have danced'.

JEWISH COMMENTARY

Jewish literature from the early Middle Ages falls into two categories: legal discussion and scriptural interpretation. Legal discussion can be found in the Mishnah, which was finalized in the early third century CE, and then over the next few centuries in the two Talmuds, the Palestinian or Jerusalem Talmud (*Yerushalmi*), finished by the late fourth century CE, and the Babylonian Talmud (*Bavli*), completed two centuries or so later. The Mishnah and the Talmuds – which are extensive commentaries on the Mishnah – consist mostly of *halakhah*, but also contain stories, fables and speculative passages more characteristic of *aggadah*. There is also a certain amount of scriptural interpretation within the talmudic tradition, but the arrangement is topical: each tractate, as the sections are known, concerns some area of Jewish life that requires regulation.

Scriptural interpretation in its own right is to be found in the midrashim. The major collection of these is the *Midrash Rabbah* on the books of the Pentateuch and the books read at festivals (Song of Songs, Lamentations, Esther, Ruth and Ecclesiastes). A midrash is what we think of as a commentary, going through a biblical book in order and commenting on the verses as they occur. The overall tendency is aggadic, though occasional points will be made that have a bearing on *halakhah*, behaviour. One of the earliest midrashim is the *Mekhilta of Rabbi Ishmael*, and that is predominantly halakhic in character (see pp. 331–9). These texts are the foundation of Jewish interpretation throughout the Middle Ages.

The composer/compiler of midrashim, known as the *darshan*, sometimes expounds what a Christian commentator would have called the literal sense, but more often moves into more fanciful or allegorical interpretations: thus 'Edom' in the Bible is interpreted as referring to the Romans, which in turn means the Christians. As we saw, it is unusual to think in terms of allegories of otherworldly realities, as sometimes occurs in Christian interpretation; much more commonly the non-literal meaning is concerned with practice – that is, it has a halakhic tendency. But above all, midrash works by connecting the verse being commented on with other verses from anywhere in the Bible, which is treated as a kind of database of texts that are all interrelated, and questions of 'before and after', as the rabbinic authorities put it, simply do not arise. This method, defined in the previous chapter, continued to be common in Jewish reading of the Bible during the Middle Ages.

The sanctity and inspiration of the Bible made it unlike all other books: as a sage recorded in the second-century *Sayings of the Fathers* (*Pirke Aboth*) put it, 'Turn it, turn it, for everything is in it.' Every smallest detail of the text, down to the punctuation, could be pressed to yield meaning; every juxtaposition of words and sentences was exegetically significant; there was no redundancy or accident in the composition, so any repetition, or the slightest deviation from the wording that might be expected, was meaningful and important, and could be used to solve puzzles that a more superficial reading might throw up. As Eva Mroczek puts it, 'Here, we see a fixed and bounded canon, "exegetical totalization", and the claim that nothing is new but all had already been revealed on Sinai – together with irrepressible exegetical ingenuity that makes the aggressively finite text infinitely generative.'[44]

The typical procedure in rabbinic works is to notice some kind of oddity or inconsistency in the biblical text and then to account for it by an extremely 'close reading'. Take Genesis 35:22:

> While Israel [= Jacob] dwelt in that land, Reuben went and lay with Bilhah his father's concubine; and Israel heard of it. Now the sons of Jacob were twelve.

At first sight, the two sentences here appear unconnected, and indeed the text continues by listing the sons of Jacob, so that it is natural to take the second sentence as the beginning of a new section. As traditionally written in manuscripts of the Hebrew Bible, however, the two sentences are treated as though they conveyed a single idea, with a section break after, not before, the second sentence. The first question for the interpreter is therefore why this is so. The second arises from the odd clause, 'and Israel heard of it', which does not – as we should expect – report any consequence of what on the face of it was a grave offence. A modern reader is likely simply to note that the text appears to lack coherence. But for writers of midrashim, this was not an option. The solution, which is preserved already in the book called *Jubilees*, is this: there *was* a consequence. Jacob had no further relations with Bilhah, his concubine, since his son had 'defiled' her; consequently there were no more children, so 'the sons of Jacob were twelve' – not more. Thus this passage of Genesis is really perfectly coherent, and implicitly tells us much more about Jacob than it appears to. We discover this additional information by refusing to treat odd gaps and inconsequentialities in the text as such: each of them proves, on analysis, to be full of important information.[45]

This kind of interpretation is entirely dependent on having a very accurate text of the Bible, which records even such indications as sentence and section divisions, absent in early manuscripts such as those at Qumran. Jewish Bibles in the Middle Ages fall into two categories. One is the traditional scroll used in worship in the synagogue, in which the text is written without vowels or other marks beyond the consonants of the text, and for liturgical reading serves primarily as an aide-mémoire for the reader. This remains the case for scrolls read in the synagogue today. The other type is the codex. Though the use of the codex was apparently a Christian innovation (see Chapter 10), Jews had adopted it by the early Middle Ages (probably around 700[46]) as the preferred format for Bibles intended for study. Hebrew was originally written without vowels; by the tenth century CE or so it was felt necessary to devise ways of recording them, lest the tradition of reading the text accurately be lost. In Jewish codices the vowels were indicated by a complex system of dots and dashes above and below the letters (which stand for consonants), and there were also indications of punctuation, and (unlike in Greek and Latin) spaces between words.

Around the text of the biblical books there came to be a whole paratextual element known as the small Masorah (Hebrew for tradition), which indicated places where the text was uncertain or liable to misreading, and which provided information about unusual words and their frequency of occurrence, as well as little mnemonics to help the scribe to copy out the text accurately. Thus there are several places in the Bible where we find a list of the nations whom the Israelites were supposed to eject from the Promised Land,[47] but the order in which they are listed varies, and the names are not always the same. (The first occurrence, Genesis 15:19–21, lists them as 'the Kenites, the Kenizzites, the Kadmonites, the Hittites, the Perizzites, the Rephaim, the Amorites, the Canaanites, the Girgashites, and the Jebusites', but several of the lists are shorter.) A scribe might easily write the list from memory and make a mistake in a given verse. So the Masorah often provides a *sîman*, a 'sign', which lists the first letter of each nation to make an acronym that can be used to check that what has been copied is correct.

The small Masorah also marks places where what is traditionally read differs from the written text, indicating the reading tradition by writing the word as read over the letter *qoph* (q) for *qere*, meaning 'read'. The purpose of marking the distinction between the *qere* and the *ketîb* ('written') is disputed, but it may have been, again, to help the scribe not to be distracted by the reading tradition into 'correcting' the written form of the text.[48] The marginal notes in the small Masorah also point out places where letters have an odd shape or size, or are upside down. Some of these features may originally have been mistakes, but they are lovingly preserved, never corrected, and the scribe's attention is drawn to them to ensure that they survive.

There is also a great Masorah, which appears at the head and foot of the page and consists of a discussion of grammatical and linguistic points, a count of the number of verses, even of words, in a particular book, and comments on other details relevant to copying the text. The result is that a medieval Hebrew Bible – our earliest nearly complete example being the Aleppo Codex from the tenth century CE – looks not unlike a Christian Bible with the *Glossa Ordinaria*: a basic text surrounded by comments. But the comments are not interpretative: they concentrate on features of the text as a piece of writing, not on its meaning. They are the work of various groups of Masoretes, of whom the most famous were five generations of the family of Ben Asher, from the second half of the eighth century and based at Tiberias on the Sea of Galilee. The Cairo Codex of the Prophets, the oldest Hebrew codex still extant, claims to have been written by Moses ben Asher in 895. The Leningrad or St Petersburg Codex (L), from the eleventh century, still represents the Tiberian tradition in its vowel points and Masoretic notes.[49]

Thus a great deal of information beyond the plain text is provided in a Hebrew Bible codex, and much of this continues to be present today in standard Hebrew Bibles, though the great Masorah is now usually produced in a volume of its own. In the Middle Ages there was plentiful information for interpreters to be able to comment not on the general gist of a passage, but on details as small as the shape of letters or the divisions between verses.

In the midrashim, opinions of many different rabbis are juxtaposed, with no more concern for temporal sequence than is the case for biblical quotations. It is as if all the rabbinic authorities were contemporaries, discussing points of interpretation with each other, even though they often lived in different centuries. The compiler of each midrash himself remains anonymous. But in the Middle Ages there came to be commentators who

7 שָׂרַ֔י וַתִּבְרַ֖ח מִפָּנֶֽיהָ׃ 7 וַֽיִּמְצָאָ֞הּ מַלְאַ֧ךְ יְהוָ֛ה עַל־עֵ֥ין הַמַּ֖יִם בַּמִּדְבָּ֑ר
8 עַל־הָעַ֖יִן בְּדֶ֥רֶךְ שֽׁוּר׃ 8 וַיֹּאמַ֗ר הָגָ֞ר שִׁפְחַ֥ת שָׂרַ֛י אֵֽי־מִזֶּ֥ה בָ֖את וְאָ֣נָה
9 תֵלֵ֑כִי וַתֹּ֕אמֶר מִפְּנֵי֙ שָׂרַ֣י גְּבִרְתִּ֔י אָנֹכִ֖י בֹּרַֽחַת׃ 9 וַיֹּ֤אמֶר לָהּ֙ מַלְאַ֣ךְ
10 יְהוָ֔ה שׁ֖וּבִי אֶל־גְּבִרְתֵּ֑ךְ וְהִתְעַנִּ֖י תַּ֥חַת יָדֶֽיהָ׃ 10 וַיֹּ֤אמֶר לָהּ֙ מַלְאַ֣ךְ
11 יְהוָ֔ה הַרְבָּ֥ה אַרְבֶּ֖ה אֶת־זַרְעֵ֑ךְ וְלֹ֥א יִסָּפֵ֖ר מֵרֹֽב׃ 11 וַיֹּ֤אמֶר לָהּ֙
מַלְאַ֣ךְ יְהוָ֔ה

הִנָּ֥ךְ הָרָ֖ה וְיֹלַ֣דְתְּ[a] בֵּ֑ן וְקָרָ֤את שְׁמוֹ֙ יִשְׁמָעֵ֔אל
כִּֽי־שָׁמַ֥ע יְהוָ֖ה אֶל־עָנְיֵֽךְ׃
12 וְה֤וּא יִהְיֶה֙ פֶּ֣רֶא אָדָ֔ם יָד֣וֹ בַכֹּ֔ל וְיַ֥ד כֹּ֖ל בּ֑וֹ
וְעַל־פְּנֵ֥י כָל־אֶחָ֖יו יִשְׁכֹּֽן׃

13 וַתִּקְרָ֤א שֵׁם־יְהוָה֙ הַדֹּבֵ֣ר אֵלֶ֔יהָ אַתָּ֖ה אֵ֣ל רֳאִ֑י[a] כִּ֣י אָֽמְרָ֗ה הֲגַ֥ם 13
14 הֲלֹ֛ם רָאִ֖יתִי[b] אַחֲרֵ֥י רֹאִֽי[c]׃ 14 עַל־כֵּן֙ קָרָ֣א לַבְּאֵ֔ר בְּאֵ֥ר לַחַ֖י רֹאִ֑י[a]
15 הִנֵּ֥ה[b] בֵין־קָדֵ֖שׁ וּבֵ֥ין בָּֽרֶד׃ 15 וַתֵּ֧לֶד הָגָ֛ר לְאַבְרָ֖ם בֵּ֑ן וַיִּקְרָ֨א אַבְרָ֧ם
16 שֶׁם־בְּנ֛וֹ אֲשֶׁר־יָלְדָ֥ה הָגָ֖ר יִשְׁמָעֵֽאל׃ 16 וְאַבְרָ֕ם בֶּן־שְׁמֹנִ֥ים שָׁנָ֖ה וְשֵׁ֣שׁ
שָׁנִ֑ים בְּלֶֽדֶת־הָגָ֥ר אֶת־יִשְׁמָעֵ֖אל לְאַבְרָֽם׃ ס

17 1 וַיְהִ֣י אַבְרָ֔ם בֶּן־תִּשְׁעִ֥ים שָׁנָ֖ה וְתֵ֣שַׁע שָׁנִ֑ים וַיֵּרָ֨א יְהוָ֜ה[a] אֶל־
2 אַבְרָ֗ם וַיֹּ֤אמֶר אֵלָיו֙ אֲנִי־אֵ֣ל שַׁדַּ֔י הִתְהַלֵּ֥ךְ לְפָנַ֖י וֶהְיֵ֥ה[a] תָמִֽים׃ 2 וְאֶתְּנָ֥ה
3 בְרִיתִ֖י בֵּינִ֣י וּבֵינֶ֑ךָ וְאַרְבֶּ֥ה אוֹתְךָ֖ בִּמְאֹ֥ד מְאֹֽד׃ 3 וַיִּפֹּ֥ל אַבְרָ֖ם עַל־
4 פָּנָ֑יו וַיְדַבֵּ֥ר אִתּ֛וֹ אֱלֹהִ֖ים לֵאמֹֽר׃ 4 אֲנִ֕י הִנֵּ֥ה בְרִיתִ֖י אִתָּ֑ךְ וְהָיִ֕יתָ לְאַ֖ב
5 הֲמ֥וֹן גּוֹיִֽם׃ 5 וְלֹא־יִקָּרֵ֥א ע֛וֹד אֶת[a]־שִׁמְךָ֖ אַבְרָ֑ם וְהָיָ֤ה שִׁמְךָ֙ אַבְרָהָ֔ם
6 כִּ֛י אַב־הֲמ֥וֹן גּוֹיִ֖ם נְתַתִּֽיךָ׃ 6 וְהִפְרֵתִ֤י אֹֽתְךָ֙ בִּמְאֹ֣ד מְאֹ֔ד וּנְתַתִּ֖יךָ לְגוֹיִ֑ם
7 וּמְלָכִ֖ים מִמְּךָ֥ יֵצֵֽאוּ׃ 7 וַהֲקִמֹתִ֨י אֶת־בְּרִיתִ֜י בֵּינִ֣י וּבֵינֶ֗ךָ וּבֵ֨ין זַרְעֲךָ֧
אַחֲרֶ֛יךָ לְדֹרֹתָ֖ם לִבְרִ֣ית עוֹלָ֑ם לִהְי֤וֹת לְךָ֙ לֵֽאלֹהִ֔ים וּֽלְזַרְעֲךָ֖ אַחֲרֶֽיךָ׃
8 וְנָתַתִּ֣י לְ֠ךָ וּלְזַרְעֲךָ֨ אַחֲרֶ֜יךָ אֵ֣ת ׀ אֶ֣רֶץ מְגֻרֶ֗יךָ אֵ֚ת כָּל־אֶ֣רֶץ כְּנַ֔עַן 8

[9]Ru 2,12. [10]Jer 4,29. [11]Mm 22. [12]Mm 1480. [13]Mm 1231. [14]Mm 3560. [15]Mm 104. [16]Mm 1989. Cp 17 [1]Mm 1227. [2]Mm 541. [3]Mm 109. [4]Mm 959. [5]Mm 2563. [6]Mm 17. [7]Mm 108. [8]Mm 260. [9]Mm 105.

11 [a] forma mixta ex וְיֹלֶדֶת et וְיָלַדְתְּ? cf ad Jdc 13,5 || 13 [a] ש ראה 𝔊(𝔙) ὁ ἐπιδών με = רֹאִי || [b–b] prp אֱלֹהִים ר׳ וָאֶחִי || [c] ש ראה 𝔊 ὀφθέντα μοι || 14 [a] ש[Mss] ראה 𝔊 εἶδον = רָאִיתִי || [b] 𝔗[J] + hj', frt ins הִיא || Cp 17,1 [a] ש והוי cf 12,2[a] || 5 [a] > nonn Mss ש.

A modern Hebrew Bible: the story of Abraham in the *Biblia Hebraica Stuttgartensia*.

produced continuous commentaries on the Bible in their own names, which were not compilations but independent books. The twelfth century is as important for the production of these Jewish commentaries as it is for the work of the glossators in the Christian schools, and northern France is again the primary place where the work was undertaken.

The late eleventh century saw the writings of Rashi (Rabbi Solomon ben Isaac of Troyes, 1040–1105), who wrote a complete commentary on the Pentateuch.[50] Like the midrashists, he sometimes allows the text to have an allegorical or at least metaphorical sense, for example treating references to Edom or to the 'Kittim' in the text as allusions to the Romans (by now the Christians), just as the midrashim had done. But he also emphasized the importance of what in Hebrew is called the *peshat* or 'plain sense'. While this may sound like the 'literal' sense in the Christian scheme of four senses, it is more complicated than that. Raphael Loewe has argued persuasively that *peshat* in early texts means 'a reading in accordance with the usual interpretation', as opposed to a more far-fetched one that is proposed idiosyncratically by a particular rabbi.[51] David Weiss Halivni has argued that in the Talmud it actually means something like 'context' (from its etymological sense, 'extension'), so that the principle that 'no text can be deprived of its *peshat*'[52] means that texts must not be interpreted without regard to their context.[53]

In the Middle Ages *peshat* did eventually come to mean something nearer to the literal sense, and that is how it is generally used today. But it is still rarely literal in the way that modern critical readings are. It is concerned much more with the application of the text to Jewish life – i.e. having a halakhic interest – than with penetrating the literal meaning. Halivni comments:

> Our sense and the rabbis' sense of what constitutes simple, literal meaning do not always agree. Their sense of the simple, literal meaning was more inclusive. They felt less committed to our limited sense of peshat, seeing it instead as larger and wider in scope. To the rabbis, there was less of a distinction between simple and applied meaning with respect to both scope and primacy of peshat than there is to us . . . Thus the rabbis did not equate peshat with simple, literal meaning as we know it, but with a wider scope of expositions.[54]

I doubt whether a literal/allegorical distinction does justice to the many readings and uses of the Bible in Judaism.[55] As we saw, Christian distinctions between the literal and the various kinds of non-literal meaning are also complex, in that the most literal meaning of a text can sometimes be allegorical.[56] In the work of medieval Jewish commentators such as Abraham ibn Ezra (1089–1167) and David Kimchi (1160–1235, known acronymically as Radak), there is often a polemical element in the identification of the *peshat*: it is the Jewish meaning of the text, as opposed to the meaning Christians find in it. Thus readings of the Psalms that see in them references to Jesus are, unsurprisingly, rejected. The idea that some of them do refer to the Messiah is not necessarily contested in itself: it is just that the identity of the Messiah is differently conceived, Jews of course believing that he is still to come. But often a supposedly messianic text is interpreted as referring to a historical figure, one of the kings of Israel, just as is common in modern commentaries. *Peshat* readings are thus sometimes, but not always, what we might call literal.

The primary focus for Jewish commentators is not so much literality as an interpretation of the Hebrew Bible that endorses and undergirds Jewish belief and practice, and rules out the tenets of any other religion (specifically Christianity and Islam). Erwin Rosenthal writes that the task of Jewish interpretation

> was twofold. Its principal object was to explain the tenets of biblical religious culture to each generation in order to give the life of the community and the individual member guidance and direction, and to strengthen their faith in the existence and absolute, simple unity of God, his revelation in history through the Torah, his promise of the kingdom of God on earth and the final redemption at the end of days through the Messiah, son of David. The second objective was the defence of these concepts against Muslims and Christians in so far as these two daughter-religions claimed to have superseded Judaism.[57]

In other words, Jewish interpreters developed reading techniques that would enable the Bible to provide the kind of religious and moral instruction that their system of religious belief and practice required, and to counter other ways of taking it. Both *peshat* and *derash* readings could serve this purpose at times, but it is probable that extensive Christian use of what a Jew would term *derash* – a quest for the allegorical, tropological, anagogical sense, or whatever it might be called – predisposed Jewish commentators to prefer 'plain' readings, ones that contemporaneous Christian writers tend, indeed, to call 'Jewish' readings. Christians such as Andrew of St Victor, who followed literality to the extent of denying a Christological meaning even in such well-loved passages as Isaiah 52:13–53:12 (see above), were suspected of 'Judaizing'.

For all their similarity, Christian and Jewish interpretations have a different flavour: Christian readings tend to focus on theological meanings, Jewish on practical applications. Consider, for example, this interpretation of the famous speech of the Moabite, Ruth, to her mother-in-law, Naomi, in the book of Ruth, where she promises that she will stay with Naomi and never leave her side even in death, despite the fact that she is a foreigner and Naomi is an Israelite (Ruth 1:16–17). Christian readers were often interested in the story of Ruth because she was the ancestress of King David, and hence of Jesus Christ: she appears in Matthew's genealogy of Jesus (Matthew 1:5). For Jews, by contrast, she was an ideal convert to Judaism. Nicholas of Lyra commented on the interpretation of Ruth's speech in a way that is very close to that of Rashi, explicitly referring to 'the Hebrews' as the source of this interpretation:

> Here the Hebrews say that willing converts to the God of Judaism must be told the most difficult parts of the Law . . . Therefore, they say that Naomi, seeing Ruth's wish to convert to Judaism, told her some of the burdens of the Law: and first she told her that it was not lawful for Jews to go outside the land of Israel, except in great necessity. And then Ruth answered her, '*Wherever you go, I shall go*, and nowhere else.' Again, she said to her, 'It is not lawful for a woman to be alone with a man, unless he is her husband', and Ruth answered, '*Wherever you lodge, I shall lodge*, unwilling to be with another man without you.' Again, she said, 'The Hebrew people is subject to the burdens of the Law, in which there are 613 precepts.' Then she answered, '*Your people are my people*', which is to say, 'I wish to be subject to that Law.' Again, she said, 'It is forbidden to us to worship other gods.' And she answered, '*Your God is my God*', which is to say, 'I do not wish to worship any other god.' Again she said to her, 'In some cases a fourfold penalty of death (by stoning, burning, strangulation by hanging, or death by the sword) is imposed on transgressors of our Law, as is clear in Exodus and Deuteronomy.' And then Ruth answered, '*Whichever land takes you at death, there shall I die*', which is to say, 'I am prepared to receive whatever death penalty I should merit, just like you.'[58]

This makes the story of Ruth into a homily on obedience to the Torah, and in Christian terms is tropological or moral, rather than literal. But it displays what we may call the horizontal interest in Jewish reading of Scripture, by contrast with the frequently vertical concern of Christian commentators: they look for heavenly meanings, where Jewish teachers see parallels with other scriptural texts and thus build up a pattern of moral teaching. Christians read the biblical text within the framework of the theological message they found in the Bible, the message of creation, fall, redemption and final consummation. We can see an elaborated version of the Christian scheme in the writings of Hugh of St Victor. Hugh described the 'letter', that is, the basic literal sense, of the Bible as a foundation on which to erect a building of faith:

> For this building, Hugh used an extended metaphor of Noah's ark. Erecting this 'ark' was a kind of mental exercise, aimed at building up one's faith. The keel of the ark was the temporal framework of salvation history: Creation, Fall, Redemption, and Completion, as related in the history of the Old and New Testaments. At its center was the salvation of Mankind in Christ's passion; all the doctrines of the Christian faith were to be spiritually built on this historical framework.[59]

Jews read the Bible just as much within a framework, but that framework was the moral and practical structures of Judaism as a religion focused more on action than on doctrine.

Thus Christian and Jewish readers in the Middle Ages might arrive at different, sometimes even opposite, conclusions from their study of Scripture; but what drove them was essentially the same aim: to get the Bible to support their own system of thought and practice. Their problem was that the Bible only partly overlaps with Judaism, just as it only partly overlaps with Christianity, as these two religions have developed. If one insists that the overlap is to be seen as total, then necessarily rather ingenious techniques of interpretation will have to be devised; and this happened in both religions, in similar though not identical forms.

Medieval commentators, Jewish and Christian, for all that they polemicized against each other, at times recognized themselves as brothers beneath the skin. They talked to each other and read each other's works.[60] Nicholas of Lyra was not alone in consulting and being influenced by Jewish teachers, and some Christian writers even tried to learn Hebrew, as Jerome was known to have done successfully so many centuries before. Already in the ninth century Theodulf of Orleans, a contemporary of Alcuin, with whom this chapter began, consulted Hebrew manuscripts in order to correct the Latin of the Vulgate Bible.[61] But more common was the attempt to learn Greek in order to be able to read the New Testament in its original language, and there are Graeco-Latin manuscripts, such as a Psalter written in Sankt Gallen (now in

Switzerland) in 909 with Latin and Greek texts in parallel columns.[62] Even so, few western Christian scholars in the early Middle Ages knew either Greek or Hebrew, whereas Jewish commentators could read Latin as well as Hebrew and Aramaic, and so had the advantage when disputing over the meaning of the Old Testament/Hebrew Bible. In the twelfth century, however, the study of Hebrew revived: Herbert of Bosham, a student of Andrew of St Victor who went on to be secretary to Thomas Becket (1118–70), Archbishop of Canterbury, was a notable Hebraist, and may mark the high point of knowledge of Hebrew in the Latin west.[63]

THE BIBLE IN EAST AND WEST

In this chapter our focus of attention has moved west. The centre of gravity for earlier, patristic study and exposition of the Bible lies in the eastern churches of what are now Greece, Turkey and Syria; but in the Middle Ages the Latin west came into its own. The rise of universities, such as Bologna, Paris and Oxford, contributed to a style of biblical study that was enquiring rather than meditative; and the orders of friars, Dominican and Franciscan, sought to integrate it into the growing interest in philosophical thought that reached its climax in the work of Thomas Aquinas.

There is a reason for the comparative neglect of medieval eastern biblical study by scholars, which is that in the east there developed no tradition of academic biblical study such as we see in the west. Instead there was a continuation of the patristic tradition that biblical exposition belonged in homilies, in the context of the Church's liturgy. This tended to favour the old Alexandrian approach of the quest for the spiritual or allegorical sense, rather than the Antiochene method or that of its western medieval successors. Undergirding this is the fact that the Old Testament, in particular, was little read in the Eucharistic liturgies of what became the Orthodox churches. In the west, Old Testament readings, it is true, were found almost entirely in the Divine Office (the non-Eucharistic services throughout the day, and especially Matins or Vigils, celebrated during the night or in the early morning), rather than in the Eucharist. But in the east the Old Testament was scarcely read liturgically at all. The consequence was that most laypeople virtually never heard a reading from the Old Testament; what they did hear were hymns and chants in which images from the Old Testament were woven into complex allegories, in many cases Mariological in character.[64] The Song of Songs figured largely in such hymns in both east and west, in the choice of texts for feasts of the Blessed Virgin Mary.

But if actual readings from the Old Testament were comparatively few, people in both east and west came to know its stories through art (stained glass and paintings in the west, icons in the east) and through preaching; while the New Testament they heard anyway, in the readings at Mass from the Epistles and Gospels which were then expounded in homilies, and acted out through such customs as mystery plays. In the eastern churches the readings were in Greek or Old Church Slavonic, comprehensible to the congregation, but in the west they were in Latin, which few laypeople understood and which they mostly could not read. As we shall see, there were vernacular Bibles in the west too, but they were not used liturgically until the revolution in liturgy initiated at the Reformation. The picture of a laity wholly uninformed about the contents of the Bible is certainly an exaggeration, but the average Christian in the Middle Ages is unlikely to have known the Scriptures in much detail, and would have been guided primarily by the scheme of salvation history I outlined in Chapter 13 – just as Jews would have treated the Bible as essentially a source for *torah*, communicated chiefly through rabbinic teachings.

Thus the Bible could serve as a basis for faith even for the many who could not read it in Latin, but only as interpreted through this basic idea of salvation history. In the Middle Ages, as at most other times, the Bible was understood within an interpretative framework: individuals were not seen as free to make anything they chose of the text. That idea arrived only with the Reformation and the Enlightenment, as we shall see in the next two chapters.

16

The Reformation and Its Readings

There was no moment at which the Protestant Reformation of the sixteenth century definitively began.[1] The thirty-first of October 1517, when Martin Luther is said to have posted his ninety-five theses against indulgences on the door of the Castle Church in the small town of Wittenberg in Saxony, has traditionally been seen as decisive; and this is so, in the sense that from that point on there was no going back. But Luther's initiative did not come out of the blue. There were anticipations of the call for the reform of the Church in the Middle Ages, and one has only to read Dante (1265–1321) to see how excoriating could be the criticism of Church authorities, up to and including popes, even in the work of a perfectly orthodox Catholic.

ANTICIPATIONS OF THE REFORMATION

Three movements in particular can be seen as paving the way for Luther. The Waldensians, still in existence in Piedmont in Italy today, as well as in other parts of Europe and South America, often describe themselves as the first Protestants. They derive from the activity of a teacher called Petrus Waldes, who died in about 1217.[2] Waldes started a lay movement of travelling preachers, not initially condemned by the Church authorities but later regarded as heretical. Waldensians were not only critical of the Church, but took their stand on the Bible, which they interpreted freely without reference to official Church authorities, and had at least excerpts in their various vernaculars, rather than in Latin. In Waldensian writing we find what may be the earliest statement of the principle which was to become a central part in Luther's teaching: that Scripture is its own interpreter. A former Waldensian, Durandus of Huesca (1160–1224), commenting on Daniel, reports that for the Waldensians the words of Daniel are absolutely limpid (*luculentissima*) and require no interpretation (*responsio*).[3] None of the Fathers, none of the medieval interpreters we have discussed would have been likely to say that. Protestants were to say it forcefully, even of texts (such indeed as Daniel) that strike the average reader as very much in need of an interpreter.

In England, John Wyclif (1330–84; sometimes spelled Wycliffe), a teacher at Oxford, represents an early anticipation of the Reformation, arguing that the true Church was an invisible reality that did not depend on clergy and an ecclesiastical hierarchy. He was the inspiration for the so-called Lollard movement ('lollard' was a term of abuse, meaning babbler). The Lollards ran into trouble with the authorities for their minimalist interpretation of the Eucharist: they denied the medieval doctrine that the bread and wine of the Eucharist or Mass become literally the body and blood of Christ. 'Literally' here is a highly sophisticated term, not implying a magical change, but defined as meaning that the bread and wine change in substance (essential nature) while retaining all the appearance and normal functions ('accidents') of bread and wine. Lollards were burned by English monarchs from Henry IV (r. 1399–1413) to Henry VIII (r. 1509–47). More important for our purposes, Wyclif also had a particularly exalted view of the Bible and wanted it to be available to ordinary laypeople, which led him to produce his own translation into English (see Chapter 18). At least towards the end of his life, Wyclif came to assert that Scripture alone was necessary for human salvation, without the mediation of the Church authorities, priests and popes.

Anticipations of Luther's attack on the ecclesiastical hierarchy can also be found in the work of the teacher Jan Hus, from whom the Hussite churches take their name. Hus (1369–1415) came from Bohemia, now the Czech Republic, and was the Dean of the Philosophical Faculty at the University of Prague. He became familiar with the works of Wyclif, and argued for similar changes to the Church, in particular seeking a vernacular (Czech) liturgy and the administration of both bread and wine to the people at Mass, rather than bread alone, as had become the custom (and as remains the custom in the Roman Catholic Church). Hus was burned at the stake in 1415 after being condemned at the Council of Konstanz, at which he had been given a safe-conduct to defend his position – a treacherous act that outraged his followers. A Hussite church nevertheless emerged from this debacle; its main body even established a somewhat tense relationship of communion with Rome, and survived as the main church in Bohemia until the seventeenth century.

All these movements, which with hindsight can be seen as anticipations or forerunners of the Reformation, seemed in their day to threaten the Church more than did the theses of an academic Augustinian friar in Wittenberg. Luther's theses primarily attacked the sale of indulgences, and he was hardly the first person to have seen them as a corrupt method of funding the Church. Chaucer (1343–1400) in *The Canterbury Tales* takes pot-shots at them in his presentation of the Pardoner. Like his forerunners, Luther was concerned to appeal over the head of the ecclesiastical authorities to the Bible, and this was more novel. But it was linked to a quite particular idea of what the Bible actually taught. And for this we have to go back to what perhaps can be seen as the real beginning of the Reformation, which happened not in the centre of Wittenberg, but in Luther's head.

LUTHER'S REFORMATION

Luther himself[4] identified a short period in which he realized the truth of the message the rest of his life was to be dedicated to proclaiming, a time of spiritual wrestling in 'the tower' of his monastery. His thinking centred on a single biblical text, which he became convinced was not to be interpreted as the Church of his day did, but in a wholly new way. The text is in Paul's Letter to the Romans: 'the righteousness of God is revealed through faith for faith; as it is written "The one who is righteous will live by faith"' (Romans 1:17, quoting Habakkuk 2:4). The 'righteousness' of God, Luther realized, did not mean God's righteous judgement on sinners, but rather the righteousness which God gave or 'imputed' to Christians, which Luther described as 'passive' righteousness – righteousness that is not a matter of doing good works so as to earn salvation, but of being in the right with God by God's own action alone. This righteousness was to be accepted through faith rather than worked at by striving to perform good actions. Luther immediately added that it would then lead to good actions; but such actions were not a prerequisite, since it was by God's grace alone that men and women were accepted as righteous.

This had huge implications for the practice of piety, given how focused the late medieval Church was on 'good works', that is, acts such as pilgrimages, attending Mass, and above all paying into the coffers of the Church, for example by buying indulgences. These acts, rather than good works in the more general sense of living a moral life, were mainly what Luther had in his sights. He was developing an idea that is certainly there in Romans (though see the discussion of the New Perspective on Paul in Chapter 7), and that had been further elaborated by Augustine, who to this extent is one of the fathers of the Reformation. But he saw the idea as the key to the whole of theology, and indeed to the whole of life, so that 'justification by grace through faith alone' became the central plank of the Lutheran Reformation.

The idea brought theological difficulties in its wake, as was quickly seen. It could easily lead to antinomianism, the theory that once one has been justified through faith it does not matter how one behaves – a consequence Luther was quick to deny, but which could easily be levelled at him as it was at Paul ('why not say (as some people slander us by saying that we say), "Let us do evil so that good may come"? Their condemnation is deserved!', Romans 3:8).[5] It could lead to a theory of double predestination, the belief that God had chosen certain people as the recipients of his righteousness and thus must have rejected others, without regard for their moral character – a conclusion drawn consistently by Luther's younger contemporary, John Calvin (1509–64). And it could lead to individualism, detaching the believer from any need to belong to the Church as a visible body of people, since the Church was no longer a necessary context for the (already justified) believer. All these dangers lurked, and as the Reformation developed they appeared and had to be either accepted or, somehow, rebutted. But for Luther himself the idea of justification by grace through faith brought a sense of relief from moral scruples, to which he had been greatly subject, and showed God to be gracious and loving. Gratitude for salvation replaced scrupulous moral striving, assurance replaced anxiety about salvation. Nothing human beings could do, however good in itself, could please God; but nothing needed to, since he granted salvation freely and without price. Here lies the original heart of the Lutheran Reformation.

Luther's idea had two major effects on the study and interpretation of the Bible. First, it meant that a major text in Scripture had the power to dethrone the authority of the Church, in so far as the Church was not teaching in accordance with that text. So long as the Church insisted on good works as the necessary condition for salvation, it was out of step with Scripture, and one of the two must be wrong. Luther was in no doubt that it was the Church that was mistaken. The idea of setting the word of the Bible against the teaching of the Church in this way had scarcely arisen in the Middle Ages. Secondly, Romans 1:17 provided a new criterion for interpreting the whole of Scripture, a new hermeneutical principle akin to the patristic rule of faith, almost a kind of new creed (though Luther by no means rejected the traditional creeds). The Bible was to be read in the light of the principle of justification.

Soon, Luther developed other principles that stood alongside justification by faith. One was a dialectic between law and gospel, which seems to have emerged in his thinking between 1515 and 1518.[6] This was not an opposition between the Old Testament and the New, or not primarily so, and it did not suggest that the gospel had simply replaced the law. Rather, law – the demands God makes on the human race – is evident in both Testaments; but, also in both, the Bible insists that law is never God's last word. The law, meaning all the rules God gives in both Old Testament laws such as the Ten Commandments and in New Testament passages such as the Sermon on the Mount (Matthew 5–8), has two primary functions. One is to regulate human life in society, and this function is never to be set aside. But, in many ways more important theologically, it also has the function of showing up human moral impotence for what it is. God's demands can never in practice be fulfilled; humankind always falls short of them. However, the Bible contains such despair-inducing moral teachings not to reduce us to a sense of desperation, but to open the way for us to receive the gospel: the good news that God freely justifies (makes righteous) the sinner who accepts his grace through faith. Once one has accepted this, one will continue to profit from biblical moral teachings, but not as an inexorable demand that must be fulfilled to the letter by ever more moral striving, or (and here we come back to Luther's criticism of the Church of his day) by doing more and more 'good works' in an attempt to stave off divine judgement. God, as Luther often says in relation to the text 1 Samuel 2:6, 'kills, yet brings to life'. His law reduces us to a near-death experience of hopelessness, but his gospel then raises us up to hope and joy.

The tension between law and gospel is for Luther the centre of the Bible. In this perspective, the whole Bible is about Christ: not in the sense that Christ must be found in all the texts through an allegorical reading, but in the sense that the whole of Scripture witnesses to the freely given salvation from deserved judgement that Christ brings about.[7] In a way, Luther's scheme is an extension of the ancient Christian scheme, observed in Chapter 13, which read the entire Bible as a story of disaster followed by salvation, a history of the way God had rescued the human race from the plight into which its sin had cast it. Luther's version operates along similar lines, only more at the existential than the historical level. Failure to obey God, followed by God's miraculous decision not to punish this, but to forgive freely, operates not simply at the level of the historical development of the human race, but for each individual believer. The old 'rule of faith' is thus reaffirmed against late-medieval tendencies to turn Christianity into a religion of 'works' (to 're-Judaize' it, as Luther would have seen the matter); but it is reaffirmed as valid for every Christian. It thus acquires a psychological aspect that had not been so evident in the early Church. It concerns the way the believer feels about the law and the gospel, and about appropriating the blessings of the gospel through an act of faith.

Read in this way, the Bible is not a source of allegories about the Church, but a guide for the life of the individual. Not that Luther neglected matters of liturgy, moral teaching and all the other things that go to make up Christian life, though he was uninterested in Church order, and did not produce a liturgy for ordination until 1535. The heart of the faith, and hence (for him) of the Bible, lay in the relation of law and gospel. Luther's reading of Scripture is in some ways akin to the medieval tropological or moral one, but the moral teaching that emerges is focused much less on obedience to commandments – even the overarching commandment of mutual love – than on faith as the proper reaction to the goodness of God manifested in the life, death and resurrection of Jesus Christ. The Bible is not there primarily to make us good, but to reveal to us how bad we are, and then to show us how God nevertheless saves us through Christ. This is a complete hermeneutic, or interpretative scheme, for reading the Bible.

If Luther's theology led to a new way of interpreting the Scriptures, it also depended on some new information about them. This was the result of the recovery in the west of the Greek text of the New Testament, and a renewed awareness of the meaning of certain Greek words. Until then, we recall, western Christians knew the Bible only through the Vulgate. Though there were some scholars in the Middle Ages who gained at least a basic knowledge of Hebrew, very few in the west could read the New Testament in Greek. A crucial figure here is Desiderius Erasmus (1466–1536) of Rotterdam, who worked in a number of centres of learning in Europe, including Cambridge and Basel, but who was essentially an independent scholar rather than a university professor, and also an ex-monk, eventually dispensed by the pope from his vows. Erasmus compiled a Greek New Testament on the basis of the best manuscripts he could find (many not, in fact, very good), and published it in 1516. Luther, who was an excellent linguist, learned Greek and read Erasmus' New Testament. There he discovered, among other things, that the word translated in the Latin as *paenitentia*, and interpreted by the contemporary Church as referring to 'penance' – that is, acts done to display penitence such as building churches or, for the poor, contributing to the coffers of the Church in smaller ways – really meant repentance as an inward state, *contrition* as we might say. This appeared to fit well with Luther's psychological emphasis on the inner life of the believer rather than on external acts of piety.

Erasmus' promotion of the Greek Bible was controversial, since many thought that Jerome had worked under divine inspiration in translating it into Latin and so no reference back to the Greek original was desirable or even licit. The supremacy of the Vulgate Bible was indeed reasserted at the Council of Trent, and it is only in recent times that Catholic scholars have been encouraged to work from the Hebrew and Greek texts rather than from the Latin. But Luther at once embraced the principle that one should study the Bible in its original languages, and when he produced his own translations into German it was from the Hebrew and Greek texts that he worked.

Further important hermeneutical principles followed. Luther argued that the Bible should be seen as its own interpreter. The principle is also sometimes referred to as the principle of the clarity of Scripture: that there is nothing obscure in the Bible that requires an authoritative person or group to illuminate it for the simple believer, but that the Bible speaks for itself. This probably strikes the average reader today as deeply counter-intuitive. It is obvious that there are many obscure individual passages in the Bible, and that even on a macro level there are whole books whose exact meaning is hard to grasp. Why else does the genre of biblical commentary exist at all? Indeed, Luther himself spent hours and days on biblical interpretation, lectured on biblical texts and wrote comments on disputed verses, not least the very text in Romans 1:17 that we saw represented the starting point for his whole work. How then can Scripture be said to be so clear that it interprets itself?

In fact Luther did not say that Scripture is wholly clear, but that the 'matter of Scripture' (*res scripturae*) is clear: what Scripture is really about. We can see this emerging in Luther's arguments with Erasmus, who initially had tended to support Luther – Erasmus too made many trenchant criticisms of the Church of his day – but later turned against the reformer and defended the Church against his attacks.

Luther and Erasmus disputed about the clarity or perspicuity of Scripture. This debate produced Luther's important work *On the Bondage of the Will* (*De servo arbitrio*), written in 1525. The introductory material in this treatise discusses Erasmus' argument that the Bible contains many obscurities and hence that it needs to be expounded by the authoritative organs of the Catholic Church if Christians are not to risk being misled. Erasmus was obviously correct in thinking that there are obscure places in the Bible. But, as is so often the case in theological debates, he and Luther were to some extent at cross purposes. Luther insisted against Erasmus that the Bible is not obscure or dark, but plain and clear: but by 'the Bible' or 'Scripture' he does not exactly mean this long and complicated text, just as we encounter it in its thousands of pages, but a sort of core or essence of the Bible:

> What kind of deep secret can still be hidden in the Scripture, now that the seals have been opened, the stone rolled away from the grave, and the deepest secret of all revealed: that Christ, the only Son of God, has become man, that there is one eternal God in three persons, that Christ has died for us, and that he reigns for ever in heaven?[8]

What is 'clear' here is not exactly Scripture but the gospel message – something like the rule of faith, or what the Antiochenes called the *hypothesis* of the Bible – its drift. Luther's polemic is not really directed against the idea that some places in the Bible are difficult to interpret, but against the idea that it is in biblical interpretation *guided by the authorities of the Church* that Christian truth is made known. On the contrary, he argues, the gospel has been made known by God himself: it is not *encoded* in Scripture in such a way that technical skill, regulated by the Church, is required to expound it. It is evident to the simplest person who reads the Gospels or Paul. The principle of the clarity of Scripture, and of Scripture as its own interpreter, is thus not a literal statement about the Bible but a call to arms: a call to grasp the Bible's central message, which would exist even if there were no Bible, and is summed up in the principle of justification by grace, through faith in the saving death and resurrection of Jesus Christ.

But even if this is the essence, in some sense, of the Gospels and Pauline letters, can it really apply to the whole of the Bible? Are the books of Joshua, say, or Proverbs, or Revelation, exemplifications of the essential gospel message? As we have seen, throughout Christian use of the Bible this problem had been acknowledged, at least dimly, and its solution had lain through allegorization. For Luther, that could not be the answer; the biblical books must be taken at face value and evaluated in the light of the basic gospel message. Notoriously, he went further than almost any Christian before or since in concluding that certain books were not an authentic expression of the gospel, and when he translated the Bible he removed them to an appendix. The books in question are Esther (demoted because it nowhere mentions God), Hebrews, James and Revelation. Conversely, Luther was prepared to say which books were the most important, the 'truest and noblest books': John, Romans, Galatians, Ephesians, 1 Peter and 1 John.[9] Lutheran tradition did not follow the reformer closely in this. But for Luther himself the principle that one can assess the value of even biblical books in the light of an overarching or more fundamental message was extremely important.

> Since Luther placed Christ at the heart of Scripture he could be critical of the Bible as a book in a manner which would have scandalized later Lutherans: the chapters of Isaiah are out of order; James is 'a good book but it is not an apostolic book'; Revelation is neither apostolic nor prophetic and resembles the dreams of the Abbot Joachim; the Book of Kings is a Jewish calendar; it does no harm to say that the Pentateuch could not have been written by Moses; Paul did not write Hebrews and perhaps Apollos did.[10]

Thus Luther's criticism of authority reached even to criticism of the authority of parts of the Bible itself, in the name of principles derived from what he took to be the Bible's overall drift.

It is of a piece with this that Luther generally avoided what he saw as allegorization. The Bible was meant to speak with its own voice, rather than having a meaning imposed upon it by interpreting it in whatever way would yield an acceptable sense. Luther saw medieval allegorizing as a means of twisting the text to fit the interpreter's presuppositions – already Alan of Lille in the twelfth century had warned against this, using a figure of speech that became proverbial: 'authority has a wax nose, that is, it can change the meaning in a diversity of ways'.[11] From a modern perspective, some of Luther's allegedly literal meanings themselves seem quite allegorical. The Song of Songs is a case in point. He altogether rejects the 'spiritual' interpretation according to which the lovers represent Christ and the Church (or the individual believer); but he does not anticipate the modern tendency to read the text literally as an account of a human love affair. For him, the lovers stand for God and the political order, and the whole book is about good government – which probably strikes most modern readers as even more counter-intuitive. He does not, however, see this as allegorization: it represents the plain sense of the text, which is metaphorical (compare comments on this idea in Chapter 15).

Similarly, Luther takes Psalm 19:4, 'their voice goes out through all the earth, and their words to the end of the world', to be about the preaching ministry of the apostles and hence of their successors, the Church's ministers. This is a traditional interpretation, enshrined in the Catholic liturgy, where Psalm 19 is set for feasts of apostles, perhaps precisely because of this verse. This interpretation ignores the obvious meaning, namely that the heavens in their movements give praise to God, and substitutes an ecclesiastical one: and we should have no hesitation in calling this an allegorical or metaphorical reading. But for Luther it is what the psalm plainly means.[12] Similarly, he treats the traditional prophecies of Christ such as Isaiah 9:2–7 and 11:1–9 as literal predictions of Jesus, and does not think of these interpretations as allegorical: there was no historical reference in such prophecies other than to him. The suggestion that they referred to a king of Judah was simply a Jewish misunderstanding, not a 'literal' reading, even if it had been accepted by Andrew of St Victor and, before him, by the Antiochene theologians of the fourth and fifth centuries. Luther also applied some prophecies in Scripture to events of his own day, just as the first Christians and the Qumran sect had done: thus Ezekiel 38–39 was about the Turks.[13]

Luther argued strongly that the biblical text itself was the only authority in matters of faith, and that its meaning in that context was entirely lucid. It can be seen, however, that he was apt to impose his own beliefs on the text as much, or almost as much, as his predecessors in the Middle Ages who had read their own convictions into it by means of allegorical interpretation. The doctrine of justification by grace through faith, the principle of the dialectic of law and gospel, and even the clarity of Scripture itself were ideas that did not derive clearly from the Bible taken on its own terms. At most we could say that they were ideas occurring in some places in the Bible which Luther generalized into an overall hermeneutical scheme.

The gap between the Bible and Lutheran doctrine is perhaps even more obvious when it comes to the uses of the law. From the Old Testament one would have the impression that God's laws are given to be observed, and woe betide anyone who breaks them. From Paul one could conclude that the law is abrogated for Christians, who are free to act simply out of love and are under no other precepts (see Romans 13:8, 'Owe no one anything, except to love one another'). These two ideas are clearly hard to reconcile, and medieval writers had on the whole downplayed the more antinomian-sounding aspects of Paul. For Luther, reconciliation is achieved by a different route. Paul is his guiding star, and so the abrogation of the law is central. Yet the basic moral laws in the Old Testament are not dispensed with: in so far as they correspond to the natural laws understood by all peoples (the Ten

Commandments, for example), they are still in force, and this use of the law is to keep society properly ordered. Another use, however, as we have seen, is to bring us to our knees in recognition of failure and abjection: the unbearably demanding commands in the Sermon on the Mount exist to show us just how far any human being is from being able to please God. Some Lutherans argued that there is also a third use of the law, and that is to offer guidance to those who have accepted God's passive righteousness and are now in a state of justification. Such people need advice for the path ahead, and this the law, in its third use, provides. Whether Luther himself believed in the third use of the law is much disputed among Luther specialists. If there is such a third use, this does go some way towards answering the charge of antinomianism; though both Catholics and Reformed Christians tend to suspect that antinomian tendencies always lurk in Lutheranism.

Is the theory of the two or three uses of the law itself a biblical theory? Certainly the Bible can be read in its light, and in a way that many Christians have found illuminating – though to Jews it seems a travesty of what the Hebrew Bible means when it offers us God's laws, failing to take seriously the divine demand for obedience. But to claim that a neutral, unbiased reading of the Bible would lead one to the theory – that Scripture simply teaches it 'clearly', once the clouds of Catholic allegorizing have been removed – is audacious. In 1630, a century after Luther, William Chillingworth in England declared that 'the Bible only is the religion of Protestants'; but already for Luther that religion is the Bible read in accordance with principles such as the uses of the law, not the Bible read without presuppositions (if such a thing were possible). Elements of these principles are drawn from the Bible, just as is justification by grace through faith. But all such general principles result from taking a biblical insight and then applying it to the Bible as a whole, and this the Bible itself, in its huge variety and shapelessness, tends to resist. The reformed Christian faith overlaps with the Bible but is not identical with it. Protestants judge that their reading does better justice to the Bible than a Catholic one, taken overall. If they did not, they would not be Protestants – but the fit remains imperfect.

Though Luther claimed that there was gospel in the Old Testament just as there was law in the New, and that the dialectic of law and gospel was not an Old/New contrast, he seems at times at best ambivalent about the Old Testament, and he was hostile in the extreme towards Judaism as a contemporary phenomenon. The Nazis later exploited Luther's anti-Jewish polemic, but there was plenty to exploit. Most Jews accordingly have a low view of Luther, and see his whole theology, and hence his approach to interpreting the Bible, as tainted by anti-Semitism. This extends to an adverse judgement on modern biblical scholars in the Lutheran tradition, who at least until recently were apt to refer to Jewish 'legalism' as opposed to the freedom of the Christian gospel, thus tacitly conceding the accusation that Lutheranism is antinomian while at an explicit level usually denying it.[14] Those such as myself who feel a great affinity to Lutheran theology have to recognize the danger of anti-Semitism that lurks beneath the surface emphasis on freedom and joy.

One example of Luther's attitude to the Jewish law can be found in his treatment of the Ten Commandments. In general he regards them as part of natural law, binding therefore on all peoples. But the prohibition of images he treats as given only to the Jews – the Lutheran Reformation was not iconoclastic in the way more Reformed movements were in England. When he summarized the Commandments in his catechisms he did not even mention the prohibition of images, and he followed Catholic practice in enumerating the Commandments in such a way that 'you shall not make a graven image' is not a separate, second Commandment but merely an appendage to the first ('you shall have no other gods before me'; the Tenth Commandment is then split in two to make up the number). The law against images is for him 'merely Jewish'.

Erasmus, incidentally, had been even harsher in his judgement on the Old Testament than Luther. He hated Judaism, and feared that Christian interest in the Old Testament could lead to 'Judaizing', to him a self-evidently wrong path. The Old Testament in his view was far too important in the Church, and should fade in the light of Christ and his new revelation. It had been intended 'only for a limited time', and was now superannuated.[15] It could be fruitful in the Church only if it was read allegorically, with the New Testament providing the principles for its interpretation; and even this, he thought, was a mere rescue mission for a text that it would really be better to abandon.

THE REFORMED TRADITION*

Reformers in France and Switzerland, such as Calvin and Huldrych (Ulrich) Zwingli (1484–1531), had a less dialectical understanding of

* 'Reformed', with a capital R, refers to reformers other than Luther, and especially to those active in France and Switzerland rather than Germany, who also greatly influenced the progress of the Reformation in England and Scotland.

the Bible, and tended to treat the Old and New Testaments in a smoother and more equal way as two parts of a single revelation. Calvin wrote extensive commentaries on the Old Testament, which he saw as a history of the divine education of the human race that could still instruct Christians in righteous living. He shared Luther's dislike of allegorization, and preferred John Chrysostom to Origen among the Fathers because he, like the Antiochene school in general, had been less inclined to allegorize.[16] This is one of many ways in which Calvin's biblical commentaries can have a rather modern air.

There is little that could be called antinomian in Calvin. He accepted Luther's principle of justification by grace through faith, and the consequent idea that those who were saved owed this only to the mercy of God; but he took the logical step of asking about those who did not accept God's grace through faith: they, he argued, were damned by God's decision alone just as the saved were saved only through his mercy. This is arguably implied in Luther's position, but Luther was not so given to following his own insights to their ultimate conclusion, enjoying paradox and mystery rather than strictly logical reasoning. Hence Calvin produced a doctrine of double predestination, in which God not only saves without human desert but also damns without human fault. One might think that this would eliminate the law altogether and result in an even more antinomian system than that of Luther, and there were some on the more extreme fringes of the Reformation who took precisely that view. But in Calvin the law makes a triumphant re-entry: the ability to keep the law is a sure indication that one is among the saved. Hence moral striving becomes important, almost as important, it might be said, as it had been for medieval Catholicism, though now manifested not in pilgrimages and indulgences but in sobriety, industry and probity in secular affairs. Like Luther, Calvin was able to point to Paul as a basis for his own doctrines; for Romans teaches something approaching double predestination:

> Even before they [Jacob and Esau] had been born or had done anything good or bad (so that God's purpose of election might continue, not by works but by his call) she was told, 'The elder shall serve the younger.' As it is written, 'I have loved Jacob, but I have hated Esau.' What then are we to say? Is there injustice on God's part? By no means! For he says to Moses, 'I will have mercy on whom I have mercy, and I will have compassion on whom I have compassion.' So it depends not on human will or exertion, but on God who shows mercy. For the scripture says to Pharaoh, 'I have

> raised you up for the very purpose of showing my power in you, so that my name may be proclaimed in all the earth.' So then he has mercy on whomsoever he chooses, and he hardens the heart of whomsoever he chooses.
>
> (Romans 9:11–18)

In Reformed Christianity the Old Testament becomes critical, read literally, in forming the Christian character. Calvin expounded the laws in the Pentateuch, and even rearranged them to make them easier to grasp, rather in the same way others made harmonies of the four Gospels. He did not permit himself to sit in judgement on any books in the Bible as Luther had done, but emphasized that all the books were helpful to the Christian. Unlike later fundamentalists, however, he sat quite loosely to the traditional ascriptions of authorship, and had no problem with the idea that some of the Psalms were not by David (Psalm 74, for example, for him clearly reflects the destruction of the Temple in the sixth century BCE), or that editors had arranged the prophetic books out of individual oracles. A number of the assumptions of modern biblical criticism on its more literary-historical side thus have their roots in Calvin, just as more theological critiques of biblical books can often claim Luther as their inspiration.

Calvin criticized forced, over-orthodox interpretations, such as the use of Isaiah 64:6 ('all our righteous deeds are like a filthy cloth') to show that all human good works are really evil, or of Isaiah's 'Holy, Holy, Holy' (Isaiah 6:3) as a proof of the doctrine of the Trinity:

> The ancients quoted this passage when they wished to prove that there are three persons in one essence of the Godhead. I do not disagree with their opinion; but if I had to contend with heretics, I would rather choose to employ stronger proofs; for they become more obstinate, and assume an air of triumph, when inconclusive arguments are brought against them.[17]

And, like Luther, he was content to see the Bible as approximately true, not necessarily as perfect in every detail: the writers were as accurate as their purpose required, which did not mean that they had to get every number or detail exactly right. 'It is well known that the Evangelists were not scrupulous in their time sequences, nor even in keeping to details of words and actions.'[18] Where there are minor variations between the Gospels, we should not make a fuss over nothing. Occasionally Calvin even 'corrects' the text: 'Calvin was neither the first nor the last to defend the accuracy of the Bible by rewriting it.'[19]

SOLA SCRIPTURA

The belief that Scripture is its own interpreter, and that the Church's magisterium (official teaching function) is not required in order for the Christian to make sense of it, lies at the base of another Reformation principle: *sola scriptura*, 'Scripture alone'. Only what may be proved from the Bible can be regarded as binding on Christians; hence much of the apparatus of late-medieval piety is excluded, since according to the Reformers there is no biblical warrant for indulgences, pilgrimages, some of the so-called sacraments or penitential acts. All these are human inventions, and cannot be demanded as necessary for the Christian. But there was a division among the Reformers as to whether things not commanded in Scripture are simply unnecessary, or actually forbidden. On the whole the Lutheran arm of the Reformation took the first option, arguing that there were customs in the Church that were not scriptural but were good and harmless provided they were not treated as essential: they were known as *adiaphora*, 'indifferent matters'. The Reformed wing tended more to the view that what was not mentioned in the Bible (or provable from it) was actually not to be done. The belief that anything that mattered must be mentioned somewhere in Scripture had the perhaps predictable result that interpreters took to reading into the Bible things they regarded as important: an extreme example would be the Spanish biblical scholar Benito Arias Montano (1527–98), who was perplexed that the New World was apparently not mentioned in the Bible and so listed place names in the Old Testament that did, so he argued, correspond to places in the Americas.[20]

This may seem a relatively small difference, but in the English Reformation it became a matter of considerable importance in controversies about the Book of Common Prayer. By the end of the sixteenth century attitudes in England had hardened and there were two distinct camps. On the one hand there were the ancestors of later Puritans, who argued that the Church should not prescribe in its liturgy anything not commanded in the Bible. They had in mind such customs as kneeling to receive Holy Communion, apparently trivial in themselves but symptomatic of a continuation of Catholic practices. On the other hand there were the defenders of the 1559 Elizabethan settlement of the Church of England, of whom the most important was Richard Hooker, whom we met in the Introduction. They maintained that it was entirely lawful for the Church to make provision for matters simply not covered by scriptural regulation. The Church must not claim any absolute authority or infallibility in such matters, but was free to exercise its reason in coming to sensible conclusions.

This is how Hooker argued for the continuation of the orders of bishop, priest and deacon in the Church of England, which gave it an old-fashioned, Catholic look when compared with the Protestant churches of Geneva or Zurich. He did not suggest that the Bible enjoined the existence of these orders – and would have struggled to do so – but reasoned that, in an area where Scripture was effectively silent, the Church was free to use its own reason to decide the matter. The threefold order, Hooker argued, had worked well enough in the past, so should not be abandoned. The Lutheran churches in Scandinavia, which accepted the Reformation en masse, followed the same logic and so continued to have bishops, as did some Lutheran churches in German-speaking lands; whereas the Reformed churches on the whole adopted a Presbyterian polity, arguing that this was required by the evidence of the New Testament – such was the case, for example, in Scotland. Paradoxically, we may say that an important difference among Protestants concerned just how important certain practices in the Church actually are. Where Catholics maintained that bishops were, and always had been, an essential part of Church order, and the Reformed that they were a post-biblical innovation which should therefore be rejected, many Lutherans, along with many in the Church of England, maintained that they were not necessary but not, on that account alone, to be abolished. They were a perfectly acceptable institution which the Bible had no opinions about, one way or the other. 'Indifferent' matters are thus not unimportant ones, but raise no issues of principle, and cannot be decided on the basis of any biblical revelation.

Here we see the working-out in practice of the rather different attitudes towards the Bible in Luther, on the one hand, and Calvin and other Reformed theologians on the other. What mattered for Luther was the core of the Bible, the *res scripturae*: the principle of justification by grace through faith, the dialectic of law and gospel, the uses of the law. The detail of Scripture fitted around these schemes of interpretation, and much of the Bible gave no particular steer on less important issues. Reformed interpreters were more inclined to take the text of the Bible in a more equal way and to resist reducing it to a few grand principles. Consequently they tended to read it in what Luther would have seen as a more 'Jewish' way, as prescribing rules for the Christian life, both individual and corporate, and covering every possible eventuality – so that where the Bible gave no ruling, we could be sure that the activity in question was not to be adopted. In practice there is a great deal of common ground between the two camps: both, for example, dropped much of medieval Catholic piety; and there are also oddities such as the Church of England, which had a largely Reformed liturgy and never regarded Luther very highly, yet retained even more features of Catholic tradition than he had – saints' days, bishops, marriage as a sacrament. But the two streams of thought persisted, and still surface today from time to time: pastors in the Reformed tradition will often hold that any significant activity in the Church needs a scriptural warrant, where Lutherans and many Anglicans happily forge ahead provided they feel sure that the Bible is not actually against it.

One issue that divided Catholic from Protestant in the Reformation period was prayers for the dead. Luther's attack on indulgences took as a given that the pope could not affect the state of the souls in purgatory by any means whatever; and once this principle was granted, questions arose about whether the prayers of anyone could actually change the state of the dead. Luther argued that the status of Christians, whether saved or damned, was determined in this life and hinged on the question of whether they had received the grace of God through faith; while for Calvin, their final state was decided by God's predestination anyway. Catholics, however, were able to point to a scriptural basis for prayers for the dead in 2 Maccabees:

> Under the tunic of each one of the dead [after a major battle] they found sacred tokens of the idols of Jamnia, which the law forbids the Jews to wear. And it became clear to all that this was the reason these men had fallen . . . Judas . . . took up a collection, man by man, to the amount of two thousand drachmas of silver, and sent it to Jerusalem to provide for a sin-offering. In doing this he acted very well and honourably, taking account of the resurrection. For if he were not expecting that those who had fallen would rise again, it would have been superfluous and foolish to pray for the dead. But if he was looking for the splendid reward that is laid up for those who fall asleep in godliness, it was a holy and pious thought.
>
> (2 Maccabees 12:40–45)

This was uncomfortable for Protestants, and it was undoubtedly one factor in the decision that 2 Maccabees, like the rest of the so-called apocryphal books, should not be regarded as genuinely scriptural. Equally, it may well have been a factor in the Catholic decision, at the Council of Trent, to retain these books as part of the Church's Bible, following the lead of Augustine and rejecting Jerome's preference for the Jewish canon (see Chapter 9). Trent ruled on the canon in 1546, making it clear for the first time that the 'deutero-canonical' books were in practice to be treated as on a par with the rest of the Old Testament and rejecting Luther's treatment of them as 'Apocrypha'. Yet Luther still regarded them as worth reading, whereas the Reformed party rejected them entirely. In England the Thirty-Nine Articles of Religion (1571) took a broadly Lutheran position, defining them as edifying but not to be used in doctrinal controversy to 'prove' any point of doctrine. They continued to be read in church in exactly the same way as the books of the Old Testament.

BIBLES

Through all these controversies among Christians, Jews continued to read the Hebrew Bible in the ways described in the previous two chapters. There were no great commentators of the stature of Rashi or Ibn Ezra, but study of the Bible was made far easier for many Jews by the advent of printing, just as it was for Christians. Northern Italy was the main focus for this activity.[21] Already in 1477 a press in Bologna produced a text of the Psalms[22] with the commentary by Kimchi, followed by a Pentateuch in 1482. The most successful press to produce Hebrew books was at Soncino near Mantua, run by Jews from the south of Germany, which published an edition of the prophetic books in 1485–6, followed by the whole Hebrew Bible in 1488. Luther used a Soncino Press Bible in translating the Old Testament into German.

The year 1517 saw the publication in Venice of the Bomberg Bible, which contained not only the Hebrew text but, arranged around it, rabbinic commentary – a so-called rabbinical Bible. Daniel Bomberg (1483–1549) was a Christian printer from Flanders, but his Bible was of use both to Jews and to the rising generation of Christian Hebraists. These were for long under a cloud, suspected of being Jewish sympathizers: certainly this accusation was levelled at Johannes Reuchlin (1455–1522), a professor of law who in 1506 published the first elementary Hebrew grammar for Christians wishing to learn that language. Reuchlin described himself as the first Christian Hebrew scholar in the west. Though Nicholas of Lyra, Herbert of Bosham and others had known some Hebrew, his claim was probably not an empty one, since he possessed a better grasp of the language than those before him. He

The Complutensian Polyglot: the upper-left column contains the Septuagint with interlinear Latin, with the Hebrew on the right and the Vulgate in the centre. The lower-left column is the Aramaic Targum, and on the right is its Latin translation.

also helped to promote Hebrew studies by encouraging rulers to establish chairs of Hebrew at the universities of Europe. After Reuchlin, Sebastian Münster of Basel (1488–1552) advanced the study of Hebrew, and in 1527 even published a grammar of Aramaic. He also translated the grammatical works of Elias Levita (1469–1549), a German Jew working in Italy, whose Hebrew grammar had appeared at Rome in 1508. Christian Hebraists sometimes got diverted from biblical studies into reading Jewish esoteric works belonging to the traditions of the *kabbalah*, the mystical side of Judaism about which Orthodox Jews were often sceptical; nevertheless, there was enough Christian work on the Hebrew Bible to make for fruitful dialogue with Jewish scholars, though the latter had to be careful to avoid being suspected of trying to convert their Christian interlocutors to Judaism.

Christian work on the Hebrew Bible continued, around the same time that Luther was formulating and publishing his theses, with the printing in 1514–17 and publication in 1522 of the Complutensian Polyglot at Alcalá in Spain (known in Latin as *Complutum*). In volumes 1–4 this set out the Latin Old Testament in the centre of the page, the Septuagint in an inside column, and the Hebrew in the outside one, with marginal notes identifying the roots of the Hebrew words. (Volume 5 contains the New Testament, in both Greek and Latin.) The Christian bias can be seen from the decision to centre the Latin; nevertheless, the Polyglot represents an enormous contribution to biblical scholarship. In 1524–5 there appeared a second edition of the Bomberg Bible, which included the Masorah, the marginal notes on the Hebrew text that had been designed to ensure exact copying of the manuscript text, described in Chapter 15. The Bomberg Bible became the basis for printed Hebrew Bibles into the twentieth century.[23]

Where the New Testament is concerned, Erasmus had produced his Greek New Testament in 1516, and this caused controversy, not only because so many regarded the Latin as the authoritative text and resisted the implication that the original Greek was superior, but also because of specific textual decisions made by Erasmus. Of these the most salient concerns the so-called 'Johannine comma' (comma here meaning a short piece of text, rather than a punctuation mark). This is a passage in the first letter of John:

> There are three that testify in heaven, the Father, the Son, and the Holy Spirit, and these three are one.
>
> (1 John 5:7)

If it were genuinely part of the letter of John, this would be a remarkably early explicit reference to the doctrine of the Trinity, the only one in the New Testament apart from Matthew 28:19. We would now probably think of it as coming from the early second century CE, which is already very early; but in the sixteenth century 1 John was assumed to have been written by Jesus' 'beloved disciple', John son of Zebedee, and that would push it back well into the first century, not long after Jesus himself. Erasmus knew that the comma did not appear in any early manuscripts of the Greek New Testament – it is in fact an insertion into the Latin Bible, subsequently translated into Greek and inserted in its present position. So Erasmus omitted it, as all critical editions of the New Testament have done, though that did not prevent its appearing in the King James Version (and as a footnote even in the NRSV). This brought much criticism of his work, and he backpedalled, reinstating the comma in the third edition of his New Testament in 1522, as he had discovered that there was a manuscript in Dublin that contained it. It is one of the most egregious of the 'orthodox corruptions of Scripture', bringing a biblical book more closely into line with later doctrinal orthodoxy, but in the process falsifying the text.[24]

After various other editions of the New Testament, mostly indebted to Erasmus, Robert Estienne published the fourth edition of his small-scale, portable Greek New Testament – the first New Testament to be divided into numbered verses. The verse-numbering has lasted to this day, even though there have been many subsequent critical editions. An important edition soon after Estienne's was that of Theodore Beza (1519–1605), Calvin's successor in Geneva, who compared a number of manuscripts, including two he owned himself, the *Codex Bezae* and *Codex Claromontanus*, to produce a critical text, published in 1565. He too occasionally adjusted the text when he felt it necessary to make it accord with orthodox belief. Thus in Acts 2:47 we read that the Lord added to the Church 'those who were being saved', but Beza changed this to 'those who were to be saved', thus implying predestination. But this is not typical of Beza, whose work was mostly conservative.

The Reformation could thus draw on new critical thinking about the text of the Bible as well as about its interpretation. The roots of work on the Hebrew and Greek texts go back into the Middle Ages, but the early modern period saw it burgeon, and it bore fruit in providing the Reformers with more reliable texts of the Bible to translate and interpret. Printing, as we have seen, made an enormous difference to the circulation of Bibles. The press in Wittenberg alone published 100 editions of Luther's Bible between 1534 and 1620, amounting to some 200,000 copies – without counting single Testaments and individual biblical books, for which there was also a ready market.[25] (Even Erasmus' Greek New Testament sold 3,000 copies.) The availability of Bibles also made a difference to how the biblical text was appropriated: no longer only through public reading and proclamation in the liturgy, but by reading in private, which encouraged Christians to think their own thoughts about the Bible. Reformers made up a tiny portion of the population – learned men who knew the Bible almost by heart; but they encouraged laypeople to read it where they could, as the late-medieval Church had not. Actually forbidding people access to the Bible was not common in the Middle Ages, despite the widespread belief that it was; but in the nature of the case only those with a good degree of literacy in Latin could read the text for themselves. The provision of vernacular translations, which occurred all over Europe in both Protestant and Catholic countries, would make a great contribution to this, as we will see in Chapter 18.

Despite all the continuities between the Reformers and their medieval heritage, they introduced a new idea into the interpretation of the Bible: the possibility of criticizing the Church's teaching in the light of what the Bible appeared to be saying – and, in Luther's case, even of criticizing parts of the Bible itself in the light of what he took to be its overall drift. This was a revolutionary idea, which would feed into the premium on independent thought that would come to characterize the European Enlightenment. For the first time it opened up a gap between the Bible and the faith which hermeneutical ingenuity could not bridge.

17
Since the Enlightenment

SPINOZA

Baruch (later Benedict de) Spinoza was born in 1632 in what is now the Netherlands, of Portuguese Jewish (Sephardic) descent. He lived much of his life in Amsterdam, where he was eventually expelled from the synagogue for his unorthodox beliefs. He is generally regarded as one of the first rationalists of the period, and thus a founding father of the European Enlightenment. Where study of the Bible is concerned, he was a crucial figure in casting doubt on the reality of biblical miracles, which he thought to be either fictitious or descriptions of natural processes, and in opening up questions about the authorship of biblical books. He notoriously suggested that the Pentateuch was written not by Moses but by Ezra. Spinoza was not a professional academic – he made a living by grinding lenses – but his influence on later Enlightenment thinkers such as Voltaire make him a central figure in seventeenth-century philosophy. His major work is usually reckoned to be his (posthumously published) *Ethics*, but for the biblical specialist the central book is his *Theological-Political Treatise* (*Tractatus Theologico-politicus*) of 1670.[1]

On miracles, Spinoza was certainly sceptical in a way that anticipates the attacks on the notion by David Hume (1711–76). He thought that biblical stories of miraculous events were either records of visions and dreams, or else were susceptible of a naturalistic explanation. Joshua 10 and Isaiah 38 both record moments at which the sun is said to have stopped in heaven, or even to have moved backwards:

> The sun stopped in mid-heaven, and did not hurry to set for about a whole day. There has been no day like it before or since, when the LORD heeded a human voice; for the LORD fought for Israel.
>
> (Joshua 10:13–14)

> [Isaiah said,] 'This is the sign to you from the LORD, that the LORD will do this thing that he has promised [that is, heal King Hezekiah]. See, I will make the shadow cast by the declining sun on the dial of Ahaz turn back ten steps.' So the sun turned back on the dial the ten steps by which it had declined.
>
> (Isaiah 38:7–8)

Spinoza explains this in terms of parhelia (mock suns), an accumulation of ice in the air causing an unusual kind of refraction.[2] Nothing can ever happen contrary to the laws of nature, understood as mechanistic in character, and God does not intervene in natural events. In this Spinoza is an antecedent of the British deists later in the seventeenth and eighteenth centuries. Deism is the belief that, though there is a God, his activity is confined to the creation of the universe, after which he takes no part in its running. (Matthew Tindal's *Christianity as Old as the Creation* of 1730 was sometimes called 'the deist's Bible', as an exemplary statement of this principle.) People had of course doubted the truth of the biblical miracles before, but they would have been seen as simply atheists: Spinoza combined a belief that God existed with a conviction that God did not do anything to change the natural order of events. Later theologians and biblical scholars, rather than rejecting such a view out of hand, found that they had to cope with its implications for the writing and transmission of the Bible, and for the biblical account of history in both Testaments.

On the authorship of biblical books Spinoza was highly innovative. He noted inconsistencies between them, and saw that the authors were often in fact compilers piecing together older sources. While he accepted some traditional attributions, for example of Qoheleth (Ecclesiastes) to King Solomon, he was sceptical of others. He drew attention to a cryptic comment by the medieval Jewish commentator Abraham ibn Ezra in his commentary on Deuteronomy (1:5), who had pointed to a number of references in the Pentateuch that make it impossible that this work was actually written by Moses. For example, Genesis 12:6 says that 'At that time the Canaanites were in the land', which must have been written at a time when they no longer were – long after Moses, therefore. Moses is also often referred to in the third person; and, indeed, Deuteronomy 34 records his death.[3] Ibn Ezra did not make explicit the implication that the Pentateuch was not by Moses, probably because it could have scandalized his readers, but Spinoza had no hesitation in doing so. His proposal of a non-Mosaic origin for the Pentateuch (already known before the *Treatise* was published) was undoubtedly one of the heresies for which the Amsterdam synagogue expelled him. He did not rest content, however, with this negative conclusion, but argued carefully for Ezra as the actual compiler of the 'books of Moses'. Modern biblical scholarship, while generally refraining from postulating any specific person as the editor,[4] tends to agree with Spinoza that the age of Ezra is when the Pentateuch reached its present form (see Chapter 2).[5]

As we saw in the previous chapter, Reformation writers had not always been dogmatic about the authorship of biblical books. Calvin was perfectly relaxed about the idea that some of the Psalms were not by David, arguing, for example, that Psalm 74 reflected the destruction of Jerusalem in 587 BCE by the Babylonians, or else the events of the Maccabean age: he saw clearly that there was no context in the lifetime of David that would make sense of it. The notion that the notice of the death of Moses had been added to the Pentateuch, perhaps by Joshua, was also a commonplace. Luther was clear, for stylistic reasons, that the Letter to the Hebrews was not by Paul (as Origen had already shown in the third century), and doubted whether James was really by the apostle of that name, permitting himself to be sharply critical of its contents. But in general there remained a consensus that the books were by the people they had traditionally been attributed to, and no one had approached the question of authorship as a completely open one, as Spinoza did. He did not pay any attention to the attribution of New Testament books, trusting himself less with Greek literature than with Hebrew. If he had, the effect would have been even more explosive for Christians than his conclusions about the Hebrew Bible were for Jews, given that in any case the Catholic Church placed his works on the Index of Prohibited Books.

Spinoza was not the first to challenge accepted ideas about the authorship of documents. In the Renaissance there had already been the earthquake in thinking caused by Lorenzo Valla (1407–57), who had shown that the so-called 'Donation of Constantine' was a late forgery. This was the document that purported to be the fourth-century Emperor Constantine's edict transferring authority over Rome and the western part of the Roman Empire to the pope, thus making the pope the superior of secular rulers. Valla, himself a priest, argued on philological grounds that the work could not be from the fourth century and was more probably from the eighth – hence certainly not by Constantine.[6] Such investigations were part of the enhanced historical acumen of

Renaissance thinkers, with their greater awareness of anachronism and historical context. But to apply similar strategies to the books of the Bible was, perhaps, even more radical, and in that Spinoza had few if any precursors.

If a rationalistic approach to miracles and scepticism about the traditional attribution of biblical books were novelties, there are features of Spinoza's approach that turned out to be even more far-reaching, and formed part of a revolution in the study of the Bible. One is his attention to the historical context not just of events and writings, but of ways of thinking. As we saw above, when he discusses the miracle of the sun standing still for Joshua, he argues (as any rationalist of his day would have done) that the miracle is a literal impossibility, and speculates that it may have resulted from some freakish trick of the refraction of the light. More far-reaching in its implications, however, is his explanation of how the mistaken belief in the miracle was possible:

> Nothing in the Bible is clearer than that Joshua, and perhaps the author who wrote his history, thought that the sun moves round the earth and the earth is at rest and the sun stood still for a period of time. Some are unwilling to allow that there can be any change in the heavens and hence interpret this passage in such a way that it will not seem to say anything like that. Others who have learnt to philosophize more accurately and recognize that the earth moves and the sun is at rest, or does not move around the earth, make great efforts to derive this from this passage even though it obviously will not permit such a reading . . . Both explanations seem utterly ridiculous to me. I prefer to say frankly that Joshua was ignorant of the true cause of that longer-lasting light. He and all the people with him believed both that the sun moves in a daily motion around the earth and that on this day it stood still for some time, and they believed that this was the cause of the longer-lasting light.[7]

Spinoza will not go so far as to say that nothing happened at all and that the story is simply a legend, as a modern critic might think. But he is clear that the interpretation of whatever it was that actually occurred depended on the mindset of the people who experienced it – on their pre-Copernican cosmology, as we might put it.[8] The implication, that people in biblical times *thought* differently from modern people, had not been made clearly before. It is an idea that all biblical scholars now take for granted, but in its day it was a real innovation.[9]

A second feature of Spinoza's approach to the Bible was not entirely new, but was novel in being carried through consistently: his attention to the genre of biblical texts. This is striking enough when he applies the question of genre to well-known biblical stories. When he tries to draw out the lasting meaning of the story of Adam and Eve, he notes that 'many people do not concede that this history is a parable, but insist it is a straightforward narrative'.[10] Clearly, then, for Spinoza himself it *is* a 'parable'. This, perhaps, is not altogether different from what patristic or medieval interpreters would have meant if they had said a story was to be read allegorically – though this story, above most others, was normally read as a piece of literal history. Spinoza, however, goes far beyond this kind of analysis, and discusses the contents of the New Testament from the point of view of its genre, in such a way as to open up deep questions of biblical authority and inspiration.

Paul's letters, and the other letters in the New Testament, are to be seen as actual letters rather than as inspired Scripture. They contain not law-giving, like the Pentateuch, but persuasion and argument. The apostles who wrote them did so as 'teachers' rather than as 'prophets' – that is, they did not bring oracles from God, but their own teaching, never preceded by the formula, 'Thus says the Lord' as we find in prophetic books. Indeed, on one occasion (1 Corinthians 7:40) Paul even gives his own opinion and explicitly says that it is *not* a message from the Lord:

> Actually, ambiguous meanings and tentative expressions are found in many passages as, for example, 'we therefore think' (Epistle to the Romans 3.28) and 'for I think' (8.18), and many more. There are other turns of phrase which stand far removed from prophetic authoritativeness as, for example, 'and this I say as a weak man and not by command' (see 1 Corinthians 7.6), 'I give my advice as a man who by the grace of God is trustworthy' (see 1 Corinthians 7.25), and many others of the sort.[11]

Even Jesus' teaching is not given as law: 'he was not laying down ordinances as a legislator. Rather he was offering doctrine as a teacher'.[12] For Spinoza, this means that the teaching of Jesus (which, though Spinoza was a Jew, he seems to have revered) is to be understood as advice from a supremely wise source, but not as legislation.

One of the distinctive features of some Reformation interpretation had been a greater sensitivity to genre. Luther's disciple Matthias Flacius Illyricus (Matija Vlačić-Ilirik, 1520–75) insisted that in reading a text one must decide 'whether it deals with a narrative or history, a piece of teaching or instruction, a text offering consolation or an accusation, the description of something, or a speech or something similar'.[13] (He did not, as Spinoza was to do, raise any questions about the *truth* of any type of text.) Richard Hooker makes distinctions of the same kind when he accuses his opponents of having mistaken the genre of parts of the Bible, so that they have pressed narratives as though they were legislation:

> That which they took for an oracle, being sifted, was repelled. True it is concerning the Word of God, whether it be by misconstruction of the sense, or by falsification of the words, wittingly to endeavour that any thing may seem divine which is not, or any thing not seem which is, were plainly to abuse and even to falsify divine evidence; which injury offered but unto men, is most worthily counted heinous. Which point I wish they did well observe, with whom nothing is more familiar than to plead in these causes, the Law of God, the Word of the Lord; who notwithstanding, when they come to allege what Word and what Law they mean, their common ordinary practice is, to quote by-speeches in some historical narration or other, and to urge them as if they were written in most exact form of Law. What is to add to the Law of God, if this be not? When that which the Word of God doth but deliver historically, we construe without any warrant, as if it were legally meant, and so urge it further than we can prove it was intended; do we not add to the Laws of God, and make them in number seem more than they are?[14]

This takes the religious high ground by insisting that it is actually disrespectful to the Bible to mistake the genre of books. But early modern writers before Spinoza did apply such genre distinctions to Paul, or even to Jesus, in order to reduce their teaching from binding law to mere practical advice, as Spinoza did. Spinoza inaugurated a change from seeing books as parts of a uniform 'Scripture' to becoming aware of them (as the very earliest Christians had been) as a collection of books of different sorts. To find real parallels, and those only partial, we would need to go back to the Antiochenes (see Chapter 14). Their training in rhetoric made them sensitive to differences between types of text, as also to the flow of argument, within works such as Paul's letters – whereas other contemporary interpreters, like many later ones, saw a collection of fragmentary aphorisms that could be taken out one by one as proof texts divorced from their context. After Spinoza, that was no longer possible for responsible Bible readers, though there remained (and remain) plenty of irresponsible ones.

Perhaps the greatest novelty in Spinoza's work is the distinction between the *meaning* and the *truth* of texts. There were people before him who had denied that what the biblical text affirmed was true; but they were atheists or heretics. Christians or Jews took it for granted that in interpreting the Bible they were discovering truth. For someone to profess to believe in God, as Spinoza did, but then simply to deny that something asserted in the Bible was true – as when he says, quite plainly, that the sun did *not* stand still for Joshua – was surprising, indeed shocking. For Spinoza it is a point of principle that establishing the meaning of a text and enquiring into the truth of what it affirms are two absolutely separate procedures. To understand the Bible, one needs to assemble the opinions expressed in it, he argues. To do this one must distinguish between passages whose meaning is clear and ones which are obscure; but 'I am not now speaking of how easily or otherwise their truth is grasped by reason; for we are concerned here only with their meaning, not with their truth.'[15] He gives as an example the assertion that God is fire, which is implied in many places in the Hebrew Bible. To discover whether Moses (say) believed this literally, we must not ask whether it is, as a matter of fact, literally true, but only whether that is compatible with other things that Moses asserted (whether true or false). We must be prepared to say that Moses believed things that we cannot believe, if we find that he did so:

> Moses plainly teaches that God is jealous and nowhere teaches that God lacks emotions or mental passions. Hence, we must evidently deduce that this is what Moses believed, or at least what he wanted to teach, however much we may think this statement conflicts with reason. For, as we have already shown, we are not permitted to adjust the meaning of Scripture to the dictates of our reason or our preconceived opinions.[16]

A theological conservative would deduce from this that if we find Moses saying things that contradict our preconceived opinions, then those opinions must be changed. But, as his contemporaries immediately saw, Spinoza sensed that we must be prepared to recognize a lack of fit between the Bible and what we actually believe; and, in such cases, to declare that the Bible is mistaken. The methodological point is that we must keep the search for the meaning of texts separate from the search for theological or philosophical truth.

This blows apart centuries of biblical interpretation, patristic and medieval, Protestant and Catholic, and spells the death of allegorization as a way of reconciling meaning and truth. It refuses to read our own convictions into the Bible, and the price of this is a willingness to recognize when the Bible is in error. Few faith communities today, Jewish or Christian, have been willing to pay it. Even biblical commentators tend to look for ways of reconciling the text with their own beliefs, or at least to interpret the text so that it is capable of being believed. In the years after Spinoza, however, a good many biblical interpreters took his arguments to heart, and were willing to face the possibility that the Bible was erroneous in at least some respects, as we shall see.

Another way of putting Spinoza's point is to say that the Bible is to be read, as the nineteenth-century Oxford scholar Benjamin Jowett (1817–93) would put it, 'like any other book'.[17] When we read ordinary books, we do not interpret them in such a way that they have to conform to what we already believe, nor indeed on the assumption that they will contain only truth: their truth is an open question. What we are seeking is their meaning. The question of truth comes afterwards. Spinoza was simply applying to the Bible this basic principle of reading. Technically speaking, there is a general hermeneutic for reading books – a way of trying to establish their meaning – but no special hermeneutic that applies uniquely to the Bible. Most religious believers, including many biblical scholars, hold on the contrary that the Bible does need a special hermeneutic; for we know in advance that what we shall find in it is the truth, and so we need a way of ensuring that the meanings we do find are compatible with truth. In the past, allegorization was one way of providing this special hermeneutic; nowadays it is more likely to be what is called a theological reading of Scripture (see below). But heirs of Spinoza, whether believers or not, rule out such approaches, and are concerned simply with extracting the meaning of the text, whether palatable or unpalatable. Like him, they may sometimes mischievously enjoy showing just how unpalatable it is, for impishly challenging other people's beliefs can be a pleasure. As we shall see, there have been plenty of imps in the subsequent history of biblical study.

Spinoza's own solution to the problem raised by inaccuracies in Scripture is structurally rather like Luther's way of dealing with obscurities: to stress that there is a centre or heart to the Bible that remains untouched by detailed errors or difficulties. Luther spoke of the *res scripturae*, the central theme that the Bible was about: the gracious God who justifies the unrighteous through grace, appropriated by faith. The rest was mere detail, though not therefore unimportant. For Spinoza the heart of the Bible was the moral appeal to love God and neighbour, and beside this specific problems faded into insignificance. Indeed, to read the Bible with any other objective than to love God and others, in practical ways, was worthless; one might as well, he remarked, read the

Qur'an, or Greek tragedies.[18] Like Luther, Spinoza did not think the exact compass of the biblical canon mattered very much. We lack some books referred to in the Old Testament, such as the Book of the Wars of the Lord (see Numbers 21:14–15), from which perhaps we could learn much if we had them; and we have books which are in the Bible that are of relatively small value. God is the author of Scripture 'owing to the true religion that it teaches and not because he wanted to present human beings with a certain number of books'.[19] This true religion is essentially a moral one: 'the ultimate teaching of Scripture, whether the Hebrew Bible or the Christian Gospels . . . is, in fact, a rather simple one: Practice justice and loving kindness to your fellow human beings.'[20]

It is possible to see Spinoza as purely destructive, as one who undermined the authority and inspiration of the biblical text and laid the foundation for Enlightenment scepticism about the Bible – the scepticism of Voltaire (1694–1778) and the other *philosophes* such as Denis Diderot (1713–84). It is even possible to see his endorsement of the central teaching of Scripture as no more than a cynical way of trying to avoid censure for his views – an aim, if it was indeed his aim, in which he certainly did not succeed. But it is also possible to see him as both a pioneer of biblical criticism and as one who kept a firm hold on the essentials of biblical faith, while stripping away the whole scaffolding of interpretative subtlety that had tried to bring every last word of the Bible into an orthodox structure and, in the process, had lost the heart of the matter.

AFTER SPINOZA

In the eighteenth century the negative side of Spinoza's work seemed to come to the fore. Especially in Great Britain, rationalism generally prevailed, and the biblical text was much depreciated as crude and bloody, with the nobler sentiments of some of the New Testament seen as overlaid with inconsistency and falsehood: these denunciations reached a climax in Thomas Paine's *The Age of Reason* (1794), but can be found in many writers of the earlier part of the century such as Hume and Edward Gibbon (1737–94). An egregious example is Thomas Woolston (1668–1733), who published his six *Discourses on the Miracles of our Saviour* between 1727 and 1729, for which he was fined and imprisoned. He argued that we need to allegorize the miracle stories in the Gospels since, taken as literal history, they are so incredible that no sane person would believe them. Jesus behaves like a 'strolling fortune-teller', at the wedding in Cana he was probably drunk, and the resurrection was a staged event, managed by the disciples. Like many rationalist writers, Woolston claimed to be an orthodox Christian, but this appears to have been an unsuccessful ploy to evade prosecution, or else a remarkable piece of self-deception. Few rationalist writers went as far as Woolston, but he captures a certain widespread mood. Of course there were many staunch defenders of biblical orthodoxy, such as William Whiston and Anthony Collins,[21] but they shared a great deal of common ground with rationalism, and would have assented to much of the negative side of Spinoza's work. The deist Matthew Tindal (1657–1733) saw, as we still can, the essential circularity of many defences of the authority of Scripture: 'it's an odd Jumble, to prove the Truth of a Book by the Truth of the Doctrines it contains, and at the same Time conclude those Doctrines to be true, because contain'd in that Book'.[22] There are modern parallels to this.[23]

The more purely critical side of Spinoza's work continued and flourished, with much investigation into the origin and authorship of the biblical books. Just eight years after Spinoza's *Treatise* a French Oratorian priest, Richard Simon (1638–1712), published his *Critical History of the Old Testament*,[24] followed in the next few years by works on the text of the New Testament. The argument of these books was ingenious: by showing that the biblical books had not been written by their supposed authors – much as Spinoza had done – Simon argued that Protestants were in error in thinking that they could rely on the Bible alone as the foundation of the Christian faith. The Bible was unreliable, and hence the Church's tradition and magisterial authority were needed if faith was to be securely grounded. The Church authorities, in the person of Cardinal Richelieu, quickly saw that this gave too many hostages to fortune, and that it demoted the Bible below what was tolerable. Simon was suspended from the Oratory.

In spite of this unwise use of biblical criticism in the service of anti-Protestant polemic, Simon's arguments about biblical authorship were in themselves sound enough, and rested, like Spinoza's, on principles that went back to the Renaissance and to the work of people such as Lorenzo Valla. His position as one of the founders of modern biblical criticism, alongside the Jewish Spinoza, is a reminder that this was not in origin a purely Protestant movement, even though it would be Protestants, especially in German-speaking lands, who subsequently developed the study of the Bible to become a major industry.[25] The methods employed were essentially the same as those used in secular criticism – and this, naturally, led many to think that there was an anti-religious agenda. Sometimes there certainly was; but Simon was motivated by religious concerns, and Spinoza himself, as we have seen, was a complicated case.

Such work, which is traditionally called 'higher' criticism, that is, the study of the authorship and origins of the biblical books, was accompanied by blossoming study of 'lower', that is, textual, criticism, which attempted to establish the original text of both Old and New Testaments by a detailed attention to the best manuscripts that could be found – the kind of work surveyed in Chapter 12. A major British contribution was the work of Brian Walton (1600–61), who compiled the London Polyglot Bible (1653/4–7), with different ancient versions in parallel columns, including Syriac and Arabic translations of the New Testament together with Ethiopic and Persian versions, and an appendix of variant readings. In the next century, important contributions were made by J. A. Bengel (1687–1752), who published a critical edition of the New Testament in 1734, and J. J. Wettstein (1693–1754), whose two-volume edition of the New Testament appeared in Amsterdam in 1751–2. Wettstein invented the system, still in use today, of indicating the earlier uncial manuscripts by capital letters (A for *Codex Alexandrinus*, for example), and the later minuscule ones by numerals – see pp. 285–7.

SEMLER

Higher criticism acquired a reputation for being anti-religious. To say that Moses did not write the Pentateuch (even though the Pentateuch itself does not claim that he did) seemed blasphemous: Jesus, after all, had often referred to Pentateuchal texts as 'Moses' (see Matthew 19:8, where Jesus, in discussing divorce, says: 'It was because you were so hard-hearted that Moses allowed you to divorce your wives'). One of the first writers to try to rebut this accusation of blasphemy was Johann Salomo Semler (1725–91), whose *Free Research on the Canon* (1771–6, four volumes) sought to distinguish between the essential message of the Bible, which was supernatural, and the detail of biblical exegesis, which belonged to the sphere of normal secular literary enquiry and on which no issue of faith turned. What is more, Semler argued that this distinction could be traced back to Luther – which it arguably can, as we have seen. 'With Semler, Luther became the patron saint of free enquiry into matters of biblical origins and authorship.'[26] The essential thing was the word of assurance to believers that God accepted them by his free grace; who wrote this or that book was a secondary matter, on which Christian faith had nothing to say. This was challenging to many orthodox Christians, but it laid the foundations for free enquiry into the Bible in Protestant Germany for the next 200 years. It led to some startling conclusions: Semler like Luther prioritized some New Testament books above others (the Gospel of John and the major letters of Paul had pre-eminence), but he also questioned the value for Christians of much of the Old Testament, while seeing it as still valuable for Jews.[27]

Semler's position is arguably over-optimistic about the possibility of separating faith from criticism. While it is easy enough to argue that faith in God is not affected if someone else added the notices about Moses' death to the end of Deuteronomy, or if one or other of the several attested endings of Mark's Gospel is spurious, believers find it rather less comfortable to contemplate some of Paul's letters being pseudonymous or 'forgeries'.[28] Even though this may not compromise the basic faith asserted by the letters of Paul put forward, it is disturbing to think that later writers may have taken on his persona. Furthermore, accepting this leads inevitably to the question of whether all of Paul's letters are inauthentic, or the Gospels are inventions from the second century – however unlikely it seems – and then, surely, a clash between criticism and faith is real and undeniable. The fundamentalist who argues that suggesting even the smallest discrepancy in the Bible is the thin end of a wedge, because the very possibility of it calls in question the foundation of faith, may be exaggerating, but has a point. It makes a difference how much one has invested in the inspiration and inerrancy of the Bible in the first place, and Semler was correct in thinking that his own position was compatible with that of Luther; but it is doubtful whether it is compatible with a more Reformed approach, and it clearly clashes with a modern conservative evangelical or, arguably, traditionalist Catholic stance.

REIMARUS AND STRAUSS

I said above that there have been imps in the history of biblical criticism, and two such were important in establishing Spinozan-style study of the text, though in each case people reacted as though such issues were being brought forward for the first time. The first is H. S. Reimarus (1694–1768). Reimarus is remembered as the father of the 'quest of the historical Jesus'[29] and in particular as the first to show that Jesus' message was through and through eschatological – that he believed he was inaugurating the 'last days'. But Reimarus' importance goes beyond this. Parts of his writings on Jesus were published posthumously in 1774–8 by G. E. Lessing (1729–81), and they were an examination of a number of Gospel miracles. Like Spinoza, Reimarus argued that the biblical miracles – including, crucially, the resurrection of Jesus – were susceptible of a naturalistic explanation. He was a deist, and could not allow that God intervened in the world. In the case of the resurrection he argued that the disciples had stolen Jesus' body to make it appear that he had risen. Then the later evangelists invented predictions of the resurrection, which they placed on Jesus' lips. 'Having stolen the body they then proclaimed that this had indeed happened, as he had foretold. They reinforced their claims by twisting some Old Testament texts into supporting the case, and gave it bite by adding that the world would shortly end and that anyone who had not accepted their message would burn in hell.'[30]

A second imp, who acknowledged his debt to Reimarus, yet argued that the effect of such historical criticism of the Bible was positive rather than negative, was David Friedrich Strauss (1808–74). In 1835–6 Strauss, then a junior lecturer in the Protestant seminary at Tübingen, published his *Life of Jesus, Critically Examined*[31] – a book which cost him his post. It is 1,400 pages long, and it examines every alleged incident and saying in the life of Jesus from the same perspective as Reimarus, asking rational and historical questions which take as an assumption that miracles do not happen. Strauss similarly dismisses the miracle stories with naturalistic explanations. But, entirely unlike Reimarus, he argues that this is ultimately a vindication of Christianity, since it clears the ground of false assumptions about a miraculous faith and makes possible an attachment instead to eternal truths. Jesus was not divine in any unique sense, yet his story, rightly understood, discloses the divine in all humanity. 'Let an audacious criticism attempt what it will, all which the Scriptures declare, and the Church believes of Christ, will still subsist as eternal truth, nor needs one iota of it to be renounced. Thus at the conclusion of the criticism of the history of Jesus, there presents itself this problem: to re-establish dogmatically that which has been destroyed critically.'[32] 'Dogmatically' here means 'theologically', 'at the level of faith'. Strauss is not the first, and will surely not be the last, to argue that what seems to most readers a devastating attack on the Christian faith is actually a defence of it; but no one believed him anyway. In 1839 he was offered a chair in Zurich, but there was a popular rebellion against the very idea, which brought down the government, and he was pensioned off.

Strauss's work, however, had lasting effects, and may be said to have initiated the modern quest for the historical Jesus, which I shall discuss later. Crucially, he distinguished between questions of history and questions of faith, much as Spinoza had done. A belief in the divine nature or inspiration of Jesus does not answer, indeed does not at all bear on, the question whether this or that event recorded in the Gospels actually happened: the two issues simply occupy different spaces on the map. It can be argued that this is a mistake: that it was only because of miraculous events that the disciples were brought to believe in Jesus in the first place, or (conversely) that the divine nature of Jesus makes it *possible* to believe of him actions that we could not believe of anyone else – hence historical enquiry and theological formulation walk hand in hand. But for Strauss that would have been wishful – and, indeed, muddled – thinking.

VATKE, WELLHAUSEN AND BAUR

The kind of critical enquiry represented by Strauss, once awakened, could not be put to sleep, and biblical study down to the present is his – as also Spinoza's and Reimarus' – heir, even though many biblical critics today are much nearer to traditional Christian orthodoxy in their faith than this pedigree would suggest. Rational enquiry into the Old Testament in many ways followed similar lines. In the same year as the first volume of Strauss's *Life of Jesus* (1835), Wilhelm Vatke (1806–82) published his *Biblical Theology: The Religion of the Old Testament*. The inspiration for this was the philosophy of Hegel, but on the historical level it was highly innovative in arguing that the order of the books in the Hebrew Bible was not a correct guide to the development of theological thinking in ancient Israel. The religion of the prophets, Vatke proposed, was older than that enshrined in the Pentateuch. It stood at the beginning of the development of a system of thought that had been read back into the Pentateuch from later times. In essence this anticipates the arguments of Julius Wellhausen, examined in Chapter 2, but its time had not yet come: it could all too easily be dismissed as merely an application of Hegelian ideas of spiritual development to material – the Old Testament – that they did not fit. Vatke largely disappeared from view until Wellhausen revived his theory (shorn of its Hegelianism) in 1878. Summed up in the formula *lex post prophetas*, 'the law came after the prophets', Vatke's and Wellhausen's theory would have been a gift to Spinoza, since it was highly compatible with his theory that it is to Ezra (as late as the fifth century BCE) that we owe the 'books of Moses'.[33]

Ferdinand Christian Baur (1792–1860), like Strauss, taught at Tübingen where, by contrast, he had a long and distinguished career.[34] He laid the foundations of the study of Gnosticism (see Chapter 11), and his work on the New Testament was also innovative. He dated much of it to the second century CE – much later than on the modern consensus – and argued that in it could be seen a struggle between two versions of Christianity, one ultimately indebted to Paul and the other to Peter. The former stressed the Gentile mission; Petrine Christianity was concerned with a Jewish version of the faith, rooted in the Jerusalem community under James. Compare what Paul says in Galatians 2:11–12:

> But when Cephas [= Peter] came to Antioch, I opposed him to his face, because he stood self-condemned; for until certain people came from James, he used to eat with the Gentiles. But after they came, he drew back and kept himself separate for fear of the circumcision faction.

Baur saw Acts as hopelessly unhistorical, an early-second-century attempt to reconcile Pauline with Jewish Christianity.

Arguably even more radical was Baur's insistence that each of the four Gospels had its own theme or 'tendency' (*Tendenz*). This is commonplace in New Testament studies now, but at the time it caused alarm because it separated the Gospels from the accurate recording of history and saw them as deliberately composed to make a particular point – which calls into question their historical veracity. (I showed in Chapter 8 that modern redaction criticism has a similar effect.) It also means that they do not map directly onto a unified system of Christian doctrine, since there is diversity among them.

This diversity can be seen especially between John and the Synoptic Gospels, and operates at both the theological and the historical level. The Jesus of Mark, for example, does not seem very like the Jesus of John: the former is a clearly human figure who sharply distinguishes himself from God, while the latter is 'one with the Father' and is described as the Word of God who came down from heaven. Once one gets each Gospel into focus in its own right, the difficulty of reconciling their pictures of Jesus becomes apparent. At the historical level, as we have already seen, the narrative frameworks of John and the Synoptics are not compatible: in the latter, Jesus makes only one trip to Jerusalem as an adult, whereas John implies that he was there on several occasions.

What all these critics made clear, above all, was that the New Testament does not unequivocally support traditional Christian doctrines such as the doctrine of the Trinity or the divinity of Christ, any more than the Old Testament, studied critically, supports a traditional picture of the Mosaic origins of Israel. If we apply their critical approach to this same issue of Christology – the nature of Jesus Christ – then the New Testament as a whole gives a mixed message. No book in the New Testament explicitly says that Jesus is God, and some of his own words seem to deny it (recall his question, 'Why do you call me good? No one is good but God alone', in Mark 10:18). Even in John, which has a high Christology, Jesus prays to God. In Paul the risen Jesus clearly has a highly exalted status:

> God . . . gave him the name that is above every name, so that at the name of Jesus every knee should bend.
>
> (Philippians 2:9–10)

His status is even more exalted in Colossians, which may or may not be genuinely Pauline. But Paul also seems to see Jesus as lower in status than God himself:

> When all things are subjected to him, then the Son himself will also be subjected to the one who put all things in subjection under him, so that God may be all in all.
>
> (1 Corinthians 15:28)

> Christ is the head of every man, and the husband is the head of his wife, and God is the head of Christ.
>
> (1 Corinthians 11:3)

The New Testament thus supports at most a subordinationist Christology, that is, one in which Jesus as the Son is of lower status than God the Father. This is at odds with the later doctrine of the Trinity, in which Father and Son (and the Holy Spirit) are of equal status. Furthermore, the Trinity is referred to explicitly only once in the New Testament, at the end of Matthew:

> [Jesus said], 'Go therefore and make disciples of all nations, baptizing them in the name of the Father and of the Son and of the Holy Spirit.'
>
> (Matthew 28:19)

But this passage is widely suspected of being a later addition to the Gospel (see p. 327).[35]

All this has been well known to biblical scholars at least since the work of Strauss, Baur and other nineteenth-century writers, though it remains unfamiliar to most Christians. The tendency of parish clergy, who learn it during their training, to soft-pedal or even ignore it when it comes to preaching and teaching in the Church, was already noted by Adolf von Harnack (1851–1930), who purportedly remarked, 'I bleach my students with historical criticism, but once ordained they gradually discolour again.' It remained possible to think that Jesus Christ is indeed God, and that God is a Trinity, and that the New Testament is moving gradually in that direction, though some New Testament books do not reflect such a move clearly, if at all. But in the wake of the nineteenth-century critics it became impossible to say that the New Testament clearly teaches these doctrines in anything like their later, developed form. If the Bible is read in its own terms, it presents a range of ideas about Jesus and about God that cannot be systematized. That plurality of ideas is the clear implication of nineteenth-century biblical criticism.

Extending that critique to another area in which Christians often look for biblical guidance, the organization of ordained ministry in the Church, produces similar results. Catholic and Orthodox Christianity both insist that the orders of bishops, priests and deacons are the only correct way to arrange ministry. They have been clearly attested since the writings of Ignatius of Antioch (35–108) in the early second century CE, though a bishop is for Ignatius something like the presiding minister in a single local congregation, a deacon is his assistant, and priests or presbyters are a council of elders, rather like a Church council of the kind that exists in many Christian denominations today – not quite the arrangement regarded as normative by Catholic and Orthodox Christians. But, try as we may, it is impossible to show that even this system was already in place in the earliest churches, those established by Paul and other apostles. In the Pauline Epistles we hear of *episkopoi* and *diakonoi*, which later come to mean 'bishops' and 'deacons'. As for *presbuteroi*, these sometimes seem to be elders in a technical sense, but at others simply old men – this is a difficulty in interpreting 1 Peter, for example, where the author describes himself as a co-presbyter with the presbyters he is addressing, which may mean that he too occupies this role in the Church – in which case it must surely mean something like 'bishop' – or simply that he too is now old (see 1 Peter 5:1–5). Paul suggests a bewildering variety of types of ministry, which cannot be correlated with the later threefold 'orders' at all:

> God has appointed in the church first apostles, second prophets, third teachers; then deeds of power, then gifts of healing, forms of assistance, forms of leadership, various kinds of tongues.
>
> (1 Corinthians 12:28)

This has not proved to be a major problem for Catholic or Orthodox believers, who think that Church tradition has an authority alongside the Bible and in some measure independent of it – though that has not prevented them from trying in vain to show that the later system is anticipated in the New Testament. For Protestants, who regard the Bible alone as the source of authority, it is disturbing. Perhaps the plurality of types of ministry in the New Testament authorizes pragmatism about what system to implement. To turn to my own favourite Anglican Reformer, Richard Hooker, we can see this approach. He famously argued that the traditional threefold system of orders should be retained in the reformed Church of England because it worked well, not on the grounds that it was revealed in Scripture. In his day members of the Church of England regarded themselves as in communion with Continental churches of the Reformation, both Lutheran and Reformed. Only later did Anglicans adopt the Catholic argument, and seek to uphold the threefold system as of divine appointment, even maintaining that 'it is evident unto all men diligently reading Holy Scripture and ancient Authors, that from the Apostles' time there have been these Orders of Ministers in Christ's Church, Bishops, Priests, and Deacons.'[36] This arguing in the teeth of the evidence that the New Testament presents a clear system identical with later tradition is surely untenable.[37] Equally, an insistence that only a Presbyterian system is compatible with the New Testament evidence founders, once the New Testament material is actually inspected. Yet the churches remain divided by their ideas about ministry as much as by any other doctrinal matters, and appeal in support of their ministerial systems to a scriptural basis that is manifestly unable to sustain it. A dose of biblical criticism ought to reveal how uncertain its foundations are, and persuade the churches not to divide over a matter on which the New Testament gives no clear guidance at all. Different kinds of 'ecclesiastical polity', to use Hooker's expression, could be regarded as equally valid. Some might be more effective than others, but none has any divine sanction – if attestation in the New Testament is regarded as providing such a sanction.

We have strayed a long way from the sorts of issues that occupied Strauss and Baur, let alone Spinoza, who were not interested in questions of Church order. But the question focuses the kinds of implication that follow once one approaches the New Testament in a historical-critical spirit. To follow Spinoza's way of reasoning: we cannot use our belief about what kind of ministry is correct to decide what the New Testament meant, because that is to confuse questions of truth with questions of meaning. The evidence must be investigated coolly and dispassionately, without attention to what might or might not follow from it for us, and only after that may we attend to its possible implications. If we do so, we shall almost certainly arrive at a position some of the Reformers (including Luther and Hooker) reached, namely that the New Testament does not prescribe any determinate system for ministry because it speaks with so many different voices. As Luther argued, this does not mean that we should necessarily abolish the Catholic system; but if we adopt it, we should do so for pragmatic reasons, not on the basis that it is God-given.

Such can be the effects of biblical criticism. Since the nineteenth century biblical critics and theologians have danced around each other, trying to establish how a critical spirit can be reconciled with a desire to develop doctrine in a way that is true to the Bible. There has been a sort of concordat, under which those studying theology have to learn about biblical criticism, but the two areas have never coalesced, nor is it clear how they could. We shall go on shortly to examine the modern (and postmodern) state of biblical studies.

THE BIBLE AND SCIENCE

First, however, we must take note of one of the issues encountered by students of the Bible in the nineteenth century: its conflict with science. On the face of it, the Hebrew Bible implies that the world was created in the fifth millennium BCE: Archbishop James Ussher (1581–1656) calculated, using the figures in various books of the Bible, that the creation occurred on 23 October 4004 BCE. This is still believed by so-called young-earth creationists, but in the nineteenth century its conflict with a scientific evaluation of the age of the universe became entirely obvious in the light of scientific discoveries. The same century saw the assertion in Genesis 1 that God created each species of plant and animal separately challenged by evolutionary science, through the work of Charles Darwin (1809–82). As Owen Chadwick put it:

> The Christian church taught what was not true. It taught the world to be 6,000 years old, a universal flood, and stories in the Old Testament like the speaking ass or the swallowing of Jonah by a whale which ordinary men (once they were asked to consider the question of truth or falsehood) instantly put into the category of legends.[38]

As Philip Kennedy comments:

> The consequences of Darwin's work are very far from being appropriated by officially sanctioned Christian doctrines. For example, the current *Catechism of the Catholic Church* solemnly teaches that the biblical story of Adam and Eve, or rather the third chapter of the Book of Genesis, 'affirms a primeval event, a deed that took place at the beginning of the history'. This teaching is solemnly declared. It is also false. Chapter 3 of Genesis is a myth. It does not provide any reliable information about the historical genesis of a human species. What it does say about human origins is false. To regard it as factually true is to violate its literary form as a myth.[39]

The last sentence here points to the practical effect of scientific knowledge on biblical study: it made readers see that the Bible contained myths and legends, which might be full of wisdom and insight of many kinds but which did not provide any scientific information or historical account of human origins. The effect was not limited to claims made in the Old Testament. When Paul affirms that death entered the world because of sin (the sin of Adam: Romans 5:12), this too is rendered clearly untrue through the observation that human beings, and their hominid predecessors, have always been mortal, as are all other organisms. Incidentally, this challenges a major plank in the Christian story as outlined in Chapter 13 – the story of God's rescue mission, as I there called it, in which Adam's sin plays a central role. This too, and not just Genesis, has to be understood in a non-literal way or relinquished. On the whole, by the end of the nineteenth century biblical critics had made this transition, with varying degrees of enthusiasm; but ecclesiastical authorities, and Christians of a conservative disposition, have in many cases still not made it today. Biblical fundamentalists, as we saw in the Introduction, continue to defend the historicity of Adam and Eve,

Jonah's big fish and Balaam's talking donkey, to the delight of atheist critics of Christianity.

MODERN BIBLICAL STUDY

In the early twentieth century a kind of calm descended on the study of the Bible. The more radical approaches of Spinoza, Reimarus and Strauss had been assimilated by many of those who led the churches, and it was discovered that they could be lived with. Judaism too had passed through its Enlightenment (the *haskalah* movement of the eighteenth and nineteenth centuries, which made its peace with rationalism and a degree of assimilation to western European ideas). Though Orthodox Jews, like conservative Christians, refused (as they still do) to have any truck with doubts about the Mosaic authorship of the Pentateuch or with the idea that the prophets were not divinely inspired, more liberal Jews were willing to enter the critical dialogue. After all, the spirit of biblical criticism is not defined by its conclusions, which are always only hypotheses, but by its willingness to be open to the evidence wherever it leads. Plenty of scholars in both Judaism and Christianity accept this challenge but believe, on the basis of rational argument, that the evidence points to rather conservative conclusions: that the Pentateuch is old enough to be by Moses, or that the Gospels present a substantially accurate picture of Jesus. It is possible to be critical and yet to draw conclusions that are what has been called 'maximally conservative'.[40] And there were plenty of scholars in both religions who saw ways of reconciling faith with critical insights into the origins and development of the Bible, even if these were conceived in less conservative terms.

Among Christian scholars, by the early years of the twentieth century the sorts of conclusions examined in the first eight chapters of this book would have been regarded as entirely reasonable. It is not that they are obvious or uncontroversial in every case, but they would have been regarded as safely on the critical map, not extraordinary or wild. Old Testament scholars accepted that the Pentateuch and other books were composite, the product of a long history of composition and redaction; New Testament specialists generally believed in the two-source theory of the origin of the Synoptic Gospels (Mark + Q as the basis for Matthew and Luke), the idea that John was later than the Synoptics, and that not all the Pauline letters were genuinely by Paul. It had been found possible to accept all this while still remaining committed to the

Christian faith. The gradual composition of the Old Testament books – and even the brutality of some of the early stories – were given a positive spin by the theory of progressive revelation, which argued that God had guided Israel's understanding in gradual stages rather than at one decisive moment, and that this was a good and beneficial way of working on God's part.

In the case of the Gospels, many scholars picked up the heritage of Strauss by pursuing various 'quests for the historical Jesus', as they are known: the attempt to establish what Jesus really did and said in contradistinction to what the Church had made of him. An attempt to discover what may be known about Jesus as a historical figure, shorn of religious claims about him, is generally reckoned to have passed through a number of phases, most recently one in which his Jewishness is stressed.[41] But the conclusions of these quests have been many and various. Albert Schweitzer (1875–1965), the missionary doctor and organist who was also a leading New Testament scholar, was the founder of the modern quest. Differentiating himself from liberal nineteenth-century pious retellings of the life of Jesus based on a face-value reading of the Gospels, he proposed that the original Jesus had been an eschatological prophet, whose message mostly concerned the imminent arrival of the end of time and the inauguration of the kingdom of God. Many scholars arrived at far less disturbing pictures of Jesus, more consonant with the rather liberal Jesus that many in the period before Schweitzer had believed in, whose message was mostly about peace and love, 'the fatherhood of God and the brotherhood of man', as it was sometimes put. Later in the twentieth century images of Jesus emerged that were less compatible with a comfortable liberal religion, and in recent times the apocalyptic prophet has come to be proposed again, alongside theories in which Jesus was essentially a wisdom teacher.[42] All these results of the quest have been critical, in the sense that they have asked what can be known about Jesus if we bracket out questions of faith and simply examine him as a historical figure. But many of the questers have been Christian believers, who wholly lack the desire of someone such as Reimarus to debunk Christianity as a religion.

Thus, as I suggested above, there developed a concordat between criticism and religion. This was still apparent in the years after the Second World War, when it was assumed, for example, that meetings of the Society for Old Testament Study in Britain and Ireland would begin with Christian prayers. It was not felt that criticism threatened the foundations of faith. In more recent years, however, this amicable state of affairs has been replaced by developments that recapture some of the sharpness of Spinoza's critiques. There have been others that return to a pre-critical style of Bible-reading, apparently untouched by Spinozan concerns.

On the one hand there are those who, like Spinoza, emphasize the late date of much in the Hebrew Bible. In the scheme established by Julius Wellhausen, which we examined in the context of Hebrew narrative (Chapter 2), the J source of the Pentateuch at least was of pre-exilic origin, that is, from the ninth or eighth century BCE at the latest. It was P that came from post-exilic times and could perhaps be associated with the work of Ezra, as Spinoza had argued for the origin of the whole Pentateuch. This scheme by no means conceded that even J was by Moses, but in the days of what I have called the concordat it was felt that, at any rate, J was early enough not to rock the foundations of faith in the essential validity of the Old Testament. Especially in North America, it was argued from archaeological evidence that the stories underlying J were very old indeed, probably going back into the second millennium BCE. By 1960, when John Bright's influential *A History of Israel* was published,[43] it was possible to write as though the Old Testament was a genuinely historical document faithfully preserving the oldest traditions of Israel. This was not a fundamentalist position in any sense. Bright thought that we needed to reconstruct what lay behind the text, not to accept it just as it was; but it was a conservative position, which Spinoza would surely have regarded as a fudge.

In the 1970s Pentateuchal studies took a radical turn to the left. Scholars in both the USA and the German-speaking world started to experiment with theories that placed J, like P, in the post-exilic age, seeing its picture of Moses, for example, as deriving from the delineation of the prophets in books such as Isaiah or Jeremiah.[44] Thus the Yahwist, as the author of J is known, became a figure from the post-exilic reconstruction of Israel. About what had happened in pre-exilic times the Pentateuch gave us no information at all. This scepticism went hand in hand with a tendency to assign late dates to other parts of the Old Testament, Deuteronomy being seen as a law code for the post-exilic community rather than as the book discovered in the Temple by King Josiah, and the wisdom books such as Proverbs no longer possible evidence for activity at the court of kings such as Solomon and his successors, but as equally post-exilic works – just as had been thought in the nineteenth century.[45] In more recent years there has even been a move to date much of the Hebrew Bible in the Hellenistic age – in the third or even second century BCE[46] – though most probably regard this as extreme. But the idea so prevalent in the 1940s and 1950s that the Hebrew Bible was, one might say, respectably old, and thus in some vague sense reliable, has broken down.

New Testament study has not shown quite the same degree of scepticism; but here too positions have been considered that hark back to philosophers such as Reimarus. One development in the years after the Second World War was a greater willingness to believe that the Gospel of John contained genuinely historical material and was not simply a rehash of the Synoptics in a slightly Gnostic form. C. H. Dodd (1884–1973) in Cambridge pioneered this movement,[47] which meant that traditions in John could once again contribute to establishing a historical picture of Jesus. Confidence in such a move has evaporated in more recent years, and the current quests for the historical Jesus, as seen for example in the work of E. P. Sanders (1937–), generally eschew any use of the Fourth Gospel. Developments in the study of Paul are surveyed in Chapter 7 above; here the radical newness of Paul's message has been qualified, and he has come to be seen as more typical of his environment than in previous scholarship, so that an older consensus in which he was the linchpin in establishing the Christian faith (conceived along rather Lutheran lines) has been abandoned.

Thus, on the one hand, biblical study at present has entered a new phase, in which the concordat with doctrinal theology is no longer so apparent, and the Bible's lack of fit with the traditional understanding of Christianity has come to be more accentuated than it was for much of the twentieth century. Critical questions have come to be even more sharply focused than they were in the past, with quite radical conclusions being drawn. Yet on the other hand there is another development that tends in the opposite direction, and sometimes actually identifies itself as 'post-critical'. This is an interest in the biblical text as it presents itself to the reader, without attention to any possible history of composition that may lie behind it. 'The final form of the text' is the slogan under which this movement operates, but it has two distinct branches.

One is theologically driven. It is argued that the present form of the text is the form that Judaism (in the case of the Hebrew Bible) and Christianity (in the case of both Old and New Testaments) have canonized, and that it is this form – the Bible just as it is – that interpreters ought to be studying and interpreting. This movement has been associated above all with the American scholar Brevard S. Childs (1923–2007), who spoke of the imperative to interpret the Bible 'as Scripture', using what he described as a 'canonical approach'.[48] This seeks to draw out the meaning of the finished product rather than the putative sources of a biblical book. Thus we should ask about the meaning of the book of Isaiah, or the Gospel of Matthew, as part of the whole canon of the Bible, not treating them as free-standing works, still less as a conglomeration of bits of text. We should certainly not spend our time on the theology of conjectural sources such as J or Q. Whatever the history of the books may be – and Childs was interested in that, but regarded it as a purely historical (even antiquarian) question, irrelevant to interpretation – what we now have as part of Scripture is a complete book alongside other books, and it is this that the Church/Synagogue has handed down to us as Holy Scripture.

This approach is deeply attractive to many Christians, and connects with a widespread sense that the critics have taken the text apart and that someone ought to put it together again. It clearly has affinities with biblical interpretation before the rise of the kind of criticism associated with Spinoza and those who followed him. It is also in keeping with attitudes towards the Bible among some doctrinal theologians, who have sought to establish what is sometimes called (as a technical term) 'theological interpretation of Scripture'. This has its roots in the work of two Yale colleagues of Childs's, George Lindbeck (1923–2018) and Hans W. Frei (1922–88), both of whom thought that Scripture should be treated as a finished whole that provides what Lindbeck calls the 'grammar' of Christian faith – the categories and narratives that make Christianity what it is. For such an approach, delving back into the text and trying to get behind the surface that now presents itself to us, while of course of great interest for the historian, is less relevant to the theologian. Theological interpretation of Scripture is not so far removed from the way in which ordinary Christians tend to approach the Bible, asking not how it came to be, and when, and where, but rather what it has to say to the modern believer.[49]

The other branch of 'final form' interpretation is more literary in character, and arises from engagement with the Bible by literary critics. An older generation of literary scholars regarded the Bible as off-limits, either because it was too sacred for secular critics to handle, or because they simply found it deficient from a literary point of view (as Jerome and Augustine had both complained already in the fifth century). But from the 1960s onwards literary scholars started taking an interest in the Bible. To begin with this was an aesthetic interest: critics began to observe that there were in fact texts in the Bible of high poetic quality (as indeed Robert Lowth had already suggested in his lectures *On the*

Sacred Poetry of the Hebrews (see pp. 113–16). Pioneers were Robert Alter (1935–) in the USA[50] and Frank Kermode (1919–2010) in the United Kingdom,[51] who collaborated in editing *The Literary Guide to the Bible*.[52] (This was anticipated in 1937 by E. S. Bates's *The Bible Designed to be Read as Literature*.[53]) Kermode's study of the Gospel of Mark in *The Genesis of Secrecy* draws parallels with James Joyce; Alter's many books on the Hebrew Bible similarly bring in modern literature and draw analogies with the biblical text. But he also shows parallels with rabbinic readings of the text, and in this he connects biblical studies with pre-critical interpretation.

Neither Kermode nor Alter suggests that critical methods (which Alter dubs 'excavative') are illegitimate in themselves, but they argue that for the modern reader a literary approach is far more interesting and productive. But literary readings of text do not necessarily have to take the style of Anglo-American literary criticism. There are also Continental European approaches. In the 1960s French structuralism started to be applied to the Bible, and then the whole range of post-structuralist and postmodernist interpretation of texts. Leading writers such as Jacques Derrida (1930–2004) began to take an interest in the Bible, again often connecting with ancient rabbinic approaches. This kind of criticism soon stopped being 'aesthetic', in the sense of admiring the beauty of the biblical text, and began to be interested in how the text subverts both ancient and modern culture, challenges colonial power and embraces and empowers non-elite groups.[54] Here it joins again with theological interests, such as the concerns of liberation theology, which pays attention to how the text can enable oppressed groups to express their longing for freedom.

At the moment there is a flourishing industry of post-critical biblical study, informed by political, social-scientific and postmodernist insights, which leaves behind the older critical concerns with the dates and the literary development of texts, in order to pursue an agenda defined by what is often called simply Theory.[55] Like the canonical approach, but with quite different concerns, this focuses on the text as we have it, and is more or less indifferent to what lies beneath the surface. Some of the most sophisticated literary readings can be found in the work of Paul Ricoeur (1913–2005).[56] Ricoeur sees traditional criticism as concerned to get behind the text; his own interest is in reading 'in front of the text', that is, in such a way that the text engages with contemporary issues and interests.

All these types of post-critical interpretation may remind us of patristic, rabbinic and medieval Christian readings. In a way the wheel has come full circle, taking us back to where we were before free spirits such as Spinoza, Reimarus and Strauss got to work on the Bible. By no means all biblical scholars are content with post-critical reading of any kind, and traditional critical styles continue to flourish: even the four-source (JEDP) theory of the composition of the Pentateuch is acquiring a new lease of life in North America and in Israel, with no sense at all that this is an outdated interest.[57] Biblical studies has entered a highly pluralistic stage.

18
Translating the Bible

How shall men meditate in that which they cannot understand? How shall they understand that which is kept close in an unknown tongue? . . . Translation it is that openeth the window, to let in the light.[1]

The year 2011 marked the four-hundredth anniversary of the publication of the King James Version of the Bible. Events organized to celebrate the anniversary tended to concentrate on the excellence of the English of this version, and its contribution to the development of the English language.[2] This occasionally went to absurd lengths: I heard the suggestion that it is to the King James translators that we owe the wonderful phrase, 'Let there be light!', when it is hard to think of any other way the Hebrew sentence could be adequately translated. Sometimes I suspected that there were people who thought the translators actually *wrote* the Bible, as though it were a product of the Jacobean age in England, rather than an ancient text that they were rendering into English. The King James Bible has exerted a tremendous influence on literature in English, but we should remind ourselves that the Bible existed long before anyone in England thought of translating it.

The idea that some of the New Testament might be a Greek translation of an Aramaic original has occasionally been mooted,[3] but is generally dismissed as very unlikely. The Letters were all clearly written in Greek, and the Gospels, though they often use Semitic constructions in their Greek and so appear to have been written by people who also spoke Aramaic, show no signs of having been translated from a Semitic language. Of course, the sayings of Jesus will originally have been uttered in Aramaic, as we saw in Chapter 6. When people wish to press the exact detail of a saying, for example those on divorce and remarriage, they need to remember that these must have an Aramaic origin (see Chapter 12). Paul occasionally quotes Aramaic words that were evidently still in use in the churches he founded, such as *abba*, meaning 'father' (Galatians 4:6), and *maranatha*, 'our Lord is coming' (1 Corinthians 16:22). But the New Testament as a collection of books existed first in Greek, so it is not, as a whole, a translation.

GREEK TRANSLATIONS OF THE HEBREW BIBLE

The tradition of biblical translation, however, antedates the writing of the New Testament. The first translation of the Hebrew Bible occurred in the third century BCE, in Egypt. Jews in the communities of Egypt – descendants of those who had fled after the sack of Jerusalem in the sixth century BCE – had become fluent in Greek but many no longer read Hebrew with any ease, and they required a Greek version of at least the Pentateuch (the Torah), to read in their synagogues alongside, or even instead of, the Hebrew original. We can be confident only that the Pentateuch was translated then; the other books may come from the following century, though all were clearly available in Greek by the time the New Testament writers were quoting the Old Testament in that language.

The practical needs of a sizeable Jewish community in Alexandria that was no longer fluent in Hebrew are probably sufficient to explain the origins of the Greek version of the Hebrew Bible. But there exists a somewhat legendary account of its origins, in the document known as *The Letter of Aristeas to Philocrates*, dating from the second century BCE. This claims to be an eyewitness account of the process of translation. It maintains that the Egyptian ruler Ptolemy II Philadelphus decided to collect all the books in the world into a library in Alexandria (the library at Alexandria was indeed in later times one of the wonders of the world, a kind of research university). Among these he wished to possess the books of the Jews, translated from their original 'strange language' into Greek. To this end he wrote a letter to the high priest Eleazar in Jerusalem, asking him to send learned men to make the translation, and in the process to correct errors that had crept into the text of the Torah. Six people were chosen from each of the twelve tribes of Israel and sent to Egypt; these seventy-two translators completed their work in seventy-two days, and reached complete agreement among themselves. It is from the Greek for 'seventy' that their version came to be known as the Septuagint (often abbreviated in modern times using the Roman numeral for seventy, LXX). (See also Chapters 12 and 14.) *Aristeas* does not explicitly claim divine inspiration for the translation, but probably implies it: 'The outcome was such that in seventy-two days the business of translation was completed, just as if such a result were achieved by some deliberate design' (*Aristeas*, 307). (An addition to the letter actually claims that each of the scholars translated the entire Bible, and that when compared their versions were found, miraculously, to be identical.)

Aristeas seems to have modelled its account of the translation on the early years of the Israelites in Egypt, and also on the story of Ezra. In return for the coming of the translators, Ptolemy II is said to have released many Jewish slaves – surely an echo of the escape of the Hebrews from Egypt in Exodus. After the translation is complete, it is read aloud to all the Jews in Egypt for their approval, probably recalling the giving of the Law at Mount Sinai, and also Ezra's reading of the Law after the return from exile (Nehemiah 8). A belief in the divine inspiration of the Septuagint soon grew up among Greek-speaking Jews, and passed into the Christian Church. It came to be seen as an improvement on the Hebrew original, a kind of new Law. That is why for many New Testament writers it was the Septuagint that functioned as the Bible, rather than the Hebrew – as it also did for many early Christian writers, even in Semitic-speaking areas such as Syria, where the school of Antioch worked entirely from the Greek scriptures and paid no attention to the Hebrew original.

Despite this, even Christians today are likely to think of the Hebrew as the *real* Bible, and the Greek translation – like the King James Version – as secondary and derivative, no matter how influential. In a sense this is obviously the case, though there are two aspects of the Septuagint that qualify this impression.

One is that the LXX does not always reflect the Hebrew text we are familiar with. We tend to assume that the translators were rendering what we now find in a printed Hebrew Bible, since the Hebrew is the original text. But this is not always so. There are several books in which the Greek cannot be explained as a translation of what we now find in *Biblia Hebraica Stuttgartensia*, the standard modern edition of the Hebrew Bible, but seems rather to be translated from an older, or at least different, Hebrew text. This is true for Joshua, Judges, Samuel and Kings – the major historical books – and for several of the prophets, most notably Jeremiah, where the Septuagint version is a sixth shorter than the current Hebrew text, and many oracles appear in a different location. There are places where the Greek translators could have been altering the Hebrew deliberately, but with Jeremiah in particular this seems not to have been the case: a shorter version in Hebrew resembling the LXX has now appeared among the Dead Sea Scrolls,[4] which are centuries older than the manuscripts from which our present Hebrew text derives (the Aleppo and Leningrad or St Petersburg Codices, discussed in Chapter 12). This means that the Greek, though undoubtedly a translation from a Hebrew original, is not necessarily a version of what we nowadays think of as the Hebrew Bible. As we have seen, there was in reality no unified Hebrew Bible in the third century BCE, only a loose collection of texts that overlap, but are not coterminous with, what we now call 'The Bible'.[5]

An example of a passage for which the LXX may reflect an older Hebrew original than what we now find in a standard Hebrew Bible is Deuteronomy 32:8–9, where the text now reads:

> When the Most High apportioned the nations,
>   when he divided humankind,
> he fixed the boundaries of the peoples
>   according to the number of the children of Israel;
> the LORD's own portion was his people,
>   Jacob his allotted share.

Here 'the Most High' and 'the LORD' are assumed to be identical, and the text presumably means that God delineated as many peoples as there were sons of Israel (here another name for Jacob), i.e. twelve, but retained the nation of Israel itself as a special possession of his own (a thirteenth nation?) The Septuagint gives an entirely different impression:

> When the Most High apportioned the nations,
>   when he divided humankind,
> he fixed the boundaries of the peoples
>   according to the number of the gods;
> the LORD's portion was his people,
>   Jacob his allotted share.

Implicit here is a polytheistic context, in which the Most High (Hebrew *elyon*) is distinguished from the LORD (Yahweh). Elyon apportioned the nations one per god, implying no specific number, and Israel fell to Yahweh. It is easy to see why a later scribe might have changed this to avoid the polytheistic implications, much harder to see why anyone should have emended the version that now appears in the Hebrew Bible to make it more polytheistic. On these grounds, most modern commentators think that the Greek must rest on an older version of the Hebrew than that which has come down to us, and that is why the NRSV, together with most other modern translations, renders the LXX rather than the current Hebrew in this verse.

A second problem is that there are places where the Septuagint translators may have deliberately changed the sense of the Hebrew to produce what was from their point of view a theologically more satisfactory version. Translation is always necessarily influenced by the translator's own context, but the Septuagint goes further. We can see this clearly in its attitude to life after death. The Hebrew Bible is noticeably reticent about any kind of afterlife, tending to portray the world of the dead as shadowy and mysterious and as lacking in any positive features, very much like Hades in Homer. Sheol, as that world is known, is a place where the praise of God has ceased and where people can no longer enjoy fellowship with him. In the Psalms, particularly, the worshipper prays to be delivered from Sheol, not in the sense of rising from the dead, but of being rescued in time to avoid going there:

The snares of death encompassed me;
  the pangs of Sheol laid hold on me;
  I suffered distress and anguish.
Then I called on the name of the LORD:
  'O LORD, I pray, save my life!'

For you have delivered my soul from death,
  my eyes from tears,
  my feet from stumbling.
I walk before the LORD
  in the land of the living.

(Psalm 116:3–4, 8–9)

The Greek version sometimes changes this, understanding the prayer to be released from the power of Sheol as a prayer for resurrection. In Psalm 16, in verses 9–10 the Hebrew speaks of God saving the suppliant from untimely death: 'you do not give me up to Sheol, or let your faithful one see the Pit'. In the Greek we find instead that God will save him from Hades, into which he *has already fallen*, just as is implied in the way the psalm is read in Acts 2:31, where it is applied to the resurrection of Jesus.

The Septuagint also introduces resurrection language where there is no hint of it in the Hebrew. For example, at Psalm 1:5 we read in the

Hebrew that the ungodly 'will not stand in the judgement', which means they will not be able to stand up in court and be judged to be in the right – it is a concern wholly of this world. The ungodly will not be accorded any standing among righteous people, in particular in the town assembly. But the Greek translates 'stand' with the word that usually means 'rise from the dead' (*anastesontai*, rather than the more literal *stesontai*): 'the ungodly will not rise to take part in the council of the righteous', understood to mean their assembly in heaven after death. This gives an entirely different flavour to the psalm – one that Christians, understandably, came to prefer. The Church developed readings of the Greek Psalter that stressed the future hope of resurrection in many psalms. Psalms 1, 2 and 3 were all seen as foretelling the resurrection of Christ and so were recited at Easter, as they traditionally have been, and still are, in the Divine Office of the Roman Rite. It could fairly be said that it is the Septuagint, rather than the Hebrew, that is here functioning as 'The Bible'.[6]

In both ancient Judaism and early Christianity the divergences between Hebrew and Greek were probably not the kind of problem that they may seem to us, used as we are to accuracy in proof-reading and precision in translation. The book of Jeremiah existed in two forms, a longer and a shorter one and with the chapters in different orders, but hardly anyone would have been familiar with both, and 'Jeremiah' meant whichever version a particular community happened to possess. The overall message of the book is not much affected by the differences; and even where, as with the Psalms just discussed, there are different meanings in Hebrew and Greek versions, people will not have been aware of them. Even Paul, who was clearly competent to read both the Hebrew and the Greek Scriptures, never comments on the differences, and picks whichever will serve his argument or will be familiar to his readers. So the Septuagint was, for a Greek speaker, equivalent to the Hebrew Bible, even though its message might in fact at some points diverge. This can serve as a reminder that we still perceive our translations as though they were the actual Bible, and are usually unaware of the ways in which they may sometimes skew the original message.

Over time the Greek Bible expanded to include other books besides the Pentateuch. How that happened is not known, but the process must have been more or less complete by the first century BCE, since the other books (what Judaism would later call the Prophets and the Writings) start to be cited in other Hellenistic works, not only in the first–second-century CE New Testament. But among them were some books that had never existed in Hebrew at all (Wisdom of Solomon), and others of which the Hebrew original was lost until recent times (Sirach, Tobit) – the books that eventually, in Protestant reckoning, became the Apocrypha. Most in the early Church accepted them as Scripture (see Chapter 9), and were wholly ignorant of the fact that later Judaism had rejected them. The Jewish community in Alexandria, however, must at least in the beginning have regarded them as worthy to be set beside the books that are also in the Hebrew Bible, or we would not possess them now; but, as we have seen, the rabbinic canon of Scripture eventually excluded them.

Once Christians took up the Septuagint as their Scriptures in the first century CE, Jews began to suspect that they had tampered with it and taken it further from the original Hebrew. There were at least three attempts in the second century to bring the translation more in line with the Hebrew. Three scholars, traditionally called Aquila, Symmachus and Theodotion, attempted a major revision of the Septuagint, on the whole making a more literal translation of the Hebrew (see Chapters 12 and 14). In the case of Aquila this sometimes resulted in barely comprehensible Greek, with a number of invented words to mirror the Hebrew, whereas Symmachus in effect produced a fresh translation, in much more stylish Greek. Origen recorded their versions in his Hexapla. Theodotion's version is closer to a Greek text found at Nahal Hever by the Dead Sea (not so very far from Khirbet Qumran), of the Twelve Minor Prophets, probably from the first century BCE. This text preserves a distinctive style of translation that is also rather literal, and shows that attempts to revise the Septuagint in a more literal direction preceded the concern for possible Christian contamination of the text. There was evidently a feeling that the Greek ought to reflect the Hebrew, not only in sense but in external features of the text such as spellings and unusual constructions.[7] But in the end a reasonably uniform text of the Septuagint established itself, though in three different recensions (editions) that differ on points of detail, and were used in different areas: in Alexandria and the rest of Egypt an edition produced by Hesychius, in Constantinople and Antioch that of Lucian, and in between the version in Origen's Hexapla, as we learn from Jerome.[8]

ARAMAIC TRANSLATIONS

If Jews in Egypt needed to be able to read the Bible in Greek, those in Palestine and in the diaspora communities further east were mostly

Aramaic speakers; and from roughly the same time as the Bible was being translated into Greek, Aramaic versions began to appear too. There may be a reference to interpretations of the biblical text in Aramaic at the time of Ezra, when the Torah was read and Levites 'gave the sense' (Nehemiah 8:8). For a long time Aramaic renderings were apparently oral in character: indeed, until much later times, well into the Christian era, it was held (at least in theory) that the Aramaic version must be produced ad hoc after the scriptural lessons had been read in the synagogue, and that it must not be done by the same person who read the scriptural lection, to maintain the distinction between the divine word and the translator's and avoid any impression that the latter was the inspired text. Nevertheless, Aramaic versions, known as targums, were in due course to be written down.[9] Three main ones have come down to us. These are Targum Onkelos, a rendering of the Pentateuch, which by the third century CE had become the official version, and may rest on considerably older versions; Targum Jonathan, a translation of the prophetic books, from about the same period;[10] and Targum Neofiti, which covers the whole Pentateuch. Targum Neofiti, which is probably from the fourth century CE and of Palestinian origin, rather than from Babylonia like Targum Onkelos, was discovered only in the sixteenth century CE, and is now in the Vatican. It was published and translated in the 1960s, once it was realized that it was not identical to Targum Onkelos, as had previously been thought. There are also some more fragmentary targums, and it is clear that all of the Hebrew Bible was covered, though the targums on the Writings are the worst preserved, probably because many of the Writings are not used at all in Jewish liturgy. The targums have clearly been edited over an extended period, and contain references to events long after the scriptural stories and sayings they are translating: for example, there are occasional references to Islam. They can also be quite 'loose' translations, that is, they often expand, elaborate or even contradict the words of the Hebrew text. For example, Isaiah 19:24–5 reads:

> On that day Israel will be the third with Egypt and Assyria, a blessing in the midst of the earth, whom the LORD of hosts has blessed, saying, 'Blessed be Egypt my people, and Assyria the work of my hands, and Israel my heritage.'

This remarkably universalistic message clearly did not appeal to the targumist, who translated it so as to refer to the Israelites living in Egypt and Assyria, who will triumph when Egypt and Assyria fight each other.[11]

A dialect of Aramaic spoken in Edessa (now Urfa in south-east Turkey) also acquired its own Christian version of both Old and New Testaments, known as the Peshitta, probably in the second or third century CE: the dialect is normally called Syriac. This survives as the Bible of the Syriac-speaking churches (the Church of the East, the Syrian Orthodox Church and the Maronite Church in Lebanon).

LATIN TRANSLATIONS

Greek was the lingua franca of the whole Hellenistic world – that is, of the Mediterranean region, together with most of what we now call the Middle East – from the time of Alexander the Great in the late fourth century BCE until the beginnings of the Roman Empire 300 years later; and even then Romans of high social standing were expected to know Greek. Latin did not replace it until well into the Christian era in the east. Even a work such as the Letter to the Hebrews, which many think was actually written in Rome, naturally adopts Greek as its language; and early Christian worship was conducted in Greek even in Rome, bequeathing to the modern Church (as we saw in Chapter 6) the occasional Greek expression such as *kyrie eleison* ('Lord, have mercy'). Nevertheless, in the west Latin did eventually replace Greek as the language of high and low alike, and a need was clearly felt to possess the Bible in Latin. From about the late first century CE onwards, especially in North Africa, Christian translations into Latin began to be produced, normally known as the Old Latin (or *Vetus Latina*). The best witness to the *Vetus Latina* is the *Codex Bezae*, a fifth-century manuscript of the whole Bible in Greek and Latin, presented to the University of Cambridge in 1581 by Theodore Beza (see Chapter 12).[12] As with all early Latin translations, both the Old and New Testaments were made from the Greek, not from the Hebrew: Christian knowledge of Hebrew was extremely rare in the first few centuries CE. (The New Testament was of course in Greek anyway.)

The first translation of the Bible into Latin made on the basis of the Hebrew text of the Old Testament was that of Jerome (347–420 CE),[13] at the instigation of Pope Damasus. Jerome was initially commissioned, when he was in Rome, to revise the Latin New Testament in the light of the oldest manuscripts available. These, none of which is extant any longer, were extremely diverse, and suffered, as New Testament manuscripts often do, from a scribal tendency to bring the Gospels into

The Vulgate: the beginning of John's Gospel in the Gospel Book of St Augustine, brought to England from Italy in 597 or 601 in Augustine's mission and still used at the installation of archbishops of Canterbury.

harmony with each other by assuming that any omission in a Gospel of a saying or incident that appears in one or more of the others is an error. This then leads the scribe to insert the 'missing' material, so that in the end the Gospels become more and more similar to each other. Jerome understood this, and corrected the 'corrections'. On the basis of his experience he went on to revise the entire Latin Bible – or, in reality, to make his own translation of it. This happened after he settled in Bethlehem in 386, where he got to know a Jewish convert to Christianity who taught him Hebrew. In the library at Caesarea he consulted Origen's Hexapla as a source for both the Hebrew and the Greek Bible (including the versions of Aquila, Symmachus and Theodotion), and produced, single-handed, a complete version of the whole of Scripture, Old and New Testament alike – which he called respectively the old and the new *instrumentum*. He tells us that he consulted a number of Jewish scholars in the course of his work on the Hebrew Bible.

Jerome's translation was not universally well received. Apparently, in Tripoli it caused a riot when it was read in church instead of the familiar Old Latin. New versions of the Bible often do provoke sharp reactions, and the Old Latin continued to be used for centuries in North Africa. But over time Jerome's version established itself, especially in Italy and thence in northern Europe, as the 'common' or 'vulgar' version, that is, the one that enjoyed the greatest currency: in Latin, the *biblia vulgata* or Vulgate. This actual title does not appear until as late as the sixteenth century in reference to Jerome's version, though it was earlier applied to the Old Latin.

> The Vulgate, as we now know it, contains Jerome's translation of the Hebrew books of the Old Testament Canon, with the exception of the Psalms; of the Hebrew and Aramaic of Esdras [Ezra-Nehemiah] and Daniel, as also of the Greek parts of the latter and Esther; and his translation from Aramaic of Tobit and Judith. The Psalms are those of the Gallican Psalter. And the remaining books, Wisdom, Ecclesiasticus [Sirach], the two Books of Maccabees and Baruch, are in the Old Latin Version. These were neither translated nor revised by Jerome. The New Testament is in the form revised by him.[14]

OTHER TRANSLATIONS

During the Middle Ages there were translations of all or part of the Bible in various languages, often as aids to study. The Hebrew Bible was translated into Arabic, probably written in Hebrew script, by Saadia

Gaon, a leader of the Jewish community in Babylonia in the tenth century CE. His version is still used by some Jews in Yemen, though there are more up-to-date Arabic versions available. Medieval Christian biblical translations also survive in Ethiopic, and many European languages. The Psalms are often to be found in translation, usually as aids to monks learning to recite them in the liturgy, and normally rendered from the Latin. In German there are Psalter fragments from the ninth century associated with the Abbey of Reichenau on Lake Constance, and from the fourteenth a whole-Bible translation by Marchwart Biberli (1265–1330), a Dominican from Zurich. There are the remains of a Bible in Gothic, an East Germanic language (now extinct), which is almost the only evidence for that language, along with a biblical commentary in Gothic known as *Skeireins*, the Gothic for commentary. The translation, by one Wulfila, dates to the fourth century, a remarkably early time for a rendering into a northern European language – though Gothic was widespread at the time and spoken in parts of Italy and France as well as in the traditional Germanic lands.

In England Bede, who died in 735, is said to have been working on an English translation of St John's Gospel at the time of his death, and King Alfred (849–99) apparently translated the Psalms, or more likely patronized their translation. Aelfric of Winchester in 1010 seems to have succinctly paraphrased, rather than exactly translated, some of the narrative books of the Old Testament, but wrote that he was hesitant about translation because of the danger of misunderstanding by ignorant people – an attitude which hardened in the later Middle Ages into a reluctance to allow laypeople to read the Bible at all, and which attracted the anger of the Reformers. A real translation (rather than a paraphrase) of the Gospels can be found in the Northumbrian Lindisfarne Gospels, where the Latin text is glossed with an interlinear, word-by-word translation in the local dialect of English.

The Bible was also translated into Slavic languages, following the missionary activity of Cyril (826–69) and Methodius (815–85) in the ninth century: this was for the purpose of using it in the liturgy, rather than for private study as with most western versions. According to the later *Life of Methodius* he translated the entire Bible into Slavonic – what is now called Old Church Slavonic – in sixth months in 884. This may be an exaggeration – he may have translated only the liturgical readings. But there is a manuscript from the following century, the *Codex Zographensis*, that does contain all four Gospels in their entirety in a Slavonic version. A complete Slavonic Bible was not produced until the fifteenth century.

REFORMATION TRANSLATIONS

The great age of biblical translation, after the achievements of Jerome, is the period of the Reformation and its immediate precursors, when the Bible came to occupy a more prominent place in the Christian system, and to be regarded as all-important. In the eight decades before Luther, the Bible had been translated into various kinds of German between 1466 and 1522; into Italian in 1471; Dutch in 1477; Spanish and Czech in 1478; and Catalan in 1492. The great impetus was the invention of the printing press by Johannes Gutenberg in 1439, which made quick dissemination possible for the first time. Diarmaid MacCulloch's argument, which suggests that the rise in translations of the Bible helped to cause, rather than was created by, the Reformation, is supported by the sheer number of fifteenth-century versions, well before the Reformation is generally reckoned to have begun in earnest.[15]

A medieval translation of the Vulgate into Middle German had been produced in 1350 and printed as early as 1466, but the translators had had no knowledge of Greek or Hebrew. Luther, however, worked from Erasmus' new Greek New Testament (see Chapter 16), and once he had acquired it he set about producing a rendering in German. He completed his work in 1522 with the help of Philip Melanchthon (1497–1560), his close associate and the heir to much of his teaching. His complete Old Testament followed in 1534. By then his New Testament had already circulated widely and itself been translated into Dutch, Danish and Swedish. One of Luther's achievements was to forge a style of German, from the many dialects of the language, which could be understood by most speakers – German was at that time far less unified than English; though for the north of the German lands it was translated into Low German, and glossaries were provided of unusual terms.

Catholics responded to Luther's Bible by producing translations of their own, though the first, by Hieronymus Emser (1477–1527), commissioned by Duke Georg of Saxony, was an adaptation of an early version of Luther's New Testament adjusted to conform more with the Vulgate. Emser's translation survived into the eighteenth century as a widely used Catholic Bible in German. Subsequent German Catholic Bibles also tended to stay close to Luther, simply changing controversial terms to underscore Catholic beliefs. Luther's Bible had so shaped the German language that it was very difficult – and has continued to be difficult – for anyone else to produce a successful alternative, whether Protestant or Catholic. Similar difficulties result from the dominance of the King James Version in English.

So far as Anglophone Bibles are concerned, the first, in Middle English, were the late fourteenth century 'Wyclifite' Bibles, associated with though probably not made by John Wyclif. Official opposition to these, aligned as they were with the Lollard movement, made the Church hierarchy in England hostile to the undertaking of biblical translation as such. More important in the long run was the later William Tyndale (1494–1536), who obtained Luther's New Testament and by 1526 had produced his own English version from the Greek. As MacCulloch remarks:

> Tyndale came from the remote west-country Forest of Dean on the borders of Wales, and it is not fanciful to see his fascination with translation as springing out of market-days in his childhood, listening to the mixed babble of Welsh and English around him. He was a gourmet of language: he was delighted that he could use two good Anglo-Saxon words, 'gospel' and 'worship', when biblical translators into other languages were stuck with versions of Greek '*euaggelion*' and Latin '*cultus*', and it also pleased him to discover – as he moved into translating the Old Testament – that Hebrew and English were so much more compatible than Hebrew and Greek.[16]

Tyndale, like nearly all translators in this period, added annotations of a distinctly Protestant kind, and rendered contentious words in a Protestant way – thus, as in Luther, the term generally then understood to mean 'penance' was translated 'repentance', undermining the entire medieval system of penitential theory and practice, including indulgences (see Chapter 16). This led to many copies being burned, and Thomas More wrote a refutation of Tyndale's translation in 1529, describing it as heretical. The accusation of heresy clung to Tyndale, who was eventually arrested and executed in 1536 in The Netherlands when he was halfway through a translation of the Old Testament from Hebrew, which he had taught himself with the help of what was already published of Luther's Old Testament.[17]

Only a year later, however, Tyndale's version, including his unfinished translations, was completed and published for the English market as the Matthew Bible, a text continued and co-ordinated by one of Tyndale's associates, John Rogers, and it was licensed by Henry VIII. So quickly did things move and change in the excitable atmosphere of the early

Reformation. Towards the end of 1539 there appeared the Great Bible, prepared by Miles Coverdale as editor-in-chief under commission from Thomas Cromwell, which became the first 'official' English Bible and was placed in all churches in many dioceses;[18] it was also a great success in Scotland. It followed Tyndale closely, but where Tyndale had not finished the translation of the Old Testament, Coverdale worked from the Latin Vulgate and from Luther's German, as well as drawing on his own earlier version of 1535,[19] rather than from the Hebrew. For the second edition, just a year later, Thomas Cranmer (1489–1556) wrote a preface. In 1560 the Geneva Bible was published, a product of the exiles in Geneva (including Coverdale) who had fled there to escape persecution by the Catholic Queen Mary. This was an important influence on subsequent English versions, supplanting the Great Bible in private or domestic use: it is the Bible of Shakespeare, John Donne and George Herbert. It was also the first vernacular Bible to be printed in Scotland, in 1579. In 1568 there was an official attempt to improve on both the Great Bible and the Geneva Bible in the form of the so-called Bishops' Bible, which in its readings and translations represented a compromise between the two, moderating the more obvious Reformed Protestantism of the latter. The Bishops' Bible did not become widely popular, but it formed the basis for the revision of 1611 that produced the King James Bible.

By 1582 there was also an official Catholic version in English, the Rheims-Douai translation of the New Testament; the Old Testament followed in 1609–10. This was an English translation of the Vulgate, made so that English-speaking Catholics might be able to reply to Protestant 'misuse' of scriptural texts, and avoid heretical translations. There were copious annotations to keep the reader on the right track – as in most Bibles of this period.

Soon there were Bibles in almost all the languages of Europe, and a complete survey would turn into a mere list. In most northern European languages there is a Protestant translation from the Reformation period: thus, for example, German has Luther's Bible (with many subsequent revisions), Dutch a translation of this published in 1526, Czech a New Testament published in 1549, and Polish a version from 1563. Translations into the Romance languages of the Catholic south appeared only a little later: the first French Catholic Bible was produced as early as 1550, and the classic Spanish one in 1559. The first Italian version to be widely read comes from 1603–7, reprinted in 1640/41, and was produced by Giovanni Diodati from the Hebrew and Greek rather than from the Latin (there had been earlier versions, however, from the 1530s). No

French version ever established itself as standard: there was no Luther in France, and biblical translation was seen as tending to heresy. Indeed, the use of vernacular Bibles, other than by papal permission, was actually prohibited by Pope Pius IV in 1564, so that Italian and other versions in Romance languages tended to be, or to be assumed to be, produced by Protestants. Where they were used by Catholics it was for study, rather than in public worship, which remained exclusively in Latin until the 1960s.[20]

In Britain a decisive move occurred in 1604, when the Puritan party in the Church of England proposed to King James (James I of England, James VI of Scotland) that there should be a new Bible translation to improve on both the Bishops' and the Geneva Bible. Where earlier versions had often been completed in haste, the King James Bible was planned with care and involved a large translation committee, working in six 'companies' based in Oxford, Cambridge and Westminster. They were to take the Bishops' Bible as their basis, but were free to draw on other versions and, indeed, to make their own translations where this was necessitated by improved knowledge of Hebrew, Aramaic and Greek. The work took six years, and the result was what came to be known as the 'Authorized Version' of 1611, though it was never formally authorized but simply became the most popular Bible version in print.[21] As the translators say in the preface:

> Truly, good Christian reader, we never thought from the beginning that we should need to make a new translation, nor yet to make of a bad one a good one ... but to make a good one better, or out of many good ones one principal good one, not justly to be excepted against; that hath been our endeavour, that our mark.

The King James Bible was thus a revision, not an innovation, and many of its most striking phrases can be traced back as far as Tyndale – though it is also important to remember that many of them are simply a natural way of rendering the original. As I pointed out at the beginning of the chapter, we do not owe to the AV translators expressions such as 'Let there be light' or 'In the beginning was the Word': these are the obvious English way of translating the Hebrew and Greek sentences in question (Genesis 1:3 and John 1:1). We owe them to writers of the sixth century BCE (the author of 'P') and the first or second century CE respectively.

Although the quality of the English in the King James Version is undeniable,[22] it was in many places already slightly archaic in 1611, in this conforming to some of the norms of the English Book of Common

Prayer, which goes back to 1549, even though the current edition was fixed in 1662. King James's translators aimed at a lofty and dignified style, rather than a colloquial one, and they removed some of the high spirits of, for example, Tyndale's version – 'The Lord was with Joseph and he was a lucky fellow' (Genesis 39:2) did not make it through into the King James Version, nor did 'Joseph was a goodly person, and well favoured' (Genesis 39:6).

The seventeenth and eighteenth centuries saw further versions of the Bible in many languages, many the work of individuals rather than in any sense official. But some established themselves in popular use: this is particularly true of the French translation by Louis-Isaac le Maistre de Sacy (1612–84) in the late seventeenth century. Sacy was a Jansenist (Jansenists shared with some Protestants a high doctrine of divine predestination) and his translation was therefore suspect to some, but it was a great success, with Protestants as well as Catholics, and it was quoted by Blaise Pascal (1623–62) in his *Pensées*, since he had seen an early version of it. No English translation of this period successfully contested the secure place quickly won by the King James Version, which held sway until the end of the nineteenth century, though as we shall see there were some innovative attempts to translate the Bible into a more contemporary idiom.

The Reformation in eastern Europe saw the translation of the Bible into Lithuanian and Slovene, and outside Europe Catholic missionaries rendered it into Japanese. In 1784 there appeared the first Bible in Korean, also a Catholic venture, but not until the nineteenth century was there a Chinese Bible, under Protestant auspices. The first complete Bible for Russia to have any success was produced in the eighteenth century and is known as the Elizabeth Bible. It is the authorized version of the Russian Orthodox Church and is in Old Church Slavonic rather than in Russian, though biblical passages were known in Church Slavonic from the time of Cyril and Methodius, who evangelized the Slavs in the ninth century. The eighteenth century also saw a translation into Eskimo.

MODERN TRANSLATIONS

The last two centuries have produced an enormous number of translations into most of the world's languages, at least those that have a written form, and biblical translators have often been in the forefront of devising scripts for those that previously were unrecorded. At the same

43 And he tooke it, and did eate before them.
44 And hee said vnto them, These
are the wordes which I spake vnto you,
while I was yet with you, ỹ all things
must be fulfilled, which were written in
the Law of Moses, & in the Prophets,
and in the Psalmes concerning me.
45 Then opened he their vnderstan-
ding, that they might vnderstand the
Scriptures,
46 And said vnto them, Thus it is
written, & thus it behoued Christ to suffer, & to rise from the dead the third day:
47 And that repentance and remis-
sion of sinnes should be preached in his
Name, among all nations, beginning
at Hierusalem.
48 And yee are witnesses of these
things.
49 ¶ *And behold, I send the pro- *Iohn 15.
mise of my Father vpon you: but tarie 26. actes
ye in the citie of Hierusalem, vntill ye be 1.4.
indued with power from on high.
50 ¶ And he led them out as farre
as to Bethanie, and hee lift vp his
hands, and blessed them.
51 *And it came to passe, while hee *Mar.16.
blessed them, hee was parted from 19. actes
them, and caried vp into heauen. 1.9.
52 And they worshipped him, and
returned to Hierusalem, with great ioy:
53 And were continually in the Temple, praising and blessing God. Amen.

¶ The Gospel according to S. Iohn.

CHAP. I.

1 The Diuinitie, Humanitie, and Office of Ie-
sus Christ. 15 The testimonie of Iohn. 39
The calling of Andrew, Peter, &c.

IN the beginning was
the Word, & the Word
was with God, and
the Word was God.
*Gen.1.1. 2 *The same was
in the beginning with
God.
*Col.1.16. 3 *All things were made by him,
and without him was not any thing
made that was made.
4 In him was life, and the life was
the light of men.
5 And the light shineth in darknesse,
and the darknesse comprehended it not.
*Mat.3.1. 6 ¶ *There was a man sent from
God, whose name was Iohn.
7 The same came for a witnesse, to
beare witnesse of the light, that all men
through him might beleeue.
8 Hee was not that light, but was
sent to beare witnesse of that light.
9 That was the true light, which
lighteth euery man that commeth into
the world.
*Heb.11.3. 10 Hee was in the world, and *the
world was made by him, and the
world knew him not.
11 Hee came vnto his owne, and his
owne receiued him not.
12 But as many as receiued him, to
them gaue hee || power to become the || Or, the
sonnes of God, euen to them that beleeue right or pri-
on his Name: uiledge.
13 Which were borne, not of blood,
nor of the will of the flesh, nor of the will
of man, but of God.
14 *And the Word was made flesh, *Mar.1.16.
and dwelt among vs (& we beheld his
glory, the glory as of the onely begotten
of the Father) full of grace and trueth.
15 ¶ Iohn bare witnesse of him, and
cried, saying, This was he of whom I
spake, He that commeth after me, is preferred before me, for he was before me.
16 And of his *fulnesse haue all wee *Col.1.19.
receiued, and grace for grace.
17 For the Law was giuen by Moses, but grace and trueth came by Ie-
sus Christ.
18 *No man hath seene God at any *1.Iohn 4.
time: the onely begotten Sonne, which 12. 1. tim.
is in the bosome of the Father, he hath 6.16.
declared him.
19 ¶ And this is the record of Iohn,
when the Iewes sent Priests and Le-
uites from Hierusalem, to aske him,
Who art thou?
20 And he confessed, and denied not:
but confessed, I am not the Christ.

The King James Bible: the first edition of 1611, showing the beginning of John's Gospel.

time, there has been a sense in the language areas that do already have Bibles that modernization is desirable. This can be illustrated from the history of the English Bible in modern times.

In 1870 there was a move in the Church of England to produce a revised version of the King James Version, which was to be more 'faithful' to the Hebrew, Aramaic and Greek by always using the same English word for the words of the original wherever possible. This is a more or less unattainable goal, since the characteristics of the 'target' language (English) mean that one cannot always follow the principle of using the same word and still produce intelligible English. Nevertheless, it was attempted, and the Revised Version (RV) appeared in 1885, after the New Testament alone had been published in 1881. The RV was largely a failure, in that it did not succeed in supplanting the AV in either private or public use, despite resting on the great strides in the knowledge of the biblical languages and manuscripts that had been made since the seventeenth century. But where it succeeded was in opening up the *idea* of revision as a real possibility. The RV translators had the help of an American panel, and in the USA the slightly different version this panel agreed on was eventually published in 1901 as the American Standard Version (ASV). This became the preferred translation of many in North America.[23]

In the twentieth century translations of the Bible into English proliferated, and the flood continues to this day. In other languages they have been less numerous on the whole, and the energies of translators have often been directed to producing versions in languages that till now had lacked any translation at all: indeed, biblical translators have often been at the forefront of recording and analysing languages previously without a writing system, in order to go on to produce a version of the Scriptures. This work is carried on by the United Bible Societies, the overarching organization that includes 146 national Bible societies in some 200 countries. Included is the British and Foreign Bible Society (now known simply as the Bible Society), founded in 1804. There are also independent translation bodies in many countries, such as Wycliffe Bible Translators, who have a clear evangelical allegiance. The linguistic skill and knowledge of biblical translators is usually enormously strong.

Revisions of older versions

Modern translations are broadly of three kinds. First, there are revisions of older versions: in English, this means revisions of the King James

Version. In 1937 the churches of the USA and Canada resolved to prepare a fresh revision of the KJV/AV to replace the ASV but to stay as close to the AV/Tyndale tradition as might be feasible, given the improved state of knowledge of biblical languages and culture. This Revised Standard Version (RSV) was published in 1952. (The RSV Apocrypha followed in 1957.[24]) It allowed for cautious emendation in places where the text was clearly corrupt, but otherwise adhered closely to the Masoretic Text of the Hebrew and Aramaic Scriptures and to a particular critical edition of the Greek New Testament. One clear innovation was that in the case of Isaiah it several times followed the Dead Sea Isaiah[a] Scroll, which had recently been discovered.

The RSV was a sober and sound revision of the KJV/AV, and soon established itself as useful alike for study and for worship: it sounds like the KJV/AV, but makes sense in places where that is obscure or even meaningless. For example, the KJV/AV has this, at 2 Thessalonians 2:6–9:

> And now ye know what withholdeth that he might be revealed in his time. For the mystery of iniquity doth already work: only he who now letteth will let, until he be taken out of the way. And then shall that Wicked be revealed, whom the Lord shall consume with the spirit of his mouth, and shall destroy with the brightness of his coming: Even him, whose coming is after the working of Satan with all power and signs and lying wonders.

The RSV renders it:

> And you know what is restraining him now so that he may be revealed in his time. For the mystery of lawlessness is already at work; only he who now restrains it will do so until he is out of the way. And then the lawless one will be revealed, and the Lord Jesus will slay him with the breath of his mouth and destroy him by his appearing and his coming. The coming of the lawless one by the activity of Satan will be with all power, and with pretended signs and wonders.

What exactly this means remains obscure: it is part of Paul's (or Pseudo-Paul's) vision of the imminent future, and concerns a major wicked figure who is to initiate the events of the last days, conceivably a Roman emperor. But at least in the RSV the reader has some chance of seeing the problem!

One significant success of the RSV was that Catholics and eastern Orthodox Christians came to see its value, and the result was an Ecumenical Edition, published in 1973, the Common Bible. This was divided into four sections: the Old Testament; the books held to be deutero-canonical by the Catholic Church (i.e. most of what Protestants call the Apocrypha); the three books placed by Protestants in the Apocrypha that do not occur in Catholic Bibles at all; and the New Testament. In 1974 the scope was widened further to include the books recognized only by the eastern Orthodox churches (Psalm 151 and 3 and 4 Maccabees).

In more recent years the RSV has itself been revised to produce the NRSV, published in 1989. The edition with the Apocrypha follows the 1974 RSV in including all the books held to be canonical by Catholics, Protestants and Orthodox. The main change is the introduction of so-called inclusive language, which avoids using masculine pronouns where it is feasible to have gender-inclusive ones. Thus 'Blessed is the man who walks not in the counsel of the wicked' (Psalm 1) is replaced with 'Happy are those who do not follow the advice of the wicked'; and in Paul's letters 'brothers' is replaced with 'brothers and sisters'. I shall consider this issue again later. Most mainstream churches in Britain and North America have adopted the NRSV, which thus has a truly ecumenical reach, and it is the preferred study version in many universities and seminaries.

As we have seen, few languages have semi-official versions of the Bible in the manner of the King James Version, but those that do so have also seen new versions in the course of the twentieth and twenty-first centuries. The German Luther Bible underwent several revisions, but all leaving the basic style intact, since to German Protestants the Luther Bible simply is 'the Bible', much as is the KJV/AV for British and North American Protestants. The latest Luther Bible was published in 2016, in time for the celebrations of the five-hundredth anniversary of the beginnings of the Reformation in October 2017. It is a conservative revision, but one that takes full account of advances in knowledge of the Bible in recent years.

Fresh translations

A second type of translation has been undertaken from scratch, without reference to any traditional renderings, and using a contemporary idiom. In English the quintessential example is the New English Bible (NEB), an ecumenical version initiated by the Church of Scotland, published in 1961 (New Testament) and then in 1970 (Old Testament and Apocrypha). A revised version of it, the Revised English Bible (REB), appeared in 1989, but – sadly, I think – has not been widely used, since the NRSV has proved so popular. The NEB/REB style attempts to render the biblical text as though it had been written yesterday, so far as that is possible given the structures of the original languages. This version is rather like that in the Penguin Classics series of translations from ancient and modern languages that appeared throughout the 1950s and 1960s, an educated, modern style of writing that avoids archaisms. The second-person singular ('thou, 'thee') forms are avoided, where the RSV had retained them for address to God, though not to humans (NRSV has also eschewed them). Even in its printed format the NEB innovated, setting the text continuously in paragraphs rather than divided into verses, and no longer having double columns. In the Old Testament in particular it was quite radical, rearranging the text where it was thought that it was muddled (for example, in Job), and introducing new meanings of Hebrew words on the basis of words in related Semitic languages. (The latter tendency was regarded by many as suspect, and the REB often reversed it.)

The idea of translating the Bible into modern speech was not an original insight of the NEB panels, but had been pioneered by a number of individuals earlier in the twentieth century. Among the most successful of these were the versions of the New Testament by James Moffatt (British, 1913; Moffatt's Old Testament appeared in 1924) and Edgar J. Goodspeed (American, 1923), and then that of J. B. Phillips (British, 1958). Phillips tried to render idioms in a style appropriate to modern culture: thus the 'holy kiss' which Paul says believers should exchange (Romans 16:16) becomes 'a hearty handshake all round', and 'Friend, go up higher' (Luke 14:10) is rendered, 'My dear fellow, we have a much better seat for you' – the latter a warning that translations can age rather fast, and are not immune to influence by the translator's social class. Here, however, is Phillips's translation of the passage from 2 Thessalonians discussed above:

> You will probably also remember how I used to talk about a 'restraining power' which would operate until the time should come for the emergence of this man. Evil is already insidiously at work but its activities are restricted until what I have called the 'restraining power' is removed. When that happens the lawless man will be plainly seen – though the truth of the Lord Jesus spells his doom, and the radiance of the coming of the Lord Jesus will be his utter destruction. The lawless man is produced by the spirit of evil and armed with all the force, wonders and signs that falsehood can devise.

This may be described as paraphrase, but it does attempt to convey the (strange) eschatological message of the original in modern English.

Moffatt could be even more successful: here, for example, is his rendering of the famous passage on love in 1 Corinthians 13:

> Love is very patient, very kind. Love knows no jealousy; love makes no parade, gives itself no airs, is never rude, never selfish, never irritated, never resentful; love is never glad when others go wrong, love is gladdened by goodness, always slow to expose, always eager to believe the best, always hopeful, always patient.

In French there was also a highly innovative translation, produced in the Dominican École biblique in Jerusalem and published in sections in 1948–55 as the Bible de Jérusalem. For this, the help of poets and literary scholars was enlisted. Verse texts, such as the Psalms, are rendered in metrical lines, while the underlying scholarship, as befits the place of origin, is of an extremely high standard, expressed in invaluable notes and introductions to the various biblical books. No attention at all is paid to earlier French versions, which was perhaps easier than in the English case because of the lack of a standard French translation that might resonate behind the new version. In 1966 an English translation of this Bible, the Jerusalem Bible (JB), was produced, and it was quickly adopted liturgically by the Catholic Church in Britain and the USA and other English-speaking countries, and widely used by students of the Bible. Its achievement was that it not only used contemporary speech, like the NEB, but also tried to imitate the rhythms and tone of the original, rendering the Gospel of John, for example, in a rather more stately style than the Synoptics, Paul in colloquial English, and passages of the prophets in a broken and breathless idiom where the text conveys urgency and fear. The Jerusalem Bible was thoroughly revised in 1985 as the New Jerusalem Bible (NJB). It remains in many ways the most innovative biblical translation in common use.

Jewish readers who wanted an English version of the Hebrew Bible were content for many years to use the King James Version or lightly revised versions of it. In the twentieth century, however, a new translation was produced by the Jewish Publication Society in the USA in 1917, called simply Tanakh, the traditional Jewish name for the Scriptures (see Chapter 1). A second, revised edition appeared in 1985. This uses fairly modern English, but adheres very closely to the Hebrew and Aramaic, and in particular does not emend the Masoretic Text at all even where it is manifestly corrupt – unlike all Christian translations. This makes it particularly useful for study purposes by those with no Hebrew or Aramaic, since it gives exactly the sense of the Masoretic

Text – provided it is used with a commentary such as that in the excellent *Jewish Study Bible*.[25]

Imitative translations

The third type of translation is represented by several versions of the Hebrew Bible prepared by Jewish scholars during the twentieth and twenty-first centuries. These are versions that seek to imitate the structure, style and vocabulary of the original by deliberately introducing alien ways of speech into the target language. This produces off-centre English (or German or French), but has the advantage of respecting the alien character of the text being translated, and avoiding the danger of domesticating it too much in modern culture (as in the translation by J. B. Phillips above).

In a way this follows in the footsteps of Tyndale, who retained Hebrew idioms such as 'stiff-necked' for 'stubborn', just as the Septuagint and Vulgate had done before him. Such idioms settled so well into English and other languages that their foreign origin is not noticed. Equally, at a syntactical level, the Hebrew tendency to begin each sentence in narrative with 'and' passed over into what we now think of as 'biblical style', so that when it fails to occur (as in JB or NEB) we feel, if we are experienced Bible readers, that something is awry. Imitative translation captures the cultural distance between ourselves and the Bible, though it fails to convey how the Bible sounded to its original readers, to whom, presumably, the style did not appear strange at all. Translation always involves a compromise between rendering the text as though it had been written in the target language, and rendering it so as to recall its alien origin. The NEB/JB tradition respects the first of these principles but can too easily elide the second. The translations now being considered do the reverse.

Four 'imitative' translations should be mentioned. All of them are by Jewish scholars. The oldest is the German version of Martin Buber (1878–1965) in association with Franz Rosenzweig (1886–1929), which began to appear in 1926 with their translation of the Pentateuch.[26] This had the stated aim of adapting the German language to mirror grammatical and syntactical features of the original Hebrew. Thus the classic '"Let there be light", and there was light' became '"Licht werde"; und Licht ward' ('"Light be"; and light was'). Many words were translated in accordance with their supposed etymological base: thus the burnt sacrifice known as the *'olah*, which derives from a verb meaning 'to go up', becomes *Darhöhung*, 'upraising'. The effect can be extremely strange, but that is the intention. Buber argued that the Hebrew Bible had its origin in oral communication rather than in writing – a dubious proposition – and that it therefore required a clipped and terse kind of German, rather than the more expansive and 'normal' German found, say, in the Luther Bible. Reading Buber's version is a refreshing and enriching experience, and it does capture something of the flavour of Biblical Hebrew in German; though of course it creates the impression that Biblical Hebrew was an odd language, rather than completely normal to its original speakers, as in fact it must have been. In translation one cannot gain the benefit of all possible insights into the original text at the same time.[27]

A French equivalent of Buber's work is that of André Chouraqui, born in Algeria in 1917, who was deputy mayor of Jerusalem under Teddy Kollek, and a great sponsor of interfaith work. His Bible appeared in 1974–9.[28] His translations of the New Testament and the Qur'an were well received, and his work was favoured by the novelist André Malraux and, among theologians, by Hans Urs von Balthasar. Even more than Buber-Rosenzweig, his translation of the Hebrew Bible is a kind of imitation of the Hebrew, and he coins even more new words. For example, 'to be angry' is *nariner*, from nostril: 'to nostrilize'. One could imagine Tyndale enjoying this.

English-language parallels can be found in the work of Everett Fox and Robert Alter. Fox, whose *Five Books of Moses* appeared in 1983,[29] makes it clear that he wants to present the Bible 'in English dress but with a Hebrew voice'. Like Buber-Rosenzweig, he often renders what are allegedly the 'root meanings' of verbs, and he repeats words when the Hebrew repeats them: thus in Genesis 32:21–2 (20–21 in NRSV):

> For he [Jacob] said to himself:
> I will wipe (the anger from) his face
> with the gift that goes ahead of my face;
> afterward, when I see his face,
> perhaps he will lift up my face!
> The gift crossed over ahead of his face . . .

Whereas, according to Fox, in modern translations 'the translators are apparently concerned with presenting the text in clear, modern, idiomatic English. For example, they [the NEB translators] render the Hebrew *yissa phanai* ["lift up my face"] as "receive me kindly". The NEB translates the *idea* of the text; at the same time it translates *out* the sound by not picking up on the repetition of *panim* words.'[30] (*Panim* is the Hebrew for face.)

Fox is right that most modern translators are concerned with what could be called the *force* of passages, not with their verbal form; whereas he is concerned with the form, though managing to retain reasonable intelligibility in the rendering. As he says, his work is a homage to Buber-Rosenzweig, but not a slavish imitation of them, and altogether less extreme and opaque.

An even more impressive version that tries to give a flavour of the Hebrew idioms is that of Robert Alter. He manages both to imitate the Hebrew and to preserve the sense, as in the rendering of *tohu wabohu* in Genesis 1:2 (KJV/AV 'without form, and void') as 'welter and waste'. From his version one certainly gets the sense that the source is a foreign and remote book, yet one also hears a text in real English. Alter retains all the 'and's at the beginning of sentences in narrative, but because we are used to them from King James's English, they sound perfectly natural. Alter's version is indeed quite close to the King James Bible, which he regards as the best model for translators, with its combination of imitation of the Hebrew and yet fluency in English style. Alter is probably the closest of all modern biblical translators to producing the kind of version a translator of any other piece of literature would aim at. He has now completed a translation of the whole Hebrew Bible.[31]

Alter aside, modern attempts to mimic the Hebrew do not seem to me to have been very successful, though there are features of it that come across perfectly well in English (such as the repeated use of 'and'). But, equally, very few translators have successfully rendered the force of the text in genuinely modern and fresh English, for all that versions such as the NEB, JB and even NRSV claim to do so. It would take a very bold translator to reconceptualize whole sections of the text in modern English in the way that is quite usual in literary translations.

SOME POINTS OF CONTENTION

Reflecting on translations of the Bible from antiquity to the present, there are four issues that connect with my overall theme of the relationship between the Bible and faith systems.

Notes

First, even the earliest Reformation versions included notes to explain the translation: translators were not content with a bare text. In antiquity Jerome's version already had introductions to many of the books; in the Middle Ages most readers encountered the Bible through the Gloss, not unadorned; and translators such as Tyndale added extensive notes, in his case tending in a generally Lutheran direction. It was probably the notes as much as the translation itself that led to his condemnation as a heretic: Tyndale hammered home the doctrine of justification by faith alone, in passages often translated from Luther, and attacked much in contemporary Catholicism. His defence of the doctrine of justification went so far as to praise the deceits and lies of the patriarchs because they proceeded from faith, and to maintain that even murder and robbery are holy works if God commands them:

> Jacob robbed Laban his uncle: Moses robbed the Egyptians: And Abraham is about to slay and burn his own son: And all are holy works, because they were wrought in faith at God's commandment. To steal, rob and murder are no holy works before worldly people: but unto them that have their trust in God: they are holy when God commandeth them.[32]

Luther's own translations were similarly accompanied by lengthy notes, and also by illustrations (by Lucas Cranach the Elder).

All Catholic translations likewise came with notes that sought to contradict Protestant ones, and to show the concord of the Bible with Catholic doctrines. No one was willing to let the text speak for itself, not even those who, like Luther, maintained that Scripture was both essentially clear and 'its own interpreter' (*suae ipsius interpres*). Even today, Catholic versions of the Bible always contain notes, however minimal. The Catholic edition of the RSV, for example, had notes to passages such as those where Jesus is said to have brothers and sisters, claiming that these were more distant relatives or half-brothers and half-sisters – because to see them as real brothers and sisters would challenge the doctrine of the perpetual virginity of Mary, the mother of Jesus alone. The Jerusalem Bible's notes were more often simply informative, but they too (and sometimes even the translation itself) contained clear hints that Catholic doctrines such as this were to be seen as shining through the biblical text. Matthew 1:25 is usually translated (e.g. NRSV): '[Joseph] had no marital relations with her until she had borne a son', but JB renders it: 'though he had not had intercourse with her, she gave birth to a son'. The appended note reads:

> Lit. 'and he did not know her until the day she gave birth'. The text is not concerned with the period that followed and, taken by itself, does not

> assert Mary's perpetual virginity, which, however, the gospels elsewhere suppose and which the Tradition of the Church affirms.

This could accurately be labelled disingenuous. The translation is unnatural, and the note gives the impression that the Gospels otherwise support the doctrine, which they do only if their references to Jesus' brothers and sisters are read in accordance with this note. It was suspicion of what could be accomplished by cunningly worded notes that led to the translators of the AV being instructed not to append any marginal notes except where essential to explain the Hebrew or Greek. Even this was in a way naive, since one person's 'purely explanatory' note is another's tendentious interpretation.

Tendentious translations

Secondly, one of the salient features of Reformation translation, and one of the things that got the translators into trouble, was the rendering of certain crucial terms so as to support their own theological stance. Thus Tyndale renders *ekklesia* (traditionally 'church') by 'congregation', and *presbyteros* (traditionally 'priest') by 'senior' – both of which seriously undermine Catholic doctrines about the Church and the ordained ministry. Even as late as the King James Version, in the early seventeenth century, the revisers were explicitly instructed to avoid these contentious renderings: 'the old ecclesiastical words to be kept, viz. the word Church not to be translated Congregation'.[33] Of course, what is contentious to some is simply obvious truth to others, and indeed most modern New Testament scholars would agree with Tyndale that *presbyteros* does not mean priest – which in Greek is *hiereus*, a word never applied in the New Testament to any form of ministry in the Church.

Modern translations try not to be partisan, but to render words within their historical context. Nevertheless, even consensus versions such as the RSV, NRSV or JB are suspected by some of serious bias. The suspicion now usually comes not from Catholics detecting a desire to promote Presbyterianism, but from conservative Protestant evangelicals who think that the legacy of Tyndale has been undone by modern translators. Consequently some avowedly evangelical translations have appeared, notably the New International Version (NIV), which seek to correct the 'anti-Protestant' bias of other versions. The NIV, immensely popular in evangelical churches in North America and Britain, is far from extreme in its renderings. One sees more overtly partisan tendencies in the Good News Bible, which translates the *episkopoi kai diakonoi* (traditionally 'bishops and deacons') in Philippians 1:1 as 'church leaders and helpers'; though it freely uses 'church', which nowadays does not have the implication 'Roman Catholic Church' that it had for such as Tyndale. Even these intentionally Protestant versions will not seriously mislead anyone about the content of the Bible, nor should Catholics avoid them, any more than Protestants should steer clear of the JB/NJB: all are responsible translations, and sectarian ideas surface only occasionally.

It is partly the number of English speakers in the world that makes so many translations of the Bible into English viable: you really can find a Bible to suit your own taste. Where other languages are concerned, there are fewer options. In German, alongside Luther the main one is the 'unity translation' (*Einheitsübersetzung*), an ecumenical version begun in 1980 but used chiefly by Catholics, despite resting on formal agreement between Protestants and Catholics as to its acceptability. (France similarly has a *Traduction Oecuménique de la Bible*, based on the Bible de Jérusalem.) In the Scandinavian languages there is mostly only one modern translation, though often of high literary quality: the new Swedish Bible, for example – *Bibel 2000* – was funded by the state, and took shape over many years, with literary as well as technical advisers. Often biblical translation has been bound up with national identity, especially where minority languages are concerned: this has been true of Welsh translations (the most recent completed in 1988 and revised in 2004) and of the Slovenian Bible (1996), associated with national independence. There are also renderings of the NIV into other languages, for an evangelical market.

'Inclusive language' can also be seen as concerned with the tendentious use of words. Until the later years of the twentieth century, writers in many languages with grammatical gender tended to use words such as 'men', 'brothers' and 'he' as including women unless it was clear that they did not: so it was not felt odd that Paul should address his congregations as 'brothers', even though they obviously contained many women. But the feminist movement highlighted the fact that, whatever a writer's or translator's intentions, many women felt excluded by such discourse. In the case of 'brothers' the simple solution was to render 'brothers and sisters' (or 'sisters and brothers'): this was not to change the meaning of the text but rather to translate it more accurately. Problems arise, however, in English when a singular noun is involved, especially because English has no word for a human being in general, irrespective of sex – nothing like German *Mensch* or Dutch *mens* (French has the same problem). One solution is pluralization: 'the man who' becomes 'those who', and 'he' becomes 'they', as we saw with Psalm 1.

My own impression is that, despite the care with which versions such as the NRSV carry out the task of 'degendering' the text, there are still problems. For example, in Proverbs the reader/hearer is addressed as 'my son' (see Proverbs 1:8, 2:1, 3:1, 5:1, etc.); 'my child', which is the preferred modern rendering (thus in NRSV), obscures the fact that the wisdom literature is almost certainly addressed to young men. That then raises the fundamental question of whether we are trying to reconstruct a historical meaning, in which case 'my son' is the only serious option, or to translate so that the text becomes relevant to people today. But if the latter, might we not be justified in changing the text still more? In other words, the issue of inclusive language lands us straight in a hermeneutical debate about how the Bible is to be appropriated and how far it can be adapted or emended to fit a modern agenda. Again, the underlying issue is the imperfect fit between what the Bible appears to say and what modern Christians or Jews believe. The question is how we react to that lack of fit.

Style

Thirdly, a shared feature of most biblical translations in any language is that they have a uniform style throughout. All the characters in the historical books of the Old Testament speak in the same way; the narrative itself reads the same, whether it is in Genesis or Kings or Acts. In the King James Version it is all in something that English speakers at once recognize as 'biblical English', whereas in the NEB it is more like a modern broadsheet newspaper; but it does not vary among the different books, because everything is meant to sound like modern English. Only the Jerusalem Bible (and the NJB) vary the style to suit the book, and even there it is standardly 'modern', never either archaizing or avant-garde. What I have called the 'imitative' translations (Buber, Chouraqui, Fox, Alter) produce a style that is distanced from modern languages, but uniformly so. No translation known to me conveys the sense that Hebrew developed over the course of time, or that Greek was known better by some New Testament authors than by others. If a translation did, we would expect some parts of the Old Testament to be slightly archaic by comparison with others, and in the New Testament some books (for example Mark, and especially Revelation) to be rendered in rather ungrammatical English, say. But this is never done.

It seems to me that it would be worthwhile to try translating some of the Bible, at least, in a more varied way. It would convey the sense, which current translation practice discourages, that the Bible is a collection of books rather than a single uniform one. It could have quite a dramatic effect in some cases. For example, Luke 1–2, the birth stories of John the Baptist and Jesus, are written in a Greek that mimics the style of the historical books in the Septuagint, whereas the rest of the Gospel of Luke is in good, rather stylish Greek of its own time. If the first two chapters were translated into KJV/AV 'biblical English', and the rest into normal modern English, the contrast would be very striking. So too would the impression that chapters 1–2 are something like a folk-tale or myth, compared with the 'normal' historical narrative of the rest of the Gospel. This might be unsettling to those who believe in the historical veracity of the infancy narratives. So a translation based on the stylistic differences in the Gospel could turn out to be rather subversive, which is perhaps one reason why such experiments have not been undertaken.

Influence of earlier versions

Finally, more attention should probably be paid to the effect on later translations of the existence of earlier ones. This is most noticeable in English and German, where the overwhelming presence of the King James Version and the Luther Bible means that new versions tend to be compared, not with the original language texts, but with these great predecessors. In Britain, it is not uncommon to hear that a modern version has 'changed the wording of the King James Bible', as though it were a modern translation of that, rather than based on the original Hebrew, Aramaic and Greek texts. When Elijah's 'still small voice' (1 Kings 19:12) became in the NEB 'a low murmuring sound', causing some derision among critics, this was because the translators thought it a more adequate way of translating the Hebrew expression *qol demamah daqqah*, not a better way of rendering 'still small voice'. The NEB here loses all the poetry in the AV version, no doubt, but if it is a better rendering of the Hebrew, then it has fulfilled its purpose. (In fact I doubt whether it is what the Hebrew means, and prefer NRSV's 'a sound of pure silence' – but not because it is more evocative.)

This argument can be resisted only on the basis of the divine inspiration of the King James Version. Alongside those who insist that the KJV/

AV is better literature than modern versions (and simply do not care about its accuracy), there are also 'King James Version fundamentalists' who really do believe that the translators were divinely inspired, just as there were those who believed in the inspiration of the Septuagint, and then in turn of the Vulgate. Several societies, such as the Dean Burgon Society in the USA and the Trinitarian Bible Society in the UK, hold that the KJV/AV is the most accurate translation that exists; but there is a popular 'King James Only' movement that goes beyond this and believes that the version is inspired and inerrant to a greater extent even than the original Hebrew, Aramaic and Greek texts. Here, as an illustration, is a notice seen outside a church in Charlotte, North Carolina:

> ATTENTION CHRISTIANS!
>
> Are you tired of hearing your pastor correct the preserved word of God (the Authorized King James Version) with the Greek or other translations?
>
> Are you interested in attending a Bible-believing Baptist church in the Charlotte area?
>
> If so, call 394-8051
> Tommy H. Heffner, Pastor
> Bible Believers Baptist Church
> 3608 Dick Road, Charlotte, NC 28216#

This could almost be taken to imply that the Greek New Testament is a translation of the King James Version. Read slightly more charitably, it is clear that the original Greek and translations other than the KJV/AV are less authoritative than King James's translators. The KJV/AV is, on this view, the 'real' Bible. There is an online Bible Believers' Church Directory which claims that the KJV/AV is 'the perfect and infallible word of God ... the Authorized Version preserves the very words of God in the form in which He wished them to be represented in the universal language of these last days: English.'[34]

This is, to put it as kindly as possible, a difficult position to maintain. What are all those who can't read English supposed to do? Presumably what they need are translations of the KJV/AV into their own language. We have seen that pressing the exact wording of the biblical text, perhaps especially of the New Testament, which exists in so many varied manuscripts, is problematic; to attempt this with the wording of the KJV/AV, unless one studies it as a document of the Tudor/Jacobean period, is a hazardous enterprise.

In cultures where a vernacular Bible has not been so formative, as for example in France, the effect of contrast with earlier versions is not so evident; but in Britain and North America the shock of new translations constitutes a considerable block to their reception. This is likely to diminish over time, as generations grow up with, say, the NRSV and are no longer sensitive to its differences from the KJV/AV. But it is a reminder that for all but professional biblical scholars (and perhaps sometimes even for them) the embeddedness of a particular translation in the wider culture means that it tends to be seen as part of the essence of the faith, and this can be misleading. If the relation of faith to the Bible is inherently complex, then to pin the Bible down to one contingent translation is inadequate.

The long and winding story of biblical translation thus raises issues about the Bible and faith. We have to ask for what purpose we are translating the Bible as well as along what lines. King James's panels were not concerned with literary excellence but with conveying what they believed to be the Word of God as accurately as possible; it just so happened that the Jacobean era proved to be a critical period in the development of the English language, and that earlier versions such as Tyndale's and Coverdale's had set an excellent literary standard. But modern versions in all languages have all aimed at being literary works as well as religious ones, and any competent translator strives to do justice to both the original text and the language of the translation. Until very recently, almost all have also been inspired by religious faith. The faith dimension of the Bible will concern us in the concluding chapter.

Conclusion: The Bible and Faith

In their preface to the King James Version, the translators gave form to the inspiration experienced by countless readers over two millennia:

> It is not onely an armour, but also a whole armorie of weapons, both offensive, and defensive; whereby we may save our selves and put the enemie to flight. It is not an herbe, but a tree, or rather a whole paradise of trees of life, which bring foorth fruit every moneth, and the fruit thereof is for meate, and the leaves for medicine. It is not a pot of *Manna*, or a cruse of oyle, which were for memorie only, or for a meales meate or two, but as it were a showre of heavenly bread sufficient for a whole host, be it never so great; and as it were a whole cellar full of oyle vessels; whereby all our necessities may be provided for, and our debts discharged. In a word, it is a Panary [pantry] of holesome foode, against fenowed [mouldy] traditions; a Physions-shop (Saint *Basill* calleth it) of preservatives against poisoned heresies; a Pandect of profitable lawes, against rebellious spirits; a treasurie of most costly jewels, against beggarly rudiments; Finally a fountaine of most pure water springing up unto everlasting life.[1]

Thomas Cranmer had similarly described the Bible as 'the fountain and well of truth'.[2] For such readers, whether Jewish or Christian, opening the Bible is a delight and a pleasure, and it feeds their faith and helps them in times of trouble.

Others, however, find parts, or even the whole, of the Bible dark and uninspiring. They reject the God of the Hebrew Bible as a harsh and unbending tyrant, and they find the New Testament message of salvation through Jesus Christ sectarian and altogether depressing. The 'New Atheism', as we saw at the beginning of this book, rejects the Bible out of hand as anything other than a monumental literary miscellany.

Faced with such contradictory responses to the Bible, is it possible to formulate any kind of idea of its status and authority that can be rationally defended? Among Jews and Christians alike there is in practice a spectrum of attitudes towards the Bible. At one end stands a 'liberal' lack of interest in, or even hostility to, biblical texts – as representing Jewish or Christian religion in the past, but now superannuated. This is not so far from a New Atheist rejection of Scripture: it emphasizes the cruel nature of some of the Old Testament (the book of Joshua, for example), and thinks the message of salvation for believers alone, found in parts of the New Testament, limited and unappealing. There are few publicly available declarations of that attitude, but in some churches and synagogues the Bible is not really held in much regard: it must be read in public worship, because such is the custom, but it does not exercise much leverage on what people believe, which derives largely from secular consensus. At the other end of the spectrum stands fundamentalism, in which there is supposed to be nothing but truth in Scripture, and everything a Christian believes and does must be dictated solely by biblical precepts. (Judaism has little fundamentalism of this kind, because no sectors of Judaism regard the Bible alone as authoritative.) We have encountered both of these extreme attitudes in surveying the history of the Bible.

The majority of Christians and Jews, as well as almost all the interesting positions in both faiths, lie between these two extremes. Most adherents of both faiths acknowledge that, on the one hand, the Bible is an essential element in their religion which cannot be simply shrugged off; and, on the other, that it is not a complete compendium of all that is to be believed, so that the relation of the Bible to the faith(s) that recognize its authority must somehow be more complicated than fundamentalists think. In this concluding chapter I shall look at some issues in the relation between the Bible and faith. The main concentration will be on Christianity, but I shall try to note similarities and differences between the two faiths where they are salient. As in the rest of this book, I do not assume that readers are themselves religious, only that they find the place of the Bible in religious faith worthy of their attention.

FAITH AND THE BIBLE

Once we look beyond fundamentalism, we find that the beliefs and practices of Christians and Jews do not map exactly onto the Scriptures to which they appeal. In general terms, the Bible is the work of Jews and Christians: a necessary but of course not sufficient reason why it is their holy book. But in detail the actual religions are not literally scriptural. Starting from the Bible, one would not predict the Christian Church or Judaism as we see them today; starting from modern Judaism or Christianity, one could not reconstruct the Bible. The Church canonized the Old and New Testaments as the official documents of a faith system different in both subtle and not-so-subtle ways from that to which these texts themselves bear witness, while perceiving it to be the same. From that many problems stem. It is not difficult to demonstrate (as Géza Vermes, for example, has done[3]) that the Jesus we meet in the New Testament is not manifestly the incarnation of the Second Person of the Trinity. Describing him as such reflects a later way of understanding him: and the argument that that is indeed what he is requires a long chain of reasoning which moves outside the realm of biblical thought. The Bible alone will not yield full-blown Trinitarian belief, though it is not incompatible with it. Judaism and Christianity do hold beliefs that can be shown to be at least inchoately present in the Bible – for example, that there is only one God, who is the creator of everything. This is a fundamental element in the faith of both Christians and Jews, and there is no doubt that the Bible affirms it. But even there the background assumptions against which this biblical belief made sense (a world of many gods of varying moral character) is not that of the religions in their later, classic form. One cannot derive modern Jewish or Christian monotheism simply and solely from the biblical text: they rest on centuries of philosophical reflection in both religions.

Similarly, to take the question of types of ministry in the Church, the New Testament shows us that even the earliest churches were 'ordered' to some extent, rather than anarchic. There is, however, no way of reconciling the evidence for the various types of ministry present in the early days of Christianity with the later pattern of bishops, priests and deacons. To believe otherwise is to indulge in a form of ecclesiastical mythology. To insist on the apostolic origin of this way of ordering the ministry is at odds with a reasoned approach to the Bible. The papacy likewise may be said vaguely to derive from Scripture, in the sense that there is the famous text, 'you are Peter, and on this rock I will build my church' in Matthew 16:18; but no reading of this would have predicted the institution as it has actually turned out or the authority it wields for believers.*

* I have referred to the way the Church is ordered several times in this book, not because I think this important in theory, but because it is for the most part what divides the churches from each other and so is highly significant in practice.

BIBLICAL GENRES

The difficulty of using the Bible within the Jewish and Christian communities extends beyond the lack of an exact fit between the religion and the biblical text. One problem is the variety of genres in the Bible, many of which do not lend themselves to providing a basis for doctrine or ethics. For example, with both narrative texts and with poems such as the Psalms, there is a serious question about how they can function as part of an authoritative religious book, since they do not on the whole give rulings or advice: the narrative books tell the story of Israel or of Jesus and the early Church, while the Psalms praise God or reflect undogmatically on human life.

In Judaism, the predominant strategy has been to treat all scriptural books as essentially *torah*. Not only the Pentateuch, but all the books in the biblical canon, are to be used for teaching people how to live as observant Jews, while also containing some wisdom even for non-Jews. The focus is on practice of the religion, and even prophecy and psalmody are assimilated to this model.

In Christianity, the traditional approach has been to foreground the prophetic, forward-looking character of the Hebrew Bible, seeing it as pointing to Christ. This has been applied even to the Pentateuch and the wisdom books and Psalms, treating David and Solomon (the supposed authors of Psalms and wisdom books, respectively) as essentially prophets. The focus is on how the Bible predicts the coming of Christ, through the Old Testament, and then explains it in the New.

In neither case are other aspects of the Bible simply neglected: Jews have taken an interest in prophecy, and Christians in law and ethical teaching. But the major emphasis has fallen respectively on *torah* and prophecy.

I have emphasized the great variety of genres in the Bible, which should I think discourage us from concentrating on one to the exclusion of the others. In the case of the Hebrew Bible, this means grasping how the books reflect many different aspects of ancient Israel's life and activity, which becomes as it were three-dimensional rather than reducible to a flat picture. In the case of the New Testament, it points us to the historical rootedness of the Gospels, Acts, Letters and Revelation, and to the difference between teaching laid down in one of Paul's letters or in the sayings of Jesus, and narrative presentation of the great events upon which the New Testament rests. These different genres cannot be reduced to examples of the same kind of literature, but remain vividly different from each other. An appreciation of genre shapes our expectations of the kind of information we can expect to derive from each book. Psalms do not lay down the law and proverbs do not make concrete predictions; the passion narratives in the Gospels do not prescribe doctrine, and Paul's letters, prompted by particular issues in the early Church, do not lay down rules for all time. Sensitivity to these differences of genre is perhaps the single most important consequence of accepting a critical attitude towards the Bible, and it conditions what we expect to get from reading it.[4]

PSEUDONYMITY

Another issue is the presence of books attributed to someone other than their actual author, and the questions of authority they raise. This is a minor matter in much of the Old Testament: one can say that the Psalms are ascribed to David as a kind of ancient sponsor of psalmody, not as a deliberate (and therefore false) claim of authorship. Daniel is more troubling to some, since it claims to come from the period of the exile (sixth century BCE), when almost all scholars would see it as actually having been written in the second century BCE, in the time of the persecutions of Antiochus IV Epiphanes. But in the New Testament the problem is acute, if we are right in thinking that the letters of James, John and Peter, and several of those ascribed to Paul, are in fact pseudonymous. This appears to reduce their authority, since the pseudonymous letters are certainly making at least one claim that is untrue.

As we have seen, there are possible ways of navigating this if one wishes to maintain that even pseudonymous texts can be authoritative. One common approach has lain in recognizing that, at the time these letters were written, people may have had different literary conventions from ours, making the false claims less objectionable. But it is definitely a problem for anyone committed to the literal truth of the Bible. The usual strategy of anyone who wishes to maintain an extremely high doctrine of scriptural authority has been to deny that such texts are pseudonymous, but this sometimes requires a degree of ingenuity in argument that undermines confidence in the conclusions. In the case of the Pastoral Letters (1 and 2 Timothy and Titus), for example, it does not really seem plausible that Paul, here apparently in old age, had changed his Greek style enough to write these texts, which are so at variance with his other major letters – which is the kind of explanation one must provide, if one wants to defend their authenticity.

As we have seen, the authority of the New Testament books was accepted gradually by the Church, with very little in the way of official declaration. When official documents that do list the canonical books do appear, they generally affirm what was by then already the case for the majority of Christians. The New Testament books were not (contrary to what is often claimed) selected from a larger corpus, but established their authority without much controversy; and the books that did not achieve canonical status are in almost every case much later than those that did, and were never widely used. There are at most two or three books that might have been included but were not, for example *The Shepherd* and *Barnabas*, which appear in some very old manuscripts of the whole New Testament such as *Codex Sinaiticus*. The idea that such works were not 'apostolic' (which is what the Muratorian Fragment argues in the case of *The Shepherd*) assumed that the books now in the New Testament are. But no one actually knew that at the time – it is a deduction from their already accepted status.

Pseudonymity in the Hebrew Bible presents a problem for Orthodox Judaism, at least as it affects the Pentateuch: the suggestion that the Pentateuch was not composed by Moses implies that 'the Torah is not from heaven', which is a heretical idea. Paradoxically, Mosaic authorship of the Pentateuch is in fact not asserted or even implied in the text, unlike the attribution of at least some of the Psalms to David, and of the books of Proverbs and Ecclesiastes (Qoheleth) to Solomon. But the imputation of pseudonymity is in general regarded by Orthodox Jews as an anti-Jewish, perhaps even anti-Semitic slur on the Bible concocted by Christian scholars. (Spinoza, who stands at the source of so much of this argumentation, is seen as a renegade from Judaism.) Reform and Liberal Jews, on the other hand, tend to be somewhat relaxed about the attributions of authorship in the Bible. One of the Orthodox complaints about the British Masorti movement and its founder, Rabbi Louis Jacobs (1920–2006), is that though it practises Judaism in an Orthodox form, it is hospitable to biblical criticism and so denies that the Torah is from heaven in the traditional sense.

TWO TESTAMENTS?

We have seen that the relation between the Testaments raises intricate issues for Christians. The Old Testament is affirmed, yet the New Testament adds to it in ways that change its meaning for Christian readers.

This is part of the wider question of the relationship of what Christians believe to what was believed in Judaism before Jesus was born. Christianity is inherently dialectical in character, committed to a tension between old and new that is symbolized and exemplified in its relationship to the Bible. The dialectic is particularly acute in Lutheran thinking and in other Christian circles influenced by Luther: unlike Calvin and Zwingli, Luther saw a sharp disjunction between law and gospel which the contrast between Old and New Testaments symbolizes. To overstress this contrast lands one in Marcionism (of which Lutherans are often suspected), yet to underplay it can result in a 'legalistic' form of Christianity, in which the New Testament is interpreted, like the Old, as mainly a repository of laws to be observed. (Catholics are sometimes – equally unfairly – suspected of that, as are Reformed Protestants.) Holding the balance is extremely difficult. Christianity claims to be in continuity with Israel before Jesus, worshipping the same, one God and revering the Hebrew Bible; yet also to be in touch with something new, a fresh input into human affairs by that same God of Israel.

The relation of Old Testament to New is thus at the heart of Christian theology, but it is a conundrum rather than a clear doctrine, a paradox. Christians find themselves wanting to say things about it that appear to be, and perhaps really are, irreconcilable. The Christian creeds affirm that God 'spake by the prophets', an affirmation that the Old Testament is still important; yet they also emphasize the centrality of Jesus Christ as the 'only Son of the Father', in a way that obviously moves beyond anything the prophets had to say. The history of Christian use of the Old Testament is a history of attempts of varying dexterity to get the text to say things that it doesn't, to try to get it to conform to the new ideas in the New Testament and in subsequent Church teaching. No simple or unequivocal affirmation of the Old Testament does justice to the paradox.

We have also seen a contradiction (or paradox) in Christian attitudes towards old and new, in that the Christian revelation in Christ was initially thought of as significant in its novelty, by contrast with what previously had been known in Israel, but soon became 'tradition', respected for its venerability. This is of course a phenomenon familiar in other spheres but especially in religion, where new movements initially impress by their novelty but then come to appeal because they are old and well established. One has only to think of, for example, the Franciscan movement, an exciting new development which, in subsequent generations, became a tradition. The relation of the Old and New

Testaments in Christian thinking is also affected by this dynamic. A leader such as Marcion was so attracted by the novelty of Christian writings (particularly those of Paul) that he abolished the Old Testament as an authority for his followers, whereas other teachers stressed the continuities between the two corpora of writing and thought.

INSPIRATION

This book has not dwelled on the idea of divine inspiration in relation to the Bible. This is partly because my main purpose has been to explain how the Bible came into existence and how it has been understood through the ages, and how we might think about its elements today. It is also partly because the language of divine inspiration occurs less, in the Bible itself, than is often assumed. In the Hebrew Bible certain people are said to be inspired by God, particularly the prophets, including Moses, but the books are not. The Pentateuch is not claimed anywhere within the Hebrew Bible to have been divinely inspired – nor, indeed, to be by Moses. The New Testament books similarly make no claim to be inspired. The chief passage relevant to the idea of the inspiration of texts (as opposed to people) is 2 Timothy 3:16–17 (see the Introduction):

> All scripture is inspired by God and is [or, Every scripture inspired by God is also] useful for teaching, for reproof, for correction, and for training in righteousness, so that everyone who belongs to God may be proficient, equipped for every good work.[5]

'Scripture' here presumably refers to the Old Testament, unless by the time of the composition of 2 Timothy some New Testament material was already so described (cf. 2 Peter 3:16, which seems to call Paul's letters scripture: 'There are some things in them hard to understand, which the ignorant and unstable twist to their own destruction, as they do the other scriptures'). 'Inspired' – literally 'God-breathed' – seems to imply God as the author of the biblical books in a way not otherwise asserted within the Bible itself. In Judaism it has been customary to see the books of the Hebrew Bible as given by the spirit of God, though the mechanism is not much discussed.

Despite the paucity of references within the Bible itself, Christians have often described the Bible as the product of divine inspiration. The term is picked up most recently in a short book published in 2014 by the Catholic Pontifical Biblical Commission, entitled *The Inspiration and Truth of Sacred Scripture: The Word that Comes from God and Speaks of God for the Salvation of the World*. The argument of this document is that God is the ultimate author of Scripture, yet the writers of the different books (and in some cases the people who produced the sources from which the books were assembled) are also true authors. Reference is made to *Dei Verbum*, one of the documents of the Second Vatican Council quoted in the Introduction, which states that 'in composing the sacred books, God chose men, and while employed by him, they made use of their powers and abilities, so that with him acting in them and through them, they, as true authors, were consigned to writing everything and only those things which he wanted.' Accordingly, 'Inspiration', the authors of *Inspiration and Truth* say, 'as an activity of God . . . directly concerns the human authors: they are the ones who are personally inspired. But then the writings composed by them are also called inspired.'[6] The 'General Conclusion' notes that:

> If, on the one hand, one is fully aware that these writings were composed by human authors who left on them the stamp of their own particular literary genius, on the other hand, one equally recognizes in them a unique divine quality variously attested by the sacred texts and variously explained by theologians over the course of history.[7]

In a striking sentence, the authors claim that 'A typical example of this is the Gospel of John, every word of which is said to manifest the style of John and at the same time to communicate faithfully what Jesus said.'[8] How, one might wonder, can it do both? (And is the uneasy phrase, 'is said to manifest' a case of the Commission distancing itself from the assertion?)

This illustrates a second paradox: the difficulty in holding a high doctrine of scriptural inspiration if one is also aware of the Bible as a fundamentally human document. The authors of *Inspiration and Truth* do not wish to say that God simply overruled the human authors, using them as mere scribes to copy out his own words. There have been such theories: in the seventeenth century the Lutheran theologian J. A. Quenstedt (1617–88) argued that the biblical writers provided 'only the pen and ink' – God dictated all the words to them:

> The Holy Spirit not only inspired in the prophets and apostles the content and sense contained in Scripture, or the meaning of the words, so that they might of their own free will clothe and furnish these thoughts with their

own style and words, but the Holy Spirit actually supplied, inspired and dictated the very words and each and every term individually.[9]

The KJV/AV translators embraced a similar theory. After describing Scripture as 'a fountaine of most pure water springing up unto everlasting life', they continue:

> And what marvel? the original thereof being from heaven, not from earth; the author being God, not man; the inditer, the Holy Spirit, not the wit of the Apostles or Prophets; the penmen, such as were sanctified from the womb, and endued with a principal portion of God's Spirit.[10]

Dictation theories are unusual today: even very conservative Christians allow that the biblical writers contributed from their own minds. But accepting this makes it difficult to exclude the possibility of error in the Bible, which biblical conservatives are concerned at all costs to avoid. Conservatism about the Bible is often popularly identified with reading the Bible *literally*, but in fact it is more concerned with *inerrancy*,[11] and will sometimes accept a metaphorical reading if that will preserve the truth of the text – just like Origen and those who followed him. Some conservative Christians do indeed hold that, since Genesis 1–2 says that the world was created in six days, it must have been so created – a literal interpretation. Many other conservatives, however, maintain that 'day' here does not literally mean a period of twenty-four hours, but some vastly longer timespan. Since God inspired the writers, they cannot have been in error; and since we know that the world formed and life evolved over billions of years, that must be what Genesis really means. Here inerrancy, not literalism, is the point at issue. The text can be interpreted in many ways, but not read as affirming anything we know to be untrue. I have often heard Christians deny that the world was made in six days but insist that there must have been six *periods* in its creation, and even that science supports this – anything but suggest that Genesis is simply wrong.

To me it seems that the language of inspiration is often seriously misleading, since it does seem to imply a dictation theory – for how can a text be inspired unless its words are? A text is made of words. Yet this is generally denied, as in *Inspiration and Truth*. A more subtle theory of inspiration was pioneered in Continental Catholicism at the beginning of the twentieth century under the slogans, 'inspiration without inerrancy' and 'the sufficiency of Scripture'.[12] It was argued that Scripture could be sufficient for its purpose without being perfect. God had ensured that the Church had a book in which all the truths necessary to bring people to salvation could be found. But this did not mean that it was free of all imperfections. Like any other book, the Bible was inevitably affected by errors of fact and opinion. And it was rooted in particular historical periods, and could not speak directly to all other periods. To claim that only a perfect book could be inspired by God would be to imply that God could not, in fact, inspire any book, for God cannot do things that are inherently impossible; as Alfred Loisy (1857–1940) said, an absolutely true book could no more exist than could a square triangle.[13] The Bible is not, and could not be, perfect. Nevertheless, it is by God's providence that we have it, so we can call it inspired and even verbally inspired, without denying that it may contain errors – which, however, are not of a kind that affects its efficacy in matters of faith and morals.

This makes an intelligible attempt to maintain the language of inspiration while denying that God actually wrote the words of the Bible. In its talk of the 'sufficiency' rather than the perfection of Scripture it comes close to Anglican ways of formulating the matter, as we shall see: not surprisingly, it was condemned as 'Modernism' in the Catholic Church. But it may be that inspiration is a term that causes more problems than it solves. To talk of the authority of the Bible may not require a belief in its divine inspiration at all.

TEXTUAL FLUIDITY

One of the difficulties in seeing the Bible as doctrinally authoritative, let alone divinely inspired, arises from its textual uncertainty. Even the Old Testament, for which there is a long-standing tradition of careful textual transmission, varies from manuscript to manuscript; but the New Testament has no fixity of text at all, and there is no one manuscript that is regarded by the churches, or certainly by scholars, as *the* New Testament. As we saw in Chapter 12, the variation can be very wide, as with Jesus' reported sayings on divorce and remarriage – which in any case differ among the three Synoptic Gospels. No exact ruling can be extracted from the text, though (as I argued above) we can conclude at least that Jesus opposed the abuse of women – no small thing. This lack of fixity is not a problem for Christians who think that ethical decision-making should draw on what evidence there is in the Bible but should also involve human judgement where the Bible gives no certain ruling.

But it is a major difficulty for anyone who believes that all decisions should be driven only by Scripture.

To possess an authoritative Scripture also implies that one's beliefs and actions should be guided by its teachings – that is part of the definition of a 'Scripture'. But we have noticed an important and paradoxical effect of recognizing certain texts as scriptural: the more central and important they are, the more likely that they will be subject to forced or strained readings. Once a text is holy in a given religion, it becomes important for believers to perceive it as teaching what that religion teaches, but in the case of the Bible we have repeatedly seen that this is sometimes not really so. The Hebrew Bible does not clearly foretell the coming of Christ, or reveal the exact tenets and practices of Orthodox Judaism; the New Testament does not clearly teach the doctrine of the Trinity, or prescribe any particular way of ordering the Church. To find these matters in the biblical text, as Christians and Jews wish to do, it has to be read in unnatural ways. In Judaism this often involves pressing sub-semantic features of the text such as spellings and redundancies, or linking together unconnected texts from all over the Bible to make a single ruling. In Christianity it frequently results in allegorizing the Old Testament or even the New so as to make them appear to teach exactly what Christians believe. The holier the text, the more likely it is that it will be subjected to such reading, and the less likely that it will be heard in its own voice.

This is useful to have in mind when we try to identify which texts are regarded as scriptural or canonical. The traditional way of investigating the growth of the canon is to look for Jewish or Christian rulings on its content; but we have seen that such rulings are few and far between – and generally only codify what is in practice already the case. More telling are the specific texts that authors in particular periods quote and discuss, since they constitute their effective, rather than theoretical, canon. Identifying which of these are read in forced ways, allegorically or midrashically, tells us which are of central importance for the writer in question. People did not allegorize trivial or unimportant texts, or assemble them into a connected series to underpin a ruling, or analyse their spelling and outward shape. Only texts that are considered holy are subjected to readings of those kinds, and where we find them we may be sure we are dealing with books that are part of the biblical canon.

A parallel phenomenon, at least in the case of Christian biblical manuscripts (whose text was not fixed), is what Bart Ehrman calls the 'orthodox corruption of Scripture' – places where an older text has been altered to ensure that it teaches sound Christian doctrine. An egregious example is the 'Johannine comma' discussed in Chapter 16; but there are subtler changes, too, such as the alteration of 'who were born' to 'who was born' in John 1:13 in order to smuggle the doctrine of Jesus' virginal conception into the Fourth Gospel, which otherwise lacks it (see Chapter 12). From such emendations we can infer what Christians believed at the time the change was made, so that they are part of the history of Christian theology, and know that the text in question must have been regarded as Scripture because, just as with strained readings, no one would have bothered to change it if it had not been centrally important. Orthodox corruption thus also confirms the high status of the text being corrupted – a third paradox.

Forced readings are not a feature of biblical study only in the ancient world, but are still prevalent today, and have the same value as evidence of the perception of the holiness of the text. *The Inspiration and Truth of Sacred Scripture*, published in 2014, argues repeatedly that the Bible should not be read 'literally', which leads, it suggests, towards fundamentalism. Thus in a passage on the earthquake that according to Matthew 28:2 followed the death of Jesus, we read that earthquakes are often symbols of significant events in both Testaments, and hence:

> It is likely ... that Matthew uses this 'literary motif'. By mentioning the earthquake, he wishes to underline that the death and resurrection of Jesus are not ordinary events but 'traumatic' events in which God acts and achieves the salvation of the human race.[14]

On the fall of Jericho to Joshua (Joshua 6), we read:

> From the outset, it is necessary to note that these narratives do not have the characteristics of a historical account: in a real war, in fact, the walls of a city do not come crashing down at the sound of trumpets (Joshua 6:20).[15]

Such readings attempt to make the biblical stories acceptable to a modern reader who does not believe in miracles. But they surely amount to a metaphorical – or, one might as well say, allegorical – method of dealing with historical difficulties in the text. They do not belong to a historical-critical style of reading, which would see the stories as reports of alleged actual events, but then go on simply to deny that such events happened, as Spinoza might have done. They inhabit the world of Origen and Augustine, not that of the modern historical critic.

Arguably, the same is true of the assertion that the story of creation in Genesis 1:1–2:4 is not meant literally, which is a complete commonplace in modern discussions of religion and science, and is picked up in *Inspiration and Truth*:

> The first creation account (Gen 1:1–2:4a), through its well-organized structure, describes not *how* the world came into being but *why* and *for what purpose* it is as it is. In poetic style, using the imagery of his era, the author of Gen 1:1–2:4a shows that God is the origin of the cosmos and of humankind.[16]

As a statement of how the faithful can best derive benefit from reading this passage, this may be accurate. But it seems to me highly likely that the original author *was* trying to describe how the world came into being, in other words that the text *is* meant literally. The problem with this way of understanding it is that, unless one is a fundamentalist, one then has to go on to admit that the author was mistaken; and this comes very hard to Christians, especially when they are producing ecclesiastical documents. The metaphorical reading of the creation story is, I suggest, a 'forced' or strained reading, designed to ensure that the narrative can continue to be seen as true in some sense. And perhaps it is indeed true in that sense – but it foists on the author what some readers believe is the best way *we* have of extracting benefit from the passage. Such readings are not a modern undertaking, but follow in the footsteps of Origen. Recall again the passage from him quoted in Chapter 14:

> Could any man of sound judgement suppose that the first, second, and third days [of creation] had an evening and a morning, when there were as yet no sun or moon or stars? Could anyone be so unintelligent as to think that God made a paradise somewhere in the east and planted it with trees, like a farmer, or that in that paradise he put a tree of life, a tree you could see and know with your senses, a tree you could derive life from by eating its fruit with the teeth in your head? When the Bible says that God used to walk in paradise in the evening, or that Adam hid behind a tree, no one, I think, will question that these are only fictions, stories of things that never actually happened, and that figuratively they refer to certain mysteries.[17]

Because the text is inspired, it must be true: hence it must be read in ways that are capable of being true, according to our understanding of how the world is and of how it came to be. But there is an alternative, which is to read it at face value, and then recognize that it is not true. If we do that, then the idea that the text is inspired becomes harder to hold on to. Perhaps it is better not to make the high claim that it is inspired – or else to understand inspiration differently.

SCRIPTURE AND TRADITION

Traditionally Catholics have said that authority in Christianity lies with both Scripture and Tradition, while Protestants have insisted on Scripture alone – *sola scriptura*. Tradition, for Catholics, includes items such as the creeds (which many Protestants in practice also affirm), and teaching down the centuries as codified by the Catholic Church – since the Middle Ages, assumed to be found in the utterances of popes and Church councils. In principle, however, Catholics would say that Tradition is wholly consonant with Scripture, while Protestants often affirm the authority of at least the first few councils of the Church, those that ruled on the definition of the doctrines of the Trinity and the Incarnation, such as the Councils of Nicaea (325 CE) and Chalcedon (451 CE). Though Protestant clergy generally preach on biblical texts, and Catholics more often on Church teachings, even here the gap has narrowed since the Second Vatican Council placed such emphasis on the exposition of Scripture in the Church's public liturgy. The difference between Catholics and Protestants is thus not so great in practice as it appears in principle, at least where the central doctrines of Christianity are concerned. Neither would ever assert that Tradition is *more* important than Scripture – though, as we have seen, the extreme importance of Scripture means that it is often read in forced ways in order to make sure that the message it delivers is in line with Tradition, and in that sense Tradition can in reality 'trump' the biblical texts which in theory are superior to, or at least equal with, it. We have seen the parallels in Judaism, where the Tradition as codified in Talmud and Midrash determines how the Hebrew Bible, which is in theory their master, is in fact read.

Studies of biblical authority seldom draw on the thought of the eastern Orthodox churches. These have produced few works on the Bible in modern times, tending to rely on the exegesis of the Fathers of the Church, described in Chapter 14. They did not pass through the Reformation and Counter-Reformation of the sixteenth century, and the controversies between Catholics and Protestants have touched them little. Nevertheless, their potential contribution to the question of the Bible and religious belief should not be underestimated.

The 1976 *Moscow Agreed Statement* between the Orthodox and Anglican Churches states that

> Any disjunction between Scripture and Tradition such as would treat them as two separate 'sources of revelation' must be rejected. The two are correlative. We affirm (1) that Scripture is the main criterion whereby the Church tests traditions to determine whether they are truly part of Holy Tradition or not; (2) that Holy Tradition completes Holy Scripture in the sense that it safeguards the integrity of the biblical message.
>
> (*Moscow Agreed Statement*, 3:9)

This seems to imply an equality, but also a mutual reference of Scripture to Tradition, in which there can never be any conflict – either a confident affirmation (as a Catholic would see it) or extreme wishful thinking (from a Protestant perspective, since for Protestants the Bible precisely *challenges* Tradition). In an important work, Eugen J. Pentiuc comments on this, however:

> The binomial 'Scripture and Tradition' used by the *Statement* is more Roman Catholic than Eastern Orthodox in tenor. To quote John Breck: 'Orthodoxy sees the relationship between the two in a way that can be described not as Scripture *or* Tradition, or Scripture *and* Tradition, but Scripture *in* Tradition. This is because Scripture is Tradition, in the sense that the New Testament writings are a part of Tradition and constitute its normative element. Those writings came forth from the Church's life and proclamation and they have continued through the ages to be the measure, rule or "canon" of Christian faith.' . . .
>
> For a better understanding of the Orthodox view on the relationship between Scripture and Tradition, I propose the following analogy: Scripture as a textbook and Tradition as a set of explanatory handouts.[18]

Pentiuc explains this analogy as follows:

> Scripture . . . may be compared to a daring and untamable textbook. Holy Tradition in all its avatars – conciliar statements, writings of church fathers, liturgy, iconography, ascetic teaching – functions as guiding handouts of the textbook. Following this analogy, one may note a certain complementarity or reciprocity. Handouts aim to summarize and explain the salient points of a textbook. Similarly, Tradition, based on Scripture, complements the latter by condensing and illuminating its content . . . the handouts always need the textbook as their irreducible point of departure and reference.[19]

In theory, again, this seems to privilege the Bible over Tradition in the last resort, and there is not much in it that a moderate Protestant might object to – remembering that Protestantism too has its own 'holy tradition', not only in the creeds accepted by nearly all Christians, eastern and western, but also in documents such as the various Confessions acknowledged by different Protestant churches. In practice it is pretty clear that Tradition as the interpretative framework tells us what the Bible means. The handouts tend to determine how we read the textbook, just as in Catholic practice Tradition in fact dictates how Scripture is understood. But Pentiuc's model is an attractive one in emphasizing that Scripture and Tradition are not two equal and opposite bodies of material, but are different *in kind*. There are many theories about the relation of Scripture and Tradition, but Pentiuc's way of approaching the question – descriptive rather than prescriptive – is unusual in concentrating on how the relationship works in practice. And an incidental merit of the model is that it may also work for a Jewish understanding of Scripture, with the Talmud as the 'handouts' that direct one as to how the Bible is to be read.

THE INDISPENSABILITY OF THE BIBLE

Neither Judaism nor Christianity is conceivable without the Bible. Without Scripture, either religion turns into simply what Christians or Jews happen to believe or do at the moment, and there is no criterion against which to measure their beliefs. The question therefore arises, how can the Bible be fruitful in both religions when it is clearly not a foundation document like the American Constitution, or even like the creeds of the Christian Church? It seems to me that this hinges on awareness of the historical particularity, diversity and development of the books that Jews and Christians call holy.

On the one hand, the Bible can exercise a control and check on the religions that claim it as their own. Christians, for example, need to beware of claims about Jesus or the Church that are clearly incompatible with the evidence of the New Testament. The Reformation call to go back to the evidence of the 'primitive' Church as reflected in the pages of the New Testament was flawed because the Reformers often lacked relevant historical knowledge, but it was justified in principle. The Bible is the basic source for information about the origins of Christianity: there is scarcely any other evidence available. Critical study of the Bible thus supports what in the sixteenth century was a Protestant thesis, though nowadays it is (at least theoretically) embraced to varying degrees by all the churches.

On the other hand, the Bible can also nourish religious faith by its very difference from what Jews or Christians instinctively believe or do: it can surprise, constructively as well as challengingly. The narrative books, both those in the Old Testament and the Gospels and Acts, do not tell their story in such a way as to direct us as to what we should believe, but set up a world into which we can enter imaginatively and have our perceptions changed. That is part of the value of having narratives in the Bible, not simply doctrinal definitions or directives. These books have been found illuminating and profound by generations of readers, and this derives from their real character – it is not simply something read into them through wishful thinking. The Bible tells us, as Lutherans sometimes put it, 'things we cannot tell ourselves', in other words there are ideas and lines of thought in the Bible that it would be surprising for unaided human reflection to have arrived at. The extreme diversity of the material in the Bible is not to be reduced by extracting essential principles, but embraced as a celebration of variety. This undermines much traditional interpretative practice, which (as we have seen) is often designed to make sure the Bible delivers an 'orthodox' message. Freeing the Bible from the control of religious authorities is of the essence of critical study, and it results in a free counterpoint between Scripture and doctrinal faith.

I want to suggest a metaphor that can help to illuminate the relation between the Bible and what Christians believe and do. We could conceive of the Christian faith and the Bible as two intersecting circles. There are matters in the Bible that scarcely bear on Christian faith at all, and which make trouble if Christians assume they must do so: the curses in the Psalms, Joshua's battles with the Canaanites, Paul's more intemperate outbursts against his converts and against Judaism as he knew it, the vindictive prophecies in Revelation, many of the laws in Leviticus. Similarly, there are matters in Christian faith that are only very faintly, or even not at all, represented in the Bible: the doctrine of the Trinity, the way the Church is to be organized, the creation of the world out of nothing, the meaning of Christ's death, the idea that after his death he descended to the underworld.[20] Only forced interpretation will find these laid down definitively in the Bible. Indeed, as I argued in Chapter 13, the story the Old Testament tells does not map easily onto the one Christians believe: the two stories can be made to coincide, but only by doing violence to the Old Testament's natural sense. Yet there is a large area of overlap, where the contents of the Bible and of the Christian faith do coincide, or at least are congruent. There can be debate about which topics this is true of, and different churches, even different individuals, will draw the diagram slightly differently. But problems arise when people insist that the Bible and the faith are simply coterminous, that there is only one circle.

We might go one stage further, and argue that the two intersecting circles illuminate what is central and what peripheral in Christianity, at least for Protestants. To quote a formulation from my own Anglican background: the Thirty-Nine Articles of Religion of the Church of England (1563) – the nearest thing Anglicans have to a Confession of Faith – state that 'the Holy Scripture containeth all things necessary to salvation'. This appears at first to advance a doctrine of high scriptural authority. It is clearly a Protestant claim, denying that Tradition is the equal of Scripture. But it is important to weigh the formulation carefully. It says that, if anything is necessary for salvation, you will find it in Scripture. It does not say that everything in Scripture is necessary for salvation, so nothing can be superfluous. In claiming that there are things in the Bible that Christians need not be much concerned with, I am thus not contradicting this Article. Nor does it say that nothing may be done or believed that is not contained in Scripture: hence arguments, for example, about Church order, or even about weightier matters of belief and practice, may appeal to other sources of insight (Tradition and reason, say), provided no one asserts that they are 'necessary to salvation'. There is an area where the Bible and the faith overlap, and within that area matters are not negotiable – that is the logic of the Article (and difficult enough, for a believer who also knows something of the variegated origins of the Bible). But outside that area, there are matters in the Bible, and in belief and practice respectively, that are not essential, but are what, during the Reformation, were called *adiaphora*, 'things indifferent'.

Adiaphora are matters of faith and practice on which reasonable people, even when properly informed by the Bible, may reasonably differ, yet on which some decision may be needed, and so must be taken in good faith – not knowing whether it is the right decision, or even if there is a single right decision. They do not belong to what C. S. Lewis famously called 'mere Christianity', the essentials. Somehow an attribution of authority to the Bible needs to leave open the way to recognizing that there are *adiaphora* in matters of religion. That there are essentials too need not be in doubt; but one cannot well live with a system in which everything is regarded as essential. That is a totalitarian delusion. It is the trap into which fundamentalism falls, as does also a certain kind of extreme Catholicism, by claiming that the whole of life can be regulated, respectively, by Scripture or by Tradition. Such hard-line theories in practice find few adherents: most conservative evangelicals are not fundamentalists, and most Catholics are not rigid extremists – the positions are the theoretical extremes of attitudes occurring in milder forms – but both are united in not believing in *adiaphora*.

The people who framed the Articles believed, as most Christians have, that the doctrines of the Trinity and the Incarnation of Christ were taught clearly in Scripture, and accordingly fell into what in our model is the area of overlap. Modern biblical scholars and theologians are often more doubtful about that, as we have seen. They see the New Testament as showing the beginnings of these doctrines – especially in the Fourth Gospel and in some of Paul's letters – but do not think the doctrines can be strictly 'proved' from Scripture. For a biblical scholar, even one who is a Christian believer, these doctrines in their classical formulation begin to look like *adiaphora*. The New Testament clearly regards absolute allegiance to Jesus Christ, and the belief that 'God was in Christ', as essential: these fall in the area of overlap. But exact descriptions of the doctrines that define the workings behind these tenets cannot be found in the Bible. That is why many modern theologians think that new ways need to be discovered, using our own categories and vocabulary, to define or explain allegiance to Christ as the self-expression of God. Such categories can change over time, and people can honestly disagree about them. They fall outside the overlap. Austin Farrer wrote:

> Of course the most conservative of us do and must rethink the theology of the saints if we are to use it or live by it. We are bound to rid St. Paul's pages of elements which we can only regard as First-Century period junk. Nor is that all: the Christian conscience has acquired certain sensitivities to which the First Century was a stranger. We are not going to feel with St. Paul about the sovereignty of husbands over wives or about the ethics of punishment.[21]

Those words were written in 1966 by a theologian with a reputation for doctrinal orthodoxy, but it is striking how forms of Christianity that still insist on the 'First-Century period junk' survive and flourish. Yet a sizeable body of Christians do think that, though the essence of what was taught by Paul remains authoritative, its expression was conditioned by its time and should be reconsidered. This may be described as a liberal form of Christianity, but it ascribes a good deal more centrality to the Bible than liberalism has often done. In any case, it does not matter how it is described, only whether it seems plausible and is fruitful.

Only with some such understanding, I would argue, is it possible to hold together two essential things. One is to be realistic about what the Bible and the Christian faith actually contain, without forcing the evidence on either side. The other is to do justice to the book that has nourished generations of Christians, without either turning it into a paper dictator on the one hand, or on the other being obliged to accept that it means whatever the religious authorities decree. Freedom of interpretation, yet commitment to religious faith, need to go hand in hand. This seems to me possible if we accept the Bible as a crucial yet not infallible document of Christian faith. Here again are the words of Richard Hooker that I quoted in the Introduction, and which seem to me to present an ideal balance:

> ... as incredible praises given unto men do often abate and impair the credit of their deserved commendation, so we must likewise take great heed, lest, in attributing unto Scripture more than it can have, the incredibility of that do cause even those things which indeed it hath most abundantly, to be less reverently esteemed.[22]

Notes

INTRODUCTION: THE BIBLE TODAY

1. Northrop Frye, *The Great Code: The Bible and Literature* (London: Routledge and Kegan Paul, 1982), pp. xviii–xix.
2. I argued this briefly in my *People of the Book? The Authority of the Bible in Christianity* (London: SPCK and Philadelphia: Westminster John Knox Press, 1988; second edition with additional chapter, 1993; third edition, with a further additional chapter, 2011). On fundamentalism see the definitive work by James Barr, *Fundamentalism* (London: SCM Press, 1977; second edition 1995).
3. I have advanced this theoretically in my *The Nature of Biblical Criticism* (Louisville, Ky.: Westminster John Knox Press, 2007), but this book will give it substance and show it in practice by the way it presents the history of the Bible.
4. See Katie Edwards, *Admen and Eve: The Bible in Contemporary Advertising* (The Bible in the Modern World 48) (Sheffield: Sheffield Phoenix Press, 2012).
5. See Gordon Campbell, *Bible: The Story of the King James Version, 1611–2011* (Oxford: Oxford University Press, 2010), p. 270. The organization known as The Gideons gives away millions of Bibles annually.
6. See Richard Dawkins, *The God Delusion* (London: Bantam Press, 2006).
7. See www.telegraph.co.uk/culture/books/9936241/Philip-Pullman-teach-all-children-fairy-tales-and-Bible-verses.html
8. Philip Pullman, *Northern Lights* (London: Scholastic, 1995); *The Subtle Knife* (London: Scholastic, 1997); *The Amber Spyglass* (London: Scholastic, 2001).
9. Cf. Martin L. Marty, 'America's Iconic Book', in G. Tucker and D. Knight (eds), *Humanizing America's Iconic Book: Society of Biblical Literature Centennial Address, 1980* (Chico, Cal.: Scholars Press, 1982), pp. 1–23.
10. Commonwealth of Pennsylvania, *Legislative Journal*, 196th General Assembly, 24 January 2012, p. 87.
11. A. Berlin and M. Z. Brettler (eds), *The Jewish Study Bible* (New York: Oxford University Press, second edition 2014).
12. *Dei Verbum*, paragraphs 11–12.

13. The Museum of the Bible in Washington, DC, which opened in 2017, is only a partial parallel, since it rests on critical biblical scholarship – though it has a heavy bias towards Christianity and is arguably unfair to Judaism.
14. See Wilfred Cantwell Smith, *What is Scripture? A Comparative Approach* (London: SCM Press, 1993).
15. See Yaakov Ariel, *An Unusual Relationship: Evangelical Christians and Jews* (New York: New York University Press, 2013); also M. A. Chancey, C. Meyers and E. M. Meyers, *The Bible in the Public Square: Its Enduring Influence in American Life* (Atlanta, Ga.: SBL Press, 2014), especially pp. 41–6 and 91; and Byron Johnson and Nancy Isserman (eds), *Uneasy Allies: Evangelical and Jewish Relations* (Lanham, Md.: Lexington Books, 2007).
16. For more detail see the best-seller by Hal Lindsey, *The Late Great Planet Earth* (Grand Rapids, Mich.: Zondervan, 1971).
17. The first novel in the series is Tim LaHaye and Jerry B. Jenkins, *Left Behind* (Wheaton, Ill.: Tyndale House, 1995).
18. See Cantwell Smith, *What is Scripture?*
19. Augustine of Hippo, a bishop in North Africa, lived from 354 to 430 CE.
20. This is argued in his treatise *On the Consensus of the Evangelists* (*De consensu evangelistarum*).
21. See the essays in C. R. Seitz and K. Greene-McCreight (eds), *Theological Exegesis: Essays in Honor of Brevard S. Childs* (Grand Rapids, Mich.: W. B. Eerdmans, 1999).
22. Richard Hooker, *Of the Laws of Ecclesiastical Polity* (1594), 2:8.
23. C. W. Goodwin, 'On the Mosaic Cosmogony', in Henry B. Wilson (ed.), *Essays and Reviews* (London: Longman, Green, Longman, Roberts & Green, twelfth edition 1865), p. 302.

1. ANCIENT ISRAEL: HISTORY AND LANGUAGE

1. The quotation is in inverted commas here because it claims to be a decree issued by Cyrus, though the fact that it refers to Yahweh ('the LORD') must make this doubtful.
2. For example, I. Provan, V. P. Long and T. Longman III, *A Biblical History of Israel* (Louisville, Ky.: Westminster John Knox Press, 2003).
3. For example, T. L. Thompson, *The Bible in History: How Writers Create a Past* (London: Jonathan Cape, 1999).
4. Thus, classically, Martin Noth, *A History of Pentateuchal Traditions* (Atlanta, Ga.: Scholars Press, 1981) (German original 1948).
5. This argument is summarized in John Bright, *A History of Israel* (London: SCM Press, 1960); several subsequent editions.
6. The case for a much later date was argued by John Van Seters, *Abraham in History and Tradition* (New Haven and London: Yale University Press, 1975), and is now generally accepted.
7. See William G. Dever, *Who Were the Early Israelites and Where Did They Come From?* (Grand Rapids, Mich. and Cambridge: W. B. Eerdmans, 2003),

and Israel Finkelstein, *The Archaeology of the Israelite Settlement* (Jerusalem: Israel Exploration Society, 1988) for a survey of the relevant evidence.

8. See Nadav Na'aman and Israel Finkelstein, *From Nomadism to Monarchy: Archaeological and Historical Aspects of Early Israel* (Jerusalem: Israel Exploration Society, 1994); Israel Finkelstein and N. A. Silberman, *The Bible Unearthed: Archaeology's New Vision of Ancient Israel and the Origin of its Stories* (London: Simon & Schuster, 2001). An excellent guide to the question of balancing the biblical evidence with the findings of archaeology is H. G. M. Williamson (ed.), *Understanding the History of Ancient Israel* (Oxford: Oxford University Press, 2007).
9. See Israel Finkelstein, *The Forgotten Kingdom: The Archaeology and History of Northern Israel* (Atlanta, Ga.: Society of Biblical Literature, 2013).
10. On this see C. L. Crouch, *The Making of Israel* (Leiden and Boston: Brill, 2014). How far back the name Israel goes is unclear, but as it contains the divine name El it must derive from a time when the people were in the land of Canaan, to which that name is native.
11. See the discussion in H. G. M. Williamson, *Studies in Persian Period History and Historiography* (Tübingen: Mohr Siebeck, 2004).
12. On this see Martin Hengel, *Judaism and Hellenism: Studies in their Encounter in Palestine during the Early Hellenistic Period* (London: SCM Press, 1974).
13. For a lively defence of the opposite position see E. W. Heaton, *Solomon's New Men: The Emergence of Ancient Israel as a National State* (London: Thames and Hudson, 1974). But few would now agree with this.
14. See, for example, A. Lemaire, *Les écoles et la formation de la Bible dans l'ancien Israël* (OBO, 39) (Fribourg: Éditions Universitaires; Göttingen: Vandenhoeck & Ruprecht, 1981); D. W. Jamieson-Drake, *Scribes and Schools in Monarchic Judah: A Socio-Archaeological Approach* (JSOTSup 109) (Sheffield: Almond Press, 1991); P. R. Davies, *Scribes and Schools: The Canonization of the Hebrew Scriptures* (Louisville, Ky.: Westminster John Knox Press, 1998); W. M. Schniedewind, *How the Bible Became a Book: The Textualization of Ancient Israel* (Cambridge: Cambridge University Press, 2004); D. M. Carr, *Writing on the Tablet of the Heart: Origins of Scripture and Literature* (Oxford: Oxford University Press, 2005); K. van der Toorn, *Scribal Culture and the Making of the Hebrew Bible* (Cambridge, Mass: Harvard University Press, 2007); and C. A. Rollston, *Writing and Literacy in the World of Ancient Israel: Epigraphic Evidence from the Iron Age* (Atlanta, Ga.: Society of Biblical Literature, 2010).
15. For a justification of my usage see John Barton, *The Old Testament: Canon, Literature and Theology: Collected Works of John Barton* (Aldershot: Ashgate, 2007), pp. 83–9.
16. William Caslon, the typographer, included Syriac in his type samples in the 1740s, and others did so in the nineteenth century.
17. The passages in question are Ezra 4:8–6:18 and 7:12–26, and Daniel 2:4b–7:28.

2. HEBREW NARRATIVE

1. Prose appears in Mesopotamian writing in the official annals of kings, but not so much in literary or religious texts. We have no literature from pre-Israelite Canaan; the nearest are the mythological texts from Ras Shamra in Syria, which go back to the second millennium BCE and are all in verse.
2. Erich Auerbach famously wrote that Hebrew narrative is 'fraught with background'; see E. Auerbach, *Mimesis: Dargestellte Wirklichkeit in der abendländischen Literatur* (Bern: Francke Verlag, second edition 1959), p. 10; English version *Mimesis: The Representation of Reality in Western Literature* (Princeton: Princeton University Press, 2013).
3. This refers to a bizarre incident recorded in 1 Samuel 18:20–29.
4. Jonathan Magonet, *Bible Lives* (London: SCM Press, 1992), p. 91.
5. Meaning the Temple.
6. NRSV has: 'In the beginning when God created the heavens and the earth', which is also a possible rendering of the Hebrew, though I think a less likely one.
7. Martin Noth, *Überlieferungsgeschichtliche Studien* (Halle: M. Niemeyer, 1943); English version *The Deuteronomistic History* (Sheffield: JSOT Press, 1991).
8. In Judaism, Joshua, Judges, Samuel and Kings are known collectively as the Former Prophets (the Latter Prophets being the books Christians call simply 'the prophets' – Isaiah, Jeremiah, Hosea, and so on).
9. This is an ancient conjecture already found in the work of St Jerome, but was given its modern form by W. M. L. de Wette, *Dissertatio critica qua a prioribus Deuteronomium Pentateuchi libris diversum, alius cuiusdam recentioris auctoris opus esse monstratur* (Berlin: G. Reimer, 1830).
10. For an exceptionally clear presentation of the interweaving of sources in the Flood narrative see R. E. Friedman, *Who Wrote the Bible?* (London: Jonathan Cape, 1987), pp. 53–60.
11. See Stephanie Dalley, *Myths from Mesopotamia: Creation, the Flood, Gilgamesh, and Others* (Oxford: Oxford University Press, revised edition 2008).
12. To the French physician Jean Astruc, *Conjectures sur les mémoires originaux dont il paroit que Moyse s'est servi pour composer le livre de la Genèse* (1753); reprinted in P. Gibert, *Conjectures sur la Genèse* (Paris: Éditions Noêsis, 1999). See various discussions in John Jarick (ed.), *Sacred Conjectures: The Context and Legacy of Robert Lowth and Jean Astruc* (New York and London: T&T Clark, 2007).
13. Wellhausen's major works on the sources of the Pentateuch are *Die Composition des Hexateuchs und der historischen Bücher des Alten Testaments* (Berlin: G. Reimer, third edition 1899), and *Geschichte Israels I* (Marburg, 1878); second edition as *Prolegomena zur Geschichte Israels*, English version *Prolegomena to the History of Israel* (Edinburgh: Adam & Charles Black, 1885).
14. See the discussion in Joel Baden, *The Composition of the Pentateuch: Renewing the Documentary Hypothesis* (New Haven and London: Yale University Press, 2012).

15. See especially Erhard Blum, *Studien zur Komposition des Pentateuch* (Berlin: W. de Gruyter, 1990), building on Rolf Rendtorff, *The Problem of the Process of Transmission in the Pentateuch* (Sheffield: Sheffield Academic Press, 1977).
16. For an overview of Pentateuchal criticism in the period after Wellhausen see the extensive discussion in E. W. Nicholson, *The Pentateuch in the Twentieth Century: The Legacy of Julius Wellhausen* (Oxford: Clarendon Press, 1998).
17. See John Van Seters, *The Life of Moses: The Yahwist as Historian in Exodus-Numbers* (Louisville, Ky.: Westminster John Knox Press, 1994).
18. See R. N. Whybray, *The Succession Narrative* (London: SCM Press, 1968); David M. Gunn, *The Story of King David: Genre and Interpretation* (Sheffield: JSOT Press, 1978); L. Rost, *Die Überlieferung von der Thronnachfolge Davids* (Stuttgart: Kohlhammer, 1926); English version *The Succession to the Throne of David* (Sheffield: Almond Press, 1982).
19. Also sometimes called the Succession Narrative.
20. This was first proposed by Richard D. Nelson, *The Double Redaction of the Deuteronomistic History* (Sheffield: JSOT Press, 1981).
21. See Rudolf Smend, *Die Entstehung des Alten Testaments* (Stuttgart: Kohlhammer, 1978; third edition 1984).
22. There is a good discussion of this in David M. Carr, *The Formation of the Hebrew Bible: A New Reconstruction* (Oxford and New York: Oxford University Press, 2011).
23. See Herbert Donner, 'Der Redaktor: Überlegungen zum vorkritischen Umgang mit der Heiligen Schrift', *Henoch*, 2 (1980), pp. 1–30, for one of the most persuasive accounts of this explanation.
24. See H. G. M. Williamson, *1 and 2 Chronicles* (Eugene, Ore.: Wipf & Stock, 2010).
25. See Francesca Stavrakopoulou, *King Manasseh and Child Sacrifice: Biblical Distortions of Historical Realities* (Berlin: W. de Gruyter, 2004).
26. Lawrence M. Wills, *The Jewish Novel in the Ancient World* (Ithaca, NY and London: Cornell University Press, 1995).
27. See again Baden, *The Composition.*
28. The work of Robert Alter is outstanding here: see his *The Art of Biblical Narrative* (London: George Allen and Unwin, 1981).
29. Franz Stuhlhofer, *Der Gebrauch der Bibel von Jesus bis Euseb: Eine statistische Untersuchung zur Kanongeschichte* (Wuppertal: Brockhaus, 1988).
30. See John Barton, 'Historiography and Theodicy in the Old Testament', in R. Rezetko, T. H. Lim and W. B. Aucker (eds), *Reflection and Refraction: Studies in Biblical Historiography in Honour of A. Graeme Auld* (Leiden and Boston: Brill, 2006), pp. 27–33.

3. LAW AND WISDOM

1. Excellent guides to biblical wisdom literature are J. L. Crenshaw, *Old Testament Wisdom: An Introduction* (Louisville, Ky.: Westminster John Knox

Press, third edition 2010), and Katharine J. Dell, *Get Wisdom, Get Insight: An Introduction to Israel's Wisdom Literature* (London: Darton, Longman & Todd, 2000).

2. This was argued strongly by William McKane in *Proverbs: A New Approach* (London: SCM Press, 1970).
3. For this term see Tzvetan Todorov, *Mikhail Bakhtin: The Dialogical Principle* (Manchester: Manchester University Press, 1984); Carol A. Newsom, *The Book of Job: A Contest of Moral Imaginations* (Leiden and Boston: Brill, 2004).
4. Heaton, *Solomon's New Men*, pp. 124–6.
5. See Wilfred G. Lambert, *Babylonian Wisdom Literature* (Winona Lake, Ind.: Eisenbrauns, 1996).
6. Sheol is understood in much the same way as Hades in Greek literature – not a place of torment but a dim, shadowy realm in which there is no meaningful activity, memory or life.
7. For the idea that the narratives refer to incidents in biblical history see Jennifer Barbour, *The Story of Israel in the Book of Qohelet: Ecclesiastes as Cultural Memory* (Oxford: Oxford University Press, 2012).
8. The title of a poem modelled on the thinking of Ecclesiastes by Samuel Johnson (1709–84).
9. Voltaire, *Candide ou l'optimisme* (1749).
10. See Jan Assmann, *Ma'at: Gerechtigkeit und Unsterblichkeit im alten Ägypten* (Munich: C. H. Beck, second edition 2006).
11. Compare Joseph Blenkinsopp, 'The Intellectual World of Judaism in the Pre-Hellenistic Period', in his *Essays on Judaism in the Pre-Hellenistic Period* (BZAW 495) (Berlin: W. de Gruyter, 2017), pp. 84–100, especially pp. 95–6.
12. Mary Douglas in particular devoted several books to an analysis of Pentateuchal law from an anthropological perspective: see *Purity and Danger: An Analysis of Concepts of Pollution and Taboo* (New York: Routledge, 2003, originally published in 1966); *In the Wilderness: The Doctrine of Defilement in the Book of Numbers* (Sheffield: JSOT Press, 1993); *Leviticus as Literature* (Oxford: Oxford University Press, 1999).
13. For example, ritual purification after menstruation already appears in the story of David and Bathsheba – see 2 Samuel 11:4.
14. Assnat Bartor, *Reading Law as Narrative: A Study in the Casuistic Laws of the Pentateuch* (Atlanta, Ga.: Society of Biblical Literature, 2010).
15. The Hebrew is unclear: the NRSV translation, used here, follows a widely accepted interpretation.
16. NRSV says: 'If it was not premeditated'.
17. Bartor, *Reading Law as Narrative*, pp. 28–9.
18. To one of the three 'cities of refuge' that were prescribed as places of sanctuary for innocent homicides.
19. Jeremy Waldron, 'Thoughtfulness and the Rule of Law', *British Academy Review*, 18 (2011), pp. 1–11; the quotation is from p. 5.
20. Bernard S. Jackson, *Wisdom-Laws: A Study of the Mishpatim of Exodus 12:1–22:16* (Oxford: Oxford University Press, 2006).

21. See the discussion in Joseph Blenkinsopp, 'Was the Pentateuch the Constitution of the Jewish Ethnos in the Persian Period?', in his *Essays on Judaism in the Pre-Hellenistic Period*, pp. 101–18, with reference to the work of Erhard Blum, Frank Crüsemann and Ernst Axel Knauf. Blenkinsopp is sceptical.
22. See the discussion in Molly M. Zahn, 'Rewritten Scripture', in Timothy H. Lim and John J. Collins (eds), *The Oxford Handbook of the Dead Sea Scrolls* (Oxford: Oxford University Press, 2010), pp. 323–36; also her 'New Voices, Ancient Words: The *Temple Scroll*'s Reuse of the Bible', in John Day (ed.), *Temple and Worship in Biblical Israel*, Library of the Hebrew/Old Testament Studies 422 (London: T&T Clark, 2005), pp. 435–58.
23. Blenkinsopp, 'The Intellectual World of Judaism', p. 96.

4. PROPHECY

1. See Nicholas R. M. de Lange, *Modern Judaism: An Oxford Guide* (Oxford: Oxford University Press, 2005) for a survey of the various types of Judaism current today, with some historical background.
2. See Timothy Lim, *The Dead Sea Scrolls: A Very Short Introduction* (Oxford: Oxford University Press, second edition 2017), Chapter 9.
3. To understand this interpretation one needs to know quite a lot about the life of the community at Qumran which produced the scrolls. The Commentary on Habakkuk (1 QpHab) probably comes from the first century BCE; the Liar and the Teacher of Righteousness are figures in the history of the community. (The title is to be understood as follows: 1 designates Cave 1 at Khirbet Qumran in the Judaean wilderness (hence Q). The p stands for *pesher*, Hebrew for 'commentary', and Hab for Habakkuk, the biblical book being commented on. The number 2 is the chapter.)
4. Judaism also refers to the historical books as Prophets, and they do contain stories about prophets among other things; but in this chapter I shall concentrate mainly on the Major and Minor Prophets just listed: see again Chapter 9.
5. Augustine, *Confessions*, book 5, chapter 9.
6. See especially Martti Nissinen (ed.), *Prophecy in its Ancient Near Eastern Context: Mesopotamian, Biblical, and Arabian Perspectives* (Atlanta, Ga.: Society of Biblical Literature, 2000). A useful collection is John Day (ed.), *Prophecy and the Prophets in Ancient Israel: Proceedings of the Oxford Old Testament Seminar* (New York and London: T&T Clark, 2010).
7. In Martti Nissinen, with contributions by C. L. Seow and Robert K. Ritner, *Prophets and Prophecy in the Ancient Near East*, ed. Peter Machinist (Atlanta, Ga.: Society of Biblical Literture, 2003).
8. See Jonathan Stökl, *Prophecy in the Ancient Near East: A Philological and Sociological Comparison* (Leiden: Brill, 2012).
9. See Jo Ann Hackett, *The Balaam Text from Deir Allah*, Harvard Semitic Monographs 31 (Chico, Cal.: Scholars Press, 1980).

10. The most famous examples are Elijah and Elisha: see 1 Kings 17–21, 2 Kings 1–9. But another major figure is Samuel, 1 Samuel 1–16, and there are numerous more Minor Prophets in the historical books.
11. On Amos see John Barton, *The Theology of the Book of Amos* (New York and Cambridge: Cambridge University Press, 2012).
12. The detail here is blurry, but the general tone is clear. The people being condemned are probably those with responsibilities for the justice system, since they have the power to impose fines, and 'sell' the poor for money, i.e. take bribes to convict them. They also oppress those of lower social rank – the 'girl' is probably a slave.
13. See especially Reinhard G. Kratz, *The Prophets of Israel* (Winona Lake, Ind.: Eisenbrauns, 2015).
14. Thus, classically, Rudolf Smend, 'Das Nein des Amos', *Evangelische Theologie*, 23 (1963), pp. 404–23; reprinted in Rudolf Smend, *Die Mitte des Alten Testaments* (Munich: Kaiser Verlag, 1986), pp. 85–103.
15. There are excellent treatments of apocalyptic in John J. Collins, *The Apocalyptic Imagination: An Introduction to Jewish Apocalyptic Literature* (Grand Rapids, Mich. and Cambridge: W. B. Eerdmans, third edition 2016), and Christopher Rowland, *The Open Heaven: A Study of Apocalyptic in Judaism and Early Christianity* (London: SPCK, 1982). See also John Barton, *Oracles of God: Perceptions of Ancient Prophecy in Israel after the Exile* (Oxford and New York: Oxford University Press, second edition 2007).
16. On the development of the book of Isaiah see my short book *Isaiah 1–39*, Old Testament Guides (London: T&T Clark, 2003).
17. H. G. M. Williamson, *The Book Called Isaiah: Deutero-Isaiah's Role in Composition and Redaction* (Oxford: Oxford University Press, 1994) argues the general case for Deutero-Isaiah as the editor of Isaiah 1–39; the present example is discussed on pp. 119–21.

5. POEMS AND PSALMS

1. *Biblia Hebraica Stuttgartensia* (Stuttgart: Würtembergische Bibelanstalt, 1968).
2. Robert Lowth, *Lectures on the Sacred Poetry of the Hebrews* (London: second edition 1816). There are important discussions of parallelism in Robert Alter, *The Art of Biblical Poetry* (New York: Basic Books, revised edition 2011), and James L. Kugel, *The Idea of Biblical Poetry: Parallelism and Its History* (New Haven and London: Yale University Press, 1981).
3. See the comments on this by C. S. Lewis in his short book *Reflections on the Psalms* (London: Geoffrey Bles, 1958), Chapter 1.
4. See the discussion in E. W. Nicholson, *Preaching to the Exiles: A Study of the Prose Tradition in the Book of Jeremiah* (Oxford: Blackwell, 1970), as well as the argument by Robert P. Carroll, *From Chaos to Covenant: Uses of Prophecy in the Book of Jeremiah* (London: SCM Press, 1981), that Jeremiah was a

poet and that all prose sections of the book that bears his name are indeed additions by later writers.

5. A useful guide to the Psalms is William P. Brown (ed.), *The Oxford Handbook of the Psalms* (Oxford: Oxford University Press, 2014), which deals comprehensively with most of the topics covered in this chapter. See also Susan E. Gillingham, *The Poems and Psalms of the Hebrew Bible* (Oxford: Oxford University Press, 1994).
6. Lewis, *Reflections on the Psalms*, Chapter 6.
7. See Hermann Gunkel, *An Introduction to the Psalms: The Genres of the Religious Lyric of Israel* (Macon, Ga.: Mercer University Press, 1998, from German original of 1933).
8. See Sigmund Mowinckel, *The Psalms in Israel's Worship* (Grand Rapids, Mich.: W. B. Eerdmans, 2004, originally published in 1962), which rests on his much more technical *Psalmenstudien* (Kristiania [Oslo]: Skrifter utgitt av Det Norske Videnskaps-Akademi, 1921–4, 2 vols).
9. See especially Erich Zenger, *The Composition of the Book of Psalms* (Leuven: Peeters, 2010), and Susan E. Gillingham, 'The Levites and the Editorial Composition of the Psalms', in Brown (ed.), *Oxford Handbook of the Psalms*, pp. 201–28.
10. The two psalms are also treated as one in the Babylonian Talmud, Berakhot 9b–10a.
11. Zion is the name used to refer to Jerusalem considered as a sacred city, though originally it probably referred to part of what later became Jerusalem.
12. Jerusalem is not 'in the far north' from the point of view of anyone living in the Land. But the Hebrew for 'north' is *zaphon*, and Mount Zaphon was the holy mountain of the gods (analogous to Olympus for the Greeks) in the Ugaritic texts from Syria. Almost certainly the mythological overtones of Zaphon have here been applied to Zion, leaving this curious reference to the north in the psalm.
13. See Artur Weiser, *The Psalms: A Commentary* (London: SCM Press, 1962).
14. See Susan Gillingham (ed.), *Jewish and Christian Approaches to the Psalms: Conflict and Convergence* (Oxford: Oxford University Press, 2013).

6. CHRISTIAN BEGINNINGS

1. Tacitus, *Annals*, 15:44.
2. For the history of the period see Martin Goodman, *Rome and Jerusalem: The Clash of Ancient Civilizations* (London: Allen Lane, 2007). The details of the distribution of the Land to Herod's successors can be found on pp. 422–44. The main, in many cases the only, source for the period is the Jewish writer Flavius Josephus (37–*c.* 100 CE) in his *Jewish Antiquities* (see also Chapter 1).
3. E. P. Sanders, *The Historical Figure of Jesus* (London: Allen Lane, 1993), p. 294.
4. Ibid., p. 28.

5. See Goodman, *Rome and Jerusalem*, pp. 456–8, and Steve Mason, *A History of the Jewish War, AD 66–74* (Cambridge: Cambridge University Press, 2017).
6. See Hengel, *Judaism and Hellenism*.
7. On the life of Josephus see Tessa Rajak, *Josephus: The Historian and his Society* (London: Duckworth, 2002).
8. Goodman, *Rome and Jerusalem*, p. 10.
9. Still a standard work on Philo is Harry A. Wolfson, *Philo: Foundations of Religious Philosophy in Judaism, Christianity, and Islam* (Cambridge, Mass.: Harvard University Press, 1947, reprinted 1968).
10. Josephus, *Antiquities*, pp. 18–20.
11. See John Muddiman, 'The Greek Language', in John Barton (ed.), *The Biblical World* (London and New York: Routledge, 2002), pp. 25–32.
12. See the discussion in W. Smelik, 'The Languages of Roman Palestine', in C. Hezser (ed.), *The Oxford Handbook of Daily Life in Roman Palestine* (Oxford: Oxford University Press, 2010), pp. 122–44; also Sean Freyne, *The Jesus Movement and Its Expansion: Meaning and Mission* (Grand Rapids, Mich.: W. B. Eerdmans, 2014), pp. 16–22. There is evidence for knowledge of Greek at Qumran, and at Nahal Hever, some twenty-five miles away, where a Greek scroll of the Minor Prophets was discovered.
13. It is generally agreed that Jesus spoke Aramaic, but this does not rule out the possibility that he knew some Greek. For a discussion see James Barr, 'Which Language Did Jesus Speak? Some Remarks of a Semitist', *Bulletin of the John Rylands Library*, 53 (1970–71), pp. 9–29; also in John Barton (ed.), *Bible and Interpretation: The Collected Essays of James Barr*, vol. 2: *Biblical Studies* (Oxford: Oxford University Press, 2013), pp. 231–46. See also the important article by Joseph Fitzmyer, 'Presidential Address: The Languages of Palestine in the First Century A.D.', *Catholic Biblical Quarterly*, 32 (1970), pp. 501–31. Jesus' trial may have been conducted in a mixture of Greek and Aramaic, using interpreters.
14. Max Weber, *The Protestant Ethic and the Spirit of Capitalism* (London: Allen & Unwin, 1930); Ernst Troeltsch, *The Social Teaching of the Christian Churches* (Louisville, Ky.: Westminster John Knox Press, 1992), vol. 1, pp. 328–69 (from the original German of 1912).
15. Joseph Blenkinsopp, *Essays on Judaism in the Pre-Hellenistic Period* (BZAW 495) (Berlin: W. de Gruyter, 2017), p. 194.
16. See de Lange, *Modern Judaism: An Oxford Guide*.
17. Christopher Rowland, *Christian Origins: An Account of the Setting and Character of the Most Important Messianic Sect of Judaism* (London: SPCK, 1985), p. 70.
18. See Lim, *The Dead Sea Scrolls* for the position that the sectaries of Qumran were Essenes, and Goodman, *Rome and Jerusalem*, p. 240, for the contrary view. Goodman argues that the Essenes, as described by Josephus, seem to have been involved in Jewish political and social life in a way alien to the Dead Sea sect.

19. Thus in the document known as 4QMMT: see Freyne, *The Jesus Movement*, p. 137. For example: 'We have segregated ourselves from the rest of the people, from mingling in these affairs and associating with them in these things.'
20. The fascinating possibilities are set out by James D. G. Dunn, 'Christianity without Paul', in Daniel M. Gurtner, Grant Macaskill and Jonathan T. Pennington (eds), *In the Fullness of Time: Essays on Christology, Creation, and Eschatology in Honor of Richard Bauckham* (Grand Rapids, Mich.: W. B. Eerdmans, 2016), pp. 115–31.
21. The book clearly reflects a time of persecution, but the details remain obscure.
22. See the next chapter for a discussion of the problem of pseudonymity.
23. I have in mind the theories popularized by Dan Brown in *The Da Vinci Code* (London: Corgi, 2004).
24. Austin Farrer, *The Revelation of St John the Divine: A Commentary on the English Text* (Oxford: Clarendon Press, 1964), p.37.

7. LETTERS

1. See H.-J. Klauck, *Ancient Letters and the New Testament: A Guide to Context and Exegesis* (Waco, Tex.: Baylor University Press, 2006).
2. Paul regularly refers to fellow-Christians as 'saints' or 'holy ones'.
3. See the discussion in Douglas A. Campbell, *Framing Paul: An Epistolary Biography* (Grand Rapids, Mich.: W. B. Eerdmans, 2014), pp. 99–121.
4. Thus NRSV. The Greek says simply 'brothers', and it is a question whether the intention is to include both men and women, as this Greek term often does, or to refer only to men.
5. See the discussion in Jon D. Levenson, *Resurrection and the Restoration of Israel: The Ultimate Victory of the God of Life* (New Haven, Conn.: Yale University Press, 2006).
6. The NRSV in fact sets out the passage as verse, presumably following this theory.
7. See the discussion in Adela Yarbro Collins and John J. Collins, *King and Messiah as Son of God: Divine, Human, and Angelic Messianic Figures in Biblical and Related Literature* (Grand Rapids, Mich.: W. B. Eerdmans, 2008).
8. Cited in Goodman, *Rome and Jerusalem*, p. 200.
9. It is arguable that in the Synoptic Gospels (Matthew, Mark and Luke) Jesus' baptism is the moment at which he attains the status of Son of God.
10. John Knox, *Chapters in a Life of Paul* (London: SCM Press, second edition 1987). Some of Knox's arguments were anticipated in the nineteenth century by F. C. Baur, who assigned a second-century date to Acts: see Chapter 17.
11. Festus' accession is sometimes dated later, largely to accommodate Paul's career.
12. See E. P. Sanders, *Paul and Palestinian Judaism* (London: SCM Press, 1977); idem, *Paul, the Law and the Jewish People* (London: SCM Press, 1983);

J. D. G. Dunn, *Jesus, Paul and the Law* (London: SPCK, 1990); N. T. Wright, *Paul and the Faithfulness of God* (London: SPCK and Minneapolis: Fortress Press, 2013); and, much more briefly, idem, *What Paul Really Said* (Oxford: Lion, 1997).

13. See the seminal article by Krister Stendahl, 'The Apostle Paul and the Introspective Conscience of the West', *Harvard Theological Review*, 56 (1963), pp. 199–215.
14. David G. Horrell, *An Introduction to the Study of Paul* (London: Bloomsbury T&T Clark, third edition 2015), p. 125.
15. As argued by Heikki Räisänen, *Paul and the Law* (Tübingen: Mohr, 1983); see the discussion in Magnus Zetterholm, *Approaches to Paul: A Student's Guide to Recent Scholarship* (Minneapolis: Fortress Press, 2009), especially p. 110.
16. See Titus 1:5–9.
17. For a recent defence of its authenticity see Paul Foster, 'Who Wrote 2 Thessalonians? A Fresh Look at an Old Problem', *Journal for the Study of the New Testament*, 35(2) (2012), pp. 150–75.
18. The reasons for this, both stylistic and theological, are set out in C. Leslie Mitton, *The Epistle to the Ephesians* (Oxford: Clarendon Press, 1951).
19. See John Muddiman, *The Epistle to the Ephesians* (London: Continuum, 2001).
20. Campbell, *Framing Paul*, pp. 309–38.
21. See Bart D. Ehrman, *Forgery and Counterforgery: The Use of Literary Deceit in Early Christian Polemics* (Oxford and New York: Oxford University Press, 2013). Interestingly, however, in another place Ehrman speaks more gently about pseudonymity, when discussing the *Apostolic Constitutions* and *3 Corinthians*, second-century documents that claim apostolic authorship, forged by an author from Asia Minor. The man was condemned for it by Tertullian and deposed from his church appointment. He claimed that he had written these (orthodox) texts 'out of love for Paul', to honour the apostle's memory. See Bart Ehrman, *The Orthodox Corruption of Scripture: The Effect of Early Christological Controversies on the Text of the New Testament* (New York: Oxford University Press, 1993, second edition 2011), p. 26. We should not rule out an explanation in terms of inspiration from beyond the grave: pseudonymous writers may have believed that dead teachers were inspiring their writing.
22. See further D. G. Meade, *Pseudonymity and Canon* (Grand Rapids, Mich.: W. B. Eerdmans, 1987).

8. GOSPELS

1. See Matthew 26:26–9; Mark 14:22–5; Luke 22:14–20.
2. Now Pamukkale in Turkey.

3. Preserved in the *Ecclesiastical History* of Eusebius, in the early fourth century CE.
4. In John, Jesus dies at the time the Passover lambs are being killed, which has obvious symbolic significance, whereas in the other Gospels the crucifixion takes place on the day after Passover, so that the Last Supper is a Passover meal.
5. Which may well have been the case; see Sanders, *The Historical Figure of Jesus*, pp. 254–61.
6. The major figures in form criticism are Martin Dibelius (1883–1947) and Rudolf Bultmann (1884–1976).
7. This kind of argument belongs to what is sometimes called the criterion of dissimilarity, and has contributed to the various attempts since the early twentieth century to reconstruct what can be known of Jesus as a historical figure, the so-called 'quest(s) for the historical Jesus' (see Chapter 17). In the form of the criterion of double dissimilarity it refers to the argument that a given saying is unlike both early Christian and early Jewish teaching and thus cannot derive from either; hence, *prima facie*, it may go back to Jesus himself. The principle has been criticized as implying that Jesus was wholly unlike both Jewish contemporaries and Christian followers, which is clearly improbable, but so far as it goes it represents a reasonable position: a saying no one would have made up is probably authentic. For a full and nuanced discussion see Gerd Theissen and Dagmar Winter, *The Quest for the Plausible Jesus: The Question of Criteria* (Louisville, Ky. and London: Westminster John Knox Press, 2002).
8. This seems to have been first suggested by B. W. Bacon, *Studies in Matthew* (London: Constable, 1930), and is now widely accepted.
9. Johannes Weiss (1863–1914) seems to have been the first to use the siglum Q, though the theory it represents goes back further into the nineteenth century.
10. A. M. Farrer, 'On Dispensing with Q', in D. E. Nineham (ed.), *Studies in the Gospels in Memory of R. H. Lightfoot* (Oxford: Blackwell, 1955), pp. 55–88.
11. Mark Goodacre, *The Case against Q: Markan Priority and the Synoptic Problem* (Harrisburg, Pa.: Trinity Press International, 2002); idem, *The Synoptic Problem: A Way through the Maze* (Sheffield: Sheffield Academic Press, 2001); also Mark Goodacre and Nicholas Perrin (eds), *Questioning Q* (London: SPCK, 2004). Goodacre also runs a valuable web hub for Gospel study, the New Testament Gateway.
12. A more literal translation than the NRSV. See the discussion in Mark Goodacre, 'Ten Reasons to Question Q', www.markgoodacre.org/Q/ten.htm
13. An even clearer case of an agreement of Matthew and Luke against Mark is the 'Beelzebul controversy': Matthew 12:22–37; Mark 3:22–30; Luke 11:14–23. See the discussion by Eric Eve, 'The Devil in the Detail: Exorcising Q from the Beelzebul Controversy', in John C. Poirier and Jeffrey Peterson (eds), *Marcan Priority without Q: Explorations in the Farrer Hypothesis* (London: Bloomsbury T&T Clark, 2015), pp. 16–43.

14. See the classic textbook on the Gospels, B. H. Streeter, *The Four Gospels: A Study of Origins, Treating of the Manuscript Tradition, Sources, Authorship & Dates* (London: Macmillan, 1924).
15. Compare M. D. Goulder, 'Characteristics of the Parables in the Several Gospels', *Journal of Theological Studies*, 19(1) (1968), pp. 51–69.
16. The proto-Luke hypothesis has been discarded by most New Testament scholars. It can be found in Vincent Taylor, *Behind the Third Gospel: A Study of the Proto-Luke Hypothesis* (Oxford: Clarendon Press, 1926), and George B. Caird, *The Gospel of St Luke* (Harmondsworth: Penguin, 1963). I am not a New Testament specialist, but it seems to me still to have some plausibility.
17. First identified as such in J. Louis Martyn, *History and Theology in the Fourth Gospel* (New York: Harper & Row, 1968). A massive development of the hypothesis can be found in Raymond E. Brown, *The Gospel according to John* (Garden City, NY: Doubleday, 1966–70, 2 vols); a summary may be found in his *An Introduction to the Gospel of John* (New York: Doubleday, 2003).
18. Richard Bauckham (ed.), *The Gospel for All Christians* (Grand Rapids, Mich.: W. B. Eerdmans, 1998); see especially his own contribution, 'For Whom were the Gospels Written?', pp. 9–48.
19. It is fairly obvious that each Gospel writer took note of the character of his local church in some respects: Mark, like John, explains the occasional word of Aramaic, so his readers can be assumed not to have been Aramaic speakers; Luke changes features of Mark to make them more urban and also more realistic – the house that does not fall is secure not because it is built on rock, but because it has decent foundations; Matthew makes Jesus much more opposed to contemporary Jewish movements such as Pharisaism than he is in Mark; and so on. But this does not of itself imply that the Gospels were written *only* for a local church.
20. Bauckham has been sharply criticized by Margaret Mitchell, in her 'Patristic Counter-Evidence to the Claim that "The Gospels were Written for All Christians"', *New Testament Studies*, 51 (2005), pp. 36–79. She shows that early Christian writers often think of the Gospels as deriving from particular communities and do not describe them as written for 'all Christians'. I am not sure that this fully engages with Bauckham's point. Of course each Gospel derives from a particular setting, as all literature does, but his case is that none of them is intended only for domestic consumption: they were all published and meant to be of interest to anyone who encountered them.
21. Harry Y. Gamble, *Books and Readers in the Early Church: A History of Early Christian Texts* (New Haven and London: Yale University Press, 1995), p. 82, referring to P52 (Papyrus Ryland 457) in the Rylands Library at Manchester, UK.
22. The names are attached to the Gospels from at least the early second century. It may be that they are the real names of the writers: anyone inventing a name would hardly have decided on Mark or Luke, which do not appear in the New Testament as the names of apostles, though Matthew and John are both apostolic names. The belief that the evangelists were the very people

in the New Testament who shared their names would then have arisen later. Most scholars think, however, that the Gospels were originally anonymous, and that New Testament names were attached to them as they were to other early Christian texts such as *The Shepherd* of Hermas, a minor figure who appears in Romans 16:14.

23. The prologue (John 1:1–18) is unparalleled in the Synoptics in its claim that Jesus is identical with the Word (Greek: *logos*) of God that existed from all eternity, though as we saw in Chapter 7 there are similar claims in Paul's letters.
24. See Richard A. Burridge, *What Are the Gospels? A Comparison with Graeco-Roman Biography* (Grand Rapids, Mich.: W. B. Eerdmans, second edition 2004). On Plutarch see C. B. R. Pelling, 'Plutarch's Method of Work in the Roman Lives', *Journal of Hellenic Studies*, 99 (1979), pp. 74–96.
25. Burridge, *What Are the Gospels?*, p. 76.
26. The Gospels are 'a subtype of Greco-Roman biography', according to David E. Aune, *The New Testament in its Literary Environment* (Cambridge: James Clarke & Co., 1988).
27. The first extended example of redaction criticism is generally held to be Willi Marxsen, *Mark the Evangelist: Studies on the Redaction History of the Gospel* (Nashville, Tenn.: Abingdon Press, 1969, from original German of 1956).
28. See especially Michael D. Goulder, *Midrash and Lection in Matthew* (London: SPCK, 1974).
29. See most recently the discussion in Colin J. Humphreys, *The Mystery of the Last Supper: Reconstructing the Final Days of Jesus* (Cambridge: Cambridge University Press, 2011).
30. Robert Morgan, 'The Hermeneutical Significance of Four Gospels', *Interpretation*, 33 (1979), pp. 376–88; the quotations are from pp. 387 and 388.
31. Francis Watson, *Gospel Writing: A Canonical Perspective* (Grand Rapids, Mich. and Cambridge: W. B. Eerdmans, 2013), p. 550.

9. FROM BOOKS TO SCRIPTURE

1. Josephus, *Against Apion*, 1:38–41, quoted from John M. G. Barclay (trans. and ed.), *Against Apion*, vol. 10 of *Flavius Josephus* (Leiden: Brill, 2007).
2. By 'Scripture' is to be understood a text or texts that are accorded some kind of special and authoritative status within a given religious community, and that are not seen as casual or ephemeral. Often they are interpreted in ways that would not be found in the case of other texts – as illustrated in the Introduction.
3. For a collection of these lists see Edmon L. Gallagher and John D. Meade, *The Biblical Canon Lists from Early Christianity: Texts and Analysis* (Oxford: Oxford University Press, 2017).
4. And as understood in the current ordering of the Hebrew Bible, as seen in the list above.

5. Melito's list occurs in a letter to a bishop called Onesimus, and is cited in Eusebius' *Ecclesiastical History* 4:26: see Timothy H. Lim, *The Formation of the Jewish Canon* (New Haven and London: Yale University Press, 2013), pp. 37–8.
6. In Eusebius 6:25; see ibid., pp. 38–9.
7. b. Baba Bathra 14a–15b; see Lim, *The Formation of the Jewish Canon*, pp. 35–7. Quoted and discussed further later in this chapter.
8. 1QpHab 8; see Géza Vermes, *The Complete Dead Sea Scrolls in English* (New York and London: Allen Lane, 1997), p. 483.
9. The classic case of contagion through touch is touching a corpse, after which purification ceremonies are called for.
10. See Babylonian Talmud, Megillah 7a.
11. The most recent discussion is by Magnar Kartveit, *The Origin of the Samaritans* (Leiden: Brill, 2009).
12. The Babylonian creation epic *Enuma elish* and the *Epic of Gilgamesh* both exist in multiple copies from many dates in the second and first millennia BCE, showing that they were regarded as canonical literature. The same might be said of the Homeric epics within Hellenistic culture.
13. See John Barton, *The Spirit and the Letter: Studies in the Biblical Canon* (London: SPCK, 1997); American edition *Holy Writings, Sacred Text* (Louisville, Ky.: Westminster John Knox Press, 1997). See also Lim, *The Formation of the Jewish Canon*, pp. 1–16; also Eugene Ulrich, 'The Notion and Definition of Canon', in Lee Martin McDonald and James A. Sanders (eds), *The Canon Debate* (Peabody, Mass.: Hendrickson, 2002), pp. 21–35, and Albert C. Sundberg Jr, *The Old Testament of the Early Church* (Cambridge, Mass.: Harvard University Press, 1964); idem, 'The Bible Canon and the Christian Doctrine of Inspiration', *Interpretation*, 29 (1975), pp. 352–71.
14. See Stuart Weeks, Simon Gathercole and Loren Stuckenbruck (eds), *The Book of Tobit: Texts from the Principal Ancient and Medieval Traditions, with Synopsis, Concordances, and Annotated Texts in Aramaic, Hebrew, Greek, Latin, and Syriac* (Berlin: W. de Gruyter, 2004); Pancratius C. Beentjes, *The Book of Ben Sira in Hebrew: A Text Edition of all Extant Hebrew Manuscripts and a Synopsis of all Parallel Hebrew Ben Sira Texts* (Leiden: Brill, 1997). (Sirach is also known as the Wisdom of Jesus ben Sira, and in Latin as Ecclesiasticus – not to be confused with Ecclesiastes, that is, Qoheleth.)
15. The rejection of Sirach is mentioned in Tosefta Yadaim 2:13; the book was, however, highly esteemed in Judaism as a wise, though not canonical, work. See also Jerusalem Talmud, Sanhedrin 28a. In Pirqe Aboth 4:4 it appears to be cited as Scripture.
16. See the discussion and texts in Carolinne White, *The Correspondence (394–419) between Jerome and Augustine of Hippo* (Lewiston, NY and Lampeter: Mellen Press, 1990).
17. With one interesting exception: Bibles copied in Orleans under the direction of Theodulf (750–821 CE) had a separate section for the deutero-canonical

books: see Frans van Liere, *An Introduction to the Medieval Bible* (Cambridge: Cambridge University Press, 2014), p. 73.

18. The deutero-canonical books continued to be known and read throughout Christian history, up to the present: 'Bel and the Dragon', one of the additions to Daniel, is a fairly popular name for pubs in England.
19. This may be the first evidence for the equation of the snake in the garden of Eden with the devil.
20. *1 Enoch* is canonical in the Ethiopian Orthodox Church.
21. Examples are, again, *1 Enoch* and the *Assumption of Moses*; also the *Testaments of the Twelve Patriarchs*. See the useful list of possible allusions in Lim, *The Formation of the Jewish Canon*, pp. 195–207.
22. Sundberg Jr, *The Old Testament of the Early Church*, p. 102.
23. Stuhlhofer, *Der Gebrauch der Bibel von Jesus bis Euseb*; discussed at length in my *The Spirit and the Letter*.
24. James Barr, *Holy Scripture: Canon, Authority, Criticism* (Philadelphia: Westminster Press, 1983), p. 1.
25. Athanasius, *Festal Letter* of 367 CE.
26. Naomi G. Cohen, *Philo's Scriptures: Citations from the Prophets and Writings. Evidence for a* Haftarah *Cycle in Second Temple Judaism* (Boston and Leiden: Brill, 2007) argues, from the citations Philo makes from non-Torah material when commenting on the Torah, that he was drawing on the readings assigned as *haftarot* to accompany the Torah readings. If that could be made good, we would have evidence of a *haftarot*-cycle already in the first century CE.
27. The books of Samuel and Kings are typically known, as in the Greek Bible, as 1, 2, 3 and 4 Kingdoms.
28. b. Baba Bathra 14a–15b.
29. Martin Abegg Jr, Peter Flint and Eugene Ulrich (eds and trans.), *The Dead Sea Scrolls Bible* (San Francisco: HarperCollins, 1999).
30. See Elisha Qimron, *The Temple Scroll: A Critical Edition with Extensive Reconstructions* (Beersheva: Ben Gurion University of the Negev Press, 1996).
31. See the discussion in Zahn, 'New Voices, Ancient Words', pp. 435–58, and 'Rewritten Scripture', pp. 323–36. In the second article Zahn writes: 'When TS presents a law that conflicts with what is said in the Pentateuch, it must be presumed that the author believed his version of the law was the correct one' (p. 331).
32. As *1 Enoch* still is in the Ethiopian Church, which has preserved it in Ethiopic – it is not extant in full in Aramaic, though there are sections in that language among the Dead Sea Scrolls.
33. See James H. Charlesworth (ed.), *The Old Testament Pseudepigrapha*, vol. 1: *Apocalyptic Literature and Testaments* (London: Darton, Longman & Todd, 1984), p. 795.
34. The term 'Rewritten Bible' was coined by Géza Vermes in 1973. See the detailed discussion in Molly M. Zahn, *Rethinking Rewritten Scripture:*

Composition and Exegesis in the 4QReworked Pentateuch Manuscripts (Leiden: Brill, 2011), raising the issue of the possible canonicity of the reworked texts.

10. CHRISTIANS AND THEIR BOOKS

1. The essential orality of the proclamation of the gospel can still be found in Luther: 'Christ did not write his doctrines himself as Moses did, but he gave them orally, and commanded that they should be published abroad by preaching, and he did not command that they should be written' (John Nicholas Lenker and Eugene F. A. Klug (eds), *The Complete Sermons of Martin Luther* (Grand Rapids, Mich.: Baker, 2000), vol. 1, pt 1, p. 372; quoted in Stephen Westerholm and Martin Westerholm, *Reading Sacred Scripture: Voices from the History of Biblical Interpretation* (Grand Rapids, Mich.: W. B. Eerdmans, 2016), p. 212.
2. C. H. Cosgrove, 'Justin Martyr and the Emerging Christian Canon: Observations on the Purpose and Destination of the Dialogue with Trypho', *Vigiliae Christianae*, 36 (1982), pp. 209–32; the quotation is from p. 226.
3. It is quite possible that, before there were Gospels, there was indeed a 'sayings collection' recording simply what Jesus had said. The later *Gospel of Thomas* is of this type and may rest on older prototypes. See the illuminating discussion in Watson, *Gospel Writing*, pp. 249–71. Q would then be one example of a wider genre, whose existence would help to explain why Irenaeus speaks as though sayings and narratives were in two separate categories despite the fact that in the Gospels as he had them they were amalgamated.
4. Irenaeus, *Against Heresies*, book 2, 35:4.
5. Some think even Q contained some narrative material.
6. Remnants of the older approach still remain even today, for example in 'Red Letter Bibles', where the sayings of Jesus are picked out in red as though they had a higher authority than that of the Gospels in which they appear.
7. Watson, *Gospel Writing*, p. 418.
8. In a world before the invention of page numbers its convenience was not actually that much greater than that of a scroll.
9. The classic works here are by C. H. Roberts: 'The Codex', *Proceedings of the British Academy*, 40 (1954), pp. 169–204, and (with T. C. Skeat), *The Birth of the Codex* (London: Oxford University Press for the British Academy, 1987).
10. Van Liere, *An Introduction to the Medieval Bible*, p. 22.
11. Justin, *First Apology*, chapter 66.
12. There has been much speculation on why Christians adopted the codex for their own books: the best discussion is in Gamble, *Books and Readers in the Early Church*, pp. 42–66. Gamble's own theory is that the first Christian codex was a collection of the letters of Paul, which were too long to fit on a

scroll. The collection could even go back to Paul himself, if like most writers in antiquity he kept copies of his own letters (ibid., p. 101). But he also points out that codices were already in use for technical manuals and non-literary texts, and that Christians probably saw their own writings as more akin to those than to Jewish Scripture or Graeco-Roman literature. There was no tradition in Christianity, as there was in Judaism, of keeping books in a special shrine, called in the synagogue the 'ark', helping to confirm that 'the attitude of early Christianity toward religious texts was more practical than sacral' (ibid., p. 197).

13. For the statistics see Stuhlhofer, *Der Gebrauch der Bibel von Jesus bis Euseb*; and my *The Spirit and the Letter*, pp. 14–24.
14. See April D. DeConick, *The Original Gospel of Thomas in Translation* (London and New York: T&T Clark, 2007): see also Chapter 11.
15. See Justin, *Dialogue with Trypho*, 100:3.
16. Watson, *Gospel Writing*, especially pp. 249–85. Particularly interesting, as he shows, are the quotations of eleven sayings of Jesus in the pseudonymous *Second Letter of Clement*, from the mid second century CE, which mostly begin simply 'The Lord says', with no attribution of source.
17. See Judith Lieu, *Image and Reality: The Jews and the World of the Christians in the Second Century* (Edinburgh: T&T Clark, 1996) and idem, *Christian Identity in the Jewish and Graeco-Roman World* (Oxford: Oxford University Press, 2004); J. D. G. Dunn, *The Parting of the Ways between Christianity and Judaism and their Significance for the Character of Christianity* (London: SCM Press, 2006).
18. Stuhlhofer, *Der Gebrauch der Bibel von Jesus bis Euseb*, p. 67.
19. See Cantwell Smith, *What is Scripture?*
20. Cf. 'Christianity reinvented equivalents for the religious institutions of Israel': John Muddiman, 'The First-Century Crisis: Christian Origins', in S. Sutherland, L. Houlden, P. Clarke and F. Hardy (eds), *The World's Religions* (London: Routledge, 1988), p. 104.
21. *Didache* 8. See Andrew Louth (ed.), *Early Christian Writings: The Apostolic Fathers* (London: Penguin, second edition 1987), p. 194.
22. See again Dunn, *The Parting of the Ways* and Lieu, *Christian Identity in the Jewish and Graeco-Roman World*.
23. Krister Stendahl based on this an argument that Matthew belonged to a learned scribal school: see his *The School of St Matthew and its Use of the Old Testament* (Philadelphia: Fortress Press, 1968).
24. On this see Chapter 13.
25. Hans von Campenhausen, *The Formation of the Christian Bible* (London: A. & C. Black, 1972), p. 91.
26. *Clementine Recognitions*, 1:59.
27. *Barnabas*, 6:11–12.
28. Conversely, Justin can on occasion adjust a New Testament passage to conform more closely to the Old. Thus he claims that the disciples, when looking

for the donkey and colt on which Jesus was to enter Jerusalem (Matthew 21:1–7), found them tied to a vine – thus fulfilling the messianic prophecy (as it was held to be) in Genesis 49:10–11:

> The sceptre shall not depart from Judah,
> nor the ruler's staff from between his feet,
> until he comes to whom it belongs [see NRSV note];
> and the obedience of the peoples is his.
> Binding his foal to the vine
> and his donkey's colt to the choice vine . . .

See Justin, *First Apology*, chapter 32, and G. W. H. Lampe, 'The Exposition and Exegesis of Scripture: To Gregory the Great', in G. W. H. Lampe (ed.), *The Cambridge History of the Bible*, vol. 2: *The West from the Fathers to the Reformation* (Cambridge: Cambridge University Press, 1969), pp. 155–83. The Gospels themselves may already show this process at work; for example, details of the passion story may have been adjusted to match Psalm 22, such as the text, 'they divide my clothes among themselves, and for my clothing they cast lots' (verse 18); compare Matthew 27:35 and especially John 19:23–5. On this phenomenon see the classic study by Barnabas Lindars, *New Testament Apologetic: The Doctrinal Significance of the Old Testament Quotations* (London: SCM Press, 1961).

29. Justin also harmonized the Gospels of Matthew and Luke, or else drew on an already existing harmony, and there may be links between his work and the *Diatessaron*; see Watson, *Gospel Writing*, pp. 474–5.
30. There is an excellent discussion of *nomina sacra* in Gamble, *Books and Readers in the Early Church*, pp. 74–8. The practice of contracting sacred words continued in both Greek and Latin manuscripts into the Middle Ages.
31. The western church was suspicious of Hebrews because it teaches that there can be no second repentance after baptism, which conflicted with the growth of penitential practices, predicated on the idea that there was always a chance for repentant sinners. Revelation was suspect in the east, as it was again at the Reformation in the west, as tending to inflame apocalyptic hopes and thus ignite rebellion against authority. In both cases uncertainty about authorship played a part.

11. OFFICIAL AND UNOFFICIAL TEXTS

1. In *The Da Vinci Code* Brown builds on, but greatly exaggerates, the position established classically by Walter Bauer in *Orthodoxy and Heresy in Earliest Christianity* (Philadelphia: Fortress Press, 1971), from the second edition of the German original, published in 1934. Bauer argued that early (first- and second-century) Christianity was extremely diverse, and that much that would later be reckoned as heresy was simply part of this variety. The definitions of Church theologians and Church councils represented the views of the winners in theological controversies. This applies to definitions of the scriptural canon as well

as doctrinal matters. Bauer's thesis is in general not controversial in the academic world, where it is generally accepted that orthodoxy and heresy are not absolute terms. But so far as the biblical canon is concerned, evidence is strong for the much earlier origin and use of what would later become canonical texts, by contrast with the relative lateness of what would come to be seen as heretical books. There was indeed a great penumbra of texts that failed to make it into the canon, but it was exactly that: a penumbra – not an alternative canon.

2. See Bruce M. Metzger, *The Canon of the New Testament: Its Origin, Development, and Significance* (Oxford: Oxford University Press, 1987), pp. 312–13. The formula 'let nothing be added or taken away' is the classic expression of canonicity in the narrow sense of a closed collection of books that is exactly defined.
3. See Watson, *Gospel Writing*, pp. 482–3.
4. Metzger, *The Canon of the New Testament*, pp. 309–10, slightly adjusted and with emphasis added.
5. Not everyone, even after the time of Eusebius, was so favourably disposed to Revelation: Theodore of Mopsuestia (350–428 CE) is said to have disputed the canonicity of 2 Peter, 2 and 3 John, Jude and Revelation, and this appears to have been a common position in the church of Antioch in Syria. See M. F. Wiles, 'Theodore of Mopsuestia as Representative of the Antiochene School', in P. R. Ackroyd and C. F. Evans (eds), *The Cambridge History of the Bible*, vol. 1: *From the Beginnings to Jerome* (Cambridge: Cambridge University Press, 1970), p. 494.
6. See R. L. P. Milburn, 'The "People's Bible": Artists and Commentators', in *Cambridge History of the Bible*, vol. 2, pp. 280–308, at p. 285.
7. Metzger, *The Canon of the New Testament*, pp. 305–7.
8. According to Bishop Sozomen in Palestine in the fifth century CE the *Apocalypse of Peter* was still being read in church on Good Friday in his day: see C. S. C. Williams, 'The History of the Text and Canon of the New Testament to Jerome', in *Cambridge History of the Bible*, vol. 2, pp. 27–53, at p. 43.
9. See especially Albert C. Sundberg Jr, 'Canon Muratori: A Fourth Century List', *Harvard Theological Review*, 66 (1973), pp. 1–41, and Geoffrey Hahneman, *The Muratorian Fragment and the Development of the Canon* (Oxford: Oxford University Press, 1992), who argues for a late date; and Joseph Verheyden, 'The Canon Muratori: A Matter of Dispute', in J.-M. Auwers and H. J. de Jonge, *The Biblical Canons* (Leuven: Leuven University Press, 1993), pp. 487–556, who argues for the traditional second-century date. There is an up-to-date review of the literature in Christophe Guignard, 'The Original Language of the Muratorian Fragment', *Journal of Theological Studies*, 66 (2015), pp. 596–624.
10. J. R. Porter, *The Lost Bible: Forgotten Scriptures Revealed* (London: Duncan Baird, 2001), p. 6.
11. Serapion, Bishop of Antioch from 191 to 211, condemned the *Gospel of Peter* on the basis that parts of it contained 'additions to the faith taught by the Saviour' and therefore it could not be canonical.
12. Origen, *Commentary on John*, 1:18.

13. On this see the illuminating discussion by Morwenna Ludlow, '"Criteria of Canonicity" and the Early Church', in John Barton and Michael Wolter (eds), *Die Einheit der Schrift und die Vielfalt des Kanons/The Unity of Scripture and the Diversity of the Canon*, Beihefte zur Zeitschrift für die neutestamentliche Wissenschaft und die Kunde der älteren Kirche, 118 (Berlin: W. de Gruyter, 2003), pp. 69–93.
14. C. E. Hill, *Who Chose the Gospels? Probing the Great Gospel Conspiracy* (Oxford: Oxford University Press, 2010), p. 12.
15. Stuhlhofer, *Der Gebrauch der Bibel von Jesus bis Euseb*, p. 75: the reference to Overbeck is to Franz Overbeck, *Zur Geschichte des Kanons* (Chemnitz: E. Schmeitzner, 1880, reprinted Darmstadt, 1965, Wissenschaftliche Buchgesellschaft). The passage is quoted in my *Spirit and Letter*, p. 42.
16. Quoted from the translation of J. K. Elliott: see J. K. Elliott, *The Apocryphal New Testament: A Collection of Apocryphal Christian Literature in an English Translation Based on M. R. James* (Oxford: Oxford University Press, 1993), pp. 135–47.
17. For discussion see Elliott, *The Apocryphal New Testament*, pp. 123–35. 'The possibility that at least some of the unique sayings of Jesus preserved in Coptic Thomas may ultimately go back to Jesus is generally conceded. The probability that where there are synoptic parallels the version in Thomas may preserve an earlier witness is less widely accepted; an influential group of scholars (e.g. Quispel, Koester, Crossan, Cameron, and others) would wish to argue that the Greek *Vorlage* of the Coptic version may well be independent of the synoptic Gospels' (p. 124). See especially J. D. Crossan, *Four Other Gospels* (Minneapolis: Winston Press, 1985); Chirstopher Tuckett, 'Thomas and the Synoptics', *Novum Testamentum*, 30 (1988), pp. 132–57.
18. This seems to me an argument against suggestions that the New Testament canon should be enlarged by the inclusion of some of these works, as in Hal Taussig (ed.), *A New New Testament: A Bible for the 21st Century Combining Traditional and Newly Discovered Texts* (Boston: Houghton Mifflin Harcourt, 2013). See the excellent discussion in R. W. L. Moberly, 'Canon and Religious Truth: An Appraisal of *A New New Testament*', in Timothy H. Lim (ed.), *When Texts Are Canonized*, Brown Judaic Studies 359 (Providence, RI: Brown University, 2017), pp. 108–35.
19. Karen L. King, *The Gospel of Mary of Magdala: Jesus and the First Woman Apostle* (Santa Rosa, Cal.: Polebridge Press, 2003).
20. A full recent treatment can be found in Christopher Tuckett, *The Gospel of Mary* (Oxford: Oxford University Press, 2007).
21. Louth (ed.), *Early Christian Writings*, p. 156.
22. Quotations from *The Shepherd* are taken from *Apostolic Fathers*, vol. 2 (London: Heinemann, 1912, reprinted 1965, Loeb Classical Library), translated by Kirsopp Lake.
23. Their importance in early modern England is discussed in Keith Thomas, *Religion and the Decline of Magic: Studies in Popular Beliefs in Sixteenth and Seventeenth Century England* (London: Weidenfeld & Nicolson, 1971).

24. Van Liere, *An Introduction to the Medieval Bible*, p. 70. Note that the idea of Christ going down into hell to communicate with the dead patriarchs is already present in canonical Scripture, in 1 Peter 3:18–20, though not developed in any detail. *Nicodemus* is probably a fourth-century work, which incorporates the *Acts of Pilate*, which purports to be a record of Jesus' trial. No scholar attributes any historical value to the work.
25. Elliott, *The Apocryphal New Testament*, p. 64.
26. Other elements in the tradition that derive from the *Protevangelium* are that Mary (like Joseph) was descended from David, and that she remained a virgin even after the birth of Jesus – this last is an important doctrine in Catholic Christianity.

12. BIBLICAL MANUSCRIPTS

1. In John 8:1–11, the story of the woman taken in adultery, Jesus twice bends down and writes on the ground, though we are not told what he wrote. But this story is certainly an addition to the Gospel by a later writer – see the discussion below – and in any case does not imply that Jesus could have written a whole book.
2. A standard work on the textual transmission of the New Testament is Bruce M. Metzger, *The Text of the New Testament: Its Transmission, Corruption, and Restoration* (Oxford: Oxford University Press, third edition 1992).
3. For the details of this categorization see especially D. C. Parker, *The Living Text of the Gospels* (Cambridge: Cambridge University Press, 1997), pp. 8–30, to which my discussion is very heavily indebted.
4. Ehrman, *The Orthodox Corruption of Scripture*; for this example see pp. 69 and 115.
5. Ibid., p. xi.
6. Tertullian alleges that the singular reading was corrupted into a plural by the Valentinians, a Gnostic sect he opposed (*De carne Christi*, 24), while Irenaeus (*Against Heresies*, book 3, 16:2 and 19:2) argues from the singular verb that Jesus was no ordinary man but born miraculously, which is certainly what the change in the text was designed to affirm. As Ehrman says, what we have here is 'not a heretical tampering with the text, but an orthodox one' (*The Orthodox Corruption of Scripture*, p. 70).
7. For a fuller discussion of this verse see ibid., pp. 107–8.
8. F. C. Conybeare, *Expositor* (December 1895), p. 406; cited here from Parker, *The Living Text*, p. 99, to whom, again, the discussion of this story is greatly indebted.
9. Parker, *The Living Text*, pp. 75–94.
10. Ibid., pp. 90–91.
11. Ibid., p. 93.
12. Thus, in circumstances where men and women were more equal – under Roman law – the provisions of Jesus' teaching were also more equalized, to yield the Marcan version of the sayings.

13. Parker, *The Living Text*, p. 93.
14. On another set of texts, Parker points out that 'there are as many differences between D and B in Luke 6.1ff. as there are between the two texts in D of Mark 2.23ff. and Luke 6.1ff.' (*The Living Text*, p. 46). Thus even the borders between the Gospels can be porous, once one examines the manuscript tradition.
15. For further detail see Emanuel Tov, *Textual Criticism of the Hebrew Bible* (Minneapolis: Fortress Press, third edition 2012), pp. 44–5. Much of my discussion in this section depends on Tov. Further early manuscripts of parts of the Hebrew Bible are the British Museum manuscript Or. 4445, from the early tenth century CE; and the Cairo Codex of the prophets from 895 CE, the oldest extant manuscript, apart from the Dead Sea Scrolls, of any part of the Hebrew Bible.
16. Any fuller account of the textual history of the Hebrew Bible would also need to take account of the Samaritan Pentateuch, the holy text of the Samaritan community that still exists around Nablus (ancient Shechem). The Samaritans recognize only the Pentateuch (together with some of Joshua) as sacred, and their text of it contains variants as against MT which have to be taken into account by textual critics.
17. Tov, *Textual Criticism*, p. 30.

13. THE THEME OF THE BIBLE

1. The complete list is: Genesis 3:8–19; Genesis 22:15–18; Isaiah 9:2–7; Isaiah 11:1–9; Luke 1:26–38; Luke 2:1–7; Luke 2:8–16; Matthew 2:1–12; and John 1:1–14. (Sometimes Micah 5:2–5 is included, and two Lucan readings amalgamated.) The service has been held every year since 1918, and is based on an earlier form used at Truro Cathedral in Cornwall, England, since 1880.
2. Testimony books probably pre-existed Christianity: one of the Dead Sea Scrolls, 4QTest, lists some messianic texts, Deuteronomy 5:28–9; 18:18–19; Numbers 24:15–17; Deuteronomy 33:8–11; and Joshua 6:26. (The messianic expectations of the Qumran community included a priestly as well as a royal messiah.)
3. Migne, *Patrologia Graeca*, 9, cols 409–10.
4. The status of the apocryphal or deutero-canonical books makes some difference to the themes of the Christian Old Testament for those who, like the early Fathers, accept them as authoritative; but the Jewish Tanakh and the Christian Old Testament still contain almost the same books. For Protestants the contents are identical, even though the arrangement is different. See Chapter 10.
5. Alexander Samely, *Forms of Rabbinic Literature and Thought: An Introduction* (Oxford: Oxford University Press, 2007), p. 2.
6. 2 Esdras is made up of 5 Ezra + 4 Ezra + 6 Ezra, the first and last of these sections being of definitely Christian provenance. It must not be confused

with what the Greek Bible (the Septuagint or LXX) calls 2 Esdras, which is what western Bibles call Ezra-Nehemiah. The use of the term 'Esdras' (the Greek for Ezra) in different Bibles is immensely confusing.

7. Justin, *Dialogue with Trypho*, 72:4.
8. R. Kendall Soulen, *The God of Israel and Christian Theology* (Minneapolis: Fortress Press, 1996).
9. Exactly the four stages identified by Hugh of St Victor, as discussed in Chapter 15.
10. Soulen, *The God of Israel*, p. 65.
11. I have in mind such works as Géza Vermes, *Jesus the Jew: A Historian's Reading of the Gospels* (London: Fortuna/Collins, 1976; second edition London: SCM Press, 1983); idem, *The Religion of Jesus the Jew* (London: SCM Press, 1993); and E. P. Sanders, *Jesus and Judaism* (London: SCM Press, 1985).
12. On the use of the Bible in the synagogue liturgy see Elsie Stern, 'Concepts of Scripture in the Synagogue Service', Chapter 2 of Benjamin D. Sommer (ed.), *Jewish Concepts of Scripture* (New York and London: New York University Press, 2012); see also Berlin and Brettler (eds), *The Jewish Study Bible*, pp. 2231–3, for a table showing the readings used in the synagogue liturgy.
13. Benjamin D. Sommer, 'The Scroll of Isaiah as Jewish Scripture, or, Why Jews Don't Read Books', *Society of Biblical Literature 1996 Seminar Papers* (Atlanta, Ga.: Scholars Press, 1996), pp. 225–42.
14. Or 'earlier and later'.
15. Samely, *Forms of Rabbinic Literature*, p. 86.
16. Jeff Astley, 'Only God Can Cure and Free Us', *Church Times*, 4 March 2016, p. 19.
17. Dietrich Bonhoeffer, *Letters and Papers from Prison* (New York: Macmillan, 1972), p. 336; quoted in Soulen, *The God of Israel*, p. 149.
18. See Chapter 10.
19. See Chapter 10.
20. Eugen J. Pentiuc, *The Old Testament in Eastern Orthodox Tradition* (New York and Oxford: Oxford University Press, 2014), p. 148.
21. In the KJV/AV there is also 1 John 5:7, which reads: 'There are three that bear record in heaven, the Father, the Word, and the Holy Ghost: and these three are one.' But this is certainly a very late insertion in the text, known technically as the 'Johannine comma'. See the comments in Chapter 16.
22. Justin, *First Apology*, chapter 46. This formulation is very close to that in the later Christian creeds, such as those called the Apostles' and Nicene Creeds.
23. Howard Wettstein, 'God's Struggles', in Michael Bergmann, Michael J. Murray and Michael C. Rea (eds), *Divine Evil? The Moral Character of the God of Abraham* (Oxford: Oxford University Press, 2011), p. 331.
24. Though Acts cannot date from before the late first century CE, as the second volume of Luke, it is widely held that the speeches in it (by Paul, Peter and others) rest on genuinely early preaching in the churches; and they say a lot about Jesus as a miracle worker and teacher. See, for example, Acts 2:22 and

10:36–8. The classic work on the speeches is Martin Dibelius, 'The Speeches of Acts and Ancient Historiography', in Heinrich Greeven (ed.), *Studies in the Acts of the Apostles* (London: SCM Press, 1956).

14. RABBIS AND CHURCH FATHERS

1. See Azzan Yadin, *Scripture as Logos: Rabbi Ishmael and the Origins of Midrash* (Philadelphia: University of Pennsylvania Press, 2004).
2. See the discussion of this passage in Henning Graf Reventlow, *Epochen der Bibelauslegung, Band I: Vom Alten Testament bis Origenes* (Munich: C. H. Beck, 1990), pp. 108–9, to which I am indebted.
3. See Jacob Z. Lauterbach, *Mekhilta de-Rabbi Ishmael* (Philadelphia: The Jewish Publication Society of America, vol. 1, 1933), pp. 151–2: Tractate *Pisha* on Exodus 13. There is also a lengthy discussion justifying the decision to interpret 'hand' as 'arm'.
4. See Samely, *Forms of Rabbinic Literature*, p. 212, quoting *Genesis Rabbah* 55.
5. Ibid., p. 66.
6. An early Christian writer who sees things in rather the same way is Clement of Rome (d. *c* 100 CE), whose early-second-century *Letter to the Corinthians* could equally be described as halakhic in its interests: all the heroes of the Old Testament are assembled to serve as exemplars of the moral life.
7. Samely, *Forms of Rabbinic Literature*, p. 36.
8. For an introduction to midrash see Barry Holtz, 'Midrash', in Barry Holtz (ed.), *Back to the Sources: Reading the Classic Jewish Texts* (New York: Summit, 1984), pp. 177–211; Burt Visotzky, 'Midrash' and 'Rabbinic Interpretation', in Katharine Doob Sakenfeld (ed.), *The New Interpreter's Dictionary of the Bible* (Nashville: Abingdon, 2006–9), vol. 4, pp. 81–4 and 718–20; Rimon Kasher, 'The Interpretation of Scripture in Rabbinic Literature', in M. J. Mulder (ed.), *Mikra: Text, Translation, Reading and Interpretation of the Hebrew Bible in Ancient Judaism and Early Christianity* (Assen: Van Gorcum, 1988), pp. 547–94; at more length, H. L. Strack and G. Stemberger, *Introduction to the Talmud and Midrash* (Edinburgh: T&T Clark, 1991), especially pp. 254–393; and, most recently, Samely, *Forms of Rabbinic Literature*.
9. One will sometimes find *aggadah* referred to as *haggadah*, the former being the Aramaic term, the latter the Hebrew one.
10. *Pirḳê de Rabbi Eliezer*, translated by G. Friedlander (New York: Sepher-Hermon Press, fourth edition 1981), pp. 229–30. I have borrowed the quotation from its use by Yvonne Sherwood, 'Textual Carcasses and Isaac's Scar, or What Jewish Interpretation Makes of the Violence that Almost Takes Place on Mt Moriah', in Jonneke Bekkenkamp and Yvonne Sherwood (eds), *Sanctified Aggression: Legacies of Biblical and Post-Biblical Vocabularies of Violence* (London: T&T Clark International, 2003), pp. 22–43: the quotation is on p. 24.
11. *Mekhilta of Rabbi Ishmael*, Tractate *Beshallach*, on Exodus 14:24: Lauterbach, *Mekhilta de-Rabbi Ishmael*, pp. 237–8.

12. See Azzan Yadin-Israel, 'Concepts of Scripture in the Schools of Rabbi Akiva and Rabbi Ishmael', in Sommer (ed.), *Jewish Concepts of Scripture*, Chapter 4.
13. Benjamin D. Sommer, 'Concepts of Scriptural Language in Midrash', in ibid., Chapter 5.
14. See the discussion in Daniel Boyarin, *Intertextuality and the Reading of Midrash* (Bloomington and Indianapolis: Indiana University Press, 1990).
15. See the study by Henri de Lubac, *History and Spirit: The Understanding of Scripture according to Origen* (San Francisco: Ignatius, 2007).
16. For Origen's life and times see Jean Daniélou, *Origen* (London: Sheed and Ward, 1955); for his biblical interpretation, de Lubac, *History and Spirit*.
17. Westerholm and Westerholm, *Reading Sacred Scripture*, p. 78.
18. Rabbinic discussion of this passage takes a different tack. In *Tanhuma Mas'ei* 3 we read that the marches of the Israelites may be compared to a king whose son was ill. 'He took him to one place to cure him, and on the way back, the father began to recount all the marches [they had undertaken], saying to him: Here we slept, here we were cold, here your head hurt. So too did the Holy One, blessed be He, say to Moses: Recount for them all the places they had angered Me.' David Stern comments: 'Thus is a rather bare-bones list of camping places in the wilderness converted into an expression of God's love for Israel', in Berlin and Brettler (eds), *The Jewish Study Bible*, p. 1877.
19. See the discussion of this example in Samely, *Forms of Rabbinic Literature*, pp. 182–3.
20. Origen, *Commentary on John*, 10:18.
21. Cited in Daniélou, *Origen*, p. 180; see also the discussion in David Lawton, *Faith, Text and History: The Bible in English* (New York and London: Harvester Wheatsheaf, 1990), p. 22.
22. See Mark J. Edwards, *Origen against Plato* (Aldershot: Ashgate, 2002).
23. See the example of Philo's interpretation discussed in Chapter 6 above.
24. NRSV has 'at last'.
25. Philo, *On Drunkenness*, 144.
26. Origen, *Homily on Luke*, 34.
27. Irenaeus, *Against Heresies*, book 3, 18:2.
28. Augustine, *Quaestiones evangeliorum*, 2:19; see the discussion by C. H. Dodd, *Parables of the Kingdom* (London: Fontana, 1961).
29. Augustine, *Sermons*, 4:9. Clement of Alexandria (*c.* 150–215 CE) similarly explains that Christ 'pours wine on our wounded hearts, the blood of the vine of David', thus giving the parable a Christological interpretation: see *What Rich Man Can Be Saved?* (*Quis dives salvetur*), 28–9.
30. *Homily on Joshua*, 9:4; quoted from de Lubac, *History and Spirit*, p. 112.
31. Thus, in Isaiah 6, God is seen sitting on a throne and wearing robes.
32. In the next century John Chrysostom would agree: 'While the books are from them [the Jews], the treasure of the books now belongs to us; if the text is from them, both text and meaning belong to us' (*Second Sermon on Genesis*).

33. Rabbinic interpretation is seldom allegorical in the same way as Origen's, yet it also rests on the desire to see the text as bearing a religiously acceptable meaning: see James L. Kugel and Rowan A. Greer, *Early Biblical Interpretation* (Philadelphia: Westminster Press, 1986), especially p. 71.
34. But in a world of allegorical reading such a text could of course have been written intentionally as an allegorical or metaphorical work: see the discussion by Edmée Kingsmill, *The Song of Songs and the Eros of God* (Oxford: Oxford University Press, 2009). In that case, Origen would be interpreting it according to its original intention as an allegory, not allegorizing an essentially literal text.
35. Goodman, *Rome and Jerusalem*, p. 107.
36. See *On the Migration of Abraham*, 89–93, where he condemns those who claim to observe the spirit of the law while neglecting its letter.
37. In the original Greek, *Peri Archon*; in the Latin translation by Rufinus, *De Principiis*.
38. Origen, *Commentary on Matthew*, 15:32–4.
39. For Symmachus at least there is a detailed study: Alison Salvesen, *Symmachus in the Pentateuch*, JSS Monograph 15 (Manchester: The Victoria University of Manchester, 1991). She thinks that Symmachus was a Jew rather than a Jewish convert to Christianity, as some believe.
40. Origen, *Commentary on Romans*, 10:8:5.
41. Westerholm and Westerholm, *Reading Sacred Scripture*, p. 82.
42. *Commentary on John*, 10:4.
43. See Robert C. Hill, *Reading the Old Testament in Antioch*, The Bible in Ancient Christianity, vol. 5 (Atlanta, Ga.: Society of Biblical Literature, 2005).
44. *Theodoret of Cyrus: Commentary on the Psalms, Psalms 1–72*, Fathers of the Church, vol. 101, trans. Robert C. Hill (Washington, DC: Catholic University of America Press, 2000), book 101, pp. 187–91; quoted in William Yarchin, *History of Biblical Interpretation: A Reader* (Peabody, Mass.: Hendrickson, 2004), p. 83.
45. Frances Young, *Biblical Exegesis and the Formation of Christian Culture* (Cambridge: Cambridge University Press, 1997), p. 184.
46. Ibid., p. 176. On Antiochene interpretation see also Dimitri Z. Zaharopoulos, *Theodore of Mopsuestia on the Bible* (New York: Paulist Press, 1989) and Hill, *Reading the Old Testament in Antioch*.
47. 'Patristic' because it is the period of the Church 'Fathers', *patres* in Greek.
48. There are still conservative Bible readers who think that Jesus appeared in Old Testament times, for example in the guise of the angel who was seen by Manoah and his wife (Judges 13), just as Fathers such as Justin had taught. The exact interpretation of these passages can become quite contentious in such circles: see Andrew Malone, *Knowing Jesus in the Old Testament? A Fresh Look at Christophanies* (Nottingham: Inter-Varsity Press, 2015).
49. In the case of the New Testament, sometimes even when it is not: thus Augustine, like Origen, allegorizes the parable of the Good Samaritan as concerned with the salvation of the Christian, assigning metaphorical senses

to such things as the two coins (the sacraments). He similarly allegorizes the miracle of the feeding of the 5,000. The five loaves are the five books of the Pentateuch, and they are barley loaves because barley is harder than wheat, symbolizing the difficulty of extracting the meaning from the Old Testament. The fragments left over are the teachings that the majority of people are unable to understand; the twelve baskets are the twelve apostles. And so on. (See Augustine, tractate 24 of his *Commentary on St John's Gospel*.)

50. Augustine, *The Literal Meaning of Genesis*, 2:20.
51. Augustine, *On Christian Teaching*, 2:6:8. Thomas Aquinas would repeat and expound this idea of Augustine's centuries later.
52. See White, *The Correspondence (394–419) between Jerome and Augustine of Hippo*. See also Chapter 9.
53. R. P. C. Hanson, 'Biblical Exegesis in the Early Church', in Ackroyd and Evans (eds), *Cambridge History of the Bible*, vol. 1, p. 450.
54. Ibid., p. 452.

15. THE MIDDLE AGES

1. For the history of Bibles, considered as physical objects, see the lavishly illustrated work by Christopher de Hamel, *The Book: A History of the Bible* (London: Phaidon, 2001), to which I am deeply indebted.
2. See Beryl Smalley, *The Study of the Bible in the Middle Ages* (Notre Dame, Ind.: University of Notre Dame Press, second edition 1964), p. 37.
3. See Richard Gyug, 'Early Medieval Bibles, Biblical Books, and the Monastic Liturgy in the Beneventan Region', in Susan Boynton and Diane J. Reilly (eds), *The Practice of the Bible in the Middle Ages: Production, Reception, and Performance in Western Christianity* (New York: Columbia University Press, 2011), pp. 34–60, at p. 34.
4. On Cassiodorus see James J. O'Donnell, *Cassiodorus* (Berkeley: University of California Press, 1979).
5. See de Hamel, *The Book*, p. 76.
6. See van Liere, *An Introduction to the Medieval Bible*, pp. 248–52, and de Hamel, *The Book*, pp. 146–51.
7. It is now thought that the system, popularized by Philip the Chancellor (who worked 1225–30), may be slightly earlier than Langton, but still a British invention: see P. Saenger, 'The British Isles and the Origin of the Modern Mode of Biblical Citation', *Syntagma*, 1 (2005), pp. 77–123.
8. De Hamel, *The Book*, p. 114. The whole of his Chapter 2, 'Portable Bibles of the Thirteenth Century', provides invaluable information about the explosion in Latin Bibles in this period.
9. A standard work is Henri de Lubac, *Medieval Exegesis: The Four Senses of Scripture* (Grand Rapids, Mich.: W. B. Eerdmans; Edinburgh: T&T Clark, 2 vols, 1998 and 2000).
10. See Jean Daniélou, 'Les sources bibliques de la mystique d'Origène', *Revue d'ascétique et de mystique*, 23 (1947), p. 128; cited in Smalley, *Study*, p. 7.

11. In Gregory the Great we find three senses, literal, allegorical and moral: see Diane J. Reilly, 'Lectern Bibles and Liturgical Reform in the Central Middle Ages', in Boynton and Reilly (eds), *The Practice of the Bible*, pp. 105–25, at p. 116.
12. Allegedly composed by the Dominican friar Aage of Denmark (= Augustine of Dacia, d. 1282).
13. The moral sense is also sometimes described as 'tropological'.
14. This goes back at least to John Cassian (360–435 CE), a near-contemporary of Augustine. See Smalley, *Study*, p. 28.
15. Gregory was pope from 590 to 604. The *Moralia* are a series of lectures delivered to monks when he was the papal representative in Constantinople.
16. *The History of Christian Theology* (ed. Paul Avis), vol. 2: John Rogerson, Christopher Rowland and Barnabas Lindars, *The Study and Use of the Bible* (Basingstoke: Marshall Pickering and Grand Rapids, Mich.: W. B. Eerdmans, 1988), p. 60. Cf. Smalley, *Study*, p. 34.
17. Lampe, 'The Exposition and Exegesis of Scripture', p. 159.
18. See Chapter 14.
19. See Smalley, *Study*, p. xi.
20. On Joachim see Marjorie Reeves, *Joachim of Fiore and the Prophetic Future* (London: SPCK, 1976).
21. Hugh of St Victor, *Didascalicon*, 6:10, 807–8, quoted in Smalley, *Study*, p. 94.
22. Smalley, *Study*, Chapter 4 (pp. 112–95).
23. Ibid., pp. 163–5.
24. Ibid., p. 138.
25. Ibid., p. vii.
26. Aquinas, *Quodlibet*, 7, q. 6, a. 2, ad 5.
27. See the discussion in van Liere, *An Introduction to the Medieval Bible*, p. 135. Aquinas famously said that his immense *Summa theologiae* was a 'guide for beginners'.
28. Aquinas, *On Job* 1:6, and also *Summa theologiae*, I, 1, 10, ad 3.
29. Already in *Barnabas* we find the idea that the allegorical sense is the intended sense of the text. Thus, on his view, the food laws in the Old Testament were never intended to be taken literally, but were always a metaphor, for example as a warning that Christians should not have dealings with 'swinish' people. See Lampe, 'Exposition and Exegesis of Scripture', p. 168.
30. On Aquinas' theories about Scripture see Thomas G. Weinandy, Daniel A. Keating and John P. Yocum (eds), *Aquinas on Scripture: An Introduction to his Biblical Commentaries* (London and New York: T&T Clark International, 2005).
31. Luther got a printer to prepare copies of the Bible for his students with spaces between the lines and in the margins so that they could make notes at his lectures on biblical texts, rather as though he were reinventing the tradition of glossing from scratch.
32. Until 1949 it was generally thought that the Gloss had been started by Walafrid Strabo (808–49), but this was shown to be false by Jean de Blic, 'L'œuvre

exégétique de Walafrid Strabon et la *Glossa ordinaria*', *Recherches de théologie ancienne et médiévale*, 16 (1949), pp. 5–28. Beryl Smalley established the role played by Anselm of Laon, who had possibly been a student of Anselm of Bec (later Archbishop of Canterbury). Anselm of Laon seems to have compiled the Gloss on the Psalms and the letters of Paul – favourite texts in the schools – then on John and probably Luke, with the work being taken forward by his brother Ralph and by Gilbert of Auxerre.

33. There is, accordingly, no standard printed version of the *Glossa Ordinaria*. The nearest approximation is K. Froehlich and M. T. Gibson (eds), *Biblia Latina cum glossa ordinaria: Facsimile reprint of the editio princeps Adolph Rusch of Strassburg 1480/81* (Turnhout: Brepols, 1992). As indicated by the subtitle, this is a facsimile of an early printed version. See the discussion in Lesley Smith, *The* Glossa Ordinaria*: The Making of a Medieval Bible Commentary* (Commentaria. Sacred Texts and Their Commentaries: Jewish, Christian, and Islamic 3) (Leiden and Boston: Brill, 2009), on which much of my discussion depends heavily.
34. Smith, *The* Glossa Ordinaria, pp. 2–4.
35. Ibid., p. 85.
36. See the discussion in the Conclusion.
37. Smith, The Glossa Ordinaria, p. 11.
38. Jean Leclercq, 'The Exposition and Exegesis of Scripture: From Gregory the Great to Saint Bernard', in *Cambridge History of the Bible*, vol. 2, pp. 183–97, at p. 193.
39. See Philip D. W. Krey and Lesley Smith (eds), *Nicholas of Lyra: The Senses of Scripture*, Studies in the History of Christian Thought 90 (Leiden, Cologne and Boston: Brill, 2000); Lesley Smith, 'Nicholas of Lyra and Old Testament Interpretation', in Magne Sæbø (ed.), *Hebrew Bible/Old Testament: The History of its Interpretation*, vol. 2 (Göttingen: Vandenhoeck & Ruprecht, 2008), pp. 49–63.
40. Thus Mary Dove, 'Literal Senses in the Song of Songs', in Krey and Smith (eds), *Nicholas of Lyra*, pp. 129–46, at p. 142.
41. I referred in Chapter 14 n. 34 to the interesting work of Edmée Kingsmill, *The Song of Songs and the Eros of God*, which defends the idea that the intended meaning of the Song is indeed allegorical, or, as she more helpfully puts it, metaphorical, deriving from an ascetic community that used erotic imagery to present the relationship between themselves and God. Thus the Song never had a 'literal', in the sense of non-metaphorical, meaning as a poem about a pair of human lovers. This interpretation has not been widely accepted but seems to me plausible.
42. See van Liere, *An Introduction to the Medieval Bible*, p. 166.
43. Corrine Patton, 'Creation, Fall and Salvation: Lyra's Commentary on Genesis 1–3', in Krey and Smith (eds), *Nicholas of Lyra*, pp. 19–43, at p. 33.
44. Eva Mroczek, *The Literary Imagination in Jewish Antiquity* (New York and Oxford: Oxford University Press, 2016), p. 181.

45. For this example see the discussion in James L. Kugel, *The Ladder of Jacob: Ancient Interpretations of the Biblical Story of Jacob and his Children* (Princeton and Oxford: Princeton University Press, 2006).
46. See Page H. Kelley, Daniel S. Mynatt and Timothy G. Crawford, *The Masorah of* Biblia Hebraica Stuttgartensia*: Introduction and Annotated Glossary* (Grand Rapids, Mich. and Cambridge: W. B. Eerdmans, 1998), p. 16. This book is the best general guide available to understanding the Masorah.
47. Genesis 15:19–21; Exodus 3:8, 13:5, 23:23, 33:2, 34:11; Numbers 13:22; Deuteronomy 7:1, 20:17; Joshua 3:10, 9:1, 11:3, 12:8, 24:11; Judges 3:5; Ezra 9:1; and Nehemiah 9:8.
48. See James Barr, 'A New Look at Kethibh-Qere', *Oudtestamentische Studiën*, 21 (1981), pp. 19–37; reprinted in John Barton (ed.), *Bible and Interpretation: The Collected Essays of James Barr*, vol. 3: *Linguistics and Translation* (Oxford: Oxford University Press, 2014), pp. 445–60, especially p. 460; and my own discussion in *The Spirit and the Letter*, pp. 123–5. A standard and important treatment can be found in W. S. Morrow, 'Kethib and Qere', *Anchor Bible Dictionary* (New York: Doubleday, 1992), vol. 4, p. 25.
49. For Hebrew manuscripts see the discussion in Chapter 12.
50. Incidentally, the first Hebrew book ever to be printed, in 1475.
51. Raphael Loewe, 'The "Plain" Meaning of Scripture in Early Jewish Exegesis', in J. G. Weiss (ed.), *Papers of the Institute of Jewish Studies*, vol. 1 (Jerusalem: Magnes Press, 1964), pp. 140–85.
52. This principle occurs three times in the Babylonian Talmud, at Shabbat 63a, and at Yebamim 11b and 24a.
53. David Weiss Halivni, *Peshat and Derash: Plain and Applied Meaning in Rabbinic Exegesis* (New York and Oxford: Oxford University Press, 1991). Halivni discusses Loewe's paper briefly on p. 53.
54. Ibid., p. 12.
55. For the *peshat/derash* distinction see the (oddly named) article by Stephen Garfinkel, 'Clearing *Peshat* and *Derash*', in Magne Sæbø (ed.), *Hebrew Bible/Old Testament: The History of Its Interpretation*, vol. 1/2 (Göttingen: Vandenhoeck & Ruprecht, 2000), pp. 129–34. He suggests that *peshat* means 'examining the text on its own terms', as opposed to 'appropriating it for changing times', which is *derash*. I am not sure this really does justice to the rabbinic material either.
56. Eva De Visscher comments that for a Christian interpreter such as Herbert of Bosham, secretary to Thomas Becket, 'a literal interpretation should be fertile, in the sense that it leads to a spiritual understanding of the text' – not purely 'carnal', that is, literal in a deadly-dull sense. See Eva De Visscher, *Reading the Rabbis: Christian Hebraism in the Works of Herbert of Bosham* (Leiden and Boston: Brill, 2014), p. 189.
57. Erwin I. J. Rosenthal, 'The Exposition and Exegesis of Scripture: The Study of the Bible in Medieval Judaism', in *Cambridge History of the Bible*, vol. 2, pp. 252–79, at p. 254.

58. Quoted in Lesley Smith, 'The Rewards of Faith: Nicholas of Lyra on Ruth', in Krey and Smith (eds), *Nicholas of Lyra*, pp. 45–58, at p. 53.
59. Van Liere, *An Introduction to the Medieval Bible*, p. 127.
60. See Jane Dammen McAuliffe, Barry D. Walfish and Joseph W. Goering (eds), *With Reverence for the Word: Medieval Scriptural Exegesis in Judaism, Christianity, and Islam* (Oxford: Oxford University Press, 2003), and Michael A. Signer and John van Engen (eds), *Jews and Christians in Twelfth-Century Europe* (Notre Dame, Ind.: University of Notre Dame Press, 2001).
61. Smalley, *Study*, p. 43.
62. Ibid., pp. 43–4.
63. See De Visscher, *Reading the Rabbis*; also her article 'Cross-Religious Learning and Teaching', in Piet van Boxel and Sabine Arndt (eds), *Crossing Borders: Hebrew Manuscripts as a Meeting Place for Cultures* (Oxford: Bodleian Library, 2009), pp. 123–32.
64. See Pentiuc, *The Old Testament in Eastern Orthodox Tradition*, pp. 199–262.

16. THE REFORMATION AND ITS READINGS

1. The best general history of the Reformation in English is Diarmaid MacCulloch, *Reformation: Europe's House Divided, 1490–1700* (London: Allen Lane, 2003).
2. On Waldes see G. R. Evans, 'Scriptural Interpretation in Pre-Reformation Dissident Movements', in Sæbø (ed.), *Hebrew Bible/Old Testament*, vol. 2, pp. 295–318, especially pp. 296–302.
3. Evans, 'Scriptural Interpretation', p. 304.
4. For a recent biography and evaluation of Luther see Lyndal Roper, *Martin Luther: Renegade and Prophet* (London: The Bodley Head, 2016).
5. See Chapter 7.
6. See Siegfried Raeder, 'The Exegetical and Hermeneutical Work of Martin Luther', in Sæbø (ed.), *Hebrew Bible/Old Testament*, vol. 2, pp. 363–406, at p. 374.
7. Luther also describes the theme of the Bible as *homo peccati reus ac perditus et Deus justificans ac salvator*, 'the guilty and lost human being and God who justifies and saves'.
8. *De servo arbitrio*, 606, in E. Gordon Rupp and Philip S. Watson (eds and trans.), *Luther and Erasmus: Free Will and Salvation*, Library of Christian Classics 17 (London: SCM Press, 1969). Detailed discussion of the perspicuity of Scripture in Luther can be found in F. Beisser, *Claritas scripturae bei Martin Luther*, Forschungen zur Kirchen- und Dogmengeschichte 18 (Göttingen: Vandenhoeck & Ruprecht, 1966), and O. Kuss, 'Über die Klarheit der Schrift: Historische und hermeneutische Überlegungen zu der Kontroverse des Erasmus und des Luther über den freien oder versklavten Willen', in *Theologie und Glaube*, 60 (1970), pp. 273–321, reprinted in J. Ernst (ed.), *Schriftauslegung: Beiträge zur Hermeneutik des Neuen Testamentes und im Neuen Testament* (Munich: Schöningh, 1972), pp. 89–149.

9. Luther, *Preface to the New Testament* (1522): 'St. John's Gospel and his first epistle, St. Paul's epistles, especially Romans, Galatians, and Ephesians, and St. Peter's first epistle are the books that show you Christ and teach you all that is necessary and salvatory for you to know, even if you were never to see or hear any other book or doctrine': see Westerholm and Westerholm, *Reading Sacred Scripture*, p. 217.
10. Basil Hall, 'Biblical Scholarship: Editions and Commentaries', in S. L. Greenslade (ed.), *The Cambridge History of the Bible*, vol. 3: *The West from the Reformation to the Present Day* (Cambridge: Cambridge University Press, 1963), pp. 38–93, at p. 86.
11. Alan of Lille, *De fide catholica*, 1:30, PL 210, p. 333: see Smith, 'The Rewards of Faith', p. 57. The saying is attributed to a number of other people, too.
12. See Raeder, 'Exegetical and Hermeneutical Work', p. 375.
13. See Hans Volz et al., 'Continental Versions to *c.* 1600: German Versions', in *Cambridge History of the Bible*, vol. 3, pp. 94–140, at p. 96.
14. See especially Jon D. Levenson, *The Hebrew Bible, the Old Testament, and Historical Criticism: Jews and Christians in Biblical Studies* (Louisville, Ky.: Westminster John Knox Press, 1993).
15. Letter to Wolfgang Capito, cited in Raeder, 'Exegetical and Hermeneutical Work', p. 370.
16. Cf. Peter Opitz, 'The Exegetical and Hermeneutical Work of John Oecolampadius, Huldrych Zwingli, and John Calvin', in Sæbø (ed.), *Hebrew Bible/ Old Testament*, vol. 2, pp. 407–51, at p. 433.
17. Calvin, *Commentary on Isaiah*, at Isaiah 6:3.
18. Ibid., at Luke 8:19.
19. See Westerholm and Westerholm, *Reading Sacred Scripture*, p. 263.
20. See MacCulloch, *Reformation*, p. 704.
21. See Hall, 'Biblical Scholarship, pp. 38–93.
22. The Psalms, indeed, were the material for the earliest surviving (datable) book, printed at Mainz in 1457 in Latin: see MacCulloch, *Reformation*, p. 73.
23. The second edition formed the basis for nearly all modern printed Hebrew Bibles, including the scholarly *Biblia Hebraica* editions 1 and 2; for the third edition there was a move to the Leningrad or St Petersburg Codex as the norm.
24. This development is traced in detail in Ehrman, *The Orthodox Corruption of Scripture*.
25. For more on the printing and diffusion of Bibles during the Reformation see M. H. Black, 'The Printed Bible', in *Cambridge History of the Bible*, vol. 3, pp. 408–75.

17. SINCE THE ENLIGHTENMENT

1. See the discussion in Steven Nadler, *A Book Forged in Hell: Spinoza's Scandalous Treatise and the Birth of the Secular Age* (Princeton and Oxford: Princeton University Press, 2011).

2. See Jonathan Israel (ed.), *Spinoza: Theological-Political Treatise* (Cambridge: Cambridge University Press, 2007), pp. 33–4.
3. Such matters had been discussed by Thomas Hobbes in England in *Leviathan* (1651), but not taken as far as Spinoza presses them.
4. But see Friedman, *Who Wrote the Bible?*, especially pp. 223–5, who supports Spinoza in seeing Ezra as the compiler – though of already much-edited material.
5. Spinoza's motivation in questioning the authorship of biblical books was ultimately political: 'By showing that the Bible is not, in fact, the work of a supernatural God – "a message for mankind sent down by God from heaven", as Spinoza mockingly puts it – but a perfectly natural human document; that the author of the Pentateuch is not Moses; that Hebrew Scripture as a whole is but a compilation of writings composed by fallible and not particularly learned individuals under various historical and political circumstances; that most of these writings were transmitted over generations, to be finally redacted by a latter-day political and religious leader – in short, by naturalizing the Torah and the other books of the Bible and reducing them to ordinary (though morally valuable) works of literature, Spinoza hopes to undercut ecclesiastic influence in politics and other domains and weaken the sectarian dangers facing his beloved Republic': Nadler, *A Book Forged in Hell*, p. 111.
6. See Lorenzo Valla, *De falso credita et ementita Constantini donatione declamatio*, in Christopher B. Coleman, *The Treatise of Lorenzo Valla on the Donation of Constantine* (Toronto: University of Toronto Press in association with the Renaissance Society of America Press, 1993).
7. Israel (ed.), *Spinoza: Theological-Political Treatise*, pp. 33–4.
8. 'He contends that reconstructing the historical context and especially the belief system of a given era is always the essential first and most important step to a correct understanding of any text': Jonathan Israel, Introduction to Israel (ed.), *Spinoza: Theological-Political Treatise*, p. x.
9. Though it was anticipated by Johannes Kepler (1571–1630), who regarded the biblical texts as reflecting the thought-world of the time (and hence as offering no objection to a modern scientific understanding of the universe): see Charlotte Methuen, 'On the Threshold of a New Age: Expanding Horizons as the Broader Context of Scriptural Interpretation', in Sæbø (ed.), *Hebrew Bible/Old Testament*, vol. 2, pp. 665–90, at p. 672.
10. Israel (ed.), *Spinoza: Theological-Political Treatise*, p. 65.
11. Ibid., pp. 155–6.
12. Ibid., p. 103.
13. L. Geldsetzer (ed.), M. Flacius Illyricus, *De ratione cognoscendi sacras literas* (Düsseldorf: Stern Verlag, 1968), p. 97.
14. Hooker, *Of the Laws of Ecclesiastical Polity*, 3:5.
15. Israel (ed.), *Spinoza: Theological-Political Treatise*, p. 100.
16. Ibid., p. 101.
17. See James Barr, 'Jowett and the Reading of the Bible "Like Any Other Book"', *Horizons in Biblical Theology: An International Dialogue*, 4/2–5/1

(1983), pp. 1–44; reprinted in John Barton (ed.), *Bible and Interpretation: The Collected Essays of James Barr*, vol. 1: *Interpretation and Theology* (Oxford: Oxford University Press, 2013), pp. 169–97. Jowett thought, however, that when we did this, we should come to see that the Bible was *not* like any other book.

18. See Israel (ed.), *Spinoza: Theological-Political Treatise*, p. 78.
19. Ibid., p. 168.
20. Nadler, *A Book Forged in Hell*, p. 120.
21. See W. Neil, 'The Criticism and Theological Use of the Bible, 1700–1950', in *Cambridge History of the Bible*, vol.3, pp. 238–93, especially pp. 245–6.
22. Matthew Tindal, *Christianity as Old as the Creation* (London, 1730), p. 186.
23. See Barr, *Fundamentalism*, especially pp. 72–85.
24. Richard Simon, *Histoire critique du Vieux Testament* (Paris, 1678).
25. On the Catholic background of early biblical criticism see P. J. Lambe, 'Critics and Skeptics in the Seventeenth-Century Republic of Letters', *Harvard Theological Review*, 81 (1988), pp. 271–96.
26. John Rogerson, in Rogerson, Rowland and Lindars (eds), *The Study and Use of the Bible*, p. 107.
27. See John H. Hayes, 'Historical Criticism of the Old Testament Canon', in Sæbø (ed.), *Hebrew Bible/Old Testament*, vol. 2, pp. 985–1005, esp. pp. 995–1005.
28. See above, Chapter 7.
29. Albert Schweitzer, *The Quest of the Historical Jesus* (Minneapolis: Fortress Press, 2001; the original was called *Von Reimarus zu Wrede: Eine Geschichte der Leben-Jesu-Forschung* ['From Reimarus to Wrede: a history of research into the life of Jesus'], Tübingen: Mohr Siebeck, 1906).
30. Robert Morgan with John Barton, *Biblical Interpretation*, The Oxford Bible Series (Oxford: Oxford University Press, 1988), p. 55.
31. Translated into English by the novelist George Eliot.
32. Quoted from the 1973 English edition of D. F. Strauss, *The Life of Jesus, Critically Examined* (London: SCM Press), p. 757; see Morgan with Barton, *Biblical Interpretation*, p. 45.
33. See Lothar Perlitt, *Vatke und Wellhausen: Geschichtsphilosophische Voraussetzungen und historiographische Motive für die Darstellung der Religion und Geschichte Israels durch Wilhelm Vatke und Julius Wellhausen* (Berlin: A. Töpelmann, 1965).
34. Baur is associated with the rise of a distinctive 'Tübingen school' in New Testament studies, whose other members included Eduard Zeller, Albrech Ritschl and Adolf Hilgenfeld, all taking their cue from Strauss's anti-supernaturalism. Baur's argument, in 1885, that the Pastoral Letters (1 and 2 Timothy and Titus) were non-Pauline was seen as an attack on biblical inspiration. See Horton Harris, *The Tübingen School: A Historical and Theological Investigation of the School of F. C. Baur* (Oxford: Oxford University Press, 1975; second edition Leicester: Apollos, 1990).
35. On 1 John 5:7–8, containing the so-called Johannine comma, see Chapter 16.

36. From the Preface to *The Form and Manner of Making, Ordaining, and Consecrating of Bishops, Priests, and Deacons according to the Order of the Church of England*, usually bound together with the 1662 Book of Common Prayer.
37. On the argument that episcopacy is essential to the Church see Mark D. Chapman, *The Fantasy of Reunion* (Oxford: Oxford University Press, 2014).
38. Owen Chadwick, *The Victorian Church, Part Two: 1860–1901* (London: SCM Press, 1972), p. 2.
39. Philip Kennedy, *A Modern Introduction to Theology: New Questions for Old Beliefs* (London and New York: I. B. Tauris, 2006), p. 235.
40. See Barr, *Fundamentalism*, pp. 85–9.
41. See Sanders, *The Historical Figure of Jesus* for a masterly survey of the whole issue. For earlier phases, see Robert Morgan, 'Jesus', in Barton (ed.), *The Biblical World*; for recent developments, Theissen and Winter, *The Quest for the Plausible Jesus*. There is a brief summary in my own *The Bible: The Basics* (Abingdon and New York: Routledge, 2010).
42. For the eschatological prophet, the work of E. P. Sanders is central: see also Gerd Theissen, *The Shadow of the Galilean: The Quest of the Historical Jesus in Narrative Form* (London: SCM Press, 1982), and the many works of N. T. Wright, who argues that Jesus' role was to initiate the kingdom of God – understood in earthly terms – but involving such a transformation of society that it represented the breaking in of a new divine order. In Jesus, the destiny of Israel was finally to be fulfilled. For Jesus as a wisdom teacher, entirely unconcerned with eschatology, see John Dominic Crossan, *In Parables: The Challenge of the Historical Jesus* (New York: Harper & Row, 1973). For a survey of the debate see Marcus Borg, *Jesus in Contemporary Scholarship* (Valley Forge, Pa.: Trinity Press International, 1994).
43. Bright, *A History of Israel*.
44. See Hans Heinrich Schmid, *Der sogenannte Jahwist: Beobachtungen und Fragen zur Pentateuchforschung* (Zurich: Theologischer Verlag, 1976); Van Seters, *Abraham in History and Tradition*.
45. See the discussion in Ernest Nicholson, *Deuteronomy and the Judaean Diaspora* (Oxford: Oxford University Press, 2014).
46. This is especially characteristic of the so-called Copenhagen school: Niels Peter Lemche, Thomas L. Thompson and Philip R. Davies. See especially Thompson, *The Bible in History*.
47. C. H. Dodd, *The Interpretation of the Fourth Gospel* (Cambridge: Cambridge University Press, 1953), and especially *Historical Tradition in the Fourth Gospel* (Cambridge: Cambridge University Press, 1963).
48. This line of thought began in his *Biblical Theology in Crisis* (Philadelphia: Westminster Press, 1970), and continued in a long line of further publications, including the influential *Introduction to the Old Testament as Scripture* (London: SCM Press, 1979).
49. Theological interpretation, in this technical sense, has had its own journal, the *Journal of Theological Interpretation*, since 2007.

50. Alter, *The Art of Biblical Narrative*; *The Art of Biblical Poetry*.
51. Frank Kermode, *The Genesis of Secrecy: On the Interpretation of Narrative* (Cambridge, Mass. and London: Harvard University Press, 1979).
52. Robert Alter and Frank Kermode (eds), *The Literary Guide to the Bible* (Cambridge, Mass.: Harvard University Press, 1987).
53. E. S. Bates, *The Bible Designed to Be Read as Literature* (London: Heinemann, 1937).
54. See Yvonne Sherwood (ed.), *Derrida's Bible (Reading a Page of Scripture with a Little Help from Derrida)* (New York and Basingstoke: Palgrave Macmillan, 2004).
55. See Terry Eagleton, *Literary Theory: An Introduction* (Oxford: Blackwell, 2008, anniversary edition).
56. On whom see especially Anthony C. Thiselton, *New Horizons in Hermeneutics: The Theory and Practice of Transforming Biblical Reading* (Grand Rapids, Mich.: Zondervan, twentieth anniversary edition 2013).
57. See particularly Joel S. Baden, *J, E, and the Redaction of the Pentateuch* (Tübingen: Mohr Siebeck, 2009) for a survey of current trends as well as an argument for the continuing importance of the traditional Pentateuchal sources.

18. TRANSLATING THE BIBLE

1. *The Translators to the Reader*, preface to the King James Version of the Bible (1611); composed by Miles Smith.
2. I think, for example, of David Mach's exhibition *Precious Light* in Edinburgh in 2011.
3. See especially Matthew Black, *An Aramaic Approach to the Gospels and Acts* (Oxford: Clarendon Press, third edition 1967; first edition 1946).
4. 4QJerb, d.
5. On the Greek Bible see the very accessible book by Timothy Michael Law, *When God Spoke Greek: The Septuagint and the Making of the Christian Bible* (New York and Oxford: Oxford University Press, 2013).
6. On all this see J. Schaper, *Eschatology in the Greek Psalter*, Wissenschaftliche Untersuchungen zum Neuen Testament 2:76 (Tübingen: Mohr Siebeck, 1995).
7. On these developments see Law, *When God Spoke Greek*, pp. 77–9.
8. See E. F. Sutcliffe, 'Jerome', *Cambridge History of the Bible*, vol. 2, pp. 80–101, at p. 95.
9. See Étan Levine, 'The Targums: Their Interpretative Character and Their Place in Jewish Text Tradition', in Magne Sæbø (ed.), *Hebrew Bible/Old Testament: The History of Its Interpretation*, vol. 1/1 (Göttingen: Vandenhoeck & Ruprecht, 1996), pp. 323–31.
10. Not to be confused with Targum Pseudo-Jonathan, a probably much later targum of the Pentateuch originally known as Targum Yerushalmi ('the Jerusalem Targum').

11. See J. Stenning, *The Targum of Isaiah* (Oxford: Clarendon Press, 1949).
12. See van Liere, *Introduction to the Medieval Bible*, p. 83. Another recently discovered witness to the Old Latin is the commentary of Fortunatianus of Aquileia on the Gospels, from the first half of the fourth century CE. It was found by Lukas J. Dorfbauer in the cathedral library in Cologne, and is now available in an English translation: see H. A. G. Houghton (trans.) in association with Lukas J. Dorfbauer, *Fortunatianus of Aquileia: Commentary on the Gospels* (Berlin: W. de Gruyter, 2017). The text on which Fortunatianus comments is the Old Latin – he wrote before Jerome's translation was made.
13. Some other early Christian scholars knew at least some Hebrew: see Pentiuc, *The Old Testament in Eastern Orthodox Tradition*, p. 323. As well as Origen, Theodoret of Cyrus (393–457 CE) and Procopius of Gaza (465–528 CE) may have known some Hebrew, and both show awareness that the Greek Bible is a translation.
14. Sutcliffe, 'Jerome', pp. 99–100. The Gallican Psalter is Jerome's translation of the Psalms from the Greek, sometimes corrected with reference to the Hebrew. Jerome did indeed revise the whole New Testament, but it was probably only the Gospels to which he made extensive changes in the light of the Greek: the rest of the New Testament is widely thought to be substantially the Old Latin version, only lightly revised.
15. MacCulloch, *Reformation*, p. 73, following a suggestion by Bernard Cottret.
16. Ibid., p. 203.
17. Jacob van Liesfeldt of Antwerp suffered the same fate for his Dutch translation, largely based on Luther, of 1526, again mainly because of the many Protestant notes he added.
18. 'Whereas on [the title page of] the Coverdale Bible a small Henry VIII distributed Bibles to the clergy, in the Great Bible a large Henry VIII distributes Bibles to clergy and laity alike' (Campbell, *Bible*, p. 23), indicating the decisive shift towards seeing the Bible as reading matter for all during the few years involved.
19. One section of Coverdale's Bible remains in use to this day, the Psalms, which have been printed in the English Book of Common Prayer from 1549 to the present, and continue to be sung in the Church of England, especially in cathedrals, and in Anglican churches throughout the world. The translation is often inaccurate, but the language is evocative and rhythmically excellent.
20. For details of early Reformation-period translations into European languages see the article 'Continental Versions to *c.* 1600' (by various authors), in *Cambridge History of the Bible*, vol. 3, pp. 94–140.
21. Nevertheless, its royal patronage caused it to be disliked by the Pilgrim Fathers, who tended to use the Geneva Bible, the marginal notes of which in any case better suited their theology: see Harry S. Stout, 'Word and Order in Colonial New England', in N. O. Hatch and M. A. Noll (eds), *The Bible in America: Essays in Cultural History* (New York: Oxford University Press, 1982), pp. 19–38.

22. It is often said that the KJV/AV had a large impact on subsequent English, as Luther's Bible did on German; but in fact this is questionable, as argued persuasively by C. S. Lewis, 'The Literary Impact of the Authorized Version', in his collection *They Asked for a Paper* (London: Geoffrey Bles, 1962), pp. 26–50 – originally the Ethel M. Wood Lecture, delivered in London in 1950. Even where the Bible had some such influence, it was not the KJV/AV specifically that did so.
23. For the details of these developments see Campbell, *Bible*, pp. 212–35.
24. The absence of the Apocrypha from most editions of the KJV/AV that are readily available results ultimately from the decision of the British and Foreign Bible Society in 1826 to stop printing it, on religious grounds. Until then it had been normal for Bibles to include it, and readings from it were prescribed in the Church of England until the late twentieth century, when the custom arose of providing alternatives from the canonical Old Testament when the Apocrypha occurred in the Church lectionary. So far as I know, this momentous change took place silently and without debate.
25. Berlin and Brettler (eds), *The Jewish Study Bible*.
26. See Martin Buber and Franz Rosenzweig, *Die fünf Bücher der Weisung* (Cologne and Olten: Hegner, 1968).
27. There is an anticipation of modern 'imitative' translation in the work of Sebastian Castellio, published in 1555 at Basel. He too invents (in his case, French) words to capture the foreignness of the original languages – thus *arrière-femme* for 'concubine'. One could even say that Aquila, early in the Common Era, was practising imitative translation in his extreme literalism.
28. See André Chouraqui, *La Bible* (Paris: Desclée de Brouwer, 2003).
29. Everett Fox, *The Five Books of Moses* (New York: Schocken Books, 1983).
30. Ibid., p. xi.
31. See Robert Alter, *The Five Books of Moses: A Translation with Commentary* (New York: Norton, 2004); *Ancient Israel: The Former Prophets – Joshua, Judges, Samuel, and Kings – A Translation with Commentary* (New York: Norton, 2013); *The David Story: A Translation with Commentary of 1 and 2 Samuel* (New York: Norton, 1999); *Strong as Death is Love: The Song of Songs, Ruth, Esther, Jonah, and Daniel – A Translation with Commentary* (New York: Norton, 2015).
32. See S. L. Greenslade, 'English Versions of the Bible, 1525–1611', *Cambridge History of the Bible*, vol. 3, pp. 141–74, at p. 146.
33. Ibid., p. 165.
34. See the discussion in Campbell, *Bible*, pp. 264–70.

CONCLUSION: THE BIBLE AND FAITH

1. *The Translators to the Reader*, composed by Miles Smith.
2. Thomas Cranmer, *A Fruitful Exhortation to the Reading and Knowledge of Holy Scripture*, published in the *First Book of Homilies*, of which the most

recent edition is London: SPCK, 1908. See the use made of this image in John Muddiman, *The Bible: Fountain and Well of Truth* (Oxford: Blackwell, 1983).

3. See Géza Vermes, *Christian Beginnings: From Nazareth to Nicaea, AD 30–325* (London: Allen Lane, 2012).
4. See my discussion of this in Barton, *The Nature of Biblical Criticism.*
5. In 2 Peter 1:21 we also read that 'no prophecy ever came by human will, but men and women moved by the Holy Spirit spoke from God'.
6. Pontifical Biblical Commission, *The Inspiration and Truth of Sacred Scripture: The Word that Comes from God and Speaks of God for the Salvation of the World* (Collegeville, Minn.: Liturgical Press, 2014), p. 2.
7. Ibid., p. 157.
8. Ibid., p.5.
9. J. A. Quenstedt, *Theologia didactico-polemica* (1685), 1:72; quoted in J. K. S. Reid, *The Authority of Scripture: A Study of the Reformation and Post-Reformation Understanding of the Bible* (London: Methuen, 1957), p. 85.
10. See note 1 above.
11. See Barr, *Fundamentalism*, pp. 40–55.
12. See James T. Burtchaell, *Catholic Theories of Biblical Inspiration since 1810: A Review and Critique* (Cambridge: Cambridge University Press, 1969), pp. 164–229.
13. Ibid., p. 223.
14. *Inspiration and Truth*, p. 140.
15. Ibid., p. 146.
16. Ibid., p. 74.
17. Cited in Daniélou, *Origen*, p. 180: see also the discussion in Lawton, *Faith, Text and History*, p. 22.
18. Pentiuc, *The Old Testament in Eastern Orthodox Tradition*, pp. 164–5, quoting John Breck, *Scripture in Tradition: The Bible and Its Interpretation in the Orthodox Church* (Crestwood, NY: St Vladimir's Seminary Press, 2001).
19. Pentiuc, *The Old Testament in Eastern Orthodox Tradition*, p. 165.
20. This idea appears in 1 Peter 3:19–20 but nowhere else in the Bible; yet it is one of the articles of the so-called Apostles' Creed, used in many Christian churches.
21. Austin Farrer, *A Science of God?* (London: SPCK, 2009, originally published in 1966), p. 119.
22. Hooker, *Of the Laws of Ecclesiastical Polity*, 2:8.

Further Reading

An overall guide to the history of the Bible is provided by the three volumes of *The Cambridge History of the Bible*, ed. P. R. Ackroyd, C. F. Evans, G. W. H. Lampe and S. L. Greenslade (Cambridge: Cambridge University Press, 1963–1970). An update is available in the four volumes of *The New Cambridge History of the Bible*, ed. J. C. Paget, J. Schaper, R. Marsden, E. A. Matter, E. Cameron and J. Riches (Cambridge: Cambridge University Press, 2012–17). These are invaluable guides to how the Bible was ordered, canonized and read, but offer only sketchy material about its origins, which I have dealt with in more detail. For guides to the Bible's faiths see M. Goodman, *A History of Judaism* (London: Allen Lane, 2017), and D. MacCulloch, *A History of Christianity: The First Three Thousand Years* (London: Allen Lane, 2009).

K. Armstrong, *The Bible: The Biography* (London: Atlantic Books, 2007) provides an excellent and highly readable introduction to the contents and formation of the Bible as well as its influence. A. N. Wilson, *The Book of the People: How to Read the Bible* (London: Atlantic Books, 2015) presents some of the Bible's major themes and reflects on its relation to history. It is particularly interesting on the quest for the historical Jesus, on which it is sceptical, but in a constructive way.

INTRODUCTION: THE BIBLE TODAY

The place of the Bible in modern culture was discussed in J. Barr, *The Bible in the Modern World* (London: SCM Press, 1973), which is still not out of date; for a useful reader of relevant authors see R. A. Harrisville and W. Sundberg, *The Bible in Modern Culture* (Grand Rapids, Mich. and Cambridge: W. B. Eerdmans, second edition 2002). For popular culture see K. Edwards, *Admen and Eve: The Bible in Contemporary Advertising* (The Bible in the Modern World 48) (Sheffield: Sheffield Phoenix Press, 2012) and, edited by K. Edwards, *Rethinking Biblical Literacy* (London and New York: Bloomsbury, 2015). For a brief introduction to critical and traditional ways of reading the Bible see J. Barton, *The Bible: The Basics* (Abingdon and New York: Routledge, 2010).

I. ANCIENT ISRAEL: HISTORY AND LANGUAGE

There are many histories of ancient Israel, from the very traditional (e.g. I. Provan, V. P. Long and T. Longman III, *A Biblical History of Israel* (Louisville, Ky.:

Westminster John Knox Press, 2003)) to the frankly revisionist (e.g. T. L. Thompson, *The Bible in History: How Writers Create a Past* (London: Jonathan Cape, 1999)). In this chapter I have tried to take an intermediate position, following such works as H. G. M. Williamson (ed.), *Understanding the History of Ancient Israel* (Oxford: Oxford University Press, 2007).

For ancient literacy, a good guide is W. M. Schniedewind, *How the Bible Became a Book: The Textualization of Ancient Israel* (Cambridge: Cambridge University Press, 2004).

An excellent treatment of the development of Hebrew can be found in A. Sáenz-Badillos, *A History of the Hebrew Language* (Cambridge: Cambridge University Press, 1993).

The question of terminology (Old Testament, Hebrew Bible, or something else) is much discussed, and an accessible account is J. J. Collins, *Hebrew Bible or Old Testament? Studying the Bible in Judaism and Christianity* (Notre Dame, Ind.: University of Notre Dame Press, 1990). My own thoughts on it can be found in J. Barton (ed.), *The Hebrew Bible: A Critical Companion* (Princeton and Oxford: Princeton University Press, 2016), pp. 5–6, and also in J. Barton, *The Old Testament: Canon, Literature and Theology: Collected Works of John Barton* (Aldershot: Ashgate, 2007), pp. 83–9.

2. HEBREW NARRATIVE

A useful guide to narrative, focused on recent investigations, is T. B. Dozeman, T. Römer and K. Schmid (eds), *Pentateuch, Hexateuch, or Enneateuch? Identifying Literary Works in Genesis through Kings* (Ancient Israel and its Literature 8) (Atlanta: Society of Biblical Literature, 2011). For a readable introduction to the study of the Pentateuch there is J. L. Ska, *Introduction to Reading the Pentateuch* (Winona Lake, Ind.: Eisenbrauns, 2006); even more reader-friendly is J. Blenkinsopp, *The Pentateuch: An Introduction to the First Five Books of the Bible* (New Haven, Conn.: Yale University Press, 1992).

For other narrative works in the Old Testament a general guide, in touch with modern literary theory, is D. M. Gunn and D. N. Fewell, *Narrative in the Hebrew Bible* (Oxford: Oxford University Press, 1993). S. Japhet, *The Ideology of the Book of Chronicles and Its Place in Biblical Thought* (Frankfurt am Main: Peter Lang, 1997) offers an account of the religious ideas in the often-neglected books of 1 and 2 Chronicles. Readers with a more literary bent will find much of interest in the lively work by C. J. Sharp, *Irony and Meaning in the Hebrew Bible* (Bloomington, Ind.: Indiana University Press, 2009). A more popular account of biblical narrative, attractively presented, is J. Magonet, *Bible Lives* (London: SCM Press, 1992).

There is an enormous literature on the 'Deuteronomistic History' (Joshua, Judges, Samuel and Kings), beginning with the seminal study by M. Noth, *The Deuteronomistic History* (Sheffield: JSOT Press, 1991, from the German of 1943); a sound guide to the debate is T. Römer, *The So-Called Deuteronomistic History:*

A Sociological, Historical and Literary Introduction (London: T&T Clark and New York: Continuum, 2007). See also T. Römer, 'The Narrative Books of the Hebrew Bible', in J. Barton (ed.), *The Hebrew Bible: A Critical Companion* (Princeton and Oxford: Princeton University Press, 2016), pp. 109–32.

3. LAW AND WISDOM

An excellent guide to the wisdom literature of the Hebrew Bible is K. J. Dell, *Get Wisdom, Get Insight: An Introduction to Israel's Wisdom Literature* (London: Darton, Longman & Todd, 2000). The classic work, still very useful, especially on the theological aspects of wisdom, is G. von Rad, *Wisdom in Israel* (London: SCM Press, 1972). The ancient Near Eastern background can be studied in R. J. Clifford, *The Wisdom Literature* (Nashville, Tenn.: Abingdon Press, 1998). P. S. Fiddes, *Seeing the World and Knowing God: Hebrew Wisdom in a Late-Modern Context* (Oxford: Oxford University Press, 2013) makes connections with 'wisdom' today. A good short introduction to wisdom is J. Grillo, 'The Wisdom Literature', in J. Barton (ed.), *The Hebrew Bible: A Critical Companion* (Princeton and Oxford: Princeton University Press, 2016), pp. 182–205. There are useful articles on various aspects of the wisdom literature in J. Jarick (ed.), *Perspectives on Israelite Wisdom: Proceedings of the Oxford Old Testament Seminar* (London: Bloomsbury T&T Clark, 2016).

Law in the Hebrew Bible is well introduced in R. Westbrook and B. Wells (eds), *Everyday Law in Biblical Israel: An Introduction* (Louisville, Ky.: Westminster John Knox Press, 2009). A particularly important study of Deuteronomy, drawing parallels with wisdom, is M. Weinfeld, *Deuteronomy and the Deuteronomic School* (Winona Lake, Ind.: Eisenbrauns, 1992, reprinted from 1972), and such parallels are also drawn out in respect of Exodus in B. S. Jackson, *Wisdom-Laws: A Study of the Mishpatim of Exodus 21:1–22:16* (Oxford: Oxford University Press, 2006).

Ancient Near Eastern law codes and wisdom texts can be found conveniently in J. B. Pritchard (ed.), *Ancient Near Eastern Texts Relating to the Old Testament* (Princeton: Princeton University Press, third edition 1969); a more up-to-date version is W. W. Hallo and K. L. Younger, *The Context of Scripture: Canonical Compositions, Monumental Inscriptions, and Archival Documents from the Biblical World* (Leiden and Boston: Brill, 2003, 3 vols).

For understanding the meaning of *torah* in ancient Israel and in Judaism, a helpful guide is Yochanan Muffs, *Love and Joy: Language and Religion in Ancient Israel* (New York: Jewish Theological Seminary of America, 1992). For an anthropological perspective on law in the Hebrew Bible the work of Mary Douglas is significant: see especially the classic *Purity and Danger: An Analysis of Concepts of Pollution and Taboo* (New York: Routledge, 2003, originally published in 1966) and *Leviticus as Literature* (Oxford: Oxford University Press, 1999).

A helpful short guide to law in the Hebrew Bible is A. Bartor, 'Legal Texts', in Barton (ed.), *The Hebrew Bible: A Critical Companion*, pp. 160–81.

4. PROPHECY

The most up-to-date book on prophecy in the Hebrew Bible is M. Nissinen, *Ancient Prophecy: Near Eastern, Biblical, and Greek Perspectives* (Oxford: Oxford University Press, 2017); see also M. Nissinen (ed.), *Prophecy in its Ancient Near Eastern Context: Mesopotamian, Biblical, and Arabian Perspectives* (Atlanta, Ga.: Society of Biblical Literature, 2000). Nissinen's work stresses the continuities between biblical and other ancient prophecy, and this is the general trend in modern study of the prophets. This can be seen in a short format in R. G. Kratz, *The Prophets of Israel* (Winona Lake, Ind.: Eisenbrauns, 2015), in which a strong distinction is also made between the prophets and the prophetic books – a point also emphasized in his short introduction 'The Prophetic Literature', in J. Barton (ed.), *The Hebrew Bible: A Critical Companion* (Princeton and Oxford, 2016), pp. 133–59. For an older view, that Israelite prophets were highly distinctive against their ancient background, see some of the essays in John Day (ed.), *Prophecy and Prophets in Ancient Israel: Proceedings of the Oxford Old Testament Seminar*, Library of the Hebrew Bible/Old Testament Studies 531 (New York and London: T&T Clark, 2010); and also the short classic by E. W. Heaton, *The Old Testament Prophets: A Short Introduction* (Oxford: Oneworld, 2001, from 1961). One of the best accounts of the whole field is J. Blenkinsopp, *A History of Prophecy in Israel* (Louisville, Ky.: Westminster John Knox Press, second edition 1996).

How the prophets were seen in ancient Judaism is the focus of J. Barton, *Oracles of God: Perceptions of Ancient Prophecy in Israel after the Exile* (Oxford and New York: Oxford University Press, second edition 2007). And for prophecy that persisted into the Second Temple period see M. H. Floyd and R. D. Haak (eds), *Prophets, Prophecy, and Prophetic Texts in Second Temple Judaism*, Library of the Hebrew Bible/Old Testament Studies 427 (New York and London: T&T Clark, 2006).

A simple guide to the probable composition of the book of Isaiah is J. Barton, *Isaiah 1–39*, Old Testament Guides (London: T&T Clark, 2003); also J. Stromberg, *An Introduction to the Study of Isaiah* (London: T&T Clark, 2011), which is particularly lucid and helpful.

The standard introduction to apocalyptic literature is J. J. Collins, *The Apocalyptic Imagination: An Introduction to Jewish Apocalyptic Literature* (Grand Rapids, Mich. and Cambridge: W. B. Eerdmans, third edition 2016); also very valuable is C. Rowland, *The Open Heaven: A Study of Apocalyptic in Judaism and Early Christianity* (London: SPCK 1982), which also touches on Jewish mysticism.

5. POEMS AND PSALMS

An excellent guide for the general reader is S. E. Gillingham, *The Poems and Psalms of the Hebrew Bible* (Oxford: Oxford University Press, 1994); see also her short introduction 'Psalms and Poems of the Hebrew Bible', in J. Barton (ed.), *The Hebrew Bible: A Critical Companion* (Princeton and Oxford: Princeton University Press 2016), pp. 206–35. Another useful account, concentrating on the ancient Near Eastern background, is J. Day, *The Psalms*, Old Testament Guides (London: T&T Clark International, 2003).

For interpretations based on the 'cultic' line of thought the classic text is S. Mowinckel, *The Psalms in Israel's Worship* (Grand Rapids, Mich.: W. B. Eerdmans, 2004, originally published in 1962). Mesopotamian texts relevant to these theories can be found in J. B. Pritchard (ed.), *Ancient Near Eastern Texts Relating to the Old Testament* (Princeton: Princeton University Press, third edition 1969); a more up-to-date version is W. W. Hallo and K. L. Younger, *The Context of Scripture: Canonical Compositions, Monumental Inscriptions, and Archival Documents from the Biblical World* (Leiden and Boston: Brill, 2003, 3 vols).

The characteristic features of Hebrew poetry are examined in R. Alter, *The Art of Biblical Poetry* (New York: Basic Books, revised edition 2011), and J. Kugel, *The Idea of Biblical Poetry: Parallelism and Its History* (New Haven and London: Yale University Press, 1981), the latter being critical of the traditional concentration on parallelism.

An excellent commentary on the Psalms from a scholarly point of view is that by F.-L. Hossfeld and E. Zenger in the Hermeneia series (Minneapolis: Fortress Press, 2005–11); a more popular, homiletically orientated work is W. Brueggemann, *Praying the Psalms: Engaging Scripture and the Life of the Spirit* (Eugene, Ore.: Cascade Books, 2007), which rests on detailed academic study but is intended for those wishing to use the Psalms in worship. An accessible but academically credible account is offered in the three volumes of J. Goldingay's commentary, *Psalms* (Grand Rapids, Mich.: Baker Academic, 2005–9).

For the reception history of the Psalms, see S. E. Gillingham, *Psalms through the Centuries* (Oxford: Wiley Blackwell, 2008).

All aspects of the Psalms are covered in W. P. Brown (ed.), *The Oxford Handbook of the Psalms* (Oxford: Oxford University Press, 2014).

6. CHRISTIAN BEGINNINGS

An excellent guide to the origins of the Christian movement is C. Rowland, *Christian Origins: An Account of the Setting and Character of the Most Important Messianic Sect of Judaism* (London: SPCK, 1985). More idiosyncratic but significant is S. Freyne, *The Jesus Movement and Its Expansion: Meaning and Mission* (Grand Rapids, Mich.: W. B. Eerdmans, 2014). The historical background is illuminated by M. Goodman, *Rome and Jerusalem: The Clash of Ancient Civilizations* (London: Allen Lane, 2007). E. P. Sanders, *The Historical Figure of Jesus* (London: Allen Lane, 1993), offers a clear presentation of the political situation in Palestine under the Romans.

On the Hellenistic background a classic work is M. Hengel, *Judaism and Hellenism: Studies in their Encounter in Palestine during the Early Hellenistic Period* (London: SCM Press, 1974). For Philo and Josephus see M. Goodman, *A History of Judaism* (London: Allen Lane, 2017).

For some insight into the linguistic situation in Roman Palestine a good guide is W. Smelik, 'The Languages of Roman Palestine', in C. Hezser (ed.), *The Oxford*

Handbook of Daily Life in Roman Palestine (Oxford: Oxford University Press, 2010), pp. 122–44.

A straightforward introduction to the Dead Sea sect and its writings is T. H. Lim, *The Dead Sea Scrolls: A Very Short Introduction* (Oxford: Oxford University Press, second edition 2017), and a much fuller account is available in T. H. Lim and J. J. Collins (eds), *The Oxford Handbook of the Dead Sea Scrolls* (Oxford: Oxford University Press, 2010). A translation of the non-biblical texts from Qumran can be found in G. Vermes, *The Complete Dead Sea Scrolls in English* (New York and London: Allen Lane, 1997).

There is a clear account of the traditional scholarly datings and authorship of the various New Testament books in W. G. Kümmel, *Introduction to the New Testament* (London: SCM Press, second edition 1975).

7. LETTERS

Good introductions to Paul's letters are Douglas A. Campbell, *Framing Paul: An Epistolary Biography* (Grand Rapids, Mich.: W. B. Eerdmans, 2014), and J. Murphy O'Connor, *Paul: A Critical Life* (Oxford: Oxford University Press, 1997). For the difficulty of fitting Paul's letters into the framework provided by Acts the classic work is John Knox, *Chapters in a Life of Paul* (London: SCM Press, second edition 1987). An excellent guide to Paul's thought as well as to his life is D. G. Horrell, *An Introduction to the Study of Paul* (London: Bloomsbury T&T Clark, third edition 2015). Also useful, though quite complex, is M. Zetterholm, *Approaches to Paul: A Student's Guide to Recent Scholarship* (Minneapolis: Fortress Press, 2009).

Paul's theological ideas and their relationship to contemporary Judaism are the subject of E. P. Sanders, *Paul, the Law, and the Jewish People* (London: SCM Press, 1983). For a different slant, though still stressing Paul's Jewish background, see N. T. Wright, *Paul and the Faithfulness of God* (London: SPCK and Minneapolis: Fortress Press, 2013). See also H. Räisänen, *Paul and the Law* (Tübingen: Mohr, 1983). For the 'parting of the ways' between Jews and Christians a massive guide is J. D. G. Dunn, *Neither Jew nor Greek: A Contested Identity* (Grand Rapids, Mich. and Cambridge: W. B. Eerdmans, 2015).

Paul's letters were written against the background of letter-writing in the first-century world in general, and there is useful material on this in E. R. Richards, *Paul and First-Century Letter Writing: Secretaries, Composition and Collection* (Downers Grove, Ill.: InterVarsity Press, 2004), and D. Trobisch, *Paul's Letter Collection: Tracing the Origins* (Bolivar, Mo.: Quiet Waters Publications, 2001).

Pseudonymity is a highly vexed issue, as the discussion in this chapter indicates, and a standard work on it – arguing that it is simple forgery – is B. D. Ehrman, *Forgery and Counterforgery: The Use of Literary Deceit in Early Christian Polemics* (Oxford and New York: Oxford University Press, 2013). A less polemical account can be found in D. G. Meade, *Pseudonymity and Canon* (Grand Rapids, Mich.: W. B. Eerdmans, 1987).

8. GOSPELS

For anyone beginning to study the Gospels, an accessible guide is E. P. Sanders and M. Davies, *Studying the Synoptic Gospels* (London: SCM Press and Philadelphia: Trinity Press, 1989). This discusses selected passages and provides a structured study course. The classic study in English is B. H. Streeter, *The Four Gospels: A Study of Origins, Treating of the Manuscript Tradition, Sources, Authorship & Dates* (London: Macmillan, 1924), which still provides all the standard arguments in favour of the 'two-source' hypothesis. The (equally classic) study questioning the existence of Q is A. M. Farrer, 'On Dispensing with Q', in D. E. Nineham (ed.), *Studies in the Gospels in Memory of R. H. Lightfoot* (Oxford: Blackwell, 1955), pp. 55–88; the argument is developed further in M. Goodacre, *The Case against Q: Markan Priority and the Synoptic Problem* (Harrisburg, Pa.: Trinity Press International, 2002).

The Gospel according to John may be studied through R. E. Brown, *An Introduction to the Gospel of John* (New York: Doubleday, 2003), and then through his much longer *The Gospel according to John* (Garden City, NY: Doubleday, 1966–70, 2 vols). Among British contributions, C. K. Barrett, *The Gospel according to St John* (London: SPCK, second edition 1978), was an important milestone.

The question whether the Gospels represent the story of Jesus as believed only in the local community for which they were written, or rather have a universal intention, is discussed in R. Bauckham (ed.), *The Gospel for All Christians* (Grand Rapids, Mich.: W. B. Eerdmans, 1998). On the genre 'Gospel' an important guide is R. A. Burridge, *What Are the Gospels? A Comparison with Graeco-Roman Biography* (Grand Rapids, Mich.: W. B. Eerdmans, second edition 2004). F. Watson, *Gospel Writing: A Canonical Perspective* (Grand Rapids, Mich. and Cambridge: W. B. Eerdmans, 2013) is a comprehensive and well-argued guide to how the Gospels were compiled.

9. FROM BOOKS TO SCRIPTURE

An up-to-date guide to the formation of the canon of the Hebrew Bible/Old Testament is T. H. Lim, *The Formation of the Jewish Canon* (New Haven and London: Yale University Press, 2013). The relevant ancient texts for the canon of both Old and New Testaments are available in E. L. Gallagher and J. D. Meade, *The Biblical Canon Lists from Early Christianity: Texts and Analysis* (Oxford: Oxford University Press, 2017), which despite its title does also contain Jewish material. On the definition of 'canonicity' as well as reflections on the formation of both canons see J. Barton, *The Spirit and the Letter: Studies in the Biblical Canon* (London: SPCK, 1997); the American edition (Louisville, Ky.: Westminster John Knox Press, also 1997) is called *Holy Writings, Sacred Text*, but has the misleadingly restrictive subtitle *The Canon in Early Christianity.* A classic study, which dethroned the old idea that Jews in Palestine and the diaspora had different canons of the Hebrew Bible, is A. C. Sundberg Jr, *The Old Testament of the Early Church* (Cambridge, Mass.: Harvard University Press, 1964).

For a discussion of the status of various books in the community at Qumran see T. H. Lim and J. J. Collins (eds), *The Oxford Handbook of the Dead Sea Scrolls* (Oxford: Oxford University Press, 2010). A still-open question is whether we should distinguish between 'biblical' and 'non-biblical' books at Qumran – in other words, whether there was already in some sense a Bible for the sect – and this is ably discussed by M. M. Zahn, *Rethinking Rewritten Scripture: Composition and Exegesis in the 4QReworked Pentateuch Manuscripts* (Leiden: Brill, 2011).

10. CHRISTIANS AND THEIR BOOKS

For the existence of sayings collections, and on the codification of the Gospels, a good guide is F. Watson, *Gospel Writing: A Canonical Perspective* (Grand Rapids, Mich. and Cambridge: W. B. Eerdmans, 2013). The classic work on the codex form and its domination in Christian book production is C. H. Roberts with T. C. Skeat, *The Birth of the Codex* (London: Oxford University Press for the British Academy, 1987); see also the excellent discussion in H. Y. Gamble, *Books and Readers in the Early Church: A History of Early Christian Texts* (New Haven and London: Yale University Press, 1995), which also discusses the phenomenon of *nomina sacra*.

The relation of nascent Christianity to early Judaism is analysed in J. D. G. Dunn, *The Parting of the Ways between Christianity and Judaism and their Significance for the Character of Christianity* (London: SCM Press, 2006); see also J. Lieu, *Image and Reality: The Jews and the World of the Christians in the Second Century* (Edinburgh: T&T Clark, 1996). M. Goodman, *A History of Judaism* (London: Allen Lane, 2017), discusses the background of early Christianity.

An older work that examines the way in which Old Testament quotations are used, and sometimes changed, to provide backing for events in the life of Jesus or the early Church is B. Lindars, *New Testament Apologetic: The Doctrinal Significance of the Old Testament Quotations* (London: SCM Press, 1961).

For the formation of the Christian canon the standard textbook is B. M. Metzger, *The Canon of the New Testament: Its Origin, Development, and Significance* (Oxford: Clarendon Press, 1987); see also L. M. McDonald, *The Biblical Canon: Its Origin, Transmission and Authority* (Peabody, Mass.: Hendrickson, 2007), and also his more recent *The Formation of the Biblical Canon*, vol. 2: *The New Testament: Its Authority and Canonicity* (London and New York: Bloomsbury T&T Clark, 2017).

11. OFFICIAL AND UNOFFICIAL TEXTS

A thorough treatment of the Muratorian Fragment can be found in G. Hahneman, *The Muratorian Fragment and the Development of the Canon* (Oxford: Oxford University Press, 1992), which argues for a late (fourth-century) date.

There are several collections of non-canonical texts, one of the best being J. K. Elliott, *The Apocryphal New Testament: A Collection of Apocryphal Christian Literature in an English Translation Based on M. R. James* (Oxford: Oxford University Press, 1993). The *Gospel of Thomas* and other texts from Nag Hammadi can be found in M. Meyer, *The Nag Hammadi Scriptures: The Revised and Updated Translation of Sacred Gnostic Texts* (New York: HarperCollins, 2007). The *Gospel of Mary* is translated and annotated by C. Tuckett, *The Gospel of Mary* (Oxford: Oxford University Press, 2007).

The Apostolic Fathers are available in translation in A. Louth (ed.), *Early Christian Writings* (London: Penguin, second edition 1987).

12. BIBLICAL MANUSCRIPTS

The textual transmission of the New Testament is presented in detail in B. M. Metzger, *The Text of the New Testament: Its Transmission, Corruption, and Restoration* (Oxford: Oxford University Press, third edition 1992). But for a lively introduction to the issues, with worked examples, an excellent guide is D. C. Parker, *The Living Text of the Gospels* (Cambridge: Cambridge University Press, 1997). Bart Ehrman has studied ways in which orthodox scribes changed the biblical text to make it more 'sound', in B. Ehrman, *The Orthodox Corruption of Scripture: The Effect of Early Christological Controversies on the Text of the New Testament* (New York and London: Oxford University Press, second edition 2011).

The textual transmission of the Old Testament/Hebrew Bible can be studied in E. Tov, *Textual Criticism of the Hebrew Bible* (Minneapolis: Fortress Press, third edition 2012).

13. THE THEME OF THE BIBLE

Traditional Christian readings of the Bible (developed further in subsequent chapters) can be studied in F. van Liere, *An Introduction to the Medieval Bible* (Cambridge: Cambridge University Press, 2014). Eastern Orthodox Christian concerns appear in E. J. Pentiuc, *The Old Testament in Eastern Orthodox Tradition* (New York and Oxford: Oxford University Press, 2014).

Traditional Jewish approaches are described and illustrated in A. Samely, *Forms of Rabbinic Literature and Thought: An Introduction* (Oxford: Oxford University Press, 2007). For an account of a modern Jewish approach to the Bible a particularly stimulating work is B. D. Sommer, *Revelation and Authority: Sinai in Jewish Scripture and Tradition* (New Haven and London: Yale University Press, 2015).

On the possibility of a shared Jewish and Christian approach, see R. Kendall Soulen, *The God of Israel and Christian Theology* (Minneapolis: Fortress Press, 1996), which offers a Christian understanding of the Hebrew Bible that tries to avoid supersessionism. T. Frymer-Kensky et al., *Christianity in Jewish Terms* (Boulder, Co.: Westview Press, 2000), discusses how a Christian reading of the Bible looks when seen through Jewish eyes, and is a significant contribution to the attempt to find themes in the Hebrew Bible.

14. RABBIS AND CHURCH FATHERS

There is a good introduction to rabbinic methods of interpretation in A. Samely, *Forms of Rabbinic Literature and Thought: An Introduction* (Oxford: Oxford University Press, 2007). A guide to the main genres of rabbinic literature is also provided by the older work by J. Bowker, *The Targums and Rabbinic Literature: An Introduction to Jewish Interpretations of Scripture* (Cambridge: Cambridge University Press, second edition 1979). Also valuable is H. L. Strack and G. Stemberger, *Introduction to the Talmud and Midrash* (Edinburgh: T&T Clark, 1991). The Mekhilta can be found in J. Z. Lauterbach, *Mekhilta de-Rabbi Ishmael* (Philadelphia: The Jewish Publication Society of America, vol. 1, 1933).

J. Daniélou, *Origen* (London: Sheed and Ward, 1955), is an intellectual biography of Origen; for Origen's theology of the Bible an important guide is H. de Lubac, *History and Spirit: The Understanding of Scripture according to Origen* (San Francisco: Ignatius, 2007). There is much of value for the study of all the Fathers' approach to Scripture in S. Westerholm and M. Westerholm, *Reading Sacred Scripture: Voices from the History of Biblical Interpretation* (Grand Rapids, Mich.: W. B. Eerdmans, 2016); and see also H. Graf Reventlow, *History of Biblical Interpretation* (Leiden: Brill, 2010) and J. L. Kugel and R. A. Greer, *Early Biblical Interpretation* (Philadelphia: Westminster Press, 1986), which compares Christian and Jewish attitudes to the interpretation of Scripture. W. Yarchin, *History of Biblical Interpretation: A Reader* (Peabody, Mass.: Hendrickson, 2004), provides excerpts from writers of many periods, including the patristic.

On the Alexandrian and Antiochene schools a valuable study is F. Young, *Biblical Exegesis and the Formation of Christian Culture* (Cambridge: Cambridge University Press, 1997).

15. THE MIDDLE AGES

The classic study here is still B. Smalley, *The Study of the Bible in the Middle Ages* (Notre Dame, Ind.: University of Notre Dame Press, second edition 1964), on which subsequent scholarship often depends. The Bible as a physical object is the subject of C. de Hamel, *The Book: A History of the Bible* (London: Phaidon, 2001), which contains many illustrations of beautiful medieval Bibles. An introduction to medieval biblical reception and interpretation is provided by F. van Liere, *An Introduction to the Medieval Bible* (Cambridge: Cambridge University Press, 2014).

On medieval interpretation a standard work is H. de Lubac, *Mediaeval Exegesis: The Four Senses of Scripture* (Grand Rapids, Mich.: W. B. Eerdmans;

Edinburgh: T&T Clark, 2 vols, 1998 and 2000). A readable introduction to the Gloss can be found in L. Smith, *The* Glossa Ordinaria*: The Making of a Medieval Bible Commentary* (Commentaria. Sacred Texts and Their Commentaries: Jewish, Christian, and Islamic 3) (Leiden and Boston: Brill, 2009). There is no readily available edition of the Gloss itself.

E. Mroczek, *The Literary Imagination in Jewish Antiquity* (New York and Oxford: Oxford University Press, 2016), tells the story of Jewish biblical exegesis from antiquity into the Middle Ages. A guide to the complexities of the Masorah, for those with Hebrew, is P. H. Kelley, D. S. Mynatt and T. G. Crawford, *The Masorah of* Biblia Hebraica Stuttgartensia*: Introduction and Annotated Glossary* (Grand Rapids, Mich. and Cambridge: W. B. Eerdmans, 1998).

There are some good studies of Christian and Jewish readings of the Bible in J. Dammen McAuliffe, B. D. Walfish and J. W. Goering (eds), *With Reverence for the Word: Medieval Scriptural Exegesis in Judaism, Christianity, and Islam* (Oxford: Oxford University Press, 2003).

16. THE REFORMATION AND ITS READINGS

An excellent recent biography of Martin Luther is L. Roper, *Martin Luther: Renegade and Prophet* (London: The Bodley Head, 2016). For Luther's biblical exegesis there are good insights in S. Westerholm and M. Westerholm, *Reading Sacred Scripture: Voices from the History of Biblical Interpretation* (Grand Rapids, Mich.: W. B. Eerdmans, 2016). A strident criticism of Lutheran-inspired approaches to the Bible from a Jewish point of view, which anyone attracted to Luther's readings should read, is J. D. Levenson, *The Hebrew Bible, the Old Testament, and Historical Criticism: Jews and Christians in Biblical Studies* (Louisville, Ky.: Westminster John Knox Press, 1993).

There is much to be learned from D. MacCulloch, *Reformation: Europe's House Divided, 1490–1700* (London: Allen Lane, 2003), which explains the theological and political background to Reformation approaches to Scripture. *The Cambridge History of the Bible* and *The New Cambridge History of the Bible* both clarify how the Bible was read in the Reformation and Counter-Reformation.

For the Bible as a book in the Reformation context see O. O'Sullivan and E. N. Herron, *The Bible as Book: The Reformation* (New Castle, Del.: Oak Knoll Press, 2000).

On Richard Hooker's ideas about the Bible a good source is D. Eppley, *Reading the Bible with Richard Hooker* (Minneapolis: Fortress Press, 2016).

17. SINCE THE ENLIGHTENMENT

S. Nadler, *A Book Forged in Hell: Spinoza's Scandalous Treatise and the Birth of the Secular Age* (Princeton and Oxford: Princeton University Press, 2011), explains the background and essential arguments of Spinoza's *Theological-Political Treatise*. I examine some of the Enlightenment roots of modern biblical criticism in

J. Barton, *The Nature of Biblical Criticism* (Louisville, Ky.: Westminster John Knox Press, 2007), while arguing that it is not only an Enlightenment project but goes back further into antiquity. See also J. Rogerson, C. Rowland and B. Lindars, *The Study and Use of the Bible: The History of Christian Theology*, vol. 2 (Basingstoke: Marshall Pickering and Grand Rapids, Mich.: W. B. Eerdmans, 1988).

For developments in the eighteenth and nineteenth centuries see R. Morgan with J. Barton, *Biblical Interpretation*, The Oxford Bible Series (Oxford: Oxford University Press, 1988), and H. Harris, *The Tübingen School: A Historical and Theological Investigation of the School of F. C. Baur* (second edition, Leicester: Apollos, 1990).

An invaluable source for understanding attitudes to the Bible in Britain in the later nineteenth century is O. Chadwick, *The Victorian Church, Part Two: 1860–1901* (London: SCM Press, 1972). P. Kennedy, *A Modern Introduction to Theology: New Questions for Old Beliefs* (London and New York: I. B. Tauris, 2006), Chapter 11, explains the challenge of science to biblical belief succinctly.

The quests for the historical Jesus can be studied in M. Borg, *Jesus in Contemporary Scholarship* (Valley Forge, Pa.: Trinity Press International, 1994), and in E. P. Sanders, *The Historical Figure of Jesus* (London: Allen Lane, 1993).

On 'minimalism' in biblical study, an extreme, and hence very clear, statement of the issues is T. L. Thompson, *The Bible in History: How Writers Create a Past* (London: Jonathan Cape, 1999).

The best introduction to 'literary' readings of the Bible is probably R. Alter and F. Kermode (eds), *The Literary Guide to the Bible* (Cambridge, Mass.: Harvard University Press, 1987). For the more postmodern turn in such readings the clearest guide is Yvonne Sherwood: see Y. Sherwood (ed.), *Derrida's Bible (Reading a Page of Scripture with a Little Help from Derrida)* (New York and Basingstoke: Palgrave Macmillan, 2004). Hermeneutical questions are expertly handled in A. C. Thiselton, *New Horizons in Hermeneutics: The Theory and Practice of Transforming Biblical Reading* (Grand Rapids, Mich.: Zondervan, twentieth anniversary edition 2013).

18. TRANSLATING THE BIBLE

For the Greek translation of the Bible a very readable guide is T. M. Law, *When God Spoke Greek: The Septuagint and the Making of the Christian Bible* (New York and Oxford: Oxford University Press, 2013). On other versions *The Cambridge History of the Bible* provides masses of information, and on the targums see J. Bowker, *The Targums and Rabbinic Literature: An Introduction to Jewish Interpretations of Scripture* (Cambridge: Cambridge University Press, second edition 1979).

Medieval and Reformation translations are described in *The Cambridge History of the Bible* and *The New Cambridge History of the Bible*.

A number of books were published to mark the four-hundredth anniversary of the King James Bible in 2011, of which the best is G. Campbell, *Bible: The Story of the King James Version, 1611–2011* (Oxford: Oxford University Press, 2010). On American developments a good study is N. O. Hatch and M. A. Noll (eds), *The Bible in America: Essays in Cultural History* (New York: Oxford University Press, 1982).

A. Berlin and M. Z. Brettler (eds), *The Jewish Study Bible* (New York: Oxford University Press, second edition, 2014), provides a comprehensive guide to a Jewish perspective on the Hebrew Bible, together with a wealth of cultural and theological information; it uses the Jewish Publication Society translation.

CONCLUSION: THE BIBLE AND FAITH

A brief but profound guide from a Christian standpoint can be found in J. Muddiman, *The Bible: Fountain and Well of Truth* (Oxford: Blackwell, 1983). A standard work on the authority of Scripture is J. K. S. Reid, *The Authority of Scripture: A Study of the Reformation and Post-Reformation Understanding of the Bible* (London: Methuen, 1957). See also my own book, J. Barton, *People of the Book? The Authority of the Bible in Christianity* (London: SPCK, third edition, 2011).

Bibliography

Abegg Jr, Martin, Flint, Peter and Ulrich, Eugene (eds and trans.), *The Dead Sea Scrolls Bible* (San Francisco: HarperCollins, 1999).

Alter, Robert, *The Art of Biblical Narrative* (London: George Allen and Unwin, 1981).

—— *The David Story: A Translation with Commentary of 1 and 2 Samuel* (New York: Norton, 1999).

—— *The Five Books of Moses: A Translation with Commentary* (New York: Norton, 2004).

—— *The Art of Biblical Poetry* (New York: Basic Books, revised edition 2011).

—— *Ancient Israel: The Former Prophets – Joshua, Judges, Samuel, and Kings – A Translation with Commentary* (New York: Norton, 2013).

—— *Strong as Death is Love: The Song of Songs, Ruth, Esther, Jonah, and Daniel – A Translation with Commentary* (New York: Norton, 2015).

—— *The Hebrew Bible: A Translation with Commentary* (New York: Norton, 2018).

—— and Kermode, Frank (eds), *The Literary Guide to the Bible* (Cambridge, Mass.: Harvard University Press, 1987).

Apostolic Fathers, vol. 2, translated by Kirsopp Lake (London: Heinemann, 1912, reprinted 1965, Loeb Classical Library).

Ariel, Yaakov, *An Unusual Relationship: Evangelical Christians and Jews* (New York: New York University Press, 2013).

Assmann, Jan, *Ma'at: Gerechtigkeit und Unsterblichkeit im alten Ägypten* (Munich: C. H. Beck, second edition 2006).

Astley, Jeff, 'Only God Can Cure and Free Us', *Church Times*, 4 March 2016, p. 19.

Astruc, Jean, *Conjectures sur les mémoires originaux dont il paroit que Moyse s'est servi pour composer le livre de la Genèse* (1753); reprinted in P. Gibert, *Conjectures sur la Genèse* (Paris: Éditions Noésis, 1999).

Auerbach, Erich, *Mimesis: Dargestellte Wirklichkeit in der abendländischen Literatur* (Bern: Francke Verlag, second edition 1959); English version *Mimesis: The Representation of Reality in Western Literature* (Princeton: Princeton University Press, 2013).

Aune, David E., *The New Testament in Its Literary Environment* (Cambridge: James Clarke & Co., 1988).

Avis, Paul (ed.), *The History of Christian Theology*, vol. 2: John Rogerson, Christopher Rowland and Barnabas Lindars, *The Study and Use of the Bible* (Basingstoke: Marshall Pickering and Grand Rapids, Mich.: W. B. Eerdmans, 1988).

Bacon, B. W., *Studies in Matthew* (London: Constable, 1930).

Baden, Joel S., *J, E, and the Redaction of the Pentateuch* (Tübingen: Mohr Siebeck, 2009).

—— *The Composition of the Pentateuch: Renewing the Documentary Hypothesis* (New Haven and London: Yale University Press, 2012).

Barbour, Jennifer, *The Story of Israel in the Book of Qohelet: Ecclesiastes as Cultural Memory* (Oxford: Oxford University Press, 2012).

Barclay, John M. G. (trans. and ed.), *Against Apion*, vol. 10 of *Flavius Josephus* (Leiden: Brill, 2007).

Barr, James, 'Which Language Did Jesus Speak? Some Remarks of a Semitist', *Bulletin of the John Rylands Library*, 53 (1970–71), pp. 9–29; also in Barton (ed.), *Bible and Interpretation*, vol. 2: *Biblical Studies*, pp. 231–46.

—— *Fundamentalism* (London: SCM Press, 1977, second edition 1995).

—— 'A New Look at Kethibh-Qere', *Oudtestamentische Studiën*, 21 (1981), pp. 19–37, reprinted in Barton (ed.), *Bible and Interpretation*, vol. 3: *Linguistics and Translation*, pp. 445–60.

—— *Holy Scripture: Canon, Authority, Criticism* (Philadelphia: Westminster Press, 1983).

—— 'Jowett and the Reading of the Bible "Like Any Other Book" ', *Horizons in Biblical Theology: An International Dialogue*, 4 (1983), pp. 1–44, reprinted in Barton (ed.), *Bible and Interpretation*, vol. 1, pp. 169–97.

Barton, John, *People of the Book? The Authority of the Bible in Christianity* (London: SPCK and Philadelphia: Westminster John Knox Press, 1988; second edition with additional chapter 1993; third edition with a further additional chapter 2011).

—— *Isaiah 1–39*, Old Testament Guides (London: T&T Clark, 2003).

—— *The Spirit and the Letter: Studies in the Biblical Canon* (London: SPCK, 1997); American edition *Holy Writings, Sacred Text* (Louisville, Ky.: Westminster John Knox Press, 1997).

—— (ed.), *The Biblical World* (London and New York: Routledge, 2002)

—— 'Historiography and Theodicy in the Old Testament', in R. Rezetko, T. H. Lim and W. B. Aucker (eds), *Reflection and Refraction: Studies in Biblical Historiography in Honour of A. Graeme Auld* (Leiden and Boston: Brill, 2006), pp. 27–33.

—— *The Nature of Biblical Criticism* (Louisville, Ky.: Westminster John Knox Press, 2007).

—— *The Old Testament: Canon, Literature and Theology: Collected Works of John Barton* (Aldershot: Ashgate, 2007).

—— *Oracles of God: Perceptions of Ancient Prophecy in Israel after the Exile* (Oxford and New York: Oxford University Press, second edition 2007).

—— *The Bible: The Basics* (Abingdon and New York: Routledge, 2010).

—— *The Theology of the Book of Amos* (New York and Cambridge: Cambridge University Press, 2012).

—— (ed.), *Bible and Interpretation: The Collected Essays of James Barr* (Oxford: Oxford University Press, 2013–14, 3 vols).

Bartor, Assnat, *Reading Law as Narrative: A Study in the Casuistic Laws of the Pentateuch* (Atlanta, Ga.: Society of Biblical Literature, 2010).

Bates, E. S., *The Bible Designed to Be Read as Literature* (London: Heinemann, 1937).

Bauckham, Richard (ed.), *The Gospel for All Christians* (Grand Rapids, Mich.: W. B. Eerdmans, 1998).

Bauer, Walter, *Orthodoxy and Heresy in Earliest Christianity* (Philadelphia: Fortress Press, 1971, from the second edition of the German original of 1934).

Beentjes, Pancratius C., *The Book of Ben Sira in Hebrew: A Text Edition of all Extant Hebrew Manuscripts and a Synopsis of all Parallel Hebrew Ben Sira Texts* (Leiden: Brill, 1997).

Beisser, F., *Claritas scripturae bei Martin Luther*, Forschungen zur Kirchen- und Dogmengeschichte 18 (Göttingen: Vandenhoeck & Ruprecht, 1966).

Biblia Hebraica Stuttgartensia (Stuttgart: Würtembergische Bibelanstalt, 1968).

Black, M. H., 'The Printed Bible', in *The Cambridge History of the Bible*, vol. 3, pp. 408–75.

Black, Matthew, *An Aramaic Approach to the Gospels and Acts* (Oxford: Clarendon Press, third edition 1967; first edition 1946).

Blenkinsopp, Joseph, *Essays on Judaism in the Pre-Hellenistic Period* (BZAW 495) (Berlin: W. de Gruyter, 2017).

—— 'The Intellectual World of Judaism in the Pre-Hellenistic Period', in Blenkinsopp, *Essays on Judaism in the Pre-Hellenistic Period*, pp. 84–100.

—— 'Was the Pentateuch the Constitution of the Jewish Ethnos in the Persian Period?', in Blenkinsopp, *Essays on Judaism in the Pre-Hellenistic Period*, pp. 101–18.

Blum, Erhard, *Studien zur Komposition des Pentateuch* (Berlin: W. de Gruyter, 1990).

Bonhoeffer, Dietrich, *Letters and Papers from Prison* (New York: Macmillan, 1972).

Borg, Marcus, *Jesus in Contemporary Scholarship* (Valley Forge, Pa.: Trinity Press International, 1994).

Boyarin, Daniel, *Intertextuality and the Reading of Midrash* (Bloomington and Indianapolis: Indiana University Press, 1990).

Breck, John, *Scripture in Tradition: The Bible and Its Interpretation in the Orthodox Church* (Crestwood, NY: St Vladimir's Seminary Press, 2001).

Bright, John, *A History of Israel* (London: SCM Press, 1960); several subsequent editions.

Brown, Dan, *The Da Vinci Code* (London: Corgi, 2004).

Brown, Raymond E., *The Gospel according to John* (Garden City, NY: Doubleday, 1966–1970, 2 vols).

—— *An Introduction to the Gospel of John* (New York: Doubleday, 2003).

Buber, Martin and Rosenzweig, Franz, *Die fünf Bücher der Weisung* (Cologne and Olten: Hegner, 1968).

Burridge, Richard A., *What Are the Gospels? A Comparison with Graeco-Roman Biography* (Grand Rapids, Mich.: W. B. Eerdmans, second edition 2004).

Burtchaell, James T., *Catholic Theories of Biblical Inspiration since 1810: A Review and Critique* (Cambridge: Cambridge University Press, 1969).

Caird, George B., *The Gospel of St Luke* (Harmondsworth: Penguin, 1963).

The Cambridge History of the Bible, vol. 1: *From the Beginnings to Jerome*, ed. P. R Ackroyd and C. F. Evans (Cambridge: Cambridge University Press, 1970).

The Cambridge History of the Bible, vol. 2: *The West from the Fathers to the Reformation*, ed. G. W. H. Lampe (Cambridge: Cambridge University Press, 1969).

The Cambridge History of the Bible, vol. 3: *The West from the Reformation to the Present Day*, ed. S. L. Greenslade (Cambridge: Cambridge University Press, 1963).

Campbell, Douglas A., *Framing Paul: An Epistolary Biography* (Grand Rapids, Mich.: W. B. Eerdmans, 2014).

Campbell, Gordon, *Bible: The Story of the King James Version, 1611–2011* (Oxford: Oxford University Press, 2010).

Cantwell Smith, Wilfred, *What Is Scripture? A Comparative Approach* (London: SCM Press, 1993).

Carr, D. M., *Writing on the Tablet of the Heart: Origins of Scripture and Literature* (Oxford: Oxford University Press, 2005).

—— *The Formation of the Hebrew Bible: A New Reconstruction* (Oxford and New York: Oxford University Press, 2011).

Carroll, Robert P., *From Chaos to Covenant: Uses of Prophecy in the Book of Jeremiah* (London: SCM Press, 1981).

Chadwick, Owen, *The Victorian Church, Part Two: 1860–1901* (London: SCM Press, 1972).

Chancey, M. A., Meyers, C. and Meyers, E. M., *The Bible in the Public Square: Its Enduring Influence in American Life* (Atlanta, Ga.: SBL Press, 2014).

Chapman, Mark D., *The Fantasy of Reunion* (Oxford: Oxford University Press, 2014).

Charlesworth, James H. (ed.), *The Old Testament Pseudepigrapha*, vol. 1: *Apocalyptic Literature and Testaments* (London: Darton, Longman & Todd, 1984).

Childs, Brevard S., *Biblical Theology in Crisis* (Philadelphia: Westminster Press, 1970).

—— *Introduction to the Old Testament as Scripture* (London: SCM Press, 1979).

Chouraqui, André, *La Bible* (Paris: Desclée de Brouwer, 2003).

Cohen, Naomi G., *Philo's Scriptures: Citations from the Prophets and Writings. Evidence for a* Haftarah *Cycle in Second Temple Judaism* (Boston and Leiden: Brill, 2007).

Collins, John J., *The Apocalyptic Imagination: An Introduction to Jewish Apocalyptic Literature* (Grand Rapids, Mich. and Cambridge: W. B. Eerdmans, third edition 2016).

Commonwealth of Pennsylvania, *Legislative Journal*, 196th General Assembly, 24 January 2012.

Cosgrove, C. H., 'Justin Martyr and the Emerging Christian Canon: Observations on the Purpose and Destination of the Dialogue with Trypho', *Vigiliae Christianae*, 36 (1982), pp. 209–32.

Crenshaw, J. L., *Old Testament Wisdom: An Introduction* (Louisville, Ky.: Westminster John Knox Press, third edition 2010).

Crossan, John Dominic, *In Parables: The Challenge of the Historical Jesus* (New York: Harper & Row, 1973).

—— *Four Other Gospels* (Minneapolis: Winston Press, 1985).

Crouch, C. L., *The Making of Israel* (Leiden and Boston: Brill, 2014).

Dalley, Stephanie, *Myths from Mesopotamia: Creation, the Flood, Gilgamesh, and Others* (Oxford: Oxford University Press, revised edition 2008).

Dammen McAuliffe, Jane, Walfish, Barry D. and Goering, Joseph W. (eds), *With Reverence for the Word: Medieval Scriptural Exegesis in Judaism, Christianity, and Islam* (Oxford: Oxford University Press, 2003).

Daniélou, Jean, 'Les sources bibliques de la mystique d'Origène', *Revue d'ascétique et de mystique*, 23 (1947).

—— *Origen* (London: Sheed and Ward, 1955).

Davies, P. R., *Scribes and Schools: The Canonization of the Hebrew Scriptures* (Louisville, Ky.: Westminster John Knox Press, 1998).

Dawkins, Richard, *The God Delusion* (London: Bantam Press, 2006).

de Blic, Jean, 'L'oeuvre exégétique de Walafrid Strabo et la *Glossa Ordinaria*', *Recherches de théologie ancienne et médiévale*, 16 (1949), pp. 5–28.

DeConick, April D., *The Original Gospel of Thomas in Translation* (London and New York: T&T Clark, 2007).

de Hamel, Christopher, *The Book: A History of the Bible* (London: Phaidon, 2001).

de Lange, Nicholas R. M., *Modern Judaism: An Oxford Guide* (Oxford: Oxford University Press, 2005).

de Lubac, Henri, *Medieval Exegesis: The Four Senses of Scripture* (Grand Rapids, Mich.: W. B. Eerdmans; Edinburgh: T&T Clark, 2 vols, 1998 and 2000, from the French original of 1959–64).

—— *History and Spirit: The Understanding of Scripture According to Origen* (San Francisco: Ignatius, 2007, from the French original of 1950).

de Wette, W. M. L., *Dissertatio critica qua a prioribus Deuteronomium Pentateuchi libris diversum, alius cuiusdam recentioris auctoris opus esse monstratur* (Berlin: G. Reimer, 1830).

Dell, Katharine J., *Get Wisdom, Get Insight: An Introduction to Israel's Wisdom Literature* (London: Darton, Longman & Todd, 2000).

Dever, William G., *Who Were the Early Israelites and Where Did They Come From?* (Grand Rapids, Mich. and Cambridge: W. B. Eerdmans, 2003).

Dibelius, Martin, 'The Speeches of Acts and Ancient Historiography', in Heinrich Greeven (ed.), *Studies in the Acts of the Apostles*, (London: SCM Press, 1956).

Dodd, C. H., *The Interpretation of the Fourth Gospel* (Cambridge: Cambridge University Press, 1953).

—— *Parables of the Kingdom* (London: Fontana, 1961).

—— *Historical Tradition in the Fourth Gospel* (Cambridge: Cambridge University Press, 1963).

Donner, Herbert, 'Der Redaktor: Überlegungen zum vorkritischen Umgang mit der Heiligen Schrift', *Henoch* 2 (1980), pp. 1–30.

Douglas, Mary, *In the Wilderness: The Doctrine of Defilement in the Book of Numbers* (Sheffield: JSOT Press, 1993).

—— *Leviticus as Literature* (Oxford: Oxford University Press, 1999).

—— *Purity and Danger: An Analysis of Concepts of Pollution and Taboo* (New York: Routledge, 2003, originally published in 1966).

Dove, Mary, 'Literal Sense in the Song of Songs', in Krey and Smith (eds), *Nicholas of Lyra*, pp. 129–46.

Dunn, J. D. G., *Jesus, Paul and the Law* (London: SPCK, 1990).

—— *The Parting of the Ways between Christianity and Judaism and their Significance for the Character of Christianity* (London: SCM Press, 2006).

—— 'Christianity without Paul', in Daniel M. Gurtner, Grant Macaskill and Jonathan T. Pennington (eds), *In the Fullness of Time: Essays on Christology, Creation, and Eschatology in Honor of Richard Bauckham* (Grand Rapids, Mich.: W. B. Eerdmans, 2016), pp. 115–31.

Eagleton, Terry, *Literary Theory: An Introduction* (Oxford: Blackwell, 2008, anniversary edition).

Edwards, Katie, *Admen and Eve: The Bible in Contemporary Advertising*, The Bible in the Modern World 48 (Sheffield: Sheffield Phoenix Press, 2012).

Edwards, Mark J., *Origen against Plato* (Aldershot: Ashgate, 2002).

Ehrman, Bart D., *The Orthodox Corruption of Scripture: The Effect of Early Christological Controversies on the Text of the New Testament* (New York: Oxford University Press, 1993, second edition 2011).

—— *Forgery and Counterforgery: The Use of Literary Deceit in Early Christian Polemics* (Oxford and New York: Oxford University Press, 2013).

Elliott, J. K., *The Apocryphal New Testament: A Collection of Apocryphal Christian Literature in an English Translation Based on M. R. James* (Oxford: Oxford University Press, 1993).

Evans, G. R., 'Scriptural Interpretation in Pre-Reformation Dissident Movements', in Sæbø (ed.), *Hebrew Bible/Old Testament*, vol. 2, pp. 298–318.

Eve, Eric, 'The Devil in the Detail: Exorcising Q from the Beelzebul Controversy', in John C. Poirier and Jeffrey Peterson (eds), *Marcan Priority without Q: Explorations in the Farrer Hypothesis* (London: Bloomsbury T&T Clark, 2015), pp. 16–43.

Farrer, A. M., 'On Dispensing with Q', in D. E. Nineham (ed.), *Studies in the Gospels in Memory of R. H. Lightfoot* (Oxford: Blackwell, 1955), pp. 55–88.

—— *A Science of God?* (London: SPCK, 2009, originally published in 1966).

Finkelstein, Israel, *The Archaeology of the Israelite Settlement* (Jerusalem: Israel Exploration Society, 1988).

—— *The Forgotten Kingdom: The Archaeology and History of Northern Israel* (Atlanta, Ga.: Society of Biblical Literature, 2013).

—— and Silberman, N. A., *The Bible Unearthed: Archaeology's New Vision of Ancient Israel and the Origin of its Stories* (London: Simon & Schuster, 2001).

Fitzmyer, Joseph, 'Presidential Address: The Languages of Palestine in the First Century A.D.', *Catholic Biblical Quarterly* 32 (1970), pp. 501–31.

Flacius Illyricus, M., ed. L. Geldsetzer, *De ratione cognoscendi sacras literas* (Düsseldorf: Stern Verlag, 1968).

Foster, Paul, 'Who Wrote 2 Thessalonians? A Fresh Look at an Old Problem', *Journal for the Study of the New Testament*, 35(2) (2012), pp. 150–75.

Fox, Everett, *The Five Books of Moses* (New York: Schocken Books, 1983).

Freyne, Sean, *The Jesus Movement and Its Expansion: Meaning and Mission* (Grand Rapids, Mich.: W. B. Eerdmans, 2014).

Friedman, R. E., *Who Wrote the Bible?* (London: Jonathan Cape, 1987).

Froehlich, K. and Gibson, M. T. (eds), *Biblia Latina cum glossa ordinaria: Facsimile reprint of the editio princeps Adolph Rusch of Strassburg 1480/81* (Turnhout: Brepols, 1992).

Frye, Northrop, *The Great Code: The Bible and Literature* (London: Routledge and Kegan Paul, 1982).

Gallagher, Edmon L. and Meade, John D., *The Biblical Canon Lists from Early Christianity: Texts and Analysis* (Oxford: Oxford University Press, 2017).

Gamble, Harry Y., *Books and Readers in the Early Church: A History of Early Christian Texts* (New Haven and London: Yale University Press, 1995).

Garfinkel, Stephen, 'Clearing *Peshat* and *Derash*', in Sæbø (ed.), *Hebrew Bible/Old Testament*, vol. 1/2, pp. 129–34.

Gillingham, Susan E., *The Poems and Psalms of the Hebrew Bible* (Oxford: Oxford University Press, 1994).

—— (ed.), *Jewish and Christian Approaches to the Psalms: Conflict and Convergence* (Oxford: Oxford University Press, 2013).

—— 'The Levites and the Editorial Composition of the Psalms', in *The Oxford Handbook of the Psalms*, pp. 201–28.

Goodacre, Mark, 'Ten Reasons to Question Q', www.markgoodacre.org/Q/ten.htm

—— *The Synoptic Problem: A Way through the Maze* (London: Sheffield Academic Press, 2001).

—— *The Case against Q: Markan Priority and the Synoptic Problem* (Harrisburg, Pa.: Trinity Press International, 2002).

—— and Perrin, Nicholas (eds), *Questioning Q* (London: SPCK, 2004).

Goodman, Martin, *Rome and Jerusalem: The Clash of Ancient Civilizations* (London: Allen Lane, 2007).

Goodwin, C. W., 'On the Mosaic Cosmogony', in Henry B. Wilson (ed.), *Essays and Reviews* (London: Longmans, Green, Longman, Roberts & Green, twelfth edition 1865).

Goulder, M. D., 'Characteristics of the Parables in the Several Gospels', *Journal of Theological Studies*, 19 (1) (1968).

—— *Midrash and Lection in Matthew* (London: SPCK, 1974).

Guignard, Christophe, 'The Original Language of the Muratorian Fragment', *Journal of Theological Studies*, 66 (2015), pp. 596–624.

Gunkel, Hermann, *An Introduction to the Psalms: The Genres of the Religious Lyric of Israel* (Macon, Ga.: Mercer University Press, 1998, from the German original of 1933).

Gunn, David M., *The Story of King David: Genre and Interpretation* (Sheffield: JSOT Press, 1978).

Gyug, Richard, 'Early Medieval Bibles, Biblical Books, and the Monastic Liturgy in the Beneventan Region', in Susan Boynton and Diane J. Reilly (eds), *The Practice of the Bible in the Middle Ages: Production, Reception, and Performance in Western Christianity* (New York: Columbia University Press, 2011), pp. 34–60.

Hackett, Jo Ann, *The Balaam Text from Deir Allah*, Harvard Semitic Monographs 31 (Chico, Cal.: Scholars Press, 1980).

Hahneman, Geoffrey, *The Muratorian Fragment and the Development of the Canon* (Oxford: Oxford University Press, 1992).

Hall, Basil, 'Biblical Scholarship: Editions and Commentaries', in *The Cambridge History of the Bible*, vol. 3, pp. 38–93.

Hanson, R. P. C., 'Biblical Exegesis in the Early Church', in *The Cambridge History of the Bible*, vol. 1, pp. 412–53.

Harris, Horton, *The Tübingen School: A Historical and Theological Investigation of the School of F. C. Baur* (Leicester: Apollos, second edition, 1990).

Hayes, John H., 'Historical Criticism of the Old Testament Canon', in Sæbø (ed.), *Hebrew Bible/Old Testament*, vol. 2, pp. 985–1005.

Heaton, E. W., *Solomon's New Men: The Emergence of Ancient Israel as a National State* (London: Thames and Hudson, 1974).

Hengel, Martin, *Judaism and Hellenism: Studies in their Encounter in Palestine during the Early Hellenistic Period* (London: SCM Press, 1974).

Hill, C. E., *Who Chose the Gospels? Probing the Great Gospel Conspiracy* (Oxford: Oxford University Press, 2010).

Hill, Robert C., *Reading the Old Testament in Antioch*, The Bible in Ancient Christianity, vol. 5 (Atlanta, Ga.: Society of Biblical Literature, 2005).

Holtz, Barry, 'Midrash', in Barry Holtz (ed.), *Back to the Sources: Reading the Classic Jewish Texts* (New York: Summit, 1984), pp. 177–211.

Horrell, David G., *An Introduction to the Study of Paul* (London: Bloomsbury T&T Clark, third edition 2015).

Houghton, H. A. G. (trans), in association with Dorfbauer, Lukas J., *Fortunatianus of Aquileia: Commentary on the Gospels* (Berlin: W. de Gruyter, 2017).

Humphreys, Colin J., *The Mystery of the Last Supper: Reconstructing the Final Days of Jesus* (Cambridge: Cambridge University Press, 2011).

Israel, Jonathan (ed.), *Spinoza: Theological-Political Treatise* (Cambridge: Cambridge University Press, 2007).

Jackson, Bernard S., *Wisdom-Laws: A Study of the Mishpatim of Exodus 12:1–22:16* (Oxford: Oxford University Press, 2006).

Jamieson-Drake, D. W., *Scribes and Schools in Monarchic Judah: A Socio-Archaeological Approach* (JSOTSup, 109) (Sheffield: Almond Press, 1991).

Jarick, John (ed.), *Sacred Conjectures: The Context and Legacy of Robert Lowth and Jean Astruc* (New York and London: T&T Clark, 2007).

The Jewish Study Bible, ed. A. Berlin and M. Z. Brettler (Oxford and New York: Oxford University Press, 2004, second edition 2014).

Johnson, Byron and Isserman, Nancy (eds), *Uneasy Allies: Evangelical and Jewish Relations* (Lanham, Md.: Lexington Books, 2007).

Kartveit, Magnar, *The Origin of the Samaritans* (Leiden: Brill, 2009).

Kasher, Rimon, 'The Interpretation of Scripture in Rabbinic Literature', in M. J. Mulder (ed.), *Mikra: Text, Translation, Reading and Interpretation of the Hebrew Bible in Ancient Judaism and Early Christianity* (Assen: Van Gorcum, 1988), pp. 547–94.

Kelley, Page H., Mynatt, Daniel S. and Crawford, Timothy G., *The Masorah of* Biblia Hebraica Stuttgartensia*: Introduction and Annotated Glossary* (Grand Rapids, Mich. and Cambridge: W. B. Eerdmans, 1998).

Kennedy, Philip, *A Modern Introduction to Theology: New Questions for Old Beliefs* (London and New York: I. B. Tauris, 2006).

Kermode, Frank, *The Genesis of Secrecy: On the Interpretation of Narrative* (Cambridge, Mass. and London: Harvard University Press, 1979).

King, Karen L., *The Gospel of Mary of Magdala: Jesus and the First Woman Apostle* (Santa Rosa, Cal.: Polebridge Press, 2003).

Kingsmill, Edmée, *The Song of Songs and the Eros of God* (Oxford: Oxford University Press, 2009).

Klauck, H.-J., *Ancient Letters and the New Testament: A Guide to Context and Exegesis* (Waco, Tex.: Baylor University Press, 2006).

Knox, John, *Chapters in a Life of Paul* (New York: Abingdon Press, 1950; second edition London: SCM Press, 1987).

Kratz, Reinhard G., *The Prophets of Israel* (Winona Lake, Ind.: Eisenbrauns, 2015).

Krey, Philip D. W. and Smith, Lesley (eds), *Nicholas of Lyra: The Senses of Scripture*, in Heiko A. Oberman (ed.), Studies in the History of Christian Thought, 90 (Leiden, Cologne and Boston: Brill, 2000).

Kugel, James L.,*The Idea of Biblical Poetry: Parallelism and Its History* (Baltimore and London: Johns Hopkins University Press, 1998).

—— *The Ladder of Jacob: Ancient Interpretations of the Biblical Story of Jacob and his Children* (Princeton and Oxford: Princeton University Press, 2006).

—— and Greer, Rowan A., *Early Biblical Interpretation* (Philadelphia: Westminster Press, 1986).

Kuss, O., 'Über die Klarheit der Schrift: Historische und hermeneutische Überlegungen zu der Kontroverse des Erasmus und des Luther über den freien oder versklavten Willen', in *Theologie und Glaube*, 60 (1970), pp. 273–321, reprinted in J. Ernst (ed.), *Schriftauslegung: Beiträge zur Hermeneutik des*

Neuen Testamentes und im Neuen Testament (Munich: Schöningh, 1972), pp. 89–149.

LaHaye, Tim and Jenkins, Jerry B., *Left Behind* (Wheaton, Ill.: Tyndale House, 1995).

Lambe, P. J., 'Critics and Skeptics in the Seventeenth-Century Republic of Letters', *Harvard Theological Review*, 81 (1988), pp. 271–96.

Lambert, Wilfred G., *Babylonian Wisdom Literature* (Winona Lake, Ind.: Eisenbrauns, 1996).

Lampe, G. W. H., 'The Exposition and Exegesis of Scripture: To Gregory the Great', in *The Cambridge History of the Bible*, vol. 2, pp. 155–83.

Lauterbach, Jacob Z., *Mekhilta de-Rabbi Ishmael* (Philadelphia: The Jewish Publication Society of America, 1933).

Law, Timothy Michael, *When God Spoke Greek: The Septuagint and the Making of the Christian Bible* (New York and Oxford: Oxford University Press, 2013).

Lawton, David, *Faith, Text and History: The Bible in English* (New York and London: Harvester Wheatsheaf, 1990).

Leclercq, Jean, 'The Exposition and Exegesis of Scripture: From Gregory the Great to Saint Bernard', in *The Cambridge History of the Bible*, vol. 2, pp. 183–97.

Lemaire, A., *Les écoles et la formation de la Bible dans l'ancien Israël* (OBO, 39) (Fribourg: Éditions Universitaires; Göttingen: Vandenhoeck & Ruprecht, 1981).

Levenson, Jon D., *The Hebrew Bible, the Old Testament, and Historical Criticism: Jews and Christians in Biblical Studies* (Louisville, Ky.: Westminster John Knox Press, 1993).

—— *Resurrection and the Restoration of Israel: The Ultimate Victory of the God of Life* (New Haven and London: Yale University Press, 2006).

Levine, Étan, 'The Targums: Their Interpretative Character and Their Place in Jewish Text Tradition', in Sæbø (ed.), *Hebrew Bible/Old Testament*, vol. 1, pp. 323–31.

Lewis, C. S., *Reflections on the Psalms* (London: Geoffrey Bles, 1958).

—— 'The Literary Impact of the Authorized Version', in C. S. Lewis, *They Asked for a Paper* (London: Geoffrey Bles, 1962), pp. 26–50.

Lieu, Judith, *Image and Reality: The Jews and the World of the Christians in the Second Century* (Edinburgh: T&T Clark, 1996).

—— *Christian Identity in the Jewish and Graeco-Roman World* (Oxford: Oxford University Press, 2004).

Lim, Timothy H., *The Formation of the Jewish Canon* (New Haven and London: Yale University Press, 2013).

—— *The Dead Sea Scrolls: A Very Short Introduction* (Oxford: Oxford University Press, second edition 2017).

Lindars, Barnabas, *New Testament Apologetic: The Doctrinal Significance of the Old Testament Quotations* (London: SCM Press, 1961).

Lindsey, Hal, *The Late Great Planet Earth* (Grand Rapids, Mich.: Zondervan, 1971).

Loewe, Raphael, 'The "Plain" Meaning of Scripture in Early Jewish Exegesis', in J. G. Weiss (ed.), *Papers of the Institute of Jewish Studies*, vol. 1 (Jerusalem: Magnes Press, 1964), pp. 140–85.

Louth, Andrew (ed.), *Early Christian Writings: The Apostolic Fathers* (London: Penguin, second edition 1987).

Lowth, Robert, *Lectures on the Sacred Poetry of the Hebrews* (London: second edition 1816).

Ludlow, Morwenna, ' "Criteria of Canonicity" and the Early Church', in John Barton and Michael Wolter (eds), *Die Einheit der Schrift und die Vielfalt des Kanons/The Unity of Scripture and the Diversity of the Canon*, Beihefte zur Zeitschrift für die neutestamentliche Wissenschaft und die Kunde der älteren Kirche, 118 (Berlin: W. de Gruyter, 2003), pp. 69–93.

The Complete Sermons of Martin Luther, ed. John Nicholas Lenker and Eugene F. A. Klug (Grand Rapids, Mich.: Baker, 2000).

MacCulloch, Diarmaid, *Reformation: Europe's House Divided, 1490–1700* (London: Allen Lane, 2003).

Magonet, Jonathan, *Bible Lives* (London: SCM Press, 1992).

Malone, Andrew, *Knowing Jesus in the Old Testament? A Fresh Look at Christophanies* (Nottingham: Inter-Varsity Press, 2015).

Marty, Martin L., 'America's Iconic Book', in G. Tucker and D. Knight (eds), *Humanizing America's Iconic Book: Society of Biblical Literature Centennial Address, 1980* (Chico, Cal.: Scholars Press, 1982), pp. 1–23.

Martyn, J. Louis, *History and Theology in the Fourth Gospel* (New York: Harper & Row, 1968).

Marxsen, Willi, *Mark the Evangelist: Studies on the Redaction History of the Gospel* (Nashville, Tenn.: Abingdon Press, 1969, from the German original of 1956).

Mason, Steve, *A History of the Jewish War, AD 66–74* (Cambridge: Cambridge University Press, 2017).

McKane, William, *Proverbs: A New Approach* (London: SCM Press, 1970).

Meade, D. G., *Pseudonymity and Canon* (Grand Rapids, Mich.: W. B. Eerdmans, 1987).

Methuen, Charlotte, 'On the Threshold of a New Age: Expanding Horizons as the Broader Context of Scriptural Interpretation', in Sæbø (ed.), *Hebrew Bible/Old Testament*, vol. 2, pp. 665–90.

Metzger, Bruce M., *The Canon of the New Testament: Its Origin, Development, and Significance* (Oxford: Oxford University Press, 1987).

—— *The Text of the New Testament: Its Transmission, Corruption, and Restoration* (Oxford: Oxford University Press, third edition 1992).

Milburn, R. L. P., 'The "People's Bible": Artists and Commentators', in *The Cambridge History of the Bible*, vol. 2, pp. 280–308.

Mitchell, Margaret, 'Patristic Counter-Evidence to the Claim that "The Gospels were Written for All Christians" ', *New Testament Studies*, 51 (2005), pp. 36–79.

Mitton, C. Leslie, *The Epistle to the Ephesians* (Oxford: Clarendon Press, 1951).

Moberly, R. W. L., 'Canon and Religious Truth: An Appraisal of *A New New Testament*', in Timothy H. Lim (ed.), *When Texts Are Canonized*, Brown Judaic Studies, 359 (Providence, RI: Brown University, 2017), pp. 108–35.

Morgan, Robert, 'The Hermeneutical Significance of Four Gospels', *Interpretation*, 33 (1979), pp. 376–88.

—— 'Jesus', in Barton (ed.), *The Biblical World*, pp. 223–57.

—— with Barton, John, *Biblical Interpretation*, The Oxford Bible Series (Oxford: Oxford University Press, 1988).

Morrow, W. S., 'Kethib and Qere', in David Noel Freedman (ed.), *Anchor Bible Dictionary* (New York: Doubleday, 1992), vol. 4, p. 25.

Mowinckel, Sigmund, *Psalmenstudien* (Kristiania [Oslo]: Skrifter utgitt av Det Norske Videnskaps-Akademi, 1921–4, 2 vols).

—— *The Psalms in Israel's Worship* (Grand Rapids, Mich.: W. B. Eerdmans, 2004, originally published in 1962, 2 vols).

Mroczek, Eva, *The Literary Imagination in Jewish Antiquity* (New York and Oxford: Oxford University Press, 2016).

Muddiman, John, *The Bible: Fountain and Well of Truth* (Oxford: Blackwell, 1983).

—— 'The First-Century Crisis: Christian Origins', in S. Sutherland, L. Houlden, P. Clarke and F. Hardy (eds), *The World's Religions* (London: Routledge, 1988).

—— *The Epistle to the Ephesians* (London: Continuum, 2001).

—— 'The Greek Language', in Barton (ed.), *The Biblical World*, pp. 25–32.

Na'aman, Nadav and Finkelstein, Israel, *From Nomadism to Monarchy: Archaeological and Historical Aspects of Early Israel* (Jerusalem: Israel Exploration Society, 1994).

Nadler, Steven, *A Book Forged in Hell: Spinoza's Scandalous Treatise and the Birth of the Secular Age* (Princeton and Oxford: Princeton University Press, 2011).

Neil, W., 'The Criticism and Theological Use of the Bible, 1700–1950', in *The Cambridge History of the Bible*, vol. 3, pp. 238–93.

Nelson, Richard D., *The Double Redaction of the Deuteronomistic History* (Sheffield: JSOT Press, 1981).

Newsom, Carol A., *The Book of Job: A Contest of Moral Imaginations* (Leiden and Boston: Brill, 2004).

Nicholson, E. W., *Preaching to the Exiles: A Study of the Prose Tradition in the Book of Jeremiah* (Oxford: Blackwell, 1970).

—— *The Pentateuch in the Twentieth Century: The Legacy of Julius Wellhausen* (Oxford: Clarendon Press, 1998).

—— *Deuteronomy and the Judaean Diaspora* (Oxford: Oxford University Press, 2014).

Nissinen, Martti (ed.), *Prophecy in Its Ancient Near Eastern Context: Mesopotamian, Biblical, and Arabian Perspectives* (Atlanta, Ga.: Society of Biblical Literature, 2000).

—— in John Day (ed.), *Prophecy and the Prophets in Ancient Israel: Proceedings of the Oxford Old Testament Seminar* (New York and London: T&T Clark, 2010).

—— with contributions by C. L. Seow and Robert K. Ritner, *Prophets and Prophecy in the Ancient Near East*, ed. Peter Machinist (Atlanta, Ga.: Society of Biblical Literature, 2003).

Noth, Martin, *A History of Pentateuchal Traditions* (Atlanta, Ga.: Scholars Press, 1981, from the German original of 1948).

—— *Überlieferungsgeschichtliche Studien* (Halle: M. Niemeyer, 1943); English version *The Deuteronomistic History* (Sheffield: JSOT Press, 1991).

O'Donnell, James J., *Cassiodorus* (Berkeley: University of California Press, 1979).

Opitz, Peter, 'The Exegetical and Hermeneutical Work of John Oecolampadius, Huldrych Zwingli, and John Calvin', in Sæbø (ed.), *Hebrew Bible/Old Testament*, vol. 2, pp. 407–51.

Overbeck, Franz, *Zur Geschichte des Kanons* (Chemnitz: E. Schmeitzner, 1880, reprinted Darmstadt: Wissenschaftliche Buchgesellschaft, 1965).

The Oxford Handbook of the Psalms, ed. William P. Brown (Oxford: Oxford University Press, 2014).

Parker, D. C., *The Living Text of the Gospels* (Cambridge: Cambridge University Press, 1997).

Patton, Corinne, 'Creation, Fall and Salvation: Lyra's Commentary on Genesis 1–3', in Krey and Smith (eds), *Nicholas of Lyra*, pp. 19–43.

Pelling, C. B. R., 'Plutarch's Method of Work in the Roman Lives', *Journal of Hellenic Studies*, 99 (1979), pp. 74–96.

Pentiuc, Eugen J., *The Old Testament in Eastern Orthodox Tradition* (New York and Oxford: Oxford University Press, 2014).

Perlitt, Lothar, *Vatke und Wellhausen: Geschichtsphilosophische Voraussetzungen und historiographische Motive für die Darstellung der Religion und Geschichte Israels durch Wilhelm Vatke und Julius Wellhausen* (Berlin: A. Töpelmann, 1965).

Pirḳê de Rabbi Eliezer, translated by G. Friedlander (New York: Sepher-Hermon Press, fourth edition 1981).

Pontifical Biblical Commission, *The Inspiration and Truth of Sacred Scripture: The Word that Comes from God and Speaks of God for the Salvation of the World* (Collegeville, Minn.: Liturgical Press, 2014).

Porter, J. R., *The Lost Bible: Forgotten Scriptures Revealed* (London: Duncan Baird, 2001).

Provan, Iain, Long, V. Phillips and Longman III, Tremper, *A Biblical History of Israel* (Louisville, Ky.: Westminster John Knox Press, 2003).

Pullman, Philip, *Northern Lights* (London: Scholastic, 1995).

—— *The Subtle Knife* (London: Scholastic, 1997).

—— *The Amber Spyglass* (London: Scholastic, 2001).

Qimron, Elisha, *The Temple Scroll: A Critical Edition with Extensive Reconstructions* (Beersheva: Ben Gurion University of the Negev Press, 1996).

Raeder, Siegfried, 'The Exegetical and Hermeneutical Work of Martin Luther', in Sæbø (ed.), *Hebrew Bible/Old Testament*, vol. 2, pp. 363–406.

Räisänen, Heikki, *Paul and the Law* (Tübingen: Mohr, 1983).

Rajak, Tessa, *Josephus: The Historian and His Society* (London: Duckworth, 2002).

Reeves, Marjorie, *Joachim of Fiore and the Prophetic Future* (London: SPCK, 1976).

Reid, J. K. S., *The Authority of Scripture: A Study of the Reformation and Post-Reformation Understanding of the Bible* (London: Methuen, 1957).

Reilly, Diane J., 'Lectern Bibles and Liturgical Reform in the Central Middle Ages', in Susan Boynton and Diane J. Reilly (eds), *The Practice of the Bible in the Middle Ages: Production, Reception, and Performance in Western Christianity* (New York: Columbia University Press, 2011), pp. 105–25.

Rendtorff, Rolf, *The Problem of the Process of Transmission in the Pentateuch* (Sheffield: Sheffield Academic Press, 1977).

Reventlow, Henning Graf, *Epochen der Bibelauslegung, Band I: Vom Alten Testament bis Origenes* (Munich: C. H. Beck, 1990).

Roberts, C. H., 'The Codex', *Proceedings of the British Academy*, 40 (1954), pp. 169–204.

—— with Skeat, T. C., *The Birth of the Codex* (London: Oxford University Press for the British Academy, 1987).

Rollston, C. A., *Writing and Literacy in the World of Ancient Israel: Epigraphic Evidence from the Iron Age* (Atlanta, Ga.: Society of Biblical Literature, 2010).

Roper, Lyndal, *Martin Luther: Renegade and Prophet* (London: The Bodley Head, 2016).

Rosenthal, Erwin I. J., 'The Exposition and Exegesis of Scripture: The Study of the Bible in Medieval Judaism', in *The Cambridge History of the Bible*, vol. 2, pp. 252–79.

Rost, L., *Die Überlieferung von der Thronnachfolge Davids* (Stuttgart: Kohlhammer, 1926); English version *The Succession to the Throne of David* (Sheffield: Almond Press, 1982).

Rowland, Christopher, *The Open Heaven: A Study of Apocalyptic in Judaism and Early Christianity* (London: SPCK, 1982).

Rupp, E. Gordon and Watson, Philip S. (eds and trans), *Luther and Erasmus: Free Will and Salvation*, Library of Christian Classics 17 (London: SCM Press, 1969).

Sæbø, Magne (ed.), *Hebrew Bible/Old Testament: The History of Its Interpretation*, vol. 1/2 (Göttingen: Vandenhoeck & Ruprecht, 2000).

Saenger, P., 'The British Isles and the Origin of the Modern Mode of Biblical Citation', *Syntagma*, 1 (2005), pp. 77–115.

Salvesen, Alison, *Symmachus in the Pentateuch*, JSS Monograph 15 (Manchester: The Victoria University of Manchester, 1991).

Samely, Alexander, *Forms of Rabbinic Literature and Thought: An Introduction* (Oxford: Oxford University Press, 2007).

Sanders, E. P., *Paul and Palestinian Judaism* (London: SCM Press, 1977).

—— *Paul, the Law and the Jewish People* (London: SCM Press, 1983).

—— *Jesus and Judaism* (London: SCM Press, 1985).

—— *The Historical Figure of Jesus* (London: Allen Lane, 1993).

Schaper, J., *Eschatology in the Greek Psalter*, Wissenschaftliche Untersuchungen zum Neuen Testament, 2(76) (Tübingen: Mohr Siebeck, 1995).

Schmid, Hans Heinrich, *Der sogenannte Jahwist: Beobachtungen und Fragen zur Pentateuchforschung* (Zurich: Theologischer Verlag, 1976).

Schniedewind, W. M., *How the Bible Became a Book: The Textualization of Ancient Israel* (Cambridge: Cambridge University Press, 2004).

Schweitzer, Albert, *The Quest of the Historical Jesus* (Minneapolis: Fortress Press, 2001; translation of *Von Reimarus zu Wrede: Eine Geschichte der Leben-Jesu-Forschung* (Tübingen: Mohr Siebeck, 1906).

Seitz, C. R. and Greene-McCreight, K. (eds), *Theological Exegesis: Essays in Honor of Brevard S. Childs*, (Grand Rapids, Mich.: W. B. Eerdmans, 1999).

Sherwood, Yvonne, 'Textual Carcasses and Isaac's Scar, or What Jewish Interpretation Makes of the Violence that Almost Takes Place on Mt Moriah', in Jonneke Bekkenkamp and Yvonne Sherwood (eds), *Sanctified Aggression: Legacies of Biblical and Post-Biblical Vocabularies of Violence* (London: T&T Clark International, 2003), pp. 22–43.

—— (ed.), *Derrida's Bible (Reading a Page of Scripture with a Little Help from Derrida)* (New York and Basingstoke: Palgrave Macmillan, 2004).

Signer, Michael A. and van Engen, John, *Jews and Christians in Twelfth-Century Europe* (Notre Dame, Ind.: University of Notre Dame Press, 2001).

Simon, Richard, *Histoire critique du Vieux Testament* (Paris, 1678).

Smalley, Beryl, *The Study of the Bible in the Middle Ages* (Oxford: Basil Blackwell, 1952; second edition Notre Dame, Ind.: University of Notre Dame Press, 1964).

Smelik, W., 'The Languages of Roman Palestine', in C. Hezser (ed.), *The Oxford Handbook of Daily Life in Roman Palestine* (Oxford: Oxford University Press, 2010), pp. 122–44.

Smend, Rudolf, 'Das Nein des Amos', *Evangelische Theologie*, 23 (1963), pp. 404–23, reprinted in Rudolf Smend, *Die Mitte des Alten Testaments* (Munich: Kaiser Verlag, 1986), pp. 85–103.

—— *Die Entstehung des Alten Testaments* (Stuttgart: Kohlhammer, 1978; third edition 1984).Smith, Lesley, 'The Rewards of Faith: Nicholas of Lyra on Ruth', in Krey and Smith (eds), *Nicholas of Lyra*, pp. 45–58.

Smith, Lesley, 'Nicholas of Lyra and Old Testament Interpretation', in Sæbø (ed.), *Hebrew Bible/Old Testament*, vol. 2, pp. 49–63.

—— *The* Glossa Ordinaria*: The Making of a Medieval Bible Commentary*, Commentaria. Sacred Texts and Their Commentaries: Jewish, Christian, and Islamic, 3 (Leiden and Boston: Brill, 2009).

Sommer, Benjamin D., 'Concepts of Scriptural Language in Midrash', in Sommer (ed.), *Jewish Concepts of Scripture*, Chapter 5.

—— 'The Scroll of Isaiah as Jewish Scripture, or, Why Jews Don't Read Books', *Society of Biblical Literature 1996 Seminar Papers* (Atlanta, Ga.: Scholars Press, 1996), pp. 225–42.

—— (ed.), *Jewish Concepts of Scripture* (New York and London: New York University Press, 2012).

Soulen, R. Kendall, *The God of Israel and Christian Theology* (Minneapolis: Fortress Press, 1996).

Stavrakopoulou, Francesca, *King Manasseh and Child Sacrifice: Biblical Distortions of Historical Realities* (Berlin: W. de Gruyter, 2004).

Stendahl, Krister, 'The Apostle Paul and the Introspective Conscience of the West', *Harvard Theological Review*, 56 (1963), pp. 199–215.

—— *The School of St Matthew and its Use of the Old Testament* (Philadelphia: Fortress Press, 1968).

Stenning, J., *The Targum of Isaiah* (Oxford: Clarendon Press, 1949).

Stern, Elsie, 'Concepts of Scripture in the Synagogue Service', in Sommer (ed.), *Jewish Concepts of Scripture*, Chapter 2.

Stökl, Jonathan, *Prophecy in the Ancient Near East: A Philological and Sociological Comparison* (Leiden: Brill, 2012).

Stout, Harry S., 'Word and Order in Colonial New England', in N. O. Hatch and M. A. Noll (eds), *The Bible in America: Essays in Cultural History* (New York: Oxford University Press, 1982), pp. 19–38.

Strack, H. L. and Stemberger, G., *Introduction to the Talmud and Midrash* (Edinburgh: T&T Clark, 1991).

Strauss, D. F., *The Life of Jesus, Critically Examined* (London: SCM Press, 1973).

Streeter, B. H., *The Four Gospels: A Study of Origins, Treating of the Manuscript Tradition, Sources, Authorship & Dates* (London: Macmillan, 1924).

Stuhlhofer, Franz, *Der Gebrauch der Bibel von Jesus bis Euseb: Eine statistische Untersuchung zur Kanongeschichte* (Wuppertal: Brockhaus, 1988).

Sundberg Jr, Albert C., *The Old Testament of the Early Church* (Cambridge, Mass.: Harvard University Press, 1964).

—— 'Canon Muratori: A Fourth Century List', *Harvard Theological Review*, 66 (1973), pp. 1–41.

—— 'The Bible Canon and the Christian Doctrine of Inspiration', *Interpretation*, 29 (1975), pp. 352–71. Sutcliffe, E. F., 'Jerome', in *The Cambridge History of the Bible*, vol. 2, pp. 80–101.

Taussig, Hal (ed.), *A New New Testament: A Bible for the 21st Century Combining Traditional and Newly Discovered Texts* (Boston: Houghton Mifflin Harcourt, 2013).

Taylor, Vincent, *Behind the Third Gospel: A Study of the Proto-Luke Hypothesis* (Oxford: Clarendon Press, 1926).

Theissen, Gerd, *The Shadow of the Galilean: The Quest of the Historical Jesus in Narrative Form* (London: SCM Press, 1982).

—— and Winter, Dagmar, *The Quest for the Plausible Jesus: The Question of Criteria* (Louisville, Ky. and London: Westminster John Knox Press, 2002).

Thiselton, Anthony C., *New Horizons in Hermeneutics: The Theory and Practice of Transforming Biblical Reading* (Grand Rapids, Mich.: Zondervan, twentieth anniversary edition, 2013).

Thomas, Keith, *Religion and the Decline of Magic: Studies in Popular Beliefs in Sixteenth- and Seventeenth-Century England* (London: Weidenfeld & Nicolson, 1971).

Thompson, Thomas L., *The Bible in History: How Writers Create a Past* (London: Jonathan Cape, 1999).

Todorov, Tzvetan, *Mikhail Bakhtin: The Dialogical Principle* (Manchester: Manchester University Press, 1984).

Tov, Emmanuel, *Textual Criticism of the Hebrew Bible* (Minneapolis: Fortress Press, third edition 2012).

Troeltsch, Ernst, *The Social Teaching of the Christian Churches*, vol. 1 (Louisville, Ky.: Westminster John Knox Press, 1992, from the German original of 1912).

Tuckett, Christopher, 'Thomas and the Synoptics', *Novum Testamentum*, 30 (1988), pp. 132–57.

—— *The Gospel of Mary* (Oxford: Oxford University Press, 2007).

Ulrich, Eugene, 'The Notion and Definition of Canon', in Lee Martin McDonald and James A. Sanders (eds), *The Canon Debate* (Peabody, Mass.: Hendrickson, 2002), pp. 21–35.

Valla, Lorenzo, *De falso credita et ementita Constantinia donatione declamatio*, in Christopher B. Coleman, *The Treatise of Lorenzo Valla on the Donation of Constantine* (Toronto: University of Toronto Press in association with the Renaissance Society of America Press, 1993).

van der Toorn, K., *Scribal Culture and the Making of the Hebrew Bible* (Cambridge, Mass.: Harvard University Press, 2007).

van Liere, Frans, *An Introduction to the Medieval Bible* (Cambridge: Cambridge University Press, 2014).

Van Seters, John, *Abraham in History and Tradition* (New Haven and London: Yale University Press, 1975).

—— *The Life of Moses: The Yahwist as Historian in Exodus-Numbers* (Louisville, Ky.: Westminster John Knox Press, 1994).

Verheyden, Joseph, 'The Canon Muratori: A Matter of Dispute', in J.-M. Auwers and H. J. de Jonge, *The Biblical Canons* (Leuven: Leuven University Press, 1993), pp. 487–556.

Vermes, Géza, *Jesus the Jew: A Historian's Reading of the Gospels* (London: Fortuna/Collins, 1976; second edition London: SCM Press, 1983).

—— *The Religion of Jesus the Jew* (London: SCM Press, 1993).

—— *The Complete Dead Sea Scrolls in English* (New York and London: Allen Lane, 1997).

—— *Christian Beginnings: From Nazareth to Nicaea, AD 30–325* (London: Allen Lane, 2012).

Visotzky, Burt, 'Midrash' and 'Rabbinic Interpretation', in Katharine Doob Sakenfeld (ed.), *The New Interpreter's Dictionary of the Bible* (Nashville: Abingdon, 2006–9), vol. 4, pp. 81–4 and 718–20.

Visscher, Eva De, 'Cross-Religious Learning and Teaching', in Piet van Boxel and Sabine Arndt (eds), *Crossing Borders: Hebrew Manuscripts as a Meeting Place for Cultures* (Oxford: Bodleian Library, 2009), pp. 123–32.

—— *Reading the Rabbis: Christian Hebraism in the Works of Herbert of Bosham* (Leiden and Boston: Brill, 2014).

Voltaire, *Candide, ou l'optimisme* (1749).

Volz, Hans, Foster, Kenelm, Sayce, R. A., Van der Woude, S., Wilson, E. M., Auty, R. and Noack, Bent, 'Continental Versions to *c.* 1600', in *The Cambridge History of the Bible*, vol. 3, pp. 94–140.

von Campenhausen, Hans, *The Formation of the Christian Bible* (London: A. & C. Black, 1972).

Waldron, Jeremy, 'Thoughtfulness and the Rule of Law', *British Academy Review*, 18 (2011), pp. 1–11.

Watson, Francis, *Gospel Writing: A Canonical Perspective* (Grand Rapids, Mich. and Cambridge: W. B. Eerdmans, 2013).

Weber, Max, *The Protestant Ethic and the Spirit of Capitalism* (London: Allen & Unwin, 1930).

Weeks, Stuart, Gathercole, Simon and Stuckenbruck, Loren (eds), *The Book of Tobit: Texts from the Principal Ancient and Medieval Traditions, with Synopsis, Concordances, and Annotated Texts in Aramaic, Hebrew, Greek, Latin, and Syriac* (Berlin: W. de Gruyter, 2004).

Weinandy, Thomas G., Keating, Daniel A. and Yocum, John P. (eds), *Aquinas on Scripture: An Introduction to his Biblical Commentaries* (London and New York: T&T Clark International, 2005).

Weiser, Artur, *The Psalms: A Commentary* (London: SCM Press, 1962).

Weiss Halivni, David, *Peshat and Derash: Plain and Applied Meaning in Rabbinic Exegesis* (New York and Oxford: Oxford University Press, 1991).

Wellhausen, Julius, *Geschichte Israels I* (Marburg: 1878); second edition as *Prolegomena zur Geschichte Israels*, English version *Prolegomena to the History of Israel* (Edinburgh: Adam & Charles Black, 1885).

—— *Die Composition des Hexateuchs und der historischen Bücher des Alten Testaments* (Berlin: G. Reimer, third edition 1899).

Westerholm, Stephen and Westerholm, Martin, *Reading Sacred Scripture: Voices from the History of Biblical Interpretation* (Grand Rapids, Mich.: W. B. Eerdmans, 2016).

Wettstein, Howard, 'God's Struggles', in Michael Bergmann, Michael J. Murray and Michael C. Rea (eds), *Divine Evil? The Moral Character of the God of Abraham* (Oxford: Oxford University Press, 2011).

White, Carolinne,*The Correspondence (394–419) between Jerome and Augustine of Hippo* (Lewiston, NY and Lampeter: Mellen Press, 1990).

Whybray, R. N., *The Succession Narrative* (London: SCM Press, 1968).

Wiles, M. F., 'Theodore of Mopsuestia as Representative of the Antiochene School', in *The Cambridge History of the Bible*, vol. 1, pp. 489–510.

Williams, C. S. C., 'The History of the Text and Canon of the New Testament to Jerome', in *The Cambridge History of the Bible*, vol. 2, pp. 27–53.

Williamson, H. G. M., *The Book Called Isaiah: Deutero-Isaiah's Role in Composition and Redaction* (Oxford: Oxford University Press, 1994).

—— *Studies in Persian Period History and Historiography* (Tübingen: Mohr Siebeck, 2004).

—— *1 and 2 Chronicles* (Eugene, Ore.: Wipf & Stock, 2010).

—— (ed.), *Understanding the History of Ancient Israel* (Oxford: Oxford University Press, 2007).

Wills, Lawrence M., *The Jewish Novel in the Ancient World* (Ithaca, NY and London: Cornell University Press, 1995).

Wolfson, Harry A., *Philo: Foundations of Religious Philosophy in Judaism, Christianity, and Islam* (Cambridge, Mass.: Harvard University Press, 1947, reprinted 1968).

Wright, N. T., *What Paul Really Said* (Oxford: Lion, 1997).

—— *Paul and the Faithfulness of God* (London: SPCK and Minneapolis: Fortress Press, 2013). Yadin, Azzan, *Scripture as Logos: Rabbi Ishmael and the Origins of Midrash* (Philadelphia: University of Pennsylvania Press, 2004).

—— 'Concepts of Scripture in the Schools of Rabbi Akiva and Rabbi Ishmael', in Sommer (ed.), *Jewish Concepts of Scripture*, Chapter 4.

Yarbro Collins, Adela and Collins, John J., *King and Messiah as Son of God: Divine, Human, and Angelic Messianic Figures in Biblical and Related Literature* (Grand Rapids, Mich.: W. B. Eerdmans, 2008).

Yarchin, William, *History of Biblical Interpretation: A Reader* (Peabody, Mass.: Hendrickson, 2004).

Young, Frances, *Biblical Exegesis and the Formation of Christian Culture* (Cambridge: Cambridge University Press, 1997).

Zaharopoulos, Dimitri Z., *Theodore of Mopsuestia on the Bible* (New York: Paulist Press, 1989).

Zahn, Molly M., 'New Voices, Ancient Words: The *Temple Scroll*'s reuse of the Bible', in John Day (ed.), *Temple and Worship in Biblical Israel*, LHBOTS 422 (London: T&T Clark, 2005), pp. 435–58.

—— 'Rewritten Scripture', in Timothy H. Lim and John J. Collins (eds), *The Oxford Handbook of the Dead Sea Scrolls* (Oxford: Oxford University Press, 2010), pp. 323–36.

—— *Rethinking Rewritten Scripture: Composition and Exegesis in the 4QReworked Pentateuch Manuscripts* (Leiden: Brill, 2011).

Zenger, Erich, *The Composition of the Book of Psalms* (Leuven: Peeters, 2010).

Zetterholm, Magnus, *Approaches to Paul: A Student's Guide to Recent Scholarship* (Minneapolis: Fortress Press, 2009).

Biblical References

Proverbs

Ecclesiastes

Index

The abbreviations NT and OT stand for New Testament and Old Testament respectively. References to biblical books are restricted to general discussion of the texts; those cited by chapter and verse can be found in the index of scriptural references.